W9-CYU-868

FOURTH EDITION

ORIENTATION TO COUNSELING

J. Vincent
Indiana University

Bernard Nisenholz
California State University, Northridge

Allyn and Bacon

Boston • London • Toronto • Sydney • Tokyo • Singapore

To Carolyn, Linnea, Karl, Kris, and Erik
Sybil, Adam, and Julie,
Lyle and Yoshiko

Senior Editor: Raymond Short
Series Editorial Assistant: Karin Huang
Marketing Manager: Susan E. Brown
Composition and Prepress Buyer: Linda Cox
Production Editor: Christopher H. Rawlings
Editorial-Production Service: Omegatype Typography, Inc.
Manufacturing Buyer: Megan Cochran
Cover Administrator: Jenny Hart

Copyright © 1999, 1995, 1991, 1987 by Allyn & Bacon
A Viacom Company
160 Gould Street
Needham Heights, MA 02194

Internet: www.abacon.com

All rights reserved. No part of the material protected by this copyright notice may be reproduced or utilized in any form or by any means, electronic or mechanical, including photocopying, recording, or by any information storage and retrieval system, without written permission from the copyright owner.

Library of Congress Cataloging-in-Publication Data

Peterson, J. Vincent.
    Orientation to counseling / J. Vincent Peterson, Bernard
Nisenholz. — 4th ed.
      p. cm.
    Includes bibliographical references and index.
    ISBN 0-205-27539-7
    1. Counseling. 2. Counselors. I. Nisenholz, Bernard.
II. Title.
BF637.C6P45 1999
158'.3—dc21
                         98-12731
                           CIP

Printed in the United States of America

13 12 11 10   09 08 07

CONTENTS

PREFACE

The field of counseling continues to be an increasingly significant part of the U.S health care industry. In 1996, Congress passed the Mental Health Parity Act, which helped to include mental health services with other health services. This was legislative recognition of what was already happening across the country.

As a result of being included in the total national health care picture, counselors are now experiencing firsthand the effects of managed care, such as the need to become skilled in brief therapy and the tendency for cost-conscious managed care organizations to select licensed or certified mental health counselors over psychiatrists. In this edition we have included updates on the topics of counselor licensure, counselor certification, and managed care. We also have added information about brief therapy, which is an important counseling approach.

Due to the tremendous public interest in spiritual issues, counselors and counselor educators are responding by including more work with spiritual issues in both counselor practice and education. Dealing with spiritual concerns is increasingly an accepted function of counselors. We have included faith development and spiritual issues in this book since the first edition; we continue to stay current with these issues in our coverage of the transpersonal counseling approach, which speaks directly to the broad spectrum of spiritual issues.

Being sensitive to all of the possible spiritual beliefs of clients is one of the many ways a counselor can effectively deal with issues of diversity. As the country becomes increasingly multiethnic and multiracial, counselors have to learn to relate to a wider spectrum of clients. As a major component of this approach, socioeconomic and environmental issues are extremely important as counselors strive to relate better to all clients. We have continued to infuse cultural issues throughout all of the subjects in the book. We have strengthened the chapter that deals specifically with multicultural concerns by adding Ruby Payne's work on how to relate to different social classes, which is a most valuable way to understand cultural differences.

The increased use of the Internet by members of the counseling profession has been one of the major changes since our previous edition was published. We can now search the "Net" for resources, send e-mail to colleagues, and experience actual counseling via the Internet.

A major change in this edition is the inclusion of Internet resources relating to almost every chapter in the book; in addition, we have written about how counseling students can effectively use the Net to enhance their learning. We have added an interactive website to allow faculty and students to go beyond the text to access an expanded coverage of this book's topics, to participate in on-line activities, and to interact directly with us as authors.

As many people in the United States move toward the Wholistic approach to physical and mental health, the National Institutes of Health have added a department for alternative medicine and healing. Today more and more counselors are labeling themselves as Wholistic counselors. In this edition we continue to present the Wholistic approach to counseling as perhaps the epitome of eclectic, integrative counseling, an approach that strongly encourages working with other health professionals in the best interests of the client.

We also are including the 1995 Code of Ethics and Standards of Practice of the American Counseling Association (ACA) and are reporting on other changes within the ACA, such as the addition of ACA's Association for Gay, Lesbian, and Bisexual Issues in Counseling (AGLBIC) and ACA's new website.

The Council for Accreditation of Counseling and Related Educational Programs (CACREP) has announced its guidelines for accrediting counselor education programs into the twenty-first century; The content areas covered by our book parallel CACREP's standards as well as the content areas on the National Certified Counselor (NCC) examination. Students continue to report to us how this book has not only been helpful to them in an introductory course, but as a valuable resource in subsequent courses, for comprehensive examinations, and for the NCC Exam.

The early chapters of the book focus on who counselors are and how good counselors can be distinguished from ineffective counselors, including information on stress management and burnout prevention. The book then focuses on what effective counselors can do, the skills that counselors employ in developing therapeutic relationships, and then the various other content areas that proficient counselors need to know.

Throughout the book we have included interactive opportunities where students can pause after reading and consider new ideas or take part in specific activities before continuing with their reading (*Ideas in Action*). This feature has been very well-received by our past students. To initiate this kind of activity from the beginning of the book, we have added a new introductory section which welcomes students to the field and encourages them to begin journals, assembling portfolios, and creating professional libraries from the beginning of their counseling studies.

Content and research has been updated in all chapters, and there have been major revisions to the chapters related to the origin and scope of the field, social responsibility, legal and ethical issues, and counseling theory.

SPECIAL FEATURES

- This book provides an excellent overview of the contemporary field of counseling.
- The importance of the self of the counselor in the counseling relationship is especially emphasized.
- A unique historical perspective illustrates the growth of the field as it develops concurrently with other related professions and external phenomena.

- This book focuses on multicultural issues throughout the book as well as including a separate chapter dealing with specific multicultural topics.
- Emphasis is placed on students developing a personal stress management plan at the beginning of their counselor education program.
- The need to become a socially responsible counselor is stressed.
- Transpersonal and wholistic approaches to counseling are included as part of the section on theoretical approaches.
- The book presents an overall systemic approach to the field of counseling.
- Exercises and activities are built into chapters and included at the end of chapters to help students interact with new material immediately.
- Human development (one of the eight areas evaluated for certification as a Nationally Certified Counselor) is included as part of the basic content.
- Recommended reading materials are provided at the end of each chapter in addition to the references.
- Internet sites related to chapter content are supplied.
- The book is written in independent parts allowing instructors to approach the subjects in different ways, such as by beginning a course with the second part (skills) or the third part (knowledge areas).

TERMINOLOGY/LANGUAGE

The book continues to use the terms *counseling* and *psychotherapy* interchangeably. We use the term *theory* sparingly, as there are no complete theories of counseling. We favor the term *approach*, as in "the cognitive behavioral approach." We continue to use the term *force* in conjunction with the four psychological forces: psychodynamic, behavioral, humanistic, and transpersonal. We do not refer to multicultural counseling as a fourth force, for we believe that label diminishes the importance of multicultural issues and concerns. We believe multicultural concerns must permeate all of the above counseling forces. It should not be viewed as an alternative approach. We also use the broad term *multicultural* rather than the term *cross cultural*. We continue our practice of avoiding sexist language. Finally, as you may have noticed, we choose to spell *wholistic* with a "w" to emphasize the broad, all-encompassing nature of the term.

ACKNOWLEDGMENTS

We express our sincere appreciation to all of our students for their valuable feedback and contributions on all aspects of the book. We also want to acknowledge Gerald Gudorf, Jannette Shaw, Korynne Taylor-Dunlop, and Geri Stone for their very astute input on the content of various chapters in the book. We also appreciate the excellent editorial work of Omegatype Typography, Inc. and the secretarial services of Mary Thompson and Joanne Lowery. Last, we want to acknowledge the support and encouragement we have received from Ray Short, series editor at Allyn and Bacon. They have all contributed significantly to the quality of this book.

FOR THE STUDENT

WELCOME TO AN ORIENTATION TO COUNSELING: WHAT TO EXPECT

- Can reading this book really help me become an effective professional counselor?
- Is this a book that I'll want to keep for my professional library, or is it one I'll want to get through quickly and sell?
- What perspective do the authors take in their presentation of this subject area?

Welcome to the field of counseling! Whether you are beginning an extensive formal program of counselor education—one that could involve periods of formal and informal study for the rest of your working life—or you just want an overview of the counseling field, you will find this a fascinating field of study and an exciting personal journey.

The counseling profession continues to grow both in size and scope with increasing numbers of counselors finding an ever-widening choice of counselor-related occupations. During your journey into this field you will encounter descriptions of many of the occupations that you may pursue, as well as opportunities to learn about the knowledge and skills needed to function successfully in these positions. Along the way you will encounter significant controversies, colorful personalities, and a variety of ethical and legal issues.

Because counseling is such a personal field, a good place to begin is with the study of the characteristics of counselors: who they are, what they can do, and what they know. Chapters 1 through 4 highlight the identity of the counselor, elaborate on the issues and responsibilities related to becoming a counselor, describe career opportunities in the profession, and discuss the ethical, legal, and social responsibilities of counselors. The second part of the book, Chapters 5 through 8, illustrates what counselors are able to do. The third part, Chapters 9 through 20, features what counselors need to know to be proficient in their field.

Throughout the book, we encourage you to think about whether counseling is the appropriate field for you and to make an early commitment to become the best possible counselor. Do more than just read each of the chapters in this book. Get involved with the material. Consider how the facts and ideas relate to you personally. The *Ideas in Action* feature and the questions and activities in each chapter can help facilitate your involvement. Internet resources related to each topic area will allow you to easily pursue a given topic in greater depth.

As you start your journey, begin to develop a positive professional attitude (PA) toward the counseling profession. Be aware that there is increasing acceptance in the United States of master's level therapists with degrees in counseling, marriage and family therapy, and social work. In fact, a *Consumer Reports* study (1995) found that psychotherapy clients were as satisfied with master's level practitioners (social workers) as they were with doctoral level therapists (psychologists and psychiatrists). Furthermore, managed care companies and insurance providers, who are increasingly paying more and more of mental health costs, often prefer that clients see master's level therapists who generally charge lower rates than doctoral-level practitioners (McGoldrick, 1997).

We believe that many dimensions of the counseling field will capture your imagination and encourage your commitment to a career in this field. For those who ultimately decide that they are not able to make that commitment, this book still can be a valuable personal growth experience.

The approach we have taken in this book is a global wholistic one. We believe that the counselor is the key to success in developing relationships and facilitating change. We also believe that the counselor has to be prepared to work with a highly diverse clientele and be able to work with the total person, including the dimension of spirituality and other sociocultural factors. While we present the therapy dimension of the field in great detail, we are strongly committed to the preventive and developmental dimensions of counseling.

The content of this book has been designed to correspond to the subject areas covered by the National Certified Counselor Exam, the exam that counseling program graduates are eligible to take in order to become a Nationally Certified Counselor (NCC). We are particularly proud of the fact that a great many of the students who have used this book have told us that they not only have enjoyed it when they read it in their introductory course, but that they also found it to be a valuable resource for subsequent courses, for comprehensive exams, and for the NCC examination. We hope that it will be as valuable to you.

To make the journey even more meaningful and memorable, we suggest that from the very beginning you start a process of regularly writing in a journal if you are not already doing so. We also suggest that you begin a portfolio and a professional library that you can add to as you progress.

Journal   Purchase some type of notebook so that you can begin a journal of your thoughts, feelings, experiences, and learnings throughout this course. You can begin this journal now by writing down what your definition and description of counseling is and your present attitude and approach to the field. Make entries after every class, chapter, and assignment. This will be an excellent way to record your personal journey, and if you continue in the field, you can continue to write in your journal as well. See Hugh Prather's (1970) *Notes to Myself* for an example of a published personal journal.

Portfolio.   Purchase an expandable file folder or set aside a portion of a file drawer for the storage of your collection of class notes, formal and informal papers, journals, projects, and other works. This will help you demonstrate your growth and achievement and later could be a valuable resource as you prepare for examinations or to develop a job resume.

Professional Library.   From the very beginning of your journey, you will come across books, journals, articles from the Web, audiotapes, and other materials that have significant meaning to you. Reserve a shelf or two in a bookcase where you can begin a professional library to keep the books and materials that mean so much to you.

For more ideas and suggestions about journals, portfolios, personal libraries, and other ideas and activities related to this book, be sure to check out our website (www.abacon.com). We would appreciate receiving feedback from you, so let us know your ideas, reactions, and so on by e-mail or regular mail. Bon voyage!

JVP
BN

REFERENCES

McGoldrick, J. (1997). Master's threat. *Common Boundary, 15*(4), 13.

Mental health: Does therapy work? (1995, November). *Consumer Reports, 60,* 734–739.

Prather, H. (1970). *Notes to Myself.* Lafayette, CA: Real People Press.

chapter 1

focus on

THE COUNSELOR

- What motivates people to become counselors?
- What are the personal characteristics needed to be an effective counselor?
- Are all counselors effective? If not, why not?
- What skills and knowledge would an effective counselor be expected to have?
- What are the differences between an effective and an ineffective counselor?
- Does a counselor have a particular responsibility to society?

Students enter graduate-level counselor education programs from a variety of educational backgrounds, ranging from art to zoology. Many students may already have training and experience in the helping professions, perhaps as teachers, nurses, or clergy. They often stay with their original profession on completion of counselor training and use their newly acquired knowledge and experience to enhance their work. Whatever their background, students entering this field have the opportunity to develop high levels of knowledge and skill in a field that can lead to a broad variety of employment opportunities as well as provide a springboard for advanced training.

Some job titles currently held by graduates of counselor education programs include mental health counselor, organizational development consultant, personnel development trainer, school counselor, and nurse counselor. These seemingly different occupations have much in common. They are all concerned with what has been labeled "the people problem"—helping people achieve more effective relationships between themselves and others or with the world in which they live" (Combs, Avila, & Purkey, 1971, p. 4).

Does being a nice, caring person ensure success as a counselor? Is it enough to like people and to have a desire to help them? Does the completion of a required course of study guarantee that a counselor will be a positive influence when working with people? What changes, if any, will a counseling student need to experience as part of the educational process? This chapter deals directly with these issues and more as we explore the world of the counselor.

WHY DO PEOPLE BECOME COUNSELORS?

Individuals entering the field of counseling generally believe that they can be helpful to others. With that idea in mind, an increasing number of people are entering the counseling field. Many are interested in the areas of remediation and rehabilitation. They want to help what might be called the casualties of the system: the discouraged, the disturbed, and the disturbing. Others are interested in prevention and in helping people to learn and use skills and attitudes that will help them avoid or forestall debilitation. Still others enter the field to help individuals attain the highest level of human potential.

Indeed, people become counselors due to many needs and reasons. Unless these needs and reasons are understood, they can have a negative influence on the helping process. With awareness and understanding they can be a powerful positive force for becoming an effective counselor. A few of the more common needs are the following:

1. *Need to make a difference.* Many prospective counselors would like to make a contribution to society. They want to leave their mark on the world and make a difference in people's lives. This often is a way to make their own lives important and worthwhile. When these needs are unrealistic they can often lead to frustration, disappointment, and depression. Counselors who want to make a difference in their clients' lives need to realize that their clients may not be interested in being helped or changed. "Your entire worth as a person should not be tethered to the need to make an impact on the lives of others" (Corey & Corey, 1993, p. 4).

2. *Need to be helpful and care for others.* Fritz Perls, the founder of Gestalt therapy, believed that therapists who want to be helpful are doomed from the start, because clients will do anything to make therapists feel inadequate in order to compensate for the clients' needing them. Rushing in to be helpful by comforting, giving advice, or changing the topic when a client is feeling sad or uncomfortable shows disrespect for the client's experience and competency. "Clients need to take responsibility for deciding what choices and changes they will make" (Corey & Corey, 1993, p. 5). This rushing in by a therapist may result in keeping clients from experiencing feelings which are actually painful to the counselor. Counselors may run away from their own anxiety, which diminishes their feelings of helplessness. Rescuing and comforting can also revictimize clients who often were prevented from expressing their deepest feelings in childhood. It is through fully experiencing their deepest feelings that clients can become more whole. Many clients, and some prospective counselors, come from dysfunctional families and have been caregivers since childhood. As a result they have never taken care of their own needs. Those who are always giving and not taking care of their own needs risk burnout (see chapter 2).

3. *Need to understand and solve one's own problems.* Many students enter counseling programs and even become professional counselors in order to help solve their own problems. They often encounter their own problems in the people they are helping. For example, those who have a need to be liked and needed may end up using their clients to fulfill that need in themselves.

4. *Need for power, influence, or status.* The very nature of helping relationships conveys a considerable amount of power and influence to counselors. Counselors who are not aware of this need in themselves can end up defeating the real purpose of counseling, which is to help empower clients to take charge of their own lives.

These needs can work for counselors or against them. The key is awareness. Without awareness counselors can unconsciously inflict much harm. With awareness counselors can check themselves, seek help for themselves, and possibly turn deficits into assets. Individuals who have successfully coped with physical and psychological traumas can become **wounded healers** who work with others in similar circumstances. For example, many former drug addicts become substance abuse counselors, and adults who were abused as children may specialize in treating victims of abuse. First they must personally deal with their own issues.

Ideas in

As you consider becoming a counselor, which of the counselor needs listed comes closest to fitting your situation? Are there issues that you want to take care of before you pursue a counselor education prog...

DIFFERENCES BETWEEN EFFECTIVE AND INEFFECTIVE HELPERS

People from all walks of life use a variety of what they believe to be helping behaviors in their interactions with others. However, the results of many interventions are often less than helpful, and subsequent statements such as "I was only trying to help" are hardly comforting.

What is even more discouraging is that sometimes interventions by people who have had training can be harmful rather than helpful. Carkhuff (1983) reports that "we have found that all helping and human relationships may be 'for better or for worse.' The effect depend upon the helper's level of skills in facilitating the helpee's movement through the helping process toward constructive helping outcomes. These responsive and initiative helping skills constitute the core of all helping relationships" (p. 272).

The conclusion that helping professionals can hurt as well as help was arrived at in a circuitous fashion. During the 1950s several investigators charged that counseling and psychotherapy did not make a difference (Eysenck, 1952; Levitt, 1957). These investigators found that people in control groups, those not assigned to therapists, gained as much on the average as those who were seen by professional practitioners. Approximately "two-thirds of the patients improved and remained out of the hospital a year after treatment, whether they were treated or not" (Carkhuff, 1983, p. 259).

McNeilly and Howard (1991) analyzed Eysenck's original data and found a 50% improvement rate among his subjects in about 15 sessions, compared to a 2% rate among people not treated. They concluded that Eysenck's data proved that psychotherapy can be very effective. Other studies of professionally treated clients, however, indicated that the results of therapy covered a broader range than was found in groups of potential clients who did not receive therapy. Analysis of the results of therapy on clients of professional therapists indicated that some clients got significantly better and some got worse. Counseling and psychotherapy did, in fact, make a difference; however, the disturbing conclusion was that the effect could be either helpful or harmful.

The most significant finding on the effectiveness of professional therapists was that the helpful and harmful effects could be accounted for largely by the levels of functioning of the helpers on certain interpersonal dimensions, such as the ability to listen with understanding.

Therapists who displayed high levels of the identified interpersonal dimensions facilitated the process of positive change in their clients. The clients of therapists who offered low levels of the same dimensions stayed the same or got worse (Carkhuff, 1983; Rothstein, 1989).

These findings have been confirmed by experimental studies in which the variables were controlled (Carkhuff & Alexik, 1967; Holder, Carkhuff, & Berenson, 1967; Piaget, Berenson, & Carkhuff, 1968). The findings have also been generalized to other areas of helping and human relationships: parent–child relations (Carkhuff & Pierce, 1976) and teacher–student relations (Aspy & Roebuck, 1977). In a study of leadership ability in groups, Lieberman, Yalom, and Miles (1973) found that a combination of caring and meaning attribution behaviors were directly related to positive outcomes, whereas other behaviors, such as high emotional stimulation, led to negative results.

In general, the overall conclusion of these studies is that the "less knowing" persons (clients) will move toward the levels of functioning of the more knowing persons (helpers) over time, depending on both the extensiveness and intensity of contacts. Helpees of high functioning helpers get better on a variety of process and outcome indices, while helpees of low level functioning helpers get worse. (Carkhuff, 1980, p. 216)

DESCRIBING THE EFFECTIVE COUNSELOR

What then are the attributes of an effective counselor? A number of studies conducted during the past 40 years have investigated the relationship between personality characteristics and effectiveness in counseling. One consistent finding is that the quality of the therapeutic bond has a significant impact on the outcome of the therapy (Herman, 1993; Marziali & Alexander, 1991). Based on numerous studies, Herman reported the greatest factors in determining the quality of the therapeutic bond are the counselor's personal characteristics, such as the ability to communicate empathy and concern to the client and the willingness to be vulnerable and open.

Specific interpersonal skills that have been identified include communicating empathy, respect, concreteness, confrontation, self-disclosure, and immediacy (Rothstein, 1989; Truax & Carkhuff, 1967). In a review of research related to a variety of helping professionals including teachers, school counselors, counselors-in-training, and clergy, Combs (1986) found that the helper's belief system is a significant factor in being an effective helper. Combs found five areas of belief that appear to discriminate between good and poor helpers:

1. Good helpers have the belief that it is the personal meaning of another person that is what is important, not external, behavioral data. They believe in being sensitive and empathic.
2. Good helpers have very positive beliefs about people, seeing them as dependable, able, and trustworthy.
3. Good helpers have a positive belief in self. They have a good self-concept, confidence in their abilities, and a feeling of oneness with others.
4. Good helpers have strong beliefs about purposes and priorities. Beliefs held about the purposes of society, helping, and relationships influence their goals and their interventions.

5. Good helpers have strong beliefs about appropriate methods for helping. Research has not indicated any specific methods that discriminate between effective and ineffective helpers. It appears that it may well be the values and beliefs that the helper has about the methods used that make the difference. (pp. 56–58)

Multicultural Factors

There has been a growing emphasis on the awareness and understanding of multicultural factors in counseling. For example, we might add that in the first area of belief noted above, the personal meanings of people include meanings that are their **worldviews,** the presuppositions and assumptions that people hold about their world. All worldviews have a cultural base, as well as an individual, family, and universal base (Ivey, Ivey, & Simek-Morgan 1993). One's worldview influences one's ways of thinking and one's behaviors (Ibrahim, 1991). Good helpers are able to grasp the personal meanings of another person, including meanings that are cultural in nature. They are also able to help their clients to see issues in a social context and to facilitate personal action to improve their clients' conditions.

The Three Basic Dimensions of a Counselor

In recent years emphasis in the field has shifted from focusing primarily on the counselor's personality to educating counselors to perform particular behaviors, skills, or interactions (Rothstein, 1989). Ford (1979) suggests that training efficacy can be maximized by selecting trainees with high initial proficiency levels in specific target skills. Furthermore, in studying any profession there is always a concern about what the professional knows. This question is of particular importance in the helping professions because we place a high value on self knowledge as well as on externally acquired knowledge. Thus, in describing competent and effective counselors, we are concerned with who counselors are, what they can do, and what they know. Counseling competence, as noted by Lauver and Harvey (1997), "develops from the merging of these three elements: the person [who the counselor is], counseling knowledge [what the counselor knows], and counseling skills [what the counselor can do]" (p. 4).

WHO THE COUNSELOR IS

One commonly desired outcome of counseling is to help clients become more self-actualizing, more fully functioning, or more closely approximating their highest levels of potential. If this is a goal for clients, some counselor educators (e.g., Carkhuff & Berenson, 1977) believe that it should be an objective for counselors as well. If counselors are to help a client become more fully functioning, it is reasonable to suggest that counselors be involved in the same process. Counselors may not be able to help anyone progress beyond the point that they themselves have attained.

Characteristics of the Self-Actualizing Person

In a quest to determine what was special about individuals who were functioning at high levels, Maslow (1956) studied healthy people who were judged to be using personal

resources in highly effective ways. The following 14 characteristics, as summarized by
Patterson (1985), were found generally to describe Maslow's subjects, with no individual
necessarily rating high on all of the characteristics.

1. *More efficient perception of reality and more comfortable relations with it.* The self-
   actualizing person can detect the phony and dishonest person and has an accurate perception of what exists rather than a distortion of perception by one's needs. Self-actualizing
   people are more aware of their environment. They are not afraid of the unknown and
   can tolerate the doubt, uncertainty, and tentativeness accompanying the new and the
   unfamiliar.
2. *Acceptance of self, others, and nature.* Self-actualizing persons are not ashamed of
   their human nature, with its shortcomings, imperfections, and weaknesses. Nor are
   they critical of these aspects of other people. They respect and esteem themselves and
   others. They are honest, open, genuine, without pose or facade.
3. *Spontaneity.* Self-actualizing persons are not conventional, but they do not flout it. They
   are not conformists, but neither are they anticonformist for the sake of being so. They are
   not externally motivated or even goal-directed—rather, their motivation is the internal
   one of growth and development, the actualization of their potentialities.
4. *Problem-centered.* Self-actualizing persons are not ego-centered, focusing on problems outside themselves. They are mission-oriented, often on the basis of a sense of
   responsibility or obligation rather than of personal choice.
5. *The quality of detachment; the need for privacy.* Self-actualizing persons enjoy soli-
   tude and privacy. It is possible for them to remain undisturbed by what upsets others.
   They may even appear to others as asocial.
6. *Autonomy; independence of culture and environment.* Self-actualizing persons, though
   dependent on others for satisfaction of the basic needs of love, safety, respect, and
   belongingness, "are not dependent for their main satisfactions on the real world, or
   other people or culture or means-to-ends, or in general on extrinsic satisfactions.
   Rather, they are dependent for their own development and continued growth upon their
   own potentialities and latent resources" (Maslow, 1956, p. 176).
7. *Continued freshness of appreciation.* Self-actualizing persons repeatedly, though not
   continuously, experience awe, pleasure, and wonder in their everyday world.
8. *The mystic experience; the "oceanic feeling."* At times, self-actualizing persons have
   experiences of ecstasy, awe, and wonder with feelings of limitless horizons opening
   up, followed by the conviction that the experience was important and valuable and had
   a carryover into daily life.
9. ***Gemeinschaftsgefühl*** (*Social interest or social feeling, a sense of fellowship in the
   human community*). Self-actualizing persons have a deep feeling of empathy or com-
   passion for human beings in general. This feeling is unconditional, in that it exists
   along with the recognition of the existence of negative qualities in others which provoke occasional anger, impatience, and disgust.
10. *Interpersonal relations.* Self-actualizing people have deep interpersonal relations with
    others. They are selective, however, and their circle of friends may be small, usually
    consisting of other self-actualizing persons. They attract others to them as admirers or
    disciples.

11. *Democratic character structure.* Self-actualizing persons do not discriminate on the basis of class, education, race, or color. They respect everyone as potential contributors to their knowledge but also just because they are human beings.
12. *Means and ends.* Self-actualizing persons are highly ethical. They clearly distinguish means from ends and subordinate means to ends.
13. *Philosophical, unhostile sense of humor.* Self-actualizing persons have a spontaneous, thoughtful sense of humor intrinsic to the situation. Their humor does not involve hostility, superiority, or sarcasm.
14. *Creativity.* Self-actualizing persons are all found to be creative in their own ways. The creativity involved here is not the special talent creativeness. It is a creative potentiality inherent in everyone but usually suffocated by acculturation. *"It is a fresh, naive, direct way of looking at things"* (Patterson, 1985, pp. 39–41).

Self-actualizing people would regularly experience what Csikszentmihalyi (pronounced CHICK-sent-me-high-ee) calls **flow,** moments when what we feel, think, and do are in harmony (1990, 1997). Athletes refer to these experiences as "being in the zone," religious mystics as being in "ecstasy," and artists and musicians as "aesthetic rapture." Flow is not something that just happens to a person, but rather is a result of personal attributes and the person's environment. Individuals are likely to be in flow when "they perceive both the challenges to be high in a given situation and their skills to be high" (Csikszentmihalyi, 1997, p. 118). We can learn to experience flow by becoming involved in activities where it is likely to occur, such as mental work and active leisure.

Experiencing flow requires personal involvement; there is little opportunity to exercise one's skills during periods of passive leisure and entertainment. This may well be one reason why many people are unhappy when they retire. Flow experiences are quite often found in the workplace. One woman described what her career meant to her, "To be totally absorbed in what you are doing and to enjoy it so much that you don't want to be doing anything else. I don't see how anyone can survive if they don't experience something like that..." (Csikszentmihalyi, 1997, p. 116).

Self-actualizing persons are involved with people and issues in the real world. They not selfish or self-centered, but they have the self-assurance and confidence of persons who know who they are and how they relate to other people:

> Self-actualizing people are, without one single exception, involved in a cause outside their own skin, in something outside of themselves. They are devoted, working at something, something which is very precious to them—some calling or vocation in the old sense, the priestly sense. They are working at something which fate has called them to somehow and which they work at and which they love, so that the work-joy dichotomy in them disappears. (Maslow, 1971, p. 43)

Counselors have the responsibility to monitor and evaluate their own self-actualization efforts in order to better help others pursue self-actualization (Pietrofesa, Leonard, & Van Hoose, 1978). Self-actualization is a process; it is not expected that counselors will be self-actualized, but they should be aware of where they are in the process and what they need to do to move toward their goal.

Ideas in
action

Maslow's Self-Actualizing Characteristics

Some feminists object to Maslow's criteria for self-actualization on the grounds that the criteria are based upon male values. For example, the quality of detachment; the need for privacy; and the desire for autonomy, independence of culture and environment, are especially male-oriented values, whereas women tend to value involvement, relationships, and interdependence. Crimshaw (1986) asserts,

> *Consistently,…throughout his work, Maslow identifies self-actualization or superiority with dominance, with success, with winning. (p. 151)*

Crimshaw accuses Maslow of not being egalitarian and having near-fascist views in regard to male dominance, female submission, and superior human beings.

Consider Maslow's ideas in light of Crimshaw's remarks and determine how all of this relates to characteristics desirable in a counselor.

A WHOLISTIC WELLNESS MODEL

Although Maslow's self-actualization model has been used for years, new models are being developed which attempt to be broader and more inclusive. Witmer and Sweeney (1992) propose a model consisting of five life tasks which contain 11 dimensions of healthy persons for desirable optimal health and functioning of mind, body, spirit, and community. The model includes but goes beyond many of Maslow's characteristics.

1. *Spirituality.* Spirituality is the way people see themselves in relation to others against a background of shared meaning and purpose. There are many dimensions of spirituality including oneness of persons, the desire for inner peace, and sense of wholeness. It includes religion but is not necessarily synonymous with it. It assumes certain life-enhancing beliefs about human dignity, human rights, and reverence for life.
2. *Self-regulation.* Self-regulation includes a sense of worth and control, realistic beliefs, spontaneity and emotional responsiveness, intellectual stimulation, problem solving, creativity, sense of humor, and physical fitness and health habits.
3. *Work.* Work is seen as a life-span task providing economic, psychological, and social benefits to individuals' well-being. The work of a counselor is a way of life.
4. *Friendship.* Friendship includes all social relationships with others outside of marital, sexual, or familial commitments. It includes the concepts of interpersonal relations and Alfred Adler's concept of *Gemeinschaftsgefühl.* "In the absence of friendships, illness, a shorter life expectancy, and less satisfaction in life are likely companions to those individuals who fail to master the opportunities and responsibilities of friendships" (Witmer & Sweeney, 1992, p. 145).
5. *Love.* Love includes the characteristics of intimacy, trust, self-disclosure, cooperation, long term commitment, and often sexual relations. Being able to love one's friends, wife, parents, and children are predictors of good mental health. (p. 146)

The above life tasks are influenced by life forces and global events that have an impact on all aspects of our lives. Life forces include family, religion, education, community, media, government, and business and industry. Global events include "wars, hunger, disease, poverty, environmental pollution, overpopulation, violation of human rights, economic exploitation, unemployment, and competition for limited resources." These events "are heavy clouds across the international sky. All are part of the ecology of living in a 'global village' on the planet Earth. We cannot afford to ignore these events if we wish to build a 'neighborhood village' that is committed to a life-style of wellness and prevention" (Witmer & Sweeney, 1992, p. 146).

Additional Characteristics of Counselors

Some additional characteristics that are important in becoming a counselor include personal energy level, risk-taking ability, tolerance of ambiguity, and capacity for intimacy. Again, there is no strong correlation between a given characteristic and effectiveness as a counselor. Nevertheless, an awareness of the following characteristics may help to promote a better understanding of the counseling process itself.

Level of Personal Energy.   The nature of a counselor's work is somewhat deceptive. To an outsider, a skilled counselor performing at a high level may seem to be doing so effortlessly, yet a tremendous amount of energy is expended in the process of attending, listening, and problem solving with each client. Furthermore, passive, nonenergetic counselors are not as likely to inspire the trust and confidence of clients that more dynamic, energetic counselors might generate (Cormier & Cormier, 1985).

A prospective counselor who has a high energy level to begin with, or who can develop and maintain a personal strength-building program, will be better prepared for both the rigors of a counselor training program and a career in counseling. Both physical and mental strength need to be maintained (see chapter 2). Carkhuff and Berenson (1977) suggest that "only those who are physically robust and live fully from a high level of energy are potential sources of nourishment and may be entitled to confront" (pp. 199–200).

Risk-Taking Ability.   Counseling involves taking risks, including being rejected as a helper, being confronted with a client who is hostile or who presents a problem that a counselor is totally unprepared for or not trained to handle, and having to challenge a client directly without knowing how this action will be perceived.

Counseling often includes confronting a client in a caring way, a skill that involves a high level of risk and energy. For many people, confronting another person is one of the riskiest of interpersonal behaviors. In many counseling situations, however, it is not until the client's inconsistent thoughts, feelings, and behaviors are confronted that the real work of counseling and change begins. Ultimately, as Gilbert Wrenn (1983) warns, counselors must take risks both professionally and politically or risk entering new fields of work.

Tolerance of Ambiguity.   Tolerance of ambiguity has been defined as the capacity of a counselor "to tolerate the uncertainty of not knowing exactly what the client really wishes to discuss until a relationship is established which will allow the process of counseling to continue" (Pietrofesa et al., 1978, p. 105). Pietrofesa and his colleagues stress the importance of tolerance of ambiguity in counseling by noting research evidence indicating that a significant relationship exists between tolerance of ambiguity and the effectiveness of counselor responses. Being able to weigh the meaning of a client's statements carefully may result in more accurate, effective responses.

The field of counseling is filled with ambiguities. There are no standardized diagnostic procedures guaranteed to determine quickly the exact nature of each client's problem, and there are literally hundreds of ways to approach clients and their problems. Furthermore, a basic premise of many theoretical approaches to counseling is that it is up to clients to take responsibility for the ultimate solutions to their problems. Counselors, therefore, cannot simply prescribe a proven antidote for problems the way a medical doctor might prescribe penicillin for a case of bronchitis. Counseling is as much art as it is science, and it generally tends to attract practitioners who are comfortable in this type of ambiguous setting.

Capacity for Intimacy.   A counseling relationship can be one of the most intimate personal relationships. Clients share their most personal thoughts and feelings, often telling counselors things they have never told anyone else. Counselors communicate deep levels of acceptance and understanding, make caring confrontations, and often share their own personal thoughts and feelings. The capacity for intimacy on a regular basis without being possessive is an attribute that some people seem to have naturally and some never seem to attain. Most people, however, can learn to develop their capacity for intimacy in order to be able to be psychologically close to a client who is at the depths of an existential crisis.

Counselors who have difficulty with intimacy may fear being vulnerable and the possibility of being rejected. Associated with these feelings may be a fear of closeness and affection. Counselors with these fears may create excessive emotional distance in counseling relationships and avoid challenging or confronting clients when appropriate (Cormier & Cormier, 1985). Chapter 7 further elaborates on this characteristic and the skills related to it.

It seems clear that "helpers must continually develop an understanding of themselves; they need to become aware of and clarify their own social, economic, and cultural values in order to recognize and separate their needs and problems from those of their clients" (Okun, 1997, p. 10). Corey (1996) supports this, noting that therapists' ability to look at, understand, and accept themselves as well as their clients is crucial (p. 15).

Ideas in action

The lists of desirable personal qualities can be quite overwhelming: "The various prescriptions for the ideal psychotherapist have included a litany of virtues more suited, perhaps, to the most honored biblical figures than to any of their descendants" (Parloff, Waskow, & Wolf, 1978, p. 233).

Consider how many of the counselor characteristics you have to fulfill in order to be an effective counselor.

WHAT THE COUNSELOR CAN DO

Helping Skills

What we can do may be, as Carkhuff (1983), Rothstein (1989), and others suggest, a major factor in effective helping. A person may be self-actualizing and have a high level of knowledge and yet be ineffectual in helping other people solve problems. For a few, the skills of helping may come naturally; for most people, however, it takes a great deal of study and practice to develop all the necessary skills at a high level. With these helping skills mastered, expertise and competence are clearly established (Egan, 1994; Strong, 1968). Expertise can be inferred by noting a person's title, seniority, diplomas, certificates, licenses, and reputation; however, it is the counselor's actual behaviors that ultimately determine competence.

Interpersonal skills that assist in developing and maintaining a helping relationship can be classified under three headings: attending, responding, and initiating. **Attending behaviors** serve to involve the client directly in the helping process. They include such skills as maintaining eye contact, using proper body language, and following verbally without changing the subject. Attending skills are generally seen as prerequisites to subsequent skills (Carkhuff, 1983; Egan, 1994; Ivey 1994).

Responding behaviors are useful in helping the clients explore and clarify their problems. These behaviors include responding with accurate empathy, clarification, specificity of expression, and reflection of meaning. These behaviors also include being able to listen and respond directly to the client's feelings as well as to the content expressed.

Initiating skills include probing, self-disclosure, confrontation, and direct mutual communication. The skills of initiating are particularly helpful when working in the problem solving or action phase of counseling. All of these skills will be elaborated upon in detail in chapters 5, 6, 7, and 8.

WHAT THE COUNSELOR KNOWS

External and Self-Knowledge

Two basic types of knowledge concern a prospective counselor: external knowledge and self-knowledge.

External Knowledge

External knowledge is learned from books, lectures, audiotapes and videotapes, and listening to others. Although there is little demonstrated relationship between the ability to show high levels of knowledge on tests and effectiveness in counseling, there is a legitimate expectation for sufficiently high levels of external knowledge. Entrance requirements into graduate school, specific course requirements, and exit requirements—which may include comprehensive written or oral examinations and the relatively recent requirement of the successful completion of a standardized national examination for counselor certification— all speak to the need for the counselor trainee to have a strong external knowledge base.

In general, areas of knowledge in which overall mastery is expected include an understanding of the profession itself, the helping relationship, group dynamics, human growth and development, counseling theory, career development, social and cultural foundations, appraisal of individuals, and research and evaluation. These areas are the general areas covered in the National Counseling Certification Examination. An overview of each of these areas is presented in part 3 of this book.

Knowledge of Self

Those who know others are wise, those who know themselves are enlightened.

Tao-te Ching

A large amount of external knowledge needs to be mastered, but all of it is insignificant compared to an in-depth knowledge of oneself. When working with clients who are concerned about the meaning of life, the making of moral and ethical decisions, and dealing with values and value judgments, it is essential that counselors know and are comfortable with themselves. The importance of the self and how one alters self-knowledge, are described in the next section.

Self as Instrument

A person's self is the sum total of all he can call his. The self includes, among other things, a system of ideas, attitudes, values, and commitments. The self is a person's total subjective environment; it is the distinctive center of experience and significance. The self constitutes a person's inner world as distinguished from the outer world consisting of other people and things.

Jersild (1952, p. 9)

The use of the self by the therapist is an integral part of the therapeutic process and it should be used consciously for treatment purposes.

Satir (1987, p. 23)

Simply stated, the basic tool counselors have at their disposal is themselves (Combs et al., 1971; Bugental, 1987). Pens, paper, tests, tapes and tape recorders, art materials, film, toys, and computers might be used at various times by counselors. However, these ancillary materials play a small role in the helping professions.

In applying the self as instrument concept, counselors must be willing and able to use all of their personal resources. They must

- be able to observe the total person with their eyes, ears, and intuitive senses, picking up nonverbal as well as verbal cues. For example, they should note inconsistencies among tone of voice, body posture, and verbal content.
- be comfortable and effective with culturally different clients and be able to break out of their own cultural capsules.
- have the energy to be able to enter the world of troubled clients and work within that framework to help bring about change.
- feel open and comfortable enough to be able to self-disclose in an appropriate manner. They must be disciplined enough to be able to help clients become specific in stating concerns.
- be willing to take the risks involved in confrontation.

- be able to put all of these skills together to develop direct, mutual communication (intimacy).
- be in the process of growth rather than deterioration.

The growth–deterioration process illustrated in Figure 1.1 does not mean that changes in a person are exclusively one way or the other or that a counselor should never have any negative experiences. In fact, some therapists, such as Rollo May (1984), suggest that wounded healers often can best relate to the suffering of others from their own personal experiences with pain.

The important considerations are whether counselors are aware of their problems, how they contribute to them, and how they deal with them. For example, are they willing to seek out help? Do they deny, rationalize, or blame others for their problems? As stated earlier in the chapter, those counselors who lack awareness of their own conflicts will not be effective with clients, especially those clients who have similar conflicts.

Due to varying conditions and circumstances, there will probably always be movement up and down the growth–deterioration continuum (see Figure 1.1). In general, however, it would be anticipated that the prevailing tendency of a person's becoming and being a counselor would be toward growth rather than deterioration.

To Know Oneself

And seek not the depths of your knowledge with staff or sounding line. For self is a sea boundless and measureless. Say not, "I have found the truth," but rather, "I have found a truth."

Gibran (1923, p. 61)

The ancient command of Socrates to "know thyself" is of particular importance to counselors. Because our thoughts and feelings about ourselves can directly influence how we interact with clients, it is necessary to have full knowledge of ourselves. Self-knowledge, according to Weinstein and Alschuler (1985), consists of descriptions, predictions, and management of one's inner experiences. In attaining self-knowledge, we also need to consider the terms *self-concept*, an indicator of what we think about ourselves, and *self-esteem*, an indicator of how we feel about ourselves (Hamachek, 1985). How do we go about the process of knowing ourselves? What initially sounds deceptively simple is indeed most difficult to do. The following steps are helpful in the process of getting to know oneself.

1. *Know your roots.* The first step is to know your own cultural roots, biases, beliefs, and worldviews. Then you need to acknowledge that the universe "is infinite and any assumptions or beliefs that we hold concerning its reality are subject to question" (Hulnick, 1977, p. 71) and that "in the province of the mind there are no limits" (Lilly, 1972). In effect, then, nothing is impossible. Believing that something is impossible will ensure that one will never experience it. It does not mean that the event could not happen for another person.

2. *Be open to experience.* The second step toward self-knowledge is to be open to experience.

We begin to pay close attention to what is going on within ourselves and our environment. At this point, we discover a strange awakening, and we begin the descent into

GROWTH
Level 5
Creative
Self-actualizing, spontaneous, maximally
effective in promoting positive change in
self and others

Level 4
Personally Effective
Potent, chronically constructive,
promoting positive change

Level 3
Minimally Effective
Situationally distressed, marginal support
system, capable of change and
constructive action

Level 2
Disturbed
Neuroses, chronic negative patterns,
resistant to change

Level 1
Severely Disturbed
Psychoses, ingrained destructive patterns,
immune to change
DETERIORATION

**FIGURE 1.1   Levels of growth and deterioration: Where
helping professionals may be functioning.**

Adapted from *Beyond Counseling and Therapy* (2nd ed.), by R. R. Carkhuff
and B. G. Berenson, 1977, New York: Holt, Rinehart and Winston. Copyright
© 1977 by Robert R. Carkhuff. Adapted with permission.

our inner world. We take risks; we attempt to express ourselves in spite of our fears.
Now, we may even wonder whether we were wise to have begun this journey, but
something deep within will not let us turn back. We have tasted a finer substance, and
we muster the quality of heart-felt courage and proceed in the face of fear. We plunge
downward into the very blocks themselves. We experience and confront our resent-

ment, our low self-esteem, our alienation, our bitterness, our unforgiving attitudes, but now we no longer pretend that they are not a part of us. We realize that we *are* in that, and we do not like what we see. (Hulnick, 1977, p. 1)

3. *Share your thoughts and feelings.* The third step is self-disclosure.

> I have to be free and able to say my thoughts to you, to tell you about my judgments and values, to admit to you my failures and shames, to share my triumphs, before I can really be sure what it is that I am and can become. I must be able to tell you who I am before I can know who I am. And I must know who I am before I can act truly, that is, in accordance with my true self. (Powell, 1969, p. 44)

Hearing your thoughts spoken out loud, perhaps even clarifying them as you speak, and receiving feedback from others are often revealing and rewarding. This actually is one possible outcome offered to justify the hundreds of hours teenagers spend talking on the telephone. Sharing ideas, perceptions, and feelings with significant others is a helpful way to understand oneself and to clarify beliefs and values. This is one reason that some counselor education programs advocate that counseling students participate in therapy while pursuing a degree, a requirement we strongly support.

4. *Be open to others.* Step four, closely related to step three, is to be open to others and to know them. Sydney Harris (1981) suggests that there is a paradox in this whole process of knowing oneself: "We can only know ourselves through knowing others and we can only know others through knowing ourselves" (p. 6). Niebuhr (1955) supports this when he says that "the self cannot be truly fulfilled if it is not drawn out of itself into the life of the other" (p. 31). It is difficult to know yourself by focusing only inward or by reflecting on how other people respond to your thoughts and feelings. We gain much more from discovering ways in which we are similar as well as different from others. Not only is this ability to reach out to know others necessary for self-understanding, but it is also vital to the counseling process. Another way to know more about yourself is to determine how you view other people see and describe "in the behavior of others is frequently a projection of their own drives, fears, and needs" (Hamachek, 1985, p. 137).

5. *Forgive yourself.* The fifth step is to release ourselves from previously held assumptions and misconceptions "by forgiving ourselves for having created them in the first place" (Hulnick, 1977, p. 71). Through this process we become aware of what we believe and value. As we work through the distortions and misconceptions we have, we release energy, making it easier to be open to new experiences and to know ourselves at a deeper level.

> The successful release is often experienced as a "lightening" of body weight and the lifting of a great burden from one's shoulders. Now, we can understand and feel empathy or compassion since we have confronted our own pain. (Hulnick, 1977, p. 71)

6. *Keep a journal.* Finally, to tie these five steps together, it is helpful to keep a journal (see "For the Student" at the beginning of the book). Keeping a journal is a form of self-disclosure; however, it is often not shared with others. Thoughts, feelings, descriptions of experiences, stories, poems, records of dreams, doodles, and drawings—all can be kept in

a journal. In fact, attending special journal writing workshops can help maximize the use of this vehicle. A journal is significant not only for the record of growth that it provides, but also because our written expressions are sometimes different, often in subtle ways, from our verbalizations. We can again learn more about who we are. Cormier and Cormier (1985) state that "it is just as important to keep track of our own personal growth as it is to keep track of what technique or change program we are using with a client. Otherwise we run the risk of behaving incongruently in our relationships with clients" (p. 13).

Knowing oneself and directly appreciating the unlimited potential one has are crucial in applying the self as instrument concept. One is then free to take risks and to use one's total person in the helping relationship. Both the left (cognitive, rational) side of the counselor's brain and the right (affective, intuitive) side are engaged. The body is used to demonstrate attentiveness, and the voice is used as a tool to communicate awareness of the client's feeling level. Above all, the counselor communicates authenticity. The helping relationship becomes a total experience for the counselor's complete self.

Ideas in An excerpt of an actual counseling session with special notations illustrating who the counselor is, what the counselor can do, and what the counselor knows is in Appendix A (pp. 401–404). Take a few minutes to review this case to see how these dimensions manifest themselves in the counseling session.

HELPING AS A WAY OF LIFE

Carkhuff and Berenson (1977) have stated that "helping is as effective as the helper is living effectively," and that a person entering the field of counseling enters it as a way of life. They suggest that the helper has to be a whole person, one who is in the process of becoming a self-actualizing person. They indicate that only the fully functioning whole person has the right to be a helper, only the fully functioning whole person lives in society yet is able to see society through the eyes of its victims and can discriminate between the good and the bad. Those counselors and therapists functioning below this level have no right to offer themselves as helping agents and models. The fact is that most counselors and therapists cannot successfully perform in the situations with which their helpees are failing to cope. The interaction between such a helper and the helpee can be nothing more than a fraud (p. 246).

Counselors living as whole persons believe deeply that even major adversities will not destroy their inner core. They are willing to take and will even seek risks. Impoverished persons carefully avoid all major risks, working from the personal belief that if they faced major risks they would not survive. Anyone who expects to help others cope with the vicissitudes of life needs to be able to demonstrate that capacity as well.

To become a counselor is to adopt a way of life; anything less would be to play a game, enact a role, and be phony. Helping does not take place when the latest techniques are used to demonstrate skill at manipulating clients who are less than whole. One cannot assume the role of the helper for eight hours and then become oneself again and hope to be effective.

SOCIAL RESPONSIBILITY

Neither the counselor nor the client exists in a vacuum. In keeping with the idea of gemein-schaftsgefühl, counselors may need to look beyond the walls of their offices in order to help their clients. Demonstrating social responsibility may involve serving as an advocate for clients, taking various forms of political action, participating in service organizations, and helping during crises and disasters. The responsibility of the counselor extends to the social, cultural, and economic environments of our shared global community, as indicated by the 1998 American Counseling Association (ACA) World Conference theme of "Empowerment through Social Action."

COUNSELOR EDUCATION

If counseling as a profession is a way of life that can best be undertaken by persons who are self-actualizing or in the process of becoming fully functioning whole people, what implications does this have for the selection and education of counselors?

We believe that it is important to begin with students already committed to becoming fully functioning whole persons. Rothstein (1989) suggests that students should be selected with regard to their ability to function using high-level interpersonal skills. The student must be open to and committed to personal, constructive change. Counselor education is not and should not be merely a vehicle to attain legitimacy for present beliefs and practices. Some counselor candidates believe that everything they are already doing is satisfactory but that they need a degree or certificate to make them legitimate. These people tend to be less open to personal change and, through their influence in the educational setting, can negatively influence other students. Even though counselor education involves personal growth, it should not be seen as a substitute for personal therapy.

The curricular emphasis in counselor education programs, according to Rothstein (1989), should be on the enhancement of therapeutic, facilitative functioning. Because of the importance of the counselor's belief system, Combs (1986) would like to see less emphasis on learning how to counsel and more on "becoming a counselor." To develop "a broad, accurate, personally relevant, internally consistent, and appropriate system of beliefs about self, others, purposes, and desirable ways of relating to the world, both in and out of personal practice," counselor education programs should provide a wealth of opportunities for interaction with clients as well as "continuous immersion in a process of exploration of ideas and discovery of personal meanings" (p. 59).

In the final analysis, the purpose of counselor education is to involve qualified students in a lifelong learning process that can be transmitted to their clients. The effective counselor education program should be designed to develop the belief systems, worldviews, and helping skills—repertoires necessary to help students grow and to enable them to work effectively with a variety of clients and problems.

SUMMARY

People from a variety of backgrounds enter the field of counseling with the general objective of helping people live more effectively with themselves and others. Counselors work in areas ranging from problem prevention to remediation and treatment. To become an effective counselor, caring and concern for people are helpful, but not sufficient. Effective counselors can be distinguished from ineffective counselors by their belief systems and by the nature and quality of the relationship skills they use; other personal characteristics do not seem to correlate, either positively or negatively, with being an effective counselor. Clients of ineffective counselors become worse, whereas clients of effective counselors improve.

A major premise is that it may be difficult, if not impossible, to help a client beyond the point at which, the counselor is. As part of the description of who the counselor is, the characteristics of the self-actualizing person are something of which counselors should be personally aware as they work to help others become more fully functioning. Other counselor characteristics, such as having a high level of personal energy, being willing and able to take risks, having a tolerance of ambiguity, and having a capacity for intimacy, indicate what might be expected of practitioners in the field, but they do not guarantee success.

What the counselor can do for the client is of primary importance. Expertise or competence in the execution of attending, responding, and initiating skills determines a counselor's effectiveness.

What the counselor knows is also important. Counselors are expected to have both external knowledge learned from outside sources and self-knowledge attained from enhanced personal awareness. The self as instrument concept, with the counselor being the most effective tool in the counseling relationship, has been presented along with methods to better understand oneself.

Developing the characteristics and the skills necessary to be an effective helper should be seen as part of a total way of life, with the counselor making a lifetime commitment to education, personal growth, and to the global community.

QUESTIONS AND ACTIVITIES

1. What does it mean to you to use your self as an instrument in counseling? Could you become a good counselor without doing this? What attitudes and behaviors of yours might you have to change to use this concept?

2. Where would you place yourself on the scale in Figure 1.1? Are you moving up or down the scale? Check out your perceptions with significant others in your life. If the premise is true that you would have difficulty helping someone get beyond where you are, how far might you expect to help clients grow?

3. Which characteristics of a self-actualizing person present the greatest challenge to you personally?

4. What is your worldview? What presuppositions and assumptions do you hold about your world? Include your assumptions about nature, people, things, and institutions such as government. Review your ethnic, gender, and socioeconomic background and experience. How do they influence your worldview?

5. What type of involvement do you currently have with the greater community? Is this something that you might be willing to expand? If so, how?

RECOMMENDED READINGS

Corey, G., & Corey, M. (1997). *I never knew I had a choice* (6th ed.). Pacific Grove, CA: Brooks/Cole.

Csikszentmihalyi, M. (1997). *Finding flow*. New York: Basic Books.

Jourard, S. (1971). *The transparent self.* New York: D. Van Nostrand.

Manning, M. (1995). *Undercurrents.* New York: Harper-Collins.

Powell, J. (1969). *Why am I afraid to tell you who I am?* Niles, IL: Argus Press.

Rogers, C. (1961). *On becoming a person.* Boston: Houghton Mifflin.

INTERNET RESOURCES

Websites

Abraham Maslow Page <members.aol.com/ KatharenaE/private/Philo/Maslow/maslow.html>

Maslow <www.hcc.hawaii.edu/hccinfo/facdev/ Maslow.html>

REFERENCES

Aspy, D., & Roebuck, F. (1977). *Kids don't learn from people they don't like.* Amherst, MA: Human Resource Development Press.

Bugental, J. (1987). *The art of the psychotherapist.* New York: Norton.

Carkhuff, R. (1980). *The art of helping* (4th ed.). Amherst, MA: Human Resource Development Press.

Carkhuff, R. (1983). *The art of helping* (5th ed.). Amherst, MA: Human Resource Development Press.

Carkhuff, R., & Alexik, M. (1967). The effects of the manipulation of client depth of self-exploration on high and low functioning counselors. *Journal of Clinical Psychology, 23,* 210–212.

Carkhuff, R., & Berenson, B. (1977). *Beyond counseling and therapy* (2nd ed.). New York: Holt, Rinehart & Winston.

Carkhuff, R., & Pierce, R. (1976). *Helping begins at home.* Amherst, MA: Human Resource Development Press.

Combs, A. (1986). What makes a good helper. *Person-Centered Review, 1*(1), 51–61.

Combs, A., Avila, D., & Purkey, W. (1971) *Helping relationships: Basic concepts for the helping professionals.* Boston: Allyn & Bacon.

Corey, G. (1996). *Theory and practice of counseling and psychotherapy* (5th ed.). Pacific Grove, CA: Brooks/Cole.

Corey, M. S., & Corey, G. (1993). *Becoming a helper* (2nd ed.). Pacific Grove, CA: Brooks/Cole.

Cormier, W., & Cormier, L. (1985). *Interviewing strategies for helpers* (2nd ed.). Monterey, CA: Brooks/Cole.

Crimshaw, J. (1986). *Philosophy and feminist thinking.* Minneapolis: University of Minnesota Press.

Csikszentmihalyi, M. (1990). *Flow: The psychology of optimal experience.* New York: Harper & Row.

Csikszentmihalyi, M. (1997). *Finding flow.* New York: Basic Books.

Egan, G. (1994). *The skilled helper* (5th ed.). Pacific Grove, CA: Brooks/Cole.

Eysenck, H. J. (1952). The effects of psychotherapy: An evaluation. *Journal of Consulting Psychology, 16,* 319–334.

Ford, J. (1979). Research on training counselors and clinicians. *Review of Educational Research, 49,* 87–130.

Gibran, K. (1923). *The prophet* New York: Knopf.

Hamachek, D. (1985). The self's development and age growth: Conceptual analysis and implications for counselors. *Journal of Counseling and Development, 64*(2), 136–142.

Harris, S. (1981, September 28). We must know others before knowing ourselves. *South Bend Tribune,* p. 6.

Herman, K. C. (1993, September/October). Reassessing predictors of therapist competence. *Journal of Counseling and Development, 71*(4), 29–32.

Holder, T., Carkhuff, R., & Berenson, B. (1967). The differential effects of the manipulation of therapeutic conditions upon high low functioning clients. *Journal of Counseling Psychology, 14,* 63–66.

Hulnick, H. R. (1977, September). Counselor: Know thyself. *Personnel and Guidance Journal, 56*(1), 69–72.

Ibrahim, F. A. (1991). Contribution of cultural worldview to generic counseling and development.

Journal of Counseling and Development, 70(1), 13–19.

Ivey, A. E. (1994). *Intentional interviewing and counseling* (3rd ed.). Pacific Grove, CA: Brooks/Cole.

Ivey, A. E., Ivey, M. B., & Simek-Morgan, L. (1993). *Counseling and psychotherapy: A multicultural perspective.* Boston: Allyn & Bacon.

Jersild, A. (1952). *In search of self.* New York: Teachers College Press.

Lauver, P., & Harvey, D. R. (1997). *The practical counselor* (3rd ed.). Pacific Grove, CA: Brooks/Cole.

Levitt, E. (1957). The results of psychotherapy with children. *Journal of Consulting Psychology, 21,* 189–196.

Lieberman, M., Yalom, I., & Miles, M. (1973). *Encounter groups: First facts.* New York: Basic Books.

Lilly, J. (1972). *The center of the cyclone.* New York: Julian Press.

Marziali, E., & Alexander, L. (1991). The power of the therapeutic relationship. *American Journal of Orthopsychiatry, 61*(3), 383–391.

Maslow, A. H. (1956). Self-actualizing people: A study of psychological health. In C. E. Moustakas (Ed.), *The self-explorations in personal growth* (pp. 160–194). New York: Harper & Row.

Maslow, A. H. (1971). *The farther reaches of human nature.* New York: Viking Press.

May, R. (1984, March). *The wounded healer.* Presented at American Association of Counseling and Development Convention, Houston, TX.

McNeilly, C., & Howard, K. (1991). The effects of psychotherapy: A reevaluation based on dosage. *Psychotherapy Research, 1,* 74–78.

Niebuhr, R. (1955). *The self and the dramas of history.* New York: Scribner's.

Okun, B. F. (1997). *Effective helping* (5th ed.). Pacific Grove, CA: Brooks/Cole.

Parloff, M. I., Waskow, B., & Wolf, B. (1978). Research on therapist variables in relation to process and outcome. In S. I. Garfield & A. E. Bergin (Eds.), *Handbook of psychotherapy and behavior change* (pp. 233–283). New York: John Wiley.

Patterson, C. H. (1985). *The therapeutic relationship: Foundations for an eclectic psychotherapy.* Monterey, CA: Brooks/Cole.

Piaget, G., Carkhuff, R., & Berenson, B. (1968). The development of skills in interpersonal functioning. *Counselor Education and Supervision, 2,* 102–106.

Pietrofesa, J., Leonard, G., & Van Hoose, W. (1978). *The authentic counselor.* Chicago: Rand McNally.

Powell, J. (1969). *Why am I afraid to tell you who I am?* Niles, IL: Argus Press.

Prather, H. (1970). *Notes to myself, my struggle to become a person.* Lafayette, CA: Real People Press.

Rothstein, S. (1989). *Shockwave.* Carlsbad, CA: Continental Publications.

Satir, V. (1987). The therapist story. In M. Baldwin & V. Satir (Eds.), *The use of self* (pp. 17–25). New York: Haworth.

Strong, S. R. (1968). Counseling: An interpersonal influence process. *Journal of Counseling Psychology, 15,* 215–224.

Truax, C., & Carkhuff, R. (1967). *Toward effective counseling and psychotherapy.* Chicago: Aldine.

Weinstein, G., & Alschuler, A. (1985). Educating and counseling for self-knowledge development. *Journal of Counseling and Development, 64*(1), 19–25.

Witmer, J. M., & Sweeney, T. J. (1992). A holistic model for wellness and prevention over the life span. *Journal of Counseling and Development, 71*(2), 140–148.

Wrenn, C. G. (1983). The fighting risk-taking counselor. *Personnel and Guidance Journal, 61*(6), 323–326.

chapter 2

THE PROBLEMS OF BECOMING AND BEING A COUNSELOR

Stress Management and the Prevention of Burnout

- Am I a stress seeker?
- How long will I be able to help others effectively if I don't take care of myself?
- Why should I worry about stress management now?
- Could the techniques I use to manage my own stress also be useful with my clients?

Job stress has been called "the twentieth-century disease" by the International Labor Organization (Briscoe, 1993), and it often can lead to a phenomenon called burnout. People working in the helping professions have been found to be particularly prone to the debilitating effects of stress in the workplace, and we now know that stress affects students as well, even in the elementary schools. In this chapter, we will describe the dynamics related to stress and burnout and describe ways you can manage stress and prevent burnout immediately as a student and in the future as a working professional.

STRESS AND BURNOUT DEFINED

Stress and burnout are not new. Stress has always been with us, and the term *burnout* can refer to what was once called a nervous breakdown. A major problem in understanding the dynamics of stress and burnout has been the failure to arrive at commonly accepted definitions (Moracco & McFadden, 1982). To add to the confusion, the terms are often used interchangeably; therefore, a clarification of terms is necessary from the outset.

Stress is the "experiencing of external environmental or internal environmental impingements (stimuli) or stressors" (Kutash, Schlessinger, & Associates, 1980, p. 9). A stressor is a stress-producing factor, the source of which can be either internal or external (Selye, 1980). **Burnout** is the depletion of physical and mental resources characterized by a loss of motivation, enthusiasm, energy, and interest, as well as a significantly lower level of performance (Kyriacou & Sutcliff, 1978).

Stress is not something to avoid; in fact, it is impossible to do so. Complete freedom from stress is death (Selye, 1980). Selye distinguishes between two basic types of stress: **eustress,** which is pleasant, curative, and often motivational, and **distress,** which is unpleasant or disease-producing stress (Selye, 1980, p. 128). Some people are stress seekers, searching for and participating in activities in which there may be a lot of stress involved, such as bungee jumping, hang gliding, skydiving, downhill skiing, motorcycle racing, and even sedentary competitive activities such as playing high stakes poker or duplicate bridge. People entering the field of counseling may be stress seekers, because most could probably be gainfully employed in less stressful, and higher paying occupations.

What may be distress to one person may be eustress to another. How a person responds to stress depends on a number of factors: the environment, the magnitude of the stressor, what has occurred in the past, the person's perception of the situation and self-perceived ability to handle the stressor, the person's physical condition, and the person's previous pattern in dealing with the stressor (Benjamin, 1987).

Selye also adds two other characteristics to the description of stress. These are overstress (**hyperstress**), when one has extended the limits of adaptability, and understress (**hypostress**), when one suffers from a lack of self-realization, such as physical immobility, boredom, or sensory deprivation (Selye, 1980, p. 141). Burnout can be described as experiencing the conditions of hypostress.

Figure 2.1 illustrates the relationship between the various aspects of stress and burnout. A fairly high level of eustress, for example, leads to a high rate of productivity in most cases. However, too much stress (hyperstress) can be counterproductive. Distress can result, followed in some cases by hypostress and burnout.

Stress can be either self-imposed or situational. Some people impose stress on themselves by setting unreasonably high standards or having unrealistic expectations regarding their abilities. Situational stress is often caused by time constraints, lack of resources, threats to emotional or physical well-being, interpersonal value conflicts, and overwhelming challenges.

Type A and Type B Personalities

Not only are there different types of stress but stressors affect people in different ways. Meyer Friedman and Ray Rosenman (1974) discovered a connection between certain personality traits and coronary thrombosis. They described persons who exhibit a high degree of such traits as self-control, impatience, time urgency, aggressiveness, tenseness, inability to relax, achievement orientation, and insecure status as **Type A personalities.** Type A personalities also appear more prone to stress related illnesses than do Type B personalities. **Type B Personalities** can relax without feeling guilty, move and talk more slowly, and are able to have fun and to play without having to win at any cost (Rice, 1987).

Type C Behavior

Not all Type A personalities, however, are suffering as a result of their character traits. Further analysis of individuals with Type A behavior resulted in the finding that many of these

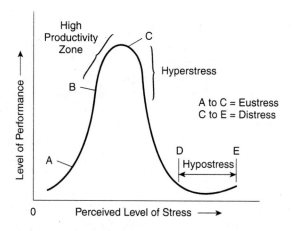

FIGURE 2.1 **The relationship between perceived level of stress and performance.**

Adapted from "How to Manage Change and Reduce Stress," by R. A. Morano, November, 1977, *Management Review*, p. 23. Reprinted by permission of the publisher, Copyright © 1977, American Management Association, New York, http://www.amanet.org. All rights reserved.

people appear to thrive on the stress they experience, manifesting none of the debilitating results experienced by others designated as Type A. In investigating this phenomenon with people from a variety of occupations, Maddi and Kobasa (1984) discovered what they call the **hardiness factor.** A distress-resistant pattern was identified, consisting of challenge, commitment, and control. Hardy individuals view stress as a challenge rather than a threat; they are strongly committed to their work, their families, and their beliefs. They believe they are able to control or influence events and their reactions to events rather than feel helpless.

A study of athletes, musicians, speakers, and other people who were able to attain peak performances while under great pressure yielded similar results (Kriegel & Kriegel, 1984). This study also identified three basic attitudes, each beginning with the letter C: challenge, control, and confidence. When the results of these two studies are combined, a picture emerges of the disease-resistant **Type C personality,** the person who seems to thrive on stress. This individual views stress as a challenge rather than as a threat, exudes confidence rather than self-doubt, has a strong sense of commitment rather than of detachment and alienation, and feels in control rather than helpless (Schafer, 1987). Each of these C attitudes or perspectives can be learned and strengthened.

Ideas in action

Examine the definitions of Type A, B, and C people and decide which type best describes your personality. How will realizing this help you prepare to deal with the stressors in the counseling field?

Three Stages of Burnout

Burnout is a dynamic process characterized by three distinct stages (Daley, 1979). Stage one is the **alarm reaction stage** during which counselors mobilize their defense mechanisms. Victims of burnout fail to respond constructively to this early warning of not being able to adapt to new or continued stressors. Burnout victims often deny that there is anything wrong. They pass off initial symptoms as minor reactions to pressures and direct their energies toward overcoming perceived obstacles. Burnout victims usually place unrealistic, perfectionist demands on themselves, often setting impossible goals.

As stressors on counselors continue to persist and increase in intensity, stage two may manifest itself. Stage two is called the **resistance stage.** It is characterized by the diversion of energies away from personal growth and professional responsibilities and directly toward managing stress. Clients suffer when their counselors begin to feel helpless and powerless and cease to care. Counselors in this stage of burnout function at a low level, both professionally and at home, as their interpersonal relations begin to deteriorate.

Finally, failure to deal effectively with the first two stages may lead to the third stage, **exhaustion.** This stage is characterized by increased cynicism, inflexibility, withdrawal, illness, depression, and possibly suicide (Nicholson & Golsan, 1983).

At each stage burnout can have physical, psychological, and behavioral effects on counselors. Some physical effects include ulcers, respiratory illness, headaches, hypertension, insomnia, and cardiovascular diseases. Psychological effects include depression, general anxiety, poor self-concept, confused thinking, and paranoid symptoms. Behavioral effects include absenteeism at work, poor relations with colleagues, inability to concentrate, and impaired interpersonal communication. Burnout results from excessive levels of stress (hyperstress) and ultimately results in exhaustion (hypostress).

CAUSES OF BURNOUT IN COUNSELOR TRAINING

Burnout is often experienced by students in counselor training programs. Many students are initially overwhelmed by the many requirements, theories, and methods presented to them and quickly become discouraged. These students believe that they will never be able to master the complex skills and approaches or attain the necessary qualities to be successful counselors. They want to become competent and polished immediately, so they become impatient with themselves. In training programs, the feeling of being overwhelmed represents a failure to see professional growth and competency as a developmental process. Students need time to contemplate new ideas. They need time to begin developing their own theoretical positions. They also need to realize that professional growth is a continuing process that goes on long after their degrees and licenses are earned. Continuous experience and supervision are essential for a counselor's professional development.

Students are often inadequately prepared to cope with negative stressors. Warnath and Shelton (1976) conclude that graduate school experiences are not positive ones for significant numbers of students and that the seeds of eventual burnout are planted there. The authors attribute this to ineffective modeling by professors who talk about the core conditions of warmth, openness, and honesty as essential characteristics for counselors, but who are themselves distant, closed, and manipulative in their contacts with students. Students soon learn to play the academic game by satisfying their professors in order to earn degrees and credentials while putting off their own need gratifications.

Contending with Relationships

Students entering graduate work in the field of counseling are not always prepared for the effect that this will have on relationships with friends and family. It is common for graduate students to experience relationship crises. Counselor education programs generally provide opportunities for students to make personal changes and to evaluate their own growth and development. Introspection is not only accepted but encouraged. This is a luxury that is generally lacking in everyday life. People rarely take the time to look at the process of their lives, because they are too busy getting things done. This opportunity for individual focus can become an integrative element in students' intrapsychic lives, affecting their interpersonal relations.

Students often report feeling confused and unsure as they examine themselves. Things that were previously taken for granted are now analyzed. As students begin to undergo growth and change, their relationships also begin to change. This process produces a great deal of pressure which, if not handled appropriately, can lead to overstress, distress, and burnout.

Students who are working to make the skills of counseling a part of their way of life may make some changes in their thinking or behavior patterns that are not acceptable to their families and friends.

Families and friends may respond in ways that cause the students to revert to former behavioral patterns. Students may experience stressful conflicts based on the possible incompatibility of their goals: striving for personal growth while trying to please significant others.

The pressures and conflicts that arise in a family as a result of one member pursuing an education are not exclusive to counseling students. This phenomenon occurs in other educational settings as well, particularly when one spouse is growing educationally and the other is not. It is important to keep family members fully aware of the nature of the work and the expectations of the counselor training program. Bringing family members to the campus library to study can be helpful in reducing some of the mystery related to studies. It also may be possible to invite one or more family members to attend a class session or two in order to meet your instructors and your classmates.

Other Outside Pressures

Embarking on a course of graduate study is a major life transition that affects almost all aspects of a student's life. Many students must have a job while attending school. The responsibilities of work, study, and family can become difficult to balance because of limited time. Students may find it difficult to establish priorities, and this may strain relationships, especially friendships. Pressures may develop to the point at which students may feel the need to cut back on their work commitments, often causing a financial strain. Sometimes power and control issues with significant others rise to the surface. Close relationships may dissolve when the people involved fail to adapt to the changes.

Family relations and friendships can also be strengthened if those involved are flexible and secure enough to adjust to the changes. Individuals who have established solid personal identities and have achieved intimate relationships are able to allow others to grow and mature without barriers or restrictions.

Ideas in action

How do you plan to keep your friends and family informed about your involvement in a counselor education program? Brainstorm a list of ways you can keep the lines of communication open.

CAUSES OF COUNSELOR BURNOUT

Striving for perfection is one cause of burnout for both the counselor-in-training and the counselor-in-service. Many counselors place unrealistic demands on themselves, interfering with their personal needs. This leads to a vicious cycle of frustration: the more that one accomplishes, then the more that remains to be accomplished. The problem is compounded when demands are not clearly defined. Sometimes the goals are unattainable, and the perfectionist counselor who equates self-worth with accomplishment is in trouble. As with academic striving, counselors must differentiate between self-defeating perfectionism and the healthy pursuit of excellence.

Work and Play

The busman's holiday syndrome (when a bus driver takes a bus trip on a vacation) is a danger in any occupation. In the counseling field, the counselor's personal and professional life merge. This causes a mind-set in which there may seem to be no opportunity to be casual or to be one's own person. Everything in a counselor's existence does not need to be scrutinized from a psychological perspective. Family and friends should be counseled by someone else. Counseling should not be the only topic of discussion in relationships. Counselors need to work to live, not live to work. When play becomes work rather than work becoming play, that is a danger signal.

Even if work is not perceived as play, if it is not what a person really wants to do and feels committed to do, the person will be more vulnerable to distress. Counselors benefit from regular examination of their work and career goals and their current satisfaction with what they are doing. When people are doing what they really want to do, they are in charge of their own lives and are less likely to become burned out regardless of the pressures involved.

Counselor–Client Interaction

Being totally immersed in the therapeutic interaction with a client can be very demanding. The content which the client may present can range from being highly emotional and possibly even dangerous, to being confusing or boring. The authors do not recommend that counselors withdraw from their clients by falling asleep when the presented material is on a superficial level, as Fritz Perls is reported to have done. Yet, as Watkins (1983) states,

> The counselor, during counseling sessions, may experience periods of phasing out with greater intensity and frequency, and the therapeutic hour can come to be regarded as just another opportunity for encounter with another human being. An ever hardening and pervasive attitude of indifference tends to develop and can have sabotaging effects on the counselor's work. (p. 208)

Phasing out, or losing contact with a client, may be due to other factors such as a defensive reaction to a client's issues with which the counselor has personal troubles. Some clients may eventually become discouraged and vent their anger toward their counselors. When this happens, counselors may develop an increased hostility toward clients and demonstrate this by veiled sarcasm or extreme silence.

Counselors must learn to pace themselves during counseling sessions and to withdraw momentarily to accumulate new energy when necessary. Counselors can resort to timely self-disclosure when appropriate. They must also seek supervision to determine whether their distortions, personal issues, and other countertransference behaviors may be impeding their counseling relationships.

Counseling is not a career in which counselors can successfully wear one hat in the counseling room and another outside; inevitably this can lead to conflict and distress. Counselors need to be concrete and genuine. Although clients may be troubled, they often are good crap detectors and can sense when the counselor is simply playing a role.

Another potential problem area exists when counselors assume responsibility for their clients and for the solution of their clients' problems. Some counselors may feel responsible for clients' lives. Not only is this behavior unhealthy and nontherapeutic, but it also places a tremendous amount of pressure on counselors. The more we attempt to become responsible for other people, the more we cheat them out of their own selfhood and foster the possibility of dependency relationships. In effect, we fail to show respect for our clients' abilities to change and grow. Perls (1969) advised counselors never to do for clients what clients are capable of doing for themselves. The help provided in such cases is, in actuality, not helpful to clients or to counselors.

Counselors also need to be aware that seeing a steady stream of troubled people over long periods of time can lead to a skewed picture of the world. It is possible to see the whole world as suffering from immense and hopeless problems from which there appears to be no escape.

Counselors in Agencies and Institutions

Counselors who work for agencies and institutions often face additional pressures. Sometimes there is no positive reinforcement on the job. Most people like to receive some recognition for work well done, but in the hectic everyday world, positive recognition is not often given. This can have a devastating effect on staff, especially when a self-support system is lacking. As counselors become more and more frustrated, they increasingly look for a reward system outside of counseling. Complicating the reward system is the difficulty of tangibly measuring success with clients.

Financial rewards are not usually adequate for counselors, and in times of budgetary crises, jobs may be in jeopardy. Agency pressures to be more efficient and take on greater case loads are often at the expense of the agency clientele. Whenever possible, counselors should work to identify and change agency policies that promote burnout (Witmer & Young, 1996).

Sometimes graduate students develop unrealistic expectations regarding the future. For example, many school counselors become disappointed when they find themselves arranging bus and class schedules and assuming other management functions. In schools, a large ratio of students per counselor leaves little time for personal counseling. Agency counselors can also find themselves doing meaningless work and, as a result, may experience diminished job satisfaction.

Many counselors work with difficult clients who would prefer not to participate in counseling. These counselors become discouraged when they see little progress being made. Counselors may experience conflict, tension, and lack of support among co-workers as well as lack of trust between counselors and supervisors. Experimentation, change, and innovation can be discouraged in an institutional bureaucracy. Sometimes no opportunities for professional renewal, such as in-service workshops and continuing education, are available.

Counselors are especially vulnerable when attempting to fulfill their parental role through their profession. Virginia Satir, the noted family therapist, reported feeling as if her whole body were covered with breasts when she entered the profession. Counselors need to free their souls and take care of themselves while giving as much as they can give. Maslach refers to this as "balance." The key to preventing burnout, according to Maslach, is to maintain a balance between giving and getting, stress and calm, work and home (1982, p. 42).

Ideas in action   Before reading further, make either mental or written notes describing how you presently prevent or reduce distress.

Are there also times when you find yourself seeking eustress (e.g., going skydiving or white-water rafting)?

STRESS MANAGEMENT

As discussed in chapter 1, the counselor needs a great amount of personal energy to perform effectively. The initial reservoirs of energy can be quickly depleted and then not renewed. From the onset of a career in counseling, the counselor-in-training needs a systematic approach to the renewal of personal energy. Initial stores of energy and positive motivating stressors help provide the eustress necessary for high level productivity. As suggested earlier, counselors may deliberately seek additional personal stressors for motivational purposes and to energize themselves. Stress management techniques are systematically used to provide the rest and relaxation the body and mind need and to provide the renewal of personal energy necessary for continued high level work.

Fortunately, numerous approaches to stress management and the prevention of burnout are available. Counselors need to be familiar with these various ideas and methods not only for their own functioning, but also as tools for their clients. Some people can handle a great deal of stress and thrive on it, while others can cope with very little. As noted, stress in and of itself is not the culprit. The inappropriate methods used in coping with stress are factors that lead to burnout. The emphasis here is on developing positive methods for managing stress and for developing an overall approach to personal wellness.

BE NATURAL: A Stress Management Plan

In order to prevent distress and avoid burnout one should have a stress management plan. An excellent way to pursue a multifaceted objective such as the management of stress is to employ a mnemonic device such as an acronym. The acronym that we have chosen is BE NATURAL. B stands for Breathing, E for Exercise, N for Nourishment, A for Attitude, T for Time management, U for Uniqueness, R for Relaxation, A for Associations, and L for Laughter. Putting all of these components together makes a reasonable package, one that addresses many of the negative aspects of stress. An explanation of each of these components follows.

Breathing

A common physiological response to stress or anxiety is a constriction of the muscles in the upper chest and neck. Breathing can become severely restricted. This adds to the overall feeling of discomfort and further aggravates an already unpleasant condition.

When people are under stress their breathing becomes very shallow, and fresh air seldom gets to the bottom of their lungs. They can be seen to inhale, but exhalation is difficult to detect. It is as though they are willing to take things in but not let things out.

When working with people under stress, they should take some deep breaths and exhale clearly each time before starting work on any personal issues. The awareness of breathing patterns and the practice of proper breathing before, during, and after any stressful events are important when dealing with major life stressors. Effective breathing can help increase energy levels.

 **Ideas in**   As you read this, become aware of your breathing. Take a couple of deep breaths. As you continue with the chapter, note your breathing pattern. Are your breaths shallow and quick or long and deep? Note your breathing pattern that seems to be most conducive to good studying.

Exercise

Counseling is basically a sedentary experience, and counselors need physical outlets for their mental as well as physical well-being. Certain exercises and sports can be practiced throughout life by counselors, including hiking, jogging, tennis, bowling, and aerobics. Evidence shows that the body releases certain hormones during exercise that can relieve depression and increase energy. Consult with a physician to determine the best types of exercises that would last a minimum of 20 minutes, three times per week.

Ideas in   What type of exercise could you be or are you already involved in that provides for a good physical workout at least 20 minutes, three times a week? Make an exercise plan and keep written records of your workouts. Many people find it easier to stick to an exercise plan when they keep track of their workouts.

Nutrition

Proper nutrition is important. Treatment of stress is environmental, social, mental, and physical; therefore, intervention needs to be wholistic, incorporating a wide range of strategies that lead to healthy patterns of living. Just as exercise has become accepted as an integral part of our culture, proper nutrition has also become an accepted practice. More and more people are concerned with food additives, weight control, and balanced diets. The basic guidelines are to eat food daily from the four basic food groups—dairy, meat, vegetables and fruits, and cereal and grain—with an emphasis on fish and poultry over red meat. With a balanced diet, vitamin supplements are rarely needed unless a known deficiency exists.

Ideas in   Are you eating three well-balanced meals each day? Create a list of what you have eaten over the past seven days. Analyze how successfully you have incorporated the four food groups in your meals.

Attitude

Negative attitudes are contagious. Counselors who have become cynical or depressed affect the people with whom they come in contact. Nicholson and Golsan (1983) state that the negativism fostered by a sense that we are not in control of our lives is a real enemy. Often negative feelings lead to deeper problems when counselors start feeling guilty about having them. The guilt feelings compound the original negative feelings and drive the counselor further into the burnout cycle. Ironically, counselors often spend much of their time fighting the same symptoms as their clients. Counselors need to realize that they are responsible for their attitudes, and that they must learn to make growth-enhancing choices for themselves.

Ideas in   Do you feel challenged by your work and/or studies? Do you have a strong commitment to your work? Do you generally feel in control of your life? Answering yes to these three questions suggests that you are quite hardy and are able to handle potentially distressful circumstances (Kobasa, 1985).

Time Management

Counseling students and beginning counselors often take on more than they can handle. They find themselves in over their heads. Counselors must be more selective in choosing their activities and even their clients. A very discouraging situation for counselors is to end up with full loads of clients at very low levels of functioning. If clients can be selected on the basis of probability of success, high-risk clients can be balanced by low-risk ones, thereby reducing the potential for burnout. Counselors can also help themselves by selecting clients who fit their particular skills or areas of interest. Having areas of specialization enables counselors to focus on those areas without the additional pressures of being knowledgeable on all aspects of counseling.

Counselors also need to set priorities and to delegate lower priority duties when possible. Sometimes exchanging jobs with other counselors provides for some variety and increased interest. Counselors who are burdened with interfering noncounseling activities must take the offensive with their administration. Perhaps they must redefine their jobs and suggest alternatives so that they can be free to do more counseling. Assertiveness training skills such as learning to say "no" can be invaluable when employer demands are unreasonable or unrealistic.

In order for counseling students to apply themselves fully to their studies they must be aware of the necessity to set priorities. These priorities may affect friends, family, and even their work if they are employed. The affected people should be made aware of the student's priority decisions directly and not have to discover these indirectly or by accident. Directness on the part of the student is the most beneficial approach for all concerned.

An important consideration is for counselors to have ample free time to develop activities and interests outside of work. The scheduling of enjoyable nonwork activities can enrich the counselor's life professionally and personally. Hobbies, travel, nonprofessional reading, and play allow for personal renewal. As counselors experience their own lives fully, they become more effective as counselors. Good health demands balance in all areas of living. Overinvolvement with work can strain family relationships. Overinvolvement with family prevents family members from becoming individuals. Overinvolvement with self is narcissistic. In all cases self-growth is retarded.

One particularly good use of private time is to set aside specific time for worrying. It is unrealistic to expect people not to worry, and there are occasions when worry is helpful. Worrying can, however, be overly time-consuming and induce distress. What some counselors and others have found to be helpful is to reserve time for worrying just as one reserves time for exercise and relaxation (e.g., Wednesday evening from 7 to 8 o'clock). Any worries throughout the rest of the week can be assigned to that time period.

Ideas in action   What are some activities that you really have wanted to do but have not gotten around to doing? Rank them and find a place for the most important activities in your daily or weekly schedule. For example, can you wake up 30 minutes earlier each day in order to meditate, exercise, or enter items into your journal?

Uniqueness

It is vital that you recognize and treasure your uniqueness—that which makes you different from everyone else. Examine how much of your life is influenced by others, how often you accept the problems of others as yours, and how willing you are to speak up and act on your own convictions even though they may be different from those of your colleagues. Individuals who are predominantly outer directed rather than inner directed are more likely to experience debilitating stress. They are always trying unsuccessfully to please others.

Counselors need to ask themselves "whose problem is it?" and keep the problem with the client when it is appropriate to do so. Counselors should strive to ensure that their clients take responsibility for the solution of their own problems, rather than the counselors assuming that responsibility. Not only could such behavior lead to possible dependency relationships, but it would quickly overwhelm counselors to have to take home all of the clients' problems every night.

   **Ideas in action**   Make a list of responsibilities you fulfill that really belong to someone else. Are you ready to give these up so that you can better concentrate on what is of great importance to you?

Relaxation

Counselors can use private time to their advantage by engaging in various types of contemplation and meditation. The many approaches to this include yoga, transcendental meditation (TM), biofeedback, progressive relaxation, tai chi, prayer, chanting, singing, and self-attending. Some are easy, some are difficult, but the result of these techniques is physical and mental rejuvenation. People who do not use systematic relaxation techniques are often surprised to realize how energizing the techniques can be.

   **Ideas in action**   While some individuals find exercise relaxing, it is generally quite productive to also include at least one 20 minute quiet relaxation period in each day, perhaps in place of a coffee break. Try doing this over a period of several weeks. Note any changes in your overall feeling of wellness.

Associations

Counselors, especially those who work with a regular routine of crisis counseling, need to spend time with healthy people, whether colleagues, friends, or family. Healthy people do not gossip or find fault. They are nourishing and supportive. Ironically, human service organizations often neglect human concerns within their own staff. Some organizations become so bureaucratic that their clients also suffer. Sometimes a support group of colleagues who are more fully functioning can make all the difference. Colleagues who focus only on gossip and negative griping tend to become toxic. Having highly functioning friends and family members also helps to counter adverse working conditions. Counselors can choose to be with nourishing, supportive people. Intimate personal relationships make life richer. The results of national surveys indicate that individuals who claim to have five or more friends with whom they can discuss important problems are 60% more likely to say they are "very happy" (Csikszentmihalyi, 1997, p. 43).

Ideas in 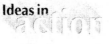   Do you have five or more people with whom you can discuss important problems? Do you have any important problems right now which you have not shared with anyone? Imagine discussing an important problem with someone. Would you feel better sharing this problem with a friend?

Laughter

An excellent source of tension relief is laughter. Wholesome, hearty laughter has been described as the music of the soul. Laughter activates chemicals in the brain called endorphins which provide a feeling of euphoria. It is extremely difficult to remain in a state of anxiety or depression when you are laughing. Humor that is self-deprecating or meant to put down other people is not appropriate. A healthy approach to stress management or the treatment of burnout requires daily doses of laughter. The act of smiling by itself can have positive effects on you (as well as on those you meet).

Ideas in   How can you arrange to have smiling and laughter be a regular part of your daily schedule? How often do you smile every day? What brings you the most laughter? The next time you laugh, examine how it makes you feel.

The BE NATURAL components, if systematically applied to the point of becoming habitual, can be invaluable in preventing excessive distress and burnout. All of these components are indeed natural and do not add any significant cost to living one's life. However, not following a program similar to this can become expensive in terms of both time and money. The various components can also be used individually to help minimize the experience of distress whenever distressing circumstances occur. Use and mastery of these concepts and skills can also be valuable in helping clients deal with their stressors.

Responsibility and Personal Therapy

Most counselors believe that we are all responsible for our behaviors. Indeed, much of what transpires in the counseling process is related to clients taking responsibility for the part they play in their problems and for changing their attitudes and behaviors as a way of coping with those problems. Counselors must also face personal responsibility for their own wellness and discover methods for maintaining it.

At the same time, counselors must avoid assuming responsibility for others. If counselors become aware of experiencing burnout symptoms and have difficulty resolving them, they may need personal therapy. Personal therapy can help counselors to develop increased understanding and insight into themselves, their clients, and their counseling behaviors. Additionally, therapy can help counselors to improve intimate interpersonal relationships which almost always suffer during burnout. Egan (1986) states,

> Ideally, [helpers] are first of all committed to their own growth—physical, intellectual, social–emotional, and spiritual—for they realize that helping often involves modeling the patterns of behavior their clients hope to achieve. They know that they can help only if, in the root sense of the term, they are "potent" human beings—that is, people with both the resources and the will to act. (p. 28)

SUMMARY

Helping counselors-in-training learn how to manage stress and prevent burnout is the theme of this chapter. The different aspects of stress have been defined and described: eustress is positive stress; distress is negative stress; hyperstress is being overstressed; and hypostress is being understressed. Because eustress can be motivating, some people (stress-seekers) may seek it out. A fair amount of stress is needed to work at a maximum productivity level. One should use a stress management plan to ensure that the stressors do not become overwhelming, lead to hyperstress, and then result in hypostress (burnout). The stages of burnout resulting from poor stress management or an abundance of negative stressors have been described.

Negative stressors that lead to burnout can occur during counselor training as a result of being overwhelmed by the material to be learned, being perfectionistic and impatient with personal progress, and experiencing relationship crises with family and friends, often as a consequence of school commitments.

Family issues can be a factor leading to burnout among practicing counselors also. Other causes include striving for perfection; setting unattainable goals; not maintaining a balance between work and play; getting overly emotionally involved with clients' problems; experiencing a lack of positive reinforcement, praise, or appreciation; and not taking care of oneself.

Basic components of a good stress management program provide for personal care, the effective management of stress, and the prevention of burnout for both counselors-in-training and practicing counselors. These components include breathing, exercise, nutrition, attitude, time management, uniqueness, relaxation, associations, and laughter (BE NATURAL). All of these components are natural, inexpensive ways to provide the nourishment, rest, and reenergizing necessary to maintain the eustress needed for high-level wellness.

A significant bonus for developing a sound personal stress management plan is that it can be used in counseling. The problems of many clients involve the ineffective management of stressors. Counselors who have been able to manage their stressors successfully will be able to serve as models for their clients and help clients develop their own stress management plans.

QUESTIONS AND ACTIVITIES

1. Are you more of a stress seeker or a stress avoider? Could it be that many people who enter the field of counselor education are stress seekers? Explore this idea with members of your class and with practicing counselors.

2. Consider the acronym BE NATURAL as one way of conceptualizing major factors that need to be considered in a stress management and burnout prevention plan. Devise your own stress management plan—one to which you will be willing to make a commitment—and come up with your own acronym to highlight the factors that are most meaningful to you. Share this plan with one or two significant others and ask them to help you monitor the plan for a given period of time.

3. How could personal counseling for a counselor or a counselor-in-training be considered an effective component of a stress management plan? Is this something that you might add to your stress management plan?

RECOMMENDED READINGS

Archer, J. (1991). *Managing anxiety and stress.* Muncie, IN: Accelerated Development.

Carlson, R. (1997). *Don't sweat the small stuff...* New York: Hyperion.

Davis, M., Robbins, E., & McKay, D. (1995). *The relaxation and stress reduction workbook* (4th ed.). Oakland, CA: New Harbinger Publications.

Travis, J., & Ryan, R. *The Wellness Workbook* (3rd ed.). Berkeley, CA: Ten Speed Press.

INTERNET RESOURCES

Websites

Wellness Web   <www.wellweb.com/preview/2pre.htm>

Virtual Meditation Center   <www.cybertowers.com/selfhelp/articles/stress/slidindx.htm>

Depression Central   <www.psycom.net/depression.central.html>

REFERENCES

Benjamin, L. (1987). Understanding and managing stress in the academic world. In ERIC Clearing House on Counseling and Personnel Services, *Highlights: An ERIC/CAPS Digest.* Ann Arbor, MI: The University of Michigan.

Briscoe, D. (1993, March 24). Job stress a global problem. *South Bend Tribune,* p. C9.

Csikszentmihalyi, M. (1997). *Finding Flow.* New York: Basic Books.

Daley, M. R. (1979). Burn out: Smoldering problem in protective services. *Social Work, 24,* 375–379.

Egan, G. (1986). *The skilled helper.* Monterey, CA: Brooks/Cole.

Friedman, M., & Rosenman, R. (1974). *Type A behavior and your heart.* Times: Knopf.

Kobasa, S. (1985). Stressful life events, personality, and health: An inquiry into hardiness. In A. Monde & R. Lazarus (Eds.), *Stress and Coping* (pp. 174–188). New York: Columbia University Press.

Kriegel, T., & Kriegel M. (1984). *The C Zone: Peak performance under pressure.* Times: Anchor/Doubleday.

Kutash, T., Schlessinger, L., & Associates. (1980). *Handbook on stress and anxiety.* San Francisco: Jossey-Bass.

Kyriacou, C., & Sutcliff, J. (1978). A model of teacher stress. *Educational Studies, 4,* 1–6.

Maslach, C. (1982). *Burnout: The cost of caring.* Englewood Cliffs, NJ: Prentice-Hall.

Moracco, J. C., & McFadden, H. (1982, May). The counselor's role in reducing teacher stress. *The Personnel and Guidance Journal, 60,* 549–552.

Morano, R. A. (1977). How to manage change or reduce stress. *Management Review, 66*(11), 21–25.

Nicholson, J., & Golsan, G. (1983). *The creative counselor.* Times: McGraw-Hill.

Perls, F. (1969). *Gestalt therapy verbatim.* Lafayette, CA: Real People Press.

Rice, P. (1987). *Stress and health: Principles and practice for coping and wellness.* Monterey, CA: Brooks/Cole.

Schafer, W. (1987). *Stress management for wellness.* New York: Holt, Rinehart & Winston.

Selye, H. (1978). On the real benefits of eustress. *Psychology Today, 2*(10), 60–64.

Selye, H. (1980). The stress concept today. In T. Kutash, L. Schlessinger, & Associates, *Handbook on stress and anxiety* (pp. 127–143). San Francisco: Jossey-Bass.

Warnath, C. F., & Shelton, J. L. (1976, December). The ultimate disappointment: The burned out counselor. *The Personnel and Guidance Journal, 55,* 172–175.

Watkins, C. E., Jr. (1983). Burnout in counseling practice: Some potential professional and personal hazards of becoming a counselor. *The Personnel and Guidance Journal, 61*(5), 304–308.

Witmer, J. M., & Young, M. E. (1996). Preventing counselor impairment: A wellness approach. *Journal of Humanist Education and Development, 34*(3), 141–153.

chapter 3

focus on

A CAREER IN THE HELPING PROFESSIONS

- Do you need to be licensed to be called a psychotherapist?
- What is the difference between counseling and psychotherapy?
- What do I have to do to be considered a professional counselor?
- Is it better to be a generalist or a specialist?
- Can counselors receive payment by insurance companies for their services?

As we continue to find out more about who the counselor is, how counselors take care of themselves, and how they become involved in the total community, we need also to look at specific details about the actual profession itself. In this chapter we will examine the nature of the different counseling job opportunities and how they relate to other human service occupations. We will also explore professional concerns such as licensure and certification and whether to become a generalist or a specialist.

THE CHANGING STRUCTURE OF THE FIELD

When considering a career in the field of counseling, it is first helpful to understand the terminology. The vocabulary of counseling has permeated our everyday life even though people are not always sure what the terms mean. **Psychotherapy** is "the systematic use of a human relationship for therapeutic purposes" (Strupp, 1993, p. 59). The American Medical Association is even more succinct: "psychotherapy is treatment by verbal means" (Kunz & Finkel, 1987, p. 303). Engler and Goteman (1992) define psychotherapy as "the general name for a variety of psychological interventions designed to help people resolve emotional, behavioral, or interpersonal problems of various kinds and improve the quality of their lives" (p. 15). Because the term is so broadly defined, it is used by a wide variety of practitioners. There is no legal or professional restriction on its use; thus, almost anyone can call oneself a psychotherapist or therapist and practice psychotherapy.

The term **counseling** is also ambiguous. The definitions offered for psychotherapy apply equally well to counseling. There have been numerous attempts to draw a precise distinction between the terms *counseling* and *psychotherapy;* the most common distinction is that counseling deals more with "normal" clients, whereas psychotherapy is used with more serious cases. For example, working with students in school would be counseling and working with patients in a mental hospital would be psychotherapy. Although the practitioner may find personal comfort in using these terms in this way, there may be little, if any, difference in the actual treatment. In either case, the process and even special techniques may be identical. Since counseling and psychotherapy are basically synonymous, we use the terms interchangeably throughout this text.

A major change in recent years in counseling degrees offered by most universities has enhanced the career opportunities for graduates. Prior to the mid-1970s, the emphasis in most counselor education programs was primarily on the training of elementary and secondary school counselors. Throughout the 1980s, counselor education programs added direct training and often specialization in such areas as community counseling and marriage and family counseling (Hollis & Wantz, 1986).

With this shift in the nature and scope of counselor education, more counselor education students are choosing fields other than school counseling. This means that virtually all agencies and institutions that provide mental health services are potential sources of employment for counselor education graduates. Also, because counselor graduates tend to have strong backgrounds in human relationships and communication skills, they are often employed by businesses in personnel, training, and development settings. This change of emphasis from a specialization in school counseling to more comprehensive training as a helping professional has been a quiet one not yet fully appreciated by professionals within the mental health field, much less by laypersons. Many people still think of a counselor as a school counselor rather than as a mental health counselor. The title *mental health counselor* was not included in the 1980 *Dictionary of Occupational Titles,* and yet in 1985 the Association of Mental Health Counselors was the largest subdivision in the American Counseling Association.

THE MENTAL HEALTH FIELD HIERARCHY

Within the mental health field is a hierarchy that is generally based on the academic degree and the length of training involved. This hierarchy is supported by government and insurance company policies. The hierarchy is headed by psychiatrists, followed by clinical psychologists, counseling psychologists, clinical social workers, and then counselors. At the bottom of the hierarchy are paraprofessionals, who have had a minimum of training and who may work at positions such as serving on a suicide prevention switchboard.

Psychiatrists are physicians who have specialized in the diagnosis and treatment of mental disorders. They qualified to use the full range of available medical techniques in treating clients, including drugs, shock therapy, and surgery. Psychiatrists differ significantly from other mental health professionals, since they are able to prescribe medication. They generally tend to emphasize treating mental disorders with medication rather than with psychotherapy. A **psychoanalyst** may be a psychiatrist, psychologist, or social worker who treats mental disorders using the ideas and approaches developed by Sigmund Freud.

Clinical and counseling psychologists usually have doctorates. All states now regulate the title *psychologist* with the general stipulation that anyone using that title has to complete a licensure process. In past years in some states, it was possible to qualify as a psychologist with a master's degree in psychology or a related field, but that is rarely the case now. Membership in the American Psychological Association (APA) is now limited to holders of doctoral degrees in psychology. The differences between a clinical and a counseling psychologist are few. Both generally require the doctorate and an APA-accredited training program with some differences in courses and internships. In practice, clinical psychologists often deal with the more serious mental and emotional disorders.

Clinical social workers are concerned about the way people's social environments affect their behavior. As a result social workers often involve community resources to help clients more than a psychologist or counselor might do. A clinical social worker has a master's degree in social work (MSW), a degree which emphasizes clinical training.

There are a number of specializations found under the broad classification of **counselors.** Generally speaking, these mental health practitioners have master's degrees in counseling and often may have particular specialties.

- **Clinical mental health counselors** typically have completed a 60 hour clinical degree program and may work with a variety of clientele depending upon their specialties.
- **Community counselors** generally have completed a 48 hour counselor education program. They too may work in a variety of settings commensurate with their training. (See Box 3.1 for further elaboration of the differences between clinical mental health counselors and community counselors.)
- **School counselors** work with prevention, development, and some remediation in school settings.
- **Substance abuse counselors** specialize in helping substance abusers learn to live without using alcohol or other drugs.
- **Rehabilitation counselors** help people with mental or other disabilities live productive lives.
- **Pastoral counselors** are clergy who have clinical training in counseling in addition to their seminary degrees.

Counselors are working to attain full recognition as professional mental health care providers. The book *Human Services in Contemporary America* (Schmolling, Youkelles, & Burger, 1997) devotes just one eight-line paragraph to counseling in its description of the contemporary human services field. Another book, *The Consumer's Guide to Psychotherapy* (Engler & Goleman, 1992), is described as "the authoritative guide for making informed choices about psychotherapy" but makes only one reference to counseling and planning services. These services are described as follows: "Often run by charitable organizations affiliated with local churches or by state and municipal departments of social services, there are counseling centers for vocational guidance, family planning, and financial advice" (p. 35). When the authors do mention the term *counselor,* they erroneously state that "the term *counselor* does not mean therapist and is not regulated by law; anyone can use it" (p. 79). In fact, counselors currently are licensed in 45 states.

If those who consider themselves to be mental health experts have difficulty recognizing and describing all those who are actively working in the field, then it should not be surprising that the general public is also confused about the similarities and differences between each profession. As an aspiring counselor this means that you will have to educate the public as you pursue your professional work.

**BOX 3.1   Differences in Training Required for Mental Health
and Community Counseling**

Council for Accreditation of Counseling and Related Educational Programs (CACREP) makes a clear distinction between the education required for certification as a mental health and as a community counselor (see Table 3.1).

In 1994, Hollis and Wantz reported that there were 82 (96%) mental health counseling programs and 127 (about 62%) community counseling programs that were not accredited. These unaccredited programs do not meet CACREP standards and often have great differences in requirements. Some com-

munity counseling programs may have as little as 32 hours required for graduation and may have little or no candidate selection criteria.

While the table suggests a difference in training emphasis between community and mental health counseling, in actuality both types of programs generally focus on diagnosis and treatment. The result is that graduates of community counseling programs, accredited or not, compete for job positions with graduates of mental health counseling programs, accredited or not.

TABLE 3.1   Programs in mental health counseling and community.

	Mental Health Counseling	Community Counseling
Clinical Requirements	1000 clock hours including practicum	700 clock hours including practicum
Graduation Requirements	60 semester hours	48 semester hours
Emphasis	Diagnostic and treatment	Preventive and developmental

Adapted from *Mental Health Counseling in the 90s,* by M. K. Altekruse and S. K. Terneus, 1997. Available: www.coe.unt.edu/cdhe/ALTKRS/Ethics.htm. Copyright 1997 by Michael Altekruse. Adapted with permission.

Altekruse, M. K., & Terneus, S. K. (1997). *Mental Health Counseling in the 90s.* Available: www.coe.unt.edu/cdhe/ALTKRS/Ethics.htm
Hollis, J., & Wantz, R. (1994). *Counselor Preparation: Status, Trends, and Implications* (Vol. 2). Muncie, IN: Accelerated Development.

CREDENTIALING

Licensure

The licensure of professionals in any field is a state prerogative. Toward the end of the 1970s, a number of states began to pass legislation that led to the licensing of counselors. Many people in other fields use the term *counselor* in titles such as insurance counselor, financial counselor, and fashion counselor. In an attempt to separate the professionally trained mental health counselor from people who use the title indiscriminately, professionals in the field have lobbied their state legislators to develop a set of criteria and procedures for licensing counselors. By 1986, 18 states had passed some form of licensure legislation. By 1998, counselors could attain professional licenses in 45 states and the District of Columbia. Counselors in the remaining 5 states (Alaska, Hawaii, Minnesota, New York, and Pennsylvania) are continuing to lobby for licensure legislation.

The different types of counselor licensing legislation cannot always be determined by the titles granted to professional counselors. Depending on the state, **licensure laws** can regulate the title and practice of an occupation. For example, some states use the title *licensed professional counselor* and protect the use of that title, but the states do not regulate practitioners or examine the practices of unregistered counselors. **Practice acts** are laws which specify the activities that licensed professionals can perform and are therefore true licensure. Generally speaking, licensure usually is practice protection, while certification protects the use of the title.

States may also have very specific legislation governing specialties such as school, alcohol and drug abuse, and marriage and family counseling.

Licensure bills are now under consideration in most of the remaining unlicensed states. Although the process is slow, eventually all states will have some form of licensure law for counselors. Counseling is achieving licensure at a rate similar to or faster than other professions, including social work. Despite this trend, the profession of counseling is still not included as a mental health discipline recognized in the Public Health Services Act, so consumers using federally funded or state-funded programs do not have access to a large group of qualified mental health providers.

Ideas in    What are the licensure laws in your state? If you are in a state that doesn't have licensure laws, are you willing to lobby for them?

Certification

Even though the prerogative to license belongs to the state, professional organizations can develop standards and procedures to certify professionals. The American Mental Health Counselors Association (AMHCA), a division of the American Counseling Association (ACA), began the national procedure in the late 1970s. ACA followed with a more global certification process.

The ACA certifies professional counselors in a number of ways. The ACA offers the Nationally Certified Counselor (NCC), which requires approved educational background and experience plus a written examination. The National Academy of Certified Clinical Mental Health Counselors offers the designation of Certified Clinical Mental Health Counselor (CCMHC) with approved training and experience, a written examination, and the submission of a counseling work sample. The Commission on Rehabilitation Counselor Certification certifies rehabilitation counselors (CRC). A counselor may also attain certification as a Nationally Certified Career Counselor (NCCC), a Nationally Certified School Counselor (NCSC), a Master Addictions Counselor (MAC), and a Nationally Certified Gerontological Counselor (NCGC). In addition, certification may be attained through meeting the requirements of other organizations such as the American Association of Marriage and Family Therapists (AAMFT).

Some of the benefits of certification are as follows:

- *Professional identity.* Certification as an NCC identifies the individual as a professionally certified counselor and as a professional within the mental health field; certification as a CCMHC, CRC, or NCGC indicates that the individual is a specialist within the counseling profession.

- *Visibility.* Certified counselors are listed in registers that are made available to mental health centers and to consumer, insurance, and medical organizations.
- *Credibility.* Certification procedures are consistent with established national guidelines and are backed by organizations with codes of ethics and procedures for handling consumer complaints.
- *Flexibility.* Certification is valuable to counselors who can take the certification across state lines if they should move.
- *Continued professional growth.* Because of **rectification** requirements (having to continue professional training to maintain the certificate), the skills of certified counselors are kept current in order to better serve the consumer (Messina, 1985; Stone, 1985).

Accreditation

The accreditation of counselor training programs by professional organizations is another trend that developed in the 1970s. In the accreditation process, professional organizations establish standards for training professionals and evaluate training institutions against the standards. Institutions that meet or exceed the standards are accredited. Students graduating from accredited institutions may receive benefits not given to graduates of unaccredited schools, may be exempt from certain certification or licensure requirements, and may be more employable.

The Association for Counselor Education and Supervision (ACES), a division of ACA, has developed an accreditation process for counselor education programs. This accreditation process is regulated by the Council for Accreditation of Counseling and Related Educational Programs (CACREP). CACREP evaluates school counseling, community counseling, and student personnel programs at the master's degree and doctorate levels in education programs. By 1997, 72 universities with 195 programs in 36 states and Canada had gone through the accreditation process and are now accredited as approved counselor education programs.

Three other organizations grant accreditation. The Council on Rehabilitation Education (CORE) accredits master's degree programs in rehabilitation counseling. The American Psychological Association (APA) accredits clinical and counseling psychology programs, and the Commission on Accreditation for Marriage and Family Therapy Education (CAMFM) accredits programs in marriage and family counseling through the AAMFT.

Since 1985, students from nonaccredited programs are required to have two years of approved experience after the completion of their degree before applying for certification as an NCC. The accreditation regulations and certification are linked, because the same organization is determining the standards and procedures for both. Certification is easier to attain for students who are graduates of an accredited program. This link has been criticized as leading to programs that are relatively static and noncreative. Others argue that it is important that accredited programs maintain and set high standards and that certified practitioners earn the recognition as professionals when they meet those high standards.

The trend of counselor licensure, counselor certification, and program accreditation persists, and the levels of qualification continue to be increasingly demanding. The general rule for a person entering the field is to apply for licensure and/or certification at the earliest possible time. Waiting even as little as one year may mean having to meet additional requirements.

Counseling Services Accreditation

The practice of certifying counseling centers and agencies dates back to 1962, but it gained momentum as the related credentialing activities developed. The International Association of Counseling Services (IACS), an affiliate of ACA, accredits community, junior, and technical college counseling centers; public and private counseling agencies; and university and college counseling centers in the United States and Canada. The basic purposes of certification efforts conducted on a voluntary basis are encouraging and assisting counseling service facilities to meet high professional standards, informing the public about competent and reliable services, and fostering communications among counseling services operating in a variety of settings (McDonough, 1985, p. 4). For counseling practitioners to be considered professionals, McDonough (1985) suggests that the day may not be far off when they will need to be members of a professional organization such as the ACA, be graduates of an accredited program, be licensed or certified, and also work in an approved counseling center or agency.

Continuing Education

As the counseling profession develops, counselors must continue to pursue their educational training. Though most master's level counselor training programs are approximately two years long, these programs cannot provide the depth of training and experience necessary for work in the many specialized areas of the field. Many students go on to pursue doctoral programs in counselor education, counseling, or clinical psychology; others pursue specialized forms of training at private, nonuniversity institutes such as one of the Gestalt Institutes, the Reality Therapy Institute, or the Adler Institute. Many of these training programs last approximately two years but accommodate the schedule of working professionals; for example, they may meet for two weeks every six months with weekend meetings in between.

Continuing education is generally a requirement for maintaining a license or certificate. Such continuing education requirements can usually be met in a variety of ways. Continuing Education units (CEUs) can be earned by attending professional workshops, seminars, conferences, and conventions. Such opportunities are offered by universities, professional organizations, community agencies, and independent entrepreneurs at times and locations generally convenient to most professionals.

Professional conventions are held locally, statewide, regionally, and nationally. Often professional development institutes and seminars are offered in conjunction with major conventions. Continuing education not only meets certification and licensure requirements but also may be tax deductible.

Reading professional journals is a common and inexpensive way to continue one's education. Such reading is an excellent way to keep up with the most current developments in the field. Books are also a vital way to keep up with the field, providing greater depth to a given topic. CEUs generally are not given for reading journal articles and books, but many employers expect helping professionals to keep up with one or more monthly journals on a regular basis (see Appendix C) and read several books a year that are related to the field.

Ideas in   As you think about becoming a counselor, are you ready to commit yourself to a lifetime of professional education and advocacy?

THE MARKET FOR COUNSELORS

Making predictions about the prospect of employment for trained counselors in either the near or distant future is risky at best. Nonetheless, every prospective counselor has concerns about employment, and these concerns need to be addressed directly.

Economic and Social Trends

Economic and social trends in our society indicate that employment opportunities are increasing for counselors. The service occupations and the information services are in demand as the U.S. economy shifts from a manufacturing economy to a service economy. John Naisbitt, in his book *Megatrends* (1984), sees professionals such as counselors, teachers, and social workers as being primarily information workers whose knowledge is crucial and "the creation, processing and distribution of information is the job" (p. 5).

In 1950, only about 17 percent of Americans were employed in information jobs. In 1984, more than 65 percent were information workers. This trend is expected to continue into the twenty-first century, according to the U.S. Department of Labor. Employment in the services sector of the U.S. economy is expected to rise 34 percent, making this sector the fastest growing of all the industry divisions. Employment of all counselors—including school, rehabilitation, and mental health counselors—is expected to grow faster than the average for all occupations through the year 2005. Job opportunities should increase significantly at the beginning of the twenty-first century as a large number of counselors reach retirement age. Counselors who might be planning to work for federal, state, and local government, however, could find employment opportunities limited by budget constraints (U.S. Department of Labor, 1996).

A second major social trend that may account for some of the increased need for counseling services is the changing nature of the family. Only a small proportion of the U.S. population experience their extended family living together or in close proximity. Increasing numbers of individuals are living alone. A related trend is the ever-increasing number of single-parent families. This trend toward more isolation and alienation is a factor that often results in a need for increased services of counselors and other helping professionals.

The range of human services now offered by business and industry constitutes a third major trend. Business and industry have made a strong commitment to human resource development, learning in large part from the successful example of the Japanese. Most changes involve greater employee involvement in decision making as well as in other aspects of corporate life. Helping both employers and employees to function effectively in the work environment is a task handled capably by counselors who have specialized in human relations development and organizational development. The importance of this trend, however, may be diminishing as many corporations downsize to maximize profits.

Other major trends causing growth in the field of counseling are an increased emphasis on mental health in conjunction with the treatment of physical illness, increased testing and counseling of children, the large turnover of counselors in group homes, the increased demand for services for elderly populations, and more community-based programs for the chronically mentally ill, mentally impaired, and developmentally disabled (U.S. Department of Labor, 1992).

Business and Industry

In the past, counseling graduates have been employed in business and industry in personnel departments, engaged primarily in hiring and firing employees and solving labor disputes. The scope of such departments has changed. Now, personnel or human resource departments may offer career development services, employee assistance programs, team-building workshops, leadership for quality circles, and direction for total quality management programs. The targets of these services are not only the assembly line employees, but all employees, starting with the company president.

Borrowing a term from the counseling field, Naisbitt (1984) describes "the new [business] leader as a facilitator, not an order giver" (p. 209). The overall philosophy now is "if you can develop the skills of facilitating people's involvement in decision-making processes, you can become a very effective leader in your community and in your work" (p. 209). Another concern is with the quality of work life. Many companies employ trained personnel, often with master's degrees in counseling, to develop employee leadership and participatory skills as well as organizational structure.

In conclusion, the world of business and industry has become more open to the knowledge, skills, and abilities of professionally trained counselors.

Community Opportunities

In each community, there are many potential employers of counselors. Most human service agencies, whether public or private, are prospective employers. Such agencies include publicly supported mental health centers, counseling centers supported by religious institutions, vocational rehabilitation and employment counseling agencies, hospitals, youth service bureaus, hospice organizations, correctional institutions, mental health societies, Planned Parenthood, the American Cancer Society, and welfare departments.

In most areas, the local mental health center is one of the largest potential employers. Community mental health centers were developed in the early and mid-1960s and were supported in large part by the federal government. When federal funding was reduced in the late 1970s, these agencies had to become aggressive in developing programs that would be self-sustaining. Health service providers had to be able to qualify for insurance payments. Because mental health counselors have only been able to qualify for such coverage since the late 1980s, the market for master's level counselors has been small.

The opportunities for employment in other community social service agencies depend on a number of factors. First, governmental regulations may control the employment of counselors (e.g., certain positions in nursing homes may be filled only by candidates with an MSW). Second, because of insurance company limitations, some agencies will employ only professionals who can be reimbursed directly by third parties. Third, the mental health worker hierarchical order influences employment. For example, psychologists will often try to employ only psychologists, and social workers will hire only other social workers. The professionally trained counselor does have to develop a great deal of credibility when relating to other professionals. These barriers, however, are increasingly disappearing. Initially, professional acceptance happens in the areas in which professional counselors receive their education, and their work becomes known. Also, as counselor licensure and national counselor certification are instituted, the professional acceptance process will be accelerated.

Private Practice

Some students enter the counseling field with the intent of going into private practice. Counselors in schools and agencies may develop part-time private practices separately from their full-time positions. In many cases, such practices may earn sufficient income to become full-time work. Developing and maintaining a private practice is not easy. In addition to attaining a high level of counseling skill, and appropriate certification and licensure, counselors entering private practice require managerial talent, financial acumen, and marketing ability.

Private practitioners need to contact physicians, attorneys, schools, and agencies for sources of referrals. They also need to pay for liability insurance, find a good location for an office, advertise, and find other ways to become known in the community. This would include doing volunteer work, joining service organizations, and speaking before school and other community groups.

Counselors in private practice may find themselves spending as much time managing the business as they are practicing counseling. Marketing skills have become so essential for the private practitioner that many counselors hire marketing consultants to develop and maintain the practice.

Partnerships are often established to help share the financial risks and the managerial duties. Also, since typical master's degree programs in counseling do not provide the specialized training in all the areas necessary to establish a private practice, partnerships can make available practitioners with different specialized interests and training.

Many beginning private practitioners seek new mentors to replace their university instructors. Some enter supervision groups established by experienced practitioners in order to receive assistance in processing cases and dealing with countertransference issues. Some join professional support groups in order to share common values and interests. Others enter training groups, or they attend institutes such as the Institute for Rational Emotive Therapy, and the Gestalt Institute in order to become experts in particular approaches. Many work to revise and evolve their own theoretical models of practice by receiving counseling for themselves on a periodic basis; studying videotapes, audiotapes, or transcripts of counselors they admire; reading; attending workshops, seminars, and professional meetings; and experiencing a variety of different clients.

Ideas in action   Consider the career possibilities available to a prospective counselor. Which seem the most appealing to you at this point?

PROFESSIONALISM

What Does It Mean to Be a Professional Counselor?

The field of counseling is a professional occupation. Sociologically speaking, a profession has six basic features (Ohlsen, 1983):

1. *A profession determines its own preparation and training standards.* This is being done in the field of counseling through ACA accreditation procedures.
2. *A profession is recognized legally via licensure and certification using criteria defined by the members of the group.* The various national certification and state licensure efforts are examples of developments toward this objective.
3. *A unique role for the profession in general and for each specialty within the profession must be determined by the members of the group.* ACA and the members of its various divisions have worked to develop these unique role definitions. This is also being done through the licensure process.
4. *A profession has its own professional ethics.* Ethical standards for the professional conduct of counselors have been developed and widely disseminated. ACA has a well-developed, concise code of ethics initially established in 1961 (see Appendix B). Divisions of ACA such as the Association of Specialists in Group Work (ASGW) have formulated supplemental codes of ethics in areas of specialization.
5. *A profession has procedures for disciplining members who behave unethically.* The ethical guidelines of the ACA provide procedures for the recognition and the disciplining of practitioners who violate approved ethical principles.
6. *Generally, a profession is considered a terminal occupation, where a practitioner may be gainfully and productively employed throughout his or her career.* Career patterns of school and mental health counselors support this criterion.

Becoming a Professional Counselor

Since counseling is a profession, how does one become a professional counselor? Becoming a professional counselor is an involved, enriching process. It includes developing a high level of competence in six major areas:

1. An overall understanding of the scope of the field, its historical heritage, its purpose, and its organizational structure.
2. Extensive knowledge of relevant subject matter.
3. A diversity of supervised clinical field experiences.
4. Knowledge and understanding of ethical codes and principles.
5. Developing an attitude of professionalism.
6. Active participation in the profession, through organizational work, lobbying, research, and writing.

This book provides a strong foundation in areas 1, 2, 4, and 5. Participation in an entire counselor education program should result in developing a high degree of mastery in all six areas.

Professional Attitude (PA)

To make a commitment to the counseling field and to make the role of counselor your way of life, note that more than knowledge and skill are involved. An additional factor is necessary: a **professional attitude (PA).** Professional attitude in counseling begins with making the commitment to become a counselor. PA includes learning the content and processes of counseling as part of your being rather than as something to be forgotten after examinations. It also means making a commitment to continued growth both personally and professionally. This means regularly looking for new ideas and skills so that you can do your work better, rather than going to a seminar because you need more continuing education units (CEUs) to maintain your National Counselor Certificate (NCC). PA means accepting and following the professional code of ethics even when it is difficult, such as when reporting a colleague for a violation. In addition, PA means doing the research necessary to find ways to deal with challenging clients and to make appropriate referrals when you are not qualified to handle a given case. PA includes working to improve your profession by participating in professional organizations; attending conventions; holding office; making presentations to peers; and sharing your experience, research, and ideas by writing articles or making presentations at conferences, conventions, and workshops. Also, PA means keeping up with the literature in your field—books, journal articles, newsletters, and material in the general media. PA means being willing to devote time, energy, and money for issues that are in the best interests of the profession, ranging from signing a petition and writing letters to legislators to organizing a drive to support counselor licensure legislation in your state.

The professional counselor has a duty to promote the field and to help overcome biases and misinformation about mental health and counseling. This duty can be accomplished by giving talks, presentations, and workshops or seminars to lay groups such as the PTA, Rotary Club, and church groups. In the final analysis, professional attitude requires the fostering of your own personal growth within the field, as well as supporting and encouraging the growth of the counseling field itself.

Ideas in action   What's your professional attitude (PA)? How willing are you to develop the PA that is necessary to become a true professional in the field?

When Does Professional Life Begin?

Since counseling should be a way of life, total involvement in the field begins with the first course of a counselor education program. The better the student understands the nature of the work of a counselor, including the expectations and demands of the field, then the more likely a sound personal choice will be made when the student chooses to commit to the field. To decide not to pursue a counseling career because it does not fit your expectations is much wiser than to complete a degree and be unhappy in the work. Being unfulfilled or unhappy in your work may still occur, but if you were initially happy with the field of counseling, subsequent problems may be remediated (see chapter 2). From the very first course, you need to develop your knowledge and skills, your ethical awareness, and your PA.

As for involvement in professional organizations, student memberships are available for virtually all appropriate organizations. Membership in a professional organization generally includes at least one journal subscription and a newsletter. All professional conventions have special student registration fees and usually have a number of activities geared directly to the graduate student. Students are usually invited to all regular sessions and business meetings. Generally, students have opportunities to make presentations either individually or in collaboration with other students or with professors. Many journals and newsletters publish student contributions. Workshops, seminars, institutes, and conferences, with few exceptions, are also open to students, usually at reduced rates.

Professional Organizations

The largest professional organization for counselors in the United States is the American Counseling Association (ACA). This organization, with roots in the vocational guidance movement of the early part of the twentieth century, was created in 1952 as the American Personnel and Guidance Association (APGA), was changed to the American Association for Counseling and Development (AACD) in 1983, and was renamed the ACA in 1992.

In 1997, the organization had more than 52,000 members and 17 divisions representing the broad spectrum of the field. The ACA publishes the *Journal for Counseling and Development,* a bimonthly journal, and *Counseling Today,* a monthly newspaper. Most divisions also publish journals and newsletters related to their areas of specialization (see Table 3.2). The organization has developed a general code of ethics for the field (see Appendix B) as well as specialized codes of ethics (e.g., for group workers). The ACA has accreditation and certification procedures, as described earlier in this chapter.

The ACA lobbies Congress and state legislatures on issues related to the field of counseling. In addition to holding annual conventions, it sponsors training programs and publishes and distributes books, movies, audiocassettes and videocassettes, and other educational materials. The ACA also offers placement services for members through its newsletter and at the annual convention. The regional and state organizations also hold meetings and sponsor workshops on a regular basis. A counselor can be a member of a division or a state organization without being a member of ACA. There are student rates for membership. State and regional branches of the ACA have a wide variety of professional activities and are also open to student membership.

The ACA has a strong presence on the Web. Virtually all aspects of the organization can be accessed by the URLs provided at the end of this chapter. Surfing these sites is one good way to keep up-to-date with happenings in the field of counseling.

Another major professional organization is the American Psychological Association (APA). Its membership is restricted to psychologists, but much of its work finds its way into the counseling literature. The APA has 40 divisions that publish journals, several of which are of direct interest to counselors. Other professional organizations include the American Association of Marriage and Family Therapists (AAMFT), the American Society for Training and Development (ASTD), and the National Association of Social Workers (NASW).

TABLE 3.2   Divisions of the American Counseling Association (ACA).

Divisions	Publications
1 American College Counseling Association (ACCA)	*VISIONS*
2 Association for Counselor Education and Supervision (ACES)	*Counselor Education and Supervision* *ACES Newsletter*
3 National Career Development Association (NCDA)	*The Career Development Quarterly* *NCDA Newsletter*
4 Association for Humanistic Education and Development (AHEAD)	*Infochange Newsletter*
5 American School Counselor Association (ASCA)	*The School Counselor* *Elementary School Guidance and Counseling* *ASCA Newsletter*
6 American Rehabilitation Counseling Association (ARCA)	*Rehabilitation Counseling Bulletin* *ARCA Newsletter*
7 Association for Assessment in Counseling (AAC)	*Measurement and Evaluation in Counseling and Development* *AAS Newsnotes*
8 National Employment Counselors Association (NECA)	*Journal of Employment Counseling* *NECA Newsletter*
9 Association for Multicultural Counseling and Development (AMCD)	*Journal for Multicultural Counseling and Development* *AMCD Newsletter*
10 Association for Spiritual, Ethical, Religious, and Value Issues in Counseling (ASERVIC)	*Counseling and Values* *ASERVIC Newsletter*
11 Association for Specialists in Group Work (ASGW)	*Journal for Specialists in Group Work* *ASGW Newsletter*
12 International Association of Addictions and Offender Counselors (IAAOC)	*Journal of Addictions and Offender Counseling* *IAAOC Report/Newsletter*
13 American Mental Health Counselors Association (AMHCA)	*AMHCA Journal* *AMHCA News*
14 Association for Counselors and Educators in Government (ACEG)	*ACEG Newsletter*
15 Association for Adult Development and Aging (AADA)	*Journal of Adult Development and Aging: Practice* *Journal of Adult Development and Aging: Theory and Research* *AADA Newsletter*
16 International Association of Marriage and Family Counselors (IAMFC)	*Journal of Marriage and Family Counseling* *IAMFC Newsletter*
17 Association for Gay, Lesbian, and Bisexual Issues in Counseling (AGLBIC)	*AGLBIC Newsletter*

Adapted from *ACA Resource Catalog* (pp. 58–59), 1997, Alexandria, VA: American Counseling Association.

WHAT TYPE OF CAREER CHOICE SHOULD A PROSPECTIVE COUNSELOR MAKE?

Becoming a counselor involves making many choices. There are any number of directions that a person can deliberately choose to take, and unexpected opportunities open up as a person progresses along the career path. An early decision may be whether to become a generalist or a specialist. Then, if you were to specialize, what area(s) would you select?

Generalist or Specialist

Even though master's level counselor training programs are now designed primarily for training generalists in the field, some experts question how viable it is to be a generalist. With the field as broad and diverse as it is, and with the relentless increase of knowledge and technology, developing skills and effectiveness in all areas of the counseling field is impossible; however, being too highly specialized can be restrictive. For example, being highly trained only in sex counseling could limit employment opportunities. Some career choices occur by chance and some by design. Even though chance may influence your career choices, one should have some plans on which to focus attention and energy. Kottler and Brown (1985) suggest pursuing a **flexible specialty.** This means focusing on one or perhaps two specialty areas within the field, while continuing to become aware of other aspects of the total field. Some major specialty areas, along with occupations within each, are shown in Figure 3.1.

Note that within most areas listed are opportunities for preventive, developmental, and remedial work. These specialty areas are in addition to developing skills in given theoretical approaches, such as cognitive–behavioral therapy, or the attainment of expertise in some special treatment modality such as music therapy.

GUIDELINES FOR SELECTING A COUNSELING SPECIALTY

1. *Assess personal strengths and weaknesses.* As part of the process of developing self-knowledge described in chapter 1, consider how areas of personal strength and weakness relate to certain types of work settings and types of clients. For example, having feelings of discomfort when being around handicapped people might preclude working as a rehabilitation counselor. Interests also need to be considered at the same time. A person may be able to relate very well to children but have no interest in working with them professionally, preferring instead to work with adults. The more open and honest you are in this self-assessment, the less likely you are to make a disappointing career decision. Solicit feedback from instructors, peers, and other people who know you well. Do not argue with feedback that you have requested; listen, and check it out. If it fits, acknowledge it; if it does not fit, simply thank the person who provided the information.

2. *Clarify values related to work and lifestyle.* Examining your values early in the training process could prevent your making decisions that could be quite uncomfortable and frustrating in a few years. For example, if you value a lifestyle that requires a lot of money to maintain, you may rule out most agency work.

FIGURE 3.1   Counseling specializations and their occupations.

Adolescent Development and Counseling

Adolescent Counseling in Mental Health Agencies
Middle/High School Counseling
Psychological Education
Student Assistance Program Professional
Youth Probation Officer
Youth Work in a Residential Facility

The Aged

Gerontological Counseling
Hospice Work
Nursing Home Counseling
Preretirement Counseling

Business and Industry

Affirmative Action/Equal Opportunity Specialist
Employee Assistance Programs
Employee Career Development Personnel
Quality of Work Life/Quality Circles
Training and Development Personnel

Careers/Lifestyle

Career Development
Employment Counseling
Leisure Counseling
Occupational Therapy
Vocational Rehabilitation

Child Development and Counseling

Child Counseling in Mental Health Agencies
Counseling with Battered and Abused Children
   and Their Families
Early Childhood Education
Elementary School Counseling
Parent Education
Preschool Counseling

College and University

College Student Counseling
Counselor Educator
Resident Hall Counselor

Student Activities
Student Personnel Work

Community

Crisis Intervention Counseling
Feminist Counseling
Grief Counseling
Mental Health Counselor
Phobia Counseling/Agoraphobia
Post-traumatic Stress Disorder Counseling
Sports Counseling

Consultation

Agency and Corporate Consulting
Industrial Psychology
Organizational Development
Training

Drugs

Adult Children of Alcoholics Counseling
Alcohol Counseling
Drug Counseling
Stop Smoking Programs
Substance Abuse Counseling

Health

AIDS Counseling
Anorexia/Bulimia Counseling
Genetic Counseling
Nurse Counselor
Nutritional Counseling
Rehabilitation Counseling
Sex Education
Sexual Dysfunction Counseling
Stress Management Counseling
Wholistic Health Counseling

Marital/Relationship Counseling

Divorce Mediation
Family Counseling
Marriage Relationship Counseling
Premarital Counseling

Adapted from *Introduction to Therapeutic Counseling* by J. A. Kottler. Copyright © 1992, 1985 Brooks/Cole Publishing Company, Pacific Grove, CA 93950, a division of International Thomson Publishing Inc. By permission of the publisher.

3. *Visit as many different specialty settings as possible.* Reading about different types of specialization is helpful, but it can never give the full impact of the nature of the occupation that a person can receive by spending time in various settings, observing, asking questions, and testing the reality of the occupation.

4. *Interview as many counselors in the field as possible.* In each setting, one should interview each of the different types of counselors represented there. In a mental health center, for example, different types of counselors work in a variety of ways with different populations. One strategy that can be helpful is to arrange to shadow a counselor during a routine work day, sitting in on activities from the beginning of the day until the counselor heads home.

5. *Maximize practicum and internship experiences.* When given the opportunity to choose practicum and internship sites, select sites that will give you a variety of diversified experiences and opportunities. Select a totally different site for an internship than you had for a practicum. For example, if you worked in a university counseling center for your practicum, you might choose to work with the elderly in a nursing home for an internship. These supervised experiences allow you a significant amount of freedom to work extensively in different types of settings and with different types of populations without having to make a long-term commitment. Some students have discovered that doing an outstanding job in a practicum or internship has led to employment in that setting.

6. *Develop a "futures" orientation.* The counseling field is a continually emerging one. New positions evolve as society changes. Therefore, the counseling student should remain cognizant of this and be open to making career changes within the field as circumstances dictate (Kottler & Brown, 1985, pp. 75–76).

A major concern in selecting a specialty is that it may require additional training following the completion of the master's degree. This should be no real stumbling block, however, since being certified or licensed as a counselor already means a lifetime commitment to continuing education to maintain the credential.

Ideas in action   Review the list of counseling specialty areas (see Figure 3.1) and the guidelines for selecting a counseling specialty. Pick two or three specialty areas that are the most appropriate for you right now. How might you investigate these areas further? Will you try to schedule a relevant practicum so that you can be sure that at least one of these areas is right for you?

SUMMARY

The field of counseling has been changing, with the primary change being the shifting of emphasis in counselor education programs from a focus on school counseling to a more comprehensive focus on the mental health counseling field. The result is that counselor education graduates are now employed in a broad variety of helping profession occupations. Facing some adversity, mental health counselors are having to establish their identity alongside the previously established mental health professionals, such as psychiatrists, psychologists, and social workers. They also must work more closely with insurance companies and governmental agencies that pay for services.

The counselor credentialing process helps to create a strong identity for mental health counselors. Credentials in the forms of licensure and certification are becoming more available for counselors under governmental and organizational auspices. Counselor education programs and counseling service agencies are increasingly becoming accredited by professional organizations. Licensure, certification, and accreditation are not guarantors of counseling effectiveness; however, they do help to ensure basic standards with regard to counselor qualifications, educational competence, and training experience. Obtaining a degree and being licensed or certified are not sufficient. Ongoing continuing education is an expected part of this profession. To maintain most licenses and certificates, regular documentation of ongoing training and education is required. This continuing education includes specialized training programs, advanced courses in counseling, and workshops and seminars. Independent reading in books and journals is also an expected activity of counseling professionals.

Job prospects for counselors appear bright. Employment in service occupations in general is increasing in our society. Changes in society and in the structure of the family, with more people living alone and with increased numbers of single-parent families, appear to increase the need for counseling. The extended family is no longer readily available as a personal resource. In addition to a growing need for school counselors, there are good employment prospects in community health agencies and in business and industry. The emphases in the latter two areas of employment are on prevention, training, and development. One outcome of the emphasis on licensure and certification is that an increasing number of mental health counselors are going into private practice on either a full-time or part-time basis.

Becoming a professional in counseling requires making a career commitment to total involvement in the field. It includes nurturing a professional attitude by being an active member of local, state, and national organizations, continually striving to enhance one's own skills and education, and working to improve the profession as a whole.

One decision facing all prospective counselors is whether to be a generalist and work in almost all areas of the field or to specialize in one or two areas. The guidelines of a flexible specialty suggest that students concentrate in one or two specialty areas while continuing to maintain an awareness of techniques and developments in the whole field.

Guidelines for use in selecting a counseling specialty include assessing personal strengths and weaknesses, clarifying personal values related to work and lifestyle, being in direct contact with counselors in a broad variety of specialty settings, using practicum and internship experiences as testing grounds, and being flexible and open to change.

Counseling is a broad, challenging field. Stringent demands are made on counseling professionals, and the ultimate payoff comes from working to help people in a variety of creative ways.

QUESTIONS AND ACTIVITIES

1. Many states license more than one type of counselor (school counselors, substance abuse counselors, etc.). Find out what certification is available to you in your state and what the requirements are. Would it be to your advantage to be licensed in more than one area or specialty?

2. Investigate the rules and regulations, if any, for establishing a private practice in your state. Interview several private practitioners and find out what they see as the problems and benefits of private practice. Would this be a direction that you might seriously consider? If so, what special training do you anticipate you may need in order to ensure success as a private practitioner?

3. From the information given, which divisions of ACA would you be willing to spend money to join and actively participate in the division's work? Are there divisions in which you would just like to get the journal but not become an active member?

4. How are you determining whether to become a generalist or a specialist? Review the pros and cons of each and then share your conclusions with fellow students. What issues cause you the most difficulty in making this decision?

RECOMMENDED READINGS

Collison, B. B., & Garfield, N. J. (1990). *Careers in counseling and human development*. Alexandria, VA: American Counseling Association.

Corey, M. S., & Corey, G. (1993). *Becoming a helper* (2nd ed.). Pacific Grove, CA: Brooks/Cole.

INTERNET RESOURCES

Websites—General Interest
Pastoral Counseling and Psychology
    <www.charm.net/%7Ejlohr/pcpage.html>
Unofficial Rehabilitation Counseling Webpage
    <pages.prodigy.com/rehabilitation-counseling/index.html>
Psych Central: Differences Between Therapists' Degrees <www.coil.com/%7Egrohol/diff.html>
Licensure Links for Counselors <www.tarleton.edu/~counseling/coresour/lllpc.htm>
Council on Accreditation of Counseling and Related Educational Programs (CACREP)
    <www.uc.edu/~wilson/cacrep/index.htm>

Websites—Professional Organizations
Academy of Counseling Psychology <www.hometown.net/academy/academy.htm>
American Association of Marriage and Family Therapists
American College Personnel Association
American College Counseling Association <www.raritanval.edu/internet/acca>
American Counseling Association
American Educational Research Association <tikkun.ed.asu.edu/aera/home.html>

American Education Research Association Division E, Counseling and Human Development
    <gopher://info.asu.edu:70/11aff/aera/division/e>
American Mental Health Counselors Association <pie.org/amhca>
American Psychological Association
American Psychological Society <psych.hanover.edu/APS/>
American School Counselor Association <www.edge.net/asca>
Association for Specialists in Group Work <www.uc.edu/~wilson/asgw>
Association for Gay, Lesbian, and Bisexual Issues in Counseling
California Association of Marriage and Family Therapists
The California Career Development Association <www.csun.edu~hcpsy001/ccda.html>
International Association for Cross-Cultural Psychology <www.fit.edu/CampusLife/clubs-org/iaccp/>
International Association for Marriage and Family Therapists <www.suba.com/~jlewis/iamfc/iamfc.html>
National Career Development Association <www.uncg.edu~ericcas2/ncda>

Mailing Lists and Usenet Groups

If you have an e-mail address, you can subscribe to a mailing list or browse and post messages to a usenet group. Mailing lists are discussion groups for people with similar areas of interest; membership is free and open to anyone, but you must subscribe to each list individually. Usenet groups require no subscription; anyone with access to e-mail can participate in these discussions.

CESNET-L (Counselor Education and Supervision Network): Counselor educators, supervisors, and graduate students discuss research, theory and practice related to a wide variety of professional counseling and supervision issues. To sign on, send the message, "subscribe CESNET-L" to <Majordomo@earth.colstate.edu>.

ACCA-L (American College Counseling Association): The emphasis of this list is on counseling issues with college students and the developmental and psychological issues they face while in college. College counselors and others who deal with this age group are the primary subscribers. To sign on, send the message, "subscribe ACCA-L" to <listproc2@bgu.edu>.

ICN (International Counselor Network): This network is for counselors working in all specialty areas, with an emphasis on school counseling. Topics range widely, including such issues as self-esteem, multicultural issues, program development, career planning, play theory, professional issues, and more. To sign on, send the message "subscribe ICN" to <listserv@utkvml.utk.edu>.

EAP (Employee Assistance Counselors Net Discussion List): EAP is a list that discusses any aspect of employee assistance counseling and psychological interventions in the workplace. To sign on send the message "subscribe eap" to <majordomo@pinsight.com>.

CARDEVNET (Career Development Network Discussion List): CARDEVNET is a list for the discussion of issues relating to career development. To sign on, send the message "subscribe" to <cardevnet-request@world.std.com>.

Psychotherapy Usenet Group: <news:sci.psychology.psychotherapy>

REFERENCES

Altekruse, M. K., & Terneus, S. K. (1997). *Mental Health Counseling in the 90s* [On-line]. Available: www.coe.unt.edu/cdhe/ALTKRS/Ethics.htm

Engler, J., & Goleman, D. (1992). *The consumer's guide to psychotherapy.* New York: Simon & Schuster/Fireside.

Hollis, J., & Wantz, R. (1986). *Counselor preparation 1986–89.* Muncie, IN: Accelerated Development.

Hollis, J., & Wantz, R. (1994). *Counselor preparation: Status, trends, and implications* (Vol. 2). Muncie, IN: Accelerated Development.

Kottler, J., & Brown, R. (1985). *Introduction to therapeutic counseling.* Monterey, CA: Brooks/Cole.

Kunz, J., & Finkel, A. (Eds.). (1987). *The American Medical Association family medical guide* (Rev. ed.). New York: Random House.

McDonough, P. (1985). My view. *Guidepost, 27*(12), 4.

Messina, J. (1985). The national academy of certified mental health counselors: Creating a new professional identity. *Journal of Counseling and Development, 63*(10), 607–608.

Naisbitt, J. (1984). *Megatrends.* New York: Warner Books.

Ohlsen, M. (1983). *Introduction to counseling.* Itasca, IL: Peacock.

Schmolling, P., Youkelles, M., & Burger, W. (1997). *Human services in contemporary America* (5th ed.). Pacific Grove, CA: Brooks/Cole.

Stone, L. (1985). National board for certified counselors: History, relationships, and projections. *Journal of Counseling and Development, 63*(10), 605–606.

Strupp, H. (1993, May 24). Does psychotherapy work? *U.S. News and World Report, 114,* 56–59.

U.S. Department of Labor. (1992). *Occupational outlook handbook* (1992–93 ed.). Scottsdale, AZ: Associated Book Publishers.

U.S. Department of Labor. (1996, Spring). *Occupational Outlook Quarterly, 40*(1), 18.

chapter 4

RESPONSIBILITIES OF COUNSELORS: ETHICAL, LEGAL, AND SOCIAL

- What are the ethical guidelines for counselors?
- Of what legal issues must counselors be aware?
- Do social issues have a place in the practice of therapy?

In the counseling field, as in all professions, practitioners are expected to behave both ethically and legally. One way to determine a profession's concern for ethics is to find out if it has a code of ethics. The American Counseling Association (ACA) has a code of ethics and standards of practice (see Appendix B), and at least six of its divisions also have their own sets of standards. Codes also have been developed by other professional organizations in the field, such as the American Psychological Association (APA), the Association of Certified Social Workers (ACSW), and the American Association of Marriage and Family Therapists (AAMFT). Although there is consensus among these ethical guidelines on many issues, some circumstances may not be covered, or the codes may not be consistent with each other for some situations. We will discuss several issues for which there is consensus and then provide some principles for professionals to follow in handling situations for which the codes of ethics are not clear. This chapter also provides information on legal and social concerns of interest to counselors. Three important ethical issues highlighted in this chapter are confidentiality, professional limits, and sexual conduct.

CONFIDENTIALITY

For the counseling relationship to be successful, trust between counselor and client must be established and maintained. A genuine concern of clients, and one that leads them to have reservations about entering into counseling relationships, is that their personal problems may become known around the community. If prospective counselors have difficulty keeping to themselves what other people tell them, this should be acknowledged as early as possible and another career choice should be pursued. Even though confidentiality is the foundation of the counseling relationship, there are some exceptions to the rule. These exceptions include cases in which there is clear and imminent danger to the client or to other people and actual or suspected child abuse; in addition, records of a counselor who is not covered by **privileged communication,** the legal protection of one's records from public disclosure, may be subpoenaed by a court and could become part of the court's record.

Clear and Imminent Danger

One vital exception to the rule of confidentiality built into the ethical codes is when the client indicates that there is clear and imminent danger to the client or to other people. If this should occur, the counselor "must take reasonable personal action or inform responsible authorities" (ACA, 1995). One way to deal with such an occurrence and still maintain the counseling relationship is to follow the principle of informed consent. **Informed consent** means that at the beginning of the counseling relationship the counselor provides clients with pertinent information regarding counseling goals, services to be provided, procedures and techniques that may be used, fees, anticipated duration of counseling, limits on confidentiality, and rights of access to files (Corey, Corey, & Callanan, 1988). The licensure laws in some states may mandate informed consent.

An example of what now is referred to as *the duty to warn* is when a client informs the counselor that violent action of any kind is to be taken against an unsuspecting third party. In this case, the third party and others who might be identified in advance as potential victims would have to be notified directly of the imminent danger (Leslie, 1983).

Child Abuse

Another instance in which confidentiality cannot be guaranteed legally is when the issue of child abuse is raised. Today, in all states, a counselor who becomes aware of or even suspects a situation involving child abuse is required by law to report such information immediately to the proper authorities.

Contagious Disease

Another exception to the concept of confidentiality is when a client has a contagious disease such as AIDS. Since this is considered to be another clear and present danger, the ACA's code of ethics indicates that "a counselor who receives information confirming that a client has a disease commonly known to be communicable and fatal is justified in disclosing information to an identifiable third party" (ACA, 1995, p. 5). Such disclosure should be made only after the counselor determines that the client has not already done so and has no intention of doing so. The client should be notified of the counselor's intent to notify the third party.

PROFESSIONAL LIMITS

The ACA ethical standards state that a counselor shall neither claim nor imply professional qualifications exceeding those possessed and should only accept positions for which the counselor is professionally qualified. Even though this is not necessarily an issue of immediate concern to a beginning counselor, it is important to be aware of it throughout a counselor training program. In particular, although it may seem obvious that receiving a master's degree in counseling does not certify you as proficient in all areas of counseling, an unfamiliar issue might arise even within a practicum or internship setting. For instance, a client might be seeking sex therapy. You have had no direct training and supervision, but you need the hours to complete your course requirements. Professional responsibility and skill are required in this situation to make an appropriate referral.

SEXUAL CONDUCT

The counseling relationship can be intimate; however, the codes of ethics are clear that the relationship should not include sexual intimacies. Such behavior is harmful to the parties involved as well as to the counseling profession. The use of sexist language or other types of sexual harassment also is not condoned. In addition to codes of ethics, there are often legal restraints on sexual relationships with clients. Some states (including Colorado, Minnesota, and Wisconsin) have enacted laws that make therapist–client sexual activity a felony crime. Sexual intimacies are one of the major causes of malpractice suits. In 1994, the largest number of complaints to the ethics board of the APA (47%) involved adult sexual misconduct. Most of the complaints involved allegations of men violating women. Despite the ethical and legal restraints, however, counselors still engage in sexual relations with clients. Heiden (1993) believes the continued widespread sexual involvement of counselors with their clients demands the infusion of training strategies for prevention of this problem into the counseling curriculum and into in-service training for practicing counselors.

ETHICAL PRINCIPLES

To have a better understanding of the expectations and responsibilities of being a professional counselor, the student should read through the ACA ethical standards early in the training program. Not everything will have immediate application for prospective counselors. Students should take note of expectations which are difficult to implement, such as not counseling close friends or relatives. Students should also become aware of an area that probably will not change, such as keeping information confidential. What happens, however, if a situation arises that is not covered by the codes of ethics? One limitation of a code of ethics is that it cannot anticipate every possible situation. To handle such situations, the counselor should refer to the basic principles on which the codes of ethics themselves are based. The circumstances should be measured against each principle, ultimately resulting in a defensible decision. Kitchener (1984) offers five fundamental principles of counseling: autonomy, beneficence, nonmaleficence, justice, and fidelity:

1. **Autonomy** refers to the clients' right to choose their own course of action as long as it does not interfere with the rights of others. Counselors are expected to respect clients as autonomous individuals who are responsible for their own behavior.

2. **Beneficence,** the principle of doing good for others, is a critical factor in counseling. Counselors who are incompetent or dishonest or who otherwise do not contribute to the growth and welfare of the clients cause harm to their clients and to the profession.

3. A related principle is **nonmaleficence,** not doing harm. Included in this principle are both the avoidance of inflicting harm and the admonition to refrain from actions that risk harming others (Van Hoose, 1989, p. 169). Counselors may be legally responsible for actions taken by clients that harm other people.

4. **Justice and fairness** are principles based on the premise that all clients are equal regardless of race, sex, or creed. This entails equal access to treatment as well as equivalent services within an agency.

5. **Fidelity** refers to loyalty, faithfulness, and keeping promises. Lying and not fulfilling the counseling contract (for instance, missing appointments without notice or breaking confidentiality) are examples of violations of fidelity.

These five ethical principles provide a basis for understanding the counseling profession and the various codes of ethics and serve as guideposts for the review of ethical dilemmas not otherwise covered. Knowledge of codes of ethics and the principles on which they are based is vital; however, given the ever-increasing number and complexity of ethical issues facing the counselor, it may be as important to develop what Tennyson and Strom (1986) call "moral responsibleness" or what Wilcoxon (1987) labels an "ethical conscience."

To develop moral responsibleness or an ethical conscience, prospective counselors must be committed to rational thinking based on the five ethical principles previously described. This commitment develops through a process of critical reflection on the meaning and consequences of counseling goals, theoretical approaches, and specific interventions. This reflection, or self-confrontation, can be done as part of the review of taped counseling sessions and as part of the counselors' ongoing journal writing.

This self-confrontation needs to be supplemented by dialogue. It requires active communication with mentors and professional colleagues to clarify and test the validity of personal decisions, to learn about and examine other points of view, and to become involved in mutual problem solving (Tennyson & Strom, 1986). This professional dialogue directed toward developing moral responsibleness should be an integral part of a counselor education program. The lack of such an ongoing dialogue is a major drawback to the development of ethical consciousness when counselors receive most of their training in workshops, institutes, or poorly run counselor education programs (Wilcoxon, 1987). Collegial dialogues need to be encouraged even more when the student becomes a practicing professional. The scope and nature of the ethical issues confronted do not diminish on graduation or with the receipt of certification. Also, in many settings the counselor may not have immediate access to peer dialogues such as those held in an agency as part of case conferences. The continued development of moral responsibleness is another reason for the development and maintenance of a professional network (see chapter 2).

Ideas in action

A counselor must maintain open, active communication with professional colleagues to be able to manage ethical issues not dealt with in published codes of ethics. How are you going to make sure that this communication is part of your professional education as well as your professional practice?

LEGAL ISSUES

Ethical and legal issues are difficult to separate into distinct categories. Issues that may have been primarily ethical concerns often are addressed in legislation, such as the necessity for reporting suspected child abuse. On the other hand, counselors have been sued in court for violating ethical codes that were formulated by professional organizations but not by state or national legislative bodies. Professional counselors must be aware of a number of issues in regard to legal matters. These issues range from the possibility of being sued for malpractice, to carrying out the requirements of specific laws, to having to testify in court on behalf of a client in a child custody case. A counselor's behavior is regulated by law in two primary ways. One way is by specific laws; the other is as a result of court rulings. All states now have laws requiring counselors and other people to report actual and suspected cases of child abuse. Some other specific laws that affect the actions of counselors include the following:

- *Title IX of the Education Amendments of 1972.* As a result of this law, a school counselor is prohibited from cooperating with an outside agency, organization, or individual that discriminates against students on the basis of sex (Knox, 1977).
- *Family Education Rights and Privacy Act of 1974 (Buckley Amendment).* This law provides parents of children under the age of 18 and students over 18 the right to review records related to them that are held by an institution. Many people are familiar with this act, because on recommendation forms they have waived the right to review a particular recommendation
- *Education for All Handicapped Children Act of 1975.* This law provides guidelines for school counselors who work with handicapped children.
- *Americans with Disabilities Act of 1990.* This act prohibits job discrimination against people with disabilities. It also requires that disabled individuals have the same access to goods, services, facilities, and accommodations available to all U.S. citizens. Counselors working with disabled clients may work as an advocate on behalf of their clients.

Our society has become increasingly litigious. In cases involving professional counselors and psychologists, the issues have generally been related to violations of the professional ethical standards. The most significant case in recent years was *Tarasoff v. Board of Regents of the University of California* in 1976, when a psychologist and his employer were sued for not notifying a potential victim of imminent danger. The psychologist notified the campus police after his client threatened to do harm to a woman. The suspect was interrogated and released, but he subsequently killed the woman. The victim's family sued and won the case on the basis that the woman herself was never notified of the threat. The counselor is legally responsible for knowing what information may be relevant for assessing the real and imminent danger and taking efforts to gather that information. Therapists are usually faulted for failing to gather information that would make a reasonable effort at prediction possible—such as neglecting to obtain records of past and current treatment and not interviewing the client and significant others—not for making an inaccurate prediction (Monahan, 1993).

In terms of numbers of cases, probably the most common case is of a client suing the therapist for sexual intimacies, but it is not all that common. Such behavior on the part of a therapist is in clear violation of the ethical standards of ACA and the APA. Some therapists have claimed that sex can be therapeutic; however, such claims have not been documented, and the negative ramifications of such behavior have been determined to overshadow all possible positive effects.

Recently, a great number of lawsuits have been filed against therapists who have used repressed memory techniques to try to determine whether a client had been sexually abused as a child. In a large number of cases, the clients have recalled events that actually never happened. The results of these false memories and the ensuing lawsuits have been devastating to individuals and their families.

Liability Insurance

Every year there are numerous lawsuits against counselors, some of whom practice without any insurance. These counselors risk losing their personal assets when a court rules against them. The perceived failure to successfully treat a client's problem is another primary cause of lawsuits. Often, this is the result of clients' high expectations which are not met. The counselor may be exonerated as a result of the litigation, but the legal defense costs are very high, exceeding $50,000 in most lawsuits.

As a result of the potential danger of being sued, counselors take out professional liability insurance. Many insurance companies offer such policies, as do the ACA and the APA. An insurance policy can also be taken out by a student who is doing a practicum or internship course. Most agencies or institutions have insurance coverage for all of their working staff, but any practicum and internship student and any prospective employee should inquire about the nature and coverage of available liability insurance plans. Liability insurance is essential for counselors in private practice.

The Counselor and the Courts

A counselor may be called on to appear in court in three different situations. The most common way would be to testify in a matter regarding a client. For example, in a divorce proceeding of the parents of a child you have been counseling, you might be called as the child's counselor to give testimony regarding parental custody.

A major issue in such cases is privileged communication. State laws vary as to who has the right to privileged information. For example, Indiana school counselors have this right by law, whereas mental health counselors do not. Not having the right of privileged communication could affect the nature of record keeping. For example, being forced by a judge to reveal detailed notes of actual counseling sessions could have untold negative consequences on the client–counselor relationship and on the client's family relationship.

As part of the training process, counselor education students need to be aware of the potential legal and ethical implications of their work. The process of helping is a complex one that often affects people and institutions far beyond the individual client. These implications need to be understood from the beginning of a training program.

Expert Witness

Another way for a counselor to appear in court is as an expert witness. As a result of study and practice a counselor may develop expertise in a particular aspect of the field and be called upon to give unbiased testimony to assist a judge or a jury in making an appropriate legal decision. Financial compensation is awarded counselors for this professional service.

Malpractice

The type of court appearance counselors want to avoid is for a malpractice lawsuit. Malpractice is "any professional misconduct, unreasonable lack of skill or fidelity in professional or fiduciary duties, evil practice, or illegal or immoral conduct" (Black, 1951, p. 111). Tables 4.1 and 4.2 describe the types of malpractice suits against mental health practitioners and guidelines for avoiding such lawsuits.

Ideas in    Which of the ethical and legal issues would be of the most concern to you as a counselor? Compare your response with your classmates' responses.

If you were working in a school or agency where you would have liability insurance coverage, would you still consider purchasing your own insurance policy to protect you?

TABLE 4.1   Malpractice suits.

There are nine types of malpractice suits that have been brought against mental health practitioners in all settings.

1. Faulty diagnosis: Diagnosis of a problem of physical origin as psychological.
2. Improper certification in a commitment proceeding.
3. Failure to exercise adequate care when working with a suicidal client.
4. Breach of confidentiality.
5. Providing services for which competence has not been demonstrated, established, or proven.
6. Promise of a cure (may be the basis of a breach of contract).
7. Taking advantage of the counseling relationship for personal gains, whether monetary, sexually, or otherwise.
8. Failure to warn another person of imminent danger.
9. Engaging in behavior inappropriate to accepted standards of the profession.

Adapted from *A Professional Orientation to Counseling* (2nd ed., pp. 150–151), by N. Vacc and L. Loesch, 1994, Bristol, PA: Accelerated Development. Copyright © 1994 by Accelerated Development. Adapted with permission.

TABLE 4.2   Basic guidelines to avoid charges of malpractice.

A counselor seeking to prevent charges of malpractice is advised to follow the following guidelines:

1. Obtain medical diagnoses in virtually all cases. Be able to rule out physiological possibilities.
2. Do not break confidentiality except in cases for which you are legally required to do so. Inform clients of your constraints so that there will be no confusion as to the limits on confidentiality.
3. Only use counseling approaches for which you have appropriate training.
4. Never promise any cure.
5. Do not use sexual intercourse as a form of therapy.
6. Seek opinions of professional colleagues in questionable situations, particularly when working with dangerous clients.
7. Keep accurate records, focused on facts as opposed to subjective statements.
8. When danger to another person appears to be imminent, the counselor has a duty to warn the potential victim.
9. Know and follow the ethical code and standards of practice applicable to you (e.g., the ACA's Code of Ethics and Standards of Practice).

THE RESPONSIBILITY OF THE COUNSELOR IN THE GREATER SOCIETY

> *My personal experiences have led me to believe strongly that as counselors we must not only be agents of individual change, but of systemic change as well.*
>
> Courtland Lee, President of ACA (1997, p. 5)

Neither the counselor nor the client exists in a vacuum. Counselors need to look at society to help their clients. Counselors may help themselves and the greater society by working toward social change in keeping with the counselor characteristic of *Gemeinschaftsgefühl* described in chapter 1.

 **Ideas in action**   R. D. Laing (1967) claimed that insanity is a perfectly rational adjustment to an insane world. Part of his argument is that normal people have killed approximately 100 million of their fellow human beings in recent times (p. 12). Do you agree that the world is insane? Are there parts of society that are dysfunctional? Is it the proper duty of a counselor to make the client become a functional part of an insane world? Is it appropriate for counselors to work on changing the parts of society that are dysfunctional?

Precedence for Social Commitment

Kelly (1989) argues that the significant role of social commitment in counseling needs to be enhanced by clarifying the balance between the individual and social perspectives.

Alfred Adler was a charter member of Freud's inner circle but after a series of disagreements became the first to break with Freud. He later founded his own approach which he called Individual Psychology (see chapter 11).

A major tenet of Individual Psychology is the concept of *Gemeinschaftsgefühl* being an innate part of a person's development. Adler believed that individuals should feel themselves to be a part of a larger social whole and contribute to the common well-being. He wrote on such social issues as crime, war, and nationalism. Other noted theorists and practitioners who have advocated social consciousness include Abraham Maslow, Carl Rogers, Victor Frankl, Jerome Frank, Albert Ellis, B. F. Skinner, Robert Jay Lifton, M. Scott Peck, Erik Erikson, and Harry Stack Sullivan.

What Can the Counselor Do?

Given the various problems in the world and people's often ineffective ways of reacting to them, what can be done? First of all, you need to decide whether to become involved in social issues. If you do choose to become involved, you can work on making a difference in yourself through **inner work** (intrapsychic). At the same time, you can begin to work on **outer work** (making a difference in the environment: interpersonal, family, community, state, nation, and world).

Inner Work

The place to start making a difference is in ourselves. We achieve peace within ourselves through self-knowledge and awareness (see chapter 1). When we put an end to war in ourselves, we can be more fully functioning in all areas of our lives. Below are some suggestions for inner work.

- Be open to new possibilities.
- Learn to listen to yourself.
- Regularly and persistently affirm and imagine a positive goal of sustainable peace at all levels.
- Identify with humankind; do not preoccupy yourself with an enemy. Allow yourself to love.
- Allow yourself to be you. Get in touch with the innermost core of your being.
- Practice what you preach on a personal level, whether it be for justice, equality, concern for the environment, or peace.
- Learn to take care of yourself in terms of breathing, exercise, nutrition, attitude, time management, uniqueness, relaxation, associations, and laughter (see chapter 2).

Outer Work

It is not enough merely to work through the pain and then not act. If we see the necessity for immediate action and act, then we are taking care of our unfinished business and actualizing ourselves. Below are suggestions for taking action.

Political Action. You can participate in the political process through recruiting, nominating, campaigning for, and supporting political candidates and by contributing to political action committees (PACs). Many counselors participate in specific training workshops at the national level for ACA members, and many state ACA branches provide such training at conferences.

Service Organizations.   You can volunteer in community organizations that have interests and concerns similar to yours, such as men's and women's community service organizations, domestic violence agencies, and civil rights groups. Through networking and building coalitions with these groups, change can be brought about more rapidly than working alone.

Crises and Disasters.   Many counselors have gotten involved by responding to events that devastate communities, such as storms, floods, fires, earthquakes, and uprisings. After the Los Angeles civil unrest in 1992 as a result of the Rodney King verdict, mental health professionals established hot lines and offered counseling to those affected by the events. Many counselors assisted with flood relief efforts during the Midwest floods in 1993 and 1997, and in 1994 many helped earthquake victims in Southern California after the earthquake. Similarly, counselors offered their services to victims of Hurricane Andrew, which devastated parts of Florida in 1992. Crisis intervention research shows that if interventions are made quickly by helping professionals when these events occur, those affected will recover quickly. Many counselors have become involved in dealing with the AIDS crisis through participating in community education, starting AIDS support groups, establishing hot lines, and counseling AIDS victims.

Client Advocacy.   Often counselors engage in client advocacy for those who do not have the awareness or resources themselves or who are disenfranchised, such as rape and child abuse victims, oppressed minorities, neglected elderly populations, and homeless persons. Other counselors work on behalf of special interest groups such as gays and lesbians by educating the community, presenting in-service workshops for helping professionals, and influencing policymakers.

Personal Implications

All counselors must decide how involved to become based on personal beliefs, needs, and priorities. Counselors have a responsibility as citizens in a democracy at least to express political convictions by voting in local, state, and national elections.

Counselors also need to take care of the necessities of personal lives, including work, education, career, and family, and to leave room for leisure. Beyond this, most can occasionally find a few minutes to write a letter, make a call about an issue dear to their hearts, and to financially contribute to causes. Counselors need to be alert as to how social issues can affect clients. A counselor can create a context, offer permission, or establish a therapeutic method for dealing with social and political subjects with clients. Finally, counselor education programs should make time to deal with the ideas and concepts discussed in this chapter. If today's counselor educators give no importance to social responsibility, it is unlikely that future counselors will.

All counselors can do the necessary inner work to achieve peace within themselves, nourish themselves, and prevent burnout. Unless counselors work on themselves, the necessary outer work is difficult. Collective change in society is always the result of a process beginning with individual change. Without individual change, societal change cannot occur. As counselors, most are committed to personal growth. Counselors cannot, however, be complacent. The best way to serve clients and students is to be an excellent model, practicing what we preach.

SUMMARY

Major factors in the field of counseling are the ethical and legal issues. Becoming a professional counselor includes making a commitment to act in ethically appropriate ways, to understand legal issues in the field, to realize how much the work of a counselor is affected by the legal system, and to know how to resolve situations for which there may be no ethical or legal guidelines.

There has been much precedence for social commitment in the counseling profession. Many of the pioneers and many of the leading theorists and practitioners in the field were actively involved in social issues. Counselors can utilize many of their current skills and knowledge to incorporate a social perspective to counseling. Counselors can make a difference in themselves (inner work) and in their environment (outer work).

QUESTIONS AND ACTIVITIES

1. Are there any parts of the ACA code of ethics (see Appendix B) with which you cannot agree? Are there any areas which you do not understand? Raise questions in class. Becoming a counselor requires adherence to this code, so it is important that this be considered early in the process.

2. How confidential is the counseling relationship? With a fellow student, practice stating how you would describe the nature of confidentiality to a client coming for counseling for the first time.

3. Having to purchase liability insurance and facing the possibility of having to testify in court on behalf of clients are circumstances that prospective counselors often find somewhat discouraging. How do you react to these facts?

4. What do you think is our society's most urgent problem? the environment? drugs? crime and violence? the economy? homelessness? AIDS? Why? Discuss this question with friends and colleagues.

5. Are the issues for psychotherapeutic work determined only by the private circumstances of clients' lives? Are they determined also by the outside world and cultural community that surround clients? Can any therapy be effective that does not address the outside world?

6. A significant form of commitment to an issue is making a financial contribution. About what issue do you feel most strongly so that you are willing to contribute at least $25 to a legitimate group favoring your point of view? Affirm your conviction and send the group a check.

7. Should helping professionals be social activists? If so, to what extent? Can a counselor's social activism interfere with objectivity in dealing with intrapsychic conflicts, or does activism provide a useful role model for the client?

RECOMMENDED READINGS

Hillman, J., & Ventura, M. (1992). *We've had a hundred years of psychotherapy, and the world's getting worse.* San Francisco: Harper San Francisco.

Kelly, E. W., Jr. (1989). Social commitment and individualism in counseling. *Journal of Counseling and Development, 67*(6), 341–344.

Peck, M. S. (1987). *The different drum: Community making and peace.* New York: Simon & Schuster.

Robinson, G. (1991, December). Empowering counselors for legislative action. *Counseling and Human Development, 24*(1), 1–12.

Roszak, T. (1992). *The voice of the earth.* New York: Simon & Schuster.

Shepard, P. (1982). *Nature and madness.* San Francisco: Sierra Club Books.

INTERNET RESOURCES

Websites

Online Counseling Ethics Course (University of North Texas) <www.coe.unt.edu/cdhe/ALTKRS/Ethics.htm>

Ecopsychology by Tim Boston <www.islandnet.com/~ronnye/boston.htm>

Contacting the Congress (A listing of phone numbers, FAX numbers, e-mail addresses, and WWW home pages for members of Congress) <www.visi.com/juan/congress>

Ethics Questions and Answers from ACA <www.counseling.org/ethicsqa.htm>

ACA Code of Ethics <www.counseling.org/ethics.htm>

ACA Government Relations <www.counseling.org/gr.govaff.htm>

APA Principles and Code of Conduct <www.apa.org/ethics.code.html>

REFERENCES

American Counseling Association. (1995). Ethical standards of the ACA (4th. Rev.) [on-line]. Available: www.counseling.org/ethics.htm

Americans with Disabilities Act of 1990, Pub. L. No. 101-336, §2, 104 Stat. 327 (1991).

Corey, G., Corey, M., & Callanan, P. (1988). *Issues and ethics in the helping professions.* Pacific Grove, CA: Brooks/Cole.

Education for All Handicapped Children Act of 1975, Pub. L. No. 94-142, 20 U.S.C., 89 Stat. 773 (1975).

Family Education Rights and Privacy Act of 1974, Pub. L. No. 93-380, 20 U.S.C., 88 Stat. 484 (1974).

Heiden, J. (1993, September 1). Preview–prevent: A training strategy to prevent counselor–client sexual relationships. *Counselor Education and Supervision, 33,* 53.

Kelly, E. W., Jr. (1989). Social commitment and individualism in counseling. *Journal of Counseling and Development, 67*(6), 341–344.

Kitchener, K. S. (1984). Intuition, critical evaluation, and ethical principles: The foundation for ethical decisions in counseling psychology. *Counseling Psychologist, 12*(3), 43–55.

Knox, H. (1977). *Cracking the glass slipper: Peer's guide to ending sex bias in your school.* Washington, DC: The NOW Legal Defense and Education Fund.

Laing, R. D. (1967). *The politics of experience.* New York: Pantheon Books.

Lee, C. (1997). Empowerment through social action. *Counseling Today, 40*(7), 5.

Leslie, R. (1983, November/December). Tarasoff decision extended. *California Therapist, 14*(2), 6.

Monahan, J. (1993, March). Limiting therapist exposure to *Tarasoff* liability. *American Psychologist, 48,* 242–250.

Tarasoff v. Regents of the University of California, 17 Cal. 3d 425, 557 p. 23 334, 131 Cal. Rptr. 14 (Cal. Supreme Ct. 1976).

Tennyson, W. W., & Strom, S. M. (1986). Beyond professional standards: Developing responsibleness. *Journal of Counseling and Development, 64*(5), 298–302.

Title IX of the Education Amendments of 1972, 20 U.S.C. §1681 *et seq.*

Vacc, N., & Loesch, L. (1994). *A Professional Orientation to Counseling* (2nd ed.). Bristol, PA: Accelerated Development.

Van Hoose, W. H. (1989). Ethical principles in counseling. *Journal of Counseling and Development, 65*(3), 168–169.

Wilcoxon, S. A. (1987). Ethical standards: A study of application and utility. *Journal of Counseling and Development, 65,* 510–511.

chapter 5

THE HELPING RELATIONSHIP

- What causes people to seek help from others?
- What is a therapeutic alliance?
- Are interviewing and counseling the same thing?
- What is the counseling process?
- What are the important dynamics of the counseling process?

This chapter examines the many aspects of the helping relationship, the developmental process of helping, and the counselor's role in this process. Having considered the counselor as the major instrument in the helping relationship in chapter 1, we turn now to a description of the other important part of the relationship—the client who comes for help. This description is followed by a discussion of the helping process and the dynamics of the helping relationship.

HOW PEOPLE BECOME CLIENTS

There are three ways by which people become clients:

1. *Self-initiated action.* People often experience discomfort when they acknowledge specific problems, or they may want to enhance a relationship or improve themselves. They know of the existence of professionals trained in counseling and have a basic feeling of trust in their abilities. Such self-referred clients tend to have the greatest chance for success, because they already have some information about the general counseling process. They are usually motivated by their pain. The probability of seeking counseling is greatest if a person associates with people who know and value counseling (Kadushin, 1969).

2. *The recommendation of others.* People may recognize if they have problems but may not be able to identify them or know where to go for help. Significant others may help loved ones to identify the problems and may also make suggestions or recommendations as to where to seek help. Because the decision to seek counseling comes as a result of advice from others, the client does not generally have as high a motivation level as one who is self-referred.

3. *Coercion.* A person may be sent for counseling by legal or social coercion. A judge may give a drunk driver a sentence of six months of counseling; a teacher may send a disruptive child to a counselor for help. Business organizations may also require psychological help for some employees as a condition of continued employment. Involuntary referrals are probably the most difficult cases counselors face, because the clients are not there by choice and have little personal motivation to change any behavior; however, counselors can still be effective with these clients.

MULTICULTURAL CONCERNS

Historically, clients initiating counseling for themselves have tended to be white, middle-class or upper-class, and female, and therapists have tended to be white males. Much has been made of the fact that Sigmund Freud's theory of psychoanalysis, which was influential on counseling for all classes of men and women, resulted from his work with white middle-class and upper-class Austrian women (see chapter 11). Therapists have always had their preferences. Schofield (1964) found that psychotherapists prefer clients who fall into the YAVIS pattern—young, attractive, verbal, intelligent, and successful. Now, however, with the advent of insurance coverage for mental health problems and agencies which provide services free or on a sliding scale, personal counseling can be available to almost everyone. Prospective counselors need to be prepared to work with clients of every background and socioeconomic class.

Because it is quite unlikely that you will ever work with a client that will have exactly the same characteristics as you, from the beginning of your education as a counselor you should think of all mental health counseling as multicultural. You will continually be faced with, among other things, differences of age, gender, sexual preference, spirituality, and socioeconomic status. From the outset you must have an extremely broad perspective. As Ivey, Ivey, and Simek-Morgan (1993) state,

> If we fail to understand the unique clients before us and their cultural surrounds, particularly as manifested in their families of origin, even the most well-intentioned counseling and therapy effort is likely to fail. (p. 95)

ADDITIONAL CHARACTERISTICS OF CLIENTS

Persons who seek help often do so out of desperation. Usually they have tried to relieve their troubled feelings in numerous ways but have not been successful. Jerome Frank (1978) states that

> despite the diversity of complaints, most persons who seek or are brought to psychotherapy suffer from a single condition that assumes protean form, and all psychotherapies counteract this condition. As a first approximation this condition may be termed demoralization. Demoralization ensues when a person is unable to cope with a life situation that he and those about him expect him to be able to handle. (p. 10)

Often clients feel overwhelmed by feelings of pain, anxiety, helplessness, and hopelessness. No options seem to be open. Clients appear to have lost control of their lives. According to Ivey and Simek-Downing (1980), clients usually come for counseling because they have some degree of decisional conflict and because they are blocked in their behaviors, thoughts, and feelings. The client frequently has unfinished business and needs to broaden his perspective, break old behavior patterns, develop new behaviors, and choose fulfilling alternatives (p. 29).

The problem, as the client presents it, does not necessarily represent objective reality, but it is reality for the client. Lankton (1980) states, "How else could clients be coming into our offices with descriptions of pain, frustration, and limitations when other people find the world exciting, open-ended, and availing nothing but choices? It is not the 'world' itself that dictates unhappiness, it is each person's version of it" (p. 17). Clients coming for counseling often seem to be wearing blinders that prevent them from perceiving the options that would make their lives richer or would at least give them hope that life could be better. The desire for relief of anxiety and pain and a faint feeling of hope motivate clients to seek therapy; it is this feeling of hope that the counselor draws on and encourages.

Initially, the expectation of most clients is that the counselor can do for them what they cannot do for themselves. Perhaps the counselor can make sense out of their confusion, provide insight and meaning to their problem, and then provide the solutions; however, the trained counselor realizes that only clients can take responsibility for their own lives. With the counselor as a catalyst, clients must discover and implement their own solutions. Ineffective counselors, in their eagerness to help, often jump in and attempt to give advice, try to relieve the client's pain, and make things all better. They fail to realize that counseling is a process actively involving both the client and the counselor. A relationship must be established and the problem clearly defined and understood before action is taken toward a solution.

THE THERAPEUTIC ALLIANCE

The counselor is the most important element in the helping relationship; the next most important element is the **therapeutic alliance,** or working relationship, between the counselor and the client. Without this working relationship, little can be achieved. This relationship is so important that the effectiveness of counseling can, in large part, be correlated to its degree of development. The counselor's initial objective is to establish the core conditions of trust and respect, so a therapeutic alliance can be established with both the counselor and the client working together to achieve mutually established goals. Once these core conditions have been established, they must be maintained. Any ongoing personal relationship has to be nurtured; this is especially crucial in the case of the therapeutic alliance. With the exceptions of the personal and psychological health of the counselor and the life and safety of the client, the relationship between the counselor and the client takes precedence over any other aspect of counseling. As Teyber (1997) explains, "It is the relationship that heals" (p. 16). A review of 85 studies of the outcomes of psychotherapy were reported in the 1985 annual review of the American Psychiatric Association. The studies indicated that the strength of the alliance between the client and the counselor was a better predictor of therapeutic success than the specific kind of therapy, the qualities of the therapist, or the kind of client (Goleman, 1985). Another review of studies on the outcomes of psychotherapy indicated that the therapeutic bond between client and counselor was an extremely important influence, more important than training or experience; however, it was the personal qualities of the counselors that determined their ability to form helping alliances (Herman, 1993).

Having an effective therapeutic alliance does not mean that there is an absence of tension or an avoidance of conflict in the relationship. On the contrary, an effective therapeutic alliance is one in which confrontation can and does occur and can be satisfactorily worked through. A counselor's tasks, then, are to establish the relationship, to monitor it, and to enlist the client's assistance in keeping the alliance strong. As with any alliance, it involves a mutual responsibility for maintenance. As Rosenblatt (1975) states,

> I want to assist you, individuals, persons, to become whole, to integrate ... your lives. To do this, I need assistance from you, from the individual himself. You become my teacher and I become your student, to learn who you are, how you live your life. We become partners in an open-ended, freewheeling venture to get to know each other, to assist each other. (p. 3)

Counselors, through their training and awareness, usually notice and respond to cues that might indicate difficulties in the relationship; in addition, clients may do so as well. Some cues noted by the counselor may be quite obvious, such as when the client regularly misses appointments; others may be subtle, such as a change in the client's tone of voice. One or two such cues may be coincidental, but a pattern should be brought to the attention of the client and clarified. In general, however, as in most interpersonal relationships, focusing and dwelling on negative aspects of the relationship can be destructive. As a rule it is more productive to nourish the strengths of the relationship in positive ways. Here is an example:

COUNSELOR: "We have really been successful in coming up with several good ways that you might use to help yourself get better grades."

Innerviewing versus Interviewing

> *The [therapist] hears not only what is in the words; he hears what the words do not say. He listens with the "third ear." Reik (1952, p. 144)*

Just as there are different ways that a person may become a client, a counselor can use different approaches in establishing a therapeutic alliance with a client. Many authors of books and articles on counseling discuss the counseling interview and the interviewing of clients. The terms *interview* and *interviewing* are actually misnomers and often confuse counselor trainees, clients, and even experienced counselors. Counselors have been plagued for years with the problem of how best to describe what they do when they work with individual clients. Using different terms to refer to what counselors do would be a major step in improving communications with all involved.

The conventional concept of an interview involves a person in some authoritative position asking a variety of questions of another person; the interviewer may be taking notes or otherwise recording the transaction (for example, a prospective employee interviewing for a job or a reporter interviewing a state department official about foreign affairs). This conventional conceptualization of an interview, when applied to a helping relationship such as counseling, can have negative effects. If this interviewing method is followed, it requires the counselor to be able to come up with a steady flow of meaningful questions that are supposed to get right to the heart of the problem. When the questions do not succeed at this, the counselor (interrogator) must continue to come up with more, or at least some, successful questions. If questioning continues to be unproductive, the client may be perceived as resistant, and the counselor may be seen as ineffectual.

Even when successful, the result of such an approach is that the overall focus of the session is not on the client, but on the counselor and the effectiveness of the counselor's questioning skills. This approach also tends to set a norm for the counseling sessions themselves, with the counselor being expected to initiate and determine the content and nature of the interaction and the client taking little responsibility for what happens during the sessions.

This type of interview can be a part of legitimate helping relationship settings (for example, a counselor using the behavioral counseling technique of reciprocal inhibition [Wolpe, 1958] or a social worker taking a case history); however, most current theories and approaches to counseling do not put a great deal of emphasis on the interrogative expertise of the counselor. Patterson (1974), in fact, is quite direct when he states that "questioning by the therapist has little place in counseling or psychotherapy" (p. 112). Questions used selectively and timed appropriately can have an important role in the counseling process; however, the counselor trainee should be encouraged to learn to tune in to the client as directly as possible without the use of questions and to try to understand accurately what the actual problem is from the client's point of view. This is important because each person experiences the world differently and operates as if this experience were reality. The client who hides under the bed, believing that someone from another planet is nearby, operates from a unique perspective of the world. For the client, this experience is reality. From this experience, the client makes choices of behavior. In addition, the outside world and the words different people use to describe it are not the same. The counselor's task is to try to get an "innerview" of the world of the client. Once counselors are in touch with this innerview, they are then better able to work with clients to help change attitudes or behaviors.

Questioning is the primary tool used in interviewing, but innerviewing requires that the counselor focus more on the client, using a variety of skills including attending behavior, active and passive listening, and self-attending. Authors of articles and books on helping interviews do include discussions of these and other related skills; however, because these skills are presented in the context of conducting an interview and all that the term *interview* connotes, the importance of noninterrogative skills in the total context of counseling is not always easily grasped by the counselor trainee.

From the beginning of your education as a counselor, talk in terms of the counseling or helping session rather than an interview. Focus on your ability to establish a helping relationship and to attain an accurate *innerview* of what the client is experiencing. It is difficult to know how a client can be helped if this innerview is not attained. This process would closely resemble what Egan (1994) calls "advanced empathy." Here is an example:

CLIENT: I really like my teacher. Everybody in the whole school admits that she's about the best. She makes English and history come alive, not like the others. But still I can't talk to her the way I'd like to.

COUNSELOR: You really like her and are glad that you are in her class, but, Jim, it seems that you are a bit resentful because she doesn't show you much personal attention. (Egan, 1975, p. 137)

Another way to look at the difference between interviewing and innerviewing is through the use of the diagrams in Figures 5.1 and 5.2. In interviewing (Figure 5.1), the counselor is represented by a figure with a given cognitive–emotional configuration, or set. The client, who is experiencing a problem, has a different cognitive–emotional set. Counselors who use a predominantly interrogative interviewing approach attempt to determine the nature of the client's cognitive–emotional condition through what might be a systematic approach but is more often than not hit-or-miss questioning (step 1). Other interventions must also be used, with the ultimate desired outcome being a change in the client's attitude or behavior (step 2).

The innerviewing approach (Figure 5.2) is a process that begins with the counselor who has a particular cognitive–emotional set meeting a client who has a different cognitive–emotional set (step 1). The counselor, using systematic observation, listening, and responding skills, works to enter the phenomenological field of the client. Entering that phenomenological field requires that counselors project themselves to experience reality as the client does, to crawl into the client's skin to feel and perceive what the client feels and perceives. Most importantly, the client becomes the judge of how successfully the counselor is innerviewing. If the client does not feel that the counselor has entered the client's phenomenological field, then the counselor has not (steps 2 and 3). Working within the clients' phenomenological frameworks, counselors can help clients help themselves (step 4). The counselor and client then terminate the relationship (step 5). The counselor does not necessarily return to step 1, because in a meaningful interaction both client and counselor would be affected. Also, the client does not become a carbon copy of the counselor.

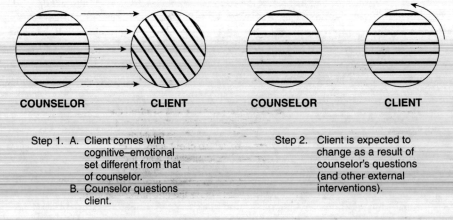

COUNSELOR   CLIENT   COUNSELOR   CLIENT

Step 1. A. Client comes with   Step 2. Client is expected to
            cognitive–emotional   change as a result of
            set different from that   counselor's questions
            of counselor.   (and other external
         B. Counselor questions   interventions).
            client.

FIGURE 5.1   Interviewing model.

From "Innerviewing vs. Interviewing: An Approach to Aid Counselors-in-Training Develop Greater Empathy Skills," by J. V. Peterson and B. Nisenholz, 1984, *New Jersey Journal of Professional Counseling, 47*(1), pp. 27–28. Copyright © 1984 by *New Jersey Journal of Professional Counseling.* Reprinted with permission.

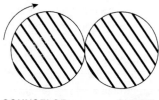

COUNSELOR   CLIENT   **COUNSELOR   CLIENT**

Step 1. Client comes with
cognitive–emotional
set different from that
of counselor.

Step 2. Counselor, using specific
attending and responding
skills, works to understand
perspective of client.

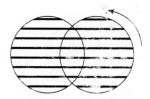

COUNSELOR   CLIENT   **COUNSELOR   CLIENT**

Step 3. Using skills such as
responding with accurate
empathy, counselor enters
client's phenomenological
field.

Step 4. Working within the
phenomenological field
of the client, changes in
thought, attitude, and
behavior occur as a result
of counselor's use of a
variety of skills.

COUNSELOR   CLIENT

Step 5. Termination occurs when the
goal of the client is attained.
Note that as the relationship
ends, the client is not a copy
of the counselor; also, the
counselor does not return to
being exactly the way he or she
was before the encounter occurred.

FIGURE 5.2   Innerviewing model.

From "Innerviewing vs. Interviewing: An Approach to Aid Counselors-in-Training Develop Greater Empathy Skills," by J. V. Peterson and B. Nisenholz, 1984, *New Jersey Journal of Professional Counseling, 47*(1), pp. 27–28. Copyright © 1984 by *New Jersey Journal of Professional Counseling.* Reprinted with permission.

The innerviewing approach requires skilled and psychologically healthy counselors to be flexible and open from the beginning of the counseling relationship. They work in every way to enter the clients' phenomenological fields and then work from there to help clients solve problems. This approach requires a significant amount of involvement and skill on the part of the counselor. Once this level of expertise is understood, it is easier to appreciate what a demanding job successful counseling is. The innerviewing steps are an integral part of the stages of the helping process; they are counseling sessions rather than interviews.

THE HELPING PROCESS

Different methods may be used to describe the helping process. **Process** can be defined as the characteristics of the ongoing counselor–client relationship—the therapeutic alliance—as it develops over time. Counseling is a continuous process, a process that may often flow smoothly without any obvious breaks. However, to study the elements of counseling directly, the process can be divided into stages. In each stage of the process certain skills, attitudes, and strategies of the counselor are prominent. Initially, for example, relationship-building skills and the engendering of hope are prominent; then, skills that facilitate client insight and awareness become important. Decision making and action strategies follow, and then the skills involved in terminating the relationship are used (or the process may be recycled). Presented here is a five-stage model of the counseling process based on the work of Carkhuff (1983); Egan (1982); Ivey, Ivey, and Simek-Morgan (1993); Hansen, Stevic, and Warner (1986); and Brammer (1993) (see Figure 5.3). There are decision points between each stage of the counseling process (Figure 5.4). These are points at which, for various rea-

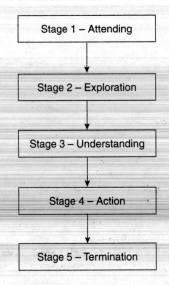

FIGURE 5.3   The helping process.

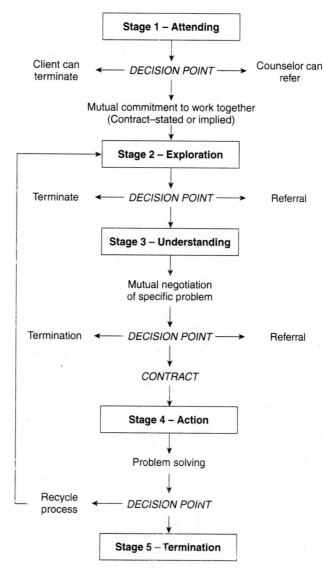

FIGURE 5.4   The helping process with decision points.

sons, counseling might be terminated before the total process is complete. In another situation, a counselor might want to move to the action stage before there was mutual agreement on what the problem is.

With the use of this model, counselors have a framework from which to function and a means to evaluate their location in the process as well as the process itself. The stages in the model are similar to those in human development, because they are flexible and overlapping. Yet each step must be passed through successfully if counseling (growth) is to be effective. If counselors are not competent, they will not be able to move through the stages and will become stuck in whatever stage they are unable to perform. As a result, every time they try to move ahead, they will be blocked by their failure to complete the necessary tasks of some previous step. They will be forced to return to that previous stage and encounter it successfully in order to move ahead in the process.

The stages apply to both short-term and long-term counseling, and they are applicable to virtually all theoretical approaches. Different theories do, however, place greater emphasis on certain stages; for example, behavioral therapists stress stages 1, 2, and 4, whereas Gestalt therapists stress stages 1, 2, and 3.

There is no time element implicit in the description of these stages. It is possible to work through all five stages in one session of 50 minutes or less. It could also take several years, depending on the nature and depth of a given problem. Upon satisfactory resolution of a problem, the entire process may be recycled to work through additional concerns.

The guidelines presented in this model are broad enough for neophyte counselors with significant differences in personality and skill levels to use as a base when they begin the process of developing personal approaches to the establishment of therapeutic alliances. In general, the core conditions for establishing a successful therapeutic alliance occur during the first three stages.

Stages of the Helping Process

The five stages of the helping process are (1) a brief initiating, attending period; (2) an exploratory period; (3) an understanding stage; (4) an action stage; and (5) termination. The stages are described below in terms of the counselor and the client characteristics, behaviors, and experiences in each stage. Table 5.1 gives a general outline of the interaction that takes place during the helping process.

The following is a brief discussion of the dynamics of each stage of the helping process along with a description of the nature of the involvement of the counselor and the client at each level.

Stage 1—Attending

The first stage of the counseling process begins when the client and the counselor first meet (for example, in the office waiting room) and begin to become acquainted.

> And so the two strangers meet. They look at each other, sniff the air between them. Their invisible antennae gently stretch out, tentatively probing, and gingerly assessing. Their intuitions working consciously and far below consciousness, take stock. One silently thinks, "Is this someone I can believe in? Someone I can trust with my secrets, my guilts and shames, my tender and deep hopes for my life, my vulnerability?" The other wonders, "Is this someone I can invest in? Someone I can stand by in pain and crisis? Someone I can make myself vulnerable to? What surprise may this person bring forth, and what may that surprise trigger within me?" (Bugental, 1978, pp. 27–28)

The initial observations are made and a first impression mentally recorded. This first stage is generally quite brief, perhaps lasting from only a couple of minutes to one session or so, with the participants meeting and quickly sizing up each other. Social amenities take place

TABLE 5.1   Counselor and client characteristics and behaviors during the five stages of the helping process.

Stage 1—Attending

Client
Checks out procedures
Tests relationship
Is cautious
States concerns
Presents problem

Counselor
Provides working environment
Clarifies process
Attends to client and self
Observes, listens, accepts client
Gives client space to state concerns
Is nonjudgmental

Stage 2—Exploration

Client
Begins to explore
Experiences counselor as helper
Is less defensive
Sees problem becoming clearer
Attains greater awareness of feelings and
    concerns
Becomes aware of self-destructive behaviors
Becomes aware of problems in the here and now
Is more self-disclosing

Counselor
Establishes trust
Shows concern and caring
Gives empathic responses
Communicates respect and warmth
Acknowledges client feelings
Focuses on here and now
Gives feedback
Mild confrontations
Helps client explore deeper meanings
Summarizes

Stage 3—Understanding

Client
Takes responsibility for problems
Strengthens commitment
Identifies discrepancies
Develops insight
Confronts impasse
Experiences release of energy
May terminate on identification and
    understanding of problem

Counselor
Helps client take responsibility for his or her
    part in problem
Deals with intensified levels of feeling
Uses advanced levels of empathy
Confronts, self-discloses
Directs, interprets, probes
Uses immediacy

Stage 4—Action

Client
Puts ideas and insights into action
Further clarifies thoughts and feelings
Sets goals, implements plan, and evaluates actions
If goals not met, revises plan; if goals met,
    moves to new problem or toward termination

Counselor
Helps generate and evaluate alternatives
Helps client decide on an alternative to test
Gives encouragement
Gives feedback to client on results of activity

Stage 5—Termination

Client
Evaluates gains
Acknowledges changes
Works with loss of relationship
Plans beyond relationship

Counselor
Helps complete unfinished business
Assesses client readiness for ending counseling
Gives feedback, affirmation
Reviews process
Arranges for follow-up

here as well as general housekeeping procedures, such as discussing issues related to confidentiality, the length of sessions, and fees. A formal case history, if required, would be part of this stage. Here, clients begin to tell their stories, with counselors attending fully to all of the clients' messages.

Stage 1—Client Process.   Clients entering therapy are concerned not only about their plight but also about how much they should reveal. What secrets should be kept? It is not uncommon that the presenting problem is not the major problem. The client often has questions and concerns: what will the counselor be like? Will counseling take a long time? Will the counselor really understand and accept me? The counseling process for the client may, in fact, begin when the appointment is made. Between the time the appointment is made and the appointment itself, much work is done by clients as they rehearse, and on occasion even write out, what they plan to discuss with the counselor.

If clients have any questions or concerns about the procedures and process, they might ask them at this point. In the best interest of the clients and of the counselor–client relationships, the clients should have as clear an understanding as possible about the counseling process. In particular, it is vital for the clients to know that counseling is not a magical process involving something done to or for them by counselors. At some point, either at the request of the counselors or spontaneously, the clients may begin to talk about why they came for counseling.

Often, the first session is like the first round in a boxing match, in which the fighters try to figure out each other's approach, testing each other out and being somewhat cautious. It is the start of what some helpers have described as a journey in which both client and helper engage each other, invest in each other, and learn from each other. As the first stage unfolds, clients start to explore their problems. They become more open and self-disclosing with the counselor and begin to reduce their defensiveness and resistance. They experience the counselor as a responsive, understanding person.

Stage 1—Counselor Process.   After introducing themselves and taking care of procedural matters, depending on their personal approach or the guidelines of their agency, counselors may ask questions to obtain background information. In some settings, a separate intake interview is scheduled to go over procedures and to obtain a case history before actual counseling begins. Other agencies request that a client come in 15 to 20 minutes early to fill out a detailed information form prior to the first session. Counseling time is not taken up then with generally routine questions.

From the beginning, counselors work to establish trust based on openness and honesty of expression. They use themselves as instruments to attend fully to the client. This means that counselors have to be aware of what is going on inside themselves as well as inside the client. Initially they give clients space to state concerns. They allow clients to initiate topics, following them verbally and nonverbally as appropriate. They attempt to develop a learner stance toward clients in order to be open to the clients' experience. In doing so, counselors observe, listen, and experience clients without judging or evaluating. Counselors strive to be attuned to all the messages clients are trying to convey. By doing this, counselors gather vital information necessary to acquire a full picture of the client's world without necessarily asking questions. Gradually, through their attitudes and behaviors, counselors establish credibility as understanding, responsive, and trustworthy persons.

The first stage of the counseling process is relatively brief. It consists mainly of helping clients become comfortable enough to begin expressing their concerns and expectations of counseling. The stage is concluded when counselors begin to make substantive interventions, such as responding empathically, clarifying, or summarizing.

Once the first session is over, clients and helpers must decide whether to go ahead. How much of a commitment are they willing to make, if any? Can they work with each other? If clients and helpers feel positively toward each other, a genuine relationship is not guaranteed; clients must trust helpers enough to bare their innermost emotions, concerns, and secrets. The helpers must be ready to accept clients as individuals who are capable of changing and growing and not be frightened by the clients' anxiety. A bond must be formed, and a respect for each other must be maintained.

Stage 2—Exploration

In the first stage of the counseling process, the emphasis is on establishing an environment in which clients can comfortably tell their stories as the counselor learns how clients experience and perceive their worlds. The counselor accumulates a basic picture of who the clients are, what the clients need and want, and how to help. The major focus in stage 2 is on the strategies and techniques needed to explore the nature of clients' basic concerns more fully.

Because of clients' failures to take ownership of their problems, the initial problems discussed are often not the real problems. For example, a college student might enter therapy complaining that his classes are boring, he feels anxious, he has difficulty concentrating, and he is failing his courses even though his previous academic achievement has been quite high. Initially, he may ask for help in concentrating and reducing anxiety so that he can pull his grades up and satisfy his parents. He might blame his professors or the academic institution. As the relationship develops, the problem begins to change. The student begins to realize that he is going to college in this major only to satisfy his parents. He would like to be in a different major or perhaps even travel and work for a while. His parents oppose this. The problem now is his difficulty in finding separateness from his parents and pursuing his own goals.

Stage 2—Client Process.   In this stage clients increase their level of exploration and self-disclosure. They move from surface structure to deep structure and gradually acquire a greater awareness of the depth of their feelings and the nature of their concerns. Ivey and Simek-Downing (1980) refer to **surface structure** as the immediate sentences clients use to share thoughts, feelings, and perceptions; **deep structure** is made up of the words, thoughts, and perceptions that underlie the surface structure sentences. In deep structure, clients become more oriented to the present in regard to their problems. There is a realization, for example, that the problems are caused not only by difficult childhoods but also by how clients continue to use their pasts to keep from taking responsibility. Clients begin to become aware of the incongruities between thoughts, feelings, and behaviors and of how many of these behaviors may be self-defeating. Clients experience the counselor as someone who will be there with them at deeper levels, and as a result they become less defensive and more open. In the process the nature of the problems become clearer. As trust in the counselor increases, the presenting problem may be phased out and an emerging—perhaps more serious—problem replaces it.

Stage 2—Counselor Process.   The specific counselor process goals for this stage include facilitating client exploration of problems and feelings in order to increase client self-awareness, focusing on the immediacy of client problems, strengthening the relationship, using selected strategies such as basic empathy as interventions to facilitate further exploration, dealing with feelings that impede progress toward selected goals, providing encouragement for client introspection at deeper levels of understanding, and making a further commitment to the counseling relationship.

Stage 2—Decision Point.   Sometimes clients feel a cathartic relief as they work through the exploratory stage and become better able to verbalize their feelings. They might believe that their problems are now solved and therapy is no longer needed; some counselors refer to this phenomenon as a **flight to health.** Often clients are reluctant to face the pain and discomfort that might come from further exploration and fear what the dark side of their personalities might be like. Some clients feel even worse as they work through their painful self-confrontations. They may become confused and discouraged. In Gestalt therapy this is called the point of impasse. It is the point at which clients are dissatisfied with their old ways of behaving but are unable to find self-support for change (Korb, Gorrell, & Van de Riet, 1989). As a result, clients implode, or retreat into themselves. They experience fear of the unknown. They have been comfortable with their old behaviors even though these behaviors do not serve them well anymore. They begin to worry whether other people will still accept them if they change or whether they will like themselves. As a result, clients may wish to terminate the counselor–client relationship. Counselors need to pay attention to their own feelings and to those of their clients in this situation. Counselors may need to terminate relationships if they are also uncomfortable, perhaps by making referrals to other counselors. On the other hand, counselors might provide the necessary encouragement at this point for clients to continue exploration to deeper levels.

Stage 3—Understanding
Stage 3 focuses on using insights and awareness to allow the clients and counselors to come to mutual understanding of client issues and problems and to set the stage for them to begin to take action to resolve those problems.

Stage 3—Client Process.   This stage is characterized by clients' awareness of the personal involvement needed for changing and specific knowledge of what needs to be done. Here, clients realize that they are responsible for their behavior and for changing it. They let go of their defenses and filters and concretely experience their role in their problems. They decide to confront the impasse and make a leap of faith. They strengthen their commitment to their goals in counseling and allow themselves to experience repressed feelings and any unfinished business. As a result, clients become more congruent in terms of feelings, attitudes, and behaviors. They have an increased awareness of self and the external world. Clients experience a different perception of the meaning of their problems in their present existence. Clients mourn their old selves which may have served them well through much of their lives but are no longer appropriate with their new perceptions and awareness.

As clients complete this mourning, they become calmer and more at peace. They begin to experience all aspects of themselves more freely, redirecting their energy away from staying rigid and safe toward being freer and more alive.

Stage 3—Counselor Process.   Counselors must feel competent to deal with a client's intensified levels of feelings. They need to offer encouragement, support, and positive reinforcement as a client strengthens a commitment to change. In addition, they must be able to offer an advanced level of accurate empathy, high level confrontation, and authenticity as a client works through the impasse. They might use interpretation or summarize the client's process. Finally, as the client achieves clarity and feels freer, counselors must be able to provide an accurate reflection of meaning in describing the client's problem.

With the increased intensity of interaction in the relationship that develops in this stage, certain strong feelings may become noticeable which may have been developing earlier on the part of the client toward the counselor and vice versa. These conditions, commonly called transference and countertransference, are discussed separately in this chapter.

Stage 3—Mutually Agreed-On Problem.   The conclusion of the understanding stage, stage 3, is reached when the client has clearly defined the problem, and it is fully acknowledged by the counselor. Without this point entirely attained, any action steps are generally doomed to failure. One reason some counseling is not effective is that problem solving and other action steps have been taken before a problem has been clearly defined and before the client has committed to change. This agreement can be considered a "therapeutic contract" (Gottman & Lieblum, 1974).

Many therapies, such as Gestalt or person-centered, may end with stage 3 as far as the formal helping relationship or therapeutic alliance is concerned. As a result of significant work in the exploration and understanding stages, the client's problem is clearly defined and, with the insights gained, the client can make change as necessary. Insight therapists often find that when the problem has been clarified, the client has an "aha!" experience, saying in effect, "That's it, and I know what to do about it. People have been telling me for years."

Stage 4—Action
Although some therapies consider the therapeutic process completed when insight and awareness have been achieved, many therapies (particularly the cognitive-behavioral approaches) move into an action-oriented fourth stage. The primary element necessary for moving into stage 4 is having a mutually agreed-on problem as a result of the exploration and understanding stages.

Stage 4—Client Process.   In this stage of the counseling process, clients have the opportunity to learn and further clarify their thoughts and feelings, to formulate alternative actions, to make decisions, to practice new behaviors, and to carry them out.

Stage 4—Counselor Process.   The counseling relationship in this stage is more of an adult-to-adult relationship than in any of the preceding stages. Decision making skills come to the forefront. Counselors help clients to generate and examine an array of potential solutions and to make a commitment to action based on evaluating solutions and their possible consequences. Counselors may initiate behavioral interventions, such as systematic desensitization, as appropriate. Counselors support and encourage clients as the clients test solutions in their home environment. The counselors attempt to reinforce client action, and in the process make themselves more and more dispensable. If necessary, counselors help clients return to earlier stages if further clarification of the problem is needed. Finally, both client and counselor assess whether the goals of counseling have been met. Accomplishments are summarized, and progress is evaluated.

Plans for termination and for the client's continued progress after counseling are formulated; however, the whole process may start again to work on another problem. Many counselors begin to wean their clients by scheduling more time between counseling sessions.

Stage 5—Termination

The fifth stage, termination, is characterized by summarizing and wrapping up any unfinished business and saying good-bye. Usually the door is left open for possible follow-up appointments or for work on other problems.

Terminating is generally not a major problem if the other stages of the counseling process have been worked through successfully. Clients are usually ready to leave, and they often begin the terminating process before the counselor does. Some clients, however, have difficulty letting go and attempt to bring up new issues in order to prolong the relationship. Counselors also have to be able to let go when the need for this type of relationship has been met. One counselor, for example, in order to make the final parting less abrupt and yet stress its finality, would have a closing ceremony in which client and counselor toasted each other with a nonalcoholic beverage.

Stage 5—Client Process.   As part of the termination process the client may learn how to conclude a short-term, positive relationship successfully and how to appraise its worth. Unfinished business, if any, should be identified and planned for, and follow-ups, if any, should be scheduled. Also, a final recapitulation of the entire process on the part of the client can be extremely helpful to acknowledge and internalize the gains made as a result of counseling.

Stage 5—Counselor Process.   An important part of the termination process is to prepare the client for the ending of the relationship. In time-limited therapy, the date of the final session is known from the onset. In other cases, however, some notice needs to be given at least one or two sessions prior to the final session. Efforts also need to be made by the counselor to assist the client in working through the process of the loss of the relationship, just as earlier the client had to grieve the loss of self-destructive behaviors.

The counselor may add to the client's recapitulation, if appropriate, and affirm the changes made and the client's responsibility and involvement in the process. Finally, negotiations may be made for follow-up sessions if mutually desirable.

Ideas in action   Imagine a scenario of meeting with a client and working through the stages of the helping process in one 50-minute session.

Dynamics That May Hinder the Helping Process

Even though the counselor may have a solid understanding of the helping process and be generally proficient in the skills necessary in the different stages, there are still interpersonal dynamics that can interfere with the process or even prevent its completion. Some of these dynamics are resistance, transference, and countertransference.

Resistance

Client Resistance.   Resistance occurs when clients use their defense systems in ways that oppose the purpose of change. A paradox that is part of many helping relationships occurs when a client comes for assistance with a personally difficult situation and then proceeds almost immediately to resist making any personal changes that could improve the circumstances. Inevitably, helpers encounter resistance during the helping process.

Teyber (1997) believes that clients usually have learned resistant behavior for good reasons. Clients' resistance originally served self-preservative and adaptive functions and was the best possible response to an irresolvable conflict given what they had available at that point in their development. As destructive and as energy-consuming as they might be, resistance tactics give clients some measure of protection. Resistance tactics do allow for survival and often become creative forces in difficult environments.

Counselor Resistance.   Counselors themselves can often manifest resistance. Some counselors, for example, may become anxious when their clients move deeply into very emotion-laden concerns. As a result, such counselors may change the topic or in some other way interrupt the client's continued exploration. They might also be reluctant to confront or challenge a client for fear of jeopardizing the relationship (Egan, 1994; Teyber, 1997).

In addition, counselors sometimes resist because they dislike their clients, lack necessary skills, or have failed to come to terms with certain issues in their own lives. Some counselors may have problems involving power and control issues. Others may have difficulty establishing the closeness or intimacy necessary to help a client work through an existential problem.

 **Ideas in**   Some therapists believe that there are no resistant clients; there are only resistant counselors, counselors who are not able to relate with the clients. The argument is that clients can only be where they are, and the counselor's labeling clients as resistant reflects the counselor's inability to work with the clients. How do you react to this idea?

Methods of Handling Resistance.   In the various theoretical approaches, resistance is treated somewhat differently. Perhaps the greatest differences exist among the psychoanalytical, humanistic, and behavioral approaches. The psychoanalytical method of dealing with resistance involves interpreting and analyzing clients' resistance to determine its presence, purpose, ramifications, historical origin, and present dynamics. Resistances are gradually worked through, and clients become less and less resistant. Among the humanistic approaches, person-centered therapists work at reducing threat in the counselor–client relationship so that clients will more readily confront themselves. Existentialists sensitively confront and point out the resistances. Gestaltists view resistance as a creative force rather than as something to be broken down, and they also focus on the resistance by pointing out how clients avoid unpleasantness. Rational–emotive therapy (RET) adherents view resistance as a failure to face reality by seeking magical solutions. RET counselors challenge their clients' need for a magical solution. Behavioral counselors might make subsequent therapy sessions contingent on clients exhibiting nonresistant behavior by completing their therapeutic homework assignments.

Teyber (1997) proposes a three-step sequence for dealing with resistance: (1) helping clients understand why they originally needed to defend themselves and how they continue to do that now in therapy, (2) validating the necessary protection that this resistance provided, and (3) demonstrating how the counselor's current responses differ from the aversive ways others have responded in the past.

Generally, counselors might ignore mild resistances, lower the anxiety level of a client through humor or diversion, reflect the resistant feeling to the client, point out the resistance, challenge it, interpret its dynamics, or consider a variety of different approaches for responding to the client. Resistance can be handled on a continuum from completely ignoring it to direct confrontation. Regardless of therapeutic approach, counselors must help clients learn to respect their resistance and not view it as a negative behavior to be broken down. Overall, resistance patterns serve as useful cues in learning about the helping process and about both client and counselor personality patterns.

Transference

Transference is the phenomenon where the client reacts to the therapist not objectively as a real person but as a virtual reincarnation of a parent or another significant figure from the client's past. More generally, transference is used to label any feelings the client expresses toward the counselor. As people move from childhood to adult life, they carry with them many feelings, values, and attitudes that take the form of fixed patterns of behavior that manifest themselves during certain interpersonal situations. For example, an adult man who may have been intimidated by a harsh, punitive father may respond to all authoritarian men in the same way he did as a little boy awaiting punishment for a misdeed. Thus, present reality is always distorted. In therapy, the client expects to be treated by the therapist in ways similar to ways the client was handled by previous authorities.

Transference can occur in all helping relationships but is more predominant in psychotherapeutic counseling because of the deeper intensity of the relationship. **Transference** is a cornerstone of Freudian therapy (psychoanalysis). Freud discovered that, if not interfered with, the client inevitably projects feelings and attitudes from the past into the therapeutic situation. Occasionally, these transference reactions become so intense that clients actually live through, with the therapist, some of their earlier traumatic experiences. Freud's name for the development of these exaggerated transference reactions is *transference neurosis*. According to Freud, these reactions enable the client to adopt new, more mature, and appropriate behaviors facilitated by a more accepting and permissive authority figure, the therapist.

There is disagreement regarding the necessity of inducing the transference relationship. Some neo-Freudians, as well as humanists and behaviorists, pay more attention to here and now problems. They believe that personality change can occur without the client regressing to infantile neuroses. In fact, many counselors consider the outbreak of transference behaviors a sign of bad therapy.

Depending on the theoretical point of view, the effect of transference in a helping relationship may range from being a helpful, necessary part of the process to being harmful. Most non-Freudian approaches to counseling tend to minimize the importance of the phenomenon.

Ideas in action   Have you reacted to someone recently in the same way that you might have reacted to one of your parents in a similar situation when you were a child? How did the other person act in return? How did your parents act in response to that behavior?

Countertransference

The counterpart of the client's transference is referred to as **countertransference**. Countertransference has to do with the counselor's personal emotional response to the client. Generally, in psychoanalytical terms, it describes situations in which the client's behavior invokes in the counselor conflicts relating to unresolved situations in the counselor's life, causing the counselor to respond to the client in a subjective way. Countertransference does not have a precise standard definition, however, even among psychoanalysts. It is generally agreed, however, that the phenomenon is not beneficial to the helping process. It could be considered as another example of resistance on the part of the counselor.

Brammer and Shostrom (1982) view countertransference as "conscious and unconscious attitudes of the counselor toward real or imagined client attitudes or overt behavior" (p. 227). Under this definition countertransference could be an expression of humanity, a genuine response to the client, or a counselor's projections.

Watkins (1985) identifies four patterns of countertransference behaviors: overprotective, benign, rejecting, and hostile. Overprotective behaviors include cushioning statements with many qualifiers in order to soften their impact; preventing clients from experiencing unpleasant emotions such as anxiety, hurt, or guilt; and talking in a very low voice in order to shield the client from verbal stimulation. In using benign behaviors, the counselor creates a bland counseling atmosphere in which the positive is accentuated and the negative is avoided as much as possible. This behavior is often used because the counselor has an intense need to be liked by the client or is frightened by any displeasure or anger on the part of the client.

Rejecting countertransference behavior involves aloofness and coolness on the part of the counselor in an effort to create considerable separateness between the counselor and the client. Often the counselor is fearful of client demands and of becoming responsible for the client's welfare. The counselor becomes intimacy-phobic. Finally, hostile behaviors might be used by counselors who are fearful of being like their clients and adapting behaviors that are personally detestable. Hostile behaviors include verbal abuse of various kinds, such as demonstrating curtness or bluntness, missing or coming late to appointments, and enjoying the turmoil of clients' experience.

The most effective weapon against countertransference is counselor awareness and growth. Videotaping or audiotaping counseling sessions in order to analyze counselor responses is highly recommended. It is also recommended that counselors undergo their own psychotherapy and participate in growth groups. A counselor can also seek out supervisory assistance from counselor educators, field supervisors, or colleagues.

SUMMARY

The primary reasons that clients seek counseling are discouragement and the inability to cope. People generally become clients in one of three ways: self-initiated action, the recommendation of others, and coercion. Once they have come for counseling, the therapeutic alliance can be developed and the counseling process can unfold. A distinction has been made between the counseling terms *interview* and *innerview* and between an *interview* and a *counseling session*. These differences are related to the counseling process itself, which is described in terms of a synergistic model.

The counseling process begins with developing the basic helping relationship or therapeutic alliance. The counselor's task in developing the alliance includes establishing and monitoring the relationship and enlisting the client's help in maintaining it. The stages of the counseling helping process begin with attending and are followed by exploration, understanding, action, and termination. A description of client and counselor behavior during each of the stages is presented.

The counseling process is often impeded by the dynamics of resistance on the part of both the client and the counselor, transference on the part of the client, and countertransference on the part of the counselor. Each of these factors is described along with its negative effects. Guidelines for working with and minimizing these factors are explained.

QUESTIONS AND ACTIVITIES

1. Listen to audiotapes and videotapes of counseling sessions. Observe the stages that are present in the examples and see if you can identify the counselor and client characteristics and behaviors.

2. How open are you to change? How do you show reluctance and resistance in your interpersonal relationships? What do you fantasize would happen if you were to let go of your resistances? How do you feel about expecting clients to change when you may be reluctant to do so?

3. What issues in your life might result in your becoming involved in countertransference with a client? How might you recognize the phenomenon? What might you do about it?

4. Are you aware of examples of transference in your observations of interactions with other people? Share examples with your classmates.

5. Counselors are confronted with a wide variety of clients: people with abused family members, drug addicts or AIDS victims, or people from different ethnic and cultural backgrounds, for example. With which type of clients do you believe you would have the most difficulty working? How would you expect to deal with a case in which you knew that you were likely to be judgmental or otherwise biased against the client?

RECOMMENDED READINGS

Baldwin, M., & Satir, V. (1987). *The use of self in therapy.* New York: Haworth Press.

Brammer, L. M. (1993). *The helping relationship: Process and skills* (5th ed.). Boston, MA: Allyn & Bacon.

Frank, J. D., & Frank, J. B. (1992). *Persuasion and healing: A comparative study of psychotherapy.* (3rd ed.). New York: Schocken Books.

Kopp, S. (1972). *If you meet the Buddha on the road, kill him.* Palo Alto, CA: Science and Behavior Books. (Also available in Bantam paperbacks.)

Teyber, E. (1997). *Interpersonal process in psychotherapy* (3rd ed.). Pacific Grove, CA: Brooks/Cole.

REFERENCES

Brammer, L. M. (1993). *The helping relationship: Process and skills* (5th ed.). Boston, MA: Allyn & Bacon.

Brammer, L. M., & Shostrom, E. (1982). *Therapeutic psychology: Fundamentals of counseling and psychotherapy* (4th ed.). Englewood Cliffs, NJ: Prentice Hall.

Bugental, J. (1978). *Psychotherapy and process.* Reading, MA: Addison-Wesley.

Carkhuff, R. (1983). *The art of helping* (5th ed.). Amherst, MA: Human Resource Development Press.

Egan, G. (1975). *The skilled helper.* Monterey, CA: Brooks/Cole.

Egan, G. (1982). *The skilled helper* (2nd ed.). Monterey, CA: Brooks/Cole.

Egan, G. (1994). *The skilled helper* (5th ed.). Pacific Grove, CA: Brooks/Cole.

Frank, J. (1978). *Psychotherapy and the human predicament.* New York: Schocken Books.

Goleman, D. (1985, August 2). Switching therapists may be best. *Indianapolis News,* p. 9.

Gottman, J., & Lieblum, S. (1974). *How to do psychotherapy and how to evaluate it.* New York: Holt, Rinehart & Winston.

Hansen, J., Stevic, R., & Warner, R. (1986). *Counseling: theory and process* (4th ed.). Boston, MA: Allyn & Bacon.

Herman, K. C. (1993). Reassessing predictors of therapist competence. *Journal of Counseling and Development, 72*(1), 29–32.

Ivey, A. E., Ivey, M. B., & Simek-Morgan, L. (1993). *Counseling and psychotherapy: A multicultural perspective.* Boston: Allyn & Bacon.

Ivey, A. E., & Simek-Downing, L. (1980). *Counseling and psychotherapy: Skills, theory, and practice.* Englewood Cliffs, NJ: Prentice-Hall.

Kadushin, A. (1969). *Why people go to psychotherapists.* New York: Atherton.

Korb, M. P., Gorrell, J., & Van De Riet, V. (1989). *Gestalt therapy practice and theory.* New York: Pergamon Press.

Lankton, S. (1980). *Practical magic.* Cupertino, CA: Meta Publications.

Patterson, C. H. (1974). *Relationship counseling and psychotherapy.* New York: Harper & Row.

Perls, F. S. (1969). *Gestalt therapy verbatim.* Lafayette, CA: Real People Press.

Peterson, V., & Nisenholz, B. (1984). Innerviewing vs. interviewing: An approach to aid counselors-in-training develop greater empathy skills. *New Jersey Journal of Professional Counseling, 47*(1), 26–29.

Reik, T. (1952). *Listening with the third ear.* New York: Farrar Strauss.

Rosenblatt, D. (1975). *Opening doors.* New York: Harper & Row.

Schofield, W. (1964). *Psychotherapy: The purchase of friendship.* Englewood Cliffs, NJ: Prentice-Hall.

Teyber, E. (1997). *Interpersonal process in psychotherapy* (3rd ed.). Pacific Grove, CA: Brooks/Cole.

Watkins, C. E. (1985). Countertransference: Its impact on the counseling situation. *Journal of Counseling and Development, 63*(2), 356–359.

Wolpe, J. (1958). *Psychotherapy by reciprocal inhibition.* Stanford, CA: Stanford University Press.

chapter 6

DEVELOPING RESPONSE/ABILITY

The Learning of Counseling Skills, Part 1

- What are the conditions that are particularly helpful in establishing and maintaining a counseling relationship?
- What is meant by psychological attending?
- Can you establish a helping relationship without asking questions?
- Is silence a helpful response?

THE COUNSELING RELATIONSHIP—CORE CONDITIONS

The time available for counseling may vary from very brief therapy (one to four sessions) to long-term therapy (more than a year) and the therapeutic approaches counselors use may vary dramatically. To assist a client in making attitudinal and behavioral changes, the counselor needs to take some time to develop what Carl Rogers (1957) identifies as the core conditions for establishing a relationship. As the research cites in chapter 1 and chapter 5, the counselor's ability to develop and implement the skills related to the core conditions may determine whether the counselor is helpful or harmful. These core conditions, initially labeled empathy, genuineness, and positive regard, have been elaborated on by theorists and researchers in the field (Brammer, 1985; Combs & Avila, 1985; Carkhuff, 1987; Danish & Hauer, 1973; Ivey, 1988; Egan, 1986; Gazda, Asbury, & Balzer, 1984).

In this chapter we describe the development of these core conditions and related response skills that have been demonstrated as important in establishing and maintaining the therapeutic alliance. Competent implementation of these skills by the counselor allows the client to move successfully through the five stages of the counseling process described in chapter 5. This chapter examines stages 1 and 2. Chapter 7 will feature the skills of stages 3, 4, and 5,

Although some skills may be associated with a given stage of the counseling process more than another, these skills can be used whenever an individual counselor deems them to be appropriate. Also, different theoretical approaches may call for different patterns of skill use. The skills for attending and exploration are important throughout the counseling process.

STAGE 1—ATTENDING SKILLS

The counselor's behaviors in stage 1 of the counseling process are critical. If the behaviors are inappropriate there may be little or no opportunity to use additional skills. The basic skills of stage 1 are attending skills and the use of encouragers. At the very beginning of the relationship the core condition of positive regard or respect is established. At this time the counselor demonstrates unconditional, nonjudgmental acceptance of the client regardless of any cross-cultural differences.

Before counselors can really help the client, they have to be able to get involved with the other person. As Egan (1994) states,

> Helping and other deep interpersonal transactions demand a certain intensity of presence. Attending, or the way you orient yourself physically and psychologically to clients, contributes to this presence. Effective attending does two things: it tells clients you are with them, and it puts you in a position to listen carefully to their concerns. (p. 91)

Physical attending refers to the posture, eye contact, and the general position that counselors take with regard to the client. Psychological attending refers to the ability to tune into the nonverbal as well as the verbal messages of the client.

A client who is coming for help from someone who is probably a total stranger is often extremely sensitive to the cues emanating from the counselor. An ambivalent client may use a counselor's nonattending behaviors as a reason to terminate the relationship after the first session. A client may, of course, decide to terminate the relationship early for a variety of other reasons even though the counselor's attending behavior is superb. The point here is that the effective counselor has an attending response repertoire that quickly forms the foundation for a solid helping relationship. From the beginning, the counselor deliberately strives to avoid behaviors that are detrimental to the relationship.

Physical Attending

Building on the self as instrument concept, the counselor must perform specific actions to adopt a posture of involvement with a client and to be physically attentive. Regardless of what problems clients may present, counselors are expected to be able to control and modify their own behavior appropriately. Some specific guidelines for effective physical attending are as follows:

- *Have no physical object between you and the client.* An object such as a desk places a clear physical barrier between you and the client. Even executives of major corporations recognize this, and when they really want to become involved in helping someone they will come out from behind their desks and work with the person face-to-face.
- *Maintain a comfortable working distance.* In general, being too close to a person while attempting to facilitate a therapeutic relationship is not very helpful. Neither is being too distant. Many individual and cultural differences are involved here; however, a distance of about three to five feet between persons in a sitting position is usually suitable.

- *Face the other person directly.* The posture that demonstrates the most involvement is facing the person squarely (Carkhuff, 1983; Egan, 1986). Squarely facing very shy or very disturbed persons, or persons from different cultural backgrounds, is often perceived as threatening behavior, however. In cases such as these, one can begin by facing the client at an angle of about 15 degrees off center so that both the counselor and the client can more comfortably look away at times. As the relationship develops, a more direct face-to-face posture may be taken.
- *Establish eye contact.* The counselor generally should initiate eye contact with the client. Again, this is to begin with some discretion. Direct, sustained eye contact can create discomfort in a shy person and can be perceived negatively by people from different cultural backgrounds. Essentially, the idea is to try to establish eye contact while also scanning the client's face and body for nonverbal cues. At times when the relationship and the interaction are particularly intense, there may be long periods of sustained eye-to-eye contact not immediately noticed by either of the participants.
- *Maintain an open-position posture.* Crossed arms and crossed legs are often signs of lessened involvement. An open posture is a sign that the counselor is open to what the client has to say and open to communicating directly to the client. It is a nondefensive position.
- *Lean toward the other.* This is another "sign of presence, availability, or involvement" (Egan, 1975, p. 65). One might lean forward as much as 20 degrees when attending from a sitting position.
- *Remain relatively relaxed.* A relaxed posture says to the client, "I am comfortable with you."
- *Become aware of your client's breathing pattern (and your own).* People who are anxious tend to virtually stop breathing. Maintaining a regular deep breathing pattern will help you and your client attain an appropriate state of relaxation.

These basic nonverbal attending behaviors can go far in helping to develop the climate necessary for creating a successful therapeutic alliance.

Psychological Attending

Counseling is usually portrayed as a predominantly verbal activity when actually it is much more than that. There may seem to be a continuous stream of words in a given counseling session; however, the counselor is attending to more than just the words. To be totally with another person, to attend to a client psychologically, incorporates appropriate physical attending along with systematic observation and listening with all of your senses.

Psychological attending helps to provide the counselor with a full picture of the client's world without interfering in the counseling relationship as psychological tests and other assessment devices could. Clients project every part of their existence in the way they talk, move, dress, act, look, feel, and think. If counselors can see and hear with all of their senses, they will discover much that will be vital to their understanding of a client's world.

Observing

Perhaps as important as any other skill is the counselor's skill of observation. Even before appropriate attending behavior is established or clients begin to speak, the counselor can begin to make important observations. As clients enter the room and take a seat, observations of their general energy level can be made in four specific areas: grooming, posture, body build, and nonverbal expressions (Carkhuff, 1983). Grooming cues include appearance of clothes, hair, hands—including fingernails—and face. Nonverbal cues to note initially are speed of movement, facial expressions, gestures, and head and eye movements (Carkhuff, 1980). The authors have found that greeting their clients with a handshake before each session is an important source of data. Cues about posture include persons' carriage as they walk and sit and whether they lean forward when interacting or sit with their head drooping. Abnormalities in weight and muscle tone are important characteristics to observe in clients' body builds. Table 6.1 depicts some nonverbal behaviors and their possible effects or meanings.

The counselor should make observations for three reasons. First, the observations "provide a basis for making helpful behavior descriptions" (Loughary & Ripley, 1979, p. 117).

TABLE 6.1   Inventory of nonverbal behavior.

Nonverbal Dimensions	Observed Behaviors	Description of Counselor–Client Interaction	Possible Effects or Meanings
Paralinguistics	Whining or lisp	Client is complaining about having a hard time losing weight; voice goes up like a whine.	Dependency or emotional emphasis
Face	Eyes strained; furrow on brow; mouth tight	Client has just reported strained situation as a child. Then client sits with lips pursed together and a frown.	Anger or concern; sadness
Eyes	Staring or fixation on person or object	Counselor has just asked client to consider consequences of a certain decision. Client is silent and gazes at a picture on the wall.	Preoccupation, possibly rigidness or uprightness
Mouth	Open mouth without speaking	It has been a long session. As counselor talks, client's mouth parts slightly.	Suppression of yawn-fatigue
Arms and hands	Arms folded across chest	Counselor has just initiated conversation. Client does not respond verbally; sits back in chair with arms crossed against chest.	Avoidance of interpersonal exchange or dislike
Total body	Facing other person squarely or leaning forward	Client shares a concern and faces counselor directly while talking; continues to face counselor while counselor responds.	Openness to interpersonal communication and exchange
Distance	Moves away	Counselor has just confronted client; client moves back before responding verbally.	Signal that space has been invaded

Adapted from *Interview Strategies from Helpers: Fundamental Skills and Cognitive Behavioral Interventions* by W. H. Cormier and L. S. Cormier. Copyright © 1998, 1991, 1985, and 1975 Brooks/Cole Publishing Company, Pacific Grove, CA 93950, a division of International Thomson Publishing Inc. By permission of the publisher.

These skillfully made observations provide a data base to enable counselors to understand clients and their problems, as well as to determine change. Thus, counselors will not be relying only on clients' verbal messages. Some practitioners, in fact, claim that the nonverbal messages are more accurate than the verbal ones (James & Jongeward, 1971). Second, these observational data can also be useful in providing accurate information that enables counselors to confront clients on the inconsistencies and contradictions between their verbal and nonverbal behaviors in the later stages of counseling. Third, observing helps in the identification of feelings. The ability to tune into and deal with a client's emotional condition is in many cases much more productive than focusing on clients' words. Words deal with the content of clients' messages. According to Mehrabian (1971), most people pick up only about 7% of a message from the content, whereas 38% is picked up from such things as tone of voice, volume, and speed of talk; 55% is picked up from facial expressions and other body language.

An effective counselor should be able to describe behavior accurately. Once observations have been made, however, care must be taken with any inferences that have been made. Any inferences made from observations must be viewed as hypotheses which need to be confirmed or denied over time by the helpee's behavioral and verbal expressions. Observations should not be taken as a valid basis for making diagnoses about a person (Carkhuff, 1980, p. 53).

Some inferences can relate directly to client levels of functioning and can significantly affect the way a counselor interacts with a client. A counselor working to develop empathy with a client might particularly notice and match the client's energy and emotional levels. For example, a counselor would not emit a high energy level with enthusiastic and rapid speech with a client who has low energy and very slow, deliberate speech.

Ideas in action   A major task for a counselor is to become an accurate describer of human behavior. Find a place on campus or at a shopping mall where you can observe people. Note differences in appearances and behavior. Consider how you might describe the characteristics of different individuals if they came to you for counseling. Consider the variety of inferences that might be made from the variety of nonverbal behaviors you see. Share your findings with a classmate.

Active Listening

Active listening is a special type of observing. Here the focus is on observing all aspects of the verbal expressions of the client. Passive listening is when a person is not involved, such as reading a newspaper while someone else talks. Guidelines for active listening include the following:

Resist Distractions.   Use your ability to be a selective listener. Stay with the client in spite of temptations to respond to various external cues. We have all experienced social situations that required the use of our powers of selective listening in order to stay with a conversation in spite of major distractions. Use this same skill in the helping relationship.

Keep the Focus on the Client.   If you are observing appropriately and attending physically, keeping the focus on the verbal output of the client should follow; however, beginning and sometimes experienced counselors can become so concerned with what they are going to say that they simply do not listen to everything that the client says. To assist in keeping the focus on the client it is helpful for the counselor to do the following:

1. *Adopt an attitude of acceptance of what the client says.* This includes being nonjudgmental even though the client may be presenting very controversial or shocking material to you.
2. *Listen to the tone of voice.* When the client speaks, listen to the context of the verbiage, or **paralinguistics.** The "music" often tells more than words do. A client could be describing a very logical straightforward problem, but the voice could have a whiny, helpless quality about it. On the other hand, people presenting very serious, personally devastating problems may not be aware of the personal strength that their voices communicate.
3. *Listen for cues to clients' feelings.* In many cases, it is more important to first help clients communicate their emotions before effectively working with the cognitive components of their problems. Sometimes working with the emotional content may be all that the counselor needs to do.
4. *Listen for common cognitive and emotional themes.* Themes may be repeated, often in different ways (Carkhuff, 1985).
5. *Listen for generalizations, deletions, and distortions.*

   a. **Generalizations:** Clients often avoid being specific, so they inaccurately represent their real experiences through generalizations. "People push me around," for example, is a generalization because the noun *people* fails to identify anyone specifically. We know that all people do not push a client around. The real experience may be, "My father pushes me around." In this statement something specific is identified in the client's experience (Harman & O'Neil, 1981).

   b. **Deletions:** Another way that clients present their experiences inadequately is by leaving things off or deleting them. When clients say, "I'm frightened," they are not including of what or whom they are frightened. The result is a communication with missing parts.

   c. **Distortions:** "By distortions, we refer to things which are represented in the client's model, but are twisted in some way [limiting] her ability to act and [increasing] her potential for pain" (Bandler & Grinder, 1975, p. 51). For example, a person may distort all critical messages received with the response, "I'm not lovable," or "I'm incapable." This personalizing of critical messages prevents the person from learning anything of value from outside feedback.

Your careful observations of the client's verbal output as well as physical appearance and behavior can be valuable in both establishing the therapeutic relationship and in helping to clearly understand the client's problem. Obviously, beginning counselors will not be able to listen for and become aware of all aspects of client communication. A counselor must be aware of the complexity and difficulty of high-level active listening and strive to attain the experience and supervision necessary to develop these skills fully.

Responding as Part of Attending Behavior

For the most part, physical and psychological attending require little verbal initiating or responding on the part of the counselor. In a few rare cases, paying close attention to another person by using the skills described may be all that is necessary to significantly help that person; however, in most cases one must make some specific responses as well as initiate interaction. The skilled counselor is one who has a broad repertoire of responses at hand. Once clients have summoned the courage to come and talk to someone about their problems, they will often let loose with a torrent of stored up thoughts and feelings. In such cases the counselors do not really have to say much but may need only to attend and express what Ivey (1988) calls "encouragers."

Encouragers

Encouragers are the many verbal and nonverbal ways a counselor has to encourage the client to continue to talk about thoughts, feelings, and behaviors without having to ask a battery of questions. Encouragers include such things as "umhum," repetition of one or two of the client's words, nods of the head, and hand gestures. Much physical and psychological attending behavior can be classified as encouraging responses to the client.

Using encouragers helps the counselor tune in to what the client is communicating. When used correctly, clients maintain control of the session by talking about what they want to discuss, and yet they are forced to elaborate, explain, and take a more in-depth look at the problem. Here are some examples of encouraging responses:

- "Tell me more;" "Go on" (perhaps accompanied by an appropriate hand gesture).
- "Um-hum;" "Uh-huh"; (often accompanied by a nod of the head).
- "And ...;" "Then ...?", "So ...?;" "Oh ...?"
- The repetition of the last few words: "...he yelled at you."
- "Give me an example;" "For instance ..."
- "And to you, that means...?"

Encouragers are accompanied by a great deal of attending behavior and have considerable power and importance, particularly in initial helping sessions. Using encouragers keeps the focus on clients and helps them tell their stories as clearly as possible.

STAGE 2—EXPLORATION SKILLS

The skills used in the exploration stage of the counseling process build on the attending skills of stage 1. Exploration skills include responding with basic empathy; reflecting meaning, probes, and questions; responding with silence; and summarizing.

Responding with Empathy

Empathy is the most important of all of the core conditions. For example, you could be very respectful and genuine, but your effectiveness would be limited if you were not an empathic listener. **Empathy** "involves listening to clients, understanding them...and communicating this understanding to them so that they might understand themselves more fully and act on their understanding (Egan, 1994, p. 106). Empathy is the counselor understanding the other person's thoughts and feelings as if the counselor were this other person, as if the counselor were attaining an innerview. Empathy includes all of the attributes of active listening.

When clients begin to tell their stories and are encouraged by attending behavior, the counselor should "communicate to the client what it is that he understands of the client's perspective of the world" (Egan, 1975, p. 73). The closer the counselor's response to the client's ideas and feelings, then the more accurate the empathy will be. Before actually beginning the work of helping a client solve a problem, both the counselor and the client should have a common understanding of what the problem really is. If the counselor and the client do not have this common understanding, they may end up working on no problem at all. This could result in an early termination of the relationship, with the counselor saying that the client was "resistant" and the client considering the counselor to be inept.

There may, of course, be the circumstance in which the client does not have a clearly identified problem even after a number of counseling sessions have taken place. The client may simply need to be with another person and may remain more or less in the exploratory stage throughout the relationship. This, too, needs to be understood and communicated empathically.

Accurate empathy is important for another major reason. Often a client will approach a counselor with a safe presenting problem, a problem that is not too threatening. The client. in fact, may use this presenting problem to test how much to trust the counselor before the client brings up the real problem. If the empathic responses are accurate, the client's real problem, whether the initial presenting problem or not, will more likely be discussed. Most importantly, the counselor's empathic understanding enables clients to become their own counselors and growth enhancers.

Empathic Responding to Content and Feelings

As noted above, clients continually communicate who they are by what they say––the tone of their voice, the words used, the speed of their speech, and their nonverbal behaviors. When experiencing this data, counselors must be able to communicate to their clients what has been picked up regarding feelings and the thoughts, behavior, and experience that underlie those feelings. It is not enough to say, "I understand;" clients need to know what it is that is understood.

In learning to communicate understanding of what has been said, it is helpful to begin by focusing on the content and to reflect this back to the client.

CLIENT: "It looks pretty bleak to me. I don't see any way out of this situation. I've about given up."

COUNSELOR: "From your perspective things really seem hopeless."

In responding to a client, the response must not be perceived as a rote parroting of a statement. There are, however, occasions (as mentioned in the discussion of encouragers) when the restatement of a word or a sentence can be helpful in allowing the client to continue to explore the nature of the problem in a productive way.

When there appears to be a natural break in the client's verbal communication, or when the client begins to be repetitive without adding new content or feelings, the counselor may make a response that lets the client know exactly what has been heard.

COUNSELOR: "So you're interested in finding out what job opportunities are available for liberal arts graduates."

Once responding to content has become comfortable, move on and practice responding to feelings using the same format.

CLIENT: (wringing her hands) "I can't get control of things. I think I have everything handled well, and then things just fall apart."

COUNSELOR: "You feel really frustrated, because everything you work for does not go right."

The statement above might be considered a carefully worded paraphrase. It describes the person's feelings and also cites a cause for these feelings. The client, hearing such a statement, is able to acknowledge it as being correct, correct it if it is erroneous, or simply continue from that point in the exploration of thoughts and feelings. If the statement is incorrect, the counselor can clarify what was misstated and then rephrase the initial statement.

COUNSELOR: "You feel scared, because you think you are losing control."

All client statements have a feeling component. The emotional content is often the most difficult to work with from both the client's and the counselor's points of view. Our society generally does not encourage the free and open expression of emotions, so clients often have a difficult time expressing the emotions that may be tying them up in knots. The counselor may have an equally difficult time trying to communicate in words the emotions with which the client appears to be struggling.

When trying to describe feelings, avoid statements such as,"You feel like you've taken on too much responsibility" or "You feel that you've been put in the wrong class." Statements beginning with "you feel like..." and "you feel that..." tend to describe thoughts or beliefs rather than emotions. Note this in the client's speech as well. "I feel like going home" is not dealing directly with an emotion. This is more an example of a person's representational mode of speech than of an emotional condition.

In order to come up with words or phrases that are interchangeable with the feelings of the client, Carkhuff (1980) suggests a helpful approach. If you have a general impression of what the client is expressing, ask yourself the following: "When I feel (general feeling), how do I feel?" If the client's term was "lonely," you could ask yourself, "How do I feel when I feel lonely?" Some of your responses might be "sad," "dejected," perhaps even "scared." You might check these out to see if they fit. Some words might be dismissed, because they clearly are not applicable; others might need modification by the client, such as in the following example.

CLIENT: "Well, when I'm feeling lonely I'm not really scared, but I do get a little frightened that maybe I'll never have any friends at this school."

Table 6.2 contains a list of general categories of both positive and negative feelings, along with different levels of intensity within each category. In terms of developing basic empathy, the counselor should communicate at least at the same general level of intensity as the client. In studying the list in Table 6.2, you may add words and phrases to each level presented. To communicate at all levels, the counselor must be able to recognize feelings and their level of intensity, as well as have a well-developed feeling vocabulary.

TABLE 6.2   Categories of feelings.

Relative Intensity of Words	Feeling Category				
	Anger	Conflict	Fear	Happiness	Sadness
Mild Feeling	Annoyed	Blocked	Apprehensive	Amused	Apathetic
	Bothered	Bound	Concerned	Anticipating	Bored
	Bugged	Caught	Tense	Comfortable	Confused
	Irked	Caught in a bind	Tight	Confident	Disappointed
	Irritated	Pulled	Uneasy	Glad	Discontented
	Peeved			Pleased	Mixed up
	Ticked			Relieved	Resigned
					Unsure
Moderate Feeling	Disgusted	Locked	Afraid	Delighted	Abandoned
	Hacked	Pressured	Alarmed	Eager	Burdened
	Harassed	Torn	Anxious	Happy	Discouraged
	Mad		Fearful	Hopeful	Distressed
	Provoked		Frightened	Joyful	Down
	Put upon		Shook	Surprised	Drained
	Resentful		Threatened	Up	Empty
	Set up		Worried		Hurt
	Spiteful				Lonely
	Used				Lost
					Sad
					Unhappy
					Weighted
Intense Feeling	Angry	Ripped	Desperate	Bursting	Anguished
	Boiled	Wrenched	Overwhelmed	Ecstatic	Crushed
	Burned		Panicky	Elated	Deadened
	Contemptful		Petrified	Enthusiastic	Depressed
	Enraged		Scared	Enthralled	Despairing
	Fuming		Terrified	Excited	Helpless
	Furious		Terror-stricken	Free	Hopeless
	Hateful		Tortured	Fulfilled	Humiliated
	Hot			Moved	Miserable
	Infuriated			Proud	Overwhelmed
	Pissed			Terrific	Smothered
	Smoldering			Thrilled	Tortured
	Steamed			Turned on	

Note: The context in which words such as these are used may result in shifting their intensity as well as changing the category in which they are used. Words are listed here only to suggest the range of options available to the helper seeking to identify feelings of the client. From *Helping Relationships and Strategies,* by D. E. Hutchins and C. G. Cole. Copyright © 1997, 1992, 1986 Brooks/Cole Publishing Company, Pacific Grove, CA 93950, a division of International Thomson Publishing Inc. By permission of the publisher.

 **Ideas in** Pair up with a classmate or friend. Have your partner tell you a personal experience. From time to time let your partner know what you have been hearing by responding with statements that include actual emotions you have observed. After about 10–15 minutes, reverse roles. Afterward, discuss how this type of responding influenced the interaction.

Reflection of Meaning

In helping clients to explore the nature of their problems, ascertain the meaning that is attributed to events and situations in clients' lives. As Frankl (1959) has pointed out, events in and of themselves are neutral; people ascribe meaning to them. A summer thunderstorm can mean joy and hope for a farmer but sadness and discouragement for a baseball player.

As clients continue to communicate verbally and nonverbally, the meaning of the various messages must be ascertained in order to help. Clients can continue to talk without any direction, which may provide cathartic relief; however, some feedback is generally helpful. As counselors work to communicate empathy with clients, they are primarily reflecting the thoughts and feelings that they have picked up with all of their senses. With all of the data collected, the counselor may or may not get a sense of what the messages mean to the client.

COUNSELOR: "I sense that it is very important for you to be the best in your class."

COUNSELOR: "Being divorced is quite confusing. On the one hand it means having a lot of freedom that you say you've never had, and yet on the other hand you are now very lonely."

Through the process of reflecting the meaning as perceived by the counselor, the client's thoughts and feelings may become clarified, which then leads to the next counseling stage—actually understanding the nature and scope of the problem. Even though Carl Rogers never included responding to meaning in the core conditions for a helping relationship, it probably should be considered as one of the fundamental conditions of Rogers's Person-Centered Therapy. Rogers's approach is often characterized as predominantly paraphrasing and reflecting feelings, "however, meaning plays an even more important part in his overall thinking and conceptualization" (Ivey, 1983, p. 136).

Yalom (1985), in describing his landmark study of group leadership (Lieberman, Yalom, & Miles, 1973), reported that two leadership functions, caring and meaning attribution, had a direct relationship to positive outcomes in counseling: "The higher the caring and the higher the meaning attribution, the higher the positive outcome" (p. 502). Caring includes such factors as offering support, affection, praise, protection, warmth, acceptance, genuineness, and concern. Meaning attribution includes clarifying, translating feelings and experiences into ideas, providing a cognitive framework for change, explaining, and interpreting. Both caring and meaning attribution are critical; however, neither alone is sufficient to ensure success. Yalom's conclusion is that "the Rogerian factors of empathy, genuineness, and unconditional positive regard thus seem incomplete; we must add the cognitive function of the leader" (p. 502).

Reflection of meaning in the exploration stage "focuses on the client's frame of reference even if the meanings and values are unclear." As a result of reflection of meaning "clients search for deeper ideas underlying their statements and behaviors and learn to interpret their experience from their own frame of reference" (Ivey, 1980, p. 137).

Summarization Responses

Summarizations, a form of empathic responding, are used to pull together material in a counseling session over a period of time, from a few minutes, to an entire session or to several sessions. Generally, the counselor summarizes selected key concepts and dimensions as accurately as possible for the client. A request to determine the degree of accuracy may be added to the summary statement.

COUNSELOR: "You've started several times in the last few minutes to talk about how angry you feel toward your mother, but each time you've wandered off on a different topic. You seem to want to deal with this anger toward your mother, but it is awfully difficult to stay with it. Does that fit?"

COUNSELOR: (at the end of the session) "You began the session today working on trying to feel better about yourself, and you worked hard. You've been able to come up with several things that you already appreciate about yourself as well as a couple of things you want to feel better about—such as your grades. You've made a plan to build yourself up and to stop putting yourself down. You've shown a lot of strength and determination as you've done this, and it really feels as though you are serious about following through on your plan. Is that all pretty accurate?"

COUNSELOR: "In each of the last three sessions now you've begun with a different problem, each time coming up with ways of solving your problem; yet you don't seem to follow through on any of these ideas. Now you bring in another new problem when it is not clear whether we're finished with the previous problems."

Summarization is important to help keep a client moving, to add more data to what has already been given, and to provide some structure and direction to what may seem to be a casual, random conversation. Accurate summarization is an empathic response; like responding to feelings or reflecting meaning, summarization is an important component of the greater skill of responding empathically.

Respect.   Adhering to the behaviors just described communicates to clients that you care for them and value them and their thoughts. This attribute is not seen as often as it should be in society and so is particularly valuable for a counselor to demonstrate.

Genuineness.   If you have attended well, displayed empathy, and have been open, honest, and respectful in your responses (and not just been a mirror, a blank screen, or an immediate advice giver), you have demonstrated genuineness. Genuineness was one of the basic conditions that Rogers (1957) described as a major characteristic in establishing the therapeutic relationship. Genuineness, or congruence, comes when your external communication matches your internal experience. Patterson (1974) describes individuals experiencing genuineness as real persons in a real encounter, not phonies playing a role. One way of responding overtly in a genuine manner would be through the use of self-disclosure (see chapter 7).

Responding Using Probes and Questions

As noted in chapter 5, the use of questions in counseling sessions is controversial. Some counselors suggest that counseling can be done effectively without questions; however, most counselors ask questions as a counseling technique. If questions are to be used, which types of questions are better than others? Are questions more appropriately used at certain stages of the counseling process? How do probes differ from questions?

Probing

A **probe** is a response that attempts to seek information or to provoke further response along a certain line (Porter, 1950). Probing responses usually take the form of direct or indirect questions. Some probes are commands or directives, such as, "Tell me more" or "Go on." These open-ended probes are especially helpful during the earlier stages of the counseling process, but they are useful in all stages. Other probes take the form of statements, such as, "I suppose you could tell me how much longer you're going to continue to do that."

Questioning

As the counselor works to establish the therapeutic relationship and to understand the client's world during the first three stages (attending, exploration, and understanding), direct questioning is usually not as effective as the other responses already described. During the third stage and throughout the action phase (stage 4) of the counseling process, the use of questions is the most effective.

After the initial intake session when some specific questions are necessary, the use of questions should be minimized in order to facilitate client exploration and understanding of thoughts and feelings. Such a procedure prevents the unproductive pattern of the counselor asking the questions and the client waiting for the next question. Instead of the focus being on the client, it is on the counselor, with the counselor feverishly trying to come up with the question that will break the case wide open. The session becomes an inquisition. An environment is established in which the counselor is clearly the authority and expert. The client may then expect that once the questions are over, the expert will have the proper solution to the problem.

Clients tend to take very little responsibility in that type of situation. Even when satisfactory solutions are found, clients do not learn to solve their own problems. The next time they are stuck, then they must seek out another authority.

Direct versus Indirect Questions

When questions are called for, it is important to know the types of questions to ask and the effectiveness of each type. **Direct questions** are to the point, without any ambiguity or vagueness. The **indirect question,** like the commanding probe, usually has no question mark at the end; however, it is generally clear that a query is being made and that an answer is expected. Such queries can be presented without ambiguity. The indirect questions are more open in nature, giving the client more room to respond and to give direction to the session content. Examples of direct and indirect questions are:

DIRECT: "How is your new school?"

INDIRECT: "I wonder how your new school seems to you."

DIRECT: "What is your opinion about getting an abortion?"

INDIRECT: "I wonder what some of your thoughts are on abortion."

DIRECT: "Your divorce is almost final. How do you feel about it?"

INDIRECT: "I'll bet you've got a lot you'd like to talk about, since your divorce is almost final."

DIRECT: "Isn't it hard to do everything you have to do with four little kids to take care of?"

INDIRECT: "I'd be interested in hearing how you manage to do everything with four young children."

Types of Direct Questions

Open, noncued questions that give no indication of the correct response can be helpful in uncovering affective and cognitive material that has not been brought out in any other way; for example, "What are your feelings about school?" With an open question, the client is free to respond in any way. Open questions usually begin with "how," "what," "could," "would," or "why" (see Table 6.3).

How and what questions solicit facts and gather information. They can also focus on client process or emotion, thus developing greater client self-awareness. For example, a counselor might ask a client, "How do you stop yourself from asking for what you want?" or "What does it do for you to act like a child?" "Could" or "would" questions facilitate client self-exploration. An example is, "Could you share some of your fears about getting

TABLE 6.3   Types of direct questions.

Exploratory Open, Noncued Questions	Exploratory Closed, Noncued Questions	Nonexploratory Closed, Cued Questions
	Examples	
"What did you think about what Bob said?"	"Did you feel hurt by what Bob said?"	"You didn't let Bob's remark get to you, did you?"
"What was your reaction when your mom walked in?"	"Were you scared when your mom walked in?"	"When your mom walked in, you were scared to death, weren't you?"
"Where would you like to begin?"	"Do you want to begin by discussing your family?"	"You wanted to begin by discussing your anger, didn't you?"
	Characteristics	
Opens doors to communication. Communicates to the respondent that the questioner wants to hear about whatever the respondent wants to say. A wide range of responses possible.	Closed because this type of question often results in simple yes or no responses with no elaboration.	Blocks open communication. Cue a desired answer; makes it difficult for respondent if the truth is in opposition to the questioner's desires.

Adapted from *The Individual and the School.* by F. Wilson, J. Lopis, and M. Radke, 1978, San Diego, CA: Collegiate Publishing. Copyright © 1978 by Collegiate Publishing.

married?" "Why" questions generally produce reasons, excuses, explanations, or intellectual history. They can also lead to client defensiveness and are rarely recommended by any theoretical orientation.

Closed, noncued questions limit the client to either affirmation or denial (see Table 6.3). To answer the question, "Do you like school?" the client needs to answer only "yes" or "no." The closed question can be useful if there is some particular information the client has not voluntarily disclosed (for example, "Are you married?"); however, if this approach is continued, the focus of the session is controlled by the questions rather than by what the client wants to work on.

A third type of question, the **closed, cued question,** clearly blocks communication. Built into the question is the cue to the desired answer (for example, "People who are really honest wouldn't lie, would they?"). Often the cues are found both in the tone of voice and the expressions on the counselor's face, as well as in the words themselves. This type of question has little known therapeutic value for a client.

Ideas in action

The "No Question Innerview"

An axiom in counseling is that "behind every question is a statement." Making statements could well be more therapeutic than continually asking questions.

Invite a colleague to share a problem with you. Begin the session by saying, "You can begin telling me what is of concern to you when you are ready." Once your colleague begins, structure all of your responses so that they are statements and not questions. Don't be concerned if you are hesitant when you do this. If you find yourself starting to ask a question, stop immediately and form a statement. You can conclude your session by providing a summary.

Get feedback from your colleague about how well this approach facilitated the exploration of the problem.

Responding with Silence

Silence as a response can often be very powerful. It can have much the same effect as that of an encourager such as "go on" or "and then…" Silence keeps the focus on the client and allows the client, rather than the counselor, to direct the content of the sessions. Goodman (1984) reports that significant changes in the helping relationship occur when the length of silence or pauses between utterances are increased even if only by a fraction of a second. "The major effect…was one of feeling less crowded or being allowed to speak freely" (pp. 278–279). Crowding the client, making very short or no pauses, and interrupting tend to reduce the disclosure of personal feelings. When the time between responses is expanded, the discloser naturally feels invited to take time to reply, to delve more deeply into feelings and to try to express it to an uncrowding listener (Goodman, 1984, p. 279).

If the client's material discussed after a silence is repetitious, then a verbal response of some sort is usually required of the counselor. In sessions when client or counselor both are talking continuously, there is not much time for the absorption of new material. Silence can help to meet this need, especially at times when some significant learning appears to be taking place. Silence can help this learning become a lasting part of the client's behavior.

SUMMARY

Virtually all theoretical approaches to counseling acknowledge the importance of the therapeutic relationship, regardless of the number of sessions with a client. This chapter has focused on the skills needed to develop the first two stages of the helping relationship, attending and exploration.

Attending skills (stage 1) relate to establishing rapport and being responsive to the client through the use of physical and psychological attending behaviors. While the attending skills involve nonverbal responding to the client, including silence, the major verbal responses stressed in stage 1 are encouragers to help the client continue to discuss a problem.

Basic empathy is the major exploration skill presented in stage 2. Responding with empathy refers to the counselor's ability to understand and to communicate accurately to the client what the counselor understands. Reflecting feelings and meaning builds empathy and helps clients to clarify their thoughts. The judicious use of probes, questions, and silence in the exploration process has also been described. Summary statements help tie together key concepts over various periods of time. They help provide structure and direction to the counseling process.

QUESTIONS AND ACTIVITIES

1. Locate a video of a counseling session and play it with the sound off. Formulate responses that you might make to the client based on your careful observations. You might tape-record or write these statements down. Be sure to include emotions as part of each response. After you have watched and responded to the client for about a period of 15 minutes, then play back the tape and see how accurate you were.

2. Check out the interviewing techniques of talk show hosts, interviewers on programs such as *Meet The Press,* and TV news reporters. Note how often they use closed, cued questions for which the answer

desired is built into the question. Keep track of how many reporters use the phrase "How do you feel about...?" when they mean what do you think about...?" Do the reporters ever get a response about feelings?

3. Make a list of five to seven "I feel..." statements, completing the sentence each time. Then go back and scratch out the word "feel" and substitute "think" or "believe" in its place. Which of your statements are now more accurate?

4. Practice attending and exploration behaviors with your family and friends. What results do you notice?

RECOMMENDED READINGS

Carkhuff, R. (1987). *The art of helping* (6th ed.). Amherst, MA: Human Resource Development Press.

Egan, G. (1994). *The skilled helper* (5th ed.). Pacific Grove, CA: Brooks/Cole.

Ivey, A., Ivey, M. B., & Simek-Morgan, L. (1997). *Counseling and Psychotherapy* (4th ed.). Boston: Allyn & Bacon.

REFERENCES

Bandler, R., & Grinder, J. (1975). *The structure of magic* (Vol. 1). Palo Alto, CA: Science and Behavior Books.

Brammer, L. (1985). *The helping relationship: Process and skills* (3rd ed.). Englewood Cliffs, NJ: Prentice-Hall.

Carkhuff, R. (1980). *The art of helping* (4th ed.). Amherst, MA: Human Resource Development Press.

Carkhuff, R. (1983). *The art of helping* (5th ed.). Amherst, MA: Human Resource Development Press.

Carkhuff, R. (1985). *The art of helping* (6th ed.). Amherst, MA: Human Resource Development Press.

Carkhuff, R. (1987). *The art of helping* (7th ed.). Amherst, MA: Human Resource Development Press.

Combs, A. W., & Avila, D. L. (1985). *Helping relationships: Basic concepts for the helping professions* (3rd ed.). Boston: Allyn & Bacon.

Cormier, W. H., & Cormier, L. S. (1991). *Interview strategies for helpers.* Pacific Grove, CA: Brooks/Cole.

Danish, S., & Hauer, A. (1973). *Helping skills: A basic training program.* New York: Behavioral Publications.

Egan, G. (1975). *The skilled helper.* Monterey, CA: Brooks/Cole.

Egan, G. (1986). *The skilled helper* (3rd ed.). Monterey, CA: Brooks/Cole.

Egan, G. (1994). *The skilled helper* (5th ed.). Pacific Grove, CA: Brooks/Cole.

Frankl, V. (1959). *Man's search for meaning: An introduction to logotherapy.* New York: Washington Square Press.

Gazda, G., Asbury, F., & Balzer, F. (1984). *Human relations development* (3rd ed.). Boston: Allyn & Bacon.

Goodman, G. (1984). SASHA tapes: Expanding options for helping intended communications. In D. Larson (Ed.), *Teaching psychological skills* (pp. 271–286). Monterey, CA: Brooks/Cole.

Harman, R., & O'Neil, C. (1981). Neurolinguistic programming for counselors. *Personnel and Guidance Journal, 59*(7), 449–453.

Hutchins, D. E., & Cole, C. G. (1992). *Helping relationships and strategies.* Pacific Grove, CA: Brooks/Cole.

Ivey, A. (1980). *Counseling and psychotherapy: Skills, theories, and practice.* Englewood Cliffs, NJ: Prentice-Hall.

Ivey, A. (1983). *Intentional interviewing and counseling.* Monterey, CA: Brooks/Cole.

Ivey, A. (1988). *Intentional interviewing and counseling.* Pacific Grove, CA: Brooks/Cole.

James, N., & Jongeward, D. (1971). *Born to win.* Reading, MA: Addison-Wesley.

Lieberman, M., Yalom, I., & Miles, M. (1973). *Encounter groups: First facts.* New York: Basic Books.

Loughary, J., & Ripley, T. (1979). *Helping others help themselves: A guide to counseling skills.* New York: McGraw-Hill.

Mehrabian, A. (1971). *Silent messages.* Belmont, CA: Wadsworth.

Patterson, C. H. (1974). *Relationship counseling and psychotherapy.* New York: Harper & Row.

Porter, E. H. (1950). *Introduction to therapeutic counseling.* Boston: Houghton Mifflin.

Rogers, C. (1957). The necessary and sufficient condition of therapeutic personality change. *Journal of Consulting Psychology, 21,* 93–103.

Wilson, F., Lopis, J., & Radke, M. (1978). *The individual and the school.* San Diego, CA: Collegiate Publishing.

Yalom, I. (1985). *The theory and practice of group psychotherapy* (2nd ed.). New York: Basic Books.

chapter 7

DEVELOPING RESPONSE/ABILITY

The Learning of Counseling Skills, Part 2

- Can there be too much empathy?
- Should counselors self-disclose?
- Why is it important for a counselor to be skilled in using confrontational responses?
- In what ways is immediacy (intimacy) considered to be an important part of the counseling process?
- What are effective ways of helping clients solve their own problems?

In this chapter we will build upon the skills which have been described as important for the Attending and Exploration stages of the helping process. Keep in mind that counselors use attending and exploration skills throughout the counseling process. We will now describe the skills related to the Understanding, Action, and Termination stages of counseling.

STAGE 3—UNDERSTANDING

After working through the first two stages of the counseling process and the basic core conditions of empathy and respect have been established, the focus of the third stage is on the client's specific problem. After the third stage, both the counselor and client should fully understand the nature of the client's concerns and agree to take action on the problem. Skills used in the third stage include advanced empathy, self-disclosure, confrontation, and immediacy.

Responding with Advanced Empathy

Egan (1994), in his approach to skill training, makes a distinction between levels of empathy. Basic empathy, as described in stage 2, is a counselor's communicated understanding of the client's shared feelings and meanings. **Advanced empathy,** a skill generally found in the third stage of the counseling process, goes beyond the surface to reach feelings and meanings that are buried, hidden, or in other ways not attainable by the client. The advanced empathy response enables clients to see the need for action and helps them attain a more objective frame of reference. With advanced empathy the counselor is able to put together both stated and unstated material.

Carkhuff (1987) uses the term *personalizing* to describe this additional depth of understanding. He maintains that when counselors accurately add to clients' expressions, they are helping clients understand where they are in relation to where they want or need to be. Personalized, empathic responses can acknowledge the significance described experiences have for the client, the feelings related to the problem, and often, the solution to the problem. A response format for making a personalized, empathic response is as follows: "You feel…because you cannot…and you want to…" (Carkhuff, 1987, p. 128). An example of this type of response is, "You feel angry, because you cannot resolve your differences with your mother, and you want to learn how to work things out with her."

Advanced empathy or personalizing helps clients to

- *See the bigger picture:* "Your problem doesn't seem to be just with your geometry class, you seem to be having trouble with almost everything connected with school."
- *See what is expressed indirectly:* "I think I'm hearing you say that you are more than disappointed—perhaps even angry."
- *See the logical conclusions of what has been said:* "Do I hear you say that, since you have lost all enthusiasm for school, you'd like to drop out, at least for a while?"
- *Open up areas that are only hinted at:* "You've brought up sexual matters a number of times. My guess is that sex is a pretty touchy issue with you—but pretty important, too."
- *See what may have been overlooked:* "I wonder if it's possible that some people take your wit too personally and that they see it as sarcasm rather than humor?"
- *Identify themes:* "You've mentioned several times, in different ways, that people you don't know make you uncomfortable and even frighten you. Is that the way you see it?"
- *Fully own feelings and behaviors:* "I'm not sure whether you are saying that you actually do want to court her."
- *Connect seemingly unrelated topics:* "I'm wondering if there isn't some relationship between your poor grades, the difficulty you are having in getting dates, and the arguments you are having with your parents."

Advanced empathy or personalized responses are hunches or hypotheses based on a fair amount of data gleaned through the preceding stages of the counseling process and which help clients to see a problem more clearly. The counselor can include some tentativeness when expressing advanced empathy or other responses that might be seen as challenging to clients; therefore, clients will not take those responses as accusations or judgments (for example, the counselor can ask, "Does that fit?" or "Is that close?"). Clients should feel comfortable enough to be able to disagree with the counselor's response (Egan, 1986).

The following example illustrates the difference between basic level and advanced empathy.

CLIENT: "I'm having a lot of problems with my parents. Just because they're paying for my college education, they want to control everything I do—like who I should date, where

I should go, even what courses I should take. I don't know how to break free of them and be my own person."

Counselor responses:

a. *Basic empathy:*

COUNSELOR: "You're really angry with your parents for trying to control you when you would like to make your own decisions."

b. *Advanced empathy:*

COUNSELOR: "I hear you wanting to stand on your own two feet and be responsible for yourself. It seems that you are not only angry with your parents, but also at yourself for still having to be dependent on them."

Ideas in action   With a classmate, practice giving basic and advanced empathy responses. Have your colleague briefly tell you a personal concern. Make a basic empathy response by giving a description of the feelings and meaning that you heard. Then follow this up with an advanced empathy response by providing some additive material that you have picked up. You can qualify this response by including a phrase such as, "Is that accurate?" Reverse roles and repeat; then discuss the effectiveness of these two types of responses.

Variation: Practice the advanced empathy response using the format suggested by Carkhuff.

Too Much Accurate Empathy?

In responding to clients, counselors may give what they consider to be accurate empathic descriptions of clients' emotional states and find that the clients reject the descriptions cold. A counselor could then work with a client to come up with a statement that is more acceptable and should also make a mental note of the first statement. In this situation the counselor observes that empathy, if it is extremely accurate, closely resembles a form of confrontation. It could be that the counselor is responding accurately to expressed or implied feelings that the client has not fully acknowledged or accepted.

COUNSELOR: "It seems to me that you're saying that you hate your mother."

CLIENT: "No, I love my mother. You're not supposed to hate your mother."

If the counselor has picked up an accurate feeling that is rejected by the client, it will quite likely be a theme that will recur. The recurring theme can be responded to in subsequent empathic response. If that response is accurate, the client may be more likely to acknowledge it when confronted with it the second or third time it occurs. If the response is not accepted even though it is a recurring theme, it is not the duty of the counselor to browbeat the client or force an interpretation on the client. Such an action would be inappropriate and unethical.

Responding with Self-Disclosure

The third core condition of the therapeutic alliance, genuineness or congruence, can be manifested in a variety of ways. Starting at the attending stage, counselors must demonstrate that they are genuine people, not phonies; being **congruent** is when nonverbal cues match verbal output. Clients are often able to identify a counselor who is trying to perform a role and play psychological games. The challenge is to be a trustworthy model for your clients and to help them learn new ways of responding in their personal lives.

Self-disclosure refers to counselors sharing personal information about themselves. These revelations may be similar to or different from the revelations of the client. Self-disclosure also includes personal statements about counselors' ideas, values, attitudes, and experiences.

What happens in the counseling relationship must be for the benefit of the client and must be related to a counseling goal. Self-disclosure must not be done simply to make the counselor feel better. When used effectively, counselor self-disclosure can be a model for client disclosure. It can set a comfortable atmosphere for client self-disclosure and exploration. When self-disclosure is inappropriate, the focus tends to shift to the counselor rather than remaining on the client. Clients also may view counselors who self-disclose inappropriately as phony or manipulative. In such cases the helping process is blocked. When self-disclosure is used too sparsely, it may hinder client disclosures, or clients may view the counselor as aloof. A middle ground developed through clinical experience is the most effective.

Most helpful counselor self-disclosure responses consist of "I" statements that are made in direct response to statements made by the client, so they are close to what the client is currently experiencing. Some clients can feel threatened or frightened by counselors' self-disclosures. Counselors need to understand their clients quite well so that self-disclosure is effective; therefore, most counselor self-disclosure is more appropriate in the later stages of the counseling process. Counselor self-disclosure can also lead to or become part of confrontation and immediacy interactions, terms described later in this chapter. Examples of appropriate self-disclosure are provided here.

CLIENT: "I'm not sure you can understand how painful it is for me, and how abandoned and empty I feel, since my wife has left me."

COUNSELOR: "I can sense your pain, hurt, and feeling of loneliness perhaps even more than you realize, since I went through a similar experience when my husband found another woman."

CLIENT: "I can't tell you how much I've gotten out of counseling. You've helped me get through a very tough time."

COUNSELOR: "I really appreciate your openness and the way in which you have decided to take charge of your life. I have learned a great deal from you."

Egan (1994) notes that self-disclosure is inappropriate when it is done too frequently or when it places burdens on clients. The clients might feel as though they have to counsel the counselor. One key to effective counselor self-disclosure is to note whether the focus of the session continues to remain on the client.

Responding with Confrontation

Confrontation is a controversial term. It is often thought of in its most negative sense as a verbal attack; however, **confrontation** is a form of advanced empathy which provides the client an opportunity to look at thoughts and behaviors that may be harmful to oneself or others and to change (Egan, 1994). To avoid what he calls the "more biting term *confrontation*," Egan now offers the word *challenge* in its place. David Augsburger (1981), on the other hand, makes a persuasive case for the use of the term *caring confrontation*. Whichever term counselors may use, counselors should understand that clients may still perceive that they have been confronted. In fact, even basic empathy responses may seem confrontational when clients hear what they have been communicating. Counseling is essentially a confrontational process, and counselors should become personally comfortable with that fact. They need to learn to offer confrontational or challenging responses skillfully.

To confront someone in a therapeutic way is to respond with a very high level of empathy. The counselor understands the client so well that the counselor is aware of some distortion in the client's perception of the world or the counselor has observed some discrepancies in the client's behavior. The counselor then responds to the client, describing what has been observed.

When counselors give a confrontation response, they are describing discrepancies they have observed in a client's behavior. There are three broad categories of confrontation responses:

1. Communicating perceived discrepancies between the client's expression of what he is and what he wants to be (real self versus ideal self)
2. Communicating perceived discrepancies between the client's verbal expressions about himself (awareness or insight) and his behavior, either as it is observed by the counselor or reported by the client
3. Communicating perceived discrepancies between the client's expressed experience of himself and the counselor's experience of him (Carkhuff, 1969, p. 191)

An observant counselor may attain sufficient data to make any or all of the three types of confrontation responses from the very beginning of the relationship; however, direct confrontation in the attending or exploration stages is not always productive. Counselors should be tentative and cautious in making early confrontation responses. "Premature direct confrontation may have a demoralizing effect on an inadequately prepared helpee" (Carkhuff, 1969, p. 93). Examples of possible early positive confrontation responses are the following: "It seems to me that you're saying two different things" or "I'd like to check something out here—a few minutes ago you said A, and now you are saying B. I'm sort of confused." While confrontational in nature, these are clarification statements.

As has been noted, confrontation can be threatening to both counselors and clients. Often, counselors are people who want to be liked and who do not want to do anything that would cause anyone to get angry or unhappy with them. One way of assuring that clients will not get upset is never to confront or challenge them. Clients usually do not like to feel uncomfortable, and being confronted directly with distortions, deletions, or discrepancies in behavior is likely to raise levels of discomfort. A change in behavior, however, rarely takes place without some discomfort. Often the ultimate choice clients have to make is whether they are more uncomfortable with their present behavior than they would be if they changed it. Often, clients would prefer to talk about how bad they feel rather than put themselves through a process of change that would possibly ease their problem. Ironically, not confronting clients could leave them frustrated with the counseling process.

Confrontations are crucial to the counseling process. As Patterson (1974) points out, "Direct communications precipitate an awareness of a crisis in the client that, when faced, leads to movement to higher levels of functioning. The goal is to enable the client to confront himself and when desirable, others" (p. 76). According to Carkhuff, confrontation is indeed essential to life itself. "Confrontation of self and others is prerequisite to the healthy individual's encounter with life" (Carkhuff, 1969, p. 93). Counselors who protect clients by not confronting them appropriately are not being helpful and are probably also protecting themselves.

In addition to being aware that appropriate confrontation is important for client growth, the counselor should realize that confrontation need not be limited to negative distortions, deletions, or discrepancies. Confrontation also can be used to describe assets and resources that are discounted or unrecognized.

COUNSELOR: "You really seem to have a number of strengths that you are reluctant to acknowledge."

The next example illustrates a high level of confrontation. Note that it is difficult to distinguish this from a high level of empathy. Note also how the counselor responds to being challenged by the client.

CLIENT: "All the way over here, I kept wondering what I would talk about. I still don't know what to say."

COUNSELOR: "You seem to be groping for something to work on."

CLIENT: "I suppose that I could talk about my mother, but I seem to be handling the situation better."

COUNSELOR: "I get the feeling that you would like me to direct you."

CLIENT: "I wouldn't mind. I'm always initiating things. Maybe you can do it today. Is that OK?

COUNSELOR: "It's OK that you ask; however, I would rather you struggle with it."

CLIENT: "You're mean. Why won't you?"

COUNSELOR: "I won't take responsibility for you. I believe that you are perfectly capable of taking responsibility for yourself."

CLIENT: "You seem to have a whole lot more faith in me than I have in myself. I wait for my mother to direct me, too, and then get angry when she does."

The following dialogue, in which the client is faced with an unrecognized or unaccepted strength, illustrates a positive confrontation.

CLIENT: "I must seem like a real victim with all my maladies. Do I come across like a victim to you?"

COUNSELOR: "I know that you seem to be running into a series of problems, and although I don't see you as coping with them very well right now, I really don't view you as a victim. You seem very sensitive and in touch with your feelings."

CLIENT: "I really don't feel like a victim, but somehow…"

COUNSELOR: "You don't like being seen as a victim."

CLIENT: "I don't want people to feel sorry for me."

COUNSELOR: "You seem to be afraid that people wouldn't like you if you honestly expressed your feelings."

Cultural Differences

While confronting is not a behavior tolerated well by many groups, it is of particular importance to be aware of how threatening it is to different ethnic groups. For example, a young counselor challenging an elderly Chinese teacher would find the relationship quickly terminated, because the client views confrontation as demonstrating a lack of respect. Native Americans and traditional Latino people are also quite sensitive to such experiences (Ivey, 1994).

Ideas in action

How can not confronting clients mean that counselors are protecting themselves? From what are they protecting themselves?

Responding with Immediacy

Immediacy is "the ability to explore with another what is happening in their relationship" (Egan, 1986, p. 232). Immediacy is perhaps the deepest level of a counseling relationship. It is an experience best friends can have, and one that some people never seem to have. It is nonsexual intimacy, what theologian Martin Buber (1958) has called the *I–Thou* relationship, when counselors are absorbed in the present with clients. Counselors can make statements that are in either the past, present, or future tense. Present tense statements tend to be the most powerful (Ivey, 1994).

Responding with immediacy, or direct mutual communication (Ivey, 1971; Ivey & Authier, 1978), integrates all of the other types of responding. It is here where the self as instrument concept can be fully implemented. Effective immediacy includes a high level of empathy and is a special case of self-disclosure. The disclosure of the counselor's view of the relationship may be perceived by the client as a confrontation, which it is. When a counselor makes an immediacy response, the relationship is brought directly into the helping process. An immediacy response can, therefore, be very powerful. Such responses, which build as they do on all of the others, tend to be most effective in the later stages of the counseling process.

Because direct mutual communication is not a common experience for many clients, it can be a threatening and demanding experience. Being aware of this, counselors work cautiously and tentatively, assisting clients in learning more about themselves without unduly frightening them. In some cases the essence of a client's problem may be a fear of intimacy and the vulnerability that accompanies it. The client may try to use previously successful approaches to sabotage the establishment of a relationship. The following dialogue is an example of an absence of immediacy.

CLIENT: "I'm not sure I should continue these sessions. I don't feel I'm getting anywhere. You—they don't seem to be helping me. I don't get the feeling you are very concerned."

COUNSELOR: "You're pretty discouraged and feel like quitting and giving up trying."

CLIENT: "Yeah…it doesn't seem worthwhile to continue."

Here, the counselor ignores the client's feelings and focuses on the general reaction of discouragement. Contrast this with the following dialogue, where the counselor responds with a high level of immediacy to the client's confused feelings of aggression. Note the elements of empathy and confrontation in the counselor's response.

CLIENT: "I'm feeling sort of low. I couldn't get out of bed this morning. I had some bad news last night. Don't know how to deal with it. I almost forgot our appointment. Anyway, I did apply for that job we had talked about. That was before my car broke down."

COUNSELOR: "I'm really feeling lost. You're jumping around from one thing to another, and I'm having a hard time following you. I am aware that you are feeling depressed about something but are not ready to share it. Like there isn't enough trust in our relationship at this point."

Ideas in action   Be aware of moments of immediacy in your life, whether you experience them directly or observe others having such moments. How often do these moments occur? What are the emotions associated with such events? How might you initiate such a moment with a significant other? Try initiating a moment of immediacy with someone important to you.

Responding Using Interpretation

Interpretation responses are perhaps the most controversial of all the various types of responses. **Interpretation** can be defined as an attempt to impart meaning about a client's behavior based on the counselor's observations and knowledge. The goal of this approach is to increase clients' insight or awareness regarding their behavior. The various therapeutic approaches used in counseling employ interpretation to one degree or another.

Person-centered counselors (see chapter 11) point out that there is no evidence that interpretation responses are effective. They also note that interpretation switches the focus from the client's frame of reference, fosters resistance, and places the therapeutic responsibility on the counselor. Brammer and Shostrom (1982) point out that even reflections of feelings (which person-centered counselors emphasize) are conservative interpretations. This is because counselors must select those feelings which they deem important from the material given to them. The counselor's experience and knowledge greatly influence what material is selected for response. A high-level reflection of feeling adds more meaning to a client's statement.

An approach such as Gestalt therapy discourages interpretation and uses it only in an indirect way. The psychoanalytic approach, on the other hand, places heavy emphasis on interpretation as a cornerstone of the therapeutic process. Fritz Perls, the founder of Gestalt therapy, declared that interpretation is a therapeutic mistake (Perls, 1969). However, one technique used in Gestalt therapy involving interpretation is called "feeding the client a sentence."

> In listening to or observing the patient, the counselor may conclude that a particular attitude or message is implied. He will then say, "May I feed you a sentence? Say it and try it on for size. Say it to several people here." He then proposes his sentence, and the patient tests out his reaction to the sentence. Typically, the counselor does not simply interpret for or to the patient. Although there is obviously a strong interpretative element here, the patient must make the experience his own through active participation. If the proposed sentence is truly a key sentence, spontaneous development of the idea will be supplied by the patient. (Levitsky & Perls, 1970, p. 148)

In any event, making an interpretation is a delicate task. It can easily confuse the client who has been taking initiative and responsibility in the relationship, to hear the counselor take a more authoritative role. Interpretation is most effective if the counseling relationship has been developed so that there is a high degree of trust and security between client and counselor.

If interpretations are used, they should be used selectively and phrased tentatively. Interpretations are for the benefit of clients, not to show the astuteness of counselors. Clients need to determine whether an interpretation fits or makes sense. A good interpretation must enable clients to understand themselves or their problems more clearly and as a result encourage them to act more effectively.

Ideas in action   Ask someone that you respect to give you an interpretation of a recent type of behavior you exhibited. What is your reaction to the interpretation? What is your reaction to the person giving the interpretation? (Keep in mind that you requested the interpretation).

MUTUALLY AGREED-ON PROBLEM— END OF UNDERSTANDING STAGE

The understanding stage comes to a close when the counselor and the client reach a mutual agreement as to the exact nature of the client's problem. It is at this point that many existential–humanistic practitioners find that their clients will have an "Aha!" experience. They are able to say, "I now know what the problem is and what I have to do to solve it. Thank you!" Such clients may have spent a great deal of time working on their problems before coming to see a counselor. They may have already received much advice from family members and friends and, therefore, have many ideas to work with once the exact nature of their problem is understood and accepted. In these cases, the action stage of counseling takes place within the clients themselves. Such clients terminate the relationship at that point, pursuing subsequent action on their own. For the clients who don't have this insight, the counseling relationship moves on to stage 4.

STAGE 4—ACTION

Stage 4 action skills focus on directives and methods of problem solving. Counselors may take charge and give directives, in effect telling the clients what to do. Counselors may also assist clients in putting their ideas and insights into some form of action through the use of solution-focused problem solving, with the clients taking the burden of responsibility for the decisions made. Question asking is heavily used in this stage.

Directives

Directives are instructions given to the client during the counseling session. They tell the client what to do, and they play a major role in some theoretical approaches, such as Gestalt therapy and cognitive–behavioral counseling. Directives may consist of guiding a client through a fantasy exercise or relaxation activity, urging repetition of certain key phrases, giving homework assignments, or directing a role-playing situation. As with questioning, appropriateness of timing is important in the use of directives. Open-ended probes and directions for a breathing exercise may be offered at any stage in the counseling process; however, homework and advice, if they are to be effective, have a better chance of success when given in the latter stages of the process.

Cognitive–behavioral counseling practitioners use direct intervention as a regular practice in the solving of problems (see chapter 11). For example, they may develop desensitization hierarchies and relaxation programs for students who have test anxiety.

Advising

Advising is a form of directive indicating what the client should do. Advising may be appropriate as long as it is tentatively suggested with no strings attached and is not perceived as a demand.

ADVICE (INAPPROPRIATE): "You should divorce your husband."

ADVICE (APPROPRIATE): "I really would like you to look at other alternatives—would you be willing to do that?"

Giving advice is often fruitless, because there is seldom any suggestion that a counselor can offer a client that the client hasn't already thought of and rejected. Counselors who want to avoid feelings of rejection tend to give advice sparingly, if at all. A helpful guideline in giving advice is never give any advice for which you are not willing to accept full responsibility. One example of advice that we give, for which we take full responsibility, is to suggest that clients have a complete, recent medical checkup to rule out any possible physical causation for their condition (e.g., in the case of a depressed client).

Before offering appropriate advice for resolving a given problem, find out what clients have already considered and then add at least two suggestions to those ideas. With this approach, even clients who have not thought of any solutions on their own will still have a minimum of two solutions from which to choose. The decision is then theirs rather than the counselor's.

Ideas in    Many clients come to counselors looking for advice, and many students entering counselor education programs believe that is what counselors are supposed to do. Try an experiment to see how effective giving advice is. When opportunities present themselves, deliberately give advice. To be safe, only offer advice for which you are willing to take full responsibility. Then do a careful follow-up. Was your advice appreciated? Was it followed? If it was followed and it turned out to be poor advice, what happened then?

Homework Assignments

Homework assignments are a special type of advice. Assignments are used as part of many therapeutic approaches for a number of reasons, including putting into practice what was learned in the counseling sessions, practicing new behaviors, and keeping a record of selected activities. Depending on the theoretical approach of the counselor, homework assignments may be given as early as the first counseling session. Homework assignments, like other types of advice, are not always carried out by clients. As a result, they can become a source of frustration within the relationship. Clients have been known not to return to counseling, because they did not do their homework.

Solution-Focused Approaches to Problem-Solving

Hutchins and Vaught (1997) have identified a number of characteristics of solution-focused approaches to problem-solving:

1. *The helper empowers the client as the source for solutions to the problem.* The client is the expert in knowing what will work.
2. *Techniques used focus on solutions, not on the problem.* One technique is to ask the miracle question. This type of question follows this pattern, "If a miracle happened tonight and you woke up tomorrow with the problem solved, what would you be doing differently?" (Walter & Peller, 1992, p. 73).
3. *A helper looks for examples of approximations of success in dealing with the problem.* A client who is a poor student may have done well on a class project.
4. *Evaluation is tied to specific changes in feelings, thoughts, and behaviors directly related to the client's problem.*

These characteristics or principles are found in the Method III approach described below, which Thomas Gordon (1974) has used in a variety of settings.

The Method III Problem-Solving Approach

Thomas Gordon, in working with parents, teachers, counselors, and others in the helping professions, has adapted the scientific method to counseling so that it can be used by virtually all populations to solve problems in a way in which everyone involved feels good. No solution is externally imposed on the participants. In what Gordon calls Methods I and II, either the counselor or the client is in control, and issues of manipulation and feelings of winning and losing are prevalent. Method III is seen as a win–win strategy and is an approach that the client can learn and use in subsequent problem situations. The six specific steps in Gordon's approach are as follows:

1. *Determine the problem.* The problem is determined by going through the attending, exploration, and understanding stages previously described.
2. *Generate possible solutions.* This is a brainstorming step with the counselor helping the client to generate as many solutions as possible. The counselor should wait until the client has thought of at least two ideas before adding at least two more ideas. No evaluation of ideas is involved at this step so that as many different ideas as possible might be generated.
3. *Evaluate possible solutions.* The various solutions generated in the preceding step are evaluated and prioritized by the client. Ideas can be combined or expanded on as part of this step.
4. *Make a decision on one possible solution.* At this point the counselor encourages the client to commit to one solution and follow through on it.
5. *Implement the decision.* This is when the client actually puts the solution into operation.
6. *Assess results.* This is an important follow-up step necessary to determine success. If the solution is not successful, it might need to be modified and attempted again, or the client might have to move to a second possible solution. The process can be repeated until the final assessment is positive.

Ideas in action   Pair up with a colleague and tell the colleague to present a problem. Go through the Method III Problem-Solving Approach to generate possible solutions, decide on a solution, and implement it. An acronym in the form of a sentence could be used to help you remember the first letters of each of the steps (e.g., Dark Green Evergreens Make Indiana Attractive—D, G, E, M, I, A). Reverse roles and repeat. Note how quickly you learn the process.

STAGE 5—TERMINATION

When the client's problem has been resolved, it is time to consider termination. The termination of individual counseling is a significant stage in the counseling process. Among other things it provides an opportunity for the client to learn how to successfully end a positive relationship. Ward (1984) states that if terminating counseling is handled effectively, the counseling outcome can be maximized, and new client learnings and behaviors will more likely be maintained. If handled inappropriately, effective change is unlikely to occur, and the client may be discouraged from seeking further help when necessary.

When Is the Time to Terminate?

There is usually no ideal situation in which the client has resolved all past and present problems and has learned to handle new problems without difficulties when they arise. In discussing the time for termination, Zaro, Barack, Nedelman, and Dreiblatt (1982) state,

> The ending of therapy usually represents a compromise between hoped for changes and limitations arising from waning motivation, the subjective discomfort of being in therapy, its cost, and a variety of other factors. (p. 142)

Knowing when to terminate is often especially difficult for beginning counselors. Sometimes counselors make a premature decision to terminate when a client exhibits the flight to health phenomenon discussed in chapter 5. Other times they extend counseling long after it is productive. Clients or counselors who have individuation–separation or dependency–independency issues, or counselors who are ignorant of how or when to make a decision to end counseling, can create particular problems at this stage. Hopefully counselors will have successfully resolved these personal issues before entering practice.

As the client successfully works through the stages of counseling, termination of the relationship begins to become an important issue. Clients often experience less need for counseling and make direct statements to that effect, or drop hints. For example, clients may speak of having made tremendous progress, or may share how they intend to solve a problem rather than ask the counselor to do it.

After reviewing the literature on the termination stage, Ward (1984) presents several client behaviors, other than direct verbal statements, that signal the approach of termination; these include decreased intensity in counseling sessions, lateness, joking, intellectualizing, missed appointments, apathy, acting out, withdrawal, denial, expression of anger, mourning, feelings of separation and loss, and regression to previous and less constructive behavior patterns. The client may engage in these behaviors in order to resist actually terminating. It is often difficult to end a close relationship. It is not uncommon for a client to manufacture new problems in order to remain in the counseling relationship. It may be necessary for the counselor to make the initial suggestion and then help the client to work through the issues relating to the termination process. The counselor must make an assessment of the client's readiness to terminate. If the client is ready, the counselor must then complete any unfinished business in the relationship with the client, aid the client in exploring feelings that arise during the termination process, and prepare the client for self-reliance and transfer of learning after counseling is terminated.

Making the Decision to Terminate

Several antecedent factors can aid the counselor in making the decision to terminate. The primary factor is whether the client has reached the therapy goals; therefore, the counselor and client should achieve an explicit understanding of the counseling goals in the beginning stage (Lanning & Carey, 1987). This is not always easy to do, as with clients who come to counseling with vague problems, such as general apathy or undefinable anxiety. In such cases, therapeutic goals are more difficult to define and progress more difficult to measure (Zaro et al., 1982). The counselor might also assess the client's coping ability, ability to relate intimately with significant others, capacity to enjoy life, productivity in work and career, increased valuing of self and others, rate of progress in reaching the goals of counseling, and confidence to live effectively without counseling (Ward, 1984). In the case of brief therapy, the number of sessions is known from the very beginning.

Once the decision to terminate is made, counseling should not end abruptly. The process may require a number of sessions in order to obtain closure. Some counselors begin to meet their clients less frequently. During this stage, counselors make fewer interventions, and clients are encouraged to assume greater responsibility for the sessions. The counselor will help the client review progress from the beginning of the relationship. The counselor might go back and review a counseling session recorded early in counseling (Ward, 1984). The counselor gradually removes formal support and structure as clients demonstrate greater readiness to function on their own.

Completing Unfinished Business and Exploring Feelings

The counselor and client must bring any relationship issues to closure through the discussion of their feelings toward one another and toward the relationship. The goal is to bring about an appropriate ending in which everything that needs expression is expressed. Clients may summarize their reactions to the counseling process and to the counselor and provide feedback as to what was and was not facilitative (Ward, 1984). Clients might also be encouraged to explore any feelings regarding termination such as loss, grief, or abandonment. For termination to be completely successful, clients should not deny or avoid such feelings. Counselors must be aware of their own feelings regarding the ending of counseling relationships. Students and interns especially should consult with their supervisors regarding all areas of termination.

Preparation for Postcounseling Self-Reliance and Transfer of Learning

The counselor can help the client formulate some specific strategies and plans for the transfer of learning from counseling to the client's everyday life situations. Ward (1984) suggests having the client make self-contracts concerning behavior after counseling has ceased, including the following activities: rehearsing new roles, renewing goal setting, using imagery to project future behaviors, and using counseling or feedback on the level of client functioning and issues that the client might anticipate later. Counselors can make it known to the client that the option of entering counseling again is acceptable and viable. Entering counseling again should not imply failure for the client.

SUMMARY

Skills vital to establishing the therapeutic alliance and to working through the last three stages of the counseling process—understanding, action, and termination—have been described.

The skills of advanced empathy, self-disclosure, confrontation, and immediacy are part of the understanding stage of the counseling process. These skills are used to help focus and clarify the nature of the client's problem. Once the client clearly understands the problem, the client may already know what to do to resolve it. If not, the process moves on to the fourth stage, the action or problem-solving stage.

With a mutually agreed-on understanding of the problem to be resolved, the counselor can use different problem-solving approaches. The solution-focused problem-solving approach of Thomas Gordon was described.

When the client has successfully pursued a course of action that results in the solving of the agreed-on problem, another problem may be focused on, with the relationship returning to the exploration stage (Stage 2). The relationship may also proceed toward termination. The preparation for and implementation of termination involves a variety of the skills used in earlier stages, with the major new skill being knowing how to comfortably say good-bye to a person with whom one has developed a close relationship.

QUESTIONS AND ACTIVITIES

1. With which of the skills in chapter 6 are you most competent? Which ones need more development? Are there any skills that particularly give you difficulty, perhaps even scare you? Why do you think this is? Discuss this in class.

2. Videotape a short conversation with another student. Play back the videotape and observe your physical and psychological attending.

3. Observe films or videotapes, or listen to audiotapes of professional counselors working with clients.

See if you can identify the various stages of counseling in each instance. Compare your findings with those of other students.

4. Think of a personal problem about which you are concerned. Apply the steps of Gordon's Method III approach to resolve the issue. Are there any steps that are particularly difficult to do?

RECOMMENDED READINGS

Carkhuff, R. (1987). *The art of helping* (6th ed.). Amherst, MA: Human Resource Development Press.

Cormier, W. H., & Cormier, L. S. (1985). *Interviewing strategies for helpers* (2nd ed.). Monterey, CA: Brooks/Cole.

Egan, G. (1994). *The skilled helper* (5th ed.). Pacific Grove, CA: Brooks/Cole.

Ivey, A. E., Ivey, M. B., & Simek-Morgan, L. (1993). *Counseling and Psychotherapy* (3rd ed.). Boston: Allyn & Bacon.

REFERENCES

Augsburger, D. (1981). *Caring enough to confront* (Rev. ed.) Ventura, CA: Regal.

Brammer, L., & Shostrom, E. (1982). *Therapeutic psychology: Fundamentals of counseling and psycho-* *therapy* (4th ed.). Englewood Cliffs, NJ: Prentice-Hall.

Buber, M. (1958). *I and thou* (2nd ed.). New York: Scribner's.

Carkhuff, R. (1969). *Helping and human relations: Practice and research* (vol. 2). New York: Holt, Rinehart & Winston.

Carkhuff, R. (1987). *The art of helping* (7th ed.). Amherst, MA: Human Resource Development Press.

Egan, G. (1986). *The skilled helper* (3rd ed.). Monterey, CA: Brooks/Cole.

Egan, G. (1994). *The skilled helper* (5th ed.). Pacific Grove, CA: Brooks/Cole.

Gordon, T. (1974). *Teacher effectiveness training.* New York: Peter Wyden.

Hutchins, D., & Vaught, C. (1997). *Helping relationships and strategies* (3rd ed.). Pacific Grove, CA: Brooks/Cole.

Ivey, A. (1971). *Microcounseling: Innovations in interviewing training.* Springfield, IL: Charles C. Thomas.

Ivey, A. E. (1994). *Intentional interviewing and counseling* (3rd ed.). Pacific Grove, CA: Brooks/Cole.

Ivey, A., & Authier, J. (1978). *Microcounseling* (2nd ed.). Springfield, IL: Charles C. Thomas.

Lanning, W., & Carey, J. (1987). Systematic termination in counseling. *Journal of Counselor Education and Supervision, 12*(2), 168–173.

Levitsky, A., & Perls, F. (1970). The rules and games of Gestalt therapy. In J. Fagan (Ed.), *Gestalt therapy now* (pp. 140–149). Palo Alto, CA: Science and Behavior Books.

Patterson, C. H. (1974). *Relationship counseling and psychotherapy.* New York: Harper & Row.

Perls, F. (1969). *Gestalt therapy verbatim.* Lafayette, CA: Real People Press.

Walter, J., & Peller, J. (1992). *Becoming solution-focused in brief therapy.* New York: Brunner/Mazel.

Ward, D. (1984). Termination of individual counseling: Concepts and strategies. *Journal of Counseling and Development, 63*(1), 21–25.

Zaro, J., Barack, R., Nedelman, D., & Dreiblatt, I. (1982). *A guide for beginning psychotherapists.* Cambridge, England: Oxford University Press.

chapter **8**

USING SKILLS: CONDUCTING A COUNSELING SESSION

- How do I put all of these skills into operation when I meet with a client?
- How can I develop a placebo effect to improve conditions for helping clients?
- What kind of structure is helpful in a counseling session?
- Can the counseling process be completed in one session?

In learning to expand your repertoire of responses to clients in a helping relationship, at least two major themes should be evident. First, we are learning to respond to the whole person: the body language and the emotions as well as the verbal content. Second, we are very sensitive to the nature of the verbal content. A sensitivity to the language used in counseling is an essential feature of the field. This can be demonstrated here in this chapter as we describe the process of a counseling session as an innerview, not an interview.

It is important to learn the various helping skills necessary to the counseling process and to be able to apply these skills effectively in counseling sessions. Knowledge of these skills does not guarantee the successful conduct of helping sessions, but not knowing them can have a detrimental effect.

In chapter 5, general guidelines for the development of a therapeutic alliance were presented. This chapter details some basic guidelines for conducting an actual counseling session including factors not directly related to the counselor's skills, focusing primarily on the first session. With the advent of managed care and the increased popularity of brief therapy strategies, increasing numbers of cases may not go beyond the first session. Nevertheless, a structure similar to that described in this chapter can be used for all subsequent sessions that may be needed.

SETTING THE STAGE: THE ENVIRONMENT

In developing a successful therapeutic alliance, there is no correct environmental setting. Effective work can be done while shooting a game of pool with a client in a day treatment center or while seated side-by-side on a transcontinental flight. When possible, however, counselors strive to set up the positive characteristics of their counseling setting, working to attain what Jerome Frank (1973) has called the placebo effect in the environment itself. A **placebo** is defined as the following:

> Any therapy or component of therapy that is deliberately used for its nonspecific, psychological, or psychophysiological effect, or that is used for its presumed specific effect, but is without specific activity for the condition being treated. A placebo, when used as a control in experimental studies, is defined as a substance or procedure that is without specific activity for the condition being evaluated. The placebo effect is defined as the psychological or psychobiological effect produced by placebos. (Shapiro & Morris, 1978, p. 371)

The objective of structuring the environment is so that the client feels comfortable and reassured from the onset of contact with the counselor.

The office location helps to establish the confidence clients need in order to be able to talk about an area of their lives in which they feel deficient or confused. For example, having an office in a relatively secluded part of a school building is preferable to one next to the school principal's office or adjoining the university commons area. There is still enough of a concern over the stigma of having mental health problems that many people needing help may not want to be seen entering or leaving a counselor's office.

The secretary's office and reception area should offer a feeling of warmth, comfort, and an overall feeling of confidentiality. This approach should be carried through to the counseling office so that client anxiety does not increase. Many practitioners decorate the walls of their offices with diplomas, licenses, and other certificates to enhance the placebo effect, suggesting that here is a place that is safe and secure with a practitioner who is highly qualified to provide the services desired. Such efforts enhance the expertness and competence of the counselor in the perception of the client (Cormier & Cormier, 1985, p. 46). In states where there is a licensure law, it is mandatory that the state license be prominently displayed.

Many professional offices have furniture that is deliberately designed to avoid a stark, institutional look. A desk, if present, is often set to the side of the room, not used during a session other than for such activities as administering a test instrument. Clients seem to work better if their chair is reasonably padded, but not overly stuffed. Clients seated in overstuffed sofas may feel almost too relaxed and may even get to the point at which they lose motivation to work on their problems. A recliner is used by many practitioners for specialized purposes, such as for giving instruction in relaxation techniques.

Another functional item that might be in an office is an easel with a pad of paper, useful for times when the counselor or the client wishes to express something that cannot be easily expressed in verbal terms alone. Many counselors use such tools to clarify or explain aspects of the counseling methods they are using, to list alternatives in the problem-solving process, or to construct a family tree when working with families. Videotape and audiotape recorders are also useful tools whether the counselor is a student in training or a fully certified professional. In addition to being excellent instruments for helping professionals review sessions and improve their skills, tape recorded sessions have been used directly in helping clients work on their problems. For example, a portion of a session may be replayed immediately, so a client can better note how whiny his voice is while he is trying to act forcefully. A recording of an entire session can be sent home with a client, so she can review the approach she took in solving a problem. An important and necessary item in any counseling office is the ubiquitous box of tissues. The presence of the tissue box indicates to the client that the expression of emotions is acceptable in this setting and that there is permission to cry if desired. A clock, located strategically so that the counselor and the client can see it, is helpful in controlling the length of sessions.

Because the major instrument in helping is the counselor, there is little need for other office equipment or supplies. Too many furnishings or decorations can prove to be distracting rather than helpful. There are, of course, specialists who have certain requirements consonant with their specialty. For example, a group or family counselor will need space and furniture available to accommodate a large number of clients, and art and music therapists usually have fairly large space requirements along with a substantial amount of supplemental equipment and material.

The characteristics of the office setting, then, can play an important part in at least the initial stage of the counseling relationship. Once human interaction has taken place and the counseling relationship has been established, environmental conditions take on a significantly reduced role.

COUNSELOR CHARACTERISTICS AND BEHAVIORS

Facilitative counselor characteristics are described in chapter 1. Additional counselor characteristics that are applicable primarily to initial or early sessions include the following:

1. *Attractiveness.* The client's perception of the counselor in terms of likability, friendliness, warmth, and similarities in attitudes and background has been considered an important aspect of influence in counseling settings (Strong, 1968). Attractiveness is a nonspecific factor that may help in initial contacts, but is not a substitute for counseling skills (Cormier & Cormier, 1985; Patterson, 1985).

One aspect of attractiveness is personal appearance. The counseling relationship is a professional one, so that generally high standards of grooming and dress are appropriate; however, it is difficult to set any uniform rules. For example, some male counselors in college counseling centers choose not to wear ties, because they believe that this sets them on a different level than their clients and possibly provides a barrier to full and open communication. Also, counselors working with special populations, such as juvenile delinquents in a detention center gymnasium, or with modalities such as dance therapy tend to dress in ways appropriate to these conditions.

2. *Punctuality.* Being on time for an appointment communicates respect for the client. As an ethical and even a legal issue, it is part of fulfilling your contract with the client.

3. *Comfortable assertiveness.* Meeting a client for the first time affords the counselor an excellent opportunity to make contact with the client on three different levels: verbal, physical, and psychological.

   a. *Verbal.* The counselor makes contact in the initial greeting with the immediate use of the client's name; for example, "Good afternoon, Mrs. Johnson. Do you prefer to be called Carol or Carolyn?"

b. *Physical.* The counselor takes the opportunity to shake hands with all participants in the session.

c. *Psychological.* Nonverbal communication is established by direct eye contact.

Care should be taken to ensure that contact can be made at these three levels during the initial meeting, because it may be helpful in collecting data about the client and for establishing general guidelines for the relationship. Care should also be taken to be aware of cultural differences that may cause you as counselor to modify your behaviors. For example, it may be desirable for you not to be concerned about making direct eye contact with a Native American client.

CONDUCTING THE FIRST SESSION

The nature of the first session may be dictated in part by what has preceded the actual meeting. Usually, personal data is available prior to the first counseling session. This can range from having the client answer a few basic questions at the time an appointment is made to having the client come in for a preliminary interview with a case manager who will gather a significant amount of preliminary data. If the client has been referred or if it is counselor-initiated as in a school setting, the counselor usually has a fairly extensive client file prior to the first session.

When a precounseling interview is not possible or appropriate, it is generally good practice to have a newly scheduled client come to the counseling office about 30 minutes prior to the appointment time to fill out information forms (and insurance forms, if applicable). Many counseling offices provide the new client with a written description of the counseling process, specific policies regarding making and breaking appointments, and information about arranging for payment. Such descriptions may include a discussion of confidentiality, noting the instances in which the counselor cannot maintain confidentiality, such as actual or suspected child abuse. The basic principle behind this preliminary information gathering and dissemination is to allow as much of the counseling hour as possible for establishment of the therapeutic relationship. In ideal settings, counselors should have virtually all the preliminary information they need before the first session begins.

Shertzer and Stone (1971) offer five general guidelines for an initial session to which we have added a sixth:

1. Establishing rapport (initiating the therapeutic alliance)
2. Providing structure
3. Helping the client talk
4. Remaining alert to the client's feelings
5. Closing the session smoothly
6. Attending to the counseling process

Rapport

Rapport has been described by Belkin (1975) as being established "when the counselor demonstrates an accepting, open attitude, when he shows interest in what the client has to say, and when he does everything in his power to make the client feel comfortable" (p. 296). This process obviously begins with the establishment of a comfortable environment and during the initial meeting with the client. This process continues throughout the session with every verbal and nonverbal response of the counselor contributing to it. Using the responding skills described in chapter 6, the counselor will genuinely be communicating the respect and warmth that are so crucial to creating an atmosphere of acceptance and understanding.

Although we have stressed that one should be empathic, in an opening session it may be helpful not to be too insightful or communicate too much understanding for the reasons Tyler (1969) describes:

> We must recognize that the people who consult us may have mixed feelings about being understood. They must be sure that understanding can in no way constitute a threat before they can welcome it. Many of us are afraid that someone will "see through us," uncovering our hidden weaknesses. We have put up strong defenses against this. Much of what we say, many of the things we do, are designed to hide rather than to reveal our underlying motives and traits. For this reason if it happens that the counselor shows by some penetrating remark that he has seen through a new client's defenses, the person may very well retreat in panic from the whole situation. It is only when he has become certain of a thoroughgoing unshakable acceptance that he can run the risk of trying to make his real feelings understood. (pp. 49–50).

Developing the relationship is a key component in the counseling process, so counselors work with patience and sensitivity during an opening session as they focus on attending, exploring, and understanding. As with any set of guidelines, there are exceptions. A client who has already gone through much of the exploration process mentally may come for help. Although the initial encounter with the counselor would be a first session, the client may be ready to work at a deep level from the outset and move quickly into the action stage. Accurate, empathic listening will help verify this readiness. Such a client could conceivably go through the five stages of the counseling process in just one session. Counselors using approaches such as solution-oriented brief therapy strive to attain this objective.

Providing Structure

Coming into a formal helping relationship is a new experience for most clients, so an additional way to help establish rapport is to provide a brief description of what will transpire during the time the counselor and the client will be together. To help make the counseling relationship less ambiguous for the client, provide this description at the beginning of the first session. When a session will be audiotaped or videotaped, permission to record needs to be obtained at the start of the session and can be included as part of other information about the structure of the session. In the case of children under age 18, permission to tape-record must be obtained from parents or guardians prior to the first session.

Some specific structural concerns counselors might want to present to the client include the length of the session, the counselor's role, the topic of confidentiality, the possible number of sessions, and the recording of the session. The client should be able to ask any questions related to the counseling process. Here is an example of how a practicum student began an initial session after the introductions were made:

COUNSELOR: "Today, we're going to spend the next 50 minutes together to work on whatever you would like to talk about. What you tell me will be held in confidence with three exceptions, and these are if you threaten to do harm to yourself, or to others, or if you indicate circumstances that might suggest child abuse. As I am a graduate student under supervision, I will be tape-recording the session. My supervisor will be the only other person to listen to the tape, and her basic concern is to help me improve my responses to you. Are you clear as to this procedure and what we will do today?"

CLIENT: "Yes."

COUNSELOR: "I would like to have you sign this paper indicating that you are aware that the session is being taped."

CLIENT: (signs document)

COUNSELOR: "Thank you. OK, now, where would you like to begin?"

Providing structure enhances perceived counselor–client similarities and increased interpersonal attractiveness. It also fulfills the ethical responsibility of informing clients of the purposes, techniques, and limitations of counseling (Cormier & Cormier, 1985, p. 53).

Helping the Client Talk: Open Invitation

The concluding question in the example above is a sample of what Ivey (1971) calls an open invitation to talk. Open invitations allow clients to select the subject matter and begin to provide their own structure to the session. Asking a question is the most common way to begin a counseling session. This opening probe could range from a very closed, cued, direct question such as, "Would you like to tell me how you get along with your mother?" to a very open, noncued, indirect statement such as, "I'm interested in knowing what concern you want to work on today." The latter statement gives much more latitude to the client to find the solution to the problem and keeps the session oriented in the present. This latter approach is clearly an open invitation to talk. Once the client has begun talking, the use of encouragers (see chapter 6) and empathic responses will help the client continue to share.

Responding to Client Questions and Requests

Initially, many clients may begin by making direct requests for solutions to their presenting problems. As noted in chapter 7, unless it is an emergency situation, there are significant concerns about giving advice early in a counseling relationship and even later as well. To avoid establishing a nontherapeutic structure, the counselor needs to become skilled at responding to requests for advice and solutions by using carefully worded empathic statements that include self-disclosure.

COUNSELOR: "You would really like me to give you an answer to this problem that's been frustrating you for years. I'm going to have to learn more about your problem, and even then I can't promise you that I will have an answer that will be sure to work for you."

Remaining Alert and Responding to the Client's Feelings

When clients present their problems, counselors often focus on the cognitive content and become almost oblivious to the emotional content. Just being able to talk with someone can have a therapeutic effect, and to have the counselor tune into, understand, and accept both positive and negative feelings is even more therapeutic. In striving for an innerview, the types of responses to clients' feelings (see chapter 6) can be implemented at an appropriate level. Lauver and Harvey (1997) suggest that the difference between a general problem and a real problem is that "part of every problematic episode is at least one unpleasant feeling—mad, bad, sad. Without unpleasant feelings, the episode would not be felt as problematic" (p. 101).

Responding to emotions, including those not necessarily stated in words, is an instance of the counselor's listening to the music and not just the words. This is often helpful; for example, "Even though you haven't said it, I can tell by the clenching of your fists and the sound of your voice that you are really quite angry!" It is possible that a client just needs to express and work through emotions in a given situation. The client may already know what action needs to be taken but needs to deal with emotional issues first. Some clients may be able to successfully work through unpleasant emotions in situations where the necessary action to be taken is clear; this may account for a significant portion of the one session counseling relationships.

Attending to the Counseling Process

Conducting a successful counseling session involves more than attending and responding to clients and the statements they make. A counselor must attend to the process of the session. Without direct awareness of what is happening during the session, the client and the counselor may drift aimlessly for the entire hour. The counselor, therefore, should mentally note what is happening during the session and communicate any observations to the client when appropriate. The use of internal and closing summaries are ways through which the counselor can communicate the nature of the counseling process during a session.

Internal Summaries

As the session progresses and the counselor uses responding skills to help the client explore a problem area, the counselor can build in an internal summary statement or two to help clarify what has been going on in terms of both content and process. A common tendency of beginning counselors is to respond directly to each statement of the client, keeping a one-to-one relationship between the client's statements and the responses. To formulate an internal summary, the counselor should pull together the various thoughts, feelings, and behaviors that have been communicated over a period of time. Summaries may refer to patterns, themes, discrepancies, or inconsistencies or may just help clarify a large amount of data from time to time during the session, for example, "You've just told me three good things that have happened to you today, and are you ever happy!"

A summary statement may be a useful response to help focus on feelings, especially if much of the material in the session has been cognitively oriented; for example, "You've described a whole list of things that have gone wrong for you, and you're really very upset."

A response relating to the process of a particular session might be, "Every time we get close to some feelings of sadness or anger, you immediately change the subject."

Internal summary statements used at different times during a counseling session help provide some structure, if only to note that "I am paying attention to all that is happening here and will report my findings from time to time." In the initial session especially, this response can be of great help. A client may have stored up great amounts of material (problems) in anticipation of the time that there would be an empathic listener. The client may go off in several different directions, and summary statements can help put all of the ideas in perspective. Internal summaries can be quite helpful in moving the client through the counseling stages.

Significance of the Presenting Problem

Another benefit of attending to the process and using internal summary statements is to help keep track of the initial presenting problem. As mentioned previously, the initial problem at the first session is often not the problem on which the client ultimately chooses to spend the bulk of the counseling time. The presenting problem can be a safe one that friends and family would not laugh about if they knew that personal help was being sought (e.g., wanting to take a career interest inventory or needing to find some information about colleges.) Such initial needs often serve as a smoke screen for more serious problems. The client uses the safe problem as a way of testing the counseling relationship and determining whether the counselor is to be trusted with more serious concerns. Many counseling centers that offer testing services find that the tests and inventories they offer serve to help the client safely begin the process of self-disclosing. If the relationship is comfortable, the client may talk about other concerns in addition to discussing the test results. In fact, in many instances the tests and their results are often ignored after the relationship becomes established and the real problem is disclosed. Hutchins and Voight (1997), advocates of brief therapy, "urge caution in moving ahead too rapidly—before the helper has a good basis for understanding what the client really wants to do and whether it will resolve the problem" (p. 150).

Occasionally a client presents a problem that is only one symptom of a greater problem. A client might complain of not having friends and want to learn ways to establish friendships, for instance. As the counseling process unfolds, the client discovers that the greater problem in establishing friendships is the fear of feeling vulnerable in close relationships. In this case, the presenting problem may well be the real issue, the one the client wants to resolve. Careful attending and accurate empathic responding will clarify this fact for both the counselor and the client.

Closing the Session

The process of closing a session begins with having a set time limit established, giving a warning signal that the time limit is near, making closing summaries, making arrangements for the next session, and then escorting the client to the door.

Time Limits

Because a counseling session is a professional service, clear boundaries are necessary including the ending of the session. A session should be kept to a fairly strict time limit. A generally standard practice is a 50 minute hour for individual sessions with adults and 20 to 30 minute sessions with young children. Group and family counseling sessions may last from 1 hour and 30 minutes to 2 hours.

The counsleor should maintain a set time limit for several reasons. First, counselors generally have other appointments which are affected by not maintaining a schedule. Second, 50 minutes of intense personal contact can be physically and psychologically draining on both parties. Third, if clients know that they only have a limited amount of time, they will see that the important issues are brought up. This, however, does not mean that a client will not test the established limits. It is not uncommon for a client to introduce a new but serious topic with just a few minutes left in the session. Fritz Perls (1969) once stated that the last 10 minutes of the therapeutic session often tend to be the most important. One reason for this is that the client, after struggling along with lesser feelings and thoughts, finally builds up the courage to move more deeply just as time is running out. This can also become an unconscious manipulation that might force the counselor to give the client more time. Handled appropriately, the counselor can suggest that the new topic might be a good place to begin the next session. Counselors must be aware that both they and their time can be manipulated and that if a topic is crucial, it should surface before the end of the session. There does not seem to be any evidence that providing extra time in such cases is beneficial. What is often likely to occur if the counselor spends additional time and energy is that a pattern of extending the allotted time will become the norm in subsequent sessions. Crisis counseling cases such as working with a client who is contemplating suicide would be an exception to this guideline.

Warning Signal

As the end of the session draws near, the counselor should give the client some indication of this by saying, "We have about 10 minutes left." Within this final block of time the client can finish up a topic and not be allowed to pursue any new topics.

Closing Summaries

At the end of the session, it is helpful and instructive for the counselor to have the client give a summary of what has been learned or experienced. The counselor could initiate this by saying something such as, "Since the session is almost over, I'm wondering if you could tell me what you learned or experienced as a result of our work together today." It is usually informative and interesting to hear what the client has focused on throughout the session. This is a major way of determining progress and evaluating the session. It is also a way of determining what might be done for homework as well as what maybe to deal with in the next session.

After the client has summarized, the counselor still has the opportunity for a final summary of the entire session. The counselor can just affirm what the client has said or add issues and decisions that the client may have overlooked.

Arranging for the Next Session

The final task in the session is to see if the client wants to continue the relationship and to then establish the time and date. Some counselors are more direct and authoritarian in this regard, telling the client when the next appointment will be rather than negotiating it.

An open-ended approach to setting the next session and giving that responsibility to the client would be to say something such as, "Is this time and day convenient for you for our next session?" If the problem is not particularly urgent—for example, a college fresh-man who has a whole year to choose a major—the counselor could say something such as, "Would you prefer that we meet next week or every other week?"

In crisis situations, one way of determining the client's feeling of crisis would be to say something such as, "How often and when do you think we should meet?" As mentioned, the number of sessions can be established at the beginning of the first session. In all cases, counselors need to make the final determination as to dates and times based on their objective view of the problem and their schedules. This format can be repeated in subsequent sessions as the counselor and client go through the various stages of the counseling process.

Performance Anxiety

Learning all of these skills and then trying to use them all during counseling sessions can lead some beginning counselors to experience **performance anxiety:** anxious feelings resulting from trying too hard to do everything perfectly. Counselors "with excessive performance anxieties are less effective because they are responding more to their own internal needs (to be helpful, competent, or liked) than they are to the client's need to be understood" (Teyber, 1988, p. 29).

Counselors can practice some of the stress management techniques (see chapter 2) to help relieve anxiety. Practicing the various counseling skills repeatedly under supervision is the best way to ensure that you will perform with a minimum of performance anxiety in the counseling session.

SUMMARY

This chapter pulls together the skills presented in earlier chapters to demonstrate how to conduct a counseling session. The emphasis here is on the first counseling session and the concern for the physical environment conditions that help set the stage for a successful session.

Counselor characteristics of particular importance during a first session include attractiveness, punctuality, and comfortable assertiveness. Personal appearance is an important factor, at least initially, becoming less of a factor as the relationship is established. Counselors should dress appropriately for the counseling settings and the clients with whom they work. They should keep appointments on time, make contact physically with the client by shaking hands, verbally through conversation, and nonverbally by establishing eye contact. These steps are part of the process of establishing rapport and beginning the development of the therapeutic alliance. The chapter describes the manner in which the counselor begins the session, provides the structure, sets limits, and gives open invitations for the client to begin talking. The counselor is encouraged to notice and respond to the feelings and emotions the client is communicating as well as to the verbal content.

While counselors are noticing the verbal and nonverbal material presented by the client, they also learn to become aware of the counseling process. They note whether the presenting problem maintains its initial importance or whether the focus has shifted to another issue. The use of internal summaries to keep the counselor and the client alert to the counseling process is encouraged.

The preparation for successfully closing a counseling session includes noting time limits at the beginning of the session, giving a few minutes' warning, and inviting the client to note specific areas covered that were of particular importance. The counselor then has the opportunity to make a final summary, reinforcing ideas and actions the client has offered and adding additional comments as appropriate. The arrangements for the next session are then made.

The format can be repeated in subsequent sessions as the therapeutic alliance develops. The beginning counselor needs to be aware of performance anxiety in conducting a counseling session and to know how to manage such anxiety should it occur.

QUESTIONS AND ACTIVITIES

1. How is a person supposed to be able to focus on the client, attend to the counseling process, and do a good job as a counselor? Which of these do you believe would cause you the most difficulty? What would you have to do to develop these particular skills?

2. In various settings, practice taking a genuine interest in another person using attending and responding skills. How easy is this for you to do? What are the positive as well as negative consequences of this type of interaction?

3. Make an appointment to see someone for some type of help, something that you may have been putting off for some time such as seeing a faculty advisor or going to a dentist. When you meet this person be aware of the environmental setting and the characteristics of the helper, such as attractiveness, punctuality, the development of rapport, and assertiveness. What characteristics seem to be helpful in establishing a helping relationship and which tend to be counterproductive? Compare notes with other class members.

4. With a fellow student or a friend, practice responding empathically to direct requests for advice. How hard is it for you to keep the focus on the other person rather than let the focus shift to you?

RECOMMENDED READINGS

Brammer, L. (1993). *The helping relationship: Process and skills* (5th ed.). Boston: Allyn & Bacon.

Carkhuff, R. (1987). *The art of helping* (6th ed.). Amherst, MA: Human Resource Development Press.

Egan, G. (1994). *The skilled helper* (5th ed.). Pacific Grove, CA: Brooks/Cole.

REFERENCES

Belkin, G. (1975). *Introduction to counseling.* Dubuque, IA: Brown.

Cormier, W., & Cormier, L. S. (1985). *Interviewing strategies for helpers.* Monterey, CA: Brooks/Cole.

Frank, J. (1973). *Persuasion and healing.* Baltimore. Johns Hopkins University Press.

Hutchins, D. E., & Vaught, C. C. (1997). *Helping relationships and strategies* (3rd ed.). Pacific Grove, CA: Brooks/Cole.

Ivey, A. (1971). *Microcounseling.* Springfield, IL: Charles C. Thomas.

Lauver, P., & Harvey, D. H. (1997). *The practical counselor.* Pacific Grove, CA: Brooks/Cole.

Patterson, C. H. (1985). *The therapeutic relationship: Foundations for an eclectic psychotherapy.* Monterey, CA: Brooks/Cole.

Perls, F. (1969). *Gestalt therapy verbatim.* Lafayette, CA: Real People Press.

Shapiro, A., & Morris, L. (1978). The placebo effect in medical and psychological therapies. In S. C. Garfield & A. E. Bergin (Eds.), *Handbook of psychotherapy and behavior change* (pp. 370–382). New York: Wiley.

Shertzer, B., & Stone, S. (1971). *Fundamentals of counseling.* Boston: Houghton Mifflin.

Strong, S. R. (1968). Counseling: An interpersonal influence process. *Journal of Counseling Psychology, 15,* 215–224.

Teyber, E. (1988). *Interpersonal process in psychotherapy: A guide for clinical training.* Chicago: Dorsey.

Tyler, L. (1969). *The work of the counselor.* New York: Appleton, Century, Crofts.

chapter 9

focus on

THE ORIGINS AND SCOPE
OF THE FIELD OF COUNSELING
AND CURRENT TRENDS

- How has psychiatry influenced the field of counseling?
- What are the different types of populations I could work with as a counselor?
- What are the differences between preventive and developmental counseling?
- What is the effect of the Internet on counselors?
- What will the counselor of the future be like?
- What technological know-how will counselors need?
- What issues confront present and future counselors?

This chapter presents an overview of the development of the counseling profession. It elaborates on the nature of the current field of counseling, including types of clients. The chapter concludes with a look at current trends influencing the future direction of counseling.

ORIGINS

Counseling is both very old and quite new. The practice of one person helping another deal with the problems of living has been going on for centuries, usually in the form of family members, friends, or clergy assisting an individual. The origins of career counseling can be traced back to ancient civilizations (Dumont and Carson, 1995). On the other hand, the practice of having an outsider, a professionally trained expert not necessarily affiliated with a religious institution, work with a person to resolve life's problems is a relatively recent phenomenon.

In the late nineteenth century, physicians such as Jean Martin Charcot and Pierre Janet in France began treating mental illness with nonmedical techniques such as hypnosis. A physician named Sigmund Freud studied with Charcot but found that hypnosis was not satisfactorily treating his patients. Freud then began experimenting with what has been called a talking cure. Patients would free-associate ideas and share their dreams, and then the therapist would provide interpretations. The insights gained through this process were judged to be therapeutic. Freud's approach to therapy, called **psychoanalysis,** was a major factor in the development of **psychiatry,** the profession in which a medically trained person attains special training related to diseases of the mind.

While Freud's work provided a basis for solving human problems by talking, psychoanalysis and psychiatry have otherwise had only an indirect influence on the early development of the present counseling profession. Many theorists influential in the development of the counseling field developed their ideas independently or in reaction to Freud rather than building directly on his work. It was not until the 1980s, when the third edition of the American Psychiatric Association *Diagnostic and Statistical Manual* (DSM) became widely used by professional counselors, that psychiatry had a major direct influence on the field.

The time line in Figure 9.1 shows some of the forces and events that have shaped the field of counseling. On the left side of the figure is a list of influential forces whose existence paralleled or coincided with the growth of the professional field of counseling. The time line at the bottom of the figure indicates the occurrence of national or world events. At different times during the twentieth century, these forces have significantly affected the growth of the counseling field. Each external influence has expanded and enriched the field. What should be evident is that the field is in the process of continual development and is incorporating ideas and strengths from related disciplines to become more comprehensive.

The influences of these ideas, methodologies, and energy continue to make the counseling field one of the most dynamic, continuously developing forces in the human services field. As a result of the ever-increasing scope of the counseling field (see Figure 9.1), counselors who were educated 20, 15, or even 10 years ago may have significant deficiencies in their training when compared to counselors who have recently graduated.

In the early part of the twentieth century, the primary precursors of the field of counseling were the vocational guidance movement, the mental health movement, and the study of individual differences in conjunction with the development of psychometry (Whiteley, 1984).

The Influence of Vocational Guidance and the Mental Health Movement

Vocational guidance dates back to the beginning of the twentieth century. The movement took hold with the work of Frank Parsons, who has been called the father of **guidance,** a directive approach in helping individuals to make choices. In 1908 Parsons established the Vocational Bureau of Boston to work primarily with improving the postschool placement of individuals. In 1909 Parsons published his landmark book, *Choosing a Vocation.* Subsequent developments in the vocational guidance movement are described in chapter 14.

The vocational guidance movement provided a cornerstone for the present counseling profession. In 1952 the National Vocational Guidance Association was one organization instrumental in founding the American Personnel and Guidance Association (APGA) which is now the American Counseling Association (ACA). The guidance movement has been an important part of the American school system for many years. School counselors

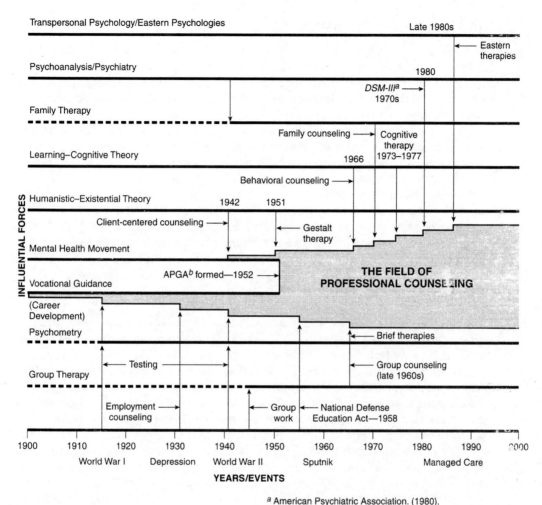

FIGURE 9.1 The development of the field of professional counseling.

are still often referred to as guidance counselors. The Vocational Guidance Association became a subdivision of the larger association and is now known as the National Career Development Association.

The mental health movement was developing in the United States at about the same time as the vocational guidance movement. Clifford Beers's *A Mind That Found Itself* (1908), a book in which he described the deplorable conditions found in mental institutions, became a major impetus in the development of the mental health movement in the United States.

The Influence of External Events

The field of counseling has been highly responsive to national and world events, and the field has benefited as a result. During the Great Depression the vocational guidance movement was strengthened because of the increased need for vocational information and job placement. World Wars I and II contributed to the development of the counseling field; personnel needs in both wars required new and improved psychological tests and testing procedures, many of which are now fully incorporated into the counseling domain. Attempts to meet the needs of disabled soldiers after World War II led to the establishment of counseling services for veterans, which included the development of group counseling procedures. Group work, however, did not make a major impact on the counseling field until the late 1960s and early 1970s. Russia's 1957 launching of the space satellite *Sputnik* prompted the U.S. Congress to enact the National Defense Education Act (NDEA), which significantly increased the numbers and the quality of training of school counselors. In the 1990s, insurance companies and other third party payers restricted the number of sessions that a client could have. This led to the growth of brief therapies.

The Influence of Different Theoretical Approaches

Over the years a number of theoretical approaches, or schools, of counseling have had a significant impact on the development of the field. Early vocational guidance counselors were influenced by the **trait factor approach,** in which counselors first try to determine what characteristics or traits a person has and then try to match those traits with the specific factors required to perform certain occupations. Carl Rogers's 1942 book, *Counseling and Psychotherapy,* gave rise to a nonmedical, humanistic approach to personal counseling called nondirective counseling. In the 1950s it became **client-centered counseling.** This approach emphasizes focusing on the client and the client's feelings rather than on characteristics and traits. **Gestalt therapy,** a humanistic approach which emphasizes here and now awareness, entered the field in the 1950s. In the 1960s **behavioral therapy,** a derivative of learning or behavioral theory that focuses on the individual's behaviors, became influential. **Cognitive therapy,** emphasizing the individual's thoughts, began making an impact in the 1970s and was often coupled with behavioral approaches to form **cognitive–behavioral therapy.** In the 1990s, the field of counseling was increasingly influenced by the Eastern psychologies. These ideas, which first entered the American awareness during the 1960s, are encompassed by **transpersonal counseling,** which emphasizes the spiritual side of humanity.

In terms of the historical impact of these theoretical conceptions on the field of counseling, the 1950s might be considered the decade of affect (client-centered therapy and Gestalt therapy); the 1960s might be the decade of behaviorism (and behavior therapy); and the 1970s might be the decade of cognition (and cognitive therapy) (Patterson, 1986, p. 562). The 1980s did not have a dominant theoretical influence. The 1990s were strongly influenced by spirituality and transpersonal counseling, along with brief therapy and managed care.

The 1980s and the early 1990s had more of a **wholistic,** eclectic emphasis, incorporating what had previously been developed. (Note that the spelling of *wholistic* is chosen deliberately to suggest a total, inclusive approach to the field.) Wholistic practitioners draw ideas from the other theoretical approaches and include an emphasis on health, wellness, and the spiritual side of human behavior. Another dimension of the wholistic approach, which was introduced in the 1970s and gained strength in the 1980s, is the **systems** perspective. This point of view suggests that a client does not have a problem in isolation. To help clients the counselor must understand them as systems and examine the nature of the interactions they have with various aspects of their environment (see chapter 13).

Group and Family Therapy

Another major influence on the field of counseling in the late 1960s and 1970s was group therapy. Group therapy had been used during World War II and before, but not until Carl Rogers's work with encounter groups was published in 1970 (*Carl Rogers on Encounter Groups*) did group work become popular. Today, proponents of most theoretical approaches tend to favor working in groups rather than individual counseling.

Developing after World War II was **family therapy,** the practice of working with the entire family rather than the individual. This began to have an increasing impact on the counseling field in the late 1970s. The systems approach has been pursued extensively by family counselors, because the family is perhaps the most important system for an individual. Many counselors today will not see a client unless they are able to involve the client's family.

Psychiatry

For years the field of counseling developed without any major direct influence from the field of psychiatry; however, this changed in the late 1970s and early 1980s at about the same time the third edition of the *Diagnostic and Statistical Manual (DSM-III)* was published by the American Psychiatric Association (1980). Increased numbers of personnel trained as counselors became employed in a wide variety of community agencies in which formal diagnoses are required for treatment plans and insurance payments, so counselor education students must now become well-versed in the fourth edition of the *Diagnostic and Statistical Manual (DSM-IV)* (American Psychiatric Association, 1994). The *DSM*, developed and published by the American Psychiatric Association, is now used in almost all mental health settings in the United States for diagnosing the problems of clients, developing treatment plans, and communicating with other professionals and insurance companies. Mental health counselors now work with psychiatrists, physicians, and psychologists to provide quality care, using the common language dictated by the *DSM-IV.* Government agencies and insurance companies generally require some type of formal diagnosis before they will pay insurance claims, so the use of the *DSM* by counselors is important.

This historical background provides a basis for a more informed discussion of the work of a contemporary professional counselor. The most common perception of a counselor is of a person talking in a one-to-one situation with a person who has a problem. This perception is incorrect because not many trained counselors spend 30 to 40 hours a week seeing clients on an individual basis. Even counselors in mental health centers who practice individual counseling on a regular basis are usually limited to 20 to 25 sessions per week, a little more than half of a 40-hour week. The field of counseling is more complex and involved than merely working with clients one-to-one. A trained counselor may regularly provide different functions geared to a variety of goals, use a number of modalities and techniques, and serve a number of populations. The second part of this chapter describes the many functions, goals, techniques, and populations involved in the field of counseling.

Ideas in action   Consider the education of counselors you know. When might they have completed their formal professional education? If they have not been maintaining a regular practice of continuing their education, in which dimensions of the current field of counseling are they likely to be weak?

THE FIELD OF COUNSELING

To describe the broad field that is open to the prospective counselor, one can use a model developed as a structural guide to the field. Morrill, Oeting, and Hurst's (1974) model of the dimensions of counseling intervention "permits the identification and classification of a variety of counseling programs or counseling approaches and thereby serves as a means of categorizing and describing the potential activities in a variety of settings" (p. 355) (see Figure 9.2). The three primary dimensions described by the model are the intervention target, the purpose, and the method. Any intervention by a counselor has these three dimensions: a person or group at whom the intervention is aimed, a reason for the intervention, and a manner of carrying it out.

Target of the Intervention

In 1957 the editor of the *Journal of Counseling Psychology* rejected an article on group counseling because "counseling is a process [involving] two persons" (Morrill, Oeting, & Hurst, 1974, p. 6). As the following description of the targets of counseling intervention indicates, the field of counseling has come a long way. Today, professionally trained counselors are as likely to target their interventions toward a group as toward an individual. Even when the intervention is targeted toward an individual, it is highly probable that the individual may be participating in group counseling.

Individual
The basic and most common form of counseling is **individual,** which is one-to-one counseling between counselor and client. Most theoretical conceptualization and direct experience of counseling have resulted from one-to-one counseling beginning with the work of Freud. Individual counseling still is dominant and is the basic modality used in training counselors.

Since the 1970s, there has been a growing emphasis on group counseling. To a great extent, **group counseling** is individual counseling within the context of a group with usually no direct effort to change the group as a functional unit. Either one-to-one or in a group, the counselor's objective is to help the individual make changes as a result of new information, altered attitudes and perceptions, and new responses and skills.

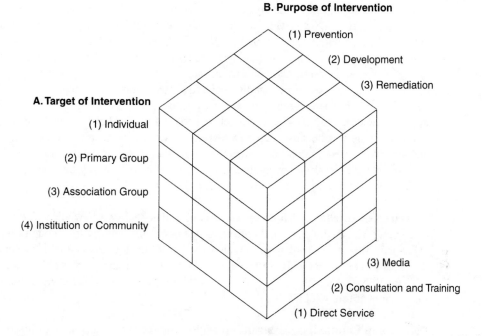

FIGURE 9.2   Dimensions of counseling interventions.

Adapted from "Dimensions of Counselor Functioning," by W. Morrill et al., 1974, *Personnel and Guidance Journal, 52*(6), pp. 354–359. Copyright © 1974 by American Counseling Association. Adapted with permission. No further reproduction authorized without written permission of the American Counseling Association.

Primary Group

Often the target of the counseling intervention is the primary group that most directly affects the individual. In the case of children, for example, a 5-year-old child may be seen on an individual basis; however, because the child's attitude and behavior are directly and continuously influenced by family members, little lasting change can take place without involving the members of the family as well.

> The **primary group** is the basic unit of social organization—that group (or groups) most influencing the individual. [They are] intimate, continuing personal associations on a face-to-face basis, determined by degree of intimacy rather than by proximity. (Morrill, Oeting, & Hurst, 1974, p. 356)

Families and peer groups are the basic primary groups. These groups have significant impact on the behavior and attitudes of individuals in the group and vice versa. When working with primary groups, counseling interventions should include working on communication patterns and improving the interaction patterns and structural relations of the group.

Family Counseling.   A specialized type of group counseling, **family counseling,** came into its own in the 1970s. Developing from a number of different sources (Ackerman, 1966; Haley, 1971; Minuchin, 1974; Satir, 1967; Watzlawick, 1966), family counseling has emerged as one of the most powerful approaches to counseling. This is largely because, as indicated above, the family is seen as a primary group.

A major drawback of both individual and group counseling is that when clients who have changed their behavior return to the family, the family members may not be willing or able to accept the change. Clients may choose to return to old behavior patterns in an effort to reduce anxiety or because their new behaviors were not reinforced. Also, in many cases changes on the part of other family members, or in family structural or communication patterns, may be necessary to bring about changes in individual family members (see chapter 12 for extended coverage of family counseling).

Marriage Counseling.   **Marriage counseling** can be seen as a specialized form of family counseling with the husband and wife seen together by the counselor, although some counselors may also see each spouse individually as part of the process. Sometimes members of the expanded family may also be brought in if deemed appropriate by marriage counselors. Ohlsen (1979) has developed a model for working with married couples in groups consisting of three or four couples.

Peer Group Counseling.   **Peer group counseling** is a type of primary group counseling that is particularly helpful with adolescents. For many young people, the primary group shifts from the family to the peer group in early adolescence. At this point the peer group often has more influence than the family on the attitudes and behavior of the adolescent. Peer group counseling is often used in high school settings, in detention homes, and with young people on probation. Much of the work done with these groups may be remedial, but a significant amount of work may he preventive and developmental.

Another form of peer group counseling includes self-help groups such as Alcoholics Anonymous and Overeaters Anonymous. These groups typically consist of people with similar problems who gather together to help each other and themselves. Typically, no outsider serves as a counselor or leader. Group counseling focusing on group rather than individual change involves association groups and an institution or a community.

Association Group.   An **association group** is an organized group that may be based on chance or choice association. Such groups could be a social studies class, a Kiwanis Club, or a college fraternity. Members of these groups have similar interests or goals and are held together by some type of organizational structure. Possible interventions with association groups include goal-setting and implementation strategies, developing communication skills, providing leadership training, and changing patterns of interaction.

Counselor interventions with association groups are primarily preventive and developmental, although there may be occasions when an organization or group may have difficulties significant enough to require remediation. Much of the work done at this level involves short workshops or long-term seminars centering on concepts such as human relations training, development of communication skills, leadership training, and organizational development. Much of the work of the developmental school counselor (see chapter 15) would consist of working with classroom association groups.

Outside of schools, a great deal of the association group work is conducted by professionals who are specifically trained in organizational development as opposed to having their primary training in counseling. The specific intervention used by organizational development professionals may be similar or even identical to counselor strategies. Large corporations often have professionals on staff who can provide preventive and developmental services to various subgroups within the organization.

Institution or Community.   An **institution** or **community** as a target group differs from association groups, because members are generally aware of being part of the institution or community but may rarely, if ever, attend any type of formal meetings; neighborhoods, religious organizations, school systems, industrial concerns, cities, states, and even nations are examples. Modes of intervention could include "attempts to alter goals, communications, system linkages, power distribution, information flow, sections, and so on" (Morrill, Oeting, & Hurst, 1974, p. 357).

In working with the larger institution or community, the interventions are generally preventive or developmental. As the groups become larger, remediation approaches become increasingly difficult to use. Most interventions described in relation to association groups apply here with a great deal of emphasis on organizational development. Community counseling has, in the last decade, become a major area of counselor activity. Much of the work here is concerned with implementation of services, interaction of the various community service agencies, short-term and long-term planning, and research and evaluation.

Ideas in

With which of the targets of intervention—individual, primary group, association group, or community (institution)—do you believe you would work best? Why?

Purpose of the Intervention

The second major dimension presented in this model deals with the purpose of a counseling intervention: (1) prevention of a potential problem, (2) development of skills to enhance personal abilities and potential, and (3) remediation of an existing problem. This dimension offers a much broader view of the purposes of counseling. Rather than providing solely a reactive, remediating function, proactive or preventive counseling interventions help to prevent problems and to foster positive personal development.

Preventive Counseling

Prevention is concerned with identifying skills that are needed now or in the future and providing a means for acquiring them. The intention is to anticipate future problems and to prevent them by providing individuals or groups with needed skills or by creating changes in the environment (Morrill, Oeting, & Hurst, 1974, p. 357).

As Albee (1977) has noted, not all of those who need care are able to obtain it, primarily for economic reasons. In addition, even though there are thousands of new psychotherapists being trained every year, there probably will never be enough to adequately help all of the people who need it. Furthermore, remediation, if obtained, is not always successful. In the final analysis, the cost of remediation is prohibitive even if such an approach is deemed desirable. Even now, the cost to society of having large numbers of people in various states of debilitation is staggering. Clearly, a different approach seems necessary. Preventive counseling is trying to meet this challenge.

Prevention is usually **proactive**—initiating, anticipating, reaching out actively—and aimed at large groups of people, in anticipation of a debilitating life problem. Groups targeted for prevention programs are generally considered to be **at risk,** or susceptible to experiencing the disorder sometime in the near future. The primary objective is to present activities and programs that will prevent or at least minimize the incidence of a disorder in the population at risk (Conyne, 1983, p. 332). An example is drug abuse prevention programs for middle school students.

Preventive programs may be offered directly by a counselor to a targeted group, or they may be offered indirectly, such as through the use of media. Much of the work that Ann Landers and Dear Abby do in the newspapers is preventive. An important site for preventive counseling is in the schools (often under the label of guidance), where counselors provide information and organize and lead programs covering a variety of topics and approaches: sex education, communication skills, the skill of saying "no," self-awareness, and career choice.

Well-designed parenting classes for expectant parents and premarital counseling can be very important in preventing future problems, perhaps even for generations. In some cases, environmental or institutional changes can be designed, such as those that might be helpful in preventing trauma for students as they move from middle school to high school life. Preventive approaches often put counselors in the position of being advocates for their client populations.

Developmental Counseling

Developmental counseling refers to "those programs designed to enhance the functioning and developmental potential of healthy individuals and groups" (Morrill, Oeting, & Hurst, 1974, p. 357). Developmental counseling focuses on helping clients achieve positive personal growth throughout the various stages of their lives. This could also be called life counseling. The importance of this area is indicated by the inclusion of the term *development* in many of the subdivisions of the American Counseling Association (for example, the Association for Adult Development and Aging and the Association for Multicultural Counseling and Development). The organization's journal is the *Journal of Counseling and Development.*

Developmental counseling involves working with children and adults who are not currently faced with a crisis or an otherwise incapacitating problem and helping them to understand themselves better and to accept themselves. The ultimate goal is to develop fully functioning, self-actualizing people.

The stages of different aspects of individual development have been described by Piaget (1952), Havighurst (1953), Erikson (1963), Kohlberg (1971), and Sheehy (1976). Much developmental counseling takes place in schools as counselors help children prepare for and go through childhood developmental stages. Gazda (1984) has formulated an extensive development group counseling approach designed to help counselors facilitate the growth of their clients across seven basic areas of human development: cognitive, emotional, moral, ego, physical-sexual, psychological, and vocational. Recently there has been increased emphasis on providing developmental counseling services for adults; this emphasis has focused on such developmental stages as midlife and retirement (see chapter 16).

Comparison of Preventive and Developmental Counseling.   Preventive and developmental counseling are similar in many ways. They are both designed for reasonably well-functioning people who are not necessarily in any current psychological crisis. The processes used often tend to be proactive and educative in nature, featuring informative experiential activities, discussions, and homework.

Both types of counseling use similar activities and can be done individually and with groups. Preventive counseling, because it often focuses more on giving information, can be used with large groups.

Preventive counseling tends to focus more on individuals or groups identified as having the potential for future problems. It also tends to be more topic-oriented and skill-oriented, centering on issues such as drug awareness and decision making. Developmental counseling deals more with promoting and encouraging positive growth for all, helping clients to progress successfully through the developmental stages in their lives.

Developmental counseling works particularly well in small groups of 8 to 12 people, which in the past may have been referred to as growth groups. On an individual basis, it might be seen as individual wellness counseling. Such counseling "is geared mainly for people who consider themselves emotionally and physically fit, yet seek to enhance their state of being. This growth-oriented approach to wellness is founded on self-responsibility. Each participant explores his or her unique path to wellness and, ultimately, peak performance" (Health and Lifestyle Center of Memorial Hospital, 1983, p. 3).

Both types of counseling can be seen as preventive in nature. Both help individuals develop to their full potential and minimize the need for future remedial counseling.

Remediation

Remediation is what most people refer to when they speak of counseling, therapy, or psychotherapy. Counseling interventions at the remediation level involve responding to an individual or group that has a felt need or problem usually involving psychological discomfort. In individuals this could include the full variety of personal, social, and vocational problems, whereas with groups it could be structural or organizational problems. The basic intervention strategy used at this level is what Pietrofesa, Hoffman, and Splete (1984) call **facilitative counseling.** "Facilitative counseling is the process of helping the client to clarify a concern; then through self understanding and acceptance, to devise a plan of action and finally to act on it in a self-responsible manner" (Pietrofesa et al., 1984, p. 11). The term facilitative counseling describes the process presented in the early chapters of this book.

The Purpose of the Intervention as a Continuum

One way to describe the purposes of the various types of intervention is to present the purpose dimension of the cube in terms of a continuum of psychological helping relationships ranging from guidance to training to therapy (see Table 9.1).

Although there are three basic intervention purposes (prevention, development, and remediation), these purposes are not distinct entities. As Table 9.1 illustrates, there is much overlap in terms of process and content. Much developmental counseling is by its nature

TABLE 9.1   The purpose of the intervention as a continuum.

	Prevention	Developmental	Remediation	
Descriptive Titles	Guidance Preventive counseling Training Teaching (subject matter instruction) Psychological education	Developmental counseling Human relations training T groups Organizational development groups	Counseling Facilitative counseling Crisis counseling	Psychotherapy Therapy
Goals	To develop awareness: skill building	To develop human potential	To develop client self-responsibility and commitment	To increase coping, change attitudes, behaviors
Time Orientation	Present (here and now)	Present	Present	Past, present, future
Time-Lines	Specific time span	Continuous (over life span)	Varies (short- to long-term)	Varies (could be brief, but more likely several months to several years)
Setting	Almost anyplace	Education, business, religion	Generally clinical —could be in other settings (e.g., milieu counseling)	Clinical
Activities of Counselor	Model, teach, information-giving, referral to other agencies	Aiding value clarification Teaching decision making	Attending, understanding, confronting, decision-making skills	Attending, understanding, confronting, decision-making skills
Clientele	Anyone	Anyone	Average individuals	Persons deficient in coping; disturbed or disturbing behavior
Possible Concerns	Drug awareness, self- and career-awareness, sex education	Developing self-concept in elementary school Midcareer change Retirement planning Acceptance of death and dying	Educational, vocational Personal, emotional, and inter-personal problems Rehabilitation	Severe emotional and personality disorders

preventive; if remediation is successful, future problems related to the target problem should be prevented.

Nevertheless, Table 9.1 offers a variety of ways to differentiate among the purposes of intervention. The left, or preventive, side of the continuum is mostly teaching and training; the right side is oriented more to therapy and treatment. From clients' points of view, however, if they are actively involved at any point along the continuum, they are learning about themselves and how to cope with life's problems. Fundamentally, all interventions involve a teaching and learning component, and this component tends to function more effectively when a positive helping relationship has been established.

On the remediation side of the continuum the terms *counseling* and *psychotherapy* are used. Over the years there has been extensive discussion regarding the differences between counseling and psychotherapy and whether there are any differences. Patterson (1974) has steadfastly maintained that the basic processes are similar, if not the same. A generally accepted difference between counseling and psychotherapy suggests that psychotherapists tend to have a longer training period. They usually have a doctorate either in psychology or in medicine specializing in psychiatry, and as a result they tend to deal with the more severe problems, particularly those requiring long-term therapy.

In actual practice, however, those distinctions have not always been maintained. Counselors and social workers may work with severely disturbed people, such as clients who manifest dangerous pathological behavior. Psychologists and psychiatrists may devote professional time working with the so-called normal population. In either case, the actual techniques and therapies used may not vary much. As noted in chapter 4, the only clear differentiation in duties involves treatments that call for medication—at the present time only the psychiatrist can legally prescribe medications. This could change if clinical psychologists are successful in their current quest to attain the privilege of prescribing medications.

The purposes or goals of intervention on this continuum are to help the person acquire knowledge and skills that will prevent future problems, to develop all aspects of the person's potential, and to teach needed coping skills. To some extent these appear to be distinct and separate purposes; however, as the client and the counselor work on any one of these goals, they may serendipitously end up attaining secondary, perhaps unstated or even unrecognized, goals in the other areas.

Ideas in  As you think of the three purposes for intervention—prevention, development, and remediation—on which of these types of intervention do you see yourself focusing?

If you selected remediation, do you see yourself more on the counseling side of the continuum in Figure 9.1 or on the therapy side?

Methods of Intervention

Professional counselors use their intervention strategies directly through face-to-face sessions with clients or indirectly by consultation, training, and the use of media. Each method is introduced here and discussed later in greater detail.

Direct Service

Direct service in the counseling field has been characterized primarily by what might be called talk therapy, which involves the client and the counselor talking and listening to each other. Chapters 5–8 have described this process.

Over the years, a number of other direct-service modes have been developed. Even though the term *therapy* is often used in conjunction with these approaches, they generally consist of a collection of activities that may be helpful with certain clients and particular types of problems. Each of these modalities, therefore, is often used as an adjunct to a theoretical approach that emphasizes talking (for example, combining art therapy with Gestalt therapy). Presented here is a partial listing of direct service therapeutic modalities currently available. Special training, in many cases including an advanced degree, is necessary for most of the following approaches.

Art Therapy. Art therapy involves the use of various art media to help clients express themselves. Often thoughts and feelings that cannot be easily expressed verbally emerge when a client is able to work freely with art techniques.

Music Therapy. Playing, singing, and listening to music can all be very evocative and can be used to help a client work through problems.

Body Therapies. These include bioenergetics, dance therapy, and different types of massage. The muscles and tissues of the body, as well as the mind, remember experiences that happened to the person. Often deep-seated emotions can be expressed through the use of various physical activities.

Hypnotherapy. Hypnosis has been used in the treatment of specific behaviors such as smoking cessation and weight-loss programs.

Phototherapy. The use of phototherapy, both the taking of new pictures and the reviewing of old family pictures, can be valuable to a number of theoretical approaches. The photos become a stimulus for communication during the counseling process.

Psychodrama. Psychodrama is a specialized structured approach used with a group in which a client uses other group members to work through family issues in the form of a play or skit.

Milieu Therapy. Milieu therapy uses the client's natural setting to conduct counseling (for example, counseling a teenager while shooting baskets on a playground).

There are, however, limitations to the provisions of direct service in terms of cost "both in money and in scarce professional time" (Morrill, Oeting, & Hurst, 1974, p. 358). Fees can be quite prohibitive, but even if money were no object there are not enough trained professionals to provide direct service to all in need. One inexpensive form of direct service is the telephone hotline service, available in many communities, which can help in crisis situations.

Consultation and Training

Consultation and training may involve direct or indirect services depending on the targeted population. An example of an indirect service is a counselor consulting with teachers on the best way to present a drug abuse program to primary grade school children. A direct service would be providing a workshop on stress management techniques to office managers.

Consultation and training activities tend to be primarily preventive and/or developmental in nature. Usually, the consultant comes in response to a need by the client. Occasionally, training programs may be required for employees by their superiors.

Consultation usually consists of a one-to-one or a group relationship over a period of time. The initial meeting centers on goals and objectives to be attained, and subsequent meetings focus on the completion of those objectives.

Training generally involves providing skill-development opportunities to adults in a variety of personal and interpersonal areas. A major organization, the American Society of Training and Development (ASTD), publishes journals and offers its own programs for trainers. Other nonuniversity organizations, such as the National Training Laboratory (NTL), offer training and certification for trainers. Training is usually offered in two basic formats: seminars and workshops.

Seminars.   Seminars are designed to be relatively small in size (18 to 20 people) so that there can be a significant degree of interaction between the counselor trainer and each participant. They are usually scheduled for relatively long periods of time—one week or four weekends, for example.

Workshops.   Workshops are generally designed to work with small to large groups of people with little or no direct interaction by the counselor trainer with individual participants. Workshops are usually scheduled for short periods of time—one day or one weekend.

The key term in the area of training is *organizational development* (see chapter 15). Whether it is a government agency, a church, a school, or a business, the organization will probably have any of a variety of organizational problems that restrict its effectiveness and productivity. Many businesses and agencies are employing their own in-house organizational development experts to provide regular training services to their employees.

Media

The most indirect method of providing counseling services is through the use of **media.** In addition to newspaper articles and services such as Ann Landers, television and radio now offer counseling services, often as part of a talk show format such as the Oprah Winfrey Show. Some radio shows encourage listeners with concerns to call in and discuss their problems. Computer networks, especially the Internet, also are now dealing with personal problems, although professionally trained counselors are not necessarily involved; this service is direct, albeit generally very brief.

Packaged, programmed counseling materials on topics such as parenting are available in workbook format, often using audiocassettes and videotapes. Perhaps the most indirect method is computer-oriented counseling. Some preliminary studies on self-help indicate that some clients would rather tell their troubles to a computer than to another human being. Counseling programs for use on home computers are available. **Bibliotherapy,** the use of books to help bring about therapeutic change, is perhaps the most successful example of providing counseling services by way of media. Self-help audiotapes and videotapes are also very popular.

The model describing the dimensions of counseling interventions can be used to describe the broad scope of the counseling profession. By creatively combining the various dimensions, new and important ways of meeting the needs of our society can be provided. Also, further elaboration of each dimension provides added awareness of the breadth and depth of the field of counseling.

A person could simply aspire to provide individual counseling in a community mental health center. The target is the individual, the purpose is remediation, and the service would be direct. A program could be designed to train Navajo paraprofessionals to work with the developmental tasks of children and parents on a Navajo reservation; the target of the intervention would be the family or primary group, the purpose of the intervention would be developmental, and the methods of intervention by the professionals would be consultation and training (Dinges, Yazzie, & Tollefson, 1974).

Crookston (1974) has proposed a design for an "intentional democratic community" to be developed for use in college residence halls (p. 382). In this example, the counselor would work with an association group (the members of the residence hall), providing a direct service in terms of group leadership, and the purpose would be developmental (to help the residents become a community).

Johnston (1974) created a college-level sex education program to help students deal with issues of sexuality and birth control. Some direct service was offered in the way of lectures, and consultation and training were offered to develop discussion leaders and train a peer counselor. The overall purpose of the program was to prevent unwanted pregnancies and other sexual problems. Individuals desiring such help were the targets of the intervention.

Ideas in action   Which method of intervention appeals the most to you: direct service, consultation and training, or media?

Now that you have explored these three dimensions, specify a target population, purpose, and method that you favor at this time. Return to Figure 9.2 and determine where on "The Cube" your particular set of interests is located.

Compare your placement on "The Cube" with placements by other students in your class.

TYPES OF CLIENTS

Many different types of clients work with professional counselors. An ongoing relationship may or may not ensue with any of these clients depending on a number of factors, particularly the level of training of the counselor.

The discussion of the target of intervention referred to clients in terms of individuals, groups, and community. Here we will consider more specific categories of clients.

Gender

The demand for gender-specific counseling has caused a large increase in the number of male counseling and support groups and the development of a strong feminist counseling movement. There also are clients who have gender identity issues.

Age

Counselors serve clients of all ages, ranging across the life span.

Children.　Children are almost always included in family therapy. Individually they may be seen in play therapy when they are quite young and as part of individual and group counseling when they have developed their communication skills. Some counselors, however, believe that the best way to help children may not be to work with them individually but to work with their families.

Adolescents.　This is an age group that is particularly amenable to group work.

Adults.　This age group includes most counseling clients and is the group for which most of the theories and treatments have been designed.

Aged.　The U.S. aged population is increasing in size and needs. The gerontological counseling specialty addresses the needs of this important group. You can now attain certification as a gerontological counselor.

Race/Ethnicity

Caucasian, Black, Latino, Native American, and Asian are the most prominent ethnic groups in the United States. These groups are described more fully in chapter 17. Note that in addition to these major racial groups, an increasing number of individuals are multiracial.

Sexual Preference

Clients may be heterosexual, homosexual, or bisexual. The importance of the needs and concerns of people with different sexual preferences has been acknowledged by the recent inclusion of Association for Gay, Lesbian, and Bisexual Issues in Counseling (AGLBIC) as the newest division of the ACA.

Health

In terms of physical health, much counseling work is now done with clients who are working on wellness, but a significant amount of counseling is done with people who have specific diseases such as AIDS, cancer, and Alzheimer's and with their families. A significant amount of counseling is done with clients who have disabilities such as blindness, deafness, epilepsy, and other physical impairments.

Socioeconomic

Many of the differences seen among people are as likely to be socioeconomic as racial, age related, or sexual (see chapter 17). Great distinctions between upper class, middle class, and the poor (lower class) are evident (Payne, 1995).

From the standpoint of mental health, counselors may meet with individuals ranging from those considered to be normal but who have a specific problem in everyday living to individuals who are having psychotic breakdowns.

A professional counselor can expect to meet clients from all of these categories. The level of training and expertise that the counselor has affects whether an ongoing professional relationship is established. In the counseling process described in chapters 5 through 8, several referral points were noted. Even after you have begun a counseling relationship you may realize that you are beyond your level of competence and must refer your client to a specialist.

Ideas in  Are there any specific types of clients that you would particularly enjoy working with at this time? With which types of clients would you expect to be the most uncomfortable? Would you refer the clients who caused you discomfort?

CURRENT TRENDS INFLUENCING THE FIELD OF COUNSELING

Increased Technological Growth and the Development of an Information Society

Progress always brings with it new sets of adjustments, many of which are related to the work of counselors. Perhaps the greatest adjustment revolves around the changes in our culture because of rapid technological development. The acceleration of knowledge is creating newer and faster technologies. Technological developments can provide benefits. Television, for example, has long been criticized for having negative effects on our society; however, as a tool both in counselor education and in counseling itself, it can be quite beneficial. Some counselors are now videotaping their counseling sessions and letting their clients view the tapes as part of the counseling process.

Perhaps the most important technological phenomenon that counselors have to learn to work with is the computer. The impact of computers on the counseling profession has been huge. Computers are used for administrative applications, for the dissemination of information in career counseling, and in skill-building such as for decision making. Computers may also be used for the development of problem-solving skills, for diagnosing client problems and cognitive styles, and for the application of appropriate intervention strategies. Further uses include networking with other counselors, creating client networks, developing games for assisting clients, and scoring and interpreting tests. Perhaps the greatest impact has come from the development of the Internet.

The Internet

Counselors, regardless of their specialization, can access a wealth of information about all aspects of the counseling profession on the **Internet,** a computer network connected to installations around the world. Computers have evolved to the point at which computer networks can link the individual to literally an entire world of electronically stored data and information. The Internet is the world's largest library, containing counseling-related bibliographies, abstracts, journal articles, lectures, research projects, assessment instruments and methods, professional issues and politics, counseling theory and practice, client problems and treatments, and funding opportunities. Through the Internet the user can utilize computers in another location, subscribe to electronic group discussion mail lists such as the Counselor Education and Supervision Network (CESNET-L), move documents and data files from one Internet-connected computer to another, send electronic mail messages, access news groups, search for documents, browse electronic library card catalogs, and download software stored in member files (Jackson & Davidson, 1996). National professional organizations such as the American Educational Research Association (AERA), the ACA, the American Association for Marriage and Family Therapists (AAMFT), and the APA, and special interest divisions such as the Association for Specialists in Group Work (ASGW), are utilizing Internet services. On the Internet they can facilitate organizational governance; advertise conventions, sponsored workshops, and official meetings; and disseminate informational announcements to association officers and members.

Internet Problems and Issues

New technologies bring new problems. One problem is individuals' excessive use of the Internet, a true addiction that can hurt relationships and impair individuals at work. Heavy on-line users meet the psychiatric criteria for clinical dependence applied to alcoholics and drug addicts. They lose control over their Net usage and cannot stop using the Internet despite harmful effects on their personal and professional lives.

Of great concern to many mental health professionals are the ethical and legal questions relating to many aspects of counseling on the Internet. There are several on-line journals that discuss psychotherapy. Many individual and group psychotherapists advertise their services on the Internet. Some mental health professionals for a fee even provide answers for people who submit questions via e-mail about personal problems. Others charge a fee for counseling sessions over the Internet. The following ethical and legal questions and issues are growing in importance:

Licensing.   Because licenses to practice counseling are granted on a state-by-state basis and the Internet often involves communication between people in different states, does the therapist's or the client's location determine which state's license is required?

Performing Psychological Evaluations over the Internet.   There are, of course, serious limitations with an evaluation performed by a counselor who does not observe the patient's appearance and behavior; however, expensive equipment and software exist that provide live video across the Internet.

Telephone Therapy.   Some therapists say counseling over the telephone is too limiting; others suggest it can be used for a brief time, such as during a patient's vacation (Miller, 1997). Voice communication over the Internet is possible with the addition of software costing less than $100, a sound card, and a microphone; however, audio communication via the

Internet is still quite primitive and more impersonal than face-to-face communication. As a response to some of these issues, the National Board for Counselor Certification has instituted a set of ethical guidelines for counseling over the Internet.

Ideas in

The Internet already has more than 200 support newsgroups where people with similar concerns, such as eating disorders, can discuss their issues.

What are the pros and cons of on-line support groups? Would you participate in one or recommend one to a friend or client? Why or why not?

NEW ROLES AND GOALS FOR THE COUNSELOR

Counselor Role

The counseling profession is in a major transition. With competition from the other mental health professionals and many states cutting mental health services, fewer doctoral positions are available. Managed care is also affecting the counseling profession as it pushes counselors to be more efficient and effective. Counselors and counselor educators need to continually monitor what is happening in the profession and to conduct outcome research to better determine their roles. Mental health counselors need to be better trained with approaches that are appropriate and effective in order to remain competitive.

Attaining the additional training may serve counselors well. Managed care organizations are turning more to master's level counselors, because the counselors are less expensive and have a consumer satisfaction rating as high as doctoral level psychiatrists and psychologists (McGoldrick, 1997; *Consumer Reports,* 1995). In fact, the "employment of counselors is expected to grow faster than the average for all occupations through the year 2005" (U.S. Department of Labor, 1996, p. 147).

Smith (1995) believes that the term *mental health counseling* will come to mean the delivery of counseling services along the full continuum of mental health services. She foresees mental health counselors articulating a diagnostic system based on developmental theories and determining appropriate intervention or treatment. She also hopes that this will lead to preventive counseling becoming respected as cost-efficient and as effective as the practice of preventive medicine.

Smith also anticipates all practicing mental health counselors having basic knowledge and skills in the diagnosis and treatment of mental disorders as well as a preventive, developmental, wholistic, and multidisciplinary emphasis as a part of their core course work. Currently, however, some states are attempting to pass laws to forbid counselors from making diagnoses based on the *DSM-IV* classifications.

An important issue is whether certain nonmedical mental health professionals should be given the right to prescribe psychotropic medications. Part of the impetus for this move is coming from health policy leaders who view the change as one way to contain escalating health care costs and to provide more coverage to underserved populations. The Public Citizens Health Research Group and the National Alliance for the Mentally Ill have already endorsed training and prescriptive authority for psychologists, physician assistants, and nurse practitioners (Wedding, 1995).

Theoretical Trends

Recent surveys of mental health practitioners indicate that loyalties to particular schools are a thing of the past (Young, 1993). Instead, there has been a growing trend toward eclecticism. General systems theory has become influential in counseling and therapy: family systems theories (see chapter 13) have been steadily gaining supporters in counselor training programs. There also is a growing emphasis (see chapter 11) on transpersonal, spiritual, and wholistic approaches.

Funding for Mental Health

The emphasis on less federal government, tax cutting, and balanced budgets has resulted in decreased funding for community-based agencies, resulting in negative effects on the job security of counselors. With growing pressure on the local governments to pay for community mental health services, a decrease in job security is likely to continue.

Managed Care

The concept of **managed care** is an idea that has been receiving much attention. It refers to a group of physical and/or mental health practitioners who contract with an employer to service employee needs, usually for a set price. Health Maintenance Organizations (HMOs) are examples of managed care providers. In mental health care, the purpose of managed care is to reduce costs by standardizing psychotherapy. While managed care has operated in medicine for some time, managed care in psychotherapy is a relatively new (1990s) and more complex phenomenon. Unlike medicine, a therapist cannot provide an X ray of depression or a personality disorder. In addition, the length or outcome of treatment cannot be predicted, no matter how standard the symptoms are or regulated the therapy is (Brave, 1994). In managed care, the practice by insurance companies or HMOs is to approve a small number of sessions (generally 3 to 5) in which a diagnosis is made and a treatment plan devised. If the diagnosis and treatment plan are found satisfactory by a case manager once they are submitted to the managed care company, a few more sessions can be approved. Managed care requires that the mental health provider give justification for the course and conduct of even the most limited treatment for each and every client.

The trend of managed care in the health care system is likely to continue. Many counselors will find themselves forced into the managed care system in order to survive. Possibly an increasing number of counselors will refuse to practice under the managed care system of insurance reimbursement and will seek other alternatives. Many counselors use such opportunities as innovative marketing, sliding fee scales calibrated to personal income, networking, collaborating with colleagues, and organizing their own group practices outside the system. On the other hand, the concurrent trend of insurance companies and government agencies to pay master's level therapists can be seen as a positive (McGoldrick, 1997).

Multicultural Emphasis

The emphasis on multiculturalism in counseling, including gender issues, continues to grow. There is a greater focus on counselor sensitivity to culturally diverse groups, culturally biased diagnoses of some mental disorders, and competence at working with culture-bound syndromes.

SUMMARY

The origins and development of the field of counseling have direct roots in the vocational guidance movement of the early twentieth century. Throughout the century, a great many external influences have contributed to and expanded the field.

A three dimensional model demonstrates the broad scope of intervention activities in which a trained counselor may become involved. The field of counseling incorporates three different dimensions: the target of the counselor's intervention, the purpose of the intervention, and the method of intervention.

The target of the intervention includes (1) individuals working in an one-to-one setting or in group settings, (2) primary groups such as family and peer groups, (3) association groups such as classes or fraternal clubs, and (4) institutions or communities. The purposes of interventions include prevention, development, and remediation. Prevention interventions emphasize the anticipation of future problems and provide the information and skill training necessary to prevent the occurrence of problems. Developmental counseling takes into consideration all the developmental stages human beings go through during a lifetime and provides the training, knowledge, and support necessary to help people successfully experience the stages of life. The similarities among and differences between preventive and developmental interventions as well as between counseling and psychotherapy are described.

Remediation is the provision of services to clients with specific problems and is commonly referred to as counseling, therapy, or psychotherapy. The facilitative counseling responses described in chapters 5, 6, and 7 of this book are illustrative of the specific interventions that occur as part of remediation.

The methods of intervention for counselors include direct and indirect service. Direct service involves meeting with individuals or groups who have specific, immediate needs. A variety of different approaches may be used to provide direct services, including techniques such as art and music therapy. Radio and television call-in shows, from which listeners can attain immediate responses to personal problems, are another form of direct service. Direct service usually applies to remediation cases. Indirect services include consultation and training for individuals or groups who have long-term needs, as in the areas of preventive and developmental work. Indirect services also include conducting workshops and seminars and working through the print and broadcast media. Packaged programmed materials in the form of books, audiotapes, and videotapes are available in most stores.

New technology is affecting the practice of counseling. Computers and the development of the Internet are providing counselors with new and challenging ways to enhance counseling work. Through the Internet, counselors can access a wealth of information about all aspects of the counseling profession regardless of their specialization.

Private practice practitioners are concerned with their future in an era of managed care. They believe that their control of the counseling process has been usurped by insurance companies whose bottom line is huge profits. Overall, the market for counselors is expected to grow well into the next century.

QUESTIONS AND ACTIVITIES

1. Much of the growth and development of counseling has come as a result of events outside of the field (for example, World Wars I and II). What current events or forces in our society are you aware of that might eventually have an impact on the field of counseling? In what ways might you predict that the field will be affected?

2. As you think of your goals in the counseling field at this time, where on the cube (Figure 9.2) do your interests fit? What part of the cube would have best represented your interests before entering this course?

3. List all the examples of counseling interventions provided by the media in your community, such as radio and television talk shows and newspaper advice columns. What is the quality of these interventions? What ethical problems are posed by these interventions?

4. Which of the current trends in the field of counseling excite you? Which concern you? How will these trends affect your future?

RECOMMENDED READINGS

Grohol, J. M. (1997). *The insider's guide to mental health resources online.* New York: Guilford.

INTERNET RESOURCES

Websites
Resources for Counselors   <www.csun.edu/ ~hfedp001/links.html>
Counselor Net   <www.plattsburgh.edu/cnet>
The Counseling Web: Counseling Psychology Programs and Resources   <seamonky.ed.asu. edu/~gail/indes.htm>

WCN (Interactive Counseling Community)

REFERENCES

Ackerman, N. (1966). *Treating the troubled family.* New York: Basic Books.

Albee, G. (1977). Does including psychotherapy in health insurance represent a subsidy from the rich to the poor? In J. Hariman (Ed.), *Does psychother-*

apy really help people? (pp. 3–8). Springfield, IL: Charles C. Thomas.

American Association for Counseling and Development. (1988). Ethical standards of the AACD 3rd revision. *Journal of Counseling and Development, 67*(9), 4–6.

American Psychiatric Association. (1980). *Diagnostic and statistical manual of mental disorders* (3rd ed.). Washington, DC: American Psychiatric Association.

American Psychiatric Association. (1994). *Diagnostic and statistical manual of mental disorders* (4th ed.). Washington, DC: American Psychiatric Association.

Beers, C. (1908). *A mind that found itself.* New York: Longman Green.

Brave, R. (1994, September 19). Psychotherapy is in turmoil over managed care. *Business Journal Serving Greater Sacramento, 11,* 35.

Conyne, R. (1983). Two critical issues in primary prevention: What it is and how to do it. *Personnel and Guidance Journal, 61*(6), 331–334.

Crookston, B. (1974). The intentional democratic community in college residence halls. *Personnel and Guidance Journal, 52*(6), 382–389.

Dinges, N., Yazzie, M., & Tollefson, G. (1974). Developmental intervention for Navajo mental health. *Personnel and Guidance Journal, 52*(6), 390–395.

Dumont, F., & Carson A. (1995, March–April). Precursors of vocational psychology in ancient civilizations. *Journal of Counseling and Development, 73*(4), 371–378.

Erikson, E. H. (1963). *Children and society* (Rev. ed.). New York: Norton.

Gazda, G. (1984). *Group counseling: A developmental approach.* Boston: Allyn & Bacon.

Haley, J. (1971). *Changing families.* New York: Grune & Stratton.

Havighurst, R. (1953). *Human development and education.* New York: Longman.

Health and Lifestyle Center of Memorial Hospital. (1983). [Brochure]. South Bend, IN.

Jackson, M. L., & Davidson, C. T. (1996, September). The web we weave: Using the Internet for counseling research—Part II. *Counseling Today, 39*(3), 22–23.

Johnston, C. (1974). Sexuality and birth control: Impact of outreach programming. *Personnel and Guidance Journal, 52*(6), 406–411.

Kohlberg, L. (1971). The stages of moral development as a basis for moral education. In C. Beck, B. Crittenden, & E. Sullivan (Eds.), *Moral education* (pp. 23–92). New York: Newman Press.

McGoldrick, J. (1997). Master's threat. *Common Boundary, 15*(4), 13.

Mental health: Does therapy work? (1995, November). *Consumer Reports, 60*(11), 734–739.

Minuchin, S. (1974). *Families and family therapy.* Cambridge, MA: Harvard University Press.

Morrill, W., Oeting, E., & Hurst, J. (1974). Dimensions of counselor functioning. *Personnel and Guidance Journal, 52*(6), 354–359.

Ohlsen, M. M. (1979). *Marriage counseling in groups.* Champaign, IL: Research Press.

Parsons, F. (1909). *Choosing a vocation.* Boston: Houghton Mifflin.

Patterson, C. H. (1974). *Relationship counseling and psychotherapy.* New York: Harper & Row.

Patterson, C. H. (1986). *Theories of counseling and psychotherapy.* (4th ed.). New York: Harper & Row.

Payne, R. K. (1995). *A framework for understanding and working with students and adults from poverty* (Rev. ed.). Baystown, TX: RFT Publishing.

Piaget, J. (1952). *The origins of intelligence in children* (M. Cook, Trans.). New York: International Universities Press.

Pietrofesa, J., Hoffman, A., & Splete, H. (1984). *Counseling: An introduction.* Boston: Houghton Mifflin.

Rogers, C. (1942). *Counseling and psychotherapy.* Boston: Houghton Mifflin.

Rogers, C. (1970). *Carl Rogers on encounter groups.* New York: Harper & Row.

Satir, V. (1967). *Conjoint family therapy* (Rev. ed.). Palo Alto, CA: Science & Behavior Books.

Sheehy, G. (1976). *Passages: Predictable crises of adult life.* New York: Dutton.

U.S. Department of Labor. (1996). *Occupational outlook handbook.* Indianapolis, IN: JIST Works.

Watzlawick, P. (1966). A structured family interview. *Family Process, 5,* 256–271.

Wedding, D. (1995). Current issues in psychotherapy. In R. J. Corsini & D. Wedding, *Current psychotherapies* (5th ed., pp. 419–431). Itasca, IL: F. E. Peacock.

Whiteley, J. M. (1984). *Counseling psychology: A historical perspective.* Schenectady, NY: Character Research Press.

Young, M. (1993). Theoretical trends in counseling: A national survey. *Guidance and Counseling, 9,* 4.

chapter 10

THEORY IN THE PRACTICE OF COUNSELING

- Does a theory of counseling help or hinder the practitioner?
- Should counselors strictly adhere to a particular theory, rely on their own experiences, or critically select combinations of techniques from the various theories?
- Are there commonalities among the various theories?
- With which of the four forces in psychology do you most identify?

Much literature in the field of counseling is related to theory. In this individualistic, idiosyncratic field, it often seems that everyone has a personal theory of counseling. This chapter discusses the nature of theories, whether they are needed, four significant theoretical forces, and an emerging major theoretical formulation—general systems theory. Finally, the process for developing a personal theory is presented.

WHAT IS A THEORY?

All of us live by a different road map of the world. This map is based on all of our past and present experiences; for us this map is reality. Our behaviors are based on this map of reality. The more structure and detail this map has, the better we are able to organize our actions. A **theory** provides a structure from which to understand what we are doing and the process of doing it. A theory is a framework on which interventions are based. It enables us to form relationships from the data we collect from our experiences and to make sense of the data. As we develop more experiences, more of the road map is filled in. Hansen, Stevic, and Warner (1986) refer to theory as an explanation for events that can be tested by events and that is useful only to the extent that it influences behavior. Patterson (1986) states that a formal theory has certain characteristics, including (1) a set of stated assumptions regarding the given field; (2) a set of definitions of the ideas and concepts in the theory stated in behavioral or observational terms so that the concepts are amenable to research; (3) concepts that bear certain relationships to one another, including cause and effect relationships; and (4) hypotheses constructed from these assumptions, definitions and relationships that can be tested through research and experimentation. Research outcomes may not validate predictions emanating from the theory, so aspects of the theory may have to be modified. The development of a theory, therefore, goes through a continual process of construction, testing, modification or reconstruction, and further testing. The theory is self-correcting and, no matter how attractive, does not need to be accepted on faith alone (Blocher, 1987). A formal theory should deal with meaningful matters; that is, however, a subjective criterion and is difficult to evaluate. Usually, a theory and its relevance are determined by whether other professionals in the field pay attention to it. A formal theory should be clear, precise, and easily understood. Concepts should be thought out and related or connected. There should be no internal inconsistencies, and the theory should be easily related to practice.

A good theory should also be comprehensive so that it takes into account numerous events in a variety of situations. The more comprehensive a theory is, then the more utility it has. A good counseling theory needs to be based in part on personality theory to provide counselors with knowledge of the development of normal and maladaptive behavior and human nature.

Currently, no counseling theory meets all of these criteria. There are more of what Blocher (1987) has labeled pseudotheories, or process models. A process model prescribes a more or less clearly defined set of actions for counselors to take in pursuit of specific goals and objectives with certain types of clients (p. 67). The field of counseling is still in its youth, and much work with regard to the development of theory lies ahead. We now examine some arguments for and against using counseling theories.

WHY HAVE A THEORY?

There is considerable debate regarding the value of psychotherapeutic theory, especially as it applies to practice. Brammer and Shostrom (1982) believe that the scientific clinical approach, as manifested by the application of counseling theory, is too difficult for counselors to use. In addition, they report a lack of strong evidence supporting a counselor's effectiveness in producing certain outcomes that correlate with the extent and explicitness of the counselor's theoretical foundations. They do believe, however, that counselors are still interested in theory as a means of enhancing their understanding of human behavior, even if this understanding does not lead to any practical results in counseling.

A case can be made both for and against the use of theory. Table 10.1 lists the main arguments for each side.

Arguments for Theory

As mentioned, a theory provides a structure or framework from which counselors can work in a systematic fashion. Hansen, Stevic, and Warner (1986) believe that the counselor cannot function in a meaningful manner without being able to place events in some order. Steffre and Grant (1973) argue that even counselors who hold an antitheoretical position are usually basing their behavior on vaguely defined but implicit theory. To them the choice between having a theory or not does not exist. The real questions are: what theory or theories should counselors have, and how should these theories be used?

TABLE 10.1   Arguments for and against the use of counseling theory.

For Theory	Against Theory
Creates order; provides a therapeutic road map.	Creates a false sense of certainty because there still is not enough psychological knowledge on which to base a complete theory.
Helps counselors understand what they are doing.	Confuses counselors because there are too many theories, many of them conflicting.
Provides knowledge from which to make choices and predictions.	Can lock counselors into a rigid format, making them inflexible.
Influences what the counselors do and how they do it.	Forces counselors to be mechanical.
Generates new ideas and approaches for testing.	Puts counselors in the position of being interpreters, thus preventing them from being individuals.
Cannot escape theorizing.	Cannot guarantee success as a counselor by having a strong theoretical approach.
May cause counselors to miss valuable data in counseling if not guided by theory.	Can lead counselors to focus on the theory rather than the here and now of the session.
May develop a reputation as a counselor more readily if you are identified with a given theory.	Makes the client conform to the counselor's theory.
May be impossible not to have a theory; having no theory is itself a theory.	Can counsel successfully without adhering to a specific theory. Cannot be completely committed to a theory that fully explains human behavior and behavioral changes, just can use approaches and techniques.

Arguments Against Theory

Many professionals in the field oppose those who favor theory. They see theory as an obstacle to being an effective therapist. For example, Carl Whitaker (1976) believes that all theories are bad and tend to constrict therapists by indoctrinating them in a narrow and rigid viewpoint. Arnold Lazarus (1981), the founder of multimodal therapy, argues that the current state of psychological knowledge does not permit the development of an accurate theory of human functioning. Brammer and Shostrom (1982) state that there is no compelling evidence proving that counseling effectiveness in producing certain outcomes definitely depends on the extent and explicitness of one's theoretical foundations. Further, there is no evidence that one particular theory of psychotherapy is superior to another. Studies that have investigated the success of counseling consistently report that theoretical orientation does not correlate to success as a counselor (Smith & Glass, 1977; Lieberman, Yalom, & Miles, 1973).

Theories of counseling also have developed in large part to explain and treat maladaptive, undesirable behavior. Even though a given approach may be of value in remediation, it is not often as useful in the preventive and developmental aspects of counseling. Probably the greatest objection cited by those who downplay the value of theory is the belief that theory forces counselors to become rigid, mechanical, and more interested in following a theoretical script than in being fully present with clients and tuning in to their processes.

Ideas in action

To function without theory is to operate without placing events in some order and thus to function meaninglessly.

Hansen, Stevic, and Warner (1986, p. 12)

All that is required of counselors is being real. The only value is authenticity. To achieve this, counselors must be willing to forsake all theories about how a good counselor should respond.

Bergantino (1978, p. 290)

With which of the above quotations do you agree? Why? If a supervisor or job interviewer asked you to describe your views regarding the necessity of having a counseling theory, how would you respond?

Types of Theories Related to the Field of Counseling

As if the counseling theory picture is not murky enough, all the different types of theories associated with the counseling field must be considered. As noted in chapter 9, the field of counseling has been influenced by a number of major factors. Most of these factors have brought with them a variety of theoretical points of view that have contributed to the richness of the field but have also been confusing to both the beginning student and the experienced practitioner. You cannot think simply of theories of counseling; you also need to consider theories of personality, theories of family counseling, and theories of career development. You then need to keep in mind that none of these theories is complete. A counseling student should view all of these approaches as a special kind of smorgasbord. Here you have the ability to explore a broad variety of ways of looking at human behavior and the possible means for bringing about significant change.

Basic Theoretical Stances

Rather than go on record as being for or against theory, many counselors compromise and call themselves eclectics. But what does eclecticism mean, and how does it relate to other conceptualizations of counseling theory?

Robinson (1965), who studied counseling approaches and labels, formulated four basic counseling orientations: pragmatic, eclectic, personality theorist, and the syncretic approach. A **pragmatic** counselor relies only on personal experience and does not adhere to any particular theory. An **eclectic counselor** critically selects concepts and techniques from a number of counseling approaches, takes research findings into account, and blends them into a consistent whole together with personal ideas and adaptations. The **personality theorist** is indoctrinated in and enamored with a particular theory and uses it exclusively with every type of client in every circumstance. **Syncretism** refers to the joining or merging of beliefs and ideas. A syncretic counselor uses ideas from two or more theories but makes no attempt to develop any coherent, consistent personal framework. Such a counselor may have a collection of techniques but does nothing to integrate their use in any logical or systematic format. Intuitive feel may be the only theory guiding the syncretic counselor.

Ideas in action

As a counselor, do you want to be creative and do what you think will work based on your own experiences and trial and error (pragmatic orientation)? Would you prefer to choose from a number of theories that interest you, that show evidence of working well together (eclectic orientation)? Instead, would you like to choose a number of theories from which to work based on your own intuition (syncretic orientation)?, or would you rather choose a specific theory from which to work and learn it well (personality orientation)?

What would be the pros and cons of each orientation? Which would make you the most effective counselor? Which would be the easiest and most difficult orientations for you?

Eclecticism is a term often used incorrectly by counselors. For example, some counselors who call themselves eclectic are often more pragmatic or syncretic. Such counselors do not necessarily have a systematically developed, research-based, consistent approach to working with clients. Their approaches may be spontaneous and idiosyncratic, with little grounding in any theoretical or research base.

The authors believe that the answer to most objections to the use of theory lies in how one uses theoretical knowledge, particularly knowledge based on research. A counselor does not have to adopt a single theory, allow theory to be a binding and constricting influence, or just have a big grab bag of techniques. A counselor can use theory creatively, humanely, and spontaneously. We advocate that counselors critically examine a number of theoretical approaches and become grounded in an approach that fits them particularly well. One can remain with that particular approach and become a specialist in it. One could also move to a more eclectic approach, working to develop a consistent, systematic theory and keeping in mind the need for research supported theoretical constructs and techniques.

The Proliferation of Theories

At one time, Sigmund Freud's psychoanalysis was the only approach to psychotherapy. Then several versions of psychoanalytic theory began fighting for dominance. The *Psychotherapy Handbook* lists more than 250 different types of therapy (Herink, 1980). Corsini (1995) reports that there are currently more than 400 approaches. Many of the lesser known approaches are offshoots of psychoanalytic, behavioral, and humanistic viewpoints.

Seemingly, each year sees a succession of new psychotherapies, each claiming to be uniquely different from its rivals and each claiming an 80% to 100% success rate. Frank (1978) states that he has yet to hear of a school that has disbanded, because it became convinced of the superiority of its rivals. Although some therapies may seem to fade from the top 40 list, they all seem to maintain a following. This proliferation of approaches has confused clients and the general public as well as students and helping professionals. How does a client or student choose? How does one really know which approach is the most effective? To confuse matters even more, there are differences within each approach. For example, there are many forms of behavior therapy, and an East Coast–trained Gestalt therapist might work differently from a West Coast–trained Gestaltist.

Commonalities Among Approaches

All of these approaches have much in common (in particular, the therapeutic relationship—see chapter 5). For example, many terms used in transactional analysis have evolved from terms used in Freudian analysis. According to Brammer and Shostrom (1982), there is a strong search for commonalities among the major therapeutic approaches today. Patterson (1986) has described commonalities in the relationship between the therapist and the client. Brabeck and Walfel (1985), after reviewing recent surveys of practitioners, reported a major shift toward a more eclectic or syncretic approach in the practice of counseling and psychotherapy.

Many approaches complement each other. For example, Gestalt therapy and person-centered therapy relate to each other in many ways. Both methodologies focus on the here and now, emphasize positive directions and goals of living, and place responsibility on the client to formulate personal solutions. Both therapies have roots in a similar philosophic frame of reference, and both use feedback. The person-centered approach emphasizes verbal interaction, however, and Gestalt therapy tends to emphasize nonverbal behavior. Viewed from a different perspective, Gestalt therapy complements transactional analysis (TA). TA employs relatively clear theoretical constructs and provides a cognitive framework for change, but Gestalt therapy provides practical approaches to help deal with the emotional aspects of change.

Goldfried (1982) cites therapists' growing discontent due to the limits of their respective approaches. He posits that although a common ground cannot be achieved among theoretical stances on either a theoretical or philosophical level, rapprochement might be achieved on a clinical strategies level. For example, most therapies offer clients direct feedback and provide clients with new, corrective experiences.

> To the extent that clinicians of varying orientations are able to arrive at a common set of strategies, it is likely that what emerges will consist of robust phenomena, as they have managed to survive the distortions imposed by the therapists' varying theoretical biases. (p. 386)

Although the means may be different, all theories carry the belief that people are capable of changing or being changed. This belief gives clients a sense of hope that acts to reverse the helpless and demoralized state that leads them to seek therapy. Most theories recognize that behavior is not entirely caused by the past but is influenced by present and future elements.

Another common element, according to Patterson (1986), is the counselor's confidence in the theory and method being used. Patterson states, "It might be hypothesized that success (or at least reports of success) bears a strong relationship to the degree of confidence the therapist has in his or her approach" (p. 547).

In a well-known study, Fiedler (1950) found that experienced helpers of different theoretical persuasions tended to have more in common than did inexperienced helpers of the same persuasion. These common elements included the relationship dimensions of genuineness, empathic understanding, respect, and acceptance of the client. Truax and Carkhuff (1967) described the same phenomenon in reporting on a number of studies comparing counselors using different approaches.

Lieberman, Yalom, and Miles (1973), in their study of group leadership, generally confirmed these conclusions. They analyzed leadership results in 10 different types of groups and found that no one type of leader was better than another; that is, a Gestalt-oriented group leader was not necessarily better than a psychoanalytically oriented group leader. The observed behavior of leaders with a similar orientation varied greatly. The conclusion reached was that "their ideological beliefs (what they believed and what they said they did) bore little relation to their actual behavior" (Yalom, 1995, p. 98). Even though the leaders' behavior was not predictable on the basis of theoretical orientation, the effectiveness of the leaders was a function of their behavior.

Patterson (1985) believes that a basic foundation of all major theories is the therapeutic relationship. After examining the research on relationship factors, he states,

> the magnitude of the evidence is nothing short of amazing. It might be ventured that there are few things in the field of psychology for which the evidence is so strong. The evidence for the necessity if not the sufficiency of the therapist conditions of accurate empathy, respect, or warmth, and therapeutic genuineness is incontrovertible. (p. 244)

Ultimately, all therapies have the common goals of helping clients reduce their suffering, improve their interpersonal relationships, and take action to live more fulfilling lives. Patterson (1986) believes that all counselors demonstrate a real concern for their clients. "They are interested in their clients, care for them, and want to help them" (p. 548). Smith, Glass, and Miller (1980), after an analysis of 475 studies of counseling outcomes, found that the average client who received therapy was better off at the end of treatment than were 80 to 85% of comparable clients who did not receive treatment regardless of the theoretical orientation of the therapist. All therapies attained comparable results for the treatment of all disorders. As Ungersma (1961) states, "All schools, given favorable conditions, achieve favorable results: the patient or client gets relief and is often enough cured of his difficulties" (p. 36).

More research needs to be conducted to discover whether certain theories and techniques work best with different counselor and client personality types. Meanwhile, some commonalities tend to reduce the confusion among theories, with more emphasis on counselors' effectiveness with clients than on counselors' theoretical orientation.

Differences Among Approaches

Probably the greatest differences among the various approaches are in the counseling process itself. Psychoanalysis focuses on developing insight in relationships through the process of skillful interpretation. Rational–emotive counselors focus on present irrational thinking by convincing clients of their faulty thought processes and teaching them more effective rational thinking. Person-centered counselors stress the building of a safe atmosphere through a nonjudgmental, accepting relationship, so that previously denied feelings will be accepted and experienced. Behavioral counselors emphasize removing undesirable or self-destructive behavior and then learning new behaviors.

Most therapies base their process on talk; the client generally decides what to talk about and does most of the talking. Behaviorists, although they use verbal interaction, base their processes on action or behavior. They are more concerned with what and how clients behave than with what they say.

MAJOR THEORETICAL APPROACHES

> *The prospect of preparing an overview of psychotherapy in America today is enough to make the most stout-hearted quail.*
>
> Frank (1978, p. 1)

The fields of counseling and psychotherapy today are dominated by three major theoretical orientations: psychoanalytic, behavioral, and humanistic-existential. A fourth force, a transpersonal approach, is making its presence felt; despite its lack of historical development, it is attracting a significant following.

Most of the various approaches to counseling emanate from one or more of these perspectives. Each perspective differs significantly in terms of its view of human nature, the process of human development, the nature of psychopathology, the role of the counselor, the techniques used, and, ultimately, the goals of counseling. Table 10.2 illustrates the four major counseling forces and lists the names of counseling approaches and theorists related to each force. Note that no boundaries exist between these forces. Some counseling approaches are difficult to categorize; for example, Jung's approach is clearly related to the psychodynamic force, but it also has much in common with the transpersonal force. A description of each of the four major forces follows.

TABLE 10.2   Four forces in psychotherapy.

Psychodynamic	Cognitive Behavioral	Humanistic	Transpersonal
Psychoanalysis Freud	*Systematic Desensitization* Wolpe	*Person Centered* Rogers	*Psychosynthesis* Assagioli
Analytic Psychotherapy Jung	*Operant Conditioning* Skinner	*Existential* May Yalom	*Zen* Watts
Individual Psychology Adler	*Modeling* Bandura	*Gestalt* Peris	*Yoga* *Sufism*
Will Therapy Rank	*Cognitive Behavioral* Beck Meichenbaum	*Logotherapy* Frankl	*Imagery*
Also: Horney Fromm Erickson Sullivan Reich Janov (Primal) Klein A. Freud Kohut (Self- Psychology)	*Reality Therapy* Glasser *Rational Emotive* Ellis *Transactional Analysis* Berne		*Meditation*

Psychodynamic Force

Psychotherapy started toward the end of the nineteenth century with the approach called **psychoanalysis** developed by Sigmund Freud (1856–1939). The influence of Freud's theoretical formulations and applications permeates many aspects of contemporary culture in addition to the fields of psychology and psychotherapy. Psychoanalysis and the psychodynamic approaches that followed it remain the most comprehensive approaches to provide insights into psychopathology.

Freud was trained as a physician and had an interest in the study of the functioning of the brain. Early work with hypnosis and awareness of a talking cure led him to look for a nonphysical structure of mental functioning. The psychoanalytic position holds a deterministic view of persons. It sees people as being driven by unconscious instincts and sees life in terms of people living out unconscious wishes and conflicts. Freud placed heavy emphasis on people's evil impulses.

Another assumption of the psychodynamic force is that the past is the main determiner of the present and the basis for understanding clients' present functioning. The term *past* refers to one's earliest childhood years, usually the first six or seven years of age. These years are the most crucial in the development of one's basic personality. The belief is that the beginnings of neuroses and other psychological difficulties are to be found in the person's childhood experiences; therefore, psychoanalytic approaches require an in-depth exploration of childhood issues.

Most psychoanalytic approaches emphasize that the forces that motivate behavior are outside of a person's conscious awareness. Freud theorized three structures of the mind; id, ego, and superego. Freud initially placed strong emphasis on the id, the most primitive and unconscious part of the psyche, as the basis for psychic energy (see chapter 11). Contemporary psychoanalytic approaches place a greater emphasis on the ego, or conscious part of the psyche, than earlier Freudian theory.

Freud established his theory on the basis of his study of the emotional disturbances of middle-class women in Vienna in the late nineteenth and early twentieth centuries. There is no strong evidence that Freudian theory is equally applicable to other cultures.

Several theorists have elaborated on Freud's work. Anna Freud, his daughter, elaborated on the concept of defense mechanisms that the ego uses to regulate unconscious drives. Melanie Klein used the concepts of psychoanalysis in working with children. Erik Erikson extended the concept of developmental stages to cover the entire life span and included a description of tasks people needed to complete to go through each life stage successfully. The concepts of psychoanalysis were applied to the study of culture and human social development by Erich Fromm.

Today's analysts are likely to believe that therapists and clients create analysis together. They are as apt to focus on the client's relationships as they are to focus intrapsychically. Today's psychoanalysts continue to delve into their clients' pasts; however, they intertwine the understanding of the past with the present. In addition to changing their theoretical orientations, analysts today are seeing a broader range of clients, from gay men and lesbians, to people of color, to the seriously mentally ill.

In keeping with present trends, many analysts today are infusing psychoanalytic approaches with more modern therapy modes, such as family-systems therapy and group therapy. They are also incorporating contemporary social issues, including class, racial, and cultural differences (DeAngelis, 1996).

Psychoanalytic Versus Psychodynamic

The terms *psychoanalytic* and *psychodynamic* are often used interchangeably; however, **psychodynamic** is a broader term reflecting all the approaches derived from psychoanalysis. Psychodynamic approaches are based on the assumptions that there are underlying, usually unconscious forces that influence current behaviors and that knowledge of clients' past developmental histories is important for clients to discover the unconscious roots of present behavior.

Cognitive–Behavioral Force

Behavior theory is often called the second force in psychology. Behavior theory includes a number of different clinical techniques related to different learning principles. In strong contrast to psychoanalysis, behavior theory is empirically and experimentally based, with principles and constructs derived as a result of research. Rather than work with abstract ideas such as the unconscious, the behaviorists (in the tradition of John Watson and other eminent experimental psychologists) emphasize observable behavior. In focusing on observable behavior, early behaviorists believed that all that can be known about people can be gained by observing their behavior and that human behavior is useful only to the extent that it can be quantified and operationally defined.

Behavior theorists have built on the work of Ivan Pavlov in respondent or classical conditioning, of Albert Bandura in terms of social modeling, and of B. F. Skinner in operant conditioning to develop a broad variety of techniques that can help people change behavior. In addition to clinical uses, behavioral methods have been used extensively in educational settings. Behaviorists emphasize the development of desirable behaviors (and the extinction of undesirable behaviors) and structure conditions in the environment so that the desired behaviors are learned and maintained.

Joseph Wolpe in the 1950s, like Freud, was concerned about the idea of neurotic anxiety; however, Wolpe considered it to be a classically conditioned, or learned, response (Spence, Carson, & Thibaut, 1976). Because anxiety is something that can be learned, a person can unlearn it. Based on this premise, Wolpe developed the technique of **systematic desensitization** to help clients overcome debilitating anxieties.

Changing behavior by reinforcing approximations toward a desired behavior, called **operant conditioning,** was developed and promulgated primarily by B. F. Skinner (1953). Techniques developed around this theoretical construct are often classified in the category of **behavior modification.** Behavior modification techniques are widely used in educational and mental health settings. In such settings the basic approach is to reinforce and strengthen behaviors desired (by the client or the caretakers) and to extinguish or not reinforce behaviors deemed undesirable. The focus is on the specific behavior and the external factors, which could lead to either strengthening or weakening the target behavior. The client's or student's thoughts and feelings were not considered to be of any consequence, because abnormal behavior could be understood and changed without regard to them (Spence et al., 1976). Children learn to manifest appropriate classroom behaviors when desirable reinforcers are appropriately presented. The children do not have to talk about how they think or feel about the situation.

Early behaviorists found it important to dissociate themselves from vague, generally untestable conceptualizations and processes of the **insight therapies**—therapies claiming that behavior would change as a result of clients' understanding of the causes and consequences of their behavior. Generally speaking, therapies associated with the psychodynamic and humanistic forces are considered to be insight therapies. Beginning in the late 1960s, however, some behaviorally oriented therapists began to consider mental processes such as thinking and imagery; they did this to acquire a better understanding of maladaptive behavior as well as to develop more effective approaches for changing behavior. Thoughts came to be viewed as behavior. This cognitively oriented conceptualization has given behavioral therapy a broader base of practitioners, including such approaches as Albert Ellis's (1962, 1989) rational–emotive therapy and Beck's (1976) and Meichenbaum's (1977) cognitive–behavioral approaches.

In most cognitive–behavioral approaches, clients are involved in defining their problems, selecting treatment objectives, and evaluating the counselor and their own success in achieving their objectives. The cognitive–behavioral clinician tends to take an approach that is didactic at times, often more in keeping with the role of a teacher than that of a counselor.

The goals of cognitive–behavioral counseling are to enable clients to function better in regard to their environment and to use more socially desirable behaviors. These goals are accomplished either through the process of changing clients' attitudes toward their environment or by teaching them more appropriate and rational ways of behaving.

Humanistic Force

Humanistic theories are often called the third force in psychology. The roots of humanistic theories are philosophical and based on the works of European existentialists such as Albert Camus (1970), John Paul Sartre (1971), Martin Buber (1958), and Soren Kierkegaard (1967). Humanists believe that problems arise when people's defenses interrupt their natural organismic growth. When this occurs, people are not able to invest their full energies and capabilities to resolve those conflicts.

Humanists such as Abraham Maslow (1954, 1970, 1971) and Carl Rogers (1951, 1980) stressed positive directions in living and the inborn tendency of all human beings to self-actualize, or develop to their full potential. This approach differs greatly from the psychoanalytic and behavioral approaches, which tend to represent mechanistic and predetermined views of the nature of people. Humanists have been influenced by researchers such as Maslow (1954), who studied the development of normal people rather than focusing on the behavior generally considered abnormal or maladaptive. The major humanistic approaches are Gestalt, person-centered (formerly client-centered), and existential.

Humanists believe that people have the ability to organize their experiences into meaningful patterns and create their own meaning of the environment in which they live. Humanists stress people's freedom to make choices and their ultimate responsibility for those choices. The goal of their counseling involves moving the clients toward self-direction, self-awareness, and improved decision making. Clients are helped to trust their own capabilities and to assume responsibility for all aspects of their lives. Humanists are strong believers in the importance of the interpersonal relationship for therapeutic success. In emphasizing the counseling relationship, some humanistic therapists stress the importance of the counselor's personal characteristics, such as openness, warmth, and empathy, and downplay the use of techniques. Other humanists, such as Gestaltists, use techniques as the context requires in order to achieve their goals.

Humanistic psychology is generally phenomenological in nature, emphasizing the actual experience of the client rather than inventing new theoretical constructs and systems. **Phenomenology,** a key concept for the humanists, is the idea that what is reality for people is what they perceive. "External events are significant for individuals only insofar as they experience them as meaningful" (Brammer & Shostrom, 1982, p. 54). To know people, the counselor must be able to understand how clients perceive events in the environment and in themselves. In working with clients, counselors need to be in tune with clients' internal frames of reference in order to understand the nature of the clients' problems. The necessity for such depth of understanding of the clients' points of view is the major reason for the heavy emphasis humanists place on the skill of empathic responding.

A major construct emanating from the phenomenological framework is the self-concept—the person's view of self. Anxiety levels become high when a person is not acting in accord with this self-concept (for example, people who consider themselves to be extremely shy trying to give a speech to a large audience). People whose concept of self is relatively close to their experience and who believe their behavior represents their ideals and values would be considered well-adjusted or psychologically whole. When people's awareness matches their experience, they are considered congruent.

Another major factor in the humanistic approach is the importance of working with feelings. Humanists are aware that emotions can interfere with thought processes and can strongly affect behavior. An existentialist would suggest that, in some cases, there may be no growth or change until clients have experienced the depth of personal despair while in the safe immediacy of the relationship with the counselor. At that point the clients realize that they are not alone and that their worst fears have failed to materialize.

The Transpersonal Force

The newest force in psychology (about four decades old) is the transpersonal approach, sometimes called the fourth force. This force has grown as society's interest in the spiritual dimension of human nature grows. The decade of the 1990s will probably be noted for its inclusion of spirituality into the mainstream of counseling. The Association of Counselor Education and Supervision (ACES) (Holden & Ivey, 1997) is working to infuse aspects of spirituality into the counselor education process, including "understanding of spiritually related phenomena, awareness of one's own spiritual belief system, understanding the client's spiritual worldview, and the appropriate use of spiritually related strategies and techniques in the counseling process" (p. 15).

Some transpersonal psychologists, such as Anthony Sutich, the founder of the Association for Transpersonal Psychology, resisted attempts at defining the transpersonal on the grounds that it was indefinable and should remain that way. Sutich wanted transpersonal psychology to be open-ended and felt that placing a definition on the transpersonal would limit its boundaries and possibly cause it to assume a rigid stance (Hendricks, 1982). Transpersonal means going beyond the personal. It refers to human development beyond the average conventional, personal, or individual levels (Scotton, 1996).

Transpersonal psychology assumes an expansionistic perspective. It incorporates the essential contributions of the first three forces and takes into account such elements as spirituality, intuition, mysticism, and psychic phenomena. Transpersonal psychology utilizes theory and methodology from both the East and the West. It is influenced by the well-established ideas and practices of meditation, yoga, sufism, biofeedback, imagery, Zen Buddhism, and psychosynthesis, and from the works of Alan Watts, Abraham Maslow, William James, Frances Vaughn, and Carl Jung (Jung first used the term *transpersonal* in 1916). Transpersonal counseling "seeks to foster development, correct developmental arrests, and heal traumas [at] all levels of development including transpersonal levels. It extends the standard biopsychosocial model of psychiatry to a biopsychosocial–spiritual one" (Scotton, 1996, p. 4).

Meditation refers to a variety of well-established practices of mental concentration which can have very positive health benefits. **Yoga** seeks to achieve union with the universal soul through deep meditation, prescribed postures, and controlled breathing. **Sufism** seeks to attain self-knowledge by going beyond the limits of reason and reaching conclusions experimentally through experience. **Biofeedback** is used to control emotional states such as anxiety by training oneself through the use of electronic devices. **Zen Buddhism** (Watts, 1957) seeks enlightenment through meditation and intuition. **Psychosynthesis** is a therapeutic process of combining individual elements of the mind to form a whole personality (Assagioli, 1965). **Imagery** is used to modify behavior through the use of mental images.

Transpersonal psychology is grounded in the premise that humans possess an inherent potential to transcend the ordinary limits of the ego and attain higher levels of consciousness (Capuzzi & Gross, 1995). It involves learning to accept and love all parts of oneself just as they are and giving oneself permission to feel whatever feelings one has without interference. It strives to explore new territories that transcend the ego. Advocates of this approach maintain that the scientific study of the ultimate dimensions of human experience provide the most comprehensive means for understanding human nature and for helping people develop their full potential.

Born in the heady days of the 1960s, transpersonal psychology has grown steadily. Graduate degrees are now available in a number of degree-granting institutions. In addition to articles published in the Journal of Transpersonal Psychology, people have been writing a substantial number of articles and dissertations featuring transpersonal topics (Chinen, 1996). Developments in transpersonal psychology are occurring both inside and outside academic institutions. One source, the Institute of Noetic Sciences, founded by the former astronaut Edgar Mitchell, has helped sponsor research in such areas as mental telepathy, extended human capabilities, and the emotional characteristics of people who are in perfect health. Some of this research is being conducted at institutions such as Stanford and Harvard Universities. A more complete description of this approach is in chapter 11.

ECLECTIC APPROACHES

In general, each of these four forces tends to focus on a relatively specific aspect of the human personality (e.g., cognitive–behavioral). Many practitioners, however, develop their own systematic blends of therapy by drawing ideas, concepts, and practices from a variety of sources to form an eclectic approach. Some of these formal eclectic approaches have become popular, such as Arnold Lazarus's Multimodal Approach (1981). Multimodal therapy has a strong body of literature and has a sizable number of adherents.

Using an existing eclectic approach or developing your own systematic approach has the advantage of taking the best features of the various theories and avoiding some of the disadvantages found in the theories. Eclectic approaches, by their very nature, tend to be wholistic. An increasing number of practitioners are using what they call a wholistic approach and advertise themselves as wholistic counselors. In chapter 11 we will explore more fully the structure of the wholistic approach.

DEVELOPING A PERSONAL APPROACH TO THEORY

Since psychotherapy is an art based on a science, becoming an effective counselor is analogous in many ways to becoming an effective singer, artist, or writer. Just like artists, counselor trainees attempt to master the core skills. Their teachers become models for them, and they learn from other established counselors by way of films, audiotapes and videotapes, and typescripts that are part of case studies.

The first attempts at practicing counseling are often characterized by a great deal of self-consciousness. Counseling students try to copy their models and often become good at it. We have often heard references, for example, of a singer who sounds just like Frank Sinatra. Eventually, as students become more knowledgeable about theory and techniques, examine their own beliefs, and become more knowledgeable about themselves, they maintain much of the style of their models with their own individual style emerging. Finally, they give up being like their models (although some influential behaviors still remain) and become entirely themselves. The singer in our example begins to develop a personal phrasing, vocal range, and choice of songs, perhaps still showing some of Sinatra's influence but performing with his own personal style. He then spends his career continually refining and perhaps even changing this style. Ivey (1980) states the following:

> Thus the task of each potential counselor and therapist is to enter the field as a lifetime silent, fully aware that a final answer to the questions which engage counseling and therapy may ultimately be unanswerable. Yet, paradoxically, the very asking of questions and the systematic study leading to answers inevitably does two things: (1) it suggests what can be done, and (2) it simultaneously opens newer and more complex questions needing further study and examination. (p. 436)

Adopting an existing theory or developing one's personal theory involves a great amount of study and effort, an inquiring, creative mind, and ongoing practical experience.

Passons (1975) suggests three key ingredients to the process of developing a personal theory of counseling: the counselor as a person, the existent theories, and the synthesizing processes counselors use in formulating a personal theory. To these three ingredients add the important dimension of the research results regarding theory effectiveness, theoretical constructs, and techniques. All beginning counselors have already lived with themselves for many years and have formulated a system of values, beliefs, needs, and feelings. They need to examine these components with a high level of awareness. These elements then become the basis for adopting an existing theoretical approach or developing a personal theoretical stance. As counselors develop greater self-awareness and knowledge of research support for various approaches, they will be better able to determine the appropriateness of particular theory for themselves. Chapter 11 describes some of the more influential approaches to counseling in order to give you an opportunity to begin your own understanding of how you might approach clients and to assist you further in the development of your own personal approach. Throughout this chapter we have emphasized that there are no complete theories; therefore, we will subsequently use the term *counseling approaches* rather than *counseling theories*.

SUMMARY

The basic components necessary for a theory of counseling include a framework on which to base counseling interventions; a continual process of theory construction, testing, modification, and further testing; and a method of dealing with meaningful matters that have relevance to life. The purposes of theory bring organization out of chaos and enhance one's understanding of human behavior.

The pros and cons of counseling theory are presented, and four basic theoretical stances are described: the pragmatic, eclectic, personality, and syncretic approaches. Commonalities among the approaches are discussed. A format for classifying counseling theories is presented based on the four major forces in psychology—psychodynamic, behavioral, humanistic, and transpersonal—along with an overview of each force.

QUESTIONS AND ACTIVITIES

1. Do people really change? If so, how? Is change based primarily on insight? manipulation? accident? What conditions help facilitate change? Is theory needed to bring about change? If so, why?

2. Should counselors adopt an existing theory, develop their own theories, or counsel without regard to theory? Examine all sides of the issue. Share your conclusions with other students.

3. How do you think a counselor can best help another person? What should be the counselor's main goal in helping someone? Which theoretical approach most closely matches your point of view?

4. Based on your present knowledge, which of these four forces intrigues you the most? Which force do you believe offers the greatest hope for helping people? Share your conclusion with your classmates.

RECOMMENDED READINGS

Frank, J. (1992). *Persuasion and healing* (2nd ed.). Baltimore: Johns Hopkins University Press.

INTERNET RESOURCES

Websites

Psychoanalytical links and resources <userpage.fu-berlin.de/albrecht/psa.html>

National Association for Cognitive Behavior Therapy

Association for Humanistic Psychology

Association for Transpersonal Psychotherapy <www.igc.org/htp/>

SEPI (Society for the Exploration of Psychotherapy Integration) <www.cyberpsych.org/sepi.htm>

Behavior On-Line: The Mental Health and Behavioral Science Meeting Place

REFERENCES

Assagioli, R. (1965). *Psychosynthesis.* New York: The Viking Press.

Beck, A. T. (1976). *Cognitive therapy and emotional disorders.* New York: International Universities Press.

Bergantino, L. (1978). A theory of imperfection. *Counselor Education and Supervision, 17*(4), 286–291.

Blocher, L. (1987). On the uses and misuses of the term theory. *Journal of Counseling and Development, 66*(2), 67–68.

Brabeck, M., & Walfel, E. (1985). Counseling theory: Understanding the trend toward eclecticism from a developmental perspective. *Journal of Counseling and Development, 63*(6), 343–348.

Brammer, L., & Shostrom, E. (1982). *Therapeutic psychology: Fundamentals of counseling and psychotherapy* (4th ed.). Englewood Cliffs, NJ: Prentice Hall.

Buber, M. (1958). *I and thou* (2nd ed.). New York: Scribner's.

Camus, A. (1970). *Lyrical and critical essays* (E. Kennedy, Trans.). New York: Vintage.

Capuzzi, D., & Gross, D. (1995). *Counseling psychotherapy: Theories and interventions.* Englewood Cliffs, NJ: Merrill.

Chinen, A. (1996). The emergence of transpersonal psychology. In B. Scotton, A. Chinen, J. Battista (Eds.), *Textbook of transpersonal psychiatrist and psychology* (pp. 9–17). New York: Basic Books.

Corsini, R. J., & Wedding, D. (1995). *Current psychotherapies.* Itasca, IL: F. E. Peacock Publishers.

DeAngelis, T. (1996, September). Psychoanalysis adapts to the 1990s [On-line], *APA Monitor Online.* Available: www.apa.org.monitor/sep96/modern.html

Ellis, A. (1962). *Reason and emotion in psychotherapy.* New York: Lyle Stuart.

Ellis, A. (1989). Rational–emotive therapy. In R. Corsini (Ed.), *Current psychotherapies* (4th ed., pp. 197–238). Itasca, IL: Peacock.

Fiedler, F. (1950). A comparison of therapeutic relationships in psychoanalytic, non-directive, and Adlerian therapeutic relationships. *Journal of Counseling Psychology, 14,* 436–445.

Frank, J. (1978). *Psychotherapy and the human predicament.* New York: Schocken Books.

Goldfried, M. (1982). Toward the delineation of therapeutic change principles. In M. Goldfried (Ed.), *Converging themes in psychotherapy* (pp. 377–393). New York: Springer.

Hansen, J., Stevic, E., & Warner, R. (1986). *Counseling theory and practice* (4th ed.). Boston: Allyn & Bacon.

Hendricks, G. (1982). An overview. In G. Hendricks & B. Weinhold (Eds.), *Transpersonal approaches to counseling and psychotherapy* (pp. 3–22). Denver: Love.

Herink, R. (Ed.). (1980). *The psychotherapy handbook.* New York: New American Library.

Holden, J., & Ivey, A. (1997, Spring). Summit on spirituality: Phase II. *ACES Spectrum Newsletter, 57*(3), 15.

Ivey, A. (with Simek-Downing, L.). (1980). *Counseling and psychotherapy: Skills, theories, and practice.* Englewood Cliffs, NJ: Prentice-Hall.

Kierkegaard, S. (1967). *Soren Kierkegaard's journals and papers.* H. Hong & E. Hong (Eds. and Trans.). Bloomington: Indiana University Press.

Lazarus, A. (1981). *The practice of multimodal therapy.* New York: McGraw-Hill.

Lieberman, M., Yalom, I., & Miles, M. (1973). *Encounter groups: First facts.* New York: Basic Books.

Maslow, A. (1954). *Motivation and personality.* New York: Harper & Row.

Maslow, A. (1970). *Motivation and personality* (Rev. ed.). New York: Harper & Row.

Maslow, A. (1971). *The farther reaches of human nature.* New York: Viking Press.

Meichenbaum, D. (1977). *Cognitive behavior modification.* New York: Plenum.

Passons, W. (1975). *Gestalt approaches in counseling.* New York: Holt, Rinehart & Winston.

Patterson, C. H. (1985). *The therapeutic relationship: Foundations for an eclectic psychotherapy.* Monterey, CA: Brooks/Cole.

Patterson, C. H. (1986). Theories of counseling and psychotherapy (4th ed.). New York: Harper & Row.

Robinson, F. (1965). Counseling orientations and labels. *Journal of Counseling Psychology, 12,* 338.

Rogers, C. (1951). *Client-centered therapy.* Boston: Houghton Mifflin.

Rogers, C. (1980). *A way of being.* Boston: Houghton Mifflin.

Sartre, J. P. (1971). *The age of reason.* New York: Knopf.

Scotton, B. (1996). Introduction and definition of transpersonal psychiatry. In B. Scotton, A. Chinen, & J. Battista (Eds.), *Textbook of transpersonal psy-*

chiatry and psychology (pp. 3–8). New York: Basic Books.

Scotton, B., Chinen, A., & Battista, J. (Eds.). (1996). *Textbook of transpersonal psychiatry and psychology.* New York: Basic Books.

Skinner, B. F. (1953). *Science and human behavior.* New York: Macmillan.

Smith, M. L., & Glass, G. V. (1977). Meta-analysis of psychotherapy outcome studies. *American Psychologist, 32*(9), 752–760.

Smith, M. L., Glass, G. V., & Miller, T. I. (1980). *The benefits of psychotherapy.* Baltimore: Johns Hopkins University Press.

Spence, J., Carson, R., & Thibaut, J. (Eds.). (1976). *Behavioral approaches to therapy.* Morristown, NJ: General Learning Press.

Steffre, B., & Grant, W. H. (1973). *Theories of counseling.* New York: McGraw-Hill.

Truax, C., & Carkhuff, R. (1967). *Toward effective counseling and psychotherapy.* Chicago: Aldine.

Ungersma, A. J. (1961). *The search for meaning.* Philadelphia: Westminster.

Washburn, M. (1988). *The ego and the dynamic ground: A transpersonal theory of human development.* Albany, NY: SUNY Press.

Watts, A. (1957). *The way of Zen.* New York: Vintage.

Whitaker, C. (1976). The hindrance of theory in clinical work. In P. J. Guerim, Jr. (Ed.), *Family therapy theory and practice* (pp. 154–164). New York: Gardner Press.

Yalom, I. (1995). *The theory and practice of group psychotherapy* (4th ed.). New York: Basic Books.

chapter **11**

focus on

SELECTED THEORETICAL APPROACHES TO COUNSELING AND PSYCHOTHERAPY

- What aspects of each theory appeal the most to you? The least?
- If a counselor's theoretical approach makes no significant difference, why spend any time studying different counseling approaches?
- How much emphasis should you place on the techniques each approach espouses?
- What do these theoretical approaches have in common?
- What seems to account for the dramatic differences between approaches?

As noted in the previous chapter, there are hundreds of formal approaches to counseling and psychotherapy and many more combinations of approaches. Because success in counseling is dependent not on the type of counseling approach used but on other factors, the question can be raised as to why time and energy should be spent pursuing particular theoretical approaches. Actually, the nature of these approaches and, in many cases, their significant differences provide much of the attractiveness, drama, and controversy found in the field. In the 1960s, one way to fill a large hall at a counseling convention was to schedule a debate between a behavioral therapist and a client-centered (Rogerian) therapist. More recently, there have been heated exchanges between proponents of rational–emotive behavior therapy and advocates of the transpersonal approach (Ellis, 1986a, 1989; Walsh, 1989b; Wilber, 1989). According to Cottone (1992), theory proponents often take strong stands and may argue that therapists trained in other approaches are poorly trained to work with certain clients or to do therapy at all.

The fact that, to date, no one approach to counseling has been universally recognized as inherently superior supports the necessity to learn different approaches. Future counselors need to explore a variety of counseling approaches in order to find an approach that will fit them and their particular style. Present and future counselors may also dream that perhaps one day they might develop the counseling theory that will meet all of the necessary qualifications for a comprehensive theory and be superior to all other approaches. Also, through the study of different approaches, the student can become more involved with some major figures in the field, including Alfred Adler, Carl Rogers, B. F. Skinner, Fritz Perls, Eric Berne, and Albert Ellis. Exploring the work of these pioneers helps provide a more human dimension to the field.

A student can pursue further study at training centers focusing on becoming an expert in a given counseling approach (for example, at a Gestalt Training Center or an Adlerian Institute). In many cases, special certification may be attained on the completion of the course of study. Being proficient in a specific theoretical orientation can be helpful in establishing one's reputation as a counselor and can be quite important for someone who plans to go into private practice. Many knowledgeable clients search out a particular type of therapist (such as Gestalt, person-centered, or behavioral) depending on the type of approach that they believe would be correct for them.

This chapter describes eight counseling approaches. These examples illustrate the diversity of counseling approaches available to prospective counselors. Representing the psychodynamic force are psychoanalysis and Adlerian counseling. The humanistic--existential force is represented by two quite distinct approaches: person-centered and Gestalt. The behavioral–cognitive force is represented by cognitive–behavioral therapy, rational–emotive behavior therapy (REBT), and transactional analysis. Brief therapies, which are most closely related to the behavioral–cognitive force, are also included. Transpersonal counseling represents the force that includes the spiritual dimension, and wholistic counseling is an eclectic approach encompassing the other forces and the environment as well. Since most university counselor education programs have one or more courses devoted specifically to the in-depth study of different theoretical approaches, we present only a general description of each approach. The applicability of each approach to culturally diverse clients is included in the strengths and weaknesses of each approach. Table 11.1 indicates how the approaches described in this chapter are similar or different based on a number of criteria. All approaches described here can be applied to individual, group, and family counseling. Additional approaches to family counseling are described in chapter 13.

PSYCHOANALYSIS

Background

Sigmund Freud (1856–1939) discovered and developed the talking cure as a result of his work with Joseph Breuer, a prominent Viennese physician. Together, they wrote *Studies on Hysteria* (1895) detailing their use of the **cathartic method,** the uncensored, undirected emotional outpouring of clients. Every approach to psychotherapy has been influenced by Freud or has been a direct reaction to Freud. Psychoanalysis and its psychodynamically derived approaches still are the most comprehensive approaches to psychotherapy. Freud spent over 40 years developing his theory of personality, and his writings encompass philosophy, religion, history, and mythology. Freud believed that humans are driven by aggressive sexual instincts, and that human behavior is determined by irrational, unconscious forces. Freud focused great emphasis on early psychosexual development. He believed that later personality problems were rooted in repressed childhood conflicts dating back to early stages of development.

One major construct of Freud's approach is that personality is a system composed of three major components: the id, the ego, and the superego. The **id** is a pleasure principle that urges a person toward drive gratification and is destructive if left unchecked. Freud saw the **ego** as the reality principle that learned practical strategies, often called defense mechanisms, to reduce tensions created by the id in order to take account of reality. The **superego** is defined as the conscience, the moral and ethical part of the person that strives to inhibit id drives. Freud viewed anxiety as the conflict created between id impulses, superego demands, and ego defenses. When the ego is unable to maintain the energy needed for its defenses against unacceptable instinctual impulses and is unable to deal adequately with the demands of the superego as well as of reality, pathology develops. If either the id or the superego becomes dominant over the other personality components, the resultant mental and behavioral aberrations are referred to as neuroses. Psychosis occurs when the ego loses all control.

Goals

The process of psychoanalysis is based on strengthening the ego and checking the id. Freud believed that logical thought and rationality should guide behavior. The goal of psychoanalysis is to totally reconstruct the personality and make the unconscious conscious. Psychoanalytic treatment acts as a second education that corrects the education of the child. The process of treatment, often called **working through,** is compared to the peeling of an onion. Layer after layer is peeled away until the client reaches the core of the problems; this core is based on some disturbance of the psychosexual stages of development. The peeling of the onion consists of dealing with the defenses people use to prevent change and growth, of analyzing fragments of the ego resistant to cure, and of discovering what is hidden in the id and why.

Techniques

The primary approach to treatment that Freud used is called transference (see chapter 5). Therapists act as a blank screen by maintaining neutrality and refraining from educating, or interjecting, their own associations. On this blank screen patients project repressed feelings related to important people in their lives; for example, patients might project their feelings of hate for their fathers onto the therapist. Working through these feelings becomes a part of the reeducative process. Freud sat in a chair outside of the patient's direct line of vision to better allow for this transference phenomenon to occur and to minimize other interaction with the patient. When the client is deemed ready, the analyst interprets the protective defense mechanisms or repressed thoughts as necessary to draw attention to the unconscious resistance impeding the analytic work.

Other methods used to uncover repressed material include the telling of dreams; the use of **free association** (the patient talks about anything that comes to mind during a session, including dreams, fantasies, urges, and concerns); and the analysis of patient forgetfulness or misstatements (Freudian slips). Freud also was interested in the symbolic nature of human communication and the meaning of symbols with regard to symptoms of abnormal behavior. When the client's fears and anxieties are brought to the surface, analyzed, and understood, the client no longer needs to use them as a signal of danger or threat.

The major cause for neurotic behavior, according to Freud, is inhibited sexual development. Freud believed that sexual development begins in infancy and proceeds through several stages until maturity; Unresolved and repressed emotions related to the person's sexual development manifest themselves in neurotic behavior and have to be treated.

Time Orientation

Psychoanalysis involves lengthy treatment often lasting for years and at great expense.

The focus of psychoanalysis is on the effects of early childhood development. The therapist makes interpretations that are aimed at teaching the client the meaning of present behavior as related to past childhood experiences.

Strengths

The influence of Freud's theoretical formulations and applications permeates many aspects of contemporary culture in addition to the fields of psychology and psychotherapy. Psychoanalysis and the psychodynamic approaches that followed are the most comprehensive approaches to provide insight into psychopathology. Psychoanalysis has had a profound influence on almost all other approaches used today, which are either extensions and adaptations of psychoanalysis or reactions against psychoanalysis.

Weaknesses

The psychoanalytic position holds a deterministic view of people, viewing them as driven by unconscious instincts and living out unconscious wishes and conflicts. Freud placed heavy emphasis on people's evil impulses. He established his theory on the basis of his study of the emotional disturbances of middle-class women in Vienna in the late nineteenth and early twentieth centuries. There is no strong evidence that Freudian theory is equally applicable to other cultures. The approach involves lengthy training for therapists. The course of treatment is long and costly for clients. Most of its concepts cannot be verified by research methods. It is based on the medical model which focuses on the mentally ill rather than healthy people. It ignores environmental and interpersonal factors.

ADLERIAN COUNSELING

Background

Alfred Adler (1870–1937) earned his medical degree from the University of Vienna. After beginning his practice in ophthalmology, he later specialized in neurology and psychiatry. He became a colleague of Freud and along with Freud cofounded and coedited the *Journal of Psychoanalysis;* however, Adler challenged some of Freud's basic concepts, resulting in permanent schism. In 1911 Adler resigned as president of the Vienna Psychoanalytic Society and a year later founded the Society for Individual Psychology.

Although Adler was well-grounded in the psychoanalytic–psychodynamic approach, his ideas and methodology today would place his approach in the cognitive–behavioral

TABLE 11.1   Comparison of counseling approaches.

Characteristics	Psychoanalytic	Adlerian	Person-Centered	Gestalt Therapy
1. Nature of People	Human behaviors are determined by psychic energy, irritational and unconscious forces, and repressed experiences. People are driven by aggressive and sexual instincts. Personality is determined by early development.	People have the capability of self-determination. Social interest is seen as a primary source of motivation. Behavior has a purpose and is goal-directed.	The individual is rational, good, trustworthy, moves in self-actualizing directions or toward growth, health, self-realization, independence, and autonomy.	Human beings are not independent from their environment but work as a whole. Individual is not a sum of parts but a coordination.
2. Major Personality Constructs	Healthy personality development is based on successful resolution of psychosexual stages of development. Psychopathology results in inadequate resolution of oral, anal, or phallic stages. Id, ego, and superego are structures of personality.	Creative self: the center from which life movement generates; lifestyle; birth order; family constellation; individual viewed wholistically; striving for significance (superiority) core motivational factor; childhood memories.	Self-concept a regulator of behavior, and perceptual field is reality for the individual, behavior a function of perceptions and organized with respect to self-concept.	Individual is considered a system in balance. He or she lives in a public (doing) level and a private (thinking) level. Imbalance is experienced as a corrective need. Awareness permits self-regulation and self-control.
3. Nature of Anxiety	Repression of basic conflicts between id and superego. Ego defenses employed to control anxiety.	Feelings of inferiority, which can lead to inferiority complex; feeling discouraged; faulty motivation. Keeps client from taking action and moving into future.	Incongruence between self-concept and experience, conditions of worth violated, and need for self-regard frustrated.	The gap between the now and the then; unfinished business.
4. Counseling Goals	Focus on client resistance, working through client's transference feelings toward counselor. Interpretation used to provide insight to client of the connection of present behavior to past experience.	Increasing client's social interest; reduce feelings of discouragement and inferiority; change faulty motivation and lifestyle.	Self-direction and full functioning of client who is congruent, mature, and open to experience.	To mature, to grow up, to take responsibility for one's life, to be in touch with one's self and with the world.

Transactional Analysis	Cognitive–Behavioral (REBT)	Transpersonal	Wholistic
Nature determined by childhood experiences but can change.	Human being subject to powerful biological and social forces, has potential for being rational. Can rid self of emotional difficulty by maximizing rational thinking.	All human beings have the same needs, feelings, and potentials, including being intuitive, psychic, and spiritual.	Seen as spiritual as well as physical, emotional, and mental. Having the potential for harmonious and total (wholistic) development.
Conceptualized as three ego states—parent, adult, child.	Psychological states largely the results of thinking illogically; thinking and reasoning are not two disparate processes; human beings are rewarded or punished by their own thinking or self-talk.	Acceptance and use of altered states of consciousness, mystical insights, paranormal powers, and the human quest for contact and unity with the divine.	The focus is on multiple systems, both internal and external to the individual.
Results from conflicts, concerts, or contaminations between ego states.	Overgeneralizing that an event will be catastrophic.	Not recognizing that we are all one; not finding that within us which gives us freedom, wholeness, and connectedness with all.	Difficulty in personal functioning as a result of conflict within internal and/or external system.
Cure presenting problem, enabling people to experience freedom of choice.	Elimination of anxiety and fears; the attainment of rational behavior, happiness, self-actualization.	To develop sense of personal unity with self and others; to live as totally free of distortion as possible.	A client who can identify and apply learned strategies as personal interventions when needed.

Continued

TABLE 11.1 *Continued*

Characteristics	Psychoanalytic	Adlerian	Person-Centered	Gestalt Therapy
5. Major Techniques	Free association, interpretation, analysis of resistance, dream analysis, analysis of transference.	Establish therapeutic alliance; use of encouragement; conduct lifestyle analysis; use of interpretation and confrontation to promote insight; helping client put insight into action.	Technique a way of communicating acceptance, respect, understanding; limited use of questioning, reassurance, encouragement, suggestion.	Confrontative: provide situations in which client experiences frustrations; focus attention on body posture, gestures, enactment of dreams.
6. Use of Tests and Appraisal Devices	Limited use.	Limited use.	Extremely limited use; tends to be seen as inimical.	Limited use.
7. History Taking	Formalized history taking is not encouraged.	In-depth lifestyle analysis conducted.	Inimical to counseling process.	Limited use.
8. Diagnosis and Prognosis	Hypotheses made based on psychoanalytic assumptions.	Limited use.	Inimical to counseling process.	Limited use.
9. Clientele	Clients must commit to spending considerable time and money and be able to perform honest self-scrutiny. Not recommended for minor problems.	No limitations noted.	Currently no restriction placed on clientele.	No limitations stated.
10. Activity of Counselor	Anonymity of therapist stressed in classical analysis; in other psychodynamic approaches therapist relates objectively with warm detachment.	Counselor active throughout relationship.	Counselor active in providing facilitative conditions.	Highly active.

Adapted by permission of Bruce Shertzer and Shelley C. Stone (1980). *Fundamentals of Counseling,* 3rd ed. (Boston: Houghton Mifflin Co.) pp. 236–237. Additional sources: Hendricks, G., & Weinhold, B. (1992). *Counseling and Psychotherapy: A Transpersonal Approach,* 2nd ed. Denver: Love. Texidor, M., Hawk, R., Thomas, F., Friedman, B., & Weiner, R. (1987).

Transactional Analysis	Cognitive–Behavioral (REBT)	Transpersonal	Wholistic
Diagnosis and analysis of transactions, games, and lifescripts.	Use of relationship techniques to establish rapport followed by teaching, suggestion, persuasion, confrontation, prescription of activities designed to rid the client of irrational ideas.	No special techniques; may use techniques from any source; likely to use imagery, intuition, meditation, dream work, and relaxation training.	Uses multiple approaches rather than singular strategies; techniques from any source may be used.
Limited use.	Limited use.	Little formal use of such tools; some personality inventories may be used.	Minimal use.
Limited use.	Relatively little use of historical clarification.	Taken as needed; generally little emphasis in this dimension.	Note is made of the nature of the internal and external systems of the individual and their interactions.
Diagnosis of ego states to determine executive power, adaptability, mentality, etc.	Used to uncover illogical ideas.	Diagnosis made in collaboration with client; the greater involvement on the part of the client, the better the prognosis.	Client invited to be participant in assessment, planning, intervention, and evaluation process.
No restriction noted.	No limitation but notes that psychotics rarely are completely cured.	No limitations; transpersonal concepts may work better with higher functioning clients.	No limitations.
Counselor very active.	Counselor warm, friendly, and highly active.	Therapy seen as partnership with counselor initiating activity at times and at other times facilitating the client's own work.	Counselor activity level varies from minimal to very active depending on the nature of the client's problem.

Statement of the Holistic Counseling Special Interest Network of the American Mental Health Counselors Assn. Washington, DC: MCD. Prochaska, J., Norcross, J. (1994). *Systems of Psychotherapy.* 3rd ed. Pacific Grove, CA: Brooks/Cole.

camp (Corey, 1991). Adler's approach is much less deterministic than Freud's, putting greater emphasis on the subjective, conscious world of the client rather than focusing on unconscious instinct. Adler called his approach **individual psychology;** it is also a social psychology in that humans are seen as being motivated primarily by social interest, or *Gemeinschaftsgefühl* (Gilliland, James, & Bowman, 1994). This approach is also significantly concerned with the effects of society and the environment on the individual. It was, very early on, a wholistic approach. In the 1920s Adler pioneered working with children when he opened child guidance clinics in Austria. He immigrated to America in the 1930s where he lectured and practiced until he died in 1937. His work was continued first by Rudolph Dreikurs, who pursued the development of child guidance clinics in the United States, and then by Don Dinkmeyer. Use of this approach began to increase in the 1980s and 1990s.

Goals

The primary goal of Adlerian counseling is to develop clients' social interest so that they will be able to live as equals in society, both giving to and receiving from others (Mosak, 1995). This may mean reeducating clients to modify their lifestyles.

Adler contributed a great number of ideas and terms to the field of counseling, many of which have become part of everyday conversation, such as empathy, lifestyle, inferiority complex, dependency, and social interest. He had a positive view of mankind, believing that people create themselves with their choices of lifestyle, as opposed to the biological and instinctual determination posited by Freud.

The term **lifestyle** refers to a person's basic orientation to life—the set of recurrent themes that will persist throughout one's existence, a pattern that is basically well established by the time the child is five years old (Dinkmeyer & Dinkmeyer, 1985). **Family constellation** refers to the overall structure of the client's family with particular emphasis on the birth order of the children. Adler's conceptualization of the differences in personality resulting from the order one is born into a family is one of his most well-known contributions. **Social interest** (*Gemeinschaftsgefühl*) refers to the "individual's awareness of the human community and to the individual's attitudes in dealing with the social world" (Corey, 1991, p. 140). Adler saw social interaction and involvement as the key human motivational force.

Techniques

The Adlerian counselor serves as a collaborator, working to establish an egalitarian relationship with the client. The counselor uses attending and listening skills to develop the mutual trust and respect deemed essential to Adlerian counseling. In addition, the counselor helps clients define their goals and determine what has prevented achievement of the goals. An Adlerian counselor may help the client to establish a contract to attain the desired goals systematically. Overall, the counselor establishes and maintains a flexible interaction process that emphasizes client responsibility (Dinkmeyer, Dinkmeyer, & Sperry, 1987).

There are four phases to Adlerian counseling. First of all, a collaborative, counselor–client relationship is established. Second, the client's lifestyle is assessed. Third, interpretations of the lifestyle are provided to promote insight. Fourth, insight is translated into action. During the first phase, the counselor establishes the therapeutic alliance using the techniques described in chapter 6 to determine the client's phenomenological point of view. During the second phase, the counselor interviews the client to determine the client's lifestyle and family constellation through the use of direct questions. Reports of the client's early memories (before the age of 7 or 8) and current dreams are gathered as part of the assessment process. The lifestyle analysis helps to identify faulty or irrational views that may be impeding the client's growth (Mosak, 1995). In phase 3, the counselor poses interpretations of what has emerged from the lifestyle analysis in the form of hunches, guesses, or hypotheses to help clients attain insights into their attitudes and behavior. Confrontation and immediacy may be used in this phase as appropriate. In the final phase, the focus is on helping the client translate insight into action to bring about desired changes.

Other than obtaining specific life history data such as the person's family constellation, birth order, and early recollections, no systematic set of techniques is used. Adlerians use basic attending skills and empathic responding, interpretation, confronting, and immediacy.

Encouragement.   Encouragement is a major method of response, one that has been found to be more effective than other social reinforcers such as praise (Gordon, 1974; Dinkmeyer & Losoncy, 1980). In the Adlerian view, clients are not sick; they are discouraged. Encouragement generally focuses on strengths that the client has but may not acknowledge or appreciate.

Asking the Question.   At some point, generally in the second phase of the counseling process, it often is productive to ask the question, "How would things be different if you didn't have this problem?" The client's response to this question can provide a great deal of valuable data, including whether the problem is physical or psychological in nature.

Spitting in the Client's Soup.   Adlerians believe that there is a payoff or reward for behaviors that are maintained; therefore, when a counselor points out the particular payoff for a negative behavior, the enjoyment may be diminished. For example, an honor roll student may tell his counselor more than once that he wants to drop out of college. The counselor might then reply, "You could do that if you wanted to. I get the feeling that you seem to enjoy having people coax you to do what you already know is the right thing for you to do." This type of response keeps the responsibility with the client.

Time Orientation

Although a historical assessment is made, the focus is on dealing with the present perceptions of the past and working to change things for the future. Adlerians take a teleological stance, viewing the individual as being pulled toward the future rather than being pushed by the past (Gilliland, James, & Bowman, 1994).

Strengths

Adler has contributed significantly to the field of counseling and human development. Many of his ideas are part of subsequent theoretical approaches and his work has transferred successfully into child and parent education. The approach is egalitarian, collaborative, and positive, putting great emphasis on encouragement and client self-responsibility.

Adlerian counseling is a developmental approach beginning with the child in the family and helping the individual work with tasks throughout the life span. It is also an approach for society designed to help individuals successfully pursue the social interest, which in the long run will be of benefit to all. Its concern for dealing with feelings of inferiority and its overall egalitarian approach make it attractive to many minority groups, including people with physical disabilities.

Weaknesses

The Adlerian approach is based mainly on a common sense, perhaps even simplistic, view of human behavior, as opposed to having a research-based foundation. Little research has been conducted to support the efficacy of the approach or of its primary theoretical constructs. Although Adlerians clearly value the family, members of some ethnic groups may not be open to the in-depth disclosure of family matters that might result from a lifestyle analysis. Clients who are looking for a brief, action-oriented approach may not be attracted to this approach.

PERSON-CENTERED COUNSELING

Background

Although there have been other early nonmedical counseling approaches such as the trait–factor approach, person-centered counseling is probably the pioneering approach that helped establish today's field of counseling. Carl Rogers (1902–1988), the founder of person-centered counseling, insisted that his work was original and not a reaction to Freud or borrowed or adapted from other precursors. The primary influences in the development of his approach were Rogers's own experiences as a therapist and his belief that people are good and ultimately have the power to solve their own problems. The theoretical rationale for change in person-centered counseling is that individuals have the capacity to understand the circumstances that cause unhappiness and can reorganize their lives accordingly. A person's ability to deal with these circumstances is enhanced if the therapist establishes a warm, accepting, and understanding relationship. Adherents of this approach believe that the quality of the interpersonal encounter is the most significant element in determining the outcome of any counseling relationship. In person-centered counseling, the emphasis is on experiencing events in the present. Searching for and trying to understand underlying causes for problems are of minor importance. The person-centered approach is noteworthy because of its evolution. It is a theoretical approach that, like the clients it has served, has grown and developed since its origin. Formulated in the 1940s, this approach was referred to as nondirective counseling, with sessions conducted accordingly. The approach evolved in the 1950s to become client-centered counseling and then changed in the 1970s to person-centered counseling. The changes in title are not cosmetic; they have come about as a direct result of changes in perspective and approach. The person-centered approach has also changed from almost exclusively focusing on a one-to-one relationship to now strongly emphasizing change within a group setting. Despite the changes in the theoretical approach, some practitioners and some critics have not kept up-to-date with these changes.

References to nondirective counseling as a contemporary approach are occasionally
in current counseling literature.

Goals

Person-centered counseling has no predetermined, explicit goals for the client. As a result
of interaction with the counselor, clients develop their own individualized goals. An ultimate, implicit goal is the client's encounter with self. Some outcomes of person-centered
counseling include greater self-acceptance, the dropping of masks (facades, roles), and positive behavior change.

Techniques

Person-centered counselors do not use formal techniques. In fact, Rogers carefully avoided
using special techniques. The development of the core conditions of empathy, genuineness,
and respect as described in chapter 6 is the only technique advocated by this approach. (See
Appendix A for an excerpt of a person-centered counseling session.

Time Orientation

The person-centered approach can be considered a moderate-term therapy, generally lasting from several months to a year or more. The approach deals almost exclusively in the
present. Even though a client's history may emerge during the counseling process, it is generally not pursued by the counselor. The counselor's response to a client's description of a
past incident would likely be in terms of the client's present emotions: "You are still very
upset and angry about what your mother said to you years ago."

Strengths

Person-centered counseling involves a positive philosophy of the person. This approach
enables the client to take responsibility for personal change, engage in behavior that actual-
izes and enhances the self, and become more accepting and trusting of the self. Substantial
research evidence supports the effectiveness of this approach. Person-centered counseling
has developed as a result of research on the process and outcomes of therapy. The principles
of person-centered counseling can be applied to all types of settings, including teaching,
organizational behavior, parenting, and human relations development. The approach
clearly focuses on the client as a person rather than on the client's problem. It is not technique centered, problem centered, or counselor centered. The attitudes and the identity of
the counselor become the primary influences that prompt the client to move toward a more
satisfying and sustaining behavior. Person-centered counseling can be individualized to the
particular needs of a client. This is a major strength of this approach. Each individual is
treated as a special case from the outset (Boy & Pine, 1982, pp. 46–56).

Weaknesses

Developing the core conditions and learning to keep the focus on the client are not easy to
master, with the result that problem-centered, counselor-centered, or technique-centered

approaches may appear more attractive to practitioners. The approach is seen as not being complete. Even though it does deal with emotional and intellectual content, it does not include the physical domains or environmental factors. Also, for many, the relationship may not be enough. Problem-solving approaches, borrowed from other systems, may be required to supplement this approach. Although a significant amount of research has been conducted on the development of this system, there has been criticism about the nature and quality of the research.

GESTALT THERAPY

Background

Frederick (Fritz) Perls (1893–1970), the founder of Gestalt therapy, was trained in psycho-analysis. However, after being rebuffed when attempting to meet with Freud, Perls began to develop his own approach to psychotherapy. He drew from a number of other sources, including Gestalt psychology, Jacob Moreno's psychodrama, and existentialism. From Gestalt psychology Perls used the concept of figure and ground perceptual organization. The process of therapy involves helping individuals make contact with their environment and themselves so that they have less rigid or incomplete figure–ground relationships. Like person-centered counseling, Gestalt therapy is concerned with insight and awareness. As a result of insights there will be a restructuring of the client's perceptual field. A major source of anxiety is the client's store of unfinished business. Gestalt therapy uses a principle known as the **Zeigarnik effect,** a person's tendency to seek closure, as an important dynamic in bringing about the restructuring of the client's awareness. A significant part of Gestalt therapy is its focus on the present. Like person-centered counseling, it is believed that little can be gained by recounting the past. The client's present awareness is of most importance and most likely to lead to change. One approach a Gestalt therapist might use to help the client stay in the present would be to have the client relate a past event in the present tense, telling and acting out the story as if it were happening right now. From his Freudian background, Perls adapted concepts such as **introjection,** which is taking on aspects of other people, particularly parents. This led to the Gestalt concepts of topdog and underdog, which might be considered similar to the superego and id. The **topdog** part of a personality has introjected all of the "shoulds" taught by parents and other sources of authority. The **underdog** part of the personality is childlike, demanding, rebellious, and evasive. A Gestalt therapist might have the client integrate these two parts of the personality through dialogue. Using an empty chair or a pillow as a focal point, the client might first speak from the perspective of the topdog: "You're so irresponsible! You always want to see what you can get away with!" The counselor would then have the client switch places and respond from the perspective of the underdog: "You're no fun. All you want to do is work, work, work." The goal of the dialogue is to make the client fully aware of these personality dimensions and to make the dimensions less polarized.

Goals

The primary goals of Gestalt therapy are to help clients become mature, grow up, take responsibility for their lives, and be in touch with themselves and the world. Another goal is to help a person deal with and accept anxiety as part of the natural order of life.

Techniques

Gestalt counselors help clients overcome barriers to awareness. The counselor's responsibility is to give full personal expression to what the client experiences in the session, live it in the present moment, and not merely talk about it by interpreting the other's behavior. The counselor confronts actual experience in the immediate environment by striving to keep everything on an I–Thou basis, talking with and not about a person, and turning questions into statements. Emphasis is placed on becoming aware of nonverbal behavior and, in particular, on inconsistencies between nonverbal and verbal behavior.

An intriguing aspect of Gestalt therapy is the number of dramatic techniques that have become associated with the approach. Gestalt techniques are extensions of basic theoretical concepts that are used to facilitate client learning and experience in interpersonal perception and communication and to bring about personal awareness. In addition to the empty chair dialogue, three other Gestalt techniques include making the rounds and exaggeration.

1. *Making the rounds.* In a group counseling setting, the counselor asks a group member to share something he or she has difficulty communicating. For example, a client who has difficulty talking in the group may go around to each member of the group and complete the sentence, "I haven't spoken up in this group because…" After this sentence is told to each group member, the client may have some valuable awareness and may even institute some personal changes.
2. *Exaggeration.* A client with a whiny way of speaking can be asked to exaggerate the whine in conversation.
3. *Dealing with inconsistencies.* Clients who smile when they say that they are angry can be asked to carry out a dialogue between the smile and the anger.

Time Orientation

Gestalt therapy strongly emphasizes the present through direct contact and expression of feelings. Although there is no ideal time frame, because of the intensity of the experience therapy can be relatively brief.

Strengths

Gestalt therapy is a positive confrontational approach. Clients become aware of discrepancies and inconsistencies in their behaviors through an experiential method that often induces change. This approach is activity-oriented, because it helps clients experience the different aspects of their problems; just talking about problems is avoided. This approach is open to the creativity of each counselor. There is no formula or prescribed set of techniques for the practitioner to follow. Unfinished business from the past is addressed in the context of the present, which is quite helpful in dealing with issues of grief and loss. The Gestalt approach is flexible and can be adapted to diverse populations. It can help people with disabilities feel whole in spite of their afflictions and bicultural individuals deal with the polarities that they experience. The Gestalt emphasis on precision in language can empower individuals who feel powerless and can help to bridge the gap between cultural groups (Gilliland, James, & Bowman, 1994).

Weaknesses

Gestalt therapy has a weak theoretical base, particularly in the area of personality development. It sometimes is combined with an approach such as transactional analysis to help compensate for this weakness. Emotion, rather than cognition, is stressed, although this is being modified by contemporary Gestalt therapists. Many Gestalt techniques are powerful, and counselors should be well-grounded in their use and should have high levels of personal development before using them (Corey, 1986). The approach is focused on individual development with limited emphasis placed on the influence of the larger community and the environment. The Gestalt approach also has a weak research base. Some ethnic clients may have difficulty with the emphasis on the expression of emotion, particularly when they may be directed to express themselves even symbolically toward their parents (Corey, 1991). Some clients are uncomfortable with the confrontational aspect of the approach. As with person-centered counseling, some clients may prefer a direct, problem-solving approach.

TRANSACTIONAL ANALYSIS

Transactional analysis (TA) is appealing to many practitioners and lay people, because it is not overly technical and complex. Basic concepts such as games; scripts; strokes; I'm OK, you're OK; and transactions are easily understood in the context of the helping relationship and can generally be used with children as well as adults.

Background

Eric Berne (1910–1970), the developer of TA, was trained in psychoanalysis, but he found that the psychoanalytic concepts were not sufficient to provide the theoretical structure appropriate for his clients. It was not until he was turned down for membership in the Psychoanalytic Institute in 1956, however, that he began pursuing the development of TA. Not surprisingly, many concepts in TA resemble psychoanalytic formulations. TA also has many other constructs that are significantly different. In 1964 Berne wrote *Games People Play;* in 1967 Thomas Harris wrote *I'm OK You're OK,* and in 1971 James and Jongeward wrote *Born to Win.* All of these books were best-sellers and served to popularize the TA approach.

The Ego States

Berne has described the human personality as consisting of three different observable ego states. An **ego state** is "a consistent pattern of feeling and experience related to a corresponding consistent pattern of behavior" (Berne, 1964, p. 364). The individual could be controlled by any of these states at any time. These states are the parent, the adult, and the child (see Figure 11.1). They are similar but not identical to the concepts of superego, ego, and id found in psychoanalytic theory. The basis for Berne's conceptualization of the human personality included his experience as a therapist and the neurological research of Dr. Wilder Penfield, which indicated that people can exist in different ego states simultaneously and that these states are connected to memories. These memories can be accessed in vivid detail and evoke sounds, smells, and feelings.

Essentially, the parent ego state consists of what is taught to people and is concerned about actions that one *ought* to do. The adult ego state is the thinking part of one's person-

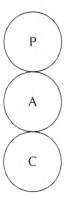

FIGURE 11.1   **Ego state structure. P represents the parent ego state; A represents the adult ego state; and C represents the child ego state.**

ality. It is the data processing computer that makes decisions. It is the fact-finding, reasoning, problem-solving, and reality-testing part of personality. In essence, the adult ego state is the cold, nonemotional, objective side of one's behavior. The child ego state is expressed in the form of feelings. It is the emotional, fun-loving, impulsive, spontaneous, sensuous, affectionate, and curious part of each person. However, the child can also be selfish, self-centered, and rebellious and can display overly aggressive behaviors. The child ego state centers on the things one *wants* to do. The three ego states are generally described as three separate, unique, and independent functions and depicted as three adjacent circles.

Goals

Transactional analysts believe that as children, individuals determine life plans for themselves and then spend the rest of their lives following these scripts. Because the initial plans, or scripts, were chosen by the clients themselves, the clients can make new decisions regarding future behaviors and the future course of their lives.

A practitioner working within the TA framework has several major goals. One is to decontaminate any damaged ego states. Contamination occurs when there is no clear distinction between the parent and adult or the adult and child ego states (for example, accepting as fact in the adult ego state that all rich people are wise.) This relates to the second goal, which is to develop the capacity to use all ego states appropriately and to develop the full use of the adult ego state. The final goal is to rid the client of poorly chosen life scripts and life position and replace them with an "I'm OK" position and a new, productive script.

Techniques

A series of progressive steps is followed in the TA approach. The first step is **structural analysis,** or the analysis of the person's ego states. This is done to help individuals understand their ego state structure, to develop fully functioning ego states that are free of contamination, and to place the adult ego state in charge of life.

The second step is **transactional analysis.** This involves developing an understanding of the transactions in which the client normally engages and then working to improve communication abilities.

The third step is **game analysis.** Working with the communication patterns learned through the previous step, the counselor proceeds to work with the interpretation of psychological games being played. Games, in this context, are repetitive interpersonal transactions that lead to bad feelings or worse (divorce, suicide, or homicide). Clients are confronted with the games they play and given permission to stop playing the games.

The final step is **script analysis.** In this step, clients review the mistakes in their life scripts that they developed as children. They are helped to gain social control, develop congruency, and revise life scripts as necessary.

TA counselors have a variety of methods at their disposal, most of a conventional nature. A fair amount of teaching is involved as the counselor helps the client understand the basic TA concepts. Most TA counselors use either a chalkboard or a flipchart to illustrate the ego states and different types of transactions.

An early task in TA counseling is to develop a counselor–client contract. This involves developing a specific statement of objectives to be attained by the client during the counseling process. The contract defines the relationship, delineating the mutual responsibilities of both the client and the counselor. Establishing a contract also lets the client know not to expect any miracle cures by the counselor.

Using material presented by the client, the counselor analyzes; interrogates; confronts; offers an anecdote, simile, or comparison to clarify the material; and then **crystallizes**—a communication at the end of therapy indicating that the client can now choose to stop game playing.

Many techniques developed by other therapists are used within the framework of transactional analysis. These include psychodrama (see chapter 5) and the broad range of Gestalt techniques.

Transactional analysis counselors function as teachers, trainers, resource persons, and facilitators. They are skilled in the analysis of ego states, interpersonal transactions, games, and life scripts. Above all, they help clients acquire the tools necessary for change. As part of this process they provide protection, give permission, and model potency. The contractual relationship they establish results in equal status. Successful TA counselors want to conclude counseling with a client by being able to work in a game-free, adult-to-adult relationship.

Time Orientation

Transactional analysis is primarily a present-oriented therapy, although TA counselors can work with both past and future material.

Strengths

TA concepts are easily understood and in some cases have become part of everyday language. The contractual approach clearly outlines the process, clarifying that the responsibility for change rests with the client, and determines when the process will be completed. The description of personality development in TA works well with techniques and procedures from other counseling approaches, such as Gestalt therapy. For individuals from minority groups, the use of contracts can be quite empowering. The establishment of the contract allows clients to determine on which issues and values they wish to work. The TA approach has been exported to other countries, which suggests that the concepts are translatable. Almost from its inception, teachers and counselors have used TA with children. TA has been used extensively with drug and alcohol abuse clients and their families, as well as with other types of abuse victims.

Weaknesses

The didactic nature of TA can serve to distance the counselor from the client. The counselor may become enamored with explaining concepts and diagnosing scripts and games to the point of losing the client in the relationship. The emphasis can easily become too heavily placed on the intellectual–cognitive factors to the exclusion of other dimensions of the personality; the use of TA concepts in conjunction with an affective approach such as Gestalt therapy is one way to deal with this. TA also has a weak research base. In working with some culturally diverse clients, the major premise that many problems are a result of parental injunctions has to be handled with extreme care. Cassius (in Gilliland, James, & Bowman, 1994) suggests that this concern can be dealt with by describing these injunctions as statements made under stress. Challenging the life scripts of ethnic minorities raises the issue of therapists imposing their values on the clients. Careful use of the contracts can help avoid this issue.

COGNITIVE–BEHAVIORAL COUNSELING

Background

Behavioral counseling, counseling with the primary goal of modifying the client's behavior, became a major addition to the counseling field in the 1960s. In the 1970s the **cognitive approach,** which focuses on changing thoughts and thought processes, became influential. Most behavioral counselors now consider thoughts to be behaviors and tend to incorporate cognitive theory and methodology in their work; therefore, the two approaches are combined. Table 11.1 describes the cognitive and behavioral approaches together. Another approach to cognitive counseling, rational–emotive therapy, is described separately.

Cognitive–behavioral counseling has evolved largely from the work emanating from university psychology departments throughout the twentieth century. The earliest formulations of these approaches focused exclusively on behavioral counseling. Behavioral counseling is the application of different principles of learning theory to the changing of human behavior and to problem resolution in a therapeutic setting. The basic premises of the behavioral approach are that (1) behavior is a function of current influences, (2) presenting problems should be defined specifically so that treatment and evaluation are possible, (3) treatment goals are to be described concretely, and (4) hypotheses about interventions are validated through research. The objective of the behavior counselor is to collaborate with the client in providing new learning experiences that allow the client to find more effective ways of behaving.

Learning theorists have determined that behavior is learned in three basic ways: through classical conditioning, operant conditioning, and imitation or modeling. As noted, behavioral theorists have now recognized the influence of cognitive factors on behaviors and have expanded their approach accordingly.

Goals

The goals of all of the approaches to cognitive–behavioral counseling are to modify maladaptive behavior patterns and learn new functional behavior.

Techniques

Over the years one major criticism of the strict behavioral approach to counseling has been its lack of concern for the personality of the clients and its emphasis on the manipulation of the external variables related to the clients' behavior. The clients' thoughts and emotions were deemed to be essentially irrelevant.

The cognitive–behavioral approach views thoughts as behaviors and suggests that what individuals say to themselves influences what they do. The emphases, therefore, in this approach are to restructure how clients think about life and to improve the quality of self-talk.

The major cognitive–behavioral techniques involve cognitive restructuring of irrational belief systems (Ellis, 1977), the restructuring of faulty thinking styles (Beck, 1976), or the teaching of problem-solving and coping skills (D'Zurilla & Goldfried, 1971). One particular technique developed by Meichenbaum (1977) is stress inoculation training. This technique is a systematic program taught to clients to help them learn how to cope with different levels of stress.

As with other approaches to counseling, the development of a strong therapeutic relationship is a crucial factor in the cognitive–behavioral approach (Brady, 1980, p. 285). The counselor helps the client eliminate specific problems and increase the client's productive behaviors and constructive interpersonal relationships. Major tasks for the counselor are to define the problem clearly, which includes understanding the antecedents and consequences that influence the problem, and to collaborate with the client in formulating treatment goals and monitoring progress toward goal achievement. Cognitive–behavioral counselors are very active. They direct client activity and reinforce goal-oriented behaviors. They teach, ask questions, give short answers, and often act as participant-observers. When working in a group setting, cognitive–behavioral counselors are generally concerned with individual rather than with group interaction.

Time Orientation

With several cognitive–behavioral techniques, there is some concern about a client's personal history in terms of the antecedent conditions related to the target behavior. Once this information has been obtained, the main focus of counseling is on the present, helping the client learn and maintain new behaviors.

Strengths

The strengths of the cognitive–behavioral approach include bringing specificity and explicitness to the field of counseling, focusing on the modification of observable behavior. Cognitive–behavioral counseling works with the modification of specific symptoms. It has been particularly successful with symptoms related to such things as conduct and phobic disorders. A broad variety of powerful techniques have been used with many different populations. Because it is a direct goal-oriented approach, focusing on thoughts and behaviors rather than emotions and self-disclosure, this approach appeals to a large number of minority clients. Finally, a significant body of research demonstrates the effectiveness of the techniques for this approach.

Weaknesses

One weakness of the cognitive–behavioral therapy is that it is essentially a teaching or training approach rather than a comprehensive approach to counseling. Because the approach focuses on specific behaviors or thoughts, practitioners tend to ignore, avoid, or downplay certain other aspects of the human personality, such as the spiritual nature. The effectiveness of this approach may be limited to pathologies with clearly defined, overt behavioral characteristics. This criticism has been tempered somewhat by recent attention by cognitive–behavioralists to emotional dimensions. When working with diverse populations, one must be aware of the contextual circumstances of the different clients. Specific cognitive–behavioral strategies may be effective for clients, but when the clients return to their systems, there may be consequences that force the clients back to their previous patterns of behavior. A sound knowledge of the client's cultural background and a direct involvement in the family or community system is helpful. This criticism may be made of the other approaches as well, however, and it is one of the reasons many practitioners prefer the practice of family therapy.

BRIEF THERAPY APPROACHES

Background

One of the most important trends in contemporary counseling is the development of brief treatments. These brief approaches have been around for some time, and many of the traditional approaches are often quite brief—Gestalt therapy has been known to be completed in two to three sessions. These can be adapted to include brief interventions; current pressures are contributing to the gaining popularity of brief cognitive–behavioral approaches. According to a survey of 850 psychologists (Sharp, 1994), more than 25% said they favored brief therapies and just 2% objected to the notion. **Brief therapies** are a group of short-term therapeutic interventions aimed at solving the client's problem in the shortest amount of time possible. Most of them have a cognitive–behavioral orientation and form an umbrella that includes time-limited therapy, short-term therapy, solution-focused therapy, and solution-oriented therapy. **Time-limited therapy** refers to any theoretical approach that is short-term. It is, from the outset, planned to last a certain number of sessions. The time limit is determined, in general, by managed care systems. In brief therapy approaches, only those issues defined as problems by the client become the focus of change. These problems are specified in clear behavioral terms, as are the desired outcomes of the counseling.

Goals

The focus of brief approaches is treating symptoms, not changing personalities. Due to its short time span, these approaches are problem-focused and goal-oriented. Brief therapy seeks to address the factors that keep clients in their present situation, that affect the here and now problem that brought them to counseling.

Techniques

Although brief therapy techniques vary greatly, they tend to be concrete and goal-oriented. The techniques build on people's resources—what they are already doing right—rather than analyzing their deficits. The emphasis is on identifying and expanding existing solution behaviors. The counselor is held accountable for results and is actively involved in the process.

Techniques focus on resolving one or two very specific problems or complaints. Counselors often initially ask such questions as, "How would your life be different if this problem were gone?" The answer to the question becomes the goal. Then the counselor and client work together to find actions and/or behaviors to achieve the goal. Brief therapists attempt to discover and build on people's resources. They choose to look for solutions and resources rather than etiology, pathology, and dysfunction.

Brief therapists often reframe responses to create a shift toward thinking positively and acting to resolve the problem. For example:

CLIENT: "I can't achieve intimacy."
COUNSELOR: "You haven't been able to achieve intimacy."

CLIENT: "We fight all the time."
COUNSELOR: "So you'd really like to relate to your wife without fighting so much."

Clients themselves will often point out solutions in the course of responding to positively phrased questions or statements.

Time Orientation

Brief approaches usually last fewer than 10 sessions, with the range being between 4 and 20. This range actually includes a great number of the therapies listed here. In actuality, numbers of sessions often are geared to company insurance plans and managed care programs, so the actual number of sessions is close to 4.

Strengths

The strengths of brief approaches include specificity, explicitness, and a focus on achieving concrete goals. Brief approaches attempt to make therapy more efficient. Like other cognitive–behavioral approaches, these direct goal-oriented approaches appeal to minority clients.

Weaknesses

Brief therapies contain similar weaknesses to cognitive–behavioral therapy, including a narrow teaching or training focus. Because the approach focuses on problem solving, practitioners tend to ignore, avoid, or downplay certain other aspects of the human personality, such as the spiritual nature. As with other cognitive–behavioral approaches, the effectiveness of this approach may be limited to pathologies with clearly defined, overt behavioral characteristics. They are more mechanical in nature, playing down the therapeutic alliance.

RATIONAL–EMOTIVE BEHAVIOR THERAPY

Background

One pioneer in the field of counseling and the developer of the first cognitive–behavioral approach is Albert Ellis. Ellis began private practice in 1943 and is an active counselor, writer, and lecturer. The approach he developed, rational–emotive therapy (RET), is now called rational–emotive behavior therapy (REBT). Ellis, who was trained initially as a marriage and family therapist and then as a psychoanalyst, broke away from the analytic approach because he believed it was too slow and ineffective. He used behavioral conditioning for a while; then he became convinced that it was not the person's behavior that was of concern, but rather the person's thoughts about events and behaviors. He then developed his rational, logical approach to counseling.

Ellis's approach is almost more philosophical than psychological, drawing on the work of philosophers such as Epictetus, who wrote, "Men are disturbed not by things, but by the view which they take of them" (Ellis, 1984, p. 200). In essence, this means that if people learn to think differently about what disturbs them, they will behave more rationally. It is not the activating event (A) that causes emotional dysfunctional consequences (C) in human beings. The clients' interpretations of these events and their concomitant irrational beliefs (B) cause emotional upset (p. 198). According to Ellis, people create their own emotional disturbances or psychological disorders. As this is an approach to cognitive–behavioral therapy, it is included on Table 11.1 under the cognitive–behavioral heading

Ellis believes that most problems people have result from irrational ideas that people use to indoctrinate themselves negatively. These ideas have come from parents and culture. Not only have people become indoctrinated by them, but they also continue to indoctrinate themselves again on a regular basis. Ellis (1987) has identified 11 ideas that he believes "would seem inevitably to lead to widespread neurosis" (p. 367). These ideas are as follows:

1. It is absolutely essential for an individual to be loved or approved by every significant person in his or her environment.
2. It is necessary that each individual be completely competent, adequate, and achieving in all areas if the individual is to be worthwhile.

3. Some people are bad, wicked, or villainous, and these people should be blamed and punished.
4. It is terrible and catastrophic when things are not the way an individual wants them to be.
5. Unhappiness is a function of events outside the control of the individual.
6. If something may be dangerous or harmful, an individual should constantly be concerned and think about it.
7. It is easier to run away from difficulties and self-responsibility than it is to face them.
8. Individuals need to be dependent on others and have someone stronger than themselves to lean on.
9. Past events in an individual's life determine present behavior and cannot be changed.
10. An individual should be very concerned and upset about other individuals' problems.
11. There is always a correct and precise answer to every problem, and it is catastrophic if it is not found. (p. 369)

Goals

People not only have the potential to be irrational, they also have the potential to learn to be rational. The objectives of RET are to help people learn to be rational, to stop using self-defeating behavior, and to acquire a more realistic, tolerant philosophy of life.

Techniques

No unique techniques are used in REBT. A relationship is established with the client to establish rapport. The therapist then proceeds to take an active, directive teaching stance.

Rational–emotive practitioners often employ a fairly rapid-fire active–directive persuasive–philosophic methodology. In most instances, they quickly pin the client down to a few basic irrational ideas. They challenge the client to validate these ideas; show how the ideas contain extralogical premises that cannot be validated; logically analyze these ideas and make mincemeat of them; vigorously show why they cannot work and why they will almost inevitably lead to renewed disturbed symptomatology; reduce these ideas to absurdity, sometimes in a highly humorous manner; explain how they can be replaced with more rational theses; and teach clients how to think

scientifically so that they can observe, logically parse, and minimize any subsequent irrational ideas and illogical deductions that lead to self-defeating feelings and behaviors. (Ellis, 1989, pp. 215–216)

The process of counseling in REBT is to teach the client to think rationally. Ellis believes that the various techniques other therapists use are basically inefficient and wasteful. He believes the counselor should be direct rather than indirect.

Time Orientation

According to Ellis (1995), most REBT clients are seen once a week for anywhere between 5 and 50 sessions. REBT is centered on the present and is well suited as a brief therapy approach for all but those with severe disturbances. Individuals with a specific problem can be helped in 1–10 sessions.

Strengths

REBT is an efficient, scientific process to behavioral change. REBT generally is a short-term therapy, with a language and methodology that is fairly easily understood and practiced. Research studies indicate that it is effective with a variety of clients dealing with a wide range of disorders. The approach continues to evolve and invites scientific investigation. There is a significant amount of supporting material in the form of books, tapes, and other resource material. As with the earlier description of cognitive–behavioral therapy, this approach appeals to minorities who want a direct, no-nonsense, solution-oriented approach. Of all the approaches included in this chapter, REBT is among the least concerned with developing a strong therapeutic alliance, which is attractive to members of some minority groups.

Weaknesses

REBT is a highly verbal, intellectual approach. The counselor takes the initial responsibility for diagnosing the client's irrational beliefs and strives to see that the client's thought patterns are changed, raising the possibility of developing a dependency relationship. In spite of the fact that this is a cognitive approach, REBT is not generally effective with clients with severe thought disorders, such as schizophrenics. Even though a fair amount of research supports the approach, questions have been raised about the methodology of some research studies (Patterson, 1986, pp. 29–30).

The personality and style of its founder, Albert Ellis, could perhaps also be cited as a weakness. Ellis is earthy and often controversial in his approach to selling his therapy. He has recently become embroiled in a heated discourse with adherents of transpersonal psychology over his perception of the dangers of their approach (Ellis & Yaeger, 1989; Wilber, 1989; Ellis, 1989). Ellis's antagonism toward spiritual issues may not appeal to people with strong spiritual beliefs and heritage. This highly intellectual, rational approach would be difficult for mentally challenged clients.

TRANSPERSONAL COUNSELING

As noted in chapter 10, transpersonal counseling is a relative newcomer to the field of psychotherapy; much of the literature describing this approach first appeared in the late 1960s and early 1970s. Even though the present formulation of transpersonal ideas and methods may be new, many concepts date back to the work of Carl Jung in the early 1900s and even further back with the incorporation of Eastern teachings.

Transpersonal counseling is based on the work of transpersonal psychologists who believe that there are potential cognitive, moral, and motivational stages of development beyond those reached by most adults (Walsh, 1989a). It is defined as that "aspect of therapy which goes beyond ego goals and bridges psychological and spiritual practice" (Boss, 1980, p. 161). Transpersonal counseling is "an open-ended endeavor to facilitate human growth and expand awareness beyond limits implied by most traditional Western models of mental health" (Vaughn, 1980, p. 182). The transpersonal approach brings together "the insights of the individualistic psychologies of the West with the spiritual psychologies of the East and the Middle East" (Fadiman, 1980, p. 181). Other therapies focus on emotions, behavior, and/or thoughts; transpersonal counseling adds the spiritual side of humanity as a vital dimension to be considered in fostering wellness.

Transpersonal counseling is a relatively small movement for a number of reasons. First, there is no charismatic proponent of this approach to serve as a mentor or model, such as Fritz Perls for Gestalt therapy. Second, it has not been institutionalized and taught in clinical programs, as has cognitive–behavioral counseling. Third, there have been no best-selling books related to it, as in the case of transactional analysis (*Games People Play* and *I'm OK, You're OK*). "It is an organic movement that has grown by networking, a movement that has drawn people to it who share a concern, a purpose, and a vision of what is possible for humanity... It is cross-cultural and interdisciplinary; though it has roots in ancient perennial philosophy, it makes use of modern science because science, like mysticism, is a search for truth" (Vaughn, 1984, p. 25). The growth of New Age literature, which parallels the development of transpersonal psychology, indicates a great deal of general public interest in spirituality and other aspects of transpersonal psychology. Some, but not all, of the New Age literature relates to concepts found in transpersonal psychology.

The incorporation of ideas and practices that are part of the transpersonal movement is significant. Books and articles on counseling and spirituality are now being published (Burke & Miranti, 1995; Kelly, 1995; Stirch-Stasko, 1996). The American Counseling Association (ACA) now has a major content category for its conventions entitled Spiritual, Ethical, and Moral Development. In 1993 one of ACA's divisions, the Association for Religious Values in Counseling (ARVIC), changed its name to the Association for Spiritual, Ethical, Religious, and Value Issues in Counseling (ASERVIC). Another ACA division, the Association of Counselor Educators and Supervisors (ACES), is working to add the subject of spirituality to counselor education programs (Holden & Ivey, 1997). The fourth edition of the American Psychiatric Association (APA) *Diagnostic and Statistical Manual*, the main diagnostic tool used by mental health professionals across the country, now includes spiritual and religious difficulty as a distinct mental disorder deserving treatment (APA, 1994).

Background

Transpersonal psychology has developed as an extension of humanistic psychology. Abraham Maslow, in his study of self-actualizing individuals, discovered many healthy people from different walks of life who had gone beyond the process of self-actualization. This higher level, transcendence, involved reaching even greater fulfillment of their human potential (Maslow, 1971).

In the late 1960s Maslow, Anthony Sutich, Stanislav Grof, and other psychologists created a new branch of psychology by combining aspects of humanistic psychology with Eastern concepts and traditions. Maslow and Sutich gave the name *transpersonal* to this branch of psychology, and in 1969 Sutich began the *Journal of Transpersonal Psychology* (Vaughn, 1984, p. 27). Roberto Assagioli's work with psychosynthesis (1965); the practical applications of Frances Vaughn (1980, 1984) and Roger Walsh (1996); and the theoretical contributions of Charles Tart (1992), Ken Wilber (1977, 1995), and Michael Washburn

(1995) have helped this psychology develop into a viable counseling approach (Weinhold & Hendricks, 1993; Capuzzi & Gross, 1995).

Transpersonal psychology addresses the relationship between psychotherapy and spirituality. The term **transpersonal** literally means beyond the personal, or beyond the personality. The use of this term signifies that who or what people are is not limited to being identified with their body, ego, or personality; they are and can be more than that (Vaughn, 1984, p. 26). They can, in fact, transcend to levels of which they may be unaware. Maslow (1971) has provided 35 different meanings of the term *transcendence,* and most people could recognize some aspects of transcendence in their lives. He also offered a condensed definition:

> **Transcendence** refers to the very highest and most inclusive levels of human consciousness, behaving, and relating, as ends rather than as means, to oneself, to significant others, to human beings in general, to other species, to nature, and to the cosmos. (p. 279)

Personality Development

The transpersonal approach builds on the idea that the human personality is formed by way of developmental stage processes as postulated and researched by Western psychologists (see chapter 17), including prenatal development (Weinhold, 1993). Transpersonal psychologists believe, however, that the stages identified do not go far enough to detail the full potential of human nature. The levels formulated by Westerners such as Piaget, Erikson, and Kohlberg have been termed *conventional stages.* In the exploration of Eastern psychologies, transpersonal psychologists discovered that contemplative and meditative disciplines also have stages that are "sufficiently similar to suggest an underlying common invariant sequence of stages despite vast cultural and linguistic differences as well as styles of practice" (Wilber, Engler, & Brown, 1986, p. 9).

Wilber, Engler, and Brown (1986) suggest a three-level model that combines the conventional and the contemplative approaches. The first two levels, prepersonal and personal, consist of conventional development stages such as those delineated by Piaget and Erikson. The third level, transpersonal, consists of contemplative developmental stages described primarily in Eastern literature. Particular pathologies are said to be associated with the different stages; for example, the diagnosis of psychotic would tend to correlate with the prepersonal level "because this range of development involves the stages leading up to the emergence of a rational–individuated–personal selfhood" (Wilber, Engler, & Brown, 1986, p. 12). Because transpersonal psychologists postulate a level beyond which the conventional approach leaves off, they consider a diagnosis of normalcy to be a case of developmental arrest.

Nature of People and Anxiety

With regard to the nature of people, transpersonal counselors believe that human beings not only "have the potential to reach eventually undreamt of levels of emotional, intellectual and ethical development" (Grof, 1988, p. 8), but they also are seen as "seeking to enhance and surpass [themselves] in the process of self-actualization" (Vaughn, 1980, p. 182). Anxiety is perceived as dealing with basic human problems involving values, meaning, and purpose (Vaughn, 1980, p. 161) and with the concerns of individuals who have already achieved a satisfactory coping level in their lives and are still unsatisfied because they intuitively believe there must be more; their potential is greater than what has already been achieved.

Goals

The ultimate goal in transpersonal counseling is to help clients fulfill "higher needs for self-realization for full functioning at optimal levels of health," with a basic goal being to "enable each person to meet physical, emotional, mental, and spiritual needs appropriately, in accordance with individual preferences and predispositions (Vaughn, 1980, p. 182). Additional goals include "both traditional [goals] such as symptom relief and behavior change, and where appropriate, optimal work at the transpersonal level" (Walsh & Vaughn, 1980, p. 165).

Techniques

Transpersonal therapists are eclectic, for they use techniques drawn from Eastern and Western psychologies to work with the mind, body, emotions, and spirit of clients. They use most of the traditional techniques noted in therapies described in this chapter and include different types of meditation (Boorstein, 1996), guided imagery (Foote, 1996), and breathwork (Travis & Ryan, 1988). Transpersonal strategies also are used in the fields of stress management, self-awareness, and self-acceptance (Fontana & Slack, 1996).

In transpersonal counseling, "participation by therapists in all their humanity in the therapeutic relationship [and] opening themselves fully to the client's experience and to their own reactions" (Walsh & Vaughn, 1980, p. 166) is considered to be fundamental. The transpersonal perspective adds the view that therapists consciously use the relationship to enhance their own transpersonal growth while serving the client. Because it is known that the therapists do change as a result of being with their clients in the therapeutic relationship, this conscious personal growth on the part of the counselor is performed in the context of growth through service.

> The therapist attempts to provide both an optimal environment and serve as a model for the client. Where the therapist is consciously serving the client there is no hierarchical status accorded to being a therapist. Rather the situation is held as one in which both therapist and client are working on themselves, each in the way that is most appropriate to their development. The therapist's openness and willingness to use the therapeutic process to maximize his or her own growth and commitment to service is viewed as the optimal modeling that can be provided for the client. (Walsh & Vaughn 1980, p. 166)

Transpersonal counselors first establish the therapeutic relationship and are open to working with any emerging personality and behavioral issues that emerge. If client concerns deal with issues of faith or go beyond what might be considered a dull, normal existence, the counselor can also work with these issues. Termination of the transpersonal counseling relationship occurs when clients are functioning at levels that will provide them with the fulfillment and meaning for which they have been searching.

Time Orientation

Transpersonal clients are usually seen for 4 sessions to 20 or more sessions, depending on the client's original state and what level of consciousness the client wishes to attain. Clients may first experience remediation until their nonproductive behavior is eliminated; then clients can decide to go beyond "being normal," which is held by the transpersonalists as a case of arrested development on one's way to higher levels of consciousness.

Strengths

Transpersonal counseling is concerned with the total person. Practitioners strive to help individuals fulfill their full potential, often going beyond levels sought by other therapies. Being free to draw from the broad range of concepts and techniques from both Eastern and Western disciplines provides a greater degree of flexibility and adaptability to client needs than do therapies that are more conceptually limited. Transpersonal counselors often work with experiences and perspectives generally ignored or avoided by other counselors. The transpersonal approach is particularly relevant for work with clients from different cultural backgrounds. As Hendricks (1993) has stated, "Cross-cultural counseling is transpersonal psychology in action." In 1996 ACES, in a summit on spirituality, developed a set of counselor competencies for spirituality which were similar in many respects to a set of multicultural competencies that had recently been developed. Transpersonal counselors employ concepts and techniques from a broad spectrum of cultures and generally are highly tuned to sensing and adapting to the cultural differences of clients.

Even though this approach is still in its infancy, Lu (1996) suggests that "because of the increasingly multicultural and transpersonally oriented population in the United States, [counselors] are more and more likely to encounter patients with transpersonal experiences and commitments" (p. 395). They should be prepared accordingly.

Weaknesses

Many assumptions specific to this approach have not been empirically tested; there is a substantial body of research on the value of meditation, and research related to other concepts is growing. A recent unsystematic sampling of doctoral dissertations from 1987 and 1988 yielded 516 dissertation titles related to transpersonal psychology (Fulton, 1989), and there continues to be a steady stream of such dissertations and published research articles according to the *Dissertation Abstracts and Psychological Abstracts* (Chinen, 1996). Nevertheless, because of the relatively ambiguous nature of many constructs emphasized in this approach (e.g., levels of consciousness), the prospect for rigorous, replicable studies is not good.

The transpersonal approach would probably be more effective with clients who were already functioning at a relatively high level. Clients who prefer more directive, problem-solving approaches would not be overly attracted to this approach. It definitely would not be a brief therapy. Transpersonal counselors themselves, out of necessity, need to be highly functioning individuals. They need to be well grounded in developing the therapeutic relationship, in using relevant techniques from other theoretical approaches, and in using techniques unique to the transpersonal approach. Critics of transpersonal therapy believe that some transpersonal counselors follow the teachings of extreme cults and use techniques such as "astrology, sorcery, psychic healing, [and] witchcraft" (Ellis, 1986b, p. 149) in their practices. Overall, the approach is still in an early developmental stage; much more needs to be done in the formulation of theory, process, and research.

WHOLISTIC COUNSELING

Many practitioners choose to specialize in a specific theoretical approach such as existential or cognitive–behavioral; however, a great number of counselors chose to blend ideas and practices into their own systematic formulation. Counselors can create their own eclectic approaches to counseling, and many experts in the field have offered their own special formulations. Arnold Lazarus (1989), for example, has developed a systematic approach for which he uses the acronym BASIC ID. B refers to behavior, A to affective responses, S to sensations, I to images, C to cognitions, I to interpersonal relationships, and D to drugs, biological functions, nutrition, and exercise. His is a *technical eclecticism* since multimodal therapists need to be able to competently apply techniques from other approaches and not be burdened with theoretical contradictions or inconsistencies that might also be present. Corey (1996) suggests the blending of concepts and techniques from various theories into one's own "personal integrative approach." A great many counselors, however, are choosing to go beyond these theories and present themselves as wholistic counselors.

Wholistic counseling might be considered the epitome of eclectic counseling. Approaches such as BASIC ID are eclectic, for they involve systematic borrowing of concepts or techniques from different therapies. The scope of these therapies tends to be limited (for example, focusing on the individual but not on the environmental systems), and the amount of borrowing also tends to be limited. This is not so in wholistic counseling.

Wholistic counseling works with the total person, including the spiritual dimension, and uses information and methodology from any source. The wholistic approach is grounded in the health and wellness movement and stresses prevention as much as, if not more than, remediation and cure. The wholistic approach also goes beyond most other approaches to look at more than the total individual; it looks at the total environment in which the individual lives. It is a proactive as much as a reactive approach. **Wholistic counseling,** then, consists of working with the whole person in terms of body, mind, emotions, and spirit, in the context of the person's total environment.

Background

The counterculture and human potential movements of the late 1960s and early 1970s helped bring about awareness of problems with the national health care system and of the potential value of new approaches, including Eastern practices, in dealing with human problems. The resultant wholistic movement focuses on wellness in reaction to medicine's focus on disease. "The wellness emphasis conveys that health is significantly more than the absence of physical symptoms and disease; it is a self-actualizing commitment to increase the quality of one's total self and one's relationship with his or her environment" (O'Donnell, 1988, p. 366). Many health-related problems in the United States are now recognized as being self-inflicted. They are the results of poor behavioral choices, self-destructive attitudes, and environmental factors rather than of germs or viruses; therefore, the wholistic health movement has involved members of the counseling profession from its beginning along with wholistic medical practitioners, including Don Ardell (1986), Bernie Siegel (1986), Deepak Chopra (1993), and Andrew Weil (1996).

Nature of People

To the wholistic counselor, people are seen as unitary. That is, it is not possible to divide the individual parts such as the physical, mental, psychological, cultural, and economic; these parts cannot be separated one from the other in the active and reactive life of the person. He lives, loves, works, and feels as a whole person. Arbitrary divisions of parts or functions represent but a convenient method for collecting and classifying bodies of knowledge, or organizing professions and social systems. The simplistic interpretation they reflect, however, bears little relationship to living, breathing human beings." (Goodwin, 1986, p. 30)

Human nature is perceived to be an open process that changes as people interact with their environment and with physical, psychological, and spiritual aspects of wellness (Stensrud & Stensrud, 1984, p. 422; Morrison, 1986, p. 240). The wholistic counselor believes that to consider adequately any aspect of human nature, the therapist must consider them all.

Principles

Nine basic principles or underpinnings for the wholistic health approach have been identified by O'Donnell (1988):

1. We are responsible for our health.
2. Illness is a communication from within.
3. Most healing comes from within.
4. Treatment must involve body, mind, emotions, and spirit (and in many cases, environment).
5. The wholistic practitioner is a consultant, facilitator, and advisor—not a miracle worker or a dogmatic authority figure.
6. Personalized caring and unconditional positive regard are essential to change and to healing.
7. Our physical and social environments greatly affect our health.
8. Nutrition and exercise are the cornerstones of good health.
9. Because clients are uniquely individualistic in their biochemistry and in their sociopsychological make-up, wholistic services by necessity should be eclectic and individually tailored. (pp. 366–377)

Goals

The goals of wholistic counseling emphasize developing client independence through clients taking charge of their own well-being and reaching the highest level of functioning of which they are capable (O'Donnell, 1988, p. 379). Wholistic counselors basically help clients attain their personal goals and, if the clients so choose, to help them move from "their presenting level of experience to the level of pure aliveness, and toward providing them with the information and skills necessary to maintain such a state" (Stensrud & Stensrud, 1984, p. 422).

Techniques

A wholistic counselor is a facilitator and consultant and views the "person and his/her wellness from every possible perspective, taking into account every available skill for the person's growth toward harmony and balance...treating the person, not the disease...using mild, natural methods whenever possible" (O'Donnell, 1988, p. 366).

Wholistic counselors establish the necessary core conditions for the therapeutic relationship and then personalize their approach to the unique characteristics of their clients. The involvement of wholistic counselors in their own personal growth is important in establishing themselves as models. Wholistic counselors must be well educated. They "must have the ability to develop a total understanding of the client—physically, psychologically, spiritually, and environmentally—including the ability to intervene in any one or all of these areas" (O'Donnell, 1988, p. 379). They also have to be well grounded in any of the numerous counseling interventions available to them and ethically responsible to acknowledge when they are not qualified to make a specific intervention.

Because wholistic counselors continually consider the whole person, they have an extensive network of referral sources and may in some instances work directly with a team of interdisciplinary practitioners (for example, working as a counselor in a clinic, along with a dietitian, one or more physicians, and an exercise physiologist).

Because wholistic counseling is an eclectic approach, there are no techniques that are particularly unique to it. Wholistic practitioners draw on resources from the entire field as well as from the disciplines of nutrition, exercise physiology, medicine, and others. Because they are aware of the effects of environment on clients, wholistic counselors generally take a systems approach to their cases (see chapter 13).

One major strategy of wholistic counselors is to work closely with other professionals such as dietitians and physicians. Wholistic counselors are expected to be excellent role models for their clients.

The therapeutic relationship is typically developed with the counselor's being sensitive to all dimensions of the client. The nature of the client's problem determines the scope of the counselor's responses and interventions. The problem may be such that the counselor and client need only go through the exploring and understanding stages of the process, with the client realizing how to solve the problem. At other times, the counselor may involve the client's family and significant others in working with the problem.

The counselor is generally concerned with the physical condition of the client, referring the client to a physician, dietitian, and/or exercise physiologist as appropriate. Whatever the extent of the counselor's involvement, the relationship is concluded with the client having direct responsibility for continued wellness.

Time Orientation

Clients seeing a wholistic counselor can expect from 2 sessions to 15 or more sessions, depending on the severity of the problem and the clients' goals. Because this approach is as much preventive as remedial in nature, additional time may be scheduled to teach skills necessary to becoming a self-reliant client. The client may also be referred to other experts, such as a dietician or an exercise physiologist.

Strengths

Wholistic counseling is a positive approach, focusing on the strengths of individuals and on what they can do to help themselves. All aspects of clients' lives are considered, and the broad repertoire of counseling interventions from other approaches are available to fit the needs of clients. Wholistic counseling can be seen as much as a preventive approach as it is a remedial approach. Even more than transpersonal counseling, the wholistic approach can be considered multicultural counseling in action. In addition to being aware of all of the developmental aspects of the client, the wholistic counselor considers the family and environmental systems in which the client is immersed. The wholistic counselor strives to see that interventions are compatible with clients' environments.

Wholistic counseling might best be offered as part of a total clinic setting where clients can be evaluated by a physician, dietitian, exercise physiologist, and counselor to obtain an overall health appraisal. The counselor working within this team approach would address the psychological needs of each client.

Weaknesses

Wholistic counseling is a relatively new approach, with a diffuse theoretical base and virtually no research data available. Highly skilled and knowledgeable practitioners are necessary to implement this approach. Minority and other clients seeking brief problem-solving therapy with little emphasis on a strong therapeutic alliance would probably not be attracted to this approach.

SUMMARY

A description has been provided of nine counseling approaches that are currently prominent in the field of counseling. The psychodynamic approaches focus on psychosexual development and emphasize working through unconscious conflicts. Person-centered counseling and Gestalt therapy emphasize working with the emotional dimension of clients. Rational–emotive behavior therapy and transactional analysis focus on the thoughts and beliefs of clients. The cognitive–behavioral approach views clients' thoughts and behaviors. Brief approaches focus on clients' constructions of reality. Transpersonal counseling incorporates the spiritual dimensions into the counseling process. Wholistic counseling incorporates all of the previous approaches and also works with how environmental systems affect clients.

Through further study of these and other approaches, students can determine which approaches most closely align with their personal beliefs and development. This brief overview has been presented to help make the future study of counseling approaches meaningful and exciting.

QUESTIONS AND ACTIVITIES

1. Consider your philosophy of life and your view of human nature. Which approach described in this chapter seems to fit best with your beliefs about human nature and how people change? Pursue further reading in that particular approach.

2. Interview one or more counselors about their theoretical approaches. Find out why they chose their particular approaches. How closely do these counselors adhere to their chosen approaches? Did they receive any special training in their theoretical approaches? If so, where and for how long?

3. What is your reaction to the idea presented by transpersonal theorists that being diagnosed as normal indicates that you are in a state of arrested development? Share your reactions with your classmates.

4. If you were to go for counseling at this time, what theoretical approach would you want your counselor to have? Would this approach be any different from the approach that you would employ as a counselor yourself? Compare your conclusions with those of several of your classmates.

RECOMMENDED READINGS

Bankart, C. P. (1997). *Talking cures: A history of Western and Eastern psychotherapies.* Pacific Grove, CA: Brooks/Cole.

Corey, G. (1995). *Theory and practice of counseling and psychotherapy* (5th ed.). Pacific Grove, CA: Brooks/Cole.

Corsini, R., & Wedding, D. (Eds.). (1995). *Current psychotherapies* (5th ed.). Itasca, IL: Peacock.

Patterson, C. H. (1986). *Theories of counseling and psychotherapy* (4th ed.). New York: Harper & Row.

Wedding, D., & Corsini, R. (1995). *Case studies in psychotherapy.* Itasca, IL: Peacock.

INTERNET RESOURCES

Websites—Psychoanalysis
Freud Net   <www.interport.net:80/nyspan>
Freud Resources   <paul.spu.edu/~hawk/freud.html>
Freud Index   <austria-info.at/personen/freud/index.html>
Psychoanalytical Links and Resources   <userpage.fu-berlin.de/albrecht/psa.html>
Freud Information   <austria-info.at/personen/freud/index.html>

Websites—Adlerian
Adler Institute   <ourworld.compuserve.com.80/homepages/hstein/homepage.htm>

Websites—Person-Centered
Client Centered Documents   <uhs.bsd.uchicago.edu/~matt/cct.papers.html>

Websites—Gestalt
American Association for Gestalt Therapy   <www.europa.com/~brownell/>

Gestalt Therapy Page   <gestalt.org/index.htm>
Gestalt! An E-journal of Applied Gestalt Therapy Principles   <rdz.stjohns.edu/gestalt!/>
Association for the Advancement of Gestalt Therapy   <www.europa.com~brownell/>

Websites—Transactional Analysis
TA Association   <usataa.org>

Websites—Cognitive–Behavioral
National Association for Cognitive Behavioral Therapy
What is Cognitive Behavior Therapy?   <pages.nyu.edu/~lqh6007/BehavioralAssociates/therapy.html>

Websites—Rational–Emotive Behavior Therapy
REBT Institute

Websites—Brief Therapies
Solution-Oriented Brief Therapy Bibliography   <www.helsinki.fi/~furman/books.html>

Brief Web   <home.earthlink.net/%7briefboy>
Narrative Therapy Page   <onthenet.com.au/~pict/ mentnarr.htm>

Websites—Transpersonal
Institute of Transpersonal Psychotherapy
   <www.tmn.com/itp/index.html>
International Transpersonal Association   <www. nbn.com/people/Transpersonal/itahome.html>
The Mind's Eye   <www.tmn.com/itp/mindseye. html>
Association for Transpersonal Psychotherapy
   <www.igc.org/htp/>

Websites—Wholistic
Journal of Emotional Wellness: Magic Stream
   <fly.hiwaay.net/~garson/>

Websites—Self Psychology

Websites—Jungian
C. G. Jung Anthology   <www.enteract.com/~jwalz/ Jung>
Keirsey Temperment Sorter-Jungian Personality Test   <sunsite.unc.edu/jembin/mb.pl>
The Jung Index   <www.uga.edu/~counseling/jung>
C. G. Jung Page

Websites—Logotherapy
Viktor Frankl Institute   <ara.pap.univie.ac.at/~ves/ vfi/>

Websites—Psychodrama
<csep.sunyit.edu/~joel/asgpp.html>

REFERENCES

American Psychiatric Association. (1994). *Diagnostic and statistical manual of mental disorders* (4th ed.). Washington, DC: author.

Ardell, D. (1986). *High-level wellness: An alternative to doctors, drugs, and disease.* Berkeley, CA: Ten Speed Press.

Assagioli, R. (1965). *Psychosynthesis. A manual of principles and techniques.* New York: Viking Press.

Beck, A. T. (1976). *Cognitive therapy and emotional disorders.* New York: International Universities Press.

Berne, E. (1964). *Games people play.* New York: Grove Press.

Boorstein, S. (1996). Clinical aspects of meditation. In B. Scotton, A. Chinen, & J. Battista. (Eds.), *Textbook of transpersonal psychiatry and psychology* (pp. 344–354). New York: Basic Books.

Boss, M. (1980). Transpersonal psychotherapy. In R. Walsh & F. Vaughn (Eds.), *Beyond ego: Transpersonal dimensions in psychology* (pp. 161–164). Los Angeles: J. R. Tarcher.

Boy, A., & Pine, G. (1982). *Client-centered counseling: A renewal.* Boston: Allyn & Bacon.

Brady, J. R. (1980). Some views of effective principles of psychotherapy. *Cognitive Therapy and Research, 4,* 271–306.

Breuer, J., & Freud, S. (1895). *Studies on hysteria.* Boston: Beacon Press.

Burke, M., & Miranti, J. (Eds.). (1995). *Counseling: The spiritual dimension.* Alexandria, VA: American Counseling Association.

Capuzzi, D., & Gross, C. (1995). *Counseling and Psychotherapy: Theories and Interventions.* Englewood Cliffs, NJ: Merrill.

Chinen, A. (1996). The emergence of transpersonal psychology. In B. Scotton, A. Chinen, & J. Battista. (Eds.), *Textbook of transpersonal psychiatry and psychology* (pp. 9–18). New York: Basic Books.

Chopra, D. (1993). *Ageless body, timeless mind.* New York: Crown.

Corey, G. (1986). *Theory and practice of counseling and psychotherapy* (3rd ed.). Monterey, CA: Brooks/Cole.

Corey, G. (1991). *Theory and practice of counseling and psychotherapy* (4th ed.). Pacific Grove, CA: Brooks/Cole.

Corey, G. (1996). *Theory and practice of counseling and psychotherapy* (5th ed.). Pacific Grove, CA: Brooks/Cole.

Cottone, R. R. (1992). *Theories and paradigms of counseling and psychotherapy.* Boston: Allyn & Bacon.

Dinkmeyer, D., & Dinkmeyer, D., Jr. (1985). Adlerian psychotherapy and counseling. In S. Lynn & J. Garske (Eds.), *Contemporary psychotherapies: Models and methods.* Columbus, OH: Merrill/ Macmillan.

Dinkmeyer, D., Dinkmeyer, D., Jr., & Sperry, L. (1987). *Adlerian counseling and psychotherapy.* Columbus, OH: Merrill/Macmillan.

Dinkmeyer, D., & Losoncy, L. (1980). *The encouragement book: Becoming a positive person.* Englewood Cliffs, NJ: Prentice-Hall.

D'Zurilla, T., & Goldfried, M. (1971). Problem solving and behavior modification. *Journal of Abnormal Psychology, 78,* 107–116.

Ellis, A. (1977). *The handbook of rational–emotive therapy.* New York: Springer.

Ellis, A. (1984). Rational–emotive therapy (RET) and pastoral counseling: A reply to Richard Wessler. *Personnel and Guidance Journal, 62,* 266–267.

Ellis, A. (1986a). An emotional control card for inappropriate and appropriate emotions in using rational–emotive imagery. *Journal of Counseling and Development, 65,* 205–206.

Ellis, A. (1986b). Fanaticism that may lead to a nuclear holocaust: The contributions of scientific counseling and psychotherapy. *Journal of Counseling and Development, 65,* 146–151.

Ellis, A. (1987). The impossibility of achieving consistently good mental health. *American Psychologist, 42*(4), 364–375.

Ellis, A. (1995). Rational–emotive therapy. In R. Corsini & D. Wedding (Eds.), *Current psychotherapies* (5th ed., pp. 162–196). Itasca, IL: Peacock.

Ellis, A., & Yeager, R. (1989). *Why some therapies don't work: The dangers of transpersonal psychology.* Buffalo, NY: Prometheus.

Fadiman, J. (1980). The transpersonal stance. In R. Walsh & F. Vaughn (Eds.), *Beyond ego: Transpersonal dimensions in psychology* (pp. 175–181). Los Angeles: J. P. Tarcher.

Fontana, D., & Slack, I. (1996). The need for transpersonal psychology. *Bulletin of the British Psychological Society, 9*(6).

Foote, W. (1996). Guided-imagery therapy. In B. Scotton, B. Chinen, & J. Battista (Eds.), *Textbook of transpersonal psychiatry and psychology* (pp. 355–365). New York: Basic Books.

Fulton, P. R. (1989, November/December). Recent transpersonal dissertations. *Common Boundary, 7*(6), 29–31.

Gilliland, B. E., James, R. K., & Bowman, J. T. (1994). *Theories and strategies in counseling and psychotherapy* (3rd ed.). Boston: Allyn & Bacon.

Goodwin, L. (1986). A holistic perspective for the provision of rehabilitation counseling services. *Journal of Applied Rehabilitation Counseling, 17*(2), 29–35.

Gordon, T. (1974). *Teacher effectiveness training.* New York: Wyden.

Grof, S. (Ed.). (1988). *Human survival and consciousness evolution.* Albany: State University of New York Press.

Harris, T. (1967). *I'm OK you're OK.* New York: Harper & Row.

Hendricks, K. (1993). Cross-cultural counseling: A transpersonal approach. In B. Weinhold & G. Hendricks (Eds.), *Counseling and psychotherapy: A transpersonal approach* (2nd ed., pp. 205–220). Denver: Love.

Holden, J., & Ivey, A. E. (1997, Spring). Summit on Spirituality Phase II. *Aces Spectrum Newsletter, 57*(3).

James, M., & Jongeward, D. (1971). *Born to win: Transactional analysis with Gestalt experiments.* Reading, MA: Addison-Wesley.

Kelly, E. (1995). *Spirituality and religion in counseling and psychotherapy: Diversity in theory and practice.* Alexandria, VA: American Counseling Association.

Lazarus, A. (1989). Multimodal therapy. In R. Corsini & D. Wedding (Eds.), *Current psychotherapies* (4th ed., pp. 503–544). Itasca, IL: Peacock.

Lu, F. (1996). Transpersonal psychiatry in psychiatric residency settings. In B. Scotton, A. Chinen, & J. Battista (Eds.), *Textbook of transpersonal psychiatry and psychology* (pp. 381–395). New York: Basic Books.

Maslow, A. (1971). *The farther reaches of human nature.* New York: Viking Compass.

Meichenbaum, D. H. (1977). *Cognitive and behavior modification.* New York: Plenum.

Morrison, D. A. (1986). A holistic and relational model of health and holiness. *Studies in Formative Spirituality: The Journal of Ongoing Formation, 7*(2), 239–251.

Mosak, H. H. (1995). Adlerian psychotherapy. In R. J. Corsini & D. Wedding (Eds.), *Current psychotherapies* (5th ed., pp. 51–94). Itasca, IL: Peacock.

O'Donnell, J. (1988). The holistic health movement: Implications for counseling theory and practice. In R. Hayes & R. Aubrey (Eds.), *New directions for counseling and human development* (pp. 365–382). Denver: Love.

Patterson, C. H. (1986). *Theories of counseling and psychotherapy.* New York: Harper & Row.

Sharp, D. (1994, May 1). Hurry-up harmony. *Health Magazine, 8,* 38.

Shertzer, B., & Stone, S. C. (1980). *Fundamentals of counseling* (3rd ed.). Boston: Houghton Mifflin Co.

Siegel, B. (1986). *Love, medicine, and miracles: Lessons learned about self-healing from a surgeon's experience with exceptional patients.* New York: Harper & Row.

Stirch-Stasko, M. (1996, November). Spiritually sensitive counseling: Pragmatic considerations. *Counseling and Human Development, 29,* 3.

Stensrud, R., & Stensrud, K. (1984, March). Holistic health through holistic counseling: Toward a unified theory. *Personnel and Guidance Journal, 62,* 421–424.

Tart, C. (1992). *Transpersonal psychologies.* New York: HarperCollins.

Travis, J., & Ryan, R. (1988). *Wellness Workbook* (2nd ed.). Berkeley, CA: Ten Speed Press.

Vaughn, F. (1980). Transpersonal psychotherapy: Context, content, and process. In R. Walsh & F. Vaughn (Eds.), *Beyond ego: Transpersonal dimensions in psychology* (pp. 182–189). Los Angeles: J. P. Tarcher.

Vaughn, F. (1984). The transpersonal perspective. In S. Grof (Ed.), *Ancient wisdom, modern science* (pp. 24–31). Albany, NY: State University of New York Press.

Walsh, R. (1989a). Asian psychotherapies. In R. J. Corsini & D. Wedding (Eds.), *Current psychotherapies* (5th ed., pp. 387–390). Itasca, IL: Peacock.

Walsh, R. (1989b). Psychological chauvinism and nuclear holocaust: A response to Albert Ellis and defense of nonrational–emotive therapies. *Journal of Counseling and Development, 67,* 338–339.

Walsh, R. (1996c). Meditation research: The state of the art. In B. Scotton, A. Chinen, & J. Battista (Eds.), *Textbook of transpersonal psychiatry and psychology* (pp. 167–175). New York: Basic Books.

Walsh, R., & Vaughn, E. (Eds.). (1980). *Beyond ego: Transpersonal dimensions in psychology.* Los Angeles: J. P. Tarcher.

Washburn, M. (1995). *The ego and the dynamic ground: A transpersonal theory of human development* (2nd ed.). Albany, NY: SUNY Press.

Weil, A. (1996). *Spontaneous healing.* New York: Fawcett.

Weinhold, B. (1993). Human development: A transpersonal perspective. In B. Weinhold & G. Hendricks (Eds.), *Counseling and psychotherapy: A transpersonal approach* (2nd ed., pp. 45–74). Denver: Love.

Weinhold, B., & Hendricks, G. (Eds.). (1993). *Counseling and psychotherapy: A transpersonal approach* (2nd ed.). Denver: Love.

Wilber, K. (1977). *Toward a spectrum of consciousness.* Wheaton, IL: Quest.

Wilber, K. (1989). Let's nuke the transpersonalists: A response to Albert Ellis. *Journal of Counseling and Development, 67,* 332–335.

Wilber, K. (1995). *Sex, ecology, and spirituality.* Boston: Shambala Press.

Wilber, K., Engler, J., & Brown, D. (Eds.). (1986). *Transformations of consciousness: Conventional and contemplative perspectives on development.* Boston: New Science Library.

chapter 12

focus on

GROUP WORK

- How does group counseling differ from other kinds of counseling?
- What different types of group work can counselors do?
- What are the advantages and disadvantages of working with groups?
- What skills do group counselors need?

Most of us belong to many groups for a variety of reasons. Before reading this chapter, take a few moments and list all the groups of which you are currently a member. Include on this list family, social, academic, business, athletic, religious, and ethnic groups. Without too much difficulty, you might come up with 10 or more groups to which you belong. Since groups are such an important part of our lives, it is not too surprising that in the field of counseling, working in groups is an approach used in an increasing number of ways to help people. The growth of therapeutic groups is considered by some to be an indication of our failure to provide close, meaningful relationships with our families, friends, and co-workers, and a failure of people to allow emotional contact to emerge naturally and spontaneously (Starak, 1988). On the other hand, the expanded use of group work in schools in the form of cooperative learning and in business and industry in the form of teamwork indicates the increasing awareness of the value of group work to enhance our society. Because of the increasing use of group work, the present professional charge is that "all counselors, regardless of career aspirations, should possess a set of core competencies in group work" (Conyne, Wilson, Kline, Morran, & Ward, 1993).

This chapter describes the origins of group work, the advantages and disadvantages of working in groups, the types of groups, basic group counselor competencies, group dynamics, and leadership styles. Groups in education, agencies, and business and industry are considered here. Then chapter 13 will describe a special type of group work, that of family and relationship counseling.

ORIGINS OF GROUP WORK

The origin of groups can be traced to the beginning of humankind when people banded together in tribes for survival and protection. The Greeks used the group approach as a vehicle for understanding interpersonal relations among other phenomena in the universe. Early religious sects used groups in schools, churches, and especially in monasteries to develop and teach religious doctrine. As society changed from rural and agrarian to industrial, intergroup cooperation became more of a necessity. Guilds, trades, unions, and other professional groups gradually developed. People had to work together to produce goods and trade. The pattern continues; contemporary society is composed of a multitude of groups, including economic, political, family, work, leisure, and therapy groups.

Therapy Groups—Pioneers

There is a lack of agreement as to who is the unequivocal father of group psychotherapy. Cohen and Smith (1976) list Joseph Pratt, Alfred Adler, Jacob Moreno, Trigant Burrow, and Cody Marsh as the most often cited founders of group psychotherapy. The early founders, however, did not practice group psychotherapy as it is practiced today. Most of these pioneers used groups to give inspirational talks or to present brief lectures to patients in hospital settings, approximating what is now called group guidance or psychological education.

The onset of World War II brought a dramatic increase in the use of group psychotherapy. In Great Britain, a group of psychiatrists at Northfield, a treatment center for psychiatric casualties of war, began experimenting with their patients using group psychotherapy. Some advocated an analytic group approach and looked beyond the group to the community as a whole. Others used an approach based on the group leader being tentative, evasive, and completely noncommittal. This methodology encouraged transference and created tension and frustration among group members, which gradually and subtly led the group to a resolution of its problems (Cohen & Smith, 1976). Alfred Adler was probably the first therapist to stress the importance of interpersonal relationships in mental health. Adler used interpersonal techniques in the training of therapists.

Jacob Moreno was an actor who became a therapist. He has been one of the major influences in group psychotherapy. Moreno founded a theoretical approach to groups called **psychodrama,** an approach in which clients are participants in a variety of dramatic situations leading to therapeutic outcomes (Moreno, 1983). In 1931 Moreno founded the first journal devoted to groups, *Impromptu.* It is currently published as *Group Psychotherapy.* Moreno had a profound influence on Fritz Perls, the founder of Gestalt therapy, who borrowed many of Moreno's dramatic techniques.

Birth of Laboratory Training

Kurt Lewin (1890–1947), a German-born and -educated psychologist, became director of the Massachusetts Institute of Technology's Center for Group Dynamics in 1944. Lewin developed a field theory approach to groups. **Field theory,** as defined by Lewin (1951), is a method for analyzing causal relations in the context of given situations. In 1947 Lewin and his colleague Leland Bradford received grants from the Office of Naval Research and the National Education Association to pursue the study of group dynamics. The National Training Laboratories (NTL) opened in the summer of 1947 at Bethel, Maine, shortly after Lewin's death. NTL was designed to study the factors that affect small group dynamics. **Laboratory training,** the idea that specific leadership skills can be developed to bring about interpersonal change, was one significant NTL outcome. The **T** (training) **group,** where individuals came together to learn how to work in groups to influence interpersonal change, became the most well-known type of laboratory training. Much of this work continues today in the form of organizational development and leadership training for business, industry, education, and government. In such settings, many counselors are using their group work training to improve the work environment and productivity (see chapter 16).

The Human Potential Movement

The **human potential movement** that began in the 1960s is based on the beliefs that most human beings use a very small part of their capabilities and that through a broad spectrum of techniques their potential can be released. Collectively, the practitioners of this approach and their methods and techniques have come to be known as the human potential movement. Its roots are based on the teachings of Jacob Moreno (1983), Frederick Perls (1969), Abraham Maslow (1962), Carl Rogers (1970), and William Schutz (1980), among others. Activities emanating from this movement include encounter and marathon groups.

Schutz (1980) defines an **encounter group** as a method of relating based on openness and honesty, self-awareness, self-responsibility, awareness of the body, attention to feelings, and emphasis on the here and now. Encounter groups are designed to help normal individuals remove blocks to their functioning better and to create conditions leading to a more satisfying use of human capabilities. Encounter groups use techniques from a wide variety of sources, including psychodrama, Gestalt therapy, T-groups, theater, and dance. They are often referred to as **personal growth groups.** Although aspects of encounter groups are still used in current group practice, the encounter group movement is a thing of the past (Yalom, 1995).

The marathon group is basically an intensified encounter group that meets from eight hours straight to an entire weekend, breaking at most for meals and short naps. The goals of marathon groups are to help members become aware of their masks and facades, give these up, and become more genuine. The marathon process helps participants lower their defenses and become more authentic.

BASIC TYPES OF GROUPS

Group work is defined as "a broad professional practice that refers to the giving of help or the accomplishment of tasks in a group setting" (Conyne et al., 1992, p. 12). In 1991 the Association for Specialists in Group Work (ASGW) approved a revised set of standards for training group work specialists. As part of these standards, four types of groups were delineated. These are task groups, guidance or psychoeducational groups, counseling groups, and psychotherapy groups (Conyne et al., 1992).

Task Groups

In **task groups,** or work groups, the focus "is on the application of group dynamics principles and processes to improve the practice and the accomplishment of identified goals" (Conyne et al., 1992, p. 13). This type of group includes learning groups, T-groups, community organizations, discussion groups, committees, planning groups, and task forces.

Guidance/Psychoeducational Groups

Guidance groups are generally preventive and educate group participants about potential threats such as AIDS or the consequences of drug use and abuse; however, these groups may also be developmental in nature, such as a group to help elementary students prepare for the transition to junior high school. Guidance groups may also be used to help students cope with an immediate life crisis such as the suicide of a classmate or the aftermath of a hurricane. The goal of these groups is to prevent psychological disturbances. Since these groups provide psychological education, they are often referred to as **psychoeducational groups.**

Counseling/Interpersonal Problem-Solving Groups

The goals of **counseling groups,** or interpersonal problem-solving groups, are to help participants resolve the usual, yet often difficult, problems of living through interpersonal support and problem solving and to improve problem-solving skills to better handle future problems. These groups deal with developmental and personal issues, which are not severe including educational, career, and social concerns.

Psychotherapy Groups

The goal of **psychotherapy groups,** or personality reconstruction groups, is to help individual group members remediate deep-seated psychological problems. Major personality dimensions of each individual group member may be reconstructed in a successful psychotherapy group (Conyne et al., 1992, p. 19).

Related Groups

Support groups deal with special populations and require different approaches than preventive or developmental groups. They function to provide information, comfort, and connectedness with others who are experiencing similar circumstances. Some examples include groups for relatives of substance abusers, families of Alzheimer's patients, adult children of alcoholics (ACOAs), victims of child abuse, and rape victims. Support groups generally have trained leaders who facilitate the interaction among group members.

   Self-help groups are a unique form of support group, since they generally have no formally trained or designated leaders. Self-help groups such as Alcoholics Anonymous, Overeaters Anonymous, and Gamblers Anonymous work for specific desirable changes in group members while providing support and encouragement. Self-help groups have experienced phenomenal growth in recent years.

GROUP COUNSELOR COMPETENCIES

The set of professional standards approved by ASGW in 1991 contains two levels of competencies and related training. First, the Core Group Competencies in general group work describe a minimum set of group competencies and minimal training requirements necessary for all counselors. Second, there are prescribed competencies for each of the four types of groups. The training standards in group work for all counselors are listed in Table 12.1.

Core Group Work Training Requirements

Core training in group work should include at least one course to learn the knowledge and skills competencies listed in Table 12.1. Knowledge and skills should also be attained through supervised practice. The practice domain should include observation of and participation in a group experience, which can occur in a classroom setting. The minimum amount of supervised practice should be 10 clock hours. The recommended amount of supervised practice is 20 clock hours (ASGW, 1992).

WHY WORK WITH GROUPS?

There are many advantages to working in groups; however, as in most approaches to counseling, there are trade-offs. The following are summaries of the positive and negative aspects of doing group work.

Advantages

People do not live in a vacuum—many basic human needs can be met only through involvement with other human beings. The group gives meaning to each member's existence. It provides a safe atmosphere for candid feedback, interpersonal risk, and new behaviors that can then be incorporated into members' daily lives. The group is a social milieu that parallels the milieu of a group member's real world. Group members interact with other members in the same functional and dysfunctional ways they do in the real world. The group becomes an ideal laboratory for learning about interpersonal behaviors and for facilitating the transfer of these learnings more readily to the outside lives of group members. Group members improve interpersonal skills as well as intrapersonal skills.

The group is an ideal place for reality testing, to see how each member's reality matches the perception of others and vice versa. The group allows members to go beyond their own concerns, reach out, and become concerned for others; this process is growth-engendering and therapeutic.

Groups encompass a wide range of needs for all age groups and populations. They are adaptable to many helping environments and programs, such as schools, colleges, mental health centers, correctional institutions, drug or alcohol treatment programs, and employment agencies. Practitioners can reach many persons in a group setting within a specific block of time and at less cost; the cost of group counseling is generally substantially less than individual counseling.

Groups provide a number of safety factors that facilitate individual growth and development. Initially there is a feeling of safety and security when members realize that they aren't the only ones who have a problem. Since only one or two persons are the center of attention at any given time, group members can more easily take risks. Meanwhile, a vicarious learning and identification process takes place in the other members as a result of observing the interaction of other members. Often clients are more willing to discuss feelings

TABLE 12.1   Group counselor competencies.

Knowledge Competencies

1. State for the four major group work specializations the distinguishing characteristics of each, the commonalities shared by all, and the appropriate instances of which each is to be used.
2. Identify the basic principles of group dynamics.
3. Discuss the basic therapeutic ingredients of groups.
4. Identify the personal characteristics of group workers that have an impact on members' knowledge of personal strengths, weaknesses, biases, values, and their effects on others.
5. Describe the specific ethical issues that are unique to group work.
6. Discuss the body of research on group work and how it relates to one's academic preparation in either school counseling, student personnel education, community counseling, mental health counseling, or other specialized studies.
7. Define the process components involved in typical stages of a group's development (i.e., characteristics of group interaction and group roles).
8. Describe the major facilitative and debilitative roles that group members may take.
9. State the advantages and disadvantages of group work and the circumstances for which it is indicated or contraindicated.
10. Detail therapeutic forces of group work.
11. Identify principles and strategies for recruiting and screening prospective group members.
12. Detail the importance of group and member evaluation.
13. Deliver a clear and concise definition of group work.
14. Deliver a clear, concise, and complete definition of each of the four work specialties.
15. Explain and clarify the purpose of a particular form of group work.

Skill Competencies

All counselors are able to effectively

1. Encourage participation of group members.
2. Observe and identify group process events.
3. Attend to and acknowledge group member behavior.
4. Clarify and summarize group member statements.
5. Open and close group sessions.
6. Impart information in the group when necessary.
7. Model effective group leader behavior.
8. Engage in appropriate self-disclosure in the group.
9. Give and receive feedback in the group.
10. Ask open-ended questions in the group.
11. Empathize with group members.
12. Confront group members' behavior.
13. Help group members attribute meaning to their experience.
14. Help group members integrate and apply learning.
15. Demonstrate ASGW ethical and professional standards in group practice.
16. Keep the group on task in accomplishing its goals.

Adapted from "Group Counselor Competencies," from ASG: Professional Standards for the Training of Group Workers, 1992, *Journal for Specialist in Group Work, 17*(1), p. 13–14. Copyright © 1992 by American Counseling Association. Adapted with permission. No further reproduction authorized without written permission of the American Counseling Association.

and concerns in groups of peers than in individual counseling. Learning can also be more potent in groups due to the high intensity of interactions, the support and acceptance of others, and the collective experience of group members. There usually is greater support for growth and change because of the strength in numbers and concurrently, greater acceptance and empathy. All of this gives group members a feeling of safety for them to clear their problems and concerns.

Groups can provide a sense of belonging. Group members feel part of a social network that satisfies needs of intimacy and relatedness. In effective groups there is immediate interpersonal feedback, which facilitates personal exploration, growth, and development.

Disadvantages

The group counselor has less situational control. Because there are more people, the counselor must pay more attention to what is happening. To help deal with this situation, many counselors insist on working with a colleague who cofacilitates the group. The group counselor must also balance the need for freedom with the need for structure. This balance becomes a paradox: to function well, individuals must sacrifice themselves for the good of the group; yet for groups to function well, the needs of individuals must not be forgotten (Rutan & Groves, 1989). Each group member receives less attention because of the obvious time limitations.

Confidentiality is more difficult to guarantee in a group than in individual counseling and is almost impossible to enforce. Coercion and peer pressure toward conformity are parts of every group process. Although a certain amount of peer pressure can help establish positive **norms** (guidelines and rules for the group), the process often referred to as **groupthink**—the forcing of group opinion on all members of the group—can curb individual initiative, autonomy, and creativity. There is a danger of group members' conforming to norms that may be distorted, inappropriate, or illogical. Shared reality can take precedence over individual perception. For example, a group norm emphasizing competition and one-upmanship can become established rather than individual perceptions that stress cooperation.

Group work is not for everyone in every situation. With the exception of some inpatient situations, groups are not advised for persons who are paranoid, brain-damaged, acutely psychotic, sociopathic, suicidal, hypochondriacal, or narcissistic.

Often a group will single out certain members as scapegoats. This may be a consequence of the group counselor's failure to explore hostility and may be reinforced by the failure of the group counselor to intervene when members gang up on other members.

Group leaders or group counselors may not have the proper training to lead groups. They may fail to screen members or prepare them properly for participating in a group. They may not be able to handle the complexity of group dynamics or destructive behaviors in a group such as angry aggressiveness, inappropriate rescuing, passivity, and monopolizing. Group leaders who are not properly trained can cause problems that may discourage individuals from seeking help in the future.

All in all, then, are groups a positive or a negative force? According to Rutan and Groves (1989) they can be either or both, depending on their size, composition, organization, purpose, lifetime, leadership, and capacity for intimacy. Many disadvantages of group work can be minimized or even eliminated with the use of properly trained leaders, careful planning, appropriate precautions, and good supervision.

THERAPEUTIC FORCES IN GROUPS

The many positive dynamic forces involved in groups can be called curative, healing, or therapeutic. Yalom (1995) identified 11 elements that account for change in group members, which he labeled **therapeutic factors.** According to Yalom these therapeutic factors are applicable to all of the schools of group counseling. Yalom's factors include the following:

- instillation of hope
- universality (others have similar problems and concerns)
- imparting of information
- altruism (the principle of living for the good of others)
- corrective recapitulation (of one's original family group)
- development of socializing techniques
- imitative behavior
- interpersonal learning
- group cohesiveness
- catharsis (emotional purging)
- existential factors (self-responsibility)

Corey and Corey (1997) have identified numerous forces, which they also call therapeutic factors, based on self-reports from group members. The factors are hope. commitment to change, willingness to risk and trust, caring, acceptance, empathy, intimacy, power, freedom to experiment, feedback, catharsis, meaning attribution, learning interpersonal skills, humor, self-disclosure, confrontation, and group cohesion. Corey and Corey view three of these factors as especially crucial to successful outcomes of groups: group cohesion, self-disclosure, and confrontation. The next section elaborates on group cohesion, confrontation, interpersonal skills, and universality as particularly important factors in group development; self-disclosure is discussed in chapter 7.

Cohesion

Forsyth (1983) defines **group cohesion** as the strength of forces that bind members to a group. Included in this are the attractiveness of the group as a whole as well as the attraction of each member to every other member. It is a firmly established sense of "we-ness" characterized by highly valuing commitment, diversity, and trust. Group members perceive the group as special, viable, and productive. Group members are committed not only to themselves but also to each other. Diversity is accepted, and differences are valued. Trust has been developed during early stages of the group. Group members have weathered storms together and have not only survived but also transcended. In groups in which cohesion is lacking, group members become discouraged and frustrated with members who drop out or who have poor attendance.

Universality

Universality, the idea that no one has a problem that is totally unique, can be an important factor in group work. Often people entering counseling groups perceive their own problems and concerns as strange and unique. They view themselves as different and alone in their suffering. As the group process develops, members soon realize that their problems are not so unique after all. Yalom (1995) cynically refers to this phenomenon with the cliché "misery loves company." This realization creates a strong sense of relief and lessens fears, anxieties, and feelings of alienation. Group members realize that they are human also and that other people have the same problems, concerns, fantasies, nightmares, and impulses. Yalom (1995) states that "there is no human deed or thought which is fully outside the experience of other people" (p. 8).

Interpersonal Skills

The focus in groups is often on the intrapersonal concerns of individual members. Interpersonal learning resulting from improved interpersonal skills, however, is one of the major means through which group members grow and change. Group members know a great deal about themselves—they live with themselves 24 hours a day—yet this knowledge is limited. Group members have facets of themselves about which they have little or no knowledge. Sometimes other people perceive these areas accurately, but often others' perceptions are distorted and incomplete. (Note the discussion on transference in chapter 5.) Harry Stack Sullivan (1953) used the term **parataxic distortions** to refer to peoples' tendencies to distort their perceptions of others. Parataxic distortion is similar to the Freudian concept of transference but is broader. It takes into account all interpersonal relationships and includes the distortion of interpersonal reality in response to interpersonal needs. It also includes the transferring of attitudes from real-life figures.

Through taking interpersonal risks by using the skills of self-disclosing, giving and receiving feedback, and self-observing, group members obtain insight into and awareness of their behaviors and the impact of their behaviors on others. They realize that they are responsible for their own interpersonal existence and have the option to change. They also learn how to put these changes into effect. As a result, perceptions of all group members undergo change and become more objective.

Confrontation

Perhaps the most crucial of all interpersonal skills is **confrontation,** giving both positive and negative feedback. In groups in which there is only support and empathy, stagnation often occurs, and the developmental process of the group is impeded. Egan (1970) states that mature people learn to challenge themselves and their own productive ways of relating to others. There are always areas not open to mature people's awareness and times when individuals fail to challenge themselves, but mature individuals are open to constructive confrontation from others and are appreciative of such confrontation. Some group members avoid giving negative feedback in terms of how they are perceiving others and how they are affected by others; these people cheat group members of information that would be helpful for the members' growth. Effective feedback is a skill that must be used constructively. It does not mean putting down others in a reckless manner, attacking others and then retreating, attributing motives to others' behavior (mind reading), hurting others intentionally, or pressing others to change. Egan (1975) speaks of **caring confrontation,** when the personal relationship has been established and the feedback is given with genuineness and respect. (See chapter 7 for additional information on confrontation.)

Ideas in *action*

The vast majority of patients (and therapists) are highly uncomfortable when expressing or receiving anger. The therapist's task is to harness conflict and use it in the service of growth. One important principle is to find the right level: too much or too little conflict is counterproductive.

Yalom (1995, p. 350)

How comfortable are you in dealing with confrontation and conflict? As a beginning group leader, what would you do if conflict arose in your group?

STAGES OF GROUP DEVELOPMENT

Group counseling is a developmental process just as individual counseling is (see chapter 5). Also, just as in individual counseling, there are numerous developmental models that describe different stages in the group's life. Most models encompass three to five stages.

A five-stage model of group development, based on Yalom (1995), Trotzer (1977), and Tuckman (1965), is suitable for studying all types of groups. In actual practice, the stages do not flow as neatly and orderly as presented. There is often overlap between stages. It is not uncommon for a group to remain stuck in certain stages or even to regress temporarily to an earlier stage. Group member behavior and group leader behavior for each stage are presented.

Stage 1—Orientation/Forming

The first stage of group development is the coming together, or **forming stage.** It is in this stage that group members become oriented to the beginning of the group process and to each other.

Group Member Behavior (Entry-Involvement)

The immediate concerns for group members in stage 1 usually center on the four I's—inclusion, identity, influence, and intimacy. Group members often experience generalized anxiety over intimacy and closeness, which is characterized by tentative involvement with other group members and superficial attempts at closeness. It is difficult for most people to share those deep inner parts of themselves under any circumstances, yet they join groups to do just that. Group members often are preoccupied with how they fit in. Are they liked or not liked? How much influence do they have in the group? Will they be listened to? Will they be accepted? Can they really be themselves or must they put up a front? What are the ground rules here? Where is the danger, support, or safety? Members generally need to resolve at least partially the four I issues before constructive risk taking can occur. Members usually make some initial attempts at revealing themselves to see if their concerns will be attended to. They want to assure themselves that the group is indeed a safe and secure place for them to express their thoughts and feelings. The establishment of trust is the main prerequisite for further group development.

Group Leader Behavior

The core conditions that are the basis for success in individual counseling are also the basis for success in group counseling. The counselor's self—who the counselor is—becomes a crucial factor in laying the groundwork for a successful group process. The counselor must model therapeutic behavior by being open, listening actively, and demonstrating acceptance, positive regard, and genuineness. The leader must deal with group members' four I's by making the group a secure and safe place. The leader must also be able to instill a sense of hope in group members. If the leader has self-confidence and has faith in the group process, these attitudes are communicated to the group with verbal and nonverbal behaviors and facilitate feelings of hopefulness among group members. The group leader will generally be more task oriented than relationship oriented to help the group through the first stage.

Stage 2—Transition/Storming

Yalom (1995) refers to the major themes in the **transition stage** of group development as those of dominance, control, and power. These are in contrast to the concerns of acceptance, approval, commitment, and the search for orientation, structure, and meaning of the first stage.

Group Member Behavior

In stage 2, group members continue to deal with stage 1 behaviors. Usually the impact is greater, with more anxiety and ambiguity. As the group members struggle to define themselves and establish norms, conflict begins to manifest itself. Often there are verbal attacks and challenges to the leader. Some group members might attempt to provoke the leader, shock, gain approval, or wrestle power from the leader. This type of behavior has caused this stage to often be referred to as the **storming stage** of group development. Participants observe the leader's reactions to all in order to find shortcomings in the leader. Even though group members are still concerned about safety, they also want to become more involved and committed. Group members make some tentative self-disclosures and show greater openness in discovering themselves and others. Group members seem to alternate between fight and flight, assertiveness or aggressiveness, and withdrawal or avoidance. Resistance and defensiveness are usually quite strong, and the norms and cohesiveness of the group at this stage revolve around member protection and avoidance of perceived threat.

Group Leader Behavior

In the second stage group leaders must demonstrate an attitude that is not defensive and allow group members to express their anxieties and resistant feelings fully. If the group leader is defensive or evasive in dealing with member confrontation, then trust will not develop, and the group process will not move forward. The group leader should help the group look at its own process so that the group members have a greater awareness of exactly what is going on in the group. The group leader also needs to encourage and reinforce growth-enhancing behaviors among members such as acceptance and respect, constructive feedback, expression of disagreement, self-disclosure, and self-exploration. In this stage the leader strives to become more relationship oriented. Depending on the theoretical approach used, the task orientation of the leader may begin to fade.

Stage 3—Cohesiveness/Norming

If the problems and concerns of the second stage are successfully handled, group members move into the third stage of group development, **cohesiveness** (Yalom, 1995). Cohesiveness in groups is the equivalent of a strong therapeutic alliance in individual counseling. Group members demonstrate greater self-responsibility, risk taking, and openness during this stage. A greater sense of cohesiveness is experienced after members' commitment and caring have been tested, and trust has been established in the previous stages. During this stage the **norms,** or rules for how the group will continue to function, become fixed.

Group Member Behavior

This stage is characterized by more self-disclosure on the part of group members. Often secrets which are difficult to express are revealed. There is considerable concern when any members are missing. Silent members are encouraged to interact with others. The cohesiveness established in this stage is based on a firmly established sense of we-ness with members highly valued as individuals and the group highly valued as a whole. This is different from the false sense of consensus in the earlier stages of the group process. Group members now become committed to helping themselves and each other. There is a strong sense of interdependency. Trotzer (1977) reports a study by Lindt (1958) whose findings report that only group members who take responsibility in the helping process benefit from their group experience. In this atmosphere of trust, acceptance, and cohesiveness, group members begin to examine their problems more closely and deeply.

Group Leader Behavior

The group leader in stage 3 facilitates deeper levels of self-exploration and helps members personalize their experiences. Sometimes group members develop such a strong sense of cohesiveness here that any intermember conflict or hostility is blocked. The group leader, therefore, must demonstrate high levels of immediacy and confrontation in order to help the group move into the working stage and not stagnate into what Yalom (1995) calls a "ritualistic embrace." This stage is characterized by high relationship behaviors on the part of the leader and a relatively low number of task-oriented interventions.

Stage 4—Working/Performing

The **working,** or **performing, stage** is characterized by group members' willingness to experiment with new behaviors and attitudes. The group leader is seen more objectively and is no longer viewed as a threat. As a result there is less dependence on the leader for direction and a greater egalitarian relationship among everyone in the group.

Group Member Behavior

In the working stage, group members exhibit high levels of self-disclosure, honesty, spontaneity, acceptance, and responsibility. Hostility and resentment are expressed in a constructive manner. Group members support and encourage attempts at change. Yalom (1995) refers to a group manifesting these characteristics as a "mature work group." There are occasional regressions into earlier stages, which are balanced by the present work and progress. The group has become an effective change agent.

Group Leader Behavior

The main tasks of the group leader in the fourth stage are to facilitate thorough discussions of problems, to suggest possible alternatives, and to examine consequences of those alternatives. At the same time, the group leader must help members to transfer learning to the world outside the group as well as support and encourage experimentation, risk, and change. Because the group is functioning in a cohesive manner at this stage, the leader tends to have a low profile with relatively few task or relationship interventions.

Stage 5—Adjourning/Terminating

The final stage of group development is the **adjourning, or terminating, stage.** This stage may be predetermined (for example, a group that is scheduled to meet for only eight sessions), or it may come as a result of the group's having fulfilled all of its stated purposes.

Group Member Behavior

As individual group members satisfy their goals, the usefulness of the group becomes diminished. Although group members may even realize that the group no longer serves the same purpose as it had originally, they may still attempt to cling together because of the strong group identity and close interpersonal relationships. The main tasks of the group as well as of separate individuals are to complete unfinished business, deal with feelings of loss and separation, and make future plans for interpersonal contact after the group ends. Sometimes group members will begin to distance themselves from each other as termination approaches, refusing to bring up new business and prematurely mourning their loss. Such grief behaviors need to be addressed in the group. Even though the end of the group is a great loss, the experience of a successful group will remain with the participants forever.

Group Leader Behavior

The group leader must be able to focus the group on its feelings regarding loss and separation and help the group decide how to end. Yalom (1995) states that the task of the group leader prior to the final session is "to repeatedly call the members' attention to the impending termination" (p. 374). Since the leader is a model, the leader must be willing to self-disclose about separation feelings. The group leader needs to provide time for group members to complete any unfinished business with the leader or with each other. Although all unfinished business may not get resolved, the leader can assist group members in at least providing some means for handling their unfinished business.

Finally, the group leader must help group members put in meaningful perspective what has occurred in the group and also help group members carry their learning forward.

LEADERSHIP STYLES AND FUNCTIONS

It seems as though everyone has a particular style of behavior when relating to groups of people. There also are certain leadership functions, or specialized types of interventions, that individuals tend to favor when working in group settings. The timing and nature of the styles and functions group leaders use can make a significant difference in the outcomes of group work.

Leadership Styles

In 1944 Kurt Lewin identified what for decades were considered the three basic types of leadership styles used in group work: **authoritarian,** leader centered; **democratic,** participant centered; and **laissez-faire,** no designated leadership. Research has attempted to determine which, if any, of these styles is clearly superior. Results from leadership effectiveness studies conducted at Ohio State University indicate that not one of these styles is inherently superior to the other two. What appears to be of most importance is the type of leadership style used at the different stages of group development (Stogdill & Coons 1957). Paul Hersey and Ken Blanchard (1972) have developed a leadership model based on the Ohio State studies. Following Hersey and Blanchard's model, the leader's behavior varies from stage to stage. At the beginning of a group, the forming stage, it may be advisable for a leader to take somewhat of an authoritarian role, be task centered, and not place much emphasis on developing strong relationships. As the group begins to mature through the storming and norming stages, the leader can become less task-oriented and put more emphasis on developing relationships through a more democratic leadership style. Finally, as the group develops a high level of maturity at the performing stage, the leader can reduce the emphasis on relationship skills and use a more laissez-faire style. This approach to group work of all types has been labeled the **situational leadership model** (Hersey, 1984). Becoming a situational leader means that you have to use yourself as an instrument. You have to be an astute observer of group dynamics throughout the process. You have to be flexible and skilled in adjusting your leadership style to relate more effectively to groups as they mature. You also have to be able to share and even give up responsibility for the groups with which you work. The situational leadership model is applicable in all types of group work, and it is finding a great deal of favor in group leadership programs in business and industry as well as in parenting classes helping parents learn to cope with the development of a family.

Leadership Functions

Lieberman, Yalom, and Miles (1973) conducted the first large-scale controlled research study of the effectiveness of encounter groups. One result of the study was the identification of specific leadership functions. Four distinct leadership functions were identified:

1. *Emotional stimulation:* challenging, confronting, and intrusive modeling by personal risk taking and high self-disclosure
2. *Caring:* offering support, affection, praise, protection, warmth, acceptance, genuineness, and concern

3. *Meaning attribution:* explaining, clarifying, interpreting, providing a cognitive framework for change, and translating feelings and experiences into ideas
4. *Executive function:* setting limits, rules, norms, and goals; managing time; pacing; stopping; interceding; and suggesting procedures (Yalom, 1995)

The findings indicated that these functions had a very clear and direct relationship to group member outcomes. The higher the caring and the higher the meaning attribution, then the higher the positive results. Too much or too little emotional stimulation or executive function resulted in lower positive outcome (Yalom, 1995). The most successful group leaders demonstrated high amounts of caring and meaning attribution and moderate amounts of stimulation and executive function, regardless of theoretical orientation.

GROUP LEADERSHIP TECHNIQUES

Many group leadership techniques are identical to or only slightly different from the skills of individual counseling discussed in chapters 6 and 7. All of the attending, responding, and problem-solving skills are essential in working with groups; however, because group work has a much more complex interpersonal dimension and an added group dimension, there are a great many more intervention skills involved than in individual therapy. For example, group leaders may focus their responses on the group as a whole, on an interpersonal relationship, or on one individual in the group. The following are some selected counseling skills unique to group work.

Facilitating Communications in Groups

Group leaders have a responsibility to facilitate open communication patterns and to block destructive patterns. This is particularly crucial in the early stages of group development. Later, group members begin to take on much of this responsibility. Behaviors that are generally discouraged are the overuse of questions, gossiping, storytelling, and other there and then behaviors outside of the group experience; invasion of privacy; **band-aiding** or **red-crossing** (prematurely rescuing group members from working things out with each other); and **mind reading** (trying to guess what another group member is thinking). The group leader needs to model the giving of constructive feedback so that group members do not feel attacked or judged and are able to learn how to give feedback themselves.

Group Processing

Often, group leaders need to provide commentary on the processes of the group rather than make an interpersonal intervention. In describing what has been happening within the group itself, group leaders will speak of "the group," "we," or "us." Here are some examples of group processing:

- "The group seems to be avoiding deeper issues."
- "There seems to be a norm here that none of us confront Joe."

- "I wonder whether the group is needing a scapegoat?"
- "How does her statement affect (us) the group?"

Yalom (1995) states that the main purpose of making such statements is to get through impasses in the group process. He identifies two common impasses: anxiety-laden issues and anti-therapeutic group norms. When there are anxiety-laden issues in a group, the group members often deflect their anxiety by avoiding those issues. This has been called **group flight.**

Sometimes the group may establish norms that are anti-therapeutic, such as members' taking turns being the focus whether they want to or not or keeping the focus on the first issue raised in the group even though the issue has been dealt with sufficiently. In such cases the group leader can make an effective group intervention by specifically describing the anti-therapeutic norm or behaviors and their consequences. The group leader might also imply that the group should find alternative norms. In some instances, group leaders invite group members to make group process statements by asking, for example, "What's going on in the group right now?"

Directing Focus to the Here and Now

Most theoretical approaches place a strong emphasis on the here and now. In groups, progress is a result of the ongoing dynamics of the group process rather than on the expressed content of the group participants. Aliveness and change always take place in the here and now; obsession with the past and future divert energy from living in the present. Yalom (1995) suggests that working in the here and now is the power that energizes the therapy group. The group leader should have well-developed skills in identifying here and now behaviors and in directing group members' awareness to the here and now (Wig & Carroll, 1993). Group leaders should have a here and now awareness of themselves, of group members as individuals, of the interpersonal process (transactions among members and their potential meanings), and of other factors such as the physical environment. The group leader should actively direct the group focus to the here and now through asking focused questions; shifting focus of there and then interactions to here and now ones; experimentation; and group processing. The following are some examples of how the group leader can accomplish these tasks.

Focused Questions
- "What feelings are you aware of now?"
- "What do you want to happen right now?"
- "What reaction do you have to what Jane just said?"
- "How do you feel toward Mary right now?"
- "What's missing for you right now?"
- "What would you like from Jim right this moment?"

Shifting Focus
- "John, you are saying that you are often shy with people—who do you feel most shy with here, and how do you demonstrate this?"

- "Mary, you have said that you are an angry person. What does this mean for us here?"
- "You have said you had a lot of tender warm feelings inside—if you could, who would you most want to share those with in the group?"

Experimentation

Experimentation is always a here and now operation, because the group member is trying out new attitudes or behaviors in the present; these attitudes or behaviors are generating some immediate internal and external reaction.

To someone who has difficulty allowing others to get close and intimate with him, have the person complete the sentence with a different ending for each group member: "I would like you to go around to each group member and say, 'If I were to let you get close to me, then...,' or 'I don't let you get close to me because....'" After the experiment the member should be encouraged to share personal reactions and to solicit the reactions of other group members.

Universalizing

Group members often feel greatly relieved when they discover that they are not alone and that their concerns are similar to those of other group members. The group leader can facilitate this universality by soliciting information from other group members when one group member has expressed a feeling or concern about a particular situation.

SUSAN: "I feel so strange and different in the group because of all the problems I'm having with my family."

GROUP LEADER: "I wonder if there are other people in the group who are having similar problems with their families and how they feel in the group?"

Linking

Linking is a way of connecting the various feelings and concerns expressed by group members in such a way as to universalize experience. It requires the group leader to be alert to nonverbal as well as verbal behavior.

GROUP LEADER (TO GROUP): "I noticed a lot of heads nodding when Joan stated how anxious she was feeling about her final examinations. I sense you really identify with Joan in regard to your finals."

THEORETICAL APPROACHES TO GROUP COUNSELING

There are probably as many theoretical approaches to group counseling as there are to individual counseling. Most individual theories have a theoretical framework for working in groups similar to their individual theory. Many major theoretical approaches consider the use of groups as the preferred mode of treatment. Since the late 1960s, Carl Rogers and his person-centered approach have been focused almost completely on group work in various settings. Fritz Perls, in his development of Gestalt therapy, worked almost exclusively with groups. Transactional analysis has been predominantly a group approach from its inception. William Glasser's reality therapy has been based in large part on the work he did with groups in reformatories and public schools. Alfred Adler was one of the first to work with the family as a group. Behaviorists use groups as a source of behavior to model and as a place to practice new behaviors and receive immediate reinforcement. Even psychoanalysts view groups as offering greater opportunities for transference to occur. There are a number of books available that detail the various applications of individual theories to group work, such as Corey (1990), Gladding (1991), and Vander Kolk (1985). Many of these approaches take on a different focus than the interpersonal model.

The most rapidly developing approaches are brief group therapies. They tend to be psychoeducational rather than process oriented and more focused on problem solving than on interpersonal counseling. Brief approaches to groups have been around for many years; largely due to economic pressures brought on by managed care health plans and HMOs, they have become more important and more widely used. Additionally, the dropout rate in groups is extremely high. Up to 50 percent of clients remain in groups for only 12 or fewer meetings (Yalom, 1995). The duration of brief groups varies according to their goals. They all strive for efficiency, however, and are focused on goal attainment and current behaviors and problems. The best forum for learning the important aspects of the group (therapeutic factors, dynamics, and development) is in the interpersonal group, though.

SPECIAL CONCERNS IN GROUP WORK

Group work not only involves more participants, but it differs significantly from individual work in several other ways. These differences include group size, participant selection, time and duration of sessions, and ethical issues such as maintaining confidentiality.

Group Size

Task group size can vary considerably depending on the nature of the task. In some cases a very large group can be divided into subgroups. Similarly, guidance and psychoeducational groups can vary from three or four members to several hundred people in an auditorium. Group counseling and psychotherapy generally work best with six to eight members.

Participant Selection

Because of the various types of groups, there must be some type of participant selection process to ensure the success of the group. In the case of counseling and psychotherapy groups, it is generally necessary to interview potential clients before admitting them to the group. The interview is used to explain the purpose and process of the group to the potential client and to ascertain whether the given group is appropriate for the person.

In addition to considering the nature of the potential client's problems, the group counselor also needs to be aware of the person's style of interaction. A counselor should be careful not to accept more than one or two extremely verbal clients who might have a tendency to monopolize the group, or more than one or two extremely shy, quiet individuals who might rarely or never participate.

Length and Duration of Sessions

Whereas most individual counseling sessions are 50 minutes long, group sessions can vary significantly depending on the nature of the activity. A guidance session where the primary purpose is to give information about drug use and abuse might last about 40 minutes, but a marathon group might last 60 consecutive hours. Counseling and psychotherapy groups generally last from one to two hours.

A group guidance situation may involve one session, and an open-ended psychotherapy group may use ongoing sessions lasting for years. In an **open group** new members are added when existing members leave the group. **Closed groups** are designed to last a given number of sessions and accept no new members when vacancies occur. The trend is toward short-term, goal-directed closed groups.

Ethics

The ASGW has published a set of ethics governing the conduct of the different types of groups. A primary concern with groups, and with group counseling and psychotherapy in particular, is maintaining confidentiality. With so many participants in a group, it becomes difficult to ensure confidentiality. Counselors may be faced with the prospect of having to exclude a client from the group who violates the principle of maintaining confidentiality.

Problems in Evaluation of Group Work

Most group leaders shy away from evaluation of their groups because of concern that the evaluations will be negative and show the leaders to be ineffective. Yalom (1995), George and Dustin (1988), and others advocate helping students learn how to evaluate their work and be open to change based on these evaluations. Good evaluation studies of group counseling are lacking, however, and researchers have not advanced knowledge of the field in the last three decades despite many improvements in research methods (Bednar et al., 1987). Part of the problem is the difficulty of obtaining agreed-on definitions of process and outcome so that there can be meaningful evaluations. There is a lack of process and outcome instruments related specifically to group situations.

Studying a group is a more complex task than studying an individual counseling relationship. A group involves a multiplicity of communication patterns, and the interaction among members and the impact of behaviors are more difficult to trace. It is difficult to determine whether change in groups that continue over a period of time is the result of events and relationships outside the group setting or inside the group setting.

Attention to research on the effectiveness of group counseling and family counseling has been increasing. The next few years may see improved research methods and an increased volume of research on group work.

PROFESSIONAL ORGANIZATIONS

The Association for Specialists in Group Work (ASGW), an affiliate of the ACA, is a major professional organization serving the needs of group workers. In addition to formulating and publishing ethical and training standards, the organization also publishes a quarterly journal, the *Journal for Specialists in Group Work.* Student memberships are available. There is also an American Group Psychotherapy Association (AGPA).

SUMMARY

The importance of group work as part of the helping professions has been emphasized in this chapter. In particular, counselors are encouraged to develop competence in group work. A brief history of group work includes reference to the development of laboratory training and the human potential movement. The four types of groups, task, guidance/psychoeducational, counseling, and psychotherapy, are described along with the basic competencies for doing group work. The advantages of group work include safety; sharing; sense of belonging; social interaction; reality testing in a small, safe setting; and adaptability to a broad range of environments. Among the disadvantages are less control by the group leader, less individual attention and confidentiality, danger of group members' being singled out as scapegoats, and unqualified leaders.

The 11 curative factors that act as therapeutic forces in groups include cohesion, universality, interpersonal skills, and confrontation. Five stages of group development are presented along with appropriate group leader and group member behavior for each stage and leadership styles. The situational leadership model suggests that a group leader's task and relationship behaviors (or style) should vary according to the maturity level of the group. The four clusters of leader interventions, or leadership functions, are emotional stimulation, caring, meaning attribution, and executive function. The use and timing of these leadership functions are important in conducting successful groups.

Group leadership techniques dealing with group processing and directing focus to the here and now include interpretation, focused questions, shifting the focus experimentation, universalizing, and linking. Finally, group approaches and theories are examined.

QUESTIONS AND ACTIVITIES

1. What type of group work appeals to you at this time? Does the wide variety of opportunities available in group work influence what you perceive your work as a counselor to be? Are you concerned about mastering any of the basic competencies?

2. What might be some typical problem behaviors found in group members? How might a group leader deal effectively with these problem behaviors? Which problem behaviors might cause you the most difficulty as a group leader?

3. Observe a session of an ongoing group, such as a school committee or a church Sunday school meet-ing. Analyze the group process. What group techniques does the leader use? What nonverbal cues do you notice? Is the group cohesive? In which stage of group process is the group? What are some of the group norms?

4. Many counselors prefer to be individual counselors rather than group counselors. Assuming that you have appropriate training, would you have any reservations about initiating and leading groups? What do you believe your preference will be?

RECOMMENDED READINGS

Association for Specialists in Group Work. (1989). *Ethical guidelines for group counselors.* Washington, DC: American Counseling Association.

Association for Specialists in Group Work. (1992). ASGW standards for training group workers. *Journal for Specialists in Group Work, 17*(1), 12–19.

Conyne, R., Dye, H., Kline, W., Morran, D., Ward, D., & Wilson, F. (1992). ASGW standards for training group workers. *Journal for Specialists in Group Work, 17*(1), 10–11.

Conyne, R., Wilson, F., Kline, W., Morran, D., & Ward, D. (1993). Training group workers: Implications

of the new ASGW training standards for training and practice. *Journal for Specialists in Group Work, 18*(1), 11–23.

Corey, G. (1990). *Theory and practice of group counseling* (3rd ed.). Pacific Grove, CA: Brooks/Cole.

Gladding, S. (1991). *Group work: A counseling specialty.* Columbus, OH: Merrill.

Vander Kolk, C. (1985). *Introduction to group counseling and psychotherapy.* Columbus, OH: Merrill.

Wiggins, J., & Carroll, M. (1993). Back to the basics: Perceived and actual needs of group leaders. *Journal for Specialists in Group Work, 18*(1), 2–28.

INTERNET RESOURCES

Websites
American Group Psychotherapy Association <www.social.com/health/nhic/data/hr01000/hr0119.html>
Association for Specialists in Group Work <www. uc.edu/~wilson/asgw/index.html>
International Association for Group Psychotherapy <www.psych.mcgill.ca/labs/iagp/IAGP.html>

Psychodrama   <csep.sunyit.edu/~joel/asgpp.html>

Mailing Lists and Usenet Groups
Group Psychotherapy Discussion Group:
Send e-mail to <majordomo@freud.apa.org>.

REFERENCES

Association for Specialists in Group Work. (1992). ASGW Standards for Training Group Workers. *Journal for Specialists in Group Work, 17*(1), 12–19.

Bednar, R. L., Corey, G., Evans, N. J., Garcia, G., Pistole, M. C., Stockton, R., & Robison, F. F. (1987). Overcoming obstacles to the future development of research on group work. *Journal for Specialists in Group Work, 12,* 98–111.

Cohen, A. M., & Smith, D. R. (1976). *The critical incident in growth groups: Theory and technique.* San Diego: University Associates.

Conyne, R., Dye, H., Kline, W., Morran, D., Ward, D., & Wilson, F. (1992). ASGW standards for training group workers. *Journal for Specialists in Group Work, 17*(1), 10–11.

Conyne, R., Wilson, F., Kline, W., Morran, D., & Ward, D. (1993). Training group workers: Implications of the new ASGW training standards for training and practice. *Journal for Specialists in Group Work, 18*(1), 11–23.

Corey, G. (1990). *Theory and practice of group counseling* (3rd ed.). Pacific Grove, CA: Brooks/Cole.

Corey, G., & Corey, M. S. (1997). *Groups: Process and practice* (5th ed.). Monterey, CA: Brooks/Cole.

Egan, G. (1970). *Encounter group process for interpersonal growth.* Monterey, CA: Brooks/Cole.

Egan, G. (1975). *The skilled helper.* Monterey, CA: Brooks/Cole.

Forsyth, D. R. (1983). *An introduction to group dynamics.* Monterey, CA: Brooks/Cole.

George, R., & Dustin, D. (1988). *Group counseling: Theory and practice.* Englewood Cliffs, NJ: Prentice-Hall.

Gladding, S. (1991). *Group work: A counseling specialty.* Columbus, OH: Merrill.

Hersey, P. (1984). *The situational leader.* New York: Warner.

Hersey, P., & Blanchard, K. (1972). *Management of organizational behavior: Utilizing human resources* (2nd ed.). Englewood Cliffs, NJ: Prentice-Hall.

Lewin, K. (1944). The dynamics of group action. *Educational Leadership, 1,* 195–200.

Lewin, K. (1951). *Field theory in social science.* New York: Harper.

Lieberman, M., Yalom, I. D., & Miles, M. (1973). *Encounter groups: first facts.* New York: Basic Books.

Lindt, H. (1958). The nature of therapeutic interaction of patients in groups. *International Journal of Group Psychotherapy, 8,* 55–69.

Maslow, A. (1962). *Toward a psychology of being.* Princeton, NJ: Van Nostrand.

Moreno, J. (1983). Psychodrama. In H. I. Kaplan & B. J. Sadock (Eds.), *Comprehensive group psychotherapy* (2nd ed., pp. 158–166). Baltimore: Williams & Wilkins.

Perls, F. (1969). *Gestalt therapy verbatim.* Lafayette, CA: Real People Press.

Rogers, C. (1970). *Carl Rogers on encounter groups.* New York: Harper & Row.

Rutan, J. S., & Groves, J. E. (1989). Making society's groups more therapeutic. *International Journal of Group Psychotherapy, 39,* 3–16.

Schutz, W. (1980). Encounter therapy. In R. Herink (Ed.), *The psychotherapy handbook* (pp. 177–178). New York: New American Library.

Starak, Y. (1988). Confessions of a group leader. *Small Group Behavior, 19,* 103–108.

Stogdill, R. M., & Coons, A. E. (Eds.). (1957). *Leader behavior: Its description and measurement* (Research Monograph No. 88). Columbus: Ohio State University.

Sullivan, H. S. (1953). *Conceptions of modern psychiatry.* London: Tavistock.

Trotzer, J. P. (1977). *The counselor and the group: Integrating theory and practice.* Monterey, CA: Brooks/Cole.

Tuckman, B. (1965). Developmental changes in small groups. *Psychological Bulletin, 63,* 381–399.

Vander Kolk, C. (1985). *Introduction to group counseling and psychotherapy.* Columbus, OH: Merrill.

Wiggins, J., & Carroll, M. (1993). Back to the basics: Perceived and actual needs of group leaders. *Journal for Specialists in Group Work, 18*(1), 24–28.

Yalom, I. D. (1995). *The theory and practice of group psychotherapy* (4th ed.). New York: Basic Books.

chapter 13

FAMILY COUNSELING

- If a person has a problem, why counsel the entire family?
- How are marriage and family counseling different from individual counseling?
- How does a counselor decide to see a person individually, with a significant other, or with the person's entire family?
- What are the characteristics of healthy and dysfunctional families?

During the first half of the twentieth century, the focus of intervention in counseling was on the individual. Now there are counselors who refuse to see an individual unless the whole family agrees to participate in counseling. Such counselors have a strong belief that significant changes in the individual will probably not be lasting unless the entire family is involved. Ideas such as this have helped make family counseling one of the growing areas of specialization in the field of counseling. In 1990 the American Counseling Association (ACA) chartered a new division, the International Association of Marriage and Family Counselors (IAMFC). By 1993 IAMFC was the fastest-growing division of ACA.

In addition to the excitement of learning to work with an entire family, the study of family counseling is stimulating because, as noted in chapter 9, many of the family therapy concepts, methodologies, and theories have developed from other disciplines. The infusion of ideas and strategies from disciplines such as anthropology and sociology has had a synergistic effect on the entire field of family counseling.

Family counseling is a special type of group counseling. All the dynamics of working with groups apply to working with families with the added factor of the counselor's entering into a system that already exists. Family therapists usually work with relationships and patterns of interactions within the family unit but are not limited to that role. They also work at the individual, couple, extended family, neighborhood, and societal levels as well. This chapter looks at family development and functioning and examines various theoretical approaches to working with families. Marriage or relationship counseling, a special type of family counseling, is also described.

ORIGINS

The beginnings of modern family counseling date to the 1940s. Family counseling was influenced by the work of Sigmund Freud, Alfred Adler, and Harry Stack Sullivan. Freud was aware of the importance of family relationships, but in theory and practice he dealt with intrapsychic conflict. He was firmly opposed to working with more than one family member at a time (Goldenberg & Goldenberg, 1996). Many of Freud's ideas were used by the early pioneers of family counseling such as Murray Bowen and Nathan Ackerman. Alfred Adler, an early associate of Freud, provided another major influence in the development of family counseling. Adler believed that social and environmental factors played an important role in human behavior. Although Adler did not work with entire families, his awareness of the importance of the family in shaping behavior led to the development of concepts that have almost become commonplace in family counseling. These concepts include sibling rivalry, the family constellation, and the importance of birth order within the family.

Harry Stack Sullivan was trained in psychoanalysis, but in his work with schizophrenics he noted that family relationships, especially between mother and child, were an important factor in the development of schizophrenia. He then switched from an intrapsychic to an interpersonal focus. Sullivan's ideas strongly influenced Don Jackson, who later began a school of family therapy in Palo Alto, California that emphasized communications (Foley, 1984).

Nathan Ackerman is often referred to as the grandfather of family counseling. He was a psychoanalyst who was one of the first clinicians to work with entire families. He combined his psychoanalytical thinking with family systems concepts, although he never sacrificed his interest in individuals (Nichols, 1984).

During the 1950s a number of scientific and clinical developments took place. One development was a result of the work of Gregory Bateson, Don Jackson, Jay Haley, and John Weakland (1956) working with families of schizophrenics. They discovered that if a schizophrenic family member got better, someone else in the family got worse. They also noted that there was a pattern in which family members encouraged and demanded that the patient not get better but continue to show irrational behavior. The term **family homeostasis** was coined to note the resistance of the family to change.

Other factors that influenced the growth of family therapy were concurrent developments in other clinical approaches, such as group, child, and marital counseling. Marriage, family, and child counselors began to treat family members in pairs and groups. Group therapy influenced family therapy by its emphasis on the developmental group process.

Family counseling is still relatively new and evolving. It regards problems as resting in the family and not just in the individual family member. This is true even if a family member is seen individually; the focus is on the family system. In individual counseling the focus is on insight, the counselor–client relationship, and individual behavior change; family counseling focuses on the communication processes, power balances and imbalances, influence processes, structures for conflict resolution, and the current functioning of the family as a system. The goal of family counseling is much broader than just effecting change within the individual. It includes changing the structure of the family and the behavioral patterns among its members (Okun & Rappaport, 1980).

GENERAL SYSTEMS THEORY—CYBERNETICS

With the introduction of general systems theory, credited to biologist Ludwig von Bertalanffy (1968), and cybernetics, developed by a disparate group of professionals from many disciplines, including engineering, mathematics, physiology, economics, sociology, and anthropology (Wiener, 1948), there was a major shift toward treating whole families. Von Bertalanffy's **general systems theory** provided a framework for looking at complex and seemingly unrelated patterns of behavior and seeing how they represented interrelated components of a larger system. Buckley (1967) defined a **system** as being composed of parts that are interconnected and interdependent with mutual causality. A change in one part of a system effects a change in other parts. Together these parts produce a property called wholeness. **Wholeness** refers to the fact that a system is more than and different from the sum of its parts but includes their interaction. The family is more than just a collection of individuals; therefore, it cannot be broken down into its component parts and still be adequately understood. Family members must be viewed in the context of their individual lives, especially when viewing the relationship to other family members. This belief of circular causality is that the behavior of each family member is related to and dependent on the behavior of all the others (Nichols, 1984); therefore, there is no simple cause for family dynamics. This perspective differs greatly from the previous view that families are nothing more than the sum of their individual members and that a counselor should concentrate on an individual's unresolved conflicts.

Cybernetics, the study of methods of feedback control within a system, grew out of the study of inanimate machines and how they compared with living organisms as researchers tried to understand and control complex systems. It focuses on feedback mechanisms, information processing, and patterns of communication. Although cybernetics and general systems theory developed separately (the former from engineering and the latter from biology), they are similar in nature. The term *general systems theory* eventually caught on and is the more widely used term in family counseling.

NEW DEVELOPMENTS: SECOND-ORDER CYBERNETICS AND POSTMODERN–CONSTRUCTIVISM

Many family theorists have become skeptical of current approaches to family therapy. Most current approaches define the counselor's task as helping families deal more effectively with their problems by either providing insight, promoting differentiation, clarifying boundaries, or prescribing tasks. From this perspective, counselors can be detached observers who are able to objectively understand the family dynamics (Goldenberg & Goldenberg, 1996). These approaches, critics claim, fail to deal with issues impacting the family, such as gender, ethnicity, and the impact of larger social systems including political and economic forces.

A recent reappraisal of cybernetic theorizing has led to the creation of a new model called **second-order cybernetics** (as opposed to the original cybernetics which is labeled as **first-order cybernetics**). Second-order cybernetics follows a **postmodern–constructivist** view. **Postmodern** refers to a philosophical outlook that believes in multiple views of reality ungovernable by universal laws. Postmodernists reject the idea that there is an objectively knowable universe that can be discovered by an impartial science. Instead, they believe that knowledge is relative and dependent on context. They also contend that belief systems are merely social constructions or points of view and not true reality.

Second-order cybernetics followers, like the postmodernists, contend that individuals in the family construct their own realities; therefore, no fixed truth or objective reality can be discovered and observed. There are only subjective, multiple realities. Even the therapist is not seen as an outside observer who is able to reveal the truth about the family and its members. The therapist is seen as a part of the observing system and also as a creator of the reality being observed.

Great controversy has developed between family therapists, who operate from a first-order cybernetic model in which the counselor remains apart from the system being observed and attempts to change how the family functions from the outside, and those who adhere to the second-order cybernetic view (Goldenberg and Goldenberg, 1996). These arguments revolve around the themes of hierarchy, power, the role of the counselor, and whether the belief of either a first-order or a second-order approach requires the rejection of the other.

Ideas in action

...if we are to be consistent with the fundamental assumptions of the postmodern world view, clients must be understood as possessing equally valid perspectives and we must become aware that there is no "transcendent criterion of the correct."

Becvar & Becvar (1996, p. 146)

Do you agree with the above statement? If so, what implications does this have for the counselor-client relationship? How would this stance affect a family therapist's counseling approach?

WHAT IS A FAMILY?

Goldenberg and Goldenberg (1996) describe a **family** as "a natural social system with properties all its own, one that has evolved a set of rules, roles, a power structure, forms of communication, and ways of negotiation and problem solving that allow various tasks to be performed effectively" (p. 3). All families regardless of the level of adaptivity, organization, or structure attempt to become functioning groups. Families can be traditional or nontraditional.

Individuals form families in order to satisfy some basic physical and emotional needs. Emotional needs include those of closeness and intimacy, self-expression, influence, and meaning or purpose. These needs are usually satisfied through relationships, work, and having children, which traditionally has required marriage and the formation of a family.

Families can be dysfunctional or functional. In **dysfunctional families,** members are not able to attain their goals. According to Satir (1972), common characteristics of dysfunctional families are low self-worth; indirect, vague, or dishonest communication patterns; strict, rigid, unbending, and everlasting rules; and linkages to society that are fearful, placating, and blaming. These characteristics interfere with the attainment of the needs for closeness, power, and meaning, resulting in symptomatic behaviors. Common symptomatic behaviors include acting-out children, escape into long hours of work, and involvement in an affair. Dysfunctional families often experience hopelessness, helplessness, and loneliness.

In **functional families,** the needs of individual members are met. In highly functioning families, self-worth is high; communication is direct, clear, specific, and honest; rules are flexible, human, appropriate, and subject to change; and the linking to society is open and hopeful (Satir, 1972). Satir refers to these as vital, nurturing families. No matter how stable and functional a family is, it cannot be free from the stresses and challenges of life, nor can it avoid every crisis or withstand every pressure. Each family unit has its own unique problems that must be dealt with to meet its goals; however, healthy, functioning families have the ability to cope with these stresses and challenges, because they are willing to listen to each other, consider each other's point of view, and make compromises. Dysfunctional families are unable to accomplish this.

ISSUES IN TODAY'S FAMILIES

The traditional nuclear family structure has changed. Goldenberg and Goldenberg (1996) state that there is no longer a typical family. The decrease in marriage rates and increases in divorce rates, women in the workforce, single-parent as well as remarried families, and especially new ethnic minorities have led to diverse family organizational patterns and living arrangements.

Other challenges and issues currently common in families include the increasing number of interracial marriages; alcoholism and other addictive behavior; abuse of children, spouses (partners), and elderly family members; gender differences; ethnic factors; socioeconomic considerations; and the effect of an AIDS diagnosis of a family member. All of these issues affect the family life cycle.

Ideas in action

We live in a society in which: there is a 50% divorce rate; 1.1 million children involved in divorce annually; 40% of white children and 75% of black children experiencing divorce by age 16; 6 of 10 second marriages ending in divorce; one third of all children born in the past decade living in a stepfamily before the age of 18; 1 out of 6 women in the United States being abused every year by the man with whom she lives; repeated violence occurring in 1 in 14 marriages; and an average of 35 violent incidents occurring before being reported.
Smith, Carlson, Stevens-Smith, & Dennison (1995, p. 154)

What is your reaction to the above statistics? Can family counseling help to alleviate the problems faced in today's families? If so, how? What else can be done?

FAMILY LIFE CYCLE

Chapter 17 discusses the stages of individual development, including cognitive, moral, and faith development. Families have developmental stages also. In the wholistic approach presented throughout the text, all human systems are viewed as interrelated. Families are social systems with unique operating principles.

Understanding the family life cycle can help counselors be more effective in dealing with family conflicts, crisis points, and tasks that need to be accomplished before moving to the next stage. Many family counselors assume a family life cycle approach, which views problems in the family as developmental impasses that arise when the family moves from one stage in the life cycle to another. The therapy is focused on resolving the developmental impasse and not on psychopathology.

Life Cycle Models

Becvar and Becvar (1996) synthesize information from other life cycle models (see Table 13.1) to arrive at their model, which begins with the unattached adult and continues through retirement. They also include emotional issues and critical tasks for each stage. Becvar and

TABLE 13.1   Stages of the family life cycle.

Stage	Emotion Issues	Stage-Critical Tasks
1. Unattached adult	Accepting parent–offspring separation	a. Differentiation from family of origin b. Development of peer relations c. Initiation of career
2. Newly married	Commitment to the marriage	a. Formation of marital system b. Making room for spouse with family and friends c. Adjusting career demands
3. Childbearing	Accepting new members into the system	a. Adjusting marriage to make room for a child b. Taking on parenting roles c. Making room for grandparents
4. Preschool-age child	Accepting the new personality	a. Adjusting family to the needs of specific child(ren) b. Coping with energy drain and lack of privacy c. Taking time out to be a couple
5. School-age child	Allowing child to establish relationships outside the family	a. Extending family/society interactions b. Encouraging the child's educational progress c. Dealing with increased activities and time demands
6. Teenaged child	Increasing flexibility of family boundaries to allow independence	a. Shifting the balance in the parent–child relationship b. Refocusing on midlife career and marital issues c. Dealing with increasing concerns for older generation
7. Launching center	Accepting exits from and entries into the family	a. Releasing adult children into work, college, marriage b. Maintaining supportive home base c. Accepting occasional returns of adult children
8. Middle-aged adult	Letting go of children and facing each other	a. Rebuilding the marriage b. Welcoming children's spouses, grandchildren into family c. Dealing with aging of one's own parents
9. Retirement	Accepting retirement and old age	a. Maintaining individual and couple functioning b. Supporting middle generation c. Coping with death of parents, spouse d. Closing or adapting family home

From D. S. Becvar and R. J. Becvar. (1996). *Family Therapy: A Systemic Integration* (pp. 130–131). Copyright © 1996 by Allyn and Bacon. Reprinted with permission.

Becvar have conceptualized a complex dynamic process model that is applicable to a wide variety of couples and families. This dynamic process model integrates both individual and family models and accounts for structural and cultural variations in families. Some of these nontraditional variations include communal families, families with cohabiting parents, and families with gay or lesbian parents. These families have many of the same issues as traditional families as well as their own dynamics and special challenges. For example, a lesbian couple may have to deal with conflict over one partner's desire to be more open about their relationship than the other would like (Buhrke, 1989).

THEORETICAL APPROACHES

Attempting to classify the various approaches to family counseling is as difficult and complex as classifying theories for the counseling of individuals. Many attempts have been made to classify family theories according to different variables. The following is a classification system based on the work of Foley (1984) and Goldenberg and Goldenberg (1996), representing seven major schools of family counseling in terms of a continuum ranging from the object relations theory of psychoanalysis to strategic and behavioral approaches (see Table 13.2). Object relations theorists place more emphasis on past relationships than on systems thinking, as opposed to those who emphasize present relationships and current systems functioning (Foley, 1984). Other important approaches to family counseling include group, behavioral, and communications counseling, which are subsumed under the following seven theoretical orientations: object relations, the family systems/Bowenian approach, experiential family counseling, the structural approach, the strategic intervention approach, cognitive–behavioral approaches, and postmodern–constructivist approaches.

Object Relations

Object relations is the psychoanalytic study of the origin and nature of interpersonal relationships and intrapsychic structures that grew out of past relationships and remain to influence present interpersonal relationships. Whereas Freud identified instinctual gratification as each individual's fundamental need, the object relation theorists (Melanie Klein, Ronald Fairbairn, and others) maintain that a person's need for a satisfying object relationship constitutes the fundamental motive of life (Goldenberg & Goldenberg, 1996). The term *object* in this context refers to people. The inability of an individual to make a satisfying connection with the individual's **family of origin** (the family into which one is born or adopted) carries over into later life and affects that person's new family system. The intrapsychic conflict derived from this failure to make a satisfying connection continues to be acted out or replicated with one's current relationships, such as with a spouse and children. The individual unconsciously continues to relate to these current family members in the same manner as to the family of origin. Current practitioners who use this framework include James Framo, A. C. Robin Skynner, and David and Jill Savege Scharff. Counselors who use this approach usually view the **identified patient,** the family member with the presenting symptom, in the family as the cause of the division and unacceptable impulses of other family members. Great attention is paid to past relationships during counseling sessions.

The Family Systems/Bowenian Approach

The family systems approach, or **Bowenian approach,** was developed as a result of the work of Murray Bowen (1978) and should not be confused with the general systems theory discussed earlier, which is an overall view of perceiving and understanding families. Family counselors who use the family systems approach view the dysfunctional family as trapped in repetitive, destructive games of sequences. As a result, family members are unable to free themselves from the rules and expectations that govern their relationships. The cornerstone of Bowen's theory is his conceptualization of the forces within the family that make for togetherness and the opposing forces that lead to individuality (Goldenberg & Goldenberg, 1996). The goal of Bowen's approach is to enable a person to **individuate**—to become one's own person as differentiated from the family system (Foley, 1984). Bowen believes that family members become trapped through the family system's emotionality by each acting on an emotional basis and thus being pulled into the system. In order to avoid falling victim to the family system's emotionality and to be able to separate oneself from it, one would have to be able to differentiate between emotional and intellectual functioning and make choices based on reason and not feeling (Okun & Rappaport, 1980). Some current well-known practitioners of this approach include Daniel Papero, Edwin Friedman, and Michael Kerr (Goldenberg & Goldenberg, 1996).

Experiential Family Counseling

Experiential family counseling emerged from the humanistic psychology of the 1960s. This approach draws heavily from Gestalt therapy, encounter groups, and existential, humanistic, and phenomenological thinking. Although it recognizes family systems concepts, its primary concern is with the individual within the system. Experiential counselors emphasize experience, encounter, confrontation, intuition, freedom, individuality, and personal fulfillment. Experiential counselors generally discourage theorizing in favor of being open and spontaneous. Outside of their existential-humanistic derivations, they are relatively atheoretical (Nichols, 1984).

Experiential counselors attempt to open individual family members to their inner experiences and unfreeze family interactions. They deal primarily with the present rather than trying to uncover the past. They believe that change resides in the growth experience, which manifests itself in the immediate therapeutic encounter between the family and an active caring counselor. This interpersonal experience becomes the primary stimulus to growth (Goldenberg & Goldenberg, 1996). Symptom relief, social adjustment, and work are considered secondary to greater freedom of choice, less dependence, richer experiences, and greater congruency between inner experience and outer behavior (Nichols, 1984).

This approach usually requires powerful therapeutic interventions and existential encounters. Treatment is aimed at reducing the defenses within and between family members. Leading figures in experiential family counseling have been Carl Whitaker, Walter Kempler, and Virginia Satir.

Whitaker has a reputation for being creative, intuitive, sometimes outrageous, humorous, and sarcastic. He often shocks and confuses family members by his interventions in order to move a disrupted family from its "stuckness." Walter Kempler (1981) is primarily a Gestalt counselor who deals only in the here and now. He guides family members to

TABLE 13.2   Seven approaches to family counseling.

Dimension	Psychodynamic	Experiential–Humanistic	Bowenian
1. Major time frame	Past; history of early experiences needs to be uncovered.	Present; here and now data from immediate experience observed.	Primarily the present, although attention also paid to one's family of origin.
2. Role of unconscious processes	Unresolved conflicts from the past, largely out of the person's awareness, continue to attach themselves to current objects and situations.	Free choice and conscious self-determination more important than unconscious motivation.	Earlier concepts suggested unconscious conflicts, although now recast in interactive terms.
3. Insight vs. action	Insight leads to understanding, conflict reduction, and ultimately intrapsychic and interpersonal change.	Self-awareness of one's immediate existence leads to choice, responsibility, and change.	Rational processes used to gain self-awareness into current relationships as well as intergenerational experiences.
4. Role of therapist	Neutral; makes interpretations of individual and family behavior patterns.	Active facilitator of potential for growth; provides family with new experiences.	Direct but nonconfrontational; de-triangulated from family fusion.
5. Unit of study	Focus on individual; emphasis on how family members feel about one another and deal with each other.	Dyad; problems arise from interaction between two members (for example, husband and wife).	Entire family over several generations; may work with one dyad (or one partner) for a period of time.
6. Major theoretical underpinnings	Psychoanalysis.	Existentialism; humanistic psychology; phenomenology.	Family systems theory.
7. Goals of treatment	Insight, psychosexual maturity, strengthening of ego functioning; reduction in interlocking pathologies; more satisfying object relations.	Growth, more fulfilling interaction patterns; clearer communication; expanded awareness; authenticity.	Maximization of self-differentiation for each family member.
8. Major theorists and/ or practitioners	Ackerman, Framo, Boszormenyi-Nagy, Stierlin, Skynner, Bell.	Whitaker, Kempler, Satir.	Bowen.

From *Family Therapy: An Overview*, by H. Goldenberg and I. Goldenberg. Copyright © 1996, 1991, 1985, 1980 Brooks/Cole Publishing Company, Pacific Grove, CA 93950, a division of International Thomson Publishing Inc. By permission of the publisher.

Structural	Communication–Strategic	Cognitive–Behavioral	Postmodern
Present and past; family's current structure carried over from earlier transactional patterns.	Present; current problems or symptoms maintained by ongoing, repetitive sequences between persons.	Present; maladaptive behavior in an individual is maintained by current reinforcements from others.	Past and present; current problems based on past "stories" that influence current choices and behavior.
Unconscious motivation less important than repetition of learned habits and role assignments by which the family carries out its tasks.	Family rules, homeostatic balance, and feedback loops determine behavior, not unconscious processes.	Personal functioning is determined by the reciprocal interaction of behavior and its controlling social conditions.	People use language to subjectively construct their views of reality and provide the basis for how they create "stories" about themselves.
Action precedes understanding; change in transactional patterns more important than insight in producing new behaviors.	Action-oriented; behavior change and symptom reduction brought about through directives rather than interpretations.	Actions taught to reward desired outcomes and ignore or punish undesired behavior; unconcerned with insight.	Emphasis on gaining new meaning through narrative reconstructions of stories families have told about themselves.
Stage director; manipulates family structure to change dysfunctional sets.	Active; manipulative; problem-focused; prescriptive, paradoxical.	Teacher, trainer; model of desired behavior; contract negotiator.	Collaborative; engages in therapeutic conversations; non-expert co-structuring meaning and understanding.
Triads; coalitions, subsystems, boundaries, power.	Dyads and triads; problems and symptoms viewed as interpersonal communications between two or more family members.	Monadic; symptomatic person is the problem; linear view of causality.	Triadic; family problems are stories its members have agreed to tell about themselves.
Structural family theory; systems.	Communication theory; systems, behaviorism.	Learning Theory, Social Learning Theory.	Social Construction Theory.
Change in relationship context in order to restructure family organization and change dysfunctional transactional patterns.	Change dysfunctional, redundant behavioral sequences ("games") between family members in order to eliminate presenting problem or symptom.	Modification of behavioral consequences between persons in order to eliminate maladaptive behavior and/or alleviate presenting problems.	Learning and creating new viewpoints by giving new meanings or constructions to old sets of problems.
Minuchin.	Jackson, Erickson, Haley, Madanes, Selvini-Palazzoli, Watzlawick.	Patterson; Stuart; Liberman; Alexander; Falloon.	deSazer; White; O'Hanlon; Goolishian; Hoffman; Anderson.

become aware of their defenses and self-deceptive games and to take responsibility for their behaviors. Virginia Satir (1972) was probably the most well known of all family counselors. She emphasized the importance of good communications among family members using therapeutic interventions to achieve that purpose. Strengthening each family member's self-esteem is a cornerstone of her approach (Goldenberg & Goldenberg, 1996).

The Structural Approach

The **structural approach** to family counseling is associated mainly with Salvador Minuchin (1974). The basic objective of this approach is to change structures within the family, such as realigning alliances and healing splits among family members. The theory focuses on the ways families organize themselves through their transactional patterns. These patterns include the development of boundaries between family subsystems, especially between parent and child (Foley, 1984). Emphasis is on present transactions and action as opposed to insight or understanding. All behavior, including the identified patient's symptoms, is perceived within the context of family structure (Goldenberg & Goldenberg, 1996). The major tasks of the counselor are to form a therapeutic system through joining the family as a leader; accommodating the dysfunctional system; diagnosing and eventually agreeing to a contract; and restructuring the family system through various intervention strategies. As a result, the family is able to challenge its current perceptions of reality, consider alternative possibilities and transactional patterns, and then develop new relationships and structures that are self-reinforcing (Okun & Rappaport, 1980). Minuchin's interventions are active, carefully calculated, and often manipulative in order to change the dysfunctional family structures. His approach has been particularly effective with psychosomatic disorders such as anorexia nervosa (Goldenberg & Goldenberg, 1996). Structural family counseling has become one of the most influential and widely practiced of all systems of family counseling (Nichols, 1984; Becvar & Becvar, 1996; Goldenberg & Goldenberg, 1996). Nichols attributes this popularity to the theory's simplicity, inclusiveness, and practicality. Some notable therapists associated with the structural approach include Braulio Montalvo, Harry Aponte, and Charles Fishman.

The Strategic Intervention Approach

The **strategic intervention approach** is descended from the communications model of general systems theory. It has been called problem-solving therapy, brief therapy, or systemic therapy. Goldenberg and Goldenberg (1996) state that whereas Minuchin's structural model drew the greatest attention in the 1970s, the strategic approach took center stage in the 1980s.

The main principles of strategic intervention are that the symptom presented is the problem and serves as a metaphor for the whole family; the problem is caused by a developmental impasse arising from failure to adjust to transition points in the family life cycle; and attempted solutions to the problem by family members usually have intensified the problem. The primary aim is symptom removal rather than insight and understanding. The counselor is responsible for solving the problem, and counseling is carefully planned in stages. Generally, the initial sessions are used for assessment of the family. The counselor then develops a treatment plan for solving the family's presenting problems, usually by giving directives in the form of homework assignments, advice, and teaching. The counselor's goal is to use tactics that will cause family members to behave differently (Foley, 1984).

Many tactics used in the strategic approach are in the form of therapeutic double binds or paradoxical interventions geared to changing family rules and relationship patterns (Goldenberg & Goldenberg, 1996). **Paradoxical interventions** prescribe the symptom by asking family members to continue to live their lives in such a manner as to make the symptom worse, not better (Foley, 1984). For example, the counselor might instruct a couple who continually engage in squabbles to set aside specific times each week to fight and to make their fights special events.

The most influential practitioner of the strategic intervention approach is Jay Haley (1963). Other important figures are Watzlawick, Weakland, and Fisch (1974) and Cloe Madanes (Madanes & Haley, 1977). Haley played an important role in formulating the concepts of general systems theory while working with families in the 1950s along with Bateson, Jackson, and Weakland. He was a student of Milton Erickson, a pioneering hypnotherapist who became well-known for his skill in tapping the unrecognized talents of his clients. Haley has also been influenced by Minuchin and takes a structural approach to family dynamics. He advocates the use of observers behind one-way mirrors who can consult with the counselor if necessary (Nichols, 1984).

Strategic intervention is an extremely powerful approach in which techniques must be carefully developed to fit each situation, based on the family counselor's clear understanding of family dynamics. Otherwise, the counselor will be ineffective and perhaps even do harm to the family (Nichols, 1984).

Cognitive–Behavioral Approaches

Since the 1970s, behavioral concepts have been applied to family therapy. Yet these concepts have had a strong influence on such practitioners as Jay Haley and Salvador Minuchin, who use behavioral interventions to manipulate environments and to attempt to change specific maladaptive patterns of behavior. Behavioral family therapists utilize established principles of human learning, such as classical and operant conditioning, positive and negative reinforcement, shaping, extinction, modeling, and social learning (see chapter 11). Cognitive factors (attitudes, thoughts, and expectations) are increasingly viewed by behaviorists as having a strong influence on behavior.

Cognitive–behavioral approaches are probably the most linear and the least systems-oriented. They focus on the identified patient as the person with the problem. They view family interactions as maintained by environmental events preceding and following each member's behavior. Cognitive–behaviorists attempt to increase positive interaction between family members, alter the environmental conditions that oppose such interactions, and train people to maintain their newly acquired positive behavioral changes.

Cognitive–Behavioral Models

Four behavioral models are currently prevalent: behavioral marital therapy, behavioral parent-skills training, functional family therapy, and conjoint sex therapy. **Behavioral marital therapy** blends principles of social learning theory and cognition. The counselor plays the role of educator, teaching couples how to achieve positive reciprocity so that their relationship will have more pleasing consequences for both partners. The goals are to increase the frequency of positive behaviors, decrease the frequency of negative behaviors, and increase communications and problem-solving skills.

Behavioral parent-skills training endeavors to train parents in behavioral principles of child management. Gerald Patterson's Oregon Social Learning Project has been particularly influential in focusing attention on the parent–child (usually mother–child) dyad. Unlike in systems-oriented family counseling, the parents' definition of the child as the person having the problem is accepted, and the focus of counseling is on changing the parents' response to the child in order to effect a change in the child's behavior (Becvar & Becvar, 1996).

Functional family therapy attempts to integrate the systems, behavioral, and cognitive theories in working with families. All behavior is viewed as serving the interpersonal function of creating specific outcomes in behavior sequences. Functional family therapists do not try to change these functions but instead try to change the behaviors used to maintain the functions (Goldenberg & Goldenberg, 1996).

Conjoint sex therapy is a time-limited program first developed by Masters and Johnson and elaborated by Kaplan (1974). It involves both marital partners in an effort to alleviate problems of sexual dysfunction. The behavioral sex counselor uses a variety of explicitly behavioral methods: teaching about sexual physiology and techniques, changing maladaptive behavior patterns and cognitions, using systematic desensitization to reduce anxiety, and utilizing assertive training and sexual massage to overcome inhibition and improve communication. Conjoint sex therapy in its present form may be conceptualized as a type of cognitive–behavioral therapy reeducation program applied to couples with sexual problems.

Because behavioral approaches to family counseling are basically built on assumptions characteristic of individual counseling, the summary of the background, process, counselor roles, applications, and techniques appearing in chapter 11 is applicable to this context.

Postmodern–Constructivist Approaches

The new postmodern–constructivist approaches tend to be goal-oriented or solution-focused. They emphasize the postmodernist–social–constructivist belief that there are multiple realities regarding a family's problem and that therapy should be a cooperative effort in which new meaning and understanding are formulated by all concerned, rather than imposed by the counselor. These approaches tend to be brief and solution-focused, emphasizing change rather than why the family developed its problems.

Goal-oriented, or solution-focused, therapies focus on the resolution of one or two very specific problems or complaints. The counselor usually asks family members—often as early as the first session—questions such as, "What would your life be like if this problem were gone?" and "How can we work together to help you change your situation?" The counselor and clients then set goals and work on ways to achieve the ideal state.

Two such approaches are the solution-based brief therapy of William O'Hanlon and Weiner-Davis and that of Steve de Shazer. The term *solution-based* refers to the assumption that clients usually know, in some form, the solution to their problems. The solution-focused counselor concentrates on eliciting the solution from the client rather than creating the solution for the client. This is done by helping clients feel encouraged by accomplishing small positive changes.

Two of the new approaches emphasize how problems are created through language and can be deconstructed through language. One of these is the **language systems approach** of Harry Gollishian and Harlene Anderson. There is no specific set of techniques; rather, there is caring and empathic conversation that focuses on the meaning system a family organizes around a problem. The approach attempts to evolve new meanings through an egalitarian, collaborative effort. The other is the **narrative therapy approach** of Michael White. White, an Australian, seeks to empower clients to develop their own unique stories or narratives about themselves. He is critical of Western society's concept of mental illness and family dysfunction; he believes this concept objectifies people through normative classification schemes that dictate the way people are supposed to be. This objectification, he contends, becomes a self-fulfilling prophesy as people internalize the normative classification and deny their own lived experience.

Ideas in
Which of these seven approaches most appeals to you at this time? About which approach do you want to learn more?

FEMINIST FAMILY THERAPY

With the growth of the women's movement in the 1970s and 1980s, a feminist critique of family therapy developed. Family therapists were criticized for misdiagnosing female clients who did not conform to gender-role stereotypes, for failing to consider the larger social context when describing family dysfunction, for viewing mothers as the main source of pathology in families, and for believing in the principle of circular causality (that all people involved with a problem share equal responsibility for that problem). This principle of circular causality was particularly repugnant to feminists when applied to problems such as battering, rape, and incest (Becvar & Becvar, 1996). The feminist approach does not propose a new set of therapeutic techniques but a different way of viewing therapy.

FAMILY COUNSELING TECHNIQUES

Many, if not all, of the techniques of individual and group counseling (see chapters 6, 7, and 12) are appropriate for family counseling. There are also a number of specialized techniques used by family counselors. A more thorough description of many of the following techniques can be obtained from *The Handbook of Structured Techniques in Marriage and Family Therapy* (Sherman & Fredman, 1986).

Family Sculpting

Family sculpting, developed by Duhl, Kantor, and Duhl (1973), is a nonverbal technique that examines the dimensions of closeness and power within the family. It substitutes for individual verbal descriptions, which are often difficult for family members to make. It provides a graphic representation of family structures, enabling both family members and the family counselor to understand each member's personal reality more readily and thus paving the way for change. In this procedure each family member is asked to physically arrange all the other family members according to that person's perception of family relationships. The sculptor is asked to explain the completed creation, and family members are then invited to discuss it.

Genogram

The **genogram** is a family-assessment technique designed to provide a structural diagram of a family's multigenerational relationship system (Guerin & Pendagast, 1976). It depicts the family relationship system schematically as a family tree (see Figure 13.1). Genograms are used especially by followers of the family systems theory, in which generational rules, patterns, and expectations are emphasized. The genogram provides a means for noting important issues within a family in a graphic manner. An example would be recognizing a pattern of the oldest daughter in each generation getting divorced in her late 30s. It may be discovered that the oldest daughter in the current generation of the family is already expecting that her marriage will not last past her 40th birthday.

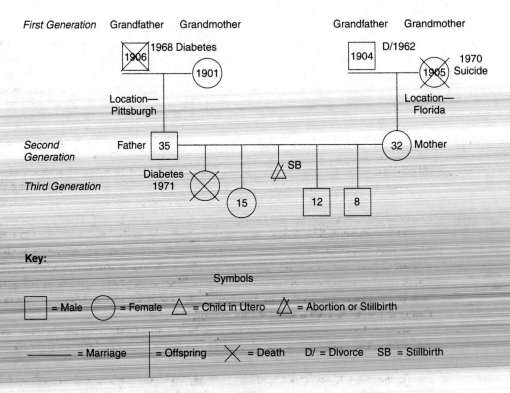

FIGURE 13.1   An example of a genogram.

Reenactment

Often family members describe a problem in general terms, such as a father complaining that the wife sabotages his attempts at disciplining their son. Rather than try to have the family members recall and explain their perceptions of the situation, the family counselor might ask the father to discipline the son in the session or reenact a discipline situation and ask the mother to intervene in the way that the father perceives as sabotaging his authority. This allows the counselor to see what is actually happening.

Paradoxical Interventions

Paradoxical interventions are powerful techniques. They are most often used by the strategic intervention theorists and are best used for long-standing, rigid, and repetitious patterns of family interaction that do not respond to other approaches. They encompass a variety of techniques for implementing change and are designed to overcome resistance by forcing family members to rebel against the counselor's directives. In doing so, they cease to act out their symptoms.

Fisher, Anderson, and Jones (1981) identified three paradoxical intervention strategies: (1) redefining the symptom by giving the behavior another meaning, (2) escalating the symptom by promoting a crisis or increasing the frequency of its expression, and (3) redirecting or changing an aspect of the symptom.

Redefinition or **relabeling** is an attempt to alter the apparent meaning or interpretation that the family places on the symptomatic behavior without changing the facts. As a result the symptomatic behavior is more amenable to change. This approach emphasizes the positive; it is like saying that a glass is half full rather than half empty. For example, a counselor might relabel a mother's behavior as trying to be helpful rather than being possessive and overprotective, thus allowing a family to view the behavior in a more hopeful and understanding way.

Escalating the symptom is often accomplished by prescribing it, thus forcing the client to either give it up or admit that it is under voluntary control. For example, a counselor might instruct a schizophrenic client to focus on hearing voices. If the client obeys the counselor's instruction, he is complying with the counselor, thus acknowledging that the symptom is voluntary. If the client does not hear voices, then he is no longer "crazy."

Redefinition and escalation both attempt to place the symptom under voluntary control. In **redirection,** however, the circumstances under which the symptom is to occur are prescribed, and the frequency is not altered. An example of redirection for a mother who continually complains about physical symptoms with no medical explanations might consist of instructing the rest of the family to listen to the mother's complaints for only 15 minutes in the evening at 6:30 P.M. The mother would be told to approach members of the family at that time even if there were not any problems.

Several techniques are utilized to have family members demonstrate how they normally deal with situations (Anderson, 1988). Some examples include the following:

- *Sequencing.* Questions are asked such as, "Who does what, and when?" and "When kids are fighting, what is your mother doing? And your father?"

- *Hypothetical questions.* These would be questions such as, "Who would be the most likely to stay home if mother got sick?" and "Which child can you visualize living at home as an adult?"
- *Scaling reports.* This technique involves the use of statements such as, "On a scale of most to least, compare one another in terms of anger, power, neediness, and happiness."
- *Tracking.* These kinds of questions help keep the focus on the family rather than on the individual: "What was it like for each of you when…?" rather than "How did you (addressed to one person) feel when…?"
- *Unbalancing.* This technique involves supporting an individual or subsystem at the expense of others. This modifies family structure and introduces the possibility of alternative ways of living together.

As stated under the strategic intervention section, these techniques require a thorough understanding of family dynamics and must be well thought out and appropriately applied. They are not intended to be used as fast and easy solutions to complex family problems.

WHEN IS FAMILY COUNSELING NEEDED?

Although therapists such as Whitaker and Napier (1978) believe that people should be seen for counseling only with the whole family present, there is no professional consensus about when family counseling is the preferred mode of treatment. Usually family counseling is called for when a problem clearly cannot be solved without the cooperation of another family member. Marital conflicts, sibling rivalry, and intergenerational conflicts are examples in which some or all of a family should be involved.

Families usually do not seek out family counseling as such. Generally an identified patient (often one of the children) is selected to be the client and serves as admission into counseling of the whole family.

A common sequence, according to Goldenberg and Goldenberg (1996), is for the entire family to initiate treatment, with various dyads or triads then being selected for further therapeutic work. The dyad most often selected at this point is the marital couple. In some instances, as many as three generations may be involved in family counseling at the same time.

Family counseling is usually contraindicated when the family is breaking up with little or no desire for reconciliation or when certain members of the family need individual help before family counseling. An example of the latter situation might be a person experiencing extreme emotional deprivation or depression (Masson & O'Byrne, 1984). Generally, counselors who prefer a systems concept tend to view many more problems as being amenable to family counseling than counselors coming from a traditional psychoanalytical background.

MARRIAGE/RELATIONSHIP COUNSELING

Marriage counseling actually was a precursor of family counseling. It was originally developed to deal with marital relationship conflicts and emphasized the marital relationship without disregarding the value of individual counseling. Family counseling, however, was started to seek alternatives to individual treatment procedures. Gradually, the two disciplines have come together. By 1970 the American Association of Marital Counseling changed its name to the American Association of Marriage and Family Therapy (Goldenberg & Goldenberg, 1996). Today, marriage and family counselors generally undergo the same training. The approaches to working with couples are pertinent to all family workers. Even when there are children involved, a counselor may focus on the parents and their relationship rather than work with the entire family. The premise in so doing is that if the relationship is functioning well between the parents, if they are cooperating with and supporting each other and are consistent in their dealings with the children, many of the problems in the family may be resolved.

The marital dyad is not the only family relationship unit, nor is the only family structure the typical married couple with dependent children living under the same roof. Axelson (1993) reports that current studies reveal that the traditional nuclear family model is difficult to attain as a result of the rise in divorces, dual-career marriages, and economic necessity. Among other important relationship units are gay and lesbian couples and **cohabitating couples** (two unmarried persons of the opposite sex who share a nonlegal, binding living relationship). These relationship units often require counseling and should be treated with the same procedures as the marital dyad.

Goldenberg and Goldenberg (1994) point out that most gay couples come for professional help not to change their sexual orientation, but for assistance with problems "quite analogous to nongay couples" (p. 213).

Premarital counseling has also been popular for some time. It is most commonly found in pastoral counseling settings. Premarital counseling is a form of preventive counseling, usually on a short-term basis (from two to eight sessions), and the basic premise is to establish a strong foundation for a long and healthy marriage.

Generally speaking, no matter what the treatment unit, marriage counseling is brief, problem-focused, and pragmatic. Marriage counseling emphasizes patterns of communication, expectations each person has of the other, role perceptions, each individual's personality, and how the couple functions together as a working unit in dealing with problems and making decisions (Cromwell, Olson, & Fournier, 1976).

Types of Marital/Relationship Counseling

Four types of counseling are used to work with couples. In each type, the focus is always on the couple relationship, even if the unit of treatment is the individual. The four types are concurrent marital counseling, collaborative marital counseling, conjoint marital counseling, and couples group counseling.

In **concurrent marital counseling,** the same counselor works separately with each partner. This method is often used when one partner has major issues of an intrapsychic nature to resolve in addition to a problem with the relationship. The major problems of this approach are remembering what has been learned from which partner, remaining impartial, and keeping confidential the secrets one partner does not wish to be revealed to the other.

In **collaborative marital counseling,** each partner is seen individually by different counselors. Sometimes this occurs when one partner prefers working on the relationship, while the other partner prefers dealing with individual problems and concerns. The counselors then collaborate with each other, compare notes, and plan compatible intervention strategies. Problems with this approach include the logistics of finding counselors who would be comfortable with such a relationship and who would be able to arrange regular collaborative sessions between counseling sessions, and the fact that each counselor would have only a narrow and limited view of the relationship and no direct awareness of the couple interaction (Bodin, 1983).

In **conjoint marital counseling,** the couple is seen together by one or more counselors. This approach is often used when both partners are motivated to work on the relationship. The emphases are on understanding and modifying the relationship. This has been a popular approach among marriage and family counselors.

In **couples group counseling,** several couples are seen together by one or more counselors (Ohlsen, 1979). This approach is sometimes used as a supplement to conjoint counseling. It can lessen an intense emotional situation between couples since people generally tend to behave more rationally in groups than individually. It can also provide the curative factors of therapeutic groups in general (see chapter 12) and can provide troubled couples with a variety of other role models (Okun & Rappaport, 1980).

Whether or not a counselor trainee intends to become a marriage and family counselor, a solid understanding of family development and dynamics and of the principles of marriage and family counseling can be valuable in any counseling setting. It is rare when clients' problems are totally separate from their family lives.

Divorce Mediation

Divorce mediation began in the United States in the early 1980s. A **divorce mediator** helps a couple that has already made the decision to divorce work out a mutually agreed-on settlement covering all of the issues of separation, including spousal and child support, custody and visitation, and the division of property, while trying to avoid or minimize bitterness, rancor, and courtroom settlements. Specialized training is available to develop the skills necessary to provide this service.

Training is provided by two groups, the Family Mediation Association and the Academy of Family Mediators. The process is based partly on the arbitration model of the American Arbitration Association and is usually handled by a trained team of counselors and lawyers (Goldenberg & Goldenberg, 1996).

Divorce mediation is a cognitively oriented activity based on facts rather than emotion. It has two primary goals: bringing about a working relationship between parents or spouses and helping families overcome financial and marital dependencies (Grebe, 1986). Grebe reports that spouses who have successfully worked through mediation usually display more self-esteem and fewer signs of stress. Other benefits include lower financial costs and better post-divorce relationships between ex-spouses and children (Goldenberg & Goldenberg, 1996).

Most separating or divorcing couples are able to use mediation successfully, especially if they have at least moderate self-esteem and reasoning ability and can comprehend a range of alternatives and possible consequences (Grebe, 1986). Divorce mediation is contraindicated if either or both partners are highly vindictive and vengeful without regard to the consequences of their behavior, or if they are alcoholic (unless in treatment), habitual liars, child abusers, spouse abusers, or victims of spouse abuse (Grebe, 1986).

The divorce mediation field is still in its infancy, but it is developing fast. Standards for practice are still in the process of development; therefore, there is no required licensing or certification yet.

MULTICULTURAL CONSIDERATIONS

Cultural factors strongly influence the practice of marriage and family counseling. Families from different cultural and ethnic backgrounds have different understandings and interpretations of the causes and symptoms of their problems and of what might be dysfunctional. They may have different attitudes about seeking counseling, about counselors, and about approaches and methods. Many ethnic groups, such as Italians, rely primarily on the family to resolve problems and only seek out counseling as a last resort. African American families rely on the church to deal with family concerns. Some ethnic groups experience family-related stress as physical symptoms and seek medical assistance (Ivey, Ivey, & Simek-Morgan, 1993).

Even the makeup of the family is defined differently across ethnic groups. The intact nuclear family is associated with Northern European culture. Italians include three to four generations, possibly including godparents and friends. Chinese include all living or deceased ancestors and descendants as family members. Native Americans consider their whole community as their family (Ivey, Ivey, & Simek-Morgan, 1993).

Family counselors need to be attuned to the different historic and cultural experiences of the ethnic groups with whom they work. For example, counselors working with African American families need to have a knowledge and awareness of racism and its effects on the family. Counselors can assist families in exploring the influence of their ethnic backgrounds on their interpersonal behaviors. Differences in counselor ethnic background from that of the family should be discussed. Counselors should be sensitive to family cultural norms and values and work in a manner that does not violate the family's sense of cultural propriety. Counselors also need to be aware of how their own values have been culturally influenced and how different these values may be from the family's cultural environment (Newlon & Arciniega, 1991). Finally, counselors need to be skilled in providing families with appropriate culture-relevant and culture-specific interventions (Ivey, Ivey, & Simek-Morgan, 1993; Goldenberg & Goldenberg, 1994).

ETHICAL CONCERNS

There are many treatment issues and ethical concerns in the field of family counseling. Because of the complex nature of working with couples and families, it is believed that more potential problems confront marriage and family counselors than individually oriented counselors (Becvar & Becvar, 1996). Both the International Association of Marriage and Family Counselors (IAMFC) and the American Association for Marriage and Family Therapy (AAMFT) have adopted a set of ethical standards for marriage and family counseling. They cover the same issues of confidentiality, dual relationships, research, training, and competence that are covered in most other codes of ethics. A number of ethical and legal considerations are unique to the area of marriage and family counseling. For example, how should the counselor handle a secret such as an affair revealed privately by an individual but unknown to the spouse? Other concerns have surfaced with the development of systems training. For example, how much concerted effort (or pressure) can therapists exert in convening all significant family members for therapy sessions? Another concern is whether willing individual marital partners or several family members seeking assistance should go untreated because one individual refuses to participate and the counselor will only work with the entire family (Huber & Baruth, 1987).

Still a new set of concerns has surfaced as a result of the growth of postmodernism and social constructivism with their emphases on ethics. For example, the *Diagnostic and Statistical Manual (DSM)* views distress in family or social contexts intrapsychically, but the view in marriage and family therapy is that such distress is due to dysfunction within the entire family system. If a counselor submits a *DSM* diagnosis of family dysfunction, insurance will not cover it.

What about the feminist contentions that the changes that most benefit the family as a whole may not always be in the best interests of all family members? Female clients could be misdiagnosed because they failed to conform to the gender-role stereotypes of the counselor. Because of the counselor's belief in circular causality, a mother may be viewed as equally responsible for her victimization. Some believe that by applying pathological classifications, counselors objectify the family system and cause it to inherit a problem it did not previously have.

Ideas in

Playing the sage and behaving like a guru is endemic to family therapy. Indeed it is prescribed in the standard textbooks in the field.
Jeffrey Moussaieff Masson (1988, p. 149)

Many family counselors believe that a position of power and influence is necessary in working with couples and families. How ethical is it for counselors to manipulate clients in order to bring about change? Do techniques such as paradoxical interventions place an inordinate share of the responsibility for change on the counselor and at the same time prevent clients from looking within and tapping their own resources to bring about change? Is there a danger that clients will attribute magical qualities to their counselors and clients will be more dependent as a result of these techniques?

LICENSURE AND CERTIFICATION

Marriage and family counselors may be regulated by individual states. Thirty-five states currently regulate the specialty of marriage and family counseling. California, for example, specifically licenses marriage and family counselors when they attain certain requirements and standards. Nationally, a counselor can be certified as a marriage and family therapist through the AAMFT. The IAMFC certifies counselors through an affiliate, the National Academy for Certified Family Therapists (NACFT). The Academy's purpose is to serve as the credentialing body for certified family therapists. The Academy has devised five options for initial certification. The main option is for someone to be certified by the National Board of Certified Counselors (NBCC) as a Nationally Certified Counselor

(NCC) or licensed as a Licensed Professional Counselor (LPC). Other options include proof of involvement in professional training, supervision, experiences working with couples and families, and avenues for providing professionals from varied disciplines with the opportunity to become credentialed (Smith, Carlson, Stevens-Smith, & Dennison, 1995).

EMPLOYMENT PROSPECTS

With the increased awareness that many problems can often be handled better through family counseling, training in family counseling is presently viewed as a decided strength in pursuing employment in the field of counseling. Even school counselors with an awareness of family dynamics and skills find that they can work more successfully with students. Receiving training and certification in marriage and family counseling is considered to be valuable in the pursuit of employment opportunities.

SUMMARY

This chapter has described family counseling, a distinct type of group counseling that has evolved from an interdisciplinary background. The term *family* has been defined as a natural social system with its own properties. Families can be traditional or nontraditional, functional or dysfunctional. Family life cycle models can be an aid to treatment planning. A number of models have been described.

A brief historical review of the development of family counseling has been presented. Family counseling mostly has developed independently of individual counseling, and its goals are much broader than just effecting change within the individual. The goals include changing family structures and behavior patterns.

Seven different theoretical approaches related to family counseling are object relations, the family systems/Bowenian approach, experiential family counseling, the structural approach, the strategic intervention approach, cognitive–behavioral approaches, and post-modern–constructivist approaches. Several techniques used in family counseling have been described, including family sculpting, genograms, reenactment, and paradoxical interventions. Marriage/relationship counseling, a special type of family counseling with different types of couples, has also been discussed along with a description of different marriage/relationship counseling approaches.

Family counseling is very complex and poses many ethical dilemmas. Divorce mediation, working with couples who are in the process of separation and divorce, has been described as an important new field for people who have counselor training. The importance of understanding relationship and family dynamics and ways of working with families is an indispensable part of being a professional counselor.

QUESTIONS AND ACTIVITIES

1. Consider how your family of origin dealt with the stages of the family life cycle. Write down your thoughts and memories. Share them with a family member or someone with whom you have a close

relationship. In what stage is your family of origin at this time? If you have left your family of origin and have started your own family, at what stage is your present family?

2. Read more about constructing a genogram (Marlin, 1989). Then construct one for your own family and consider how it might be used by a counselor working with your family. What did you learn about your family?

3. Imagine that you are a practicing counselor. A client comes to you for help in dealing with his poor grades in college. Assuming that it was possible to involve his family, would you choose to do so?

Why or why not? When would you choose to do just individual counseling? When would you insist on working with the whole family?

4. If you were to go for marriage counseling, would you choose to be part of a group of other married couples or just be with your spouse and the counselor? Would you prefer having co-counselors—a male and a female?

5. Are there any types of couples or families that you might have difficulty working with (e.g., gay couples, Asian Americans, or mothers on welfare)? What knowledge and skills would you need to work with those people successfully?

RECOMMENDED READINGS

Becvar, D. S., & Becvar, R. J. (1996). *Family therapy: A systemic integration* (3rd. ed.). Boston: Allyn and Bacon.

The Family Journal

The Family Networker

Goldenberg, I., & Goldenberg, H. (1994). *Counseling today's families* (2nd ed.). Pacific Grove, CA: Brooks/Cole.

Goldenberg, I., & Goldenberg, H. (1996). *Family therapy: An overview.* Pacific Grove, CA: Brooks/Cole.

Home, A. M., & Passmore, J. L. (1991). *Family counseling and therapy.* Itasca, IL: Peacock.

Laing, R. D. (1967). *The politics of experience.* New York: Ballantine.

Marlin, E. (1989). *Genograms.* Chicago: Contemporary Books.

Napier, A. Y., & Whitaker, C. A. (1978). *The family crucible.* New York: Harper & Row.

Satir, V. M. (1972). *Peoplemaking.* Palo Alto, CA: Science & Behavior Books.

Sherman, R., & Fredman, N. (1986). *The handbook of structured techniques in marriage and family therapy.* New York: Brunner/Mazel.

INTERNET RESOURCES

Websites

Ackerman Institute for Family Therapy

California Association of Marriage and Family Therapists   <www.camft.org>

American Association of Marriage and Family Therapists

International Association of Marriage and Family Therapists   <www.suba.com/~jlewis/iamfc/ iamfc.html>

Progress: Family Systems Research and Therapy   <www.phillips.org/progress.htm>

Solution-Oriented Brief Therapy Bibliography   <www.helsinki.fi/~furman/books.html>

Family Life Resource Center   <www.hec.ohio-state. edu/famlife/index.htm>

Facts for Families (about psychiatric disabilities affecting children and adolescents)

National Parent Information Network   <ericps.ed. uiuc.edu/npin/npinhome/html>

Legal and Ethical Issues in Marriage and Family Counseling   <www.counseling.org/enews/ volume_1/0107a.htm>

Mailing Lists and Usenet Groups

MFTC-L: This is a Listserv for discussion of issues related to marriage and family therapy and of interest to marriage and family therapists. One can register by accessing <users.aol.com/mrgary2u/MFTC.L.htm>.

IAMFCNET (International Association of Marriage and Family Counselors Network): This is a listserv for discussion of issues related to marriage and family counseling. Send e-mail with the message "subscribe iamfcnet" to <majordomo@listserver.tamu-commerce.edu>.

FAMILY THERAPY NETWORKER On-Line Mailing List: *Family Therapy Networker* magazine has a free on-line mailing list where you can discuss matters related to family therapy with practitioners and *Networker* staff. Send an e-mail with the subject "subscribe" and the message "subscribe ftnetwork@intr.net" to <ftnetwork@intr.net>.

REFERENCES

Anderson, M. (1988, December). Counseling families from a systems perspective. In ERIC Clearing House on Counseling and Personnel Services, *Highlights: An ERIC/CAPS Digest.* Ann Arbor, MI: The University of Michigan. (ERIC Document Reproduction Service No. ED304 634)

Axelson, J. A. (1993). *Counseling and development in a multicultural society* (2nd ed.). Pacific Grove, CA: Brooks/Cole.

Bateson, G., Jackson, D., Haley, J., & Weakland, J. (1956). Toward a theory of schizophrenia. *Behavioral Science, 6*(1), 251–264.

Becvar, D. S., & Becvar, R. J. (1996). *Family therapy: A systemic integration.* Boston: Allyn & Bacon.

Bertalanffy, L. von. (1968). *General systems theory: Formulations, development, applications.* New York: George Braziller.

Bodin, A. M. (1983). *Family therapy.* Unpublished manuscript.

Bowen, M. (1978). *Family therapy in clinical practice.* New York: Jason Aronson.

Buckley, W. (1967). *Sociology and modern systems theory.* Englewood Cliffs, NJ: Prentice-Hall.

Buhrke, R. A. (1989). Incorporating lesbian and gay issues into counselor training: A resource guide. *Journal of Counseling and Development, 68,* 77–80.

Cromwell, R. E., Olson, D. H. L., & Fournier, D. G. (1976). Diagnosis and evaluation in marital and family counseling. In D. H. L. Olson (Ed.), *Treating relationships* (pp. 96–108). Lake Mills, IA: Graphic.

Duhl, F. S., Kantor, D., & Duhl, B. S. (1973). Learning space and action in family therapy: A primer of sculpting. In D. Bloch (Ed.), *Techniques of family psychotherapy: A primer* (pp. 114–127). New York: Grune & Stratton.

Fisher, L., Anderson, A., & Jones, J. (1981). Types of paradoxical interventions and indications/contra-indications for use in clinical practice. *Family Process, 20*(3), 25–35.

Foley, V. (1984). Family therapy. In R. Corsini (Ed.), *Current psychotherapies* (3rd ed., pp. 447–490). Itasca, IL: Peacock.

Goldenberg, I., & Goldenberg, H. (1994). *Counseling today's families* (2nd ed.). Pacific Grove, CA: Brooks/Cole.

Goldenberg, I., & Goldenberg, H. (1996). *Family therapy: An overview* (3rd ed.). Pacific Grove, CA: Brooks/Cole.

Grebe, S. H. (1986). Mediation in separation and divorce. *Journal of Counseling and Development, 64,* 2.

Guerin, P., & Pendagast, E. (1976). Evaluation of family system and genogram. In P. Guerin (Ed.), *Family therapy* (pp. 450–464). New York: Gardner Press.

Haley, J. (1963). *Strategies of psychotherapy.* New York: Grune & Stratton.

Huber, C. H., & Baruth, L. G. (1987). *Ethical, legal, and professional issues in the practice of marriage and family therapy.* Columbus, OH: Merrill.

Ivey, A. E., Ivey, M. F., & Simek-Morgan, L. (1993). *Counseling and psychotherapy: A multicultural perspective.* Boston: Allyn & Bacon.

Kaplan, H. S. (1974). *The new sex therapy: Active treatment of sexual dysfunctions.* New York: Brunner/Mazel.

Kempler, W. (1981). *Experiential psychotherapy with families.* New York: Brunner/Mazel.

Madanes, C., & Haley, J. (1977). Dimensions of family therapy. *Journal of Nervous and Mental Disease, 165,* 88–98.

Marlin, E. (1989). *Genograms.* Chicago: Contemporary Books.

Masson, H. C., & O'Byrne, R. (1984). *Applying family therapy.* Oxford, England: Pergamon Press.

Masson, J. M. (1988). *Against therapy: Emotional tyranny and the myth of psychological healing.* New York: Atheneum.

Minuchin, S. (1974). *Families and family therapy.* Cambridge, MA: Harvard University Press.

Newlon, B. J., & Arciniega, M. (1991). Counseling minority families: An Adlerian perspective. In J. Carlson & J. Lewis (Eds.), *Family counseling: Strategies and issues* (pp. 77–88). Denver: Love.

Nichols, M. (1984). *Family therapy: Concepts and methods.* New York: Gardner Press.

Ohlsen, M. (1979). *Marriage counseling in groups.* Champaign, IL: Research Press.

Okun, D. F., & Rappaport, L. J. (1980). *Working with families: An introduction to family therapy.* North Scituate, MA: Duxbury Press.

Satir, V. (1972). *Peoplemaking.* Palo Alto, CA: Science & Behavior Books.

Sherman, R., & Fredman, N. (1986). *The handbook of structured techniques in marriage and family therapy.* New York: Brunner/Mazel.

Smith, R. L., Carlson, J., Stevens-Smith, P., & Dennison, M. (1995). Marriage and family counseling. *Journal of Counseling and Development, 74*(11), 154.

Watzlawick, P., Weakland, J., & Fisch, R. (1974). *Change: Principles of problem formation and problem resolution.* New York: Norton.

Whitaker, C., & Napier, A. (1978). *The family crucible.* New York: Harper & Row.

Wiener, N. (1948). Cybernetics. *Scientific American, 179*(5), 14–18.

chapter 14

focus on

CAREER AND
LIFESTYLE COUNSELING

- Is career counseling different from personal counseling?
- How do counseling theories differ from career development theories?
- Can you be certified as a career counselor?
- How does a job differ from a vocation?

Career counseling is one of the areas that generally distinguishes mental health and school counselors from most other mental health professionals. Most social work, psychology, and psychiatry training programs do not require study and practice in career counseling, however, as noted in chapter 4, mental health and school counseling trace their origins back to vocational guidance. These vocational guidance ideas and principles have evolved into modern day career and lifestyle counseling and are an integral part of the typical mental health and school counseling training programs. Career counseling is one of the eight areas comprising the examination to be certified as a Nationally Certified Counselor (NCC).

Career counseling is one of the oldest specialties in the field of counseling. It is also one of the most creative and exciting specialties. This dynamism is the result of career counseling's evolution, career counseling's willingness to embrace changes in the conceptualization of the specialty area, advances in psychology, and the incorporation of computer technology. Counselors no longer think about helping clients make a single occupational choice early in life; they now think in terms of **career development** and view that as a "lifelong process that encompasses maturation not only in career awareness and decision making but also in self-knowledge, life skills, and leisure pursuits" (Walz & Benjamin, 1984, p. 26).

What was once called vocational guidance has evolved to become **career and life span counseling,** encompassing a person's life span and including much more than the world of work. Now leisure, retirement, and lifestyle counseling are included under the broader title of **life planning.** This chapter describes the development of this area and its relationship to the counseling field. It also outlines the dimensions, strategies, trends, and issues that surround this specialty, one that touches all people directly.

How did you get to be the person you are? What decisions and circumstances have brought you to the place where you are now? What significant people in your life influenced your career and lifestyle choices?

HISTORICAL PERSPECTIVE

Shortly after the turn of the century, Frank Parsons wrote *Choosing a Vocation* (1909) in which he coined the term *counselor* to describe the vocational guidance practitioner. As a result of his work, Parsons is recognized as the founder of systematic vocational guidance in the United States (Borow, 1984, p. 10). The groundwork established in the field of vocational guidance has fostered the development of the entire field of counseling. In 1913 the National Vocational Guidance Association (NVGA) was formed. NVGA became the foundation for and one of several divisions of the American Personnel and Guidance Association (APGA), now the American Counseling Association (ACA). The first journal published in this field was *Occupations.* That journal has evolved through the years to become the major counseling journal for the field, the *Journal of Counseling and Development,* the official journal of ACA. Vocational guidance as practiced by Parsons emanated from an agency he established in Boston. Since then much vocational guidance and counseling has been associated with schools. As a result, the term *counselor* became almost synonymous with *school counselor.* Only in the 1980's and 1990s did counselors pursue careers in mental health and private-practice settings. Parsons's most enduring contribution was his description of the process of vocational guidance, a procedure he called "true reasoning" (Herr & Cramer, 1984). These guidelines are similar to modern principles of career counseling. The three steps of Parsons's approach are as follows:

> First, a clear understanding of yourself, aptitudes, abilities, interests, resources, limitations, and other qualities. Second, a knowledge of the requirements and conditions of success, advantages and disadvantages, compensation, opportunities, and prospects in different lines of work. Third, true reasoning on the relations of these two groups of facts. (Parsons, 1909, p. 5)

Parsons's conceptualization provided the basis for a major early theoretical approach to career counseling, the trait–factor theory. The **trait–factor approach** holds that the client has certain attributes, or traits, and that various occupations need certain skills, aptitudes, and interests. The job of the counselor following this approach is to match the client with the appropriate occupation. The trait–factor approach was influential into the 1940s and was widely used in career guidance in school settings. During the 1950s and 1960s, career counseling evolved from an emphasis on guidance—which included advice and information dissemination—to a form of psychological treatment relying on career development theory and communication and decision-making skills (Srebalus, Marinelli, & Messing, 1982).

Career Education

During the 1970s the federal government initiated and subsidized an extensive program designed to facilitate career planning and to increase career options. This program became widely known as **career education,** a term defined as "an effort aimed at refocusing American education and the actions of the broader community in ways that will help individuals acquire and utilize the knowledge, skills, and attitudes necessary for each to make work a more meaningful, productive, and satisfying part of his or her way of living" (Herr & Cramer, 1979, p. 37). In its implementation, this program involved people from all walks of life, including farmers, executives, government employees, and educators, primarily through school counseling centers.

Career education has persisted in a number of different forms throughout the 1980s and 1990s, with a major focus in the late 1990s on the school-to-work transition (Baker, 1997). In the 1980s and 1990s, at a time when career counseling was going beyond schools and universities, the career counseling specialty began taking a leadership role in the use of computer technology in career assessment and exploration. Mental health agencies have become more involved with the career counseling specialty, since they are often employed by businesses and industries to assist employees whose jobs had been terminated because of corporate downsizing.

Perhaps the most dramatic indicator of change in this field has been the expansion of career counseling from schools and vocational rehabilitation agencies to almost all agencies and to professionals in private practice. The scope and practice of career counseling is expected to increase well into the next century.

TERMINOLOGY

As this specialty has developed, the use and even the meaning of technical terms have changed. What used to be called *vocational guidance* is now referred to as *career counseling.* Terms such as *career, occupation, job,* and *position* are often used interchangeably in the popular literature. In this chapter, the use of professional terminology is in accord with the following definitions:

Job, occupation, and vocation. These terms are used interchangeably to indicate activities of employment and employment positions (Zunker, 1990).

Career. This is defined as lifelong sequence of work, educational, and leisure experiences; "Mary's career has included teaching, counseling, graduate study, foreign travel, and many volunteer activities" (Joslin, 1984, p. 261).

Lifestyle. The definition for lifestyle is an individual's aspirations for social status, a particular work climate, education, mobility, and financial security (Zunker, 1990).

Career development. This term refers to "the lifelong process of developing work values, crystallizing a vocational identity, learning about opportunities, and trying out plans in part-time, recreational, and full-time work situations" (Tolbert, 1980, p. 31).

Career guidance. This is "an organized, systematic program to help the individual develop self-understanding, understanding of societal roles, and knowledge of the world of work...[career guidance] emphasizes the process of planning, decision making, and implementation of decisions" (Srebalus, Marinelli, & Messing, 1982, p. 255). Career guidance has often been viewed as a teaching function. It increasingly includes more of the counseling process, to the point that the literature speaks more often of career counseling than of career guidance.

Career counseling. This "includes all counseling activities associated with career choices over a life span. In the career-counseling process, all aspects of individual needs (including family, work, and leisure) are recognized as integral parts of career decision making and planning" (Zunker, 1990, p. 4).

Career life planning. This is "an ongoing process that allows for change of directions as individual needs change and/or situational circumstances cause change...[allowing for] greater opportunity for fulfillment in life" (Zunker, 1990, p. 97).

CAREER COUNSELING THEORY

As noted in chapters 10 and 11, theory is a vital part of the counseling practice. Theory helps provide understanding of human behavior and offers constructs and strategies on which to base counseling decisions and interventions. It is ethically unwise to offer counseling of any type without theoretical knowledge.

The practice of career counseling can fit well within the framework of the major theoretical approaches to counseling, such as person-centered and behavioral (Crites, 1981); however, as a counseling specialty, career counseling has had a number of theoretical formulations specifically associated with it to aid in the understanding of how careers and lifestyles develop. "A **theory of career development** can be defined as a conceptual system that identifies, describes, and interrelates important factors affecting lifelong human involvement with work" (Srebalus, Marinelli, & Messing, 1982, p. 15). Career development theory tends to be multidisciplinary, combining psychological, sociological, and even economic ideas and terms.

Five major types of approaches to career development have been identified and defined by Herr and Cramer (1984):

1. **The trait–factor approach.** The trait–factor, or matching, approach relates personal traits such as aptitudes and interests to characteristics required by a given job.
2. **Decision theory.** In decision theory the person chooses between vocational alternatives by using concepts unique to this approach.
3. **Situational approaches.** In the situational, or sociological, approaches, the emphases are on situational factors such as location in space and time; political and social factors; ethnic, religious, and family beliefs; and value systems.
4. **Psychological–personality-based approach.** This perspective takes into consideration the individual's personality structure and needs.
5. **Developmental approach.** Adherents of this approach emphasize the person's long-term development.

Trait–Factor Approach

The trait–factor approach follows "the Parsonian Equation that knowledge of self + knowledge of work + counseling = ability to choose" (Srebalus, Marinelli, & Messing, 1982, p. 96). Practitioners using this approach believe that through the identification of personal characteristics or traits of a client and the matching of these traits with factors required by different occupations, correct vocational decisions can be made. Between 1910 and 1950, this approach dominated what was once called vocational counseling. As more came to be known about the career development process, competing theories were developed and now there are few, if any, advocates of a pure trait–factor approach. Vestiges of trait–factor theory can still be found in almost all the current theories of career development, however (Isaacson & Brown, 1993).

Decision Theory

A social learning approach to career decision making has been developed by Krumboltz (1976). He identifies the following four factors that influence the making of career decisions:

1. *Genetic endowment and special abilities.* A person's race, sex, physical appearance, intelligence, and musical and artistic abilities may all play a part in a person's career development. The characteristics may be helpful, as in the case of a seven-foot, physically coordinated male who desires a career in basketball. They may also be restrictive, as in the case of a person who desires a career as a musician but has only limited musical ability.
2. *Environmental conditions and events.* External factors that can affect a person's career choices can range from wars and recessions to earthquakes and floods, and from the availability of educational facilities and financial assistance to union and government regulations.
3. *Learning experiences.* A person's attitudes and interests are affected by previous learning experiences. These experiences could include active involvement, such as repairing a bicycle or observing others at work.
4. *Task-approach skills.* Work habits, emotional responses, values, and problem-solving skills are all part of what Krumboltz (1976) calls "task-approach skills."

This approach suggests that **career decision making** is more than having a good fit between personal characteristics and the requirements of a given occupation. Environmental factors, the variety and nature of personal learning experiences, and the degree of attainment of task-approach skills all need to be considered in the decision-making process.

Situational Approaches

The factors of chance, accident, and other external forces have been noted by career developmentalists. Many individuals, rather than going through a neat, orderly system of career development, have had their lives and careers directly affected by forces over which they have had little control. A major corporation moves a factory from one community to another, reducing career opportunities in one area while expanding them in another. Government regulations force the closing of a mine. A girl working in a drugstore is chosen to star in a major movie. Although luck or strokes of fate do seem to be involved in the career decisions of some people, the individual still can play a part. A girl may travel from New Jersey to Hollywood where she can get a job in a drugstore so that she might be discovered by a movie producer. An employee who is laid off because of a plant relocation might obtain retraining for a different occupation, which may be better than the original one. Advocates of the situational approach to career development suggest

> that the socio-economic structure of a society operates as a percolator and a filter of information. In essence, the position a person occupies among the social strata making up the nation has much to do with the kind of information he or she gets, the alternative actions one can take, and the kind of encouragement which accrues. (Herr & Cramer, 1979, p. 84)

There are few practitioners who give a great deal of credence to this approach. Because a purely situational approach to career development is not deemed sufficiently comprehensive and would render both the client and the counselor helpless, counselors cannot totally disregard these factors (Isaacson, 1985).

Psychological–Personality-Based Approach

According to personality-based theorists such as Holland (1973), the major factor influencing career choices is the type of personality or behavioral style of the individual. The person's personality type is an acknowledged result of genetic and environmental factors. Four major assumptions form the core of Holland's theory:

1. There are six personality types into which most individuals can be categorized: realistic, investigative, artistic, social, enterprising, or conventional.
2. Environment can be classified into the same six categories. Each environment is dominated by people of similar personality type.
3. People search for environments in which they can comfortably express their interests, skills, and abilities and take on agreeable problems and roles.
4. A person's behavior is determined by the interaction between the personal characteristics of the individual and the characteristics of the environment.

One way to use Holland's approach is to have a client respond to an instrument like the Strong-Campbell Interest Inventory. On the basis of response patterns on the inventory, the client would be categorized according to the three most dominant personality characteristics. For example, a client might be classified as RIA (realistic, investigative, and artistic). This classification would be matched to the 456 occupations that have already been classified according to the same coding system. In this case, the occupations of architectural draftsman and dental technician have the same code. The client might then explore these two occupations and related areas using a resource such as the *Occupational Outlook Handbook,* published by the U.S. Department of Labor, along with a variety of other career education materials (Herr & Cramer, 1979).

Developmental Approach

The developmental approach includes much of the previously mentioned approaches. It looks at career decision making as a lifelong process with counselor interventions varying depending on the person's life stage. The most influential developmental approach is that of

Donald Super (1957). Super developed 12 testable statements and devoted a major portion of his career to testing and researching these statements. His propositions are as follows:

1. Vocational development is an ongoing, continuous, and generally irreversible process.
2. Vocational development is an orderly, patterned, and predictable process.
3. Vocational development is a dynamic process.
4. Self-concepts begin to form prior to adolescence, become clearer in adolescence, and are translated into occupational terms in adolescence.
5. **Reality factors** (the reality of personal characteristics and the reality of society) play an increasingly important part in occupational choice with increasing age, from early adolescence to adulthood.
6. Identification with a parent or parent substitute is related to the development of adequate roles, their consistent and harmonious interrelationship, and their interpretation in terms of vocational plans and eventualities.
7. The direction and rate of the vertical movement from one occupational level to another are related to intelligence, parental socioeconomic level, status needs, values, interests, skill in interpersonal relationships, and the supply and demand conditions of the economy.
8. The occupational field the individual enters is related to interests, values, and needs; the identification with parental or substitute role models; the community resources used; the level and quality of educational background; and the occupational structure, trends, and attitudes of the community.
9. Although each occupation requires a characteristic pattern of abilities, interests. and personality traits, the tolerances are wide enough to allow both some variety of individuals in each occupation and some diversity of occupations for each individual.
10. Work satisfaction depends on the extent to which the individual can find adequate outlets in a job for his or her abilities, interests, values, and personality traits
11. The degree of satisfaction the individual attains from work is related to his or her ability to implement self-concept.
12. Work and occupations provide a focus for personality organization for most men and many women, although for some persons this focus is peripheral, incidental, or even nonexistent, and other foci such as social activities and the home are central. (Super, 1957, pp. 118–120)

Super's approach, which he calls "differential developmental–social–phenomenological psychology" (1969, p. 9), is an integrative one. It is longitudinal, with a progressive movement throughout the person's life span. Of vital concern to Super are the development of the person's self-concept and its influence in the making of career decisions. The basic theme stressed by Super is that "the individual chooses occupations that will allow him to function in a role consistent with his self-concept and that the latter conception is a function of his developmental history" (Herr & Cramer, 1979, p. 93).

> Super's approach is a wholistic one. It emphasizes four major elements: vocational life stages, vocational maturity, translating the self-concept into a vocational self-concept, and career patterns. According to this approach, the individual develops vocationally as one aspect of his or her total development at a rate determined in part by his or her

psychological and physiological attributes and in part by environmental conditions, including significant others. (Tolbert, 1980, p. 41)

Although Super indicates that all individuals go through the stages of career development, he has built on the ideas of those such as Havighurst (1953), who suggest that there are certain developmental tasks that need to be completed at different stages of life. Super's work incorporates developmental tasks along with the life stages (see Table 14.1).

Most people are aware of the career concerns that revolve around children. A child is always being asked, "What are you going to be when you grow up?" What has only recently come to light is the number of people who have major career concerns as adults. Some of these concerns manifest themselves in what has become known as the midlife crisis. Daniel Levinson (1977) has studied adult development and found that there are periods of stability and periods of transition, or instability, when some fine-tuning or adjustments are made to bring one's lifestyle in concert with needs and wants. The period of instability is followed by another period of stability. The midlife transition, described by Levinson, generally occurs in a person's late 30s or early 40s. This is a major period of evaluation, as individuals recognize that the most productive part of their lives may be over and that goals established earlier in life may never be accomplished. Events such as children leaving home, personal illness, and having to care for elderly parents contribute to this midlife malaise.

Career counseling, in view of the developmental life span concept, is not just an approach to use with high school and college students to help them find the most appropriate career. It is an activity that must be used throughout a lifetime. Even deciding what to do after retirement is a career decision.

The developmental counselor expects that career counseling will result in the client acquiring a clearer understanding of self that results in appropriate decisions in the present, compatible with client self-concept. Further, the counselor expects the client to be able to adjust or modify present decisions to fit changing circumstances in the future. (Isaacson, 1985, p. 90)

CAREER COUNSELING STRATEGIES

Career counseling, while using approaches common to other counseling specialties, also employs a number of strategies to help clients that are not often used in other counseling settings; for example, significant amounts of information dissemination, extensive use of computerized programs and testing, the use of placement services, and a direct emphasis on education.

Assessment

The use of inventories, rating scales, tests, and other assessment instruments has been linked with career counseling from its inception. The trait–factor approach requires that the client's characteristics be clearly identified with the assistance of one or more instruments in order to provide a good fit with the attributes required for a given occupation. Computers now assist in the scoring, analysis, and interpretation of results. Assessment instruments

TABLE 14.1   Super's conception of life stages and developmental tasks.

Life Stage Characteristics	Substage Characteristics	Developmental Tasks
Growth (0–14 years)		
Self-concept develops through identification with key figures in family and school; needs and fantasy are dominant early in this stage; interest and capacity become more important with increasing social participation and reality testing; behaviors associated with self-help, social interaction, self-direction, industriousness, goal setting, persistence are learned.	*Fantasy (4–10 years)* Needs are dominant; role-playing in fantasy is important. *Interest (11–12 years)* Likes are the major determinant of aspirations and activities. *Capacity (13–14 years)* Abilities are given more weight, and job requirements (including training) are considered.	Developing a picture of the kind of person one is Developing an orientation to the world of work and an understanding of the meaning of work
Exploration (14–24 years)		
Self-examination, role tryouts, and occupational exploration take place in school, leisure activities, and part-time work.	*Tentative (15–17 years)* Needs, interests, capacities, values, and opportunities all are considered, tentative choices are made and tried out in fantasy, discussion, courses, work, and so on. Possible appropriate levels of work are identified. *Transition (18–21 years)* Reality considerations are given more weight as the person enters the labor market or professional training and attempts to implement a self-concept. Generalized choice is converted to specific choice. *Trial: Little Commitment (22–24 years)* A seemingly appropriate occupation and a first job have been found, and are tried out as a potential life work. Commitment is still provisional and if the job is not appropriate, the person may reinstitute the process of crystallizing, specifying, and implementing a preference.	Crystallizing a vocational preference Specifying a vocational preference Implementing a vocational preference
Establishment (24–44 years)		
Having found an appropriate field, an effort is made to establish a permanent place in it. Thereafter changes that occur are changes of position, job, or employer, not of occupation.	*Trial-Commitment and Stabilization (25–30 years)* Settling down. Securing a permanent place in the chosen occupation. May prove unsatisfactory resulting in one or two changes before the life work is found or before it becomes clear that the life work will be a succession of unrelated jobs.	Consolidation and advancement

Continued

TABLE 14.1   *Continued*

Life Stage Characteristics	Substage Characteristics	Developmental Tasks
	Advancements (31–44 years) Effort is put forth to stabilize and make a secure place in the work world. For most persons these are the creative years. Seniority is acquired; clientele are developed; superior performance is demonstrated; and qualifications are improved.	
Maintenance (44–64 years) Having made a place in the world of work, the concern is how to hold on to it. Little new ground is broken as an established pattern continues. Concerned about maintaining present status while being forced out by competition from younger workers in the advancement stage.		Preservation of achieved status and gains
Decline (64 years–death) As physical and mental powers decline, work activity changes and in due course ceases. New roles must be developed: first, selective participant and then observer. Individual must find other sources of satisfaction to replace those lost through retirement.	*Deceleration (65–70 years)* The pace of work slackens, duties are shifted, or the nature of work is changed to suit declining capacities. Many people find part-time jobs to replace their full-time occupations. *Retirement (71–death)* Variation on complete cessation of work or shift to part-time, volunteer, or leisure activities.	Deceleration Disengagement Retirement

From *Career Guidance through the Life Span: Systematic Approaches,* (p. 95), by E. L. Herr and S. H. Cramer, 1979, HarperCollins. Copyright © 1979 by Addison Wesley Educational Publishers Inc. Reprinted with permission.

may include intelligence and aptitude tests, personality and interest inventories, and rating scales. These types of assessment instruments are described in chapter 19. Specialized training may be required to administer and interpret some assessment instruments.

Ideas in action — Make an appointment at the campus counseling center to take the assessment instruments that help clients make career decisions. Ask a counselor to help you interpret the results. Find out if you learn anything new about yourself, about assessment instruments, and about your career development. Would career counseling be something that you would like to do to help others?

Information Giving—Guidance

Much of the work of the career counselor falls under the rubric of information attainment and sharing. Clients often do not have the information they need to make informed decisions, nor do they know how to find or use appropriate data.

A significant amount of resource material and career information is available to fill the needs of clients who do not know where to turn. All major theoretical approaches use career information to some degree; however, there is a great deal of difference in emphasis. Counselors who use the trait–factor approach stress the use of career information. Person-centered counselors consider career information of less importance (Crites, 1981).

A major problem with the dissemination of career information is the sheer abundance of material. Two volumes containing 12,741 job descriptions, of which about one fifth are new or revised, are listed in the fourth edition of the *Dictionary of Occupational Titles (DOT)* (U.S. Department of Labor, 1991). Various amounts of published information for these careers are available, including books, pamphlets, audiotapes and videotapes, films, and filmstrips. It is not feasible for any counselor, school, or agency to have on hand all the available resources to satisfy the needs of every prospective client; even if they were on hand, all of that material might be overwhelming. The selection, management, and appropriate dissemination of career information is a major task for a career counselor. This is one area where having materials available on computer and on the Internet has been particularly valuable.

A great amount of information is available about occupations, but it is not always balanced. There is often an overly positive view given of occupations rather than a picture that offers negative aspects as well (Srebalus, Marinelli, & Messing, 1982, p. 100). Information may also be outdated and written at the wrong level for a particular client. Thus the use of information, which seems to be a straightforward way to help people, in fact has some serious drawbacks. Further, even if the information is written at the correct level for a client and the presentation is current and balanced, simply having the information is not enough for making a lifetime decision.

 **Ideas in action**   Use the websites listed at the end of this chapter to critically review the different types of materials that help individuals learn about occupations. Become aware of where reference books listed at the end of this chapter are located in the campus career counseling center (or library) for students to use who do not have access to the Internet. How accessible and helpful are these materials?

Career Counseling—Individual and Group

Career counseling can work well in both individual and group settings. Clients receive more direct attention in individual counseling, but working in groups has valuable features. Information giving is most often done in groups to save time and money. Group counseling is preferred for working through the stages of counseling, for all of the reasons given in chapter 12.

Srebalus, Marinelli, and Messing (1982) suggest the incorporation of Carkhuff's three-stage model (1969), as modified by Egan (1975), into the overall scheme of career counseling.

These stages are exploration, understanding, and action. The components of this model fit well into the developmental approach as well as with the counseling process described in chapter 5.

1. *Exploration.* Individuals must become more aware of the broad spectrum of work. They also begin to conceptualize the relationships among occupations. As part of this conceptualization process, distortions about occupations are reduced.
2. *Understanding.* Clients differentiate among occupations according to occupational characteristics. The comparison of self to occupations is part of the process. Increased knowledge of the components of self and improved ability to differentiate among occupations permit persons to begin making decisions about those occupations that meet their needs and whose requirements can be met.
3. *Action.* The active preparation for entry into the occupational world begins. Individuals eventually enter the occupational world in a more or less permanent manner during this period. Later in this stage, involvement in the maintenance and enrichment of their career occurs. (Srebalus, Marinelli, & Messing, 1982, p. 103)

The movement through this process is not always sequential. The client may move from the exploration to the understanding stage and then move back to the exploration stage again before moving on to complete the action stage. The process can also be recycled; for example, a client may use the exploration–understanding action process to decide on an occupation but then return to go through the process again after an injury forces a change in the initial occupational choice.

Teaching the Decision-Making Process

Following the understanding phase of counseling, the client may say, "Now that I've figured out what my problem really is, I now know what I have to do. Thank you very much!" In most cases, however, clients need to be assisted in the decision making necessary to implement previous learning. It is in the action phase that the counselor helps the client work through a decision-making model (see chapter 6). Again, the goal of the counselor is to teach a skill that is transferable to other situations.

Work Adjustment

There is more to career counseling than career choice. Every client who is unhappy with his occupation should not necessarily begin the process of making a career change. The idea of a counselor being more attuned to work adjustment problems is stressed by Hershenon (1996). A client may need to work on a number of areas, such as improving interpersonal skills or helping to change a seemingly disastrous situation into one that is very acceptable.

DOES CAREER COUNSELING DIFFER FROM PERSONAL COUNSELING?

In some settings—on a college campus, for example—a distinction can be made between career counseling and personal counseling. Srebalus, Marinelli, and Messing (1982) indicate that their review of the literature shows that it is difficult to make such a distinction consistently. The distinction could be based on the nature of training and experience that a counselor has, such as working predominantly with career counseling or working exclusively with severe psychopathology; however, decisions about an occupation, a vocation, a lifestyle, and a career are clearly personal issues. When a 55-year-old male has just found out that his employer is downsizing and his job is going to be eliminated, this is far more than making a new career choice. In fact, many personal issues dealing with loss, grief, and self-concept often need to be dealt with first before a realistic appraisal and exploration of future career decisions can be made.

Vecchione (1996) gives the example of a female client who, fighting her tears, says, "When your friends are graduating and moving on with their lives, and you are still taking out loans to survive, and have changed majors five times, and your parents are on your back, and you still don't know what to do, it's as personal as you can get" (p. 54). Most likely a client with a career problem is a client with a mental health problem. Kjos (1995) reports that of 10 personality disorders listed in the fourth edition of the *Diagnostic and Statistical Manual of Mental Disorders (DSM-IV),* (APA, 1994) 9 of them are specifically linked at least in part with occupational difficulties. With certainty one can state that all career counseling is personal, although all personal counseling is not career counseling.

Clients may often use the need for career counseling as a safe, acceptable presenting problem (see chapter 6). This is a type of counseling that family and friends would not be likely to question. The authors' experience working in a college counseling center has verified this strategy. Often when the counseling relationship has been established, the client will change the focus to another topic and may not pursue the career counseling concern again. One should not assume that all clients requesting career counseling are actually concealing a more significant problem. Legitimate career and life planning needs could be ignored.

Ideas in action   A male client comes for career counseling and reports feeling suicidal as a result of losing his job after 15 years with the same company. He questions whether he can be successful at anything else. He wonders if he chose the right profession. He feels hopeless and despondent. Should the counselor (1) first refer the client out for personal counseling and then look at career alternatives, (2) assess the suicide potential and then make a referral, (3) ignore the personal issues and concentrate on the client's career alternatives, (4) assess the suicide potential and explore how the loss of job has affected his self-concept, or (5) some other alternative?

Placement Services

Career and employment counselors do much to arrange matches between clients and employers or between clients and colleges. Their jobs include arranging job or college fairs, helping clients write resumes and practice interviewing, developing and maintaining placement files, and scheduling employer interviews. This service is most often found in high schools, universities, and state employment centers but is increasingly occurring in outside agencies.

Computer Systems

Computer-assisted programs can be used at different points in the career counseling process. According to Isaacson and Brown (1993), such programs' greatest values are helping clients attain occupational information, matching the information against various combinations of personal attributes, and relating educational and training opportunities to personal plans and characteristics. Research studies generally indicate that users of computer-assisted career guidance systems react positively, suggesting that these systems are worthwhile counseling tools that can help clients in the career exploration process.

The two basic types of computer-assisted career guidance systems are information systems and guidance systems. **Information systems** provide clients with current data on subjects such as occupational descriptions and characteristics, educational institutions, and financial aid. **Guidance systems** actively involve the client in a career decision-making process by assessing values and interests, making predictions of future success, and using decision-making strategies. Some systems combine both information and guidance approaches (Zunker, 1990).

The two most popular guidance systems currently in use are the System of Interactive Guidance and Information (SIGI) and the Discover System. Both systems are designed to assist students in high school and college and older adults in making career decisions.

ISSUES AND TRENDS IN CAREER COUNSELING

From a systems perspective, there are many important factors that influence work and career. Among these are population growth shifts, education, technological change, government legislation, racism, stereotyping women and ethnic minorities, and economic fluctuations. These factors affect the level and degree of personal accomplishment that is possible for individuals to achieve.

Educational Considerations

A National Career Development Association (NCDA) survey indicated that 44% of adults felt that schools did not devote enough attention to helping students choose careers, and 53% felt that more attention should be devoted to the development of vocational skills for people not college bound. Approximately two thirds said they would seek more information if they were to start over. The United States is the only industrialized nation without a comprehensive system to help youth acquire the necessary knowledge, skills, abilities, and information about the labor market to make an effective transition from school to work (Schwallie-Giddis, 1993). Many poor and minority people lack the education and skills necessary for employment in many occupations or for advancement once employed.

Economic Considerations

Access to education and employment opportunities is more difficult under the conditions in which many poor and minorities must live. Businesses generally avoid building in dense population centers where there may be high concentrations of poor, Latinos, African Americans, or other minorities; this limits the range of work opportunities available in these locations.

Developing a career can be expensive, and low income people have fewer resources to enable them to be educated, to commute to work, or to move to another geographical area where employment or occupational opportunities are more readily available (Axelson, 1993, p. 243).

The vast majority of research in career development has been drawn from the behaviors of middle- and upper-class white male subjects (Axelson, 1993). Career interventions based upon data related to this population will probably not be appropriate to meet the needs of individuals of differing social, economic, and cultural backgrounds.

Racism, Prejudice, and Discrimination

The traditional American worldview perceives an individual's success or failure primarily to be a result of that person's own skill and adequacy. Not having or not achieving high goals is conceptualized as a problem of internal deficiency. There is a belief that all people can better themselves if they only try harder (Axelson, 1993). This view is also basic to most philosophies of counseling (Axelson, 1993; Isaacson & Brown, 1993). Furthermore, occupational titles are culturally bound and associated with individual worth and dignity. The strengths and potential of women, people with disabilities, and many cultural minorities are often overlooked or underestimated.

Axelson (1993) states, "Most organizations do not openly refuse to hire or advance minorities, but the message is often somehow received that they are not welcome" (p. 262). Often, minority group members become hopeless, discouraged, and discontented. Career counselors working with minority clients should help clients to explore the effects of stereotypes, discrimination, and other environmental obstacles on their career aspirations and behaviors. Minority clients also need to be helped to learn more about their own strengths and environmental resources. Career counselors need to undertake a systems–wholistic perspective in which environmental factors outside the person are given as much emphasis as psychological factors within the person.

PROFESSIONAL ORGANIZATIONS AND CERTIFICATION

Counselors who specialize in career and lifestyle counseling can affiliate with two divisions of ACA: the National Career Development Association (NCDA) and the National Employment Counselors Association (NECA). In addition to holding meetings as part of the annual ACA convention, both organizations publish a newsletter and a journal. NCDA members receive the *Career Development Quarterly,* and NECA members receive the *Journal of Employment Counseling.*

The NCDA in 1981 established a certification program to recognize individuals who were qualified in the field of career counseling. Counselors can now attain certification as a Nationally Certified Career Counselor (NCCC) by meeting NCDA's minimum training, knowledge, and skill requirements and successfully completing the Career Counseling Specialty Exam administered by the National Board of Certified Counselors (NBCC). The NCCC certificate and many state counselor licensing laws, however, do not prevent untrained people from offering career counseling services. In many states career counselors are not regulated at all. As a result, in 1988 NCDA issued guidelines for assisting consumers in choosing qualified career counselors.

SUMMARY

The origin of career counseling as a specialty within the counseling profession dates back to the vocational guidance movement of the early 1900s, when the task of the counselor was to match clients with appropriate occupations. The specialty has now evolved to the point at which it is concerned with a lifelong process of career development, the learning of life skills, and the planning for leisure time.

Vocational guidance has been a major function of school counselors from the beginning of the movement. Career education programs funded by the federal government in the 1970s gave much encouragement and support to career development and counseling. The National Vocational Guidance Association (NVGA) has now become the National Career Development Association (NCDA), a division of ACA, and offers certification as a certified career counselor. Career counselors may also affiliate with the National Employment Counselors Association (NECA).

Career counseling is considered personal counseling because it emphasizes helping people work through personal career development issues. Not all personal counseling, however, is career counseling. The five major theoretical approaches to career development are the trait–factor approach, decision theory, situational approaches, the psychological–personality-based approach, and the developmental approach. The premises and components of Super's developmental approach have been described.

A number of strategies used in career counseling have been described, including assessment of client characteristics and interests, information giving, individual and group counseling, teaching the decision-making process, and the use of placement services.

From a systems–wholistic perspective many important factors influence work and career, including shifts in population growth, technological change, government legislation, racism, stereotyping women and ethnic minorities, and economic fluctuations. Career counselors need to undertake a systems perspective in which environmental factors outside the person are given as much emphasis as psychological factors within the person, especially when working with poor and minority populations.

Trends in career counseling include using ideas and approaches from other areas in counseling, such as incorporating aspects of family counseling, increased use of prepackaged programs, and assessment devices using computer technology. The use of computers is leading to improvements in the compilation and dissemination of career information. Career and lifestyle counseling continue to move from being almost exclusively aimed at children in school settings to including people of any age in almost any setting.

QUESTIONS AND ACTIVITIES

1. How do the theories of career development relate to the theories of counseling? As you select or develop a theory of counseling, do you also have to select and/or develop a compatible theory of career development?

2. Review the processes by which you have made career decisions up to this point. What developmental theories do you seem to have followed? Interview several adults about the process they experienced in their career development. If they worked with career counselors, what procedures, techniques, and assessment instruments, if any, were used? Were any of these approaches helpful? Share a summary of your learnings with the class.

3. Check with the local school system and determine how much, if anything, is being done in the way of systematic career education in the schools. Investigate different classes which might use career materials. Is career education a strong, proactive force in your community, or has it been allowed to fade from view?

4. Have a class discussion about what counseling students can do to supplement career counseling in the schools.

5. Check to see if there are any private practitioners in your community who specialize in career counseling. Visit one of them and learn as much as you can about being a private practice career counselor.

6. Visit a career center. Most college campuses have some type of career and placement center. For a complete experience, go as a client. Check out all of the resources available. If the center has a Discover or SIGI-Plus program, arrange for a session to use the program to become familiar with what it does.

RECOMMENDED READINGS

Axelson, J. A. (1993). Work and career development. In J. A. Axelson, *Counseling and development in a multicultural society* (2nd ed., pp. 224–267). Pacific Grove, CA: Brooks/Cole.

Bowless, R. (1996). *What color is your parachute* (7th ed.). Berkeley, CA: Ten Speed Press.

Isaacson, L. E., & Brown, D. (1993). *Career information, career counseling, and career development* (5th ed.). Boston: Allyn & Bacon.

INTERNET RESOURCES

Websites

California Career Development Association
<www.csun.edu/%7Ehcpsy001/ccda.html>

Careers <www.stetson.edu/~hansen/careers.html>

Careers Database Search—Career Find-O-Rama
<www.review.com/careers/find/car_search_form.html>

Career Exploration and Life Planning <www.sosc.osshe.edu/library/resour/ba272a.htm>

Career Magazine <www.careermag.com/careermag/>

Career Mosaic

Dictionary of Occupational Titles (DOT) <www.wave.net/upg/immigration/dot_index.html>

National Career Development Association

National Center for Research in Vocational Education (NCRVE)

Occupational Outlook Handbook <stat bls.gov/ocohome.htm>

Online Career Center—Career Assistance <www.iquest.net/occ/careerassist.html/>

Online Career Development Course <www.green-river.com/coutline.htm>

Riley Guide: Employment Opportunities and Job Resources on the Internet <www.jobtrak.com/jobguide/>

What Color Is Your Parachute: The Net Guide
<www.washingtonpost.com/parachute/>

REFERENCES

American Psychiatric Association. (1994). *Diagnostic and Statistical Manual of Human Disorders* (4th ed.). Washington, DC: American Psychiatric Association.

Axelson, J. A. (1993). Work and career development. In J. A. Axelson, *Counseling and development in a multicultural society* (2nd ed., pp. 224–267). Pacific Grove, CA: Brooks/Cole.

Baker, S. (1997). Helping students prepare for work and careers. *School Counselor, 44*(5), 333.

Borow, H. (1984). The way we were: Reflections on the history of vocational guidance. *Vocational Guidance Quarterly, 33,* 5–13.

Carkhuff, R. (1969). *Helping and human relations: Selection and training* (Vol. 1). New York: Holt, Rinehart & Winston.

Crites, J. O. (1981). *Career counseling.* New York: McGraw-Hill.

Egan, G. (1975). *The skilled helper: A model for systematic helping and interpersonal relating.* Monterey, CA: Brooks/Cole.

Havighurst, R. (1953). *Human development and education.* New York: Longmans, Green.

Herr, E., & Cramer, S. (1979). *Career guidance through the life span.* Boston: Little, Brown.

Herr, E., & Cramer, S. (1984). *Career guidance through the life span* (2nd ed.). Boston: Little, Brown.

Hershenson, D. B. (1996). Work adjustment: A neglected area in career counseling. *Journal of Counseling and Development, 74,* 442–446.

Holland, J. (1973). *Making vocational choices: A theory of careers.* Englewood Cliffs, NJ: Prentice-Hall.

Isaacson, L. E. (1985). *Basics of career counseling.* Boston: Allyn & Bacon.

Isaacson, L. E., & Brown, D. (1993). *Career information, career counseling, and career development* (5th ed.). Boston: Allyn & Bacon.

Joslin, L. (1984, June). Strictly speaking, vocationally. *The Vocational Guidance Quarterly,* 260–263.

Kjos, D. (1995). Linking career counseling to personality disorders. *Journal of Counseling and Development, 73,* 592–597.

Krumboltz, J. D. (1976). A social learning theory of career selection. *Counseling Psychologist, 6,* 71–80.

Levinson, D. (1977). *Seasons of a man's life.* New York: Knopf.

Parsons, F. (1909). Choosing a vocation. Boston: Houghton Mifflin.

Schwallie-Giddis, P. (1993, October). School-to-work opportunities offer new partnerships. *Guidepost, 35*(2), 23.

Srebalus, D., Marinelli, R., & Messing, J. (1982). *Career development.* Monterey, CA: Brooks/Cole.

Super, D. (1953). A theory of vocational development. *American Psychologist, 8,* 185–190.

Super, D. (1957). *The psychology of careers.* New York: Harper & Row.

Super, D. (1969). The natural history of lives and of vocations. *Perspectives on Education, 2,* 13–22.

Tolbert, E. (1980). *Counseling for career development.* Boston: Houghton Mifflin.

U.S. Department of Labor. (1991). *Occupational outlook handbook.* Scottsdale, AZ: Associated.

Vecchione, T. (1996, January). Career counseling and personal counseling: You can't have one without the other. *Counseling Today, 38*(7), 54–55.

Walz, G., & Benjamin, L. (1984). A systems approach to guidance. *Vocational Guidance Quarterly, 3*(3), 26–34.

Zunker, V. (1990). *Career counseling* (2nd ed.). Monterey, CA: Brooks/Cole.

chapter **15**

SCHOOL AND UNIVERSITY COUNSELING

- Can only certified counselors counsel in the schools?
- Is counseling in schools a necessity or luxury?
- Do counselor education programs train counselors to schedule students for classes?
- Do counselors need to be certified to work in a college setting?

Most of us first encountered a professional counselor at the middle or high school level. A few of you may have been fortunate to work with a counselor at the elementary level as well. School counseling has not only been the cornerstone of the field of counseling, but it also has been most peoples's initial contact with the field. In this chapter we will consider the emergence of comprehensive school counseling programs that necessitate a significant commitment to elementary school counseling, the redefinition of roles for middle and secondary school counselors, and the overarching developmental counseling approach that encompasses all of these levels. We also will explore counseling applications in higher education, focusing on student personnel work and college and university counseling.

Ideas in action When was the first time that you can remember working with a counselor? Did you receive the help you needed? How might your experience have been improved? How many of your ideas and attitudes about the field of counseling have been influenced by your experiences? Compare your findings with those of your classmates.

SCHOOL COUNSELING

The first school guidance program was initiated in 1889 by Jesse Davis, a high school principal in Detroit, Michigan (Wittmer, 1993b). Until the 1950s, *guidance* was the operative term in the schools and, in large part, for the entire counseling profession. *Counseling* is now the generally preferred term, although the term *guidance* is still used. In situations when the term *counseling* may still not be appropriate—for example, helping a classroom of students learn to handle test anxiety—the term *psychological education* (or *psychoeducation*) is often used now. This shift in terminology can be illustrated by the name change of the primary professional organization in the field. What was originally the American Personnel and Guidance Association (APGA) is now the American Counseling Association (ACA).

School guidance and counseling clearly dominated the counseling profession during the first three quarters of the twentieth century. Even now, when a person speaks of choosing counseling as a career, some people assume that the individual is planning to become a school counselor. The entire field of counseling has expanded dramatically in the last 25 years (see chapter 4), but school counseling is still the largest specialty. Current developments suggest that now is the golden age of school counseling. Employment projections by the U.S. Department of Labor state that

> employment of school counselors is expected to grow faster than average because of increasing secondary school enrollments, state legislation requiring counselors in elementary schools, and the expanded responsibilities of school counselors. Counselors are increasingly becoming involved in crisis and preventive counseling, helping students deal with issues ranging from drug and alcohol abuse to death and suicide. (U.S. Department of Labor, 1992, p. 134)

Although the need for all of these services is evident, the employment of all the needed counselors is clearly dependent upon the availability of adequate funding. In many parts of the country, school boards still view counseling programs as unnecessary luxuries, and as a result these programs are vulnerable when school districts have financial hardships (McGowan, 1993). Prospective school counselors may have to become politically active. They will have to help the public, the school boards, and the state and federal legislative bodies understand that school counseling must be an integral part of the school curriculum rather than treated as an expendable add-on. In addition, counselors need to promote the employment of full-time counselors at all elementary schools.

Qualifications of School Counselors

There has been a dramatic change in the qualifications for school counselors over the last quarter of the twentieth century. There may still be practicing counselors who were state certified merely by taking 18 hours in counseling courses beyond a master's degree in education; these courses may not have included even one practicum course or any group work.

Current standards for the certification of school counselors as specified in 1993 by the Council for Accreditation of Counseling and Related Educational Programs (CACREP), an affiliate of the American Counseling Association (ACA), call for a 48 hour master's program that includes extensive practice and internships, along with the content areas represented in this book (professional orientation, helping relationships, counseling theories, human development theory, social and cultural foundations, group counseling, career and lifestyle counseling, appraisal, research and evaluation, school counseling, and consultation). These current standards are beginning to have an impact on state certification guidelines and employment potential with many states requiring CACREP standards to be part of their requirements for their certified school counselors (Paisley & Hubbard, 1989). Furthermore, although there has traditionally been a distinction made between elementary and secondary counselors, some states are now requiring K–12 certification for all counselors. This means that prospective school counselors should have direct experience at the elementary, middle, and secondary levels during their practicum and internship experiences.

The Four Core Principles of Comprehensive School Counseling Programs

Of what kind of counseling program could a well-trained counselor hope to become a part? In a major review of 30 years of empirical research and professional standards, Borders and Drury (1992) found that there is widespread consensus on four core principles that characterize effective school counseling programs.

1. *School counseling must be an independent educational program.* Rather than having a loose assortment of services, there needs to be a detailed counseling curriculum that includes specific program objectives and student competencies, as well as detailed interventions, resources, and evaluation procedure (p. 488).

2. *The counseling program must be an integral part of the school district's total education program, not just a peripheral part of the teaching and learning process.* Preventive and developmental objectives should be infused into all aspects of the curriculum. For example, helping students learn about careers would be a part of any traditional curriculum area. Communication skills would be a natural part of language arts courses; problem-solving skills could be part of science and math; conflict resolution could be included as part of social studies; and health and wellness could be taught in physical education, health, and science classes. This infusion of counseling concepts and skills helps to ensure that all of the school faculty are directly involved with the counseling curriculum. This approach offers a contextualized curriculum, resulting in the skills and the specific course content having more meaning and relevance; therefore, although there is a clearly defined and independent curriculum, all faculty and staff would be instrumental in implementing the curriculum. This approach also helps to ensure that all students will be able to benefit from the counseling program.

3. *Comprehensive school counseling programs are developmental in nature.* This means that they are designed to be appropriate for the developmental stages of the students, as described in chapter 17. Borders and Drury (1992) report that research on such programs indicates positive improvement in various development dimensions as well as significant increases in self-concept and achievement scores, more positive attitudes toward school, and improved relations with other children (p. 489). This developmental principle will be discussed in more detail later in this chapter.

4. *Comprehensive programs are equitable; they serve all students equally without exception.* The history of school counseling programs was that low income students, rural students, and minorities were the least likely to receive counseling even though they needed counseling and guidance the most. Further, the Commission on Precollege Guidance and Counseling (1986) finds that in many urban schools, counselors' time was divided between students who were having a great deal of difficulty in school or

in their personal lives and the superior students who were actively pursuing post-secondary education. The result is that many of the students "in the middle" are not served (p. 41).

These four principles correspond directly with the counselor role statement developed in 1990 by the American School Counselor Association (ASCA). Role statements developed prior to 1990 specified different patterns of behavior for elementary, middle school, and high school counselors; however, the present ASCA statement focuses specifically on the five basic activities held to be common to all school counselors. These five activities are individual counseling, small group counseling, large group guidance, consultation, and coordination. These five basic services should constitute the majority of the counselor's work. Note that administrative duties such as scheduling and secretarial work are not listed.

Types of Program Interventions

Two major categories of interventions are performed by school counselors: direct and indirect services. **Direct services** include individual and group counseling and classroom guidance/psychological education. **Indirect services** include consultation with teachers and parents and coordination functions. A third type of activity, not generally considered an intervention, is clerical work. Studies of counselor workloads in schools that were rated excellent, average, and below average found that counselors at quality schools spent the majority of their time in counseling and consultation activities, whereas those working in average or below-average schools spent greater periods of time performing clerical duties (Wiggins & Moody, 1987; Miller, 1988). The ACA and the National Conference of State Legislatures recommend that elementary counselors spend 75% of their time in direct services. States such as Virginia (60%) and Florida (75%) have already mandated time allotments (Borders & Drury, 1992).

Direct Services

Individual and Group Counseling.   The basic purposes of counseling interventions in the school are to promote students' personal and social growth and to enhance their educational and career development. School counselors rarely do long-term therapy but instead work within a developmental framework to help students attain educational success. Short-term crisis counseling is provided when necessary, and referrals are made to outside agencies as needed (Gysbers & Henderson, 1988; Myrick, 1993).

Issues appropriate for school counseling include attitudes and behaviors, peer relationships, study skills, career planning, college selection, sexuality concerns, substance abuse, and family issues such as abuse, divorce, death of family member, and blended families. Counseling related to educational and career planning may often involve the administration of assessment instruments and subsequent test interpretation.

The intervention of choice in schools is small group counseling; these groups are time-limited, structured, and able to benefit from peer interaction. The powerful effects of bringing together students who share a common concern and can provide support and verification for each other cannot be underestimated. Peers are able to give and receive feedback and challenge each other to make changes more effectively than adults (Myrick, 1993).

Ideas in
action If you are thinking about becoming a school counselor, how do you react to the idea that the present approach to school counseling provides for little, if any, individual counseling with students? Will you be satisfied working primarily in the areas of preventive and developmental counseling?

Working with students in their classrooms to help them address their developmental needs is a special type of group work, an approach that provides an avenue for the counselor to be more visible. **Classroom guidance,** also referred to as **psychological education,** generally consists of a structured unit related to prevention or to the developmental needs of the children. Prepared or spontaneous units can be conducted in the classroom to respond to a particular need or to events such as the death of a student or teacher; racial conflict; or a hurricane, flood, or earthquake.

Indirect Services

Consultation.   Consultation interventions include working with consultees (teachers, staff, and parents) to help the consultees improve their interactions with children. Counselors in the consultant role may use individual conferences, seminars, or training workshops to teach specific skills or to focus on strategies for dealing with a specific problem. Even though it is an indirect service to children, consultation can have a significant impact in terms of the number of students served and as a major factor in the prevention of future problems (Borders & Drury, 1992).

Coordination.   "Coordination is a counselor-initiated leadership process in which the counselor helps organize and manage the comprehensive counseling program and related services" (Harrison, 1993, p. 140). Specific activities include planning and implementing regular programs such as student orientation, student advising, student appraisal, scheduling and placement, and special events such as a college night or a career fair.

One possible danger in performing the role of coordinator is that it may be easy to focus on these types of activities at the expense of direct services. To avoid the trap of becoming primarily a behind-the-scenes coordinator of counseling activities, one must keep in mind that to coordinate means to involve others. The role of coordinator also provides the opportunity to delegate duties in order to allow the faculty and staff greater ownership in the entire program.

Developmental School Counseling

The current trend of counseling in the schools is centered on the developmental school counseling (DSC) movement, an approach that has now been adopted, either partially or totally, by 47 states. The movement is away from the old "individual, position-oriented, one-to-one, small group counseling approach to a more preventive, wellness-oriented, proactive one" (Wittmer, 1993b, p. 5). Counselors are no longer expected to sit and wait for clients to come to their offices.

The contemporary developmental school counselor is curriculum and program oriented, is available to all, and is knowledgeable and competent to teach life skills to every student in the school regardless of race, religion, gender, or creed. (Wittmer, 1993, p. 5)

In the DSC approach, skills and experiences that students need to have as part of being successful in school and adulthood have been identified and related to specific learning behaviors and tasks. Classroom guidance/psychological education curricula designed to teach these skills and behaviors have been developed and should be implemented to complement the academic curriculum (Myrick, 1993, p. 11).

[This approach consists of a] comprehensive, planned program of sequentially presented activities as well as responsive services which address student growth and development as priority goals. It is an integral part of the total school curriculum and is designed to address the personal and social, educational, and career needs of all students at each grade level prekindergarten through senior high school. (Trotter, 1991, p. 5)

The DSC approach is significant for a number of reasons. First the traditional approach to school counseling has largely focused on scheduling, information dissemination, and reacting to crises, whereas the DSC movement offers a proactive, integrated, well-articulated structure covering the range of school experiences from preschool to high school. By design, DSC is geared to work with the developmental growth patterns (see chapter 16) of all children. It is an integral part of the total educational program of the school, not an appendage, and it is aimed at prevention as well as intervention. Above all, it is accountable, based on ongoing evaluations of the process and the products.

The major purpose of this approach is to change the role (whether real or perceived) of many school counselors from working with noncounseling administrative and clerical tasks for which they were never trained to focusing on "facilitating the personal–social (learning to live), educational (learning to learn), and the career development (learning to work) of their students" (Trotter, 1991, p. 6).

Implementing Developmental School Counseling in the Schools

There is a movement to certify school counselors from K–12, and there are now no official role distinctions made for school counselors at different levels; however, the fact remains that there are different types of activities and responsibilities at the elementary, middle, and high school levels. The comprehensive, integrated, and developmental counseling program can be implemented at these different levels.

Elementary School Counseling

Although school counseling has played a dominant role in the growth of professional counseling, elementary school counseling was not a significant part of the early history of the field. Prior to the mid-1960s, few counselors were employed at the elementary level. In 1964, however, Congress upgraded the National Defense Education Act (NDEA) that was first passed in 1958 after the Russians launched the Sputnik rocket. The 1964 version extended counseling services to the elementary level. As a result of government-funded training institutes, more than 10,000 counselors were employed at the elementary level by 1972 (Dinkmeyer, 1973). After the federal grants ended, the individual states were reluctant to increase their budgets accordingly; therefore, the numbers of elementary school counselors remained rather static until the 1980s.

Early proponents of counseling in the elementary schools stressed problem prevention and the development of human potential as primary reasons for elementary school counseling (Van Hoose, Pietrofesa, & Carlson, 1973). Now, however, the problems faced by children are better understood, and children's problems may require remediation in addition to preventive and developmental measures.

A major area of concern involves children who are considered **at risk** (a set of causal/ behavioral dynamics that places individuals in danger of a negative future event) in terms of possibly dropping out of school before graduation or graduating considerably below their potential. At-risk factors include suicide potential; poverty; incest; child pornography and other child abuse; dealing with divorce; alcohol and other drug abuse; two-career families; and single-parent families with latchkey children (Capuzzi & Gross, 1989).

The National Education Association, an organization not previously known for its support of school counselors, makes the following case for elementary school counselors:

> The new attitude in counseling is, the earlier the better. Or, don't wait for disaster. In the past, counseling was generally thought of as a task for the secondary school. Surely elementary students—cherubic, naive, still so young—could have no real problems, certainly none that would require professional help. Today's educators know better. The most serious problems of adolescence and even of adulthood—alcoholism, drug abuse, depressions, suicidal impulses, sexual conflicts—are showing up in the preteen population. And even the very young don't seem to be immune from them. These facts explain the new push to offer a variety of counseling services at the elementary level. There's clear evidence that behavioral problems are more easily identified, treated, and remedied in young children than in adolescents. What may be no more than a psychological bruise for a child at age 9 can, if untreated, easily become a gaping wound by age 16. (National Education Association, 1984, p. 52)

Because of these concerns, states such as Arkansas and Alaska began to mandate that there be at least one counselor in every elementary school. By the 1990–91 school year, a dozen states had mandated elementary school counseling (Gibson, Mitchell, & Basile, 1993). Figure 15.1 illustrates how a schedule for a modern elementary school counselor might look under ideal conditions.

Middle and High School Counseling

At the middle and high school levels, the general desirability and need for counselors has been rarely questioned. The need for counselors at these levels is acknowledged in almost every school district in the country.

A major difference at this level is the student load per counselor. The recommendation of ASCA is that there should be no more than 400 students per counselor. In comparison, the recommendation of one elementary counselor per building at the elementary school level, where there may be 800 to 1,000 or more students, is not enough. Even with the

Snyder (1993, p. 42) offers the following list of ideal counselor activities in a fully functioning, comprehensive elementary school developmental guidance program.

1. Counseling individuals
   | Scheduled | 2–5 hours per week |
   | Unscheduled | 2–3 hours per week |

2. Counseling groups — 4–6 sessions per week (6–14 hours per week)

3. Classroom guidance/ Psychological education — 6–8 sessions per week (4–8 hours per week)

4. Consultation — 1–3 hours scheduled daily

5. Coordination
Developmental guidance	Written plan, implemented and evaluated
Exceptional education program	Conducts timely meetings; clerk prepares letters, forms
Testing	Coordinates standardized testing; interprets test results

6. Administrative duties — Supervise clerical assistance; review records; participate in meetings

In addition to these generally regularly scheduled duties, elementary school counselors might also teach peer helper classes and parenting classes and be part of counseling and guidance committees (advisory boards)—all of this in addition to maintaining their own professional development. While this schedule is considered to be the ideal, it is possible. It offers the opportunity for counselors to be a major part of the team approach to working with the whole child for a significant amount of time in the child's development.

FIGURE 15.1   Guidelines for an ideal comprehensive elementary guidance program.
Adapted from "Managing an elementary school guidance program: The role of the counselor," by B. A. Snyder, 1993, *Managing Your School Counseling Curriculum: K–12 Developmental Strategies* (p. 42), by J. Wittmer, 1993, Minneapolis, MN: Educational Media Corporation. Adapted with permission.

---

reduced number of students, it is understandable why middle and high school counselors are not able to spend extended amounts of time counseling individual students.

As the developmental counseling approach continues to become established, counselors who may in the past have spent a great deal of time on administrative or even secretarial tasks will be focusing much more of their time and energies on student-oriented activities. Fully implementing all of the duties associated with the comprehensive developmental counseling approach leaves virtually no time for clerical and quasi-administrative duties that are still being performed by many school counselors. In this transition period, the school counselors and the professional organizations will have to work hard to inform administrators, school boards, parents, teachers, and students of the new way of providing student service.

Following the pattern established by elementary school counselors in the comprehensive, developmental approach, middle and high school counselors also apportion their time between counseling, classroom guidance, consulting, and coordinating (Baker, 1993; Coy & Sears, 1993). They work on skills-based programs designed to help adolescents deal with the developmental tasks of adolescence (Havighurst, 1972; Erikson, 1963), activities that are specific, student driven, and measurable rather than being vague and administrator driven (Coy & Sears, 1993).

An emphasis on career development is an integral part of the total developmental approach, and at the middle and high school levels an increasing number of ways are being created to infuse career development information, ideas, and related skills into the curriculum. There also is increased need for information services, use of interest inventories, and assistance in selecting postsecondary education, and in placement services for students not directly pursuing further education after graduation.

Ideas in action

Imagine that you have been trained to be a developmental school counselor, and you have just been hired to be a counselor in a very traditional high school. You fully believe in the developmental school counseling (DSC) principles, yet you know that there will be great pressure to do things the old fashioned way, which may include a great deal of administrative work. What steps would you take to carefully change the situation to be more in line with the DSC principles?

Student Assistance Programs

Some school districts, recognizing the need for more counseling services for their students and realizing that the regular school counselors are not always available to provide the in-depth attention necessary, are now contracting with outside agencies such as youth service bureaus and mental health centers to provide such services. Many school districts are also establishing ancillary programs in the schools. One formal program instituted in a number of U.S. schools is the Student Assistance Program (SAP), designed to focus on students who are at risk for alcohol, drug, and other substance abuse. SAPs are patterned after employee assistance programs in industry. SAPs generally have four components: group counseling sessions for students with alcoholic parents, counseling for students using drugs and alcohol, sessions for students not known to have problems with alcohol but who are performing poorly in school, and a component bringing SAPs and parent and community groups together (Schaefer, 1989).

Some schools have hired their own special counselor to establish an in-house Student Assistance Team (SAT) to supplement existing counselors. Other schools are using the team approach with existing personnel. In the state of Minnesota, SATs have been mandated by law for every public school (Moore & Forster, 1993). For such programs to be effective in the long run, it is imperative that SATs be under the umbrella of services offered and coordinated by a school counselor (Snyder, 1993).

The counselor may be a member of other teams in the school. One team may work with potential suicide cases. Another team may have the duty of appropriately handling child abuse cases (White & Flynt, 1993). A third may be trained to handle crisis counseling for the school in the event of a traumatic circumstance such as the accidental death of a student or teacher. Many schools also employ a social worker to provide a variety of other social services.

Multicultural Counseling in the Schools

The more we learn about schools, the more evident it is that they are composed of a highly diverse population and as such are representative of the nation as a whole. Other than the most obvious differences such as gender, skin color, size and shape, and physical disabili-ties, there are also many generally less obvious differences such as socioeconomic status, emotional stability, academic aptitude, psychomotor ability, learning style, sexual prefer-ence, and level of social skills. Any school, even an all-girl school or an all-Latino school, is a multicultural setting, and counselors and other school personnel have to be skilled in working with such diversity.

Developmentally oriented school counselors play a pivotal role in the life of the school in terms of working with cultural diversity. To function effectively in individual and group counseling, they need to understand the school and community environment as well as per-tinent aspects of the clientele with whom they work. (For example, is Juan a third-generation Hispanic American, or did he and his family just emigrate to America?) Counselors have to be able to work in classroom-sized groups in order to teach students to value diversity (Faubert, Locke, & McLoed, 1993) and tolerance. As students develop and mature, issues such as sexual identity arise, and the school counselor may need to help students deal with gay/lesbian issues (Wittmer, 1993a). It is estimated that up to one third of all adolescent sui-cides are related to sexual identity issues (Lacayo, 1992). Some of these incidents might be prevented with appropriate interventions.

Not to be overlooked is the counselor's work with special needs students or exceptional student education (ESE). These students range from the profoundly mentally handicapped to the highly gifted. With regard to this broad spectrum of students,

> no other educator is better equipped to assist the exceptional students themselves, their families, or their teachers to reach greater understanding of the nature of being a spe-cial needs student [than the school counselor]. It is through using the skills of both counseling and consulting that counselors reach out to all who work with this unique population. (Snyder & Offner, 1993, p. 130)

Issues in School Counseling

School counseling programs are not without their critics. Across the country there are many parent and religious groups that believe counseling activities, such as programs to help improve students' self-esteem, are contradictory to family values. The stance taken by many of these groups is that "children are being exposed to secular humanism, a person-centered philosophy that attempts to solve the problems of the world independent of God" (McCullough, 1994, p. 1). Members of these groups challenge counseling programs in a variety of ways, including participating in letter-writing campaigns to the school board, making public presentations, and serving directly on school boards themselves.

We, the authors, experienced this phenomenon firsthand when attending an ACA meet-ing in a major city. With two other colleagues, we were riding the hotel elevator on the way to a conference presentation. At one stop a group of people attending another conference in the same hotel, a religiously conservative group, got on the elevator. They looked at our convention badges and realized that we were counselors. They then began to verbally lash out at us, calling us "satans" among other things. Fortunately the elevator quickly arrived at the floor that they wanted so the confrontation was fairly brief. We, however, were quite shaken as we realized how strongly held some feelings of opposition are to counseling in the schools.

School counseling proponents, whether they have been challenged directly or not, consider such occasions as opportunities to articulate their principles and objectives in pursuing these programs and to accept valid criticism and make improvements as appropriate. Working to have an open discourse on all aspects of counseling can only serve to strengthen the position and the field as well.

Professional Status

A number of different descriptions of counseling personnel in the schools have been described in this chapter. How do they differ in terms of certification and other requirements? To begin, in all states, a school counselor has to be state certified. In almost all cases a counselor employed in a school becomes a part of the tenure-track professional education team. If the school district personnel have a professional agreement with an American Federation of Teachers or National Education Association group, the counselors would be part of the collective bargaining agreement negotiated by such a union. Other counseling personnel hired by the schools such as mental health agency counselors, SAP team members, and social workers generally have year to year contracts, are not on the tenure track, would not be represented by a union group, and would generally not have to be state certified.

All states have mandated criteria for certification or licensure as a school counselor. In some cases a counselor first must be certified as a teacher and have experience as a teacher. In many states now, however, there may be alternative methods of certification, including serving a yearlong internship in a school. Nationally, a school counselor can be certified as a Nationally Certified School Counselor (NCSC) by the National Board of Certified Counselors (NBCC).

School counselors may belong to the American School Counseling Association (ASCA), a division of ACA that publishes the *School Counselor* and the *Elementary School Counselor* journals. Student assistance professionals have their own professional organizations—the National Organization of Student Assistance Program Professionals (NOSAPP) and the National Association of Leadership for Student Assistance Programs (NALSAP).

COUNSELING AND STUDENT PERSONNEL SERVICES IN HIGHER EDUCATION

As postsecondary education has grown dramatically since World War II, there has been a significant increase in appropriately trained professionals in institutions of higher education. There are two major tracks from which counseling students wishing to pursue employment in higher education may choose. The first is working in student personnel services, which offers a variety of job opportunities, and the second is working in a college counseling center. In general, these are two separate programs at most campuses with a minimum of overlap of personnel and services.

Student Personnel Services

Student personnel services are quite diverse, and therefore there is no preferred entry point to the field. The different types of positions include admissions, recruitment, academic advising, registration, financial aid, records, retention, residence hall and food services, health services, disability and veterans services, and career and placement services. As with the K–12 school system, there is a significant emphasis on developmental work in the area of student services, so it is often referred to as student services/development.

Since the student services area covers such a broad spectrum of activities, a person could concentrate in one of three major emphases identified by the Council for Accreditation of Counseling and Related Professions (CACREP) for programs offering specialized training in Student Affairs Practice in Higher Education (SAPHE). These areas of emphasis are (1) administrative, which includes activities related to admissions, records, financial aid, food, and health (Ambler, 1989); (2) development, which includes offering students the opportunity to learn leadership skills, decision making, conflict resolution, and so on through the use of workshops and noncredit training programs; and (3) counseling from the student services perspective, which is preventive in nature and is more akin to the earlier conceptualization of guidance—that is, helping students enhance social and emotional growth in order to make sound educational, vocational, and interpersonal decisions. Activities include seminars on careers, dating, and stress management (Forrest, 1989). Students participating in these seminars who might need remediation for specific problems should be referred to the college counseling center.

A person wishing to specialize in student personnel work in higher education might pursue a number of specific student service occupations (see Figure 15.2). These include financial aid officer, career and placement director, student activities adviser, recruitment and admissions officer, and academic adviser. At schools with residence halls, there are residence hall directors, as well as the supportive personnel necessary to operate a residence hall system. For the most part, these positions are held by people with master's degrees in

---

Student Personnel Work

    Career and Placement Counselor/Director
    Student Activities Advisor
    Financial Aid Officer/Director
    Student Recruitment Officer
    Admissions Officer
    Department Program Advisors
    Graduate Program Advisors
    Resident Hall Directors
    Campus Life Director

College Counseling Centers

    Mental Health Counselors*
    Substance Abuse Counselors*
    Career Counselors
    Psychological Educators

*May need to be certified and/or licensed

FIGURE 15.2   **Jobs/job titles of college and university student personnel and college counseling employees who may hold the master's degree in counseling or a related field.**

counseling or a related field. There are no certification or licensure requirements to hold such positions.

College and University Counseling

Most colleges and universities have some type of student counseling service for the purpose of providing personal, educational, and vocational counseling to students, faculty, and staff. Campus counseling centers can range from elaborate independent facilities staffed with one or more psychiatrists, several clinical/counseling psychologists, social workers, mental health counselors, and psychometrists, to small centers attached to a department of psychology or a college of education that provides services to students primarily by practicum and internship students who are supervised by the school's faculty. Some centers serve only the campus community; others may serve the entire community.

An example of the structure of a large university counseling center would be the one at the University of Maryland. Maryland's center has five divisions: counseling service; disability support service; learning assistance service; parent consultation and child evaluation service; and the testing, research, and data processing unit. The counseling service division itself has five different components: direct service, consultation, staff development, training, and research (Westbrook et al., 1993). Note that the scope of the center includes working with children and parents in addition to the traditional college-student services. Note also the strong emphasis on research in what is primarily a service-oriented center.

Many counselors-in-training may have an opportunity to work in some type of college counseling center, as such centers are generally major practicum and internship sites. Large campuses with several different human service training programs (such as clinical psychology, counseling psychology, professional counseling, and social work) may have several such centers to provide training sites for as many students as possible.

In the past, campus counseling may have tended to be a rather narrow specialty, with counselors working primarily with 18- to 22-year-olds who often had similar religious and ethnic backgrounds. More recently, however, there has been increased diversity on most college campuses. Although there may be few schools that can match the student mix found at the University of California, Berkeley, in September of 1991, where there were 35% African American and Latino American, 35% Asian American, and 30% European American students (Faubert, Locke, & McLoed, 1993), many colleges are experiencing an increasingly diverse student body.

In colleges are greater numbers of **new majority students,** older students beginning their degrees, pursuing advanced degrees, or returning years after previously dropping out of school. There is increased ethnic and racial diversity and greater numbers of students with disabilities. At campuses with large graduate programs, as well as on campuses with large commuter populations, campus counseling centers can expect to have the full range of problems and diversity of clients found at any community mental health center and offer the same full range of services.

As in the elementary and secondary schools, many college counseling centers offer prevention and development programs. These are generally outreach programs and consultation efforts through which professional counselors offer psychological education programs in classrooms designed around such topics as stress management and test anxiety. There may be workshops and seminars open to the entire campus on topics such as racial issues. On residential campuses, much outreach work and consultation may be conducted in the residence halls (Westbrook et al., 1993).

Professional Status

Because there is such a wide diversity of interests and specialties within the field of higher education, the American College Personnel Association (ACPA), a professional organization that works to serve all of these different members, has recently experienced a major change. For several years the ACPA, one of the four groups that initially founded the American Personnel and Guidance Association (now the ACA) in 1952, held its major annual convention separate from ACA to better serve its members. Then, in 1992, ACPA voted to secede from ACA altogether and become an independent organization. A new division, the American College Counseling Association (ACCA), was then created by ACA for college counselors who wanted to maintain an affiliation with the ACA.

Other professional organizations also closely relate to the work of college counselors and student service specialists. These include the National Association of Student Personnel Administrators (NASPA) and the National Association for Women Deans, Administrators, and Counselors (NAWDAC). All of these organizations publish newsletters and professional journals and hold state and national conventions.

There are no specific certification or licensure requirements for college and university counselors. Prospective counselors planning to pursue work in the student services area might focus on attaining the NCC (Nationally Certified Counselor) and/or the NCCC (Nationally Certified Career Counselor) credentials. Those contemplating working in a college counseling center might want to pursue the Certified Clinical Mental Health Counselor (CCMHC) credential (see chapter 4).

SUMMARY

School counseling, the way most people have their first contact with a professional counselor, has undergone a major transition through the years. It has changed from primarily emphasizing guidance, with a focus on helping students make sound educational and vocational decisions, to a broader focus that emphasizes working with the total person. Terms such as *psychological education* or *psychoeducation* are often used to describe guidance functions.

School counseling has been and still is a major factor in the field of counseling, and it is in the process of becoming an increasingly important factor in the U.S. educational system; however, even though the outlook is good for the expansion of counseling in the schools, the expansion is clearly tied to the financial ability of school districts to sustain such programs. There is a need for school counselors, and aspiring school counselors, to be politically active in supporting favorable school counseling legislation at the state and national levels.

The qualifications of new school counselors are now largely determined by the Council for Accreditation of Counseling and Related Programs (CACREP), an affiliate of the American Counseling Association. A master's degree is required with a minimum of 48 credit hours. Certain courses and practicum and internship requirements are clearly required. A school counselor can become certified as a Nationally Certified School Counselor (NCSC).

Core principles of a comprehensive school counseling program include the following: (1) school counseling must be an independent educational program; (2) the school counseling program must be an integral part of the school district's total educational program and not a peripheral add-on; (3) the program should be developmental in nature and adapted to the developmental stages of children; and (4) the program should be equitable, serving all students without exception. Fully implementing this approach means that school counselors will not have time to perform noncounseling administrative and clerical tasks. They will be focusing more on direct services to children. Some states are now specifically mandating the percentage of time that counselors are to work with students and teachers.

There are two major types of program interventions that school counselors perform. Direct services include individual and group counseling and classroom guidance/psychological education. Indirect services include consultation and coordination. A developmental counseling program can be implemented at the elementary, middle, and high school levels. The Student Assistance Program, an ancillary program at the high school level that focuses on students who are at risk or who are already using alcohol and other drugs, is also described in this chapter.

Working equitably with all students in a developmental counseling program requires the counselor to be skilled at working with the broad spectrum of diverse individuals and groups. This includes working with parents who may not believe in the objectives of counseling in the schools.

Counseling services in higher education have been described. The distinction has been made between student personnel services and counseling at the college and university level. Descriptions of the variety of positions available for candidates with master's degrees in counseling have been provided as well as the professional organizations serving these occupations.

QUESTIONS AND ACTIVITIES

1. Spend all, or at least part, of a day with an elementary, a middle school, and then a high school counselor. Visit with school administrators. Ask the individuals about their ideas about fully implementing a comprehensive, developmental counseling program in the school (district). Alternative: Invite a counselor and an administrator to your class to discuss the same ideas.

2. Of which student service and counseling center activities on your campus are you already aware? Arrange to meet with personnel in each of these areas to find out the extent of the activities offered by your campus. Ask the personnel about their educational backgrounds and aspirations in the field.

3. How inclusive should a college counseling center be? Should it be open to the total community or just serve those who are directly a part of the campus itself? What issues are involved here?

4. Debate the following topic: "If we had fully implemented developmental programs from kindergarten through graduate school, we would be able to significantly reduce the number of societal problems caused by aberrant individuals. Such a benefit would more than justify the cost of such programs."

5. Make the following case: "If funds have to be cut in a school district, counselors and school counseling programs should be among the last cut."

RECOMMENDED READINGS

Myrick, R. D. (1993). *Developmental guidance and counseling.* Minneapolis, MN: Educational Media.

Wittmer, J. (Ed.). (1993). *Managing your school counseling curriculum: K–12 developmental strategies.* Minneapolis, MN: Educational Media.

INTERNET RESOURCES

Websites
American School Counseling Association
<www.edge.net/asca/>
American College Personnel Association

Student Counseling Centers on the Internet
<ub-counseling.buffalo.edu/centers.html>
School Psychology Resources On-line   <mail.bcpl.
lib.md.us/~sandyste/school_psych.html->

REFERENCES

Ambler, D. (1989). Designing and managing programs: The administrator role. In U. Delworth, G. Hanson, & Associates (Eds.), Student services: A handbook for the profession (2nd ed., pp. 247–264). San Francisco: Jossey-Bass.

American School Counseling Association. (1990). *Role statement: The school counselor.* Alexandria, VA: ACA Press.

Baker, B. (1993). Middle school counseling in the 90s: A practitioner's perspective. In J. Wittmer (Ed.), *Managing your school counseling curriculum: K–12 developmental strategies* (pp. 45–51). Minneapolis, MN: Educational Media.

Borders, L. D., & Drury, S. M. (1992). Comprehensive school programs: A review for policy makers and practitioners. *Journal of Counseling and Development, 70*(4), 487–488.

Capuzzi, D., & Gross, D. (Eds.). (1989). *Youth at risk: A resource for counselors, teachers, and parents.* Washington, DC: American Counseling Association.

Commission on Precollege Guidance and Counseling. (1986). *Keeping the options open: Recommendations.* New York: College Entrance Examination Board.

Council for Accreditation of Counseling and Related Professions. (1993). *Accreditation procedures manual.* Alexandria, VA: Council for Accreditation of Counseling and Related Professions.

Coy, D., & Sears, S. (1993). The scope and practice of the high school counselor. In J. Wittmer (Ed.), *Managing your school counseling curriculum: K–12 developmental strategies* (pp. 52–60). Minneapolis, MN: Educational Media.

Dinkmeyer, D. (1973). Elementary school counseling: Prospects and potentials. *School Counselor, 52,* 171–174.

Erikson, E. (1963). *Childhood and society.* New York: Norton.

Faubert, M., Locke, D., & McLoed, R. (1993). The counselor's role in teaching students to value cultural diversity. In J. Wittmer (Ed.), *Managing your school counseling curriculum: K–12 developmental strategies* (pp. 96–106). Minneapolis, MN: Educational Media.

Forrest, L. (1989). Guiding, supporting, and advising students: The counselor role. In U. Delworth, G. Hanson, & Associates (Eds.), *Student services: A handbook for the profession* (2nd ed., pp. 265–283). San Francisco: Jossey-Bass.

Gibson, R., Mitchell, M., & Basile, S. (1993). *Counseling in the elementary school.* Boston: Allyn & Bacon.

Gysbers, N., & Henderson, P. (1988). *Developing and managing your school guidance program.* Alexandria, VA: American Association for Counseling and Development.

Harrison, T. C. (1993). The school counselor as consultant coordinator. In J. Wittmer (Ed.), *Managing your school counseling program* (pp. 133–141). Minneapolis, MN: Educational Media.

Havighurst, R. (1972). *Developmental tasks and education.* New York: McKay.

Lacayo, R. (1992, December 14). Jack and Jack and Jill and Jill. *Time, 147*(50), 52–53.

McCullough, L. (1994). Do some school guidance programs contradict family and religious values? *Guidepost, 37*(7), 1, 12–13.

McGowan, S. (1993). Many school counseling programs cut when finances run low. *Guidepost, 36*(5), 1, 8.

Miller, G. M. (1988). Counselor functions in excellent schools: Elementary through secondary. *School Counselor, 36,* 88–93.

Moore, D. D., & Forster, J. R. (1993). Student assistance programs: New approaches for reducing substance abuse. *Journal of Counseling and Development, 77*(3), 326–329.

Myrick, R. D. (1993). *Developmental guidance and counseling: A practical approach* (2nd ed.). Minneapolis, MN: Educational Media.

National Education Association. (1984). *Today's education* (Annual edition). Washington, DC: National Education Association.

Paisley, P., & Hubbard, G. (1989). School counseling: State officials' perceptions and employment trends. *Counselor Education and Supervision, 29,* 60–70.

Schaefer, C. (1989). Student assistance programs follow lead of industry's EAPs. *Guidepost, 32*(4), 1, 3, 14.

Snyder, B. A. (1993). Managing an elementary school guidance program: The role of the counselor. In J. Wittmer (Ed.), *Managing your school counseling curriculum: K–12 developmental strategies* (pp. 33–44). Minneapolis, MN: Educational Media.

Snyder, B., & Offner, M. (1993). School counselors and special needs students. In J. Wittmer (Ed.), *Managing your school counseling curriculum: K–12 developmental strategies* (pp. 124–129). Minneapolis, MN: Educational Media.

Trotter, T. (1991). *Walking the talk: Developing a local comprehensive school counseling program.* Moscow, ID: University of Idaho.

U.S. Department of Labor. (1992). *Occupational outlook handbook* (1992–93 ed.). Indianapolis, IN: JIST Works.

Van Hoose, W., Pietrofesa, J., & Carlson, J. (Eds.). (1973). *Elementary school guidance and counseling: A composite view.* Boston: Houghton Mifflin.

Westbrook, F., Kandell, J., Kirkland, S., Phillips, P., Regan, A., MeUvene, A., & Oslin, Y. (1993). University campus consultation: Opportunities and limitations. *Journal of Counseling and Development, 72,* 684–688.

White, J., & Flynt, M. (1993). The school counselor's role in prevention and remediation of child abuse. In J. Wittmer (Ed.), *Managing your school counseling curriculum: K–12 developmental strategies* (pp. 106–117). Minneapolis, MN: Educational Media.

Wiggins, J. D., & Moody, A. H. (1987). Student evaluations of counseling programs: An added dimension. *School Counselor, 34,* 353–361.

Wittmer, J. (1993a). Counseling lesbian and gay students. In J. Wittmer (Ed.), *Managing your school counseling curriculum: K–12 developmental strategies* (pp. 118–123). Minneapolis, MN: Educational Media.

Wittmer, J. (Ed.). (1993b). *Managing your school counseling curriculum: K–12 developmental strategies.* Minneapolis, MN: Educational Media.

chapter 16

COMMUNITY COUNSELING AND CONSULTATION

- What opportunities are available for the application of counseling skills in community and business settings?
- What is the effect of managed care on community counseling?
- What are the similarities and differences between counseling and consulting?

Throughout this text we have emphasized a systems perspective based on the fact that each of us operates in the larger context of society made up of interpersonal, family, work, and community levels. These levels are interrelated. The systems approach views communities and business settings as functional units, entities unto themselves—entities that are made up of more than the sum of their members. This chapter looks at the many different types of community-based counselors and the different settings in which they work, along with the opportunities available in the business community in consulting and organizational development. Community counseling and consulting are particularly exciting because of the many roles counselors play and the wide variety of methods they use to effect change in community and organizational settings.

COMMUNITY COUNSELING

Background

The emergence of both community counseling and consulting came as a result of the final report of the Joint Commission on Mental Illness and Health in 1961 and the Community Mental Health Centers Act of 1963. These actions led, for the first time in U.S. history, to the use of federal funds for the development of an effective system of intervention in the field of mental disorders. As a result of the mental health center legislation, helping professionals were encouraged to move toward more developmental and preventive interventions and away from remedial interventions (see chapter 9) (Jackson & Hayes, 1993; Gelso & Fretz, 1992; Albee & Ryan-Finn, 1993). Major changes proposed by the legislation included the construction of 2,000 community mental health centers and the gradual reduction and elimination of the overcrowded state mental hospitals. Efforts at developmental and preventive interventions were further encouraged by Lyndon Johnson's War on Poverty during the 1960s, which had as its goal the reduction of the miserable living conditions that apparently spawned high rates of mental disorders, alcoholism, and drug use. The Commission on Mental Health appointed by President Carter included in its final report a proposal for major increases in prevention efforts (Albee & Ryan-Finn, 1993). The commission developed a formula that encompassed most mental health efforts:

$$\text{INCIDENCE} = \frac{\text{Organic factors} + \text{Stress}}{\text{Coping skills} + \text{Self-esteem} + \text{Support groups}}$$

The incidence of mental disorders in an individual is equivalent to the presence of difficult life circumstances over available resources and strengths. Problems occur whenever the numerator is greater than the denominator. Effective efforts to alter factors in the numerator or denominator alter incidence at the other side of the equation. This is rooted in the public health tradition in which incidence of a physical disease is reduced either by increasing the resistance of the host (strengthening the factors in the denominator) or by reducing or eliminating the noxious agent (reducing factors in the numerator) (Homer & McElhaney, 1993).

Definition and Goals

Community counseling is "a multifaceted approach combining direct and indirect services to help community members live more effectively and to prevent the problems most frequently faced by those who use the services" (Lewis & Lewis, 1989, p. 10). Just as the family is the identified client and target of intervention in family counseling, community counselors view the community as the client and target of intervention. Community counselors understand their clients by examining their social setting and focusing on ways of changing environmental factors that contribute to individual mental problems. Their interventions are aimed primarily at populations who are most in need of mental health services and usually most excluded from receiving them, such as ethnic minorities and the poor and elderly. Community counselors' strategies reach out to the community and include identifying and working with groups who are at risk for certain problems such as substance abuse; poor health; physical, emotional, and learning disabilities; poverty; and emotional and physical abuse in order to reduce their incidence. They also attempt to empower and increase the amount of coping skills of their target populations through education, client advocacy, and political involvement such as influencing policy makers. Counselors who have a strong sense of social responsibility (see chapter 4) may be particularly attracted to community counseling. The following are some of the ways counselors work to meet the mental health needs of the community.

Substance Abuse Counseling

An area with increasing opportunity for counselors is in the specialty of substance abuse counseling. **Substance abuse** includes the abuse of all drugs, including alcohol. The definition even includes foods such as sugar when the foods are used to alter a person's mood or psychological state, usually for the purpose of avoiding dealing with difficult situations (Schmolling, Youkelles, & Burger, 1985). Abuse often leads to psychological or physical addiction. Because this specialty usually involves physical symptoms, many treatment centers related to different types of substance abuse are located in hospitals and clinics.

Drug abuse has become recognized as a disease by insurance companies and the federal government, and substantial amounts of money are available for substance abuse counseling, one of the biggest growth areas in the counseling field.

Even though substance abuse counseling is an area of specialization by itself, counselors must be aware that many people abuse food and drugs in some form from time to time. A client seen in any agency, at almost any age, may be a substance abuser in addition to having other problems; therefore, all counselors must have an awareness of substance abuse, if only to make proper referrals.

Counseling for substance abusers can be complex because there may be other problems in a person's life in addition to chemical dependency. Although there is not total agreement among professionals that ingesting a given substance actually leads to acquiring a disease, having a disease label such as *alcoholism* has made it possible for some people to risk getting help and to have financial assistance through health insurance. In many cases the problem may be so severe that detoxification is necessary, preferably under medical supervision. Medication may also need to be provided as part of a treatment plan.

In most cases of substance abuse, medical treatment alone is not sufficient; generally many types of counseling services are offered. These services include group and family counseling, both of which may be extremely important in helping a person decide to change an undesirable behavior pattern and then to maintain the new behavior. For the best results, counseling is usually supplemented by support groups, such as Alcoholics Anonymous or Overeaters Anonymous, to help maintain the desired behavior for life. Exercise and relaxation programs are often prescribed to improve physical well-being and establish positive addictions (Glasser, 1976).

Substance abuse education as part of a prevention program is particularly important; research suggests that only 1 in 36 alcoholics receives treatment, recovers, and gets well (Ohlms, 1983). This treatment record is not impressive, and it emphasizes the need for preventive programs. Group therapies with alcoholics are regarded as more effective than individual modalities. They may be based on psychodynamic, cognitive, behavioral, or other principles. Interventions might include instructional lectures, discussions, deep analytic explorations, psychodrama, hypnosis, confrontation, and marathon sessions. The group leader establishes rules, screens and prepares members for admission, educates clients about drugs, and tries to ensure that the group norms are followed. The support of the group allows for individual resolution to give up alcohol or other drugs. Substance abuse counselors often participate in specialized programs and in some cases can receive special certification as drug and alcohol abuse counselors. The American Psychological Association (APA) has selected substance abuse as the focus of its first proficiency credential for practitioners. The association is designing a written examination to measure psychologists' proficiency in addiction treatment. The governing board of the National Association of Social Workers (NASW) recently granted provisional status to a practice section on alcohol and other drugs, an entity that will become a full-fledged section. The National Association of Alcoholism and Drug Abuse Counselors (NAADAC) has been dealing with alcohol and drug issues for over 25 years.

It is possible in some states, such as Indiana, to be certified directly as a drug abuse counselor without necessarily having a counseling degree. Marriage, family, and child counselors in California must now complete a course in substance abuse in order to be eligible for their license.

One factor that has prevailed from the earliest work with substance abuse counseling is that recovering addicts are often given preference over nonaddicts for counseling positions. This practice has occurred because presumably the addict's personal experience would make for greater empathy, and the model of being a productive recovering addict would have a positive impact on clients. The assumption that one must be a recovering addict to provide effective treatment has been challenged by research. The general conclusion is that counselors who are recovering addicts are not any more effective than counselors who are nonaddicts (LoBello, 1984).

An area of specialization related to substance abuse counseling is working with the adult children of alcoholics (ACOAs). Alcohol abuse causes problems for the abusers and their immediate families and also for the adult children of the abusers regardless of whether they drink themselves. Having been part of a dysfunctional family has left the ACOAs with deficiencies in coping and in relationship skills that have a significant impact on their personal and emotional development. Counseling processes include working with grief and shame and helping clients learn to accept themselves, express their needs, and have fun without guilt (Possum & Mason, 1986; Gravitz & Bowden, 1986; Middleton-Moz & Dwinell, 1986).

Another developing specialty for counselors is counseling driving under the influence (DUI) offenders. For those facing a DUI charge, professional counseling is often required by a court or a state's department of motor vehicles (DMV) in order to reinstate one's license. Many DUI offenders want to get their licenses back as quickly as possible, so they shop around for the most affordable treatment. In turn, an increasing number of practitioners who are wary of working with managed care companies are tapping this specialty, because clients must pay out-of-pocket when their insurance does not offer coverage (Marino, 1997).

Gerontological Counseling

Another area of growth in the counseling field is **gerontological counseling,** the counseling of older citizens. In a survey of counselor educators, Daniel and Weikel (1983) found that the primary trend identified was an increase in gerontological counseling as a specialty. This movement toward working more with the older members of society was highlighted in 1988, when the Association for Adult Development and Aging (AADA) became a division of ACA.

In 1900, life expectancy was 49 years; today it is 76. The life expectancy is expected to continue to inch up slowly. In the next 20 to 30 years we will probably see more people between 100 and 110 years of age (Schlosberg, 1995). With the increasing number of people living longer, there has been a corresponding increase in interest in working with the aged in a variety of settings (such as community centers, retirement centers, nursing homes, and hospice programs). Counselors working in these settings can be employed by the agencies or be private practitioners (Tomine, 1986).

Although older adults face multiple developmental and ecological issues and have a variety of psychosocial needs, only a small proportion of older adults seek counseling assistance (Weiss, 1995), and their needs have often been overlooked. This age group has recently found that it can exert a significant amount of political influence on issues of importance to people over age 60. Therefore, even though much effort has gone into expanding and improving the services offered to the elderly, more can be expected in the future.

Health Counseling

Another major specialty area for trained counselors is health counseling. "**Health counseling** uses the skills of the counselor to help clients make the kind of lifestyle changes that enhance their physical health" (Lewis, Sperry, & Carlson, 1993, p. 4). As Thoreson and Eagleston (1985) state, "Good health needs good counseling....Wellness depends on the ongoing integrity of thoughts, feelings, and actions" (p. 77). It is in the promotion of positive interaction between these attributes that the skills of the counselor can be most invaluable. Health counseling or behavioral health is perhaps the most predominantly preventive specialty area. Behavioral health has been defined by Matarazzo as

> an interdisciplinary field dedicated to promoting a philosophy of health that stresses individual responsibility in the application of behavioral and biomedical science knowledge and techniques to the maintenance of health and the prevention of illness and dysfunction by a variety of self-initiated individual or shared activities. (Matarazzo, 1986, p. 813)

The clients for such services may have had problems of various types, but the focus in health counseling is not to remediate old problems but to promote wellness, prevent disease, and help people learn to "care for their own 'disease' when appropriate" (Thoreson & Eagleston, 1985, p. 77). Therefore, much more is done in the way of education and training than in therapy. Rejecting the medical model that focuses on the diagnosis and treatment of disease, Thoreson and Eagleston (1985) prescribe an educational model that emphasizes training people to think, make decisions, and solve problems. These skills are deemed necessary for the ongoing prevention of disease and the maintenance of wellness. Such an approach requires an educated, informed public. Skilled counselors may be employed in a variety of settings to work with health-related issues of men, women, and children of all racial and ethnic groups to ensure that these skills are learned. Included in this area is the concept of wholistic counseling, an approach that looks at the total person and works to integrate the physical, psychological, and spiritual dimensions of a person's life (see chapter 11).

Some evidence of the changes in the proactive approaches to health can be seen in most communities, as hospitals and medical centers broaden the scope of their services. Instead of focusing only on remediation and treatment, hospitals are now adding health and lifestyle centers or wellness centers to their operations and, in general, appear to be taking a more preventive view toward health. Subspecialty areas offered at such wellness centers include nutritional counseling, exercise and health education, and stress management. Although these areas all focus on the total person, they do in some ways overlap. For example, a proper diet and a sound exercise program are considered important components of a good stress management program (see chapter 2).

Some occupations, such as nurse–counselor and physician's assistant, may be oriented to some degree toward remediation. Such practitioners tend to work with people who are experiencing one or more problems and need more time to be heard and to understand personal care procedures than is generally available from a physician. Nurse–counselors, in addition to working with patients, often are able to provide support to other nurses (for example, helping to work with the problems of stress that could lead to burnout).

Two types of eating disorders, anorexia and bulimia, are both related to using eating habits to enhance a person's self-image and often to control other people. These disorders are dealt with in group and family counseling settings, along with medical consultation. Weight-reduction programs, a form of nutritional counseling, generally offer group work to provide support and encouragement to the participants.

Helping AIDS victims and their families has also become an area of major concern to health professionals. Health professionals work with current cases and strive to prevent future occurrences through encouraging community education, starting AIDS support groups, establishing hotlines, and counseling AIDS victims and their families.

Governmental Support for Health Counseling

All of these health counseling approaches are being pursued with the full encouragement of the federal government. Research into a number of areas has produced results indicating that some chronic diseases are not as inevitable as once feared. These diseases include lung cancer, heart disease, and adult-onset diabetes. The result has been the development of the Office of Disease Prevention and Health Promotion (ODPHP) for the purpose of pursuing proactive initiatives (McGinnis, 1985).

The set of national health objectives developed by ODPHP in 1980 included, among other things, the need for measures to motivate behavior change in order to prevent debilitating problems (U.S. Department of Health and Human Services, 1980). Specific preventive initiatives include

(a) working with professional organizations with an opportunity to influence the behavior of health providers operating in clinical settings; (b) working with public and private reimbursement agencies and organizations to foster their consideration of reimbursement of preventive services; and (c) support in evaluations and studies to enhance the understanding of the effectiveness of preventive services offered in a clinical setting. (McGinnis, 1985, p. 210)

Health counseling, or the behavioral health movement, "while still in its infancy, is likely to become a professional domain of major significance during the next two decades" (Ford, 1985, p. 93). It will be exciting to see the many ways that counselors will be able to apply their special areas of knowledge and skill in conjunction with other health professionals.

Rehabilitation Counseling

Rehabilitation counselors are specialists who help clients with disabilities overcome deficits in their skills. Disabilities can manifest themselves in many different ways. Even though a major objective of a rehabilitation counselor is to help a client learn to cope with a specific mental or physical disability, such as deafness, the full goal is wholistic in nature: to help the client become fully functioning in all areas in spite of any disability or limitation.

In addition to its applicability to clients with physical disabilities such as blindness or loss of a leg, rehabilitation counseling is necessary for prisoners after release from prison, for psychiatric patients after release from mental hospitals, and for people with developmental disabilities. Much substance abuse counseling might be considered rehabilitative. People who have lost their jobs after many years of employment also need to go through a rehabilitative process. Many companies and unions have established counseling programs for workers who have lost their jobs as a result of plant closings or downsizing.

Rehabilitation counselors generally specialize within the field itself, working with specific physical disabilities, for example. A great amount of knowledge and considerable skill are essential to work with a targeted population, because the counselor needs to understand the nature of the disability itself, to establish the therapeutic alliance necessary to help the person, and to be aware of all the dynamics surrounding the situation. In many cases of rehabilitation counseling, the clients have incurred some kind of loss (for example, the loss of a leg or the loss of a job). The counselor's understanding of the grief process (Kubler-Ross, 1969), which accompanies any significant loss, is vital. Much rehabilitation work is vocational, requiring knowledge and skills in career counseling. Marriage and family counseling is often required, as well as sex counseling if the disability affects sexual functioning.

Rehabilitation counseling is often associated with hospitals such as the Veterans Administration hospitals, rehabilitation centers established by insurance companies, and state and local agencies. Although still linked to legislation and government funding, rehabilitation counseling has become less agency dominated and more centered on the individual client (Giordano, 1995).

Certification as a certified rehabilitation counselor (CRC) can be attained through the American Rehabilitation Counseling Association (ARCA), a division of ACA. Many states also have licensing requirements for rehabilitation counselors.

Crisis and Disaster Counseling

Many counselors have responded to events that devastate communities, such as storms, floods, fires, earthquakes, and riots. After the Northridge earthquake in 1994, mental health professionals established hotlines and offered counseling to those affected by the tragedy. Many counselors assisted with flood relief efforts during the Midwest floods in 1993, counseled victims of the Los Angeles riots in 1992, and offered their services to victims of Hurricane Andrew, which devastated parts of Florida in 1992.

On a smaller scale, counselors regularly become involved in local crises, such as working with the victims of a school bus accident or of a shooting at a fast food restaurant. Crisis intervention research shows that if interventions are made quickly by helping professionals when these events occur, those affected will recover quickly. One fast intervention of psychological first aid is critical incident stress management (CISM). It was originally developed to treat public service workers exposed to extreme levels of trauma. Currently it has found widespread application in a variety of settings for treating anyone exposed to natural or man-made disasters (Jackobs, 1995). One phase of the CISM team intervention is to provide a critical incident stress debriefing (CISD). This is most often a structured group session that offers educational information and psychological assistance designed to counter the effects of the trauma caused by the disaster experience. Since the value of counselors has been demonstrated in such situations, and since there seems to be almost a steady stream of crisis events, the ACA and the American Red Cross are now jointly offering special short-term training programs in crisis counseling to even better prepare future crisis counselors.

Client Advocacy

Often counselors engage in client advocacy for those who do not have the awareness or resources themselves or who are disenfranchised, such as rape and child abuse victims, oppressed minorities, neglected elderly populations, and homeless persons. Other counselors work on behalf of special interest groups such as gays and lesbians by educating the community, presenting in-service workshops for helping professionals, and influencing policy makers.

COMMUNITY COUNSELING AND MANAGED CARE

Mental health practitioners are concerned with losing control of psychotherapy, declining incomes, and at least a temporary decline in the quality of psychotherapy. In place of independent practitioners they find themselves becoming technicians implementing a series of short-term protocols under the guidance of managed-care case workers.

Mental health practitioners are also concerned with how managed care reverses the very standards of practice under which psychotherapy is conducted. Their greatest fear is the possible undermining of the therapeutic relationship by reversing the standard of confidentiality, the cornerstone of the therapeutic relationship. Most managed-care companies are requiring detailed clinical notes and histories for approval of therapy sessions. These clinical analyses are seen by the multiple persons at the managed-care company and then find their way onto microfiche or computer. There is nothing in law today preventing the release by an insurer to the employer of the names of employees using mental health services. Today, therapists are having clients under managed care sign agreements that confidentiality cannot be guaranteed (Brave, 1994, p. 35).

Many practitioners are concerned that they can no longer guarantee the adequacy of treatment. Managed-care companies have the power to simply deny use of the mental health benefit. For the most part, the decisions to approve or disapprove treatment are being made by untrained case managers. Most managed-care companies rank therapists according to their compliance with company paperwork and policy. If therapists are not found compliant, they are excluded from the system of referrals. Even with approval, a client is given only a small block of sessions, destroying a counselor's ability to plan treatment beyond three to five sessions. Cases have been reported of therapists with suicidal clients who are being denied treatment by managed care.

Mental health professionals are at a decided disadvantage when it comes to legislative redress. They are simply no match for the clout of insurance companies in the halls of state and federal governments. In the meantime, counselor educators—who are concerned with the effect of managed care on the training and supervision of their students—and many practitioners are learning how to adapt to the current situation.

Ideas in
action

These [managed care] companies are driving longtime therapists out of the field because of [the companies' commitment to the almighty bottom line instead of [a] commitment to patient health care. If we don't do something to stop it now, tomorrow may truly be too late.

John Grohol (1997)

How does the above statement affect you? Are you concerned about how managed care will impact you? What can you do about it?

CONSULTATION

One major way counselors can use their skills is through the process of consultation. As noted, much of the counselor's work in the school setting is as a consultant. The definition of *consultation* and the role of the consultant have evolved significantly from their inception (Kurpius & Fuqua, 1993a):

> Perhaps one of the most significant changes in the practice of consultation is in helping the consulted become more conceptual in understanding the multiple ways of viewing a problem and possible solutions as well as in helping him or her conceptualize the future so that a similar problem does not reoccur. Good consultants have possessed this conceptual ability for their own use but have only recently realized the power offered to the consultee if this conceptual knowledge is transferred to the client or client system. (p. 596)

The definitions, goals, and processes of consultation vary widely. Generally, **consultation** involves one person (the client) who has a problem with a person, group, organization, or community but lacks the knowledge or skill for its solution and who turns to another (the consultant), a specialist who has the requisite ability to aid in the problem's solution. The process of consultation helps those individuals, groups, organizations, and communities function more effectively and efficiently and with greater satisfaction (Korchin, 1976; Kurpius & Fuqua, 1993b). The consultant aims to improve the mental health of individuals (human services consultation such as that found in schools—see chapter 15) and the functioning of organizations (organizational development consultation). The consultant's goals are to help consultees deal with their current work problems and to provide information or teach skills that help them to deal effectively with similar problems in the future (Mendoza, 1993).

Types of Consultation

Four distinct types of consultation have been described by Caplan (1970).

Client-Centered Case Consultation

In client-centered, or clinical consultation, a referral is made to a specialist who provides direct service to the client (Gallessich, 1985). The service may be in the form of an examination and diagnosis with recommendations for treatment, or the specialist may take over full responsibility for subsequent treatment of the client (for example, a counselor referring a client to a psychiatrist for a medical evaluation and the possible need for drug therapy).

Consultee-Centered Case Consultation

In consultee-centered case consultation, the consultant works with the consultee's difficulties in dealing with a particular client or groups of clients. The consultant may work to resolve a specific problem that the consultee is having with a client, expand the consultee's overall skill in dealing with a particular type of client, or improve the consultee's skills in general. In each instance, the focus of the consultant is on the consultee's work and would rarely, if ever, involve firsthand service to a primary client. Because the consultee is directly involved, there is a distinct advantage in this approach. Consultees may learn information and skills that will allow them to work effectively with similar clients in the future without the help of consultants. This triadic arrangement is considered to be one of the "definitive orienting concepts for the field" of consulting (Mannino & Shore, 1985, p. 364). The consultant's roles include being an educator and a facilitator (Gallessich, 1985). For example, a counselor working with a teacher on classroom management skills is a consultant.

Program-Centered Administrative Consultation

In program-centered consultation, the focus is on working with a specific program or organizational structure and not on the consultee's difficulties with the program or structure. For instance, a consultant might be employed to make recommendations to a college counseling center that is contemplating making programmatic changes. Professionals performing this type of consultation are often referred to as organizational consultants and are concerned with organizational development (OD). Roles implemented by consultants working with OD include teacher–trainer, diagnostician, participant–observer, coach, facilitator, and action-researcher (Gallessich, 1985).

Consultee-Centered Administrative Consultation

In consultee-centered administrative consultation, the consultee's difficulties in working with a program or organization form the primary objective; the various components of the program or organization are secondary. For example, a consultant might work directly with an administrator on leadership or management skills. This is more of a **doctor–patient model** (Schein, 1978) or prescriptive mode (Kurpius, 1978), for which the consultant is to define or diagnose the problem, explore various solutions, and prescribe action. The consultant then supports the consultee as the action steps are implemented.

In practice it may be difficult to determine the exact type of consultation being used, especially when there is a continuation of these approaches. In the initial establishment of a consulting relationship, however, it is important to be specific about to the desired objectives. Each type of consultation generally calls for a different contract, different expectations, and different behavior. Ultimately, the determination of the effectiveness of consulting is based on the degree of success to which the contract and all objectives therein have been met.

Content and Process Consultation

Other ways of looking at consultation are based on considering different helping styles and may have profound implications on how the consultation relationship is operationalized. These styles include **purchase of expertise, doctor–patient,** and **process consultation** (Schein, 1978; Rockwood, 1993). The first two focus on the content of organizational problems; the client presents a problem to the consultant and expects the consultant to find and implement a solution. This is how the consultant–consultee role was initially perceived. In the purchase of expertise mode, the client usually identifies the specific need and contracts with the expert consultant to solve it. In the doctor–patient mode the client only recognizes that something is wrong but is not aware of what it is or how to fix it (Rockwood, 1993). The consultant collects information, makes a diagnosis, and gives direction to the consultee based on that diagnosis.

The process consultation mode focuses on how organizational problems are solved, and the client and consultant collaborate to find workable solutions. The process mode fits the wholistic–systems paradigm (see chapter 11), which emphasizes collaboration, participation, and other forms of interpersonal and intrapersonal connectedness. From this perspective consultants are neither merely experts who make interventions for all to accept nor merely processors of what exists. They, as in all effective helping relationships, use themselves as instruments in such a way as to help their clients better understand the paradigm issues, human and structural, that support and hinder growth, development, and desired change.

Each of these modes are interconnected and interactive and not an either–or situation. The choice of which mode to use depends on many factors, including the stage of the consultation process, the extent to which clients are able or willing to help themselves, and the clients' worldview.

The Roles of a Consultant

Consultants may serve in one or more roles in each consulting relationship. They may be teachers and trainers, communication facilitators, or human relations mediators, and they may serve as catalysts, helping clients brainstorm and put ideas into action (Korchin, 1976).

As **teachers and trainers,** consultants function both as technical helpers and resource personnel. They bring in relevant research literature, experience with comparable problems in other settings, and knowledge of useful techniques relevant to the concern of clients.

As **communication facilitators,** consultants may work with various members within the client's agency, between agencies, or between the client, the agency, and the larger community. When working as **human relations mediators,** consultants, as outsiders, can often diagnose and assist in the resolution of internal conflicts that affect the work of clients. In such cases they must avoid being pushed into the role of judge or referee. Finally, as **catalysts,** consultants can help inspire and even rejuvenate a client, agency, or organization by helping people to develop new ideas and to implement ideas deemed desirable. The ultimate function of the consultant is to contribute to the solution of the client's problems while at the same time developing the client's capacity to resolve future problems (Korchin, 1976, p. 512).

The Consultation Process

Like counseling, the consultation process proceeds through a series of stages. Kurpius, Fuqua, and Rozecki (1993) have described six stages, which they label (1) preentry; (2) entry, problem exploration, and contracting; (3) gathering information, problem confirmation, and goal setting; (4) solution searching and intervention selection; (5) evaluation; and (6) termination.

In the preentry stage, when consultants are contacted by clients, consultants need to do a self-assessment to determine whether they have the skills, attitudes, and time necessary to provide the requested services effectively. If the answer is no, an appropriate referral needs to be made; if the answer is yes, the consultant and client move to the entry stage, where the basic working relationship is established. The entry stage "involves the establishment of the relationship between consultant and consultees upon which the rest of the process depends" (Korchin, 1976, p. 515). It includes identifying the nature of the problem and then making a contract so that all parties know the purpose, objectives, ground rules, expectations, resources needed, and time lines.

It then is necessary to gather as much information as possible in order to define the problem accurately and determine the best interventions for solving the problem. With the problem defined and mutually agreed on by the consultant and the client, the next important step is to reach agreement on ownership of the problem: who is responsible for causing the problem, and who is responsible for problem solution? The solution of the problem becomes the goal to be reached sometime in the future. In the next stage the best possible intervention strategies need to be chosen to achieve the best solutions to the problem. The solution to the plan would then be implemented and the results evaluated. The process could then be recycled or the consulting relationship terminated.

Counseling and Consulting Compared

The consultative process is not that different from the counseling process, and that is why many counselors can take on the role of consultant easily. The two processes are different enough to warrant additional knowledge, skills, and competencies above and beyond those of a counselor, however, such as various models of consultation, methods of evaluating consultation (Brown, 1993), and concern about specific ethical issues peculiar to the consulting relationship (Robinson & Gross, 1985; Lowman, 1985; Crego, 1985; Gallessich, 1982; Brown, 1993). These issues include the consultant's having appropriate training for the services provided, proper assessment of organizational readiness for change, and the balancing of the organization's need to know with the client/employee's right to privacy (Robinson & Gross, 1985).

An important feature that distinguishes consultation from counseling is that in consultation the client is generally a professional who has particular responsibilities to other people or to an organization. An implied part of the consultative process is that the work the consultant does with the client may affect the people and the organization for which the client is responsible. The consultant's role may be an indirect one, working with what might be considered the middle level. In the long run, however, successful consultants can have a significant impact because they can reach many more people as a result of their consultations with mental health professionals, personnel officers, teachers, and administrators than they could ever reach in one-on-one settings.

Overall, there probably are many more similarities than differences between counseling and consulting. Although counseling and psychotherapy have not generally been time-limited (restricted to a set number of sessions or period of time) in the past, there are now specific time-limited approaches to counseling. Some consulting relationships are not necessarily time-limited. A psychologist, for example, may serve as an ongoing consultant with a school district, meeting weekly with school counselors to discuss difficult cases the counselors may have.

Consultants need to utilize all the counseling skills in the consulting process as well as some skills unique to consulting, such as supportive refocus (Brown, 1993). **Supportive refocus** is a skill through which the consultant can accurately understand and reflect the consultee's problem but then return the focus of the consultation to the client in order to avoid counseling the consultee. There are also numerous skills consultants need to learn for establishing and maintaining coequal relationships. Studies suggest that consultants need to be more direct than counselors by asking more questions and being more actively engaged in diagnosing both the consultee's and the client's problems (Brown, 1993).

Consulting, like counseling, requires the development of an interpersonal relationship characterized by trust and respect. The actual consulting and counseling processes closely parallel each other.

There are two major differences between counseling and consulting. Most consulting takes place in the natural environment, usually the consultee's work setting, whereas most counseling occurs in the counselor's office or work setting. The other major difference between the two is that consultation generally involves working with a middle person, one who has responsibility for working with others. As a result, consultants may have the opportunity for greater general impact because their work may, in the long run, affect many more people than they might ever see as a counselor. Egan (1986) suggests that counselors who hold client self-responsibility and self-efficacy as important values may be considered consultants hired by clients to help them face problems more effectively.

A trained professional can serve both as a counselor and as a consultant. The roles are not mutually exclusive; however, it is probably unethical for the consultant to provide counseling to the consultee in the context of the consulting relationship without renegotiating the contract (Brown, 1993). As described in chapter 15, one of the major roles and expectations of a school counselor working as part of a comprehensive, developmental K–12 school counseling program is to serve as a consultant to faculty, staff, and parents.

The school counselor as consultant does violate a general principle of having the consultant be an outsider. Many businesses also violate this principle when they employ psychologists or other human relations personnel to work with management and staff with training and various other problems. Such internal consultants have special problems to deal with in establishing relationships with their clients. There may be status conflicts, power issues, and concerns over confidentiality that must be resolved before consultant and client can begin working together effectively. The period of establishing trust in such cases may take a great deal more skill and time than an outside consultant might need. Generally speaking, an outsider is often much more easily accepted as an expert than an insider.

CONSULTING SKILLS IN BUSINESS AND INDUSTRY

Lester Thurow (1985) has indicated that one major problem with U.S. business and industry is the low level of training in its workforce. To upgrade the standards of the workforce, making it more competitive internationally, on-the-job training is required, among other things. Increasing numbers of professionals trained in the facilitation of human growth and change are finding gainful employment in the care and training of the modern workforce. Smith and Walz (1984) believe that is what makes the helping professional so appealing:

> Counselors in the privacy of their offices have successfully worked with individuals by helping them to develop, change, cope, and grow. Many of the same techniques work successfully when applied to the corporate setting. (p. 8)

Human Resource Development

The more or less generic title given to the concept of using helping skills in an organizational setting is **human resource development** (HRD). HRD consists of a process by which the employees of an organization are helped, in a continuous, planned way, to

- acquire or sharpen capabilities required to perform various functions associated with their present or expected future roles.
- develop their general capabilities as individuals and discover and exploit their own inner potentials for their own and/or organizational developmental purposes.
- develop an organizational culture in which supervisor–subordinate relationships, teamwork, and collaboration among subunits are strong and contribute to the professional well-being, motivation, and pride of employees. (Rao, 1985, p. 2)

Rao (1985) believes that HRD is needed by any organization that wants to be dynamic and growth oriented or wants to succeed in a quickly changing environment (p. 227). HRD ideas and processes can be used in virtually all types of organizations, including governmental bodies and fraternal organizations. The descriptions offered here focus on applications within business and industry.

Specific mechanisms that help develop the capabilities of the employees and units within an organization include career development programs, training, organizational development, employee assistance programs, and quality of worklife programs.

Career Development Programs
Business organizations do not deliberately remain static, and working from within an HRD framework, employees are not expected to either. Career development has been defined as "a process of human development that involves self-investigation, learning, information gathering, decision making and change on the part of the individual" (Smith & Walz, 1984, p. 38). Within the context of the business enterprise, the HRD professional helps keep individuals apprised of projected changes and helps individuals plan career moves. The basic philosophy of providing for career planning is based on the belief that employees who are working satisfactorily within their career goals and expectations are more likely to be productive.

Training and Education
The greatest growth in the field of education today is in the area of business and industry. According to Naisbitt and Aburdene (1985),

> Training and education programs within American business are so vast, so extensive, that they represent in effect an alternative system to the nation's public and private schools,

colleges and universities.... About 8 million people are learning within corporations—about the same number that are enrolled in institutions of higher learning. (p. 66)

Training includes making assessments of employee needs as far as knowledge and skills are concerned to perform specific tasks, preparing appropriate instructional materials, conducting actual training sessions, and evaluating the results of the training. As companies grow and change, and as employees move within the company and new employees are hired, there is generally a regular amount of training occurring within a medium- to large-size company.

Organizational Development

The **organization development (OD) specialist** works to maintain a psychological climate within the company that is conducive to high productivity. Experts in this area also help any department or unit within a company that is having trouble with such problems as absenteeism, low production, or interpersonal conflict. The structure of the company itself, or subdivisions thereof, may also come into the purview of experts within this area (Rao, 1985).

Employee Assistance Programs

Employee assistance programs (EAPs) are set up or contracted by companies to help employees who may be having personal difficulties that could be interfering with their productivity on the job. Personal difficulties could include money, marriage, or substance abuse problems. EAP clients are generally referred to experts outside of the company to receive assistance on their particular problems, although there may be some in-house assistance provided in some programs. EAP specialists educate all employees on the characteristics of the employee assistance plan, provide specific training to supervisory personnel so that they can help employees use the system effectively, work directly with employees who have problems, make referrals to appropriate agencies and experts, and do follow-up evaluations.

The recent focus of employee assistance has shifted from intervention to prevention. Two new concepts are *executive coaching,* and *employee enhancement.* **Executive coaching** consists almost entirely of consultation and places less of a stigma on employees seeking services. Coaching is used when there is no specific problem but an executive wishes to improve personal effectiveness. **Employee enhancement** is a wholistic concept providing stress management, smoking cessation and weight management classes, as well as brown bag seminars on job burnout and dealing with difficult people (Purnell-Bond, 1997).

Quality of Worklife Programs

Quality of worklife programs focus on making the place in which employees spend 40 hours or so a week a generally positive, attractive environment. The actual work that employees do may be tedious and monotonous; if it is done in a place they believe is safe and reasonably aesthetic and where there may be a sense of belonging and a feeling that their opinions about working conditions are heard, there is a relatively high quality of worklife.

Quality of worklife specialists may work on improving physical conditions, plan recreational facilities and activities, and help improve fringe benefit packages such as educational subsidies and health and medical benefits. An overall objective is to help develop the sense of belonging and loyalty to the company that in the long run benefits all concerned (Rao, 1985).

These descriptions indicate the variety of activities presently being undertaken in various businesses and industries by personnel trained in the helping professions. Organizations that do not have the size or capital to justify employing full-time human resource development specialists may contract with external consultants to provide the services. The need for training, development, and improved working conditions and employee services is increasing, and the job market for experts in this field appears to be expanding (Smith & Walz, 1984; Chalofsky, 1985).

A professional organization that specifically deals with the issues in this area is the Association of Specialists in Training and Development (ASTD). The organization publishes the *Training and Development Journal.* Specialized training for work in this field is offered by the National Training Laboratories (NTL) in Bethel, Maine, and University Associates (UA) in San Diego, California.

MULTICULTURAL CONSIDERATIONS

Most of the multicultural factors in individual, group, and family counseling also apply to community counseling and consulting. Consultants need to be aware that organizations and their employees may reflect different cultures with different worldviews and different concerns than the majority culture. "As the ethnic minority population of the United States continues to increase, the likelihood that more consultants will work with organizations owned or predominately populated by people of diverse cultures increases" (Jackson & Hayes, 1993, p. 144).

Each stage of the consultation process calls for certain multicultural skills and awareness on the part of the counselor. Consultants working with individuals or organizations who are culturally different from themselves should have some familiarity with their clients' culture or be able to identify sources who can help them to obtain the necessary knowledge. Consultants may have to become familiar with culturally meaningful expressions, be willing to explore issues relevant to the ethnic diversity of their clients, be willing to meet and interact in locations other than their own office, and consider how their culturally different clients respond to the implementation of written rules, agreements, and legal documents. For example, in many cultures a great deal of value is placed on an individual's word, and verbal contracts are binding. Some cultures have a different perception of time from the Western worldview. In these cultures, time is viewed not as linear (being structured, with a beginning and an end) but rather as a process (activities are not scheduled but happen more or less spontaneously). For example, an organization may not open at certain specified hours; personnel may take lunch when there seems to be a natural stopping point or when there is a consensus; the workday may extend until workers are ready to leave; or the workweek may extend into the weekend (Jackson & Hayes, 1993).

As they determine in which intervention mode to work, consultants need to incorporate consultees' cultural beliefs and experiences as well as the expectations consultees hold for the consultative relationship. For example, often ethnic minorities have felt disenfranchised by the mental health system and oppressed by the dominant culture, which they view as the source of their difficulties. These minorities might perceive that those persons from the dominant culture who have the power and expertise should act as change agents and be responsible for collecting information, making a diagnosis, providing direction for change, and challenging the offending system to bring about that change. In such a case the consultant would make an intervention using the purchase of information or doctor–patient mode. Community counseling by its very nature implies a recognition of diversity, whether dealing with the aged, homeless, or ethnic minorities.

SUMMARY

This chapter has examined the many roles counselors play and methods counselors use in helping to effect change in community and organizational settings. The focus of community counseling and consulting is on preventive and developmental interventions. Community counseling is a multifaceted approach combining direct and indirect services to help community members live more effectively and to prevent the problems most frequently faced by those who use the services. Some of the ways that counselors work in the community include the following forms of counseling: substance abuse, gerontological, health, rehabilitation, and crises and disaster. Community counselors often engage in client advocacy.

Consultants work at improving the mental health of individuals and the functioning of organizations. Their goals are to help consultees deal with current organizational problems and to provide information or teach skills that help them to deal effectively with similar problems in the future.

The consultation process has been described and compared to the counseling process. Consultation is an approach that can be used as part of a specialization, such as school counseling, or can be sustained as a separate private practice.

Finally, multicultural factors in consulting are considered. Community counselors and consultants need to be aware of the different cultures, worldviews, and issues reflected in organizations and the increasing cultural diversity throughout communities.

QUESTIONS AND ACTIVITIES

1. What practicum or internship sites are available to you in your region that might afford you the opportunity to investigate in-depth the areas of community counseling and consulting? Check with your instructor about the proper time and the approach to make in contacting these sites for practicum or internship placement.

2. Consider the following statement: "There is no difference between effective counseling and effective consulting in terms of process." Do you agree or disagree? Would your response to this question be of any influence in terms of a career decision you might make?

3. In small groups, identify a mental health problem. Then brainstorm some prevention-focused intervention strategies that might be effective for a specific population or organization. Share your ideas with the class.

RECOMMENDED READINGS

Consultation: A paradigm for helping. Consultation I: Conceptual, structural, and operational dimensions. (1993). [Special issue]. *Journal of Counseling and Development, 71*(6).

Consultation: A paradigm for helping. Consultation II: Prevention, preparation, and key issues. (1993). [Special issue]. *Journal of Counseling and Development, 72*(2).

Homan, M. (1993). *Promoting community change: Making it happen in the real world.* Pacific Grove, CA: Brooks/Cole.

Slaikeu, K. A. (1990). *Crisis intervention: A handbook for practice and research* (2nd ed.). Boston: Allyn & Bacon.

INTERNET RESOURCES

Websites

CDC National AIDS Clearinghouse
Center for Education and Drug Abuse Research
<pitt.edu/~cedar.html>
College Alcohol and Other Drug Use Counseling
<web.bu.edu/COHIS>
National Clearinghouse for Alcohol and Drug Information
National Institute on Drug Abuse

National Institute on Alcohol Abuse and Alcoholism
<www.niaa.nih.gov>
Dennis Grant Traumatic Stress Home Page
<www.long-beach.va.gov/ptsd/stress.html>
Disasters Mental Health Intervention <ourworld. compuserve.com/homepages/johndweaver>
Trauma Information Pages <gladstone.uoregon. edu/~dvb/trauma.htm>

REFERENCES

Albee, G. W., & Ryan-Finn, K. D. (1993). An overview of primary prevention. *Journal of Counseling and Development, 72*(2), 115–123.

Brave, R. (1994, September 19). Psychotherapy is in turmoil over managed care. *Business Journal Serving Greater Sacramento, 11,* 35.

Brown, D. (1993). Training consultants: A call to action. *Journal of Counseling and Development, 72*(2), 139–143.

Caplan, G. (1970). *The theory and practice of mental health consultation.* New York: Basic Books.

Chalofsky, N. (1985). HRD careers update. *Training and Development Journal, 39*(5), 64–65.

Community Mental Health Centers Act, 42 U.S.C § 33-111 (1963).

Crego, C. (1985). Ethics: The need for improved consultation training. *Counseling Psychologist, 13*(3), 473–476.

Daniel, R., & Weikel, W. (1983). Trends in counseling: A Delphi study. *Personnel and Guidance Journal, 61*(6), 327–330.

Egan, G. (1986). *The skilled helper* (3rd ed.). Monterey, CA: Brooks/Cole.

Ford, D. (1985). The behavioral health movement. *Counseling Psychologist, 13*(1), 93–104.

Gallessich, S. (1982). *The profession and practice of consultation.* San Francisco: Jossey-Bass.

Gallessich, S. (1985). Toward a meta-theory of consultation. *Counseling Psychologist, 13*(3), 336–354.

Gelso, C. J., & Fretz, B. R. (1992). *Counseling psychology.* Fort Worth, TX: Harcourt Brace Jovanovich.

Giordano, G. B. (1995, January 1). Challenge and progress in rehabilitation. *American Rehabilitation, 21, 14.*

Glasser, W. (1976). *Positive addiction.* New York: Harper & Row.

Gravitz, H., & Bowden, J. (1986). Therapeutic issues of adult children of alcoholics: A continuum of developmental stages. In R. J. Ackerman (Ed.), *Growing up in the shadow: Children of alcoholics* (pp. 187–207). Pompano Beach, FL: Health Communications.

Grohol, J. M. (1996). Managed care running the system: The editorial page [On-line]. *Mental Health Net.* Available: www.cmhc.com/

Homer, J. H., & McElhaney, S. J. (1993). Building fences: Prevention in mental health. *American Counselor, 2*(1), 17–21, 30.

Jackobs, G. A. (1995). The Development of a National Plan or Disaster Mental Health. *Professional Psychology Research and Practice, 26*(6), 543–549.

Jackson, D. N., & Hayes, D. H. (1993). Multicultural issues in consultation. *Counseling and Development, 72*(2), 144–147.

Joint Commission on Mental Illness and Health. (1961). *Action for mental health: Final report of the Joint Commission on Mental Illness and Health.* New York: Science Editions.

Korchin, S. (1976). *Modern clinical psychology.* New York: Basic Books.

Kubler-Ross, E. (1969). *On death and dying.* New York: Macmillan.

Kurpius, D. (1978). Consultation theory and process: An integrated model. *Personnel and Guidance Journal, 56*(6), 335–338.

Kurpius, D., & Fuqua, D. R. (1993a). Introduction to the special issues. *Journal of Counseling and Development, 71*(6), 596–597.

Kurpius, D., & Fuqua, D. R. (1993b). Fundamental issues in defining consultation. *Journal of Counseling and Development, 71*(6), 598–600.

Kurpius, D., Fuqua, D. R., & Rozecki, T. (1993). The consulting process: A multidimensional approach. *Journal of Counseling and Development, 71*(6), 601–606.

Lewis, J. A., & Lewis, M. D. (1989). *Community counseling.* Pacific Grove, CA: Brooks/Cole.

Lewis, J. A., Sperry, L., & Carlson, J. (1993). *Health counseling.* Pacific Grove, CA: Brooks/Cole.

LoBello, S. (1984). Counselor credibility with alcoholics and nonalcoholics: It takes one to help one? *Journal of Alcohol and Drug Education, 29*(2), 58–66.

Lowman, R. (1985). Ethical practices of psychological consultation: Not an impossible dream. *Counseling Psychologist, 13*(3), 466–472.

Mannino, F., & Shore, M. (1985). Understanding consultation: Some orienting dimensions. *Counseling Psychologist, 13*(3), 363–367.

Marino, T. W. (1997). DUI counseling becoming new niche for counselors [On-line]. *Counseling Today, 39*(8). Available: www.counseling.org/ctonline/dui/htm

Matarazzo, J. (1986). Computerized clinical psychological test interpretations: Unvalidated plus all mean and no signs. *American Psychologist, 41*(1), 14–24, 813.

McGinnis, J. M. (1985). Recent history of federal initiatives in prevention policy. *American Psychologist, 40*(2), 205–212.

Mendoza, D. W. (1993). A review of Gerald Caplan's theory and practice of mental health consultation. *Journal of Counseling and Development, 71*(6), 629–635.

Middleton-Moz, J., & Dwinell, L. (1986). *After the tears.* Pompano Beach, FL: Health Communications.

Naisbitt, J., & Aburdene, P. (1985). *Reinventing the corporation.* New York: Warner.

Ohlms, D. (1983). *The disease concept of alcoholism.* Belleville, IL: Gary Whitacker.

Possum, M. A., & Mason, M. J. (1986). *Facing shame: Families in recovery.* New York: Norton.

Purnell-Bond, C. (1997). Have you seen your EAP today? An overview of employee assistance in the 90s [On-line]. *Counseling Today, 39*(7). Available: www.counseling.org/ctonline

Rao, T. V. (1985). Integrated human resource development systems. In L. Goodstein & J. R. Pfeiffer (Eds.), *The 1985 annual: Developing human resources* (pp. 227–237). San Diego, CA: University Associates.

Robinson, S., & Gross, D. (1985). Ethics of consultation: The Centerville ghost. *Counseling Psychologist, 1*(3), 444–446.

Rockwood, G. F. (1993). Edgar Schein's process versus content consultation models. *Journal of Counseling and Development, 71*(6), 636–638.

Schein, E. H. (1978). The role of the consultant: Content expert or process facilitator? *Personnel and Guidance Journal, 56*(6), 346–350.

Schlosberg, S. (1995, May 15). Living to 100 Is Getting Easier. *Los Angeles Times,* p. E1.

Schmolling, R., Youkelles, M., & Burger, W. (1985). *Human services in contemporary America.* Monterey, CA: Brooks/Cole.

Smith, R., & Walz, G. (1984). *Counseling and human resource development.* Ann Arbor, MI: ERIC Counseling and Personnel Services Clearing House.

Thoreson, C., & Eagleston, C. (1985). Counseling for health. *Counseling Psychologist, 13*(1), 15–87.

Thurow, L. (1985). More growth ahead in '87. *Time, 126*(26), 62.

Tomine, S. (1986). Private practice in gerontological counseling. *Journal of Counseling and Development, 64*(6), 406–409.

U.S. Department of Health and Human Services. (1980). *Promoting health/preventing disease: Objectives for the nation.* (DHHS Publication No. 80-3316999). Washington, DC: U.S. Government Printing Office.

Weiss, J. (1995, April 1). Cognitive therapy and life review therapy: Theoretical and therapeutic implications for mental health counselors. *Journal of Mental Health Counseling, 17,* 157.

chapter 17

focus on

HUMAN GROWTH
AND DEVELOPMENT
FOR COUNSELORS

- Why is it important for counselors to know about human development?
- How many different developmental dimensions need to be attended to?
- How do you know how intelligent you are?
- Which is more important: nature or nurture?
- How can living in one decade make your life different from living in a different decade?

Relevance has always been a concern of students, and perhaps no chapter in this book is as relevant to the education of counselors as this one. First, a knowledge of one's personal development is an essential component of self-knowledge, as discussed in chapter 1. Second, to provide a baseline for understanding the perspective of clients and the nature of their problems, it is essential to understand the stages and processes of normal growth and development. Third, examples of direct application to the field of counseling can be made, such as in genetic counseling in hospitals and developmental counseling in the schools. Professionally, the topic of human growth and development is considered so important that it comprises one of the eight sections required on the examination counselors must take to become a Nationally Certified Counselor (NCC).

Because, as Ivey and Goncalves (1988) suggest, the primary goal of counseling is the facilitation of development, counselors must know as much about developmental processes as possible to understand where their clients are and to make interventions appropriate to their clients' developmental levels. Taking a developmental approach to counseling means that you have to start with the client rather than with your theories. The study of human development is particularly valuable in designing preventive programs because certain types of problems can be prevented by the appropriate application of current knowledge at the right time.

This chapter presents a wholistic approach to human development across the life span, considering the person as a system with body, mind, and spirit functioning as an entirety and being influenced by the environment. Here, we emphasize how human beings are similar; the following chapter on cross-cultural approaches focuses on differences between human beings.

GROWTH AND DEVELOPMENT OF THE WHOLE PERSON

The study of human development across the **life span** (from birth to death) is a relatively recent phenomenon. Much of the early work in the field has tended to focus on child and adolescent development, where the growth processes are dramatic and easy to observe. The psychosexual stages as postulated by Freud, for example, conclude with the genital stage after puberty.

The study of human development must include all of the multidimensional, interactional elements. Difficulties in any aspect of a person's life can lead to a need for intervention on the part of a counselor or other helping professional.

The basic or core elements considered here are physical–motor, cognitive–intellectual, social–emotional, and moral–spiritual (faith). Each element interacts with and influences the others (see Figure 17.1). Physical development, for example, can affect a person's social–emotional development. A physically underdeveloped adolescent boy or girl may have difficulties in peer relationships and in feelings of self-worth. Moral development is contingent on cognitive and emotional growth. While these interactions are occurring within the person, the person is interacting with the environment. These interactions are bidirectional; the person affects the environment (e.g., a 4-year-old child who is able to manipulate family members), and the environment (including the family [caregivers], peers, schools, work, religion, the mass media, and major social events and influences) affects the person (see Figure 17.3).

The physical–motor dimension includes body build, size, strength, rate of physical maturation or deterioration, motor skill coordination, and physical health. The cognitive–intellectual dimension includes memory, thinking, language, perception, problem solving, and academic achievement. The social–emotional category includes emotional development, temperament, and interpersonal relationship skills. The moral–spiritual dimension includes beliefs, values, morals, and faith development.

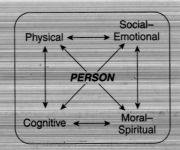

FIGURE 17.1   Basic personality dimensions.

Basic Principles of Human Growth and Development

"Growth in an organism is that structural change which increases its level of functioning in specific ways, although the potential for some different but related function may be concomitantly decreased" (Wilson, Robeck, & Michaels, 1969, p. 175); for example, as a child learns language, use of baby talk declines. The five basic principles of growth are described as the following:

1. *Growth is a continuous, lifelong process.* Beginning with the union of the ovum and the spermatozoon and continuing until death, growth is a constant process. The rate of growth may change as the person proceeds through different stages; there may even be regression at times, but the process goes on. Language illustrates this when people speak of growing up, growing in wisdom, or growing older.
2. *Growth is sequential and unique.* The spermatozoon and the ovum each contain 23 chromosomes. Each chromosome contains approximately 3,000 genes. When the spermatozoon and the ovum combine, a blueprint is formed that is both general to the species and unique to the individual. A child learns to sit, crawl, stand alone, and then walk, in predictable order. The timing of these progressions, however, varies. The metamorphosis from infancy, when the head size is one fourth of body length, to adulthood, when the head size is one eighth of body length, proceeds in an orderly fashion. The stages of growth occur at predictable times, and the result is a distinctly unique adult.
3. *Growth is the unfolding of the programmed genetic code (deoxyribonucleic acid or DNA).* This unfolding will occur at the proper time, given a generally nonhostile environment. In interaction with the environment, growth includes learning and maturation and is integrative. The human organism strives to meet basic needs, and in the process of interacting with the environment the child learns. If a child is hungry and cries, the child learns that crying can result in being fed. Some learning best occurs at critical or sensitive periods in the child's development (Piaget, 1972; Montessori, 1964).
4. *Growth is integrative in that all of the human systems work together; an integration of the cognitive, physical, emotional, and spiritual dimensions occurs.* Each system affects the others. A child may be mentally ready to ride a bicycle, but physically might not have the strength, coordination, and balance to learn.
5. *Growth occurs in stages.* The stages are identifiable within the various dimensions, but not everybody completes every stage. Also, movement through stages may be reversible. For example, a person may revert to a lower stage of moral development after having attained a higher stage at one time.

AREAS OF DEVELOPMENT

Physical and Motor Development

The most observable of the developmental processes is that of physical development. This process begins in utero at conception and is greatly influenced by the environment provided by the mother. Because of the immediate, direct consequences to children, many in the field of counseling are heavily involved with preventive counseling and education.

In the United States, approximately 250,000 babies are born every year with birth defects. Most of these defects are preventable. **Amniocentesis,** the clinical examination of cells from the womb containing the fetus to determine whether genetically or environmentally caused malformations have occurred, is an increasingly used procedure. This, along with taking genetic histories of parents, has led to the development of a very specific area of counseling; **genetic counseling** involves helping people make decisions about having children and working with families of children who have genetic problems.

Environmental factors, including nutrition, chemical agents, disease, X rays, and the emotional status of the mother, can play an important part in the development of the fetus. Both animal and human studies indicate that poor nutrition is closely linked to mental retardation (Smart & Smart, 1972, p. 29). Cigarette smoking during pregnancy increases the risk of stillbirth, premature birth, and low birth weight. Thirty-two percent of children born to mothers who are heavy drinkers are affected by **fetal alcohol syndrome (FAS).** Such children are small in size and have low birth weight, facial abnormalities, and possible mental retardation. Other drugs appear to have equally deleterious effects. Infants born to cocaine and heroin addicts and alcoholic mothers manifest all the signs of the addiction and experience withdrawal symptoms (Evans & McCandless, 1978, p. 204; Smart & Smart, 1972, p. 34). **Crack babies,** infants born to mothers who are addicted to crack cocaine, are a relatively recent phenomenon. These children, who are severely affected developmentally, become yet another burden on our hospital, mental health, and educational systems.

Children born to mothers who have AIDS will carry the HIV virus and have a strong possibility of developing AIDS. Diseases such as rubella, gonorrhea, syphilis, and poliomyelitis may result in a miscarriage or the birth of a mentally deficient, blind, or deaf child. Excessive doses of radiation during early pregnancy from repeated X rays or from radium treatment for cancer have also resulted in abnormal prenatal development (Craig, 1986, p. 77). Prolonged and severe emotional stress is also associated with pregnancy complications. In addition, the mother's age can be a problem. Older mothers, those over 35, are more likely to produce Down syndrome children.

Early Childhood

The years between birth and age 5 are the most significant. The foundation for all of the child's future growth and learning becomes well established during that period. Children attain half of their future height by the age of 2½, and by age 4, a child's IQ is stable enough to predict the IQ at age 17 (Hamachek, 1979, p. 74). By age 5, children have 75% of their maximum brain weight and 90% of it by age 6 (Hamachek, 1979, p. 82). From being almost immobile at birth, the 5-year-old is an active, energetic child, with the use of large fairly well-developed muscles. From ages 6–12, physical growth slows considerably, bodily proportions continue to change, large muscle development continues, and there is greater small muscle refinement.

Adolescence

Adolescence, from a purely physical perspective, begins with the prepubertal growth spurt and ends with the attainment of full physical maturity. Skeletal growth is complete, total height has been attained, and "the upper limits of genetic potential for endocrine development" (Hamachek, 1979, p. 137) have been reached. In terms of the quick rate of biological change, the adolescent period ranks with the fetal period and the first 2 years of life. Unlike infants, however, adolescents have both the pleasure and the pain of being direct observers of the entire process. The amount of development or lack of it is a constant concern. Comparisons with peers and the prevailing ideal, plus the horror of attendant problems like acne, make this a difficult time for adolescents and for those close to them.

During adolescence, there are several distinct periods of physical change. These are triggered by an explosion of hormones in the body. The 2 years preceding puberty are called **pubescence** or preadolescence. **Puberty** marks the onset of adolescence and is the age when secondary sex characteristics first appear and sexual organs become functional. The onset of puberty for boys is between 13 and 14. For girls, it is from about 12½ to 13 years of age. In the nineteenth century, when health care and nutrition were inferior to present standards, puberty for girls began between the ages of 14½ and 15½.

In addition to sexual changes in the body, a number of other changes take place. There is a growth spurt during which the individual's ultimate height is attained, the boys are broadening at the shoulders, and the girls are broadening at the hips. Increased activity in the sebaceous glands can cause skin problems such as acne. While the process of going through this stage of life is standard for everyone, the times and rates at which bodily changes take place differ significantly. The result is that there are early and late bloomers in addition to those who develop on a nearly normal timetable. Early maturing boys benefit from their status, whereas there is a stigma attached to the late bloomer. The reverse seems to be true for girls but not to the same degree.

Adulthood

Physical changes after adolescence center on the accumulation of fat. During adulthood there tends to be loss of muscle strength and endurance. This is partly due to age and partly due to a decline in activity level. With old age the process of deterioration continues. Body size shrinks and posture changes markedly. Loss of muscle strength is inevitable. In spite of all these changes, many older adults lead active, healthy lives, playing tennis, jogging, and swimming well into their 60s and 70s.

The major physiological change for females in their adult years is **menopause**, the time at which a woman is no longer able to conceive a child. The cessation of the menstrual cycle is brought about by a change in hormone secretions. These hormonal changes can affect the woman's total personality and result in headaches, irritability, and depression. These changes generally occur between the ages of 48 and 51 (Masters, Johnson, & Kolodny, 1982, p. 170). Menopause, or aging itself, does not necessarily lower female sexual interest or response potential (p. 170). In fact, with the fear of possible pregnancy gone, sexual interest may increase for some women.

There is no direct male equivalent to the female menopause and its major drop in sex hormone levels. Sperm production in the male, while slowing down after age 40, continues on into the 80s and 90s. A condition called the **male climacteric** affects about 5% of men over age 60. This condition results in symptoms such as tiredness, irritability, poor appetite, and impaired ability to concentrate. It is caused by decreased levels of testosterone production and can be aided by testosterone injections. The majority of men, however, do not experience this condition (Masters, Johnson, & Kolodny, 1982, p. 70).

Neurological Development

An understanding of the nature and development of the brain and the nervous system is of particular importance for all human service professionals. **Neuropsychology,** the study of the interaction between the human nervous system and behavior, continues to yield significant research indicating the correlation between the condition and development of the human neurological system and manifest human behavior. For example, there are studies which indicate that there may be nutritional deficiencies that are associated with certain types of schizophrenia and some types of depression appear to be successfully treated by drug therapy. When one client who deteriorated significantly in terms of appropriate behavior was examined fully, it was determined that he had a brain tumor. Such cases reinforce the need for professional counselors to work with medical practitioners and other human services personnel to provide the best possible care.

Cognitive–Intellectual Development

The uniquely human ability to think has long been the focus of psychological investigation. These investigations have studied both the types of cognitive abilities and their rates of development.

Intelligence

When one speaks of intellectual development or intelligence, it is difficult to speak precisely. There is no commonly accepted definition of intelligence. Terman (1916), defined intelligence as the ability to think in abstract terms. Thorndike (1913) believed that there were three kinds of intelligence: the abstract, the mechanical, and the social. Guilford (1967), in his model of the intellect, postulates 120 factors of intelligence including many factors not currently measurable.

Because it is probable that not all of the ways in which we are intelligent are known, it is best to make a distinction between intelligence and measured intelligence. **Intelligence** as a global term incorporates mental and physical processes that may or may not be measurable. **Measured intelligence** refers to specific mental and physical activities that have been demonstrated in a controlled testing situation.

Seven Types of Intelligence.   In keeping with the wholistic approach to human development, it is important to note the work of Howard Gardner (1983, 1993). After extensive research, Gardner has described seven different types of intelligence. The first two types are linguistic and logico–mathematical, which are usually thought of as the conventional types of intelligence, and are measured by intelligence and aptitude tests such as the Wechsler Adult Intelligence Scale (WAIS) and the Graduate Record Exam (GRE). These types of intelligence are associated with the left hemisphere of the brain. **Linguistic intelligence** is the ability to understand and use language. **Logico–mathematical intelligence** includes the ability to use logic and understand and apply linear types of mathematics.

Two other types of intelligence identified by Gardner are more closely associated with the right hemisphere of the brain—the musical and the spatial types of intelligence. **Musical intelligence** refers to the ability to use and conceptualize in musical terms. **Spatial intelligence** involves the ability to work in two- and three-dimensional terms, dealing with factors such as size, shape, and perspective. Students who do well in geometry tend to score high on this type of intelligence.

The body also has an intelligence of its own, which is called Kinesthetic intelligence. **Kinesthetic intelligence** refers to the body's ability to learn and master physical skills. Professional dancers and athletes demonstrate high kinesthetic intelligence.

Gardner also has included interpersonal and intrapersonal intelligence. **Interpersonal intelligence** refers to the ability to function in social situations; **intrapersonal intelligence** is the knowledge of one's self. Professional counselors might well be expected to score high in terms of these personal types of intelligence.

Gardner and his colleagues continue to explore the possibility that there may be as many as 20 different distinct types of intelligence. Meanwhile, coming from a less cognitive, analytical approach, Daniel Goleman has developed a very persuasive case for the idea of emotional intelligence (Goleman, 1995). Gardner, Goleman, and other contemporary psychologists are taking a much wider view of intelligence, working to determine what it takes to live life successfully rather than to predict success in college.

For years it has been known that a high score on the Graduate Record Exam, which measures linquistic and mathematical skills, is not a good predictor of a person's success as a counselor. The best predictors of success as a counselor probably are high scores on measures of interpersonal, intrapersonal, and emotional intelligences, of which at present there are few reliable instruments.

School districts across the country are now using curricula that are designed to develop the several types of intelligences in order to better educate the whole child. Counselors and psychometrists are now expanding their views of their clients when assessing levels of intelligence.

Figure 17.2 offers a schematic view of how professionals might picture the four major characteristics of the human being integrated with the different types of intelligence to present a three-dimensional individual. Because the individual functions as a system, the different types of intelligence interact in varying degrees to the core characteristics.

Ideas in
A friend of yours tells you that she has just been turned down for admission to a graduate counseling program because she did not have a high enough Graduate Record Exam (GRE) score. How might you respond to her?

Nature–Nurture Issue.   There is general agreement that both heredity and environment influence measured intelligence; there is, however, a continuing debate about the contribution of each. Some research suggests that measured intelligence is in large part inherited but can be affected negatively and positively by environmental influences. For example, a child with a high initial IQ raised in a negative environment may experience a loss in measured IQ, whereas a child with a low initial IQ may experience positive change as a result of specialized experiences, such as participation in a Head Start program.

Cognitive Development

One major component of the intellectual capacity of an individual is thinking ability. Thinking is a general category that includes such mental activities as forming concepts, making

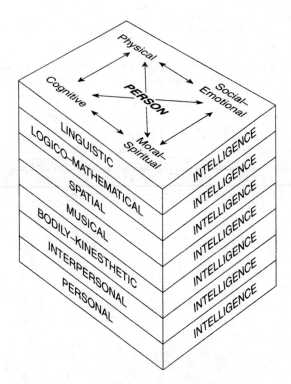

FIGURE 17.2   **The person: Integrating different intelligences and the personality dimensions.**

comparisons, solving problems, and reasoning. Thinking is often conceptualized as linear, sequential, and logical, functions of the left hemisphere of the brain. It can also be creative and intuitive, functions of the right hemisphere.

Jean Piaget, a Swiss genetic-epistemologist, as a result of observing young children give incorrect responses to intelligence tests, concluded that children think differently, rather than less, than adults do. These observations led to a lifelong study of the development of thinking and the cognitive processes.

Piaget's Stage Development Theory.   As Piaget worked with children, he noted their organized patterns of behavior or thought, which he labeled "schemas." He discovered how children adapted to their environment, assimilated new information into existing schemas, and accommodated new experiences by revising existing schemas. Piaget developed a theory that thinking processes develop in the same fixed sequence of stages. At fairly specific points in the developmental process, characteristic behaviors and abilities to conceptualize occur. Each stage builds on the accomplishments of the preceding one in a hierarchical fashion. Heredity, according to Piaget, has programmed the unfolding of these stages. The physical and social environment, however, may affect the age at which specific abilities evolve or the degree to which the abilities are developed. Table 17.1 provides a brief

TABLE 17.1   Piaget's stages of cognitive development.

Sensorimotor stage: Birth–2 years.

During the first two years of life, children acquire knowledge of the world primarily as a result of sensory impressions and motor activities. The development of organized patterns of behavior and thought (schemas) begins as newborn infants explore their own bodies and use their senses. It proceeds until, as a two-year-old, the child is able to distinguish between parents and animals, has a rudimentary sense of direction and purpose, and is beginning to use representational thought.

Preoperational stage: 2–7 years.

Children in the preoperational stage are able to think about their environment by using symbols such as words to represent their surroundings. Major accomplishments include the development of language and simple conceptualizations such as being able to distinguish among types of animals. The use of imagination is also noted; for example, the use of a cardboard box as a house. A particular characteristic of this age is that it is difficult for the child to take another person's point of view. Children at this age believe that other people see things the same way that they do. Piaget labeled this characteristic "egocentrism." Along with these characteristics, preoperational children are not able to reverse actions mentally.

Concrete-operational stage: 7–11 years.

Children in the concrete-operational stage are able to deal logically with objects. They are not yet able to work with abstract ideas. Using concrete objects, they are able to perform such operations as classifying, combining, separating, ordering, multiplying, dividing, substituting, reversing their thinking and, by the end of the stage, understanding the relationship between time and speed.

Formal operations stage: 11–15 years.

During the stage of formal operations, children develop the skill of using abstract logic to think about the process of thinking. They are able to generalize and to formulate hypotheses and test them mentally. They are able to propose alternative solutions to problems. They can check out beliefs for logical consistency. They understand metaphors and probability, and they think about the future. They synthesize materials, creating new and unique ideas. In 1972, Piaget extended the upper level of this stage to age 20. This indicated that everyone reaches the formal operation stage by this age. However, in spite of this modification, there are questions as to the number of people who attain this level. McKinnon and Renner (1971) found that only about 15–25% of college students used formal operational thinking. Piaget seems to have theorized about potential capacity for thinking in all individuals but has not accurately described attained results.

description of each cognitive developmental period. The ages for each period are meant to be used as guidelines only.

Implications of Piaget's Work.   Piaget was not a psychologist and therefore made little attempt to present his theory in psychological terms or to develop applications for his findings. Such transformations and applications have had to be made by others. Counselors working with preoperational children (up to second grade or so) need to keep in mind that words have different meanings for different children. Children are not generally able to perceive the world from the point of view of another person.

Most children under age 12 have difficulty dealing with abstract thought. They need to work with concrete objects or their own experiences. This limits the use of highly cognitive, abstract theoretical counseling approaches. Similar concerns should be considered when working with the placement of children in schools. The child's cognitive level may be a much more accurate gauge for grade placement than chronological age. Instead of looking at children as more or less miniature adults, as was the practice in the nineteenth century, Piaget's work forces people to be aware of the level at which children are when people are working with them. Parenting, teaching, and counseling should all be affected by knowledge of a child's cognitive development. A fundamental conclusion of Piaget's work in all of these areas is that one should avoid presenting material to children that is beyond their cognitive level of functioning. Much that is interpreted as resistance on the part of children may be a reaction to material that has been presented at too high a level.

The ages given for the various developmental stages are general and need to be determined individually. Also, not all children go through the four cognitive levels. Many people may not attain the level of formal operations at any time in their lives. Others may achieve little more than a threshold level at that stage. Ivey (1990) has pursued this idea and has created a systematic approach called developmental counseling and therapy (DCT). In this approach, the counselor is trained to make interventions appropriate to the developmental level of the client.

Social–Emotional Development

Human beings are social and emotional beings, and it is therefore not surprising that developmental processes occur in this dimension as well. The work of Erik Erikson in psychosocial development is perhaps the best known. Study in the development of emotions, or affect, has been rather limited, however.

Psychosocial Development.   Many of our ways of thinking about human behavior and the development of personality stem from the pioneering work of Sigmund Freud and his followers. Personality development was postulated as a result of a combination of external factors that affect the development of the ego, superego, and internal factors such as biological needs and appetites represented by and affecting the id. Freud's conceptualization of personality development centered on the process of sexual energy becoming dominant in one bodily zone after another and moving through developmental stages called oral, anal, phallic, latency, and genital (Coleman, Butcher, & Carson, 1980). Freud's psychosexual stages describe developmental processes up to adulthood but provide little data for the later stages of life.

Erik Erikson, one of Freud's followers, has been labeled an ego psychologist. In a simplification of the Freudian approach, Erikson does not focus on the superego, but rather thinks in terms of ego development. His approach is psychosocial rather than psychosexual.

Freud believed that ego development took place as a result of conflict between the id and the superego, whereas Erikson emphasizes the interaction between the self and society. This interaction occurs throughout a person's life, with the person in a "constant process of challenge and growth" (Corsini, 1977, p. 413). There is a regular need to make accommodations between experience with the environment and self-perception. The social milieu is particularly important in helping a person establish a personal identity.

Like Piaget, Erikson believes in **epigenetic development** in which the person inexorably moves from one stage to another, confronting age-specific crises along the way. Successful resolution of these crises results in a fully mature, emotionally healthy individual. Even though each stage is a particularly critical conflict, the issues of each stage are still present throughout life. For example, a child may establish a basic sense of trust during the first year or so of life and yet still have to deal with specific personal instances involving trust throughout life.

Overall, the labels for each stage are presented as extremes. It is rare that a person resolves a conflict totally in one direction or the other (e.g., total integrity or utter despair). Erikson's stages are illustrated in Table 17.2) Erikson's work is significant because he is one of the first to articulate a detailed developmental life span process. He also went beyond studying person and family to include societal impact on personality development. His

TABLE 17.2   Erikson's eight stages of life.

Conflict at Each Stage	Emerging Value	Period of Life
Basic Trust vs. Mistrust		
Consistency, continuity, and comfort produce feelings of security and predictability.	Hope	Infancy
Autonomy vs. Shame and Doubt		
Parental firmness allows for the experience of demand fulfillment with limits that produce self-control.	Will	Early Childhood
Initiative vs. Guilt		
The development of the superego and cooperation with others support the growth of planning and a sense of responsibility.	Purpose	Play Age
Industry vs. Inferiority		
Working and learning with others produces skills, such as the ability to use tools and weapons, and feelings of self-esteem.	Competence	School Age
Identity vs. Role Confusion		
The physical changes of adolescence arouse a new search for sameness and continuity and the need for a coherent sense of self.	Fidelity	Adolescence
Intimacy vs. Isolation		
A new ability to tolerate the threat of ego loss permits the establishment of mature relationships involving the fusion and counterpointing of identity.	Love	Young Adulthood
Generativity vs. Stagnation		
The adult need to care for children and to guide the next generation produces the desire to leave something of substance as a legacy.	Care	Maturity
Integrity vs. Despair		
An accrued sense of order and meaning allows one to defend one's own life cycle as a contribution to the maintenance of the human world.	Wisdom	Old Age

From *Adolescence and Early Childhood* by Judith Stevens-Long and Nancy Cobb by permission of Mayfield Publishing Company. Copyright © 1983 by Mayfield Publishing Company.

emphasis on adolescence and the identity crisis described for that stage is a particularly significant contribution. Erikson's conceptualization has provided a foundation for the growing work in the field of gerontology.

Emotional (Affective) Development.   The concept of emotion, like many of the other concepts in this chapter, is not easy to define. Santrock (1996) defines emotion "as feelings or affect that involve a mixture of physiological arousal (e.g., fast heartbeat) and overt behaviors (e.g., a smile or a grimace)" (p. 121). This definition suggests that there is some overt manifestation to virtually all feelings of emotion, which is important for counselors to be aware of as they carefully attend to their clients. Over the years older clients can become quite good at trying to conceal any overt expressions of emotions, so the task is not always easy for counselors to become aware of these emotions.

Human emotion is often thought of as an internal or intrapsychic phenomenon; however, Santrock (1996) describes a view of emotion that is wholistic. He describes emotion "as being relational in nature rather than intrapsychic, that there is a close link between emotions and the person's goals and effort, that emotional experiences can serve as social signals, and that the physiology involves much more than homeostasis and the person's interior—it also includes the ability to regulate and be regulated by the social process" (p. 172).

In describing emotional intelligence, Goleman (1995) subsumes Gardner's descriptions of personal intelligences. From Goleman's perspective, **emotional intelligence** includes the following five major abilities:

1. *Knowing one's emotions.* Regarding self-awareness, "recognizing a feeling as it is happening is the keystone to emotional intelligence" (p. 43).
2. *Managing emotions.* Handling feelings so that they are appropriate is important.
3. *Motivating oneself.* Marshalling emotion in the service of goals is essential for paying attention, for self-motivation and mastery, and for creativity.
4. *Recognizing emotions in others.* Empathy is the fundamental people skill.
5. *Handling relationships.* The art of relationships is, in large part, skill in managing emotions in others (Goleman, 1995, p. 43).

In contrast with the other areas of development, to date there are few elaborate theories of emotional, or affective, development to accompany the understanding of emotions and emotional intelligence. Affect development, which includes feelings, emotions, and values, is something all people experience, yet there is little in the way of theory or research on how this process functions.

Stages of Emotional Development

Dupont (1979) has formulated a theory of affective development which relates closely to the work of Piaget and Kohlberg. Only a portion of this theory has been confirmed by Dupont's research. Some basic tenets of Dupont's theory include

- the premise that the structural development of affect has factors in common with the structural development of cognition.
- the assumption that all thought and actions are accompanied by some change in affect.
- the belief that there are six stages of affective development. (p. 178)

The first stage in the emotional development process is the egocentric–impersonal stage (0–2 years), in which children are not able to differentiate between themselves and the world around them. Contentment or discomfort and pain are the dominant affective states at this stage. Dupont believes that affective development actually begins when affect and cognition are no longer centered on the self. In the heteronomous stage (2–7 years), children differentiate between themselves and significant adults, mainly their parents. During this time they experience and learn the names for the basic feelings of fear, anger, happiness, and sadness.

In the impersonal stage (7–12 years), children evidence feelings of mutual respect and reciprocity as relationships with peers increase and those with adults diminish. The psychological–personal stage (12–15 years) is when the adolescent develops a system of values: "These values are usually concerned with universal justice, equality under a single law, patriotic conceptions of the nation or the world, and allegiance to an abstract code of ethics, laws, or religious doctrine" (Dupont, 1979, p. 178).

Dupont suggests that few people attain the last two stages: the autonomous stage and the integritous stage. In the autonomous stage, individuals become aware of and appreciate how they are personally responsible for their own behavior. As this appreciation for self-determinism develops, so does resistance to external attempts to influence this autonomous behavior. The person at the integritous stage has a fully developed philosophy of life, and integrity is invested with affect. Integrity refers not only to consistent conduct in accordance with principle, but also to a feeling of wholeness that the individual prizes: "Integrity may become even more valued than life itself…[as demonstrated by examples such as] Socrates, Jesus Christ, and Sir Thomas More" (Dupont, 1979, p. 180).

Because the institutions of society have not dealt directly with persons' affective natures, people have developed a number of ways of handling emotions—some pleasant, some unpleasant. One of Freud's major contributions was his discovery of the defense mechanisms his patients used. Many of these mechanisms were used to handle powerful emotions. Much of what a counselor does is help people cope with their emotions and learn to handle emotionally laden material. There are assertiveness training programs that deal with the differentiation between anger, aggressiveness, and assertiveness and stress management courses that deal with boredom and anxiety. There are clinics for phobias and depression.

Howard Gardner, in describing the concept of personal intelligence, which includes emotional development, warns that when ignored and not fully developed "this kind of intelligence assumes aberrant and pathological forms. The less a person understands his own feelings, the more likely he will fall prey to them and the more likely he will misunderstand the feelings and behaviors of others and fail to secure his place in the larger community." Adults may produce a generation that is violent and self-destructive if they do not give themselves and their children the chance to be fully compassionate and self-aware (*Tarrytown Letter*, 1984, p. 6). This prognostication may well be coming true.

Moral and Spiritual Development

The moral and spiritual dimension of the human personality comes into play quite often in counseling relationships and needs to be understood by counselors. In examining these developmental processes, one must notice the interactive nature of all these dimensions and the difficulty of specifically defining terms and measuring concepts.

Moral Development

In studying how children think, Piaget also examined moral development. After listening to childrens' reactions to stories containing moral dilemmas, Piaget isolated some characteristics that distinguished different types of moral thinking (Biehler & Snowman, 1982, p. 67). Lawrence Kohlberg, as a graduate student at the University of Chicago, built on Piaget's work. He studied verbal responses by older children to moral dilemmas. As a result of his research, Kohlberg formulated a description of seven stages of moral reasoning (see Table 17.3).

Kohlberg's model was developed from his analysis of the results of structured interviews with the children in which they were asked to state how they would respond to a variety of moral dilemmas. In each instance, the children had to explain their reactions. Kohlberg and his colleagues also conducted longitudinal research that indicated there is movement from one stage level to another and that this movement is roughly correlated with age and level of cognitive development.

Some findings related to Kohlberg's work suggest that level III, (stages 5, 6, and 7) is not attained by more than a few people. Older males tend to respond at stage 4 and women at stage 3. College students tend to have higher levels of moral judgment. This may be due

TABLE 17.3   Kohlberg's stages of moral development.

Stage	Illustrative Behavior
Level I. Premoral	
Stage 1. Punishment and obedience orientation.	Obeys rules in order to avoid punishment.
Stage 2. Naive instrumental hedonism.	Conforms to obtain rewards, to have favors returned.
Level II. Morality of conventional role conformity	
Stage 3. "Good boy" morality of maintaining good relations, approval of others.	Conforms to avoid disapproval, dislike by others.
Stage 4. Authority-maintaining morality.	Conforms to avoid censure by legitimate authorities, with resultant guilt.
Level III. Morality of self-accepted moral principles	
Stage 5. Morality of contract, of individual rights, and of democratically accepted law.	Conforms to maintain the respect of the impartial spectator judging in terms of community welfare.
Stage 6. Morality of individual principles of conscience.	Conforms to avoid self-condemnation.
Stage 7. Meaningful solutions to moral questions are compatible with rational universal ethics: their essence is the sense of being a part of the whole of life and the adoption of a cosmic, as opposed to a universal, humanistic stage 6 perspective.	

From *Stages of Moral Development* [Unpublished doctorate dissertation] by L. Kohlberg, 1958, Chicago: University of Chicago. Copyright © 1958 by L. Kohlberg. Reprinted with permission.

to their high degree of independence and the necessity to resolve many value-laden issues as a result of being in a new environment on their own.

People do not necessarily remain at a given level. A regression effect can take place when a person who has attained a certain level may respond at a lower one. In fact, moral judgments may be made at two different levels within minutes of each other depending on the nature of the stimuli. There is evidence that the higher levels of moral responses can be learned through role playing and discussions (Keefe, 1975).

One area of concern related to these studies is the allegation that statements of moral judgments have been investigated and not actual moral action. Gilligan (1978, 1982) noted that Kohlberg's research involved mainly male subjects and the use of male-dominated stories. She suggests that before accurate generalizations about both sexes can be made, more concern for the reasons women make moral judgments is necessary.

Moral development is a cognitive, rational process and only indirectly related to religion or spirituality. Kohlberg's theory is clearly cognitive. Few emotions are evident in any of the children's responses.

Spiritual (Faith) Development

There is an increasing awareness in the counseling field of spirituality and its important relationship to the therapeutic process. Since it is so difficult to define and measure objectively, however, the concept is only gradually becoming a part of the mainstream counseling literature. The term *spirituality* is rarely, if ever, included in developmental psychology literature. Curiously, there is a new generation of physicians who have made an impact on the inclusion of spiritual concepts into the practice of medicine. These include medical doctors such as Siegle (1996), Weil (1996), and Benson and Proctor (1989). The medical community seems to be listening to these ideas rather than ignoring them.

Herbert Benson, who is the founder of Harvard University's Mind Body Institute and a proponent of the relaxation response (see chapter 2), notes that the aspect of spirituality and faith that is most important is belief. Belief may or may not be religious, but "belief heals" (Baker, 1997). Spirituality then, which includes such concepts as hope, meaning, purpose, beliefs, values, and faith but is not necessarily tied to religion, is becoming more an accepted part of the helping process.

As with the other dimensions of the human being, there is a developmental process associated with the spiritual area as well. James Fowler, a theologian influenced by Piaget's work in cognitive development and Kohlberg's work in moral development, has discovered and described a process that he has called "faith development."

The basic structure of the faith development process emerged as Fowler (1981) listened to the life stories of more than 200 people at the time that he was reading the work of Erik Erikson. The patterns found in the various stories led to the formulation of a six-stage process.

Faith, as defined by Fowler (1981), is "a person's way of seeing oneself in relation to others against a background of shared meaning and purpose" (p. 4). It is not always religious in its content or context. It is people's way of finding coherence in and giving meaning to events in their lives:

> Our faith orientations and our corresponding characters are shaped by three major elements, the "contents" of our faiths. First, there are the *centers of value* that claim us:

causes, concerns, and persons that consciously or unconsciously have the greatest worth to us.... Practically speaking, we worship that or those things in relation to which our lives have worth. Second, the *images of power* we hold and the *powers* with which we align ourselves to sustain us in the midst of life's contingencies. We try to align ourselves with power sufficient to sustain us and those persons and things we love. Third, the *master stories* that *we* tell ourselves and by which we interpret and respond to the events that impinge upon our lives. Our master stories are the characterizations of the patterns of power-in-action that disclose the ultimate meaning of our lives. (Fowler, 1981, pp. 276–277)

According to theologians such as Reinhold Niebuhr and Paul Tillich, faith is a universal human concern: "Prior to our being religious or irreligious...we are already engaged with issues of faith. Whether we become nonbelievers, agnostics, or atheists, we are concerned with what will make life worth living" (Fowler, 1981, p. 5).

Faith is clearly presented to be different from and not synonymous with religion and belief. "Faith can be religious faith, but it can also be centered on a career, a country, an institution, a family, money, success, or even oneself" (Fowler, 1983, p. 59). Faith is not static; it is continually growing and changing.

Fowler, working with the results of more than 350 carefully structured interviews, has identified a pre-stage and six stages of faith development (see Table 17.4). Faith stages are not to be understood as an achievement scale by which to evaluate the worth of persons. Nor do they represent educational or therapeutic goals toward which to hurry people (Fowler, 1981, p. 214).

Ideas in action   How strong is your personal faith and belief system? Can you articulate your beliefs for someone else?

Education and preventive counseling should aim to accomplish the full realization of the potential strength of faith at each stage and to keep changes in faith development current with the parallel transitional work in psychosocial areas. Remedial or therapeutic work is called for when the anachronism of a lagging faith stage fails to keep pace with psychosocial growth. Also, on occasion, when precocious faith develops, outstrips, or gets ahead of psychosocial growth, help may be needed in overcoming or reworking crippled psychosocial functions (Fowler, 1981, p. 114).

When considering all of these personal dimensions and the various descriptions of stages and sequences of development, it is easy to feel overwhelmed. Also overwhelming is when one realizes that there are additional sets of developmental stages formulated to describe other aspects of human development, such as ego development (Loevinger, 1976) and vocational development (Super, 1980) (see chapter 14).

One way to handle all of this information might be to use an approach similar to the constructive–developmental framework of Kegan (1982). Working within this framework, the emphasis is not on the developmental stages or sequences, but rather on the developmental

TABLE 17.4   Stages of faith development.

Pre-stage: Undifferentiated (Primal) Faith—Infancy (0–4 years).

The children in this stage form their basic dispositions toward the world. The beginnings of strong faith development in this stage are dependent on "the fund of basic trust and the relational experience of mutuality with the one(s) providing primary love and care" (Fowler, 1981, p. 121). The strength of this trust underlies subsequent stages of faith development. Problems develop at this level in two ways. An excessive narcissistic pattern may emerge in which "the experience of being 'central' continues to dominate and distort mutuality, or experiences of neglect or inconsistence may lock the infant in patterns of isolation and failed mutuality" (Fowler, 1981, p. 122).

The transition from the primal stage to stage 1 is facilitated by the child's use of symbols in speech and ritual play and by the concomitant development of language and thought.

Stage 1: Intuitive Projective Faith—Early Childhood (2–7 years).

Stage 1 is a period in which long-standing images and feelings, both positive and negative, in regard to faith are produced by the child as a result of the examples and modeling of significant others. Imagination emerges in this stage and is its special strength. The dangers arise from the possible possession of the child's imagination by images of terror and destructiveness; or the child, wittingly or unwittingly, may use imagination in the reinforcement of taboos and moral or doctrinal expectations. The emergence of concrete operational thinking is the primary factor influencing the transition to stage 2.

Stage 2: Mythical–Literal Faith (Childhood and Beyond).

With the ability to perform concrete operations, the child begins to reconstruct earlier imaginative views of the world, taking on a more linear, cause–effect perspective to life events as a way of achieving a personal sense of order. The child increasingly is able to understand the perspective of others. Much of personal meaning and belief comes through the stories, dramas, and myths of the community, meanings that are generally taken quite literally. The ability to note and reflect on conflicts and contradictions in stories marks a transition point leading to stage 3.

Stage 3: Synthetic–Conventional Faith (Adolescence and Beyond).

The third stage generally corresponds to the cognitive stage of formal operations. The structure of meaning emanates from beyond the family. A personal identity is developed that is reflective of responses by others. There is a personal concern for solidarity with significant others. The person is other-directed and has not yet attained the confidence or the ability to form and sustain an independent perspective. The formation of one's personal myth emerges during this stage, "the myth of one's own becoming in identity and faith, incorporating one's past and anticipated future in an image of the ultimate environment unified by characteristics of personality"(Fowler, 1981, p. 173). A significant change takes place as the individual moves from stage 3 to stage 4. There is an assumption of responsibility for personal commitments, attitudes, and beliefs that culminates in an overall personal lifestyle. This movement does not take place for all adults. Many remain at stage 3 or even stage 2.

State 4: Individuative–Reflective Faith (Young Adulthood and Beyond).

For many adults, stage 4 emerges during their mid-30s and early 40s. In this stage one's identity, or personal view of self, and one's worldview become differentiated from the views and reactions of others. A personal ownership takes place. The views of others, while considered, are not necessarily accepted. This is a period of high personal tension when choices and decisions between group identification and self-actualization are being made. This is the stage for making personal commitments in relationships and for deciding on a vocation. Commitments made in earlier stages may not need to be renewed or changed during this stage.

Continued

TABLE 17.4   *Continued*

Stage 5: Conjunctive Faith (Mid-30s and Beyond).

In this stage symbolic power is integrated with conceptual meanings. There is a reworking of one's past that includes dealing with material from stage 4 that may have been suppressed or unrecognized as a result of self-uncertainty. There is an appreciation for truths emanating from symbol, story, metaphor, and myths coming from all traditions. This stage's commitment is to justice. It goes beyond normal commitments to class, religion, community, or nation.

Stage 6: Universalizing Faith (Midlife and Beyond).

People in this stage are grounded in a oneness with the power of being. Their visions and commitments free them for a passionate, yet detached spending of the self in love. Life is devoted to overcoming division, oppression, and brutality. One loves life and yet holds it loosely. Few people attain this stage. The person in it is quite ecumenical and is ready for fellowship with individuals from other faith traditions and from other stages of faith. Gandhi, Martin Luther King, Jr., Mother Teresa, Dag Hammarskjöld, and Buckminster Fuller are some examples of stage 6 personalities.

These latter two stages characterize a searching faith guided more by the intellect than by emotions. The few people who enter these latter stages tend to be found outside of organized religion since traditional religious institutions, in general, do not focus on the needs of this population.

Adapted from *Stages of Faith: The Psychology of Human Development and the Quest for Meaning*, by J. Fowler, 1981, New York: Harper & Row; adapted from "Stages of faith," by J. Fowler (with L. Lawrence), 1983, November, *Psychology Today, 17*, pp. 50–59.

process itself, which could be considered a process of adaptation, meaning making, or evolution. The focus is therefore not on the person labeled in a certain stage, but rather on a person evolving. This idea of personal evolution or growth can be seen in another way. Each dimension presented can be perceived as sequential spirals, each interacting with the others, and together striving to maximize the growth potential of the individual. A problem or crisis is not necessarily an illness or breakdown; it could be a breakthrough or a move toward growth (Laing, 1960; Kegan, 1982). A problem affecting one spiral, such as the social–emotional, can affect one or more of the other dimensions; however, the other developmental areas can provide strength and support to the troubled area. The task of the counselor then is not to regard clients' disorders as sicknesses or as disasters, but rather as part of the pangs of their own becoming (Kegan, 1982, p. 295).

Ideas in action   Consider your own development. Was it smooth with all of the four major dimensions evolving in synchronicity as you grew to maturity? Were there times when you seemed to "spurt up," or become precocious, in one dimension while at the same time you had little or no growth in another dimension? If you plan to work with young people, how might you remember that the individual needs to attain a mature level of growth in each of the dimensions in order to become a whole person? Would you find it difficult to explain to a client that the levels of growth may be more important than looking for an illness that could be treated?

The Effects of the Environment

Much has already been noted about the effect of the environment on the development of the person. Skinner (1984) suggests that environmental influence is the most significant factor in personality development. The ingestion of toxic substances by the mother at the time of conception and afterwards has been demonstrated to have a direct effect on the child and all aspects of the child's development. The degree and type of stimulation given to a child from birth on has been found to have a marked effect on various aspects of the child's development. The influence of media, particularly television, is known to have both a positive and negative impact on the growing child as well as on the maturing adult. Other environmental factors such as air pollution and chemical pollution within the food chain can also have deleterious effects.

One purpose of schools and organized religion is to positively influence the development of the maturing person. Unfortunately, these institutions have not been as successful in fulfilling this purpose as one might desire.

The effects of peer groups, particularly in adolescence, have been well documented, and counselors working with young people need to be aware of these dynamics. For example, it may be more successful for a counselor to work with teenagers in a group setting rather than individually, in order to take maximum advantage of the interpersonal dynamics of this age group.

The importance of a person's work and its influence on developmental processes was recognized early by Freud. The world of work permeates a person's life. This world begins with the attitudes and experiences observed by a child in the home and continues with the successes and frustrations of teenagers and young adults as they begin their life's work—the work that will provide a great deal of their identity. The world of work influences the midlife crises of adults and is an obvious part of the difficulties workers have in preparing for retirement and then adjusting to retired life (see chapter 14).

Environmental effects also include social and historical events. Recessions, wars, social unrest, and periods of prosperity can affect a person differently i various formative stages of life. Living through the period of the Vietnam War had a much different effect on a person in the 18–25 year age range than it did on people in the 40–50 year age range. Adolescents and young adults are often most affected by the influence of historical events. Being aware of where a person fits in to world events can be important in understanding the person's present situation. A person who grew up during the Great Depression is less likely to consider a job change than a young person who entered the workforce during a period of prosperity. Table 17.5 illustrates different age groupings in relation to historical events. In counseling situations, awareness of these influences may be meaningful.

Baltes, Reese, and Lipsitt (1980) suggest that over the development of a life span there are three fundamental factors that interact. The first are the age-graded influences that happen normally at certain specific times in a person's life, such as menopause for women. The second are history-graded influences. These are major historical events such as wars, epidemics, and recessions that affect most people at the same time. The third are nonnormative influences. These are events that do not occur at any specific time, but when they do occur, they can have a major impact on a person's life. These influences can include divorce, death in a family, loss of job, and serious illness. Generally, it is these nonnormative influences that bring a person to counseling to learn the coping skills to deal with the unscheduled

TABLE 17.5 How historical events affect different age cohorts.*

Historical Event	Year of Birth						
	1912	1924	1936	1948	1960	1972	1984
1932 (The Depression)	20-years-old (starting out)	8-years-old (school child)					
1944 (World War II)	32 (parenting/career)	20 (starting out)	8 (school child)				
1956 (Postwar Boom)	44 (middle age)	32 (parenting/career)	20 (starting out)	8 (school child)			
1968 (Vietnam Era)	56 (preretirement)	44 (middle age)	32 (parenting/career)	20 (starting out)	8 (school child)		
1980 (Reaganism)	68 (retired)	56 (preretirement)	44 (middle age)	32 (parenting/career)	20 (starting out)	8 (school child)	
1992 (Post-Cold War Era)	80 (retirement)	68 (retired)	56 (preretirement)	44 (middle age)	32 (parenting/career)	20 (starting out)	8 (school child)

*Those starting out during the Depression were more affected than were school children, while those establishing a career during the postwar boom were more affected than were those nearing retirement.

Adapted from Grace J. Craig, *Human Development*, 5th ed., © 1989, p. 429. Reprinted by permission of Prentice-Hall, Inc. Englewood Cliffs, New Jersey.

stressors of life. For example, during the end of the 1970s and into the 1980s, there was a significant amount of counseling related to the aftereffects of the Vietnam War. A condition labeled **post-traumatic stress disorder (PTSD)** was identified, and numerous veterans of this war received psychological assistance. PTSD has now been recognized to occur after other personally traumatic events such as rape.

> Each of these [environmental] influences affect people more directly at different ages. Children and those in later adulthood are often affected most by age-graded influences. Adolescents and young adults are most affected by history-graded influences. While nonnormative events can happen at any time, their effects on a person's life can be more significant as a person grows older. (Craig, 1986, p. 393)

Figure 17.3 illustrates the individual within the environment that affects the individual's development. Figure 17.4 represents individual growth from having poorly developed per-

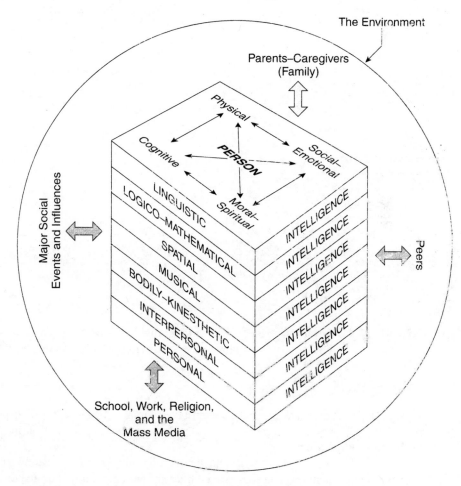

FIGURE 17.3   The person in the environmental context.

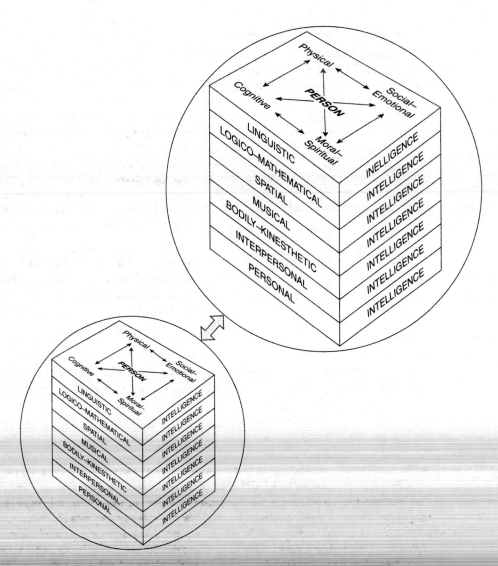

FIGURE 17.4   Developmental growth of the individual within the environment. There may be expansion or contraction of the person's world.

sonal characteristics to having enhanced attributes within a bigger world. This process is reversible. As individuals approach old age, their personal worlds begin to shrink and their skills and abilities diminish.

Figure 17.4 also serves as a schematic for the counseling process, illustrating therapeutic movement as clients expand skills and abilities and enlarge their world perspectives. The reverse process could also occur if the counseling relationship is not successful.

SUMMARY

An overview of human development throughout the life span has been presented along with implications for the practicing counselor. A wholistic, integrated, and interpersonal approach to the study of the individual has been presented with particular focus on the development of the physical, cognitive–intellectual, social–emotional, and moral–spiritual dimensions. Physical development requires excellent prenatal, preventive counseling and takes place prior to birth, during birth, and during the period of bonding after birth. Brain development has been particularly emphasized because of the significance of this primary human organ on all of the dimensions of human development. As the child matures through childhood and adolescence into adulthood, physical changes can have profound effects on overall personal development. This is generally most noticeable during adolescence and after the age of 40.

In considering cognitive and intellectual development, intelligence can refer directly to all aspects of the person including the physical and social dimensions. A description of seven different types of human intelligence has been presented along with a discussion of the relationship of these different intelligences to the total functioning of the individual. Piaget's theory of how children develop cognitively has been described along with counseling implications. Children are not miniature adults, and counselors working with children and adolescents need to be able to relate directly to the cognitive level of clients rather than expect the clients to be at an advanced level.

The psychosocial stages of Erikson aid in the understanding of social development. Erikson's stages, which cover life from birth to old age, are of particular importance because they help clarify issues related to the adolescent development as well as act as a stimulus for work in gerontology. Erikson was also aware of the interaction between the person and the environment.

Emotional or affective development, although somewhat of a stepchild as far as theory and research are concerned, is nonetheless an important personal dimension. Emotional problems are a major reason for counseling, and therefore an understanding of emotions, their development, and how people try to control them is essential for counselors.

Moral development (how individuals learn to deal with right and wrong and the making of moral judgments) is presented in terms of Kohlberg's theory. The theory is primarily cognitive with an emphasis in research on how subjects say they would act, rather than on direct action. Faith development has been presented as a representation of the concept of spirituality. Faith is not necessarily related to religion and, as in the case of cognitive and moral development, everyone does not achieve the highest developmental stages. The interaction of all of these stages is part of a wholistic growth process striving toward maximizing the growth potential of the individual. The counselor is encouraged to focus on the entire process rather than a breakdown at a given stage.

The influences of the environment on human development include family, peers, school, work, religion, mass media, and social–historical influences. The relationship between the time when events occur and the developmental level of an individual can have a profound effect on developmental growth.

The study of human growth and development is considered essential in conjunction with the study and practice of counseling. It keeps the focus on the client and the wholistic development of both the individual and the counselor.

QUESTIONS AND ACTIVITIES

1. Growth is said to be continuous. How true is this? Outside of possibly bulging at the waistline, how much actual growth can take place in the various dimensions of human existence as you grow older? Where would the limits be?

2. List local, regional, and national events that have had an effect on your personal development. Chart them on a time line. Indicate the effect each event has had on you. How many of these events have been positive for you in the long run? Share your findings with your classmates.

3. Using the developmental theories of Piaget, Erikson, Dupont, Kohlberg, and Fowler, determine where you are at this time with regard to each theory. In your journal, indicate how you were led or influenced to pass from one stage to another. Obtain feedback from others as to how they see you in accordance with each theory. Does it appear to be possible for you to move to the next stage of any of these models?

4. Consider the adage, "You cannot help a person beyond where you are." In light of your awareness of your development with regard to the various dimensions described in this chapter, where do you see yourself being the most help?

5. Given the different dimensions of each human being as presented in this chapter, consider what level of development an ideal counselor should attain in each dimension in order to be the best possible counselor. Compare your conclusions with your classmates. How realistic are these expectations?

6. Imagine that you are planning to become a gerontological counselor. Which of the developmental dimensions described in chapter 17 would be the most important in working with this population? Why?

7. Note that with almost every one of the theories of development presented in this chapter, the statement is made that few people ever attain the highest levels of a given dimension. Assuming that these statements are accurate, do they contradict the principle that all growth is continuous? What levels should you and your clients attain in each of these dimensions?

RECOMMENDED READINGS

Gardner, H. (1993). *Multiple Intelligences*. New York: Basic Books.

Goleman, D. (1995). *Emotional Intelligence*. New York: Bantam Books.

Santrock, J. W. (1996). *Child Development*. Madison, WI: Brown & Benchmark.

INTERNET RESOURCES

Websites

Classic Theories of Child Development

Nick Sushkin's Developmental Theories Page   <www.wpi.edu/~isg_501/nsushkin.html>

The Jean Piaget Archives   <www.unige.ch/piaget/ PiagetGB.html>

Changing Views on Adult Development   <www.ed. gov/databases/ERIC_Digests/ed259211.html>

REFERENCES

Baker, B. (1997). The faith factor. *Common Boundary, 15*(4), 20–27.

Baltes, P. B., Reese, H. W., & Lipsitt, L. P. (1980). Life span developmental psychology. *Annual Review of Psychology, 31*, 65–110.

Benson, H., & Proctor, W. (1989). *Your Maximum Mind*. New York: Avon.

Biehler, R., & Snowman, J. (1982). *Psychology applied to teaching* (4th ed.). Boston: Houghton Mifflin.

Coleman, J. C., Butcher, J., & Carson, R. (1980). *Abnormal psychology and modern life.* Glenview, IL: Scott, Foresman.

Corsini, R. (1977). *Current personality theories.* Itasca, IL: Peacock.

Craig, G. (1986). *Human development* (4th ed.). Englewood Cliffs, NJ: Prentice-Hall.

Dupont, H. (1979). Affective development: Stage and sequence. In R. Mosher (Ed.), *Adolescent development and education: A Janus knot* (pp. 173–183). Berkeley, CA: McCurhan.

Evans, E., & McCandless, B. (1978). *Children and youth* (2nd ed.). New York: Holt, Rinehart & Winston.

Fowler, J. (1981). *Stages of faith: The psychology of human development and the quest for meaning.* New York: Harper & Row.

Fowler, J. (with Lawrence, L.). (1983, November). Stages of faith. *Psychology Today, 17,* 52–59.

Gardner, H. (1983). *Frames of mind.* New York: Basic Books.

Gardner, H. (1993). *Multiple Intelligences.* New York: Basic Books.

Gilligan, C. (1978). In a different voice: Women's conception of the self and of morality. *Harvard Education Review, 47*(4), 481–517.

Gilligan, C. (1982). *In a different voice.* Cambridge, MA: Harvard University Press.

Goleman, D. (1995). *Emotional Intelligence.* New York: Bantam Books.

Guilford, J. P. (1967). *The nature of human intelligence.* New York: McGraw-Hill.

Hamachek, D. (1979). *Psychology in teaching, learning, growth* (2nd ed.). Boston: Allyn & Bacon.

Ivey, A. (1990). *Developmental counseling and therapy.* Monterey, CA: Brooks/Cole.

Ivey, A., & Goncalves, O. F. (1988). Developmental theory: Integrating developmental processes into clinical practice. *Journal of Counseling and Development, 66*(9), 406–413.

Keefe, D. (1975). A comparison of the effect of teacher and student led discussion of short stories and case studies on the moral reasoning of adolescents using the Kohlberg model. *Dissertation Abstracts, 3605.*

Kegan, R. (1982). *The evolving self.* Cambridge, MA: Harvard University Press.

Kohlberg, L. (1958). *Stages of moral development.* Unpublished doctoral dissertation, University of Chicago.

Laing, R. D. (1960). *The divided self.* New York: Pantheon.

Loevinger, J. (1976). *Ego development: Conceptions and theories.* San Francisco: Jossey-Bass.

Masters, W. H., Johnson, V. E., & Kolodny, R. C. (1982). *Human sexuality.* Boston: Little, Brown.

Montessori, M. (1964). *The Montessori method.* New York: Schocken.

Piaget, J. (1972). Intellectual evolution from adolescence to adulthood. *Human Development, 15,* 1–12.

Santrock, J. W. (1996). *Child Development.* Madison, WI: Brown & Benchmark.

Siegel, B. (1996). *Love, Medicine, & Healing.* New York: Harper & Row.

Skinner, B. F. (1984). The shame of education. *American Psychologist, 39*(9), 947–954.

Smart, M., & Smart, R. (1972). *Children* (2nd ed.). New York: Macmillan.

Stevens-Long, J., & Cobb, N. (1983). *Adolescence and early adulthood.* Palo Alto, CA: Mayfield.

Super, D. E. (1980). A life span, life space approach to career development. *Journal of Vocational Behavior 17*(3), 282–298.

Terman, L. (1916). *The measurement of intelligence.* Boston: Houghton Mifflin.

Thorndike, E. (1913). *Educational psychology.* New York: Teacher's College Press.

Weil, A. (1996). *Spontaneous healing.* New York: Fawcett.

Wilson, J., Robeck, M., & Michaels, W. (1969). *Psychological foundation of learning and teaching.* New York: McGraw-Hill.

chapter 18

focus on
MULTICULTURAL APPROACHES TO COUNSELING

- Could you just use the same counseling approach with everybody, even though you are fully aware of cultural differences?
- How important is it for you as a counselor to know about the various differences between cultural groups?
- How would you work with a multiracial client?
- Besides racial differences, about what other cultural concerns do professional counselors have to be concerned?
- How important are socioeconomic differences in working with clients?

Every person is like all other human beings in some ways, like others in other respects, and, finally, like no one else.

Kluckholn and Murray in Lee (1984, p. 594)

As there are multicultural considerations to all aspects of counseling, we have made reference to cultural issues throughout the book. The study of counseling's application from a multicultural perspective also, however, provides an important vehicle for understanding the origins, concepts, values, and the generalizability of the ideas and principles studied in this text. For example, whereas music may be considered a universal language, the language and practice of counseling as we know it may be limited to Western culture.

Carl Rogers visited China with the idea of testing in a distinctly different culture some of the person-centered concepts he had worked with during his career. His findings were profound:

I believe the contrast in the basic philosophy of the Chinese group and that of the person-centered workshop is obvious. They are polar opposites. The Chinese approach leads to group unity, a general contentment in conformity, and satisfaction in helping to achieve the group goals. The person-centered approach leads to a sense of freedom and power, and to the anxiety and pain of being responsible for choosing one's own life. Each represents a viable philosophy, and one cannot say that one is good, the other bad. The evaluation and choice must be personal. (Rogers, 1979, p. 15)

It is not surprising that a Western approach toward interpersonal relationships and personal development is different from an Eastern approach. What is of greater significance is that cultural differences *within our own society* can affect counseling success.

In this chapter, as we explore cultural differences and the field of counseling, we consider many questions. What are the chances for counseling success between a heterosexual, middle-class, Caucasian, Catholic, female counselor and a gay, lower-class, Jewish, male client? What problems would an affluent Latino American have in working with Native Americans on a reservation? What difficulties might an upper-middle-class African American male with a Ph.D. have in trying to help an African American elementary school dropout from Watts, a poor Los Angeles neighborhood? Do the client and the counselor have to be similar to ensure effective counseling, or can a counselor learn to counsel people effectively from different cultural backgrounds?

BACKGROUND

The concept of multicultural counseling grew out of the civil rights movement of the 1950s and 1960s as militant minorities demanded greater equity with all citizens, including the right to mental health care. At the same time, helping professionals began to write about the difficulties they encountered in counseling African American clients. In the 1970s writers in the field were discussing how culture affected counseling and the effects of race on diagnosis.

Helping professionals were initially concerned with counseling the so-called disadvantaged:increasing numbers of international students in the United States; people overseas; growing numbers of refugees from Cuba, Vietnam, Laos, and Cambodia; the rapidly increasing Hispanic population; and refugees from Haiti and China. The 1990 census indicates that by the year 2010 racial and ethnic minorities will constitute the majority of the U.S. population (Sue, 1992). Currently, 75% of the people entering the labor force are racial and ethnic minorities and women. In California the number of white students enrolled in schools has already dropped below 50%, and one in every four students lives in a home in which English is not spoken (Sue, 1992). Yet minority groups remain underrepresented as the recipients of mental health care. Most regular mental health services are not prepared to serve them adequately (Pedersen, 1994). The majority of mental health delivery services are provided by white, middle-class men, whereas a great number of clients receiving these services are nonwhite, lower-class populations with socialization and value assumptions that are different from the counselors' assumptions. These differences have resulted in culturally biased counseling with low utilization rates for mental health services by minority group members (Pedersen, 1994).

CULTURE, RACE, AND ETHNICITY

Culture has been defined as a shared pattern of learned behavior that is transmitted to others in the group (Pederson, 1994). This definition suggests that there may be cultural differences within racial or ethnic groups as well as across groups.

The United States has always been a culturally pluralistic society. Cultural pluralism is when individual ethnic groups maintain their own cultural uniqueness while sharing common elements of the dominant American culture (Atkinson, Morten & Sue, 1993, p. 11). **Cultural pluralism** has been likened to a cultural stew in which "the various ingredients are mixed together but rather than melting into a single mass, the components remain intact and distinguishable while contributing to a whole that is richer than its parts alone" (Atkinson et al., 1993, p. 7).

Race and ethnicity are two different concepts although they are often used interchangeably. **Race** refers to biological differences of physical or genetic origin that might differentiate one group of people from another (Pederson, 1994). **Ethnicity** is defined as shared social or cultural heritage and relates to customs, language, religion, or lifestyle passed on from one generation to the next (Pederson, 1994). Therefore, two persons can be from a particular race and not have the same ethnic identity. Jews are not accurately defined as a race, but more appropriately as an ethnic group. Different ethnic groups from a single racial group may have different cultures, and a single ethnic group may also represent people with different cultures.

An appreciation of the variety of cultural groups in our society and the contributions that these groups make to society is a vital factor in avoiding ethnocentrism. **Ethnocentrism** refers to the attitude that the values of the dominant culture are considered to be more important than those of minority group cultures (Atkinson et al., 1993). Differences in culture are not necessarily good or bad, or better or worse.

Minority

The term *minority* also needs some clarification because it is not always used literally. In the United States, women are often referred to as being a minority group even though statistically they make up more than one half of the population. The term *minority*, then, includes more than a numerical base. Wirth defines **minority** as a group of people who, because of physical or cultural characteristics, are singled out from the others in society in which they live for differential and unequal treatment, and who therefore regard themselves as objects of collective discrimination (in Atkinson et al., 1993, p. 8).

This definition of a minority group includes the special factor of oppression in some way by a dominant cultural group. Sue (1981) notes that "the history of minority groups in the United States is the history of oppression" (p. 11). Some people, however, object to groups being called *minority,* because they believe that the term implies a sense of inferiority. People born into a minority culture are not culturally deprived, deviant, pathological, inferior, oppressed, or disadvantaged; they simply have a different culture.

The term *minority* may not even be applicable when discussing income level or the impact of minority groups upon other minority groups (Kim, McLeod, & Shantzis, 1992; McAdoo, 1993; Paniagua, 1994; Wilkinson, 1986). As a result, the terms *multicultural* or *diversity populations/groups* are gaining more acceptance in the literature (Paniagua, 1994). From a systems perspective, in which individuals are viewed in relationship to their environments and the larger social forces such as racism and oppression, having a knowledge and understanding of the variables relating to the term *minority* can be very useful to counselors working with culturally different clients. Counselors then can distinguish if the client's problem might be, at least in part, attributable to sociopolitical circumstances rather than some personal failing on the client's part.

Multicultural Counseling

Multicultural counseling can be defined as any counseling relationship in which counselors and clients differ with respect to cultural background, values, and lifestyle. This definition reflects a broad view in which all counseling is multicultural in nature. Historically, multicultural counseling had been conceptualized as counseling relationships in which counselors are Caucasian and clients are members of racial or ethnic minority groups. The term **cross-cultural counseling** implies a comparison between two groups such as the majority group and the racial or ethnic minority group (Speight, Myers, Cox, & Highlen, 1991).

Fukuyama (1990) and others now advocate using the term *multicultural* because it reflects a broader, more inclusive view. A broad view of multiculturalism takes into consideration **ethnographic variables** (nationality, ethnicity, language, and religion), **demographic variables** (age, gender, disabilities, and geographical location), **status variables** (educational and socioeconomic background), and types of affiliations (Pedersen, 1991). This approach regards multicultural counseling as being in the mainstream of the profession, thus making it the concern of all counselors rather than the domain of a small group of specialists. As a result, increased development and refinement of existing counseling theories and practices are taking place in light of experiences with culturally diverse populations.

Some researchers, however, prefer a narrow definition, arguing that the term *culture* should be limited to reflect race and ethnicity only (Corey & Corey, 1992). They argue that defining all counseling as multicultural may maintain the status quo in which African American, Asian American, Native American, and Latino American populations are completely ignored or served poorly (Das, 1995). The authors of this book have chosen to use the broader, more inclusive term *multiculturalism*.

The Multicultural Cube

One way to understand the concerns that clients from ethnically or culturally different groups bring into counseling is through the multicultural cube, illustrated in Figure 18.1 (Cheatham, Ivey, Ivey, & Simek-Morgan, 1993). Across the horizontal dimension of the cube are the multicultural issues that clients bring to the counseling situation such as language, gender, and ethnicity. Along the vertical dimension are the possible loci of the issues brought in by clients such as individual, family, group, community, or country. Along the base of the cube are clients' levels of cultural identity development. Each of these multicultural dimensions need to be taken into consideration in order for counseling to be effective. The importance of the various dimensions may change over time.

Socioeconomic Cultural Levels

One of the multicultural issues noted in the multicultural cube is the socioeconomic situation. Ruby Payne (1995), working primarily from a framework designed to understand people

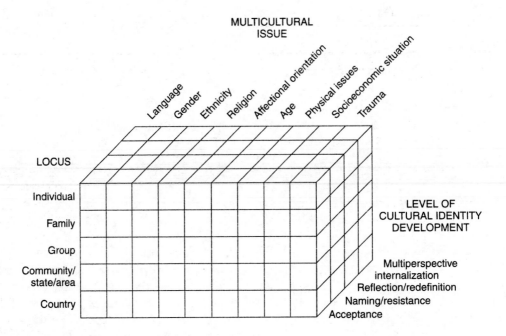

FIGURE 18.1   The multicultural cube.

From "Multicultural Counseling & Therapy: Changing the Foundations of the Field," in *Counseling and Psychotherapy: A Multicultural Perspective* (3rd ed., p. 106), by H. E. Cheatham, A. E. Ivey, M. B. Ivey, & I. Simek-Morgan, Boston: Allyn & Bacon. Copyright © 1997 by Allyn & Bacon. Reprinted by permission.

who are in poverty, has developed a structure that is helpful in understanding individuals of wealth, the middle class, and poverty. There are significant differences between people in these different economic groups when examining at least 14 different characteristics noted in Table 18.1.

Ideas in action   Test out the descriptions for each socioeconomic class with individuals you know directly or indirectly. How accurate do you find these descriptions to be? Do they, in fact, transcend race, gender, and religion? How would you adapt your counseling style to work with individuals from each of these different classes?

Multiracial Populations

Tiger Woods, the championship golfer, has often been asked about his racial background. He calls himself a Cablinasian, a term he coined to indicate that he is part *Ca*ucasian, part

TABLE 18.1   **Components of socioeconomic cultural levels.**

	Poverty	Middle Class	Wealth
1. Clothing	Clothing valued for the individual style and expression of personality.	Clothing valued for its quality and acceptance into the norm of middle class. Label important.	Clothing valued for its artistic sense and expression. Designer important.
2. Destiny	Believe in fate. Cannot do much to mitigate chance.	Believe in choice. Can change the future with good choices now.	Family status of major importance.
3. Driving Force	Survival, relationships, and entertainment.	Work and achievement.	Financial, political, and social connections.
4. Education	Valued and revered as an abstract, but not as a reality.	Crucial for climbing success ladder and making money.	Necessary tradition for making and maintaining connections.
5. Family Structure	Tends to be matriarchal.	Tends to be patriarchal.	Depends on who has the money.
6. Food	Key question: Did you have enough? Quantity important.	Key question: Did you like it? Quality important.	Key question: Was it presented well? Presentation important.
7. Gratification	Immediate gratification.	Deferred gratification very important. (Do your work, then have fun.)	Depends on the situation: Generally not necessary to defer gratification.
8. Language	Casual register. Language is about survival.	Formal register. Language is about negotiation.	Formal register. Language is about connections.
9. Love	Love and acceptance unconditional, based upon whether or not an individual is liked.	Love and acceptance conditional and based largely on achievement.	Love and acceptance conditional and related to social standing and connections.
10. Money	To be used, spent.	To be managed.	To be conserved, invested.
11. Personality	Is for entertainment. A sense of humor is highly valued.	Is for acquisition and stability. Achievement is highly valued.	Is for connections. Financial, political, social connections are highly valued.
12. Possessions	People.	Things.	One of a kind objects, legacies, pedigrees.
13. Social Emphasis	Social inclusion of the people they like.	Emphasis is on self-governance and self-sufficiency.	Emphasis is on social exclusion.
14. Time	Present most important. Decisions made for the moment based on feelings or survival.	Future most important. Decisions made against future ramifications.	Traditions and past history most important. Decisions partially made on basis of tradition/decorum.
15. Worldview	Sees the world in terms of local setting.	Sees the world in terms of national setting.	Sees the world in terms of an international view.

Adapted from *A Framework for Understanding and Working with Students and Adults from Poverty* (Rev. ed., pp. 17–18), by R. K. Payne, 1995, Baystown, TX: RFT Publishing.

*Bl*ack (African American), part *In*dian (Native American), and part *Asian.* He is definitely a minority but to try to understand him in terms of any or all of his racial characteristics would probably be very ineffective. Considering socioeconomic origins and current status (see Table 18.1) can help to better understand such a client.

The multiracial population is growing at a high rate in the United States. As a result, people are having growing difficulty with classifying individuals into specific racial groups and with trying to understand them in terms of the preestablished characteristics of the specific groups. Even the U.S. Census Bureau is struggling with this issue as it prepares for the census in the year 2000. Some people suggest having a separate choice described as multiracial, and others believe that citizens should be able to place a check mark next to every racial group that applies to them.

This situation brings into question multicultural approaches that continue to focus on racial groups as if they were pure with all members holding the same beliefs and values. A good approach is for the counselor to consider each client as culturally different, to work hard to enter the clients' worlds, to understand what clients' worldviews are, and to determine clients' socioeconomic levels. This, however, does not mean that one should not find out as much as possible about people from different cultural backgrounds. The more one finds out, then the easier it will be to understand clients' worldviews.

The Etic–Emic Continuum

Two approaches to the study of culture and the development of multicultural awareness are the etic and the emic approaches (Lee, 1984). In the **etic** approach, culture is studied and understood in terms of how it differs from or is similar to other cultures in shared dimensions such as family functions. The culture is examined from the outside or from an external viewpoint. In the **emic** approach, a culture is studied from the inside or from within the system; comparisons are made to internal structures and not to external systems or theories. The emic approach sees culture as a phenomenon to be understood from a position within the system, whereas the etic view is that cultural differences are "really only surface variations of underlying structures shared by all people" (Lee, 1984, p. 593). A counselor wishing to learn more about Native Americans could take the emic approach and become directly immersed in Native American culture by living on a reservation. Another counselor might take the etic approach to learning about Native Americans by making a comparative study of their economic, political, social, and religious characteristics. Lee (1984) points out that the process of

> gaining knowledge about another country is analogous to the process of getting to know a client. A counselor, rather than assuming that the categories used to make sense out of his or her experience are applicable to all people (etic) or that another person's experience and model of the world are so unique that there are no points of contact (emic), should settle somewhere in between in order to relate to another person. (p. 593)

Theoretical approaches gravitate toward different ends of the etic-emic continuum. Freudian psychoanalysis and Ellis's rational–emotive therapy tend toward the etic pole, with concepts that are postulated to apply to everybody; Rogers's person-centered therapy favors the emic pole. In developing an allegiance to a theory of counseling, a student might want to be wary of theories that make sweeping judgments about the behavior of people in all cultures.

BARRIERS IN MULTICULTURAL COUNSELING

Atkinson et al. (1983) suggest that the primary barrier to effective multicultural counseling may be the traditional counseling role being nonegalitarian, office bound, and intrapsychic. Feelings of helplessness and low self-esteem may only be heightened in minority clients who experience the traditional approach to counseling.

There is no conclusive evidence that the counselor and client must have shared similar experiences to be successful. "While cultural differences do result in unique experiences for both the client and the counselor, our experiences as human beings are remarkably similar" (Atkinson, Morten, & Sue, 1993, pp. 26–27). What is of critical importance is how counselors perceive and respond to the differences. Assumptions, misperceptions, and inappropriate responses can create barriers and destroy therapeutic relationships.

Intrapsychic Emphasis

A major concern in multicultural counseling is the traditional and predominant **intrapsychic** view that assumes clients' problems are due to personal disorganization rather than to some dysfunction within the institution or the society (Belkin, 1984). An example of this is the child from a minority group who has been diagnosed as hyperactive in a traditional school classroom but who behaves normally when placed in an open, less-structured classroom. Traditional counseling approaches overemphasize intrapsychic processes, resulting "in the misperception that no matter how well a person copes or works at a problem, if the problem is not resolved, the help recipient probably could do more by assuming more responsibility for her fate" (Ohlsen, 1983, p. 214). Many clients, particularly the disadvantaged and children, generally are so controlled by their environment that they are not able to change easily in constructive ways. The role of the counselor in such cases may change from that of being a facilitator, assisting the client in problem solving, to that of a **change agent,** working to modify the environment in which the client lives. The counselor may, in the earlier example, arrange to have the child moved from a traditional classroom to a classroom that is more appropriate for the child's learning style. As a change agent, a counselor may work to confront and modify institutional bureaucracies and also work "directly with majority clients in an attempt to move them toward the goal of reducing racism, sexism, and other discriminatory attitudes toward minorities" (Atkinson, Morten, & Sue, 1993, p. 240).

A particular type of change agent is the **ombudsman,** a role originating in Europe, for which the practitioner is paid to protect the citizens against bureaucratic policies and procedures. Some attempts to put this idea into practice in the United States have occurred in colleges and universities, with the practitioner being recognized as a student advocate. The idea of the counselor as an advocate for the client changes the conventional view of the counselor as a guide helping clients solve their personal problems. Judgments as to how much responsibility should be taken away from the client need to be made. One main issue in the lives of culturally different clients has been external oppression, which has left them with a feeling of helplessness. Having a counselor act on the client's behalf could continue this feeling of helplessness and may foster a sense of dependence on the counselor. Yet there are times when action must be taken, such as when any child is being physically abused by a parent. Some additional areas of concern that can interfere with effective multicultural counseling include class-bound values, culture-bound values, and language.

Class-Bound Values

The values held within a socioeconomic class can dramatically affect the counseling relationship and result in faulty diagnoses and ineffective treatment. People in lower socioeconomic classes may be less time oriented, may often be late for appointments, and may be motivated more by immediate, concrete reinforcement than by delayed gratification and planning for the future. They may be more concerned with survival than with searching for self-actualization. Research surveyed by Sue (1981) indicates that lower-class clients receive inferior treatment and are more likely to be diagnosed as having mental illness than middle-class clients. Personal awareness of class-bound values is of particular importance, since it is as difficult to counsel clients in a different socioeconomic class as it is with other cultural differences. An upper-middle-class black person may experience frustration in trying to counsel a lower-class black who is unwilling to change self-destructive behaviors. A lower-class black client may distrust a middle-class black counselor and may view the counselor as a representative of the power establishment. A middle-class white counselor may have difficulty working with a white teenaged mother who is on welfare and who is trying to find additional sources of government support. The counselors may try to influence the clients to adopt the more middle- or upper-middle-class values without working from within the framework of the clients' value structures. The clients, however, may have no desire to change their values. They may just want to know how to survive more effectively within their own cultural group.

Ideas in    Multicultural clients often have legitimate questions about the counselor that they are reluctant to address such as the following:

What makes you any different from others of your culture?

How open and honest are you about your own racism?

Will your worldviews interfere with our ability to work together?

Can I trust you?

How would you deal with these concerns and questions if you had a culturally different client? How would you respond to each of the above questions if they were asked of you?

Culture-Bound Values

The counseling profession is a reflection of the dominant cultural values of our society, values such as individuality, self-direction, and personal responsibility. It also is a profession that was developed and dominated primarily by white, middle-class males (Lee, 1984).

Specific cultural differences found in counseling settings include the amount of time necessary to establish a deep personal relationship, discomfort with disclosing very deep personal thoughts and feelings to a virtual stranger in a temporary relationship, different definitions of psychological well-being or mental health, and difficulty dealing with personal problems. Most counseling theories emphasize the analytical, verbal, left-brain functions, and this emphasis clashes with the worldviews and philosophies of many cultural groups. When Native Americans undergo counseling with traditional counselors, the approaches used may violate their basic philosophy of life (Sue, 1981, p. 41). Table 18.2 shows examples of culturally bound differences between Native Americans and representatives of the dominant U.S. culture, labeled Anglos. Similar charts could be devised for every identifiable cultural group compared with other groups. It is not realistic to expect a counselor to be aware of the cultural differences of all the cultural groups in the United States; however, it is reasonable to expect that counselors be familiar with differences within groups with whom they work on a regular basis. An Asian American counselor working with a Latino American community should understand and appreciate the cultural values of that particular group. In some cases, when the differences in cultural values are too great, referrals to counselors of the same cultural group may be necessary. Some

TABLE 18.2 Differences in Native American and Anglo values.

Native Americans	Anglos
1. Happiness—this is paramount! Be able to laugh at misery; life is to be enjoyed	1. Success—generally involving status, security, wealth, and proficiency
2. Sharing—everything belongs to others, just as Mother Earth belongs to all people	2. Ownership—indicating preference to own an outhouse rather than share a mansion
3. Tribe and extended family first before self	3. "Think of Number One!" syndrome
4. Humble—causing Indians to be passive-aggressive, gentle head hangers, and very modest	4. Competitive—believing "If you don't toot your own horn, then who will?"
5. Honor your elders—they have wisdom	5. The future lies with the youth
6. Learning through legends; remembering the great stories of the past; that's where the knowledge comes from	6. Learning is found in school; get all the schooling you possibly can because it can't be taken away from you
7. Look backward to traditional ways—the old ways are the best ways; they have been proved	7. Look to the future to things new—"Tie Your Wagon to a Star and Keep Climbing Up and Up"
8. Work for a purpose—once you have enough then quit and enjoy life, even if just for a day	8. Work for a retirement—plan your future and stick to a job, even if you don't like it
9. Be carefree—time is only relative. Work long hours if happy. Don't worry over time: "I'll get there eventually"	9. Be structured—be most aware of time. "Don't put off until tomorrow what you have to do today." Don't procrastinate
10. Discreet—especially in dating. Be cautious with a low-key profile	10. Flout an openness—"What you see is what you get." Be a "Fonz" character
11. Religion is the universe	11. Religion is individualistic
12. Orient yourself to the land	12. Orient yourself to a house, a job
13. Be a good listener—and it is better if you use your ears and listen well	13. Look people in the eye—don't be afraid to establish eye contact. It's more honest
14. Be as free as the wind	14. Don't be a "boat rocker"

Continued

TABLE 18.2   *Continued*

Native Americans	Anglos
15. Cherish your memory—remember the days of your youth	15. Don't live in the past—look ahead. Live in here-and-now
16. Live with your hands—manual activity is sacred. "Scratch an Indian—you'll find an artist." (Natives are also intelligent)	16. Live with your mind—think intelligently. Show the teacher how well you know the answers to questions he/she might ask of you. Good at books
17. Don't criticize your people	17. A critic is a good analyst
18. Don't show pain—be glad to make flesh sacrifices to the Spirits	18. Don't be tortured—don't be some kind of masochistic nut
19. Cherish your own language and speak it when possible	19. You're in America; speak English
20. Live like the animals; the animals are your brothers and sisters	20. "What are you—some kind of an animal? A pig or a jackass?"
21. Children are a gift of the Great Spirit to be shared with others	21. "I'll discipline my own children; don't you tell me how to raise mine!"
22. Consider the relative nature of a crime, the personality of the individual, and the conditions. "The hoe wasn't any good anyway"	22. The law is the law! "To steal a penny is as bad as to steal 10,000! Stealing is stealing! We can't be making exceptions."
23. Leave things natural as they were meant to be	23. "You should have seen it when God had it all alone!"
24. Dance is an expression of religion	24. Dance is an expression of pleasure
25. There are no boundaries—it all belongs to the Great Spirit. "Why should I fence in a yard?"	25. Everything has a limit—there must be privacy. "Fence in your yard and keep them off the grass!"
26. Few rules are best. The rules should be loosely written and flexible	26. Have a rule for every contingency. "Write your ideas in detail"
27. Intuitiveness	27. Empiricism
28. Mystical	28. Scientific
29. Be simple—eat things raw and natural. Remember your brother the fox and live wisely	29. Be sophisticated—eat gourmet, well prepared, and seasoned. Be a connoisseur of many things
30. Judge things for yourself	30. Have instruments judge for you
31. Medicine should be natural herbs, a gift of Mother Earth	31. Synthetic medicines—"You can make anything in today's laboratories"
32. The dirt of Mother Earth on a wound is not harmful but helpful (sun dance, mineral intake)	32. Things must be sterile and clean, not dirty and unsanitary
33. Natives are used to small things, and they enjoy fine detail (Indian fires)	33. Bigness has become a way of life with the white society (compulsion for bigness)
34. Travel light, get along without	34. Have everything at your disposal
35. Accept others—even the drinking problem of another Indian	35. Persuade, convince, and proselytize—be an evangelist/missionary
36. The price is of no concern	36. "You only get what you pay for!"
37. Enjoy simplifying problems	37. "Nothing in this world is simple."

From *Counseling the Culturally Different* (pp. 225–227), by D. W. Sue, 1981, New York: John Wiley & Sons, Inc. Copyright © 1981 by John Wiley & Sons, Inc. Reprinted by permission of John Wiley & Sons, Inc.

advocates suggest that clients should go only to counselors with the same background. Women should go to women counselors; African Americans should go to African American counselors. According to Atkinson et al. (1993), there is no evidence that this practice improves counseling outcomes. One interesting approach, in terms of preventive counseling, has been the training of members of a specific cultural group, such as a Native American tribe, in counseling skills to use with their own people.

A major cultural barrier to counseling is that many culturally diverse groups view counseling and psychology as threats to their continued existence (Pedersen & Marsella, 1982). The fear is that the minority group will be indoctrinated to become more like the dominant cultural group. This barrier may be the most difficult one for counselors to deal with successfully.

In working multiculturally, the skill of being able to conduct an *innerview* is valuable. This skill helps one to better understand the experiences, perceptions, values, and worldview of the client. A counselor's task is to work within the client's system and not to be a missionary. For example, it would be insensitive to convert Chinese clients to a belief in individualism. Chinese populations have a predisposition toward a family- and group-oriented society. The challenge for counselors-in-training is to learn to work with the broad spectrum of clients.

Ideas in action

Are there some types of clients with whom you know you might never be able to work (for example, child molesters or drug addicts)? Are there any racial or ethnic groups with whom you might have difficulty working? Why? How would you handle the situation if a client from that group came to you for help? Discuss your conclusions with several classmates.

Language Barriers

Verbal interaction is crucial in developing a therapeutic relationship; however, it cannot be developed effectively if counselor and client are not able to understand each other. A counselor who speaks only English, no matter how well-intentioned or skilled in therapeutic techniques, will have a difficult time developing a working, therapeutic relationship with a client who speaks only Spanish. Even within languages there are great differences. A middle-class African American counselor may have difficulty understanding the street talk of a lower-class African American student. A Spanish-speaking person of Puerto Rican descent may have difficulty understanding a migrant Mexican American worker in California. A deaf client using sign language will require either a translator or a counselor who is trained in the use of sign language. If a client's language is not clearly understood by the counselor, the results may be erroneous interpretations, faulty diagnoses, and negative outcomes. One reason for the emphasis on the innerviewing process advocated in this text is because this process encourages the counselor to relate to clients from the clients' frame of reference, worldview, and language. The counselor must be direct and ask a client what is meant by a given word or phrase. One of the authors was told by a Latino American client that a relative had "bought the farm." Even though the idea seemed clear in terms of the context, the client was asked directly what he meant by that. The client responded, "My uncle committed suicide." Asking for clarification in such instances can have beneficial effects, in addition to the obvious one of mutual understanding. The counselor is viewed as a person, as opposed to an omniscient, omnipotent being. When the client is able to educate the counselor, an egalitarian relationship results. This demonstrates that the client has abilities and resources and minimizes the potential development of a dependency relationship. When the client has to continually educate the counselor, however, the client may never get to adequately deal with concerns.

ISSUES IN MULTICULTURAL COUNSELING

Although multicultural counseling has actually been a specialty for some time, perhaps even since the beginning of the profession, specific study of it lacks a solid identity and a coherent conceptual framework. Even though most counselor educators and practitioners seem to acknowledge its importance, there is little agreement on many issues.

Status of Theories, Approaches, and Research

The study of multicultural counseling is expanding rapidly, resulting in a sharp increase in the number of articles on the subject in professional journals (Ponterotto & Benesch, 1988; Heath, Neimeyer, & Pedersen, 1988; Wehrly, 1995). The American Counseling Association (ACA) (1991) and the American Psychological Association (APA) (1995–1996) have both published special journal editions on multicultural counseling, and in 1992, the Association of Counselor Educators and Supervisors (ACES) held a national conference in San Antonio, Texas, devoted exclusively to the topic of multicultural counseling. There now are journals devoted exclusively to multicultural counseling, including the *Journal of Multicultural Counseling and Development,* published by a major division of the ACA called the Association for Multicultural Counseling and Development (AMCD); the *Hispanic Journal of Behavioral Sciences*; the *Journal of Black Psychology,* and the *International Journal for the Advancement of Counselling.* Many of the books on multicultural counseling first published in the mid-1970s and early 1980s are now in their third and fourth revisions, and many new books are appearing (Wehrly, 1995).

One result of all of this activity is that there has been heightened awareness of multicultural concerns on the part of practitioners, authors, researchers, and counselor educators. Any textbook that does not deal substantially with multicultural issues does not have good sales potential, and counselor education programs are expected to involve their students fully in the development of multicultural knowledge and skills.

Pedersen (1991) and Ivey, Ivey, & Simek-Morgan (1993) speak of "multiculturalism as a fourth force" in counseling, suggesting that it somehow follows after the three psychological forces of psychoanalysis, humanism, and behaviorism (see chapter 10). Multiculturalism, however, is not in competition with the different theoretical points of view; it is a factor that, of necessity, needs to be an integral part of all the different theoretical points of view (forces) and of other aspects of counseling such as assessment, research, and career development. It, therefore, may be more accurate to call multiculturalism an essential dynamic factor that permeates the entire counseling field and to view this increased activity as attempts to address the needs of minorities and the culturally different who are not being adequately served.

Research related to multicultural counseling has been accumulating slowly. Pedersen (1994); Ponterotto and Casas (1991); Sabnani, Ponterotto, & Borodovsky (1991); and Wehrly (1995) all point to the need for more research in multicultural counseling. Current models of minority and racial identity development are seen as particularly inappropriate for people of more than one racial heritage and for those experiencing multiple avenues of oppression such as gender, religion, sexual orientation, and race. There is also a lack of consensus as to what emphasis such research should have. Much of the emphasis has been on abnormal rather than on normal behavior and on symptoms rather than on interactions among people, professional institutions, and community. The research has failed to address the practical concerns of program development, service delivery, and treatment techniques. Furthermore, with regard to completed research, many ethnic minorities feel resentful because it has been white researchers who have conducted much of the research on their communities without communicating understanding or caring for their people (Parham, 1993). Finally, there has not been enough interdisciplinary collaboration. Each discipline seems to be protecting its own insulated perspective.

Multicultural Counselor Training

In light of the growing cultural diversity that characterizes the U.S. population, increased attention has been given to the training of counselors in multicultural skills (Ponterotto, et al., 1995). At present, coursework in multicultural counseling is included in roughly 90% of counselor education programs; however, there is much criticism about the quality and depth of training. Sue et al. (1992) found that few counselor education programs offer systematic training in multicultural counseling, that most of the programs do not integrate the multicultural counseling course in the overall counselor education program, and that the course is frequently taught by junior or adjunct faculty. Further, the course is often taught without a strong conceptual framework related to specific competencies. In addition, the researchers reiterate the view that multicultural counseling courses often tend to deal with cultural differences from a purely intellectual perspective without reference to the sociopolitical context of counseling, which includes oppression, discrimination, and racism (Das, 1995; Katz, 1985; Pontoretto & Casas, 1991; Ridley, 1995). There is some criticism that present multicultural counseling approaches use standard counseling theories without making any adjustments for cultural differences. Another concern is the emphasis on differences in cultural groups.

Parker's answers to many of these criticisms could readily apply to all counselors in all settings:

> Counselors in multicultural settings need to be open and flexible and should be ready to change their approach to meet the needs of the clients they are attempting to serve. Counselors need to be cautious about taking rigid positions on the likeness versus difference dichotomy. We human beings are alike and we are different. The complexity of human beings does not always give us the luxury of taking an either–or position. (Parker, 1987, p. 180)

Ideas in action   Some critics argue that an overemphasis on cultural differences can create negative consequences, such as

- the creation of renewed forms of racism or sexism.
- forgetting about clients' identities as individuals.
- fostering a situation in which there is an impression that minority clients are so different from majority counselors that only highly trained multicultural counselors with wisdom and patience far in excess of the ordinary, or only clients from the same cultural group, can counsel minority clients.
- making counselors self-conscious and defensive and therefore likely to avoid multicultural issues and minority clients.
- counselors becoming overwhelmed trying to familiarize themselves with the numerous cultural groups and the many differences between and within these groups.

Do you agree with the critics of multicultural counseling? Why or why not? If not, how would you counter their criticisms?

Das and Littrell (1989) advance several conclusions and recommendations for counselor training programs. One is the belief that problems often stem from clients' sociocultural environments and, therefore, knowledge of clients' cultural backgrounds should broaden counselors' awareness and increase understanding of their clients and their clients' problems. They recommend that students acquire a broad and sophisticated understanding of how culture shapes the values and behaviors of all people, not only those perceived as being culturally different. One means of accomplishing this is for counselor educators to provide numerous opportunities for students to meet, read about, and counsel clients from diverse cultures (see Table 18.3). They also advocate that students be ready to challenge the strong set of Western assumptions permeating counseling theories and techniques when meeting clients from other cultures who may not share the counselors' assumptions or expectations. This may require modification of certain skills. For example, all of the attending skills (chapter 5) may not be suitable for all individuals in different cultures.

Ideas in action   C. H. Patterson (1996) believes that if multicultural counseling is generic, and if all counseling is multicultural, then it becomes possible to develop a universal system of counseling. He also believes that there is a current overemphasis on cultural diversity and culture-specific counseling that is leading to the development of specific techniques or skills for each cultural group.

> ...perhaps the greatest difficulty with accepting assumptions about the characteristics and so-called needs of clients from differing cultures is that they will lead to failure, or lack of success, in counseling. The active, authoritative, directive, controlling counselor, providing answers and solutions to the client's problems, has not been considered competent or effective for many years. To provide this kind of treatment (it would not be called counseling) to clients from other cultures would be providing poor or second-class treatment.
>
> Patterson (1996, p. 227)

What is your reaction to Patterson's statement? Give your reasons for agreeing or disagreeing.

TABLE 18.3   Cultural awareness experiences.

The following experiences are suggested for readers to become more sensitive to other cultures. Choose to do one or more and share your experiences with your classmates.

1. Arrange a meeting with a professional who specializes in working with certain ethnic, cultural, or demographic groups. Ask this person to describe specific considerations in dealing with this professional's particular clientele.

2. Attend religious services at a place of worship different from your own religious orientation. Talk to people afterward. Learn what you can about the services and the people.

3. Read at least two issues, cover to cover, of an ethnic newspaper or publication, such as *Ebony*. What did you learn? Eat at a neighborhood restaurant that is frequented mainly by people of a cultural group different from your own. Talk to the waiter, chef, or owner. If possible, go with someone from that cultural group.

4. Sponsor a refugee—newly arrived refugee families often need temporary living arrangements with an individual, family, or congregation who can support them while they find more permanent employment and housing.

5. Work with a neighborhood coalition to assist the homeless.

6. Volunteer to serve with a soup kitchen or homeless shelter. Talk with some of the people.

7. Arrange to spend a weekend or several days in the home of an ethnic minority family of your choice and interest and observe their family practices, values, interests, religious beliefs, and methods of discipline.

8. Interview a person from a different cultural group. Ask permission to tape or take notes. Find out some of this person's particular problems in dealing with the majority culture and ways that the majority culture does not accept and reflect the person's values.

9. Read fiction and nonfiction books dealing with other cultures.

TOWARD A MULTICULTURAL APPROACH TO COUNSELING

In the broadest sense, counselors must think in terms of being continually oriented to a multicultural or pluralistic approach to working with clients. It would be virtually impossible to find a counseling position in which all clients were of the same sex, race, religion, socioeconomic level, ethnic background, and value system as the counselor. Therefore, it is important to know something about personality attributes, social–historical perspectives, and lifestyle characteristics of clients who have different cultural backgrounds. These differences and similarities may be either real or perceived. For example, white people in the United States are more culturally similar to African Americans than to white Russians, although whites and African Americans in the United States may not always perceive this (Jackson, 1987). Therefore, the case of a white counselor from the United States counseling a white Russian, with each perceiving the other as culturally similar, would not be labeled as multicultural counseling. On the other hand, the case of a white counselor from the United States counseling a white client from the United States, with each perceiving the other as culturally different, may be described as multicultural: "In measurement terms, the [perceived] degree of counselor–client similarity or dissimilarity in terms of cultural background, values, and lifestyles would be the key determinants in discussing multicultural counseling" (Atkinson et al., 1983, p. 262).

MULTICULTURAL COUNSELING COMPETENCY STANDARDS

The multicultural counseling competencies describe the types of professional and personal awareness, knowledge, and skills that counselors need to work effectively and ethically with people from diverse populations and backgrounds. The multicultural competencies were developed by the Association for Multicultural Counseling and Development (AMCD). They have recently been endorsed by several professional organizations including division 17 (counseling psychology) of APA and ACES of ACA. The developers of the competencies defined multiculturalism as focusing on ethnicity, race, and culture. The following lists are adaptations from the competencies.

Counselor Awareness of Their Own Cultural Values and Biases

Attitudes and Beliefs
1. Culturally skilled counselors believe that cultural self-awareness and sensitivity to one's own cultural heritage are essential.
2. Culturally skilled counselors are aware of how their own cultural background and experiences have influenced attitudes, values, and biases about psychological processes.
3. Culturally skilled counselors are able to recognize the limits of their multicultural competency and expertise.
4. Culturally skilled counselors recognize their sources of discomfort with differences that exist between themselves and clients in terms of race, ethnicity, and culture.

Knowledge
1. Culturally skilled counselors have specific knowledge about their own racial and cultural heritage and how it personally and professionally affects their definitions and biases of normality, abnormality, and the process of counseling.
2. Culturally skilled counselors possess knowledge and are understanding about how oppression, racism, discrimination, and stereotyping affect them personally and in their work. This allows individuals to acknowledge their own racist attitudes, beliefs, and feelings. Although this standard applies to all groups, for white counselors it may mean that they understand how they may have directly or indirectly benefited from individual, institutional, and cultural racism as outlined in white identity development models.
3. Culturally skilled counselors have knowledge about their social impact on others. They are knowledgeable about communication style differences and how their style may clash with or foster the counseling process with persons different from themselves based on the A, B, and C dimensions. They also know how to anticipate the impact their style may have on others.

Skills
1. Culturally skilled counselors seek out educational, consultative, and training experiences to improve their understanding and effectiveness in working with culturally different populations. Being able to recognize the limits of their competencies, they (a)

seek consultation, (b) seek further training or education, (c) refer out to more qualified individuals, or (d) engage in a combination of these.

2. Culturally skilled counselors are constantly seeking to understand themselves as racial and cultural beings and are actively seeking a nonracist identity.

Counselor Awareness of Client Worldview

Attitudes and Beliefs
1. Culturally skilled counselors are aware of their negative and positive emotional reactions toward other racial and ethnic groups that may prove detrimental to the counseling relationship. They are willing to contrast their own beliefs and attitudes with those of their culturally different clients in a nonjudgmental fashion.
2. Culturally skilled counselors are aware of their stereotypes and preconceived notions that they may hold toward racial and ethnic minority groups.

Knowledge
1. Culturally skilled counselors possess specific knowledge and information about the particular group with whom they are working. They are aware of the life experiences, cultural heritage, and historical background of their culturally different clients. This particular competency is strongly linked to the minority identity development models available in multicultural counseling literature.
2. Culturally skilled counselors understand how race, culture, and ethnicity may affect personality formation, vocational choices, manifestation of psychological disorders, help-seeking behavior, and the appropriateness or inappropriateness of counseling approaches.
3. Culturally skilled counselors understand and have knowledge about sociopolitical influences that impinge upon the lives of racial and ethnic minorities. Immigration issues, poverty, racism, stereotyping, and powerlessness may impact self-esteem and self-concept and influence the counseling process.

Skills
1. Culturally skilled counselors familiarize themselves with relevant research and the latest findings regarding the mental health and the mental disorders that affect various ethnic and racial groups. They actively seek out educational experiences that enrich their knowledge, understanding, and cross-cultural skills for more effective counseling behavior.
2. Culturally skilled counselors become actively involved with minority individuals outside the counseling setting (e.g., community events, social and political functions, celebrations, friendships, and neighborhood groups) so that their understanding of minorities is not just academic (Arredondo & D'Andrea, 1995, pp. 28–32).

Diversity Competencies

AMCD defined **diversity** as including but not limited to age, gender, sexual identity, disability, religious/spiritual identification, social and economic class background, and geographic location, and encouraged those with expertise in these diverse groups to generate their own parallel sets of competencies. Through a summit on spirituality in counseling, the Association for Spiritual, Ethical, and Religious Values in Counseling (ASERVIC) and ACES have generated a set of spiritual competencies for counselors that very closely follows the multicultural competencies. Multicultural counseling advocates have been meeting with representatives from various women and gay/lesbian counseling groups to discuss ways in which the multicultural counseling competencies might be expanded to other populations.

SUMMARY

Although multicultural counseling has existed since the counseling profession began and is important to all aspects of counseling, it has only recently been receiving the attention it deserves.

In addition to having personal and multicultural awareness of value systems and being comfortable working with differences, counselors must be able to understand and appreciate the worldviews of culturally different clients. Further, knowledge of the sociopolitical treatment of minorities may be helpful in developing approaches for assisting clients; then the counselor will know if there needs to be some societal changes only or also personal change by the client.

The definition of culture acknowledges that there are culturally diverse groups within larger racial and ethnic groups. Minority groups have been described in terms of their having a history of political oppression, rather than on the basis of group size alone. The United States is a culturally pluralistic society that includes a substantial number of minority groups; socioeconomic differences are perhaps as important as any other difference.

Counselors are encouraged to learn about cultural differences using both the etic and emic approaches: studying other cultures from a distance (the etic approach) as well as immersing themselves in other cultures (the emic approach). Barriers to multicultural counseling include the traditional counseling role, the view that clients' problems are due primarily to something within themselves, language misunderstandings, and values specific to different classes and cultures. Clients may fear conforming to the majority culture at the expense of their given culture's existence.

A coherent conceptual framework for multicultural counseling is emerging; however, there still is a lack of research to support any particular theoretical stance. Increased attention has been given to training counselors in multicultural skills. This chapter's multicultural counseling competency standards include specific objectives for the culturally skilled counselor in the areas of beliefs and attitudes, knowledge, and skills. Approaches for the development of these areas of expertise have also been described. Multicultural counseling is recognized as an important qualification for all counselors and is one of the major test areas on the National Certified Counselor (NCC) examination. The Association for Multicultural Counseling and Development (AMCD) is one division of the ACA.

QUESTIONS AND ACTIVITIES

1. What are the characteristics of your own particular cultural background? When did you become aware that you were an African American person, a European American, an Asian American, a Native

American, or a Latino American? How much influence has your racial and ethnic group membership had on you? How much have you affirmed, rejected, accepted, denied, and/or ignored your racial and ethnic identity? Do you have any mixed feelings about or unresolved conflicts with this identity? How might you deal with these conflicts?

2. What were the attitudes and feelings of your parents, friends, teachers, and other significant people in your life toward various ethnic minorities as you were growing up? What did they tell you directly? Indirectly? How did these attitudes and feelings influence your current attitudes and feelings? What generalizations do you believe other people currently make about you because of your racial and ethnic identity?

3. Think of your past and current friendships. How many of these friends are or were ethnic minorities? In what ways, if any, were these friendships different from friendships you have established within your racial and ethnic group? What other experiences have you had with minorities? How do you believe that these experiences will influence you as you try to become the best counselor possible?

4. If you were being counseled by a person who was culturally different from you, would it affect what problems or issues you would present? What would you want this person to know about you and your cultural background?

RECOMMENDED READINGS

American Counseling Association. (1991, September/ October) [Special issue].

American Psychological Association. (1995, January). Culture and Counseling [Special issue]. *Counseling Psychologist, 23*(1).

American Psychological Association. (1996, April). Multicultural challenges [Special issue]. Theory, evaluation, and training. *Counseling Psychologist, 24*(2).

Ivey, A. E., Ivey, M. B., & Simek-Morgan, L. (1993). *Counseling and psychotherapy: A multi-cultural perspective* (3rd ed.). Boston: Allyn & Bacon.

Multiculturalism as a fourth force in counseling [Special issue]. (1991). *Journal of Counseling and Development, 70*(1).

Paniagua, F. A. (1994). *Assessing and treating culturally diverse clients: A practical guide.* Thousand Oaks, CA: Sage.

Pedersen, P. (1994). *A handbook for developing multicultural awareness.* Alexandria, VA: American Association for Counseling and Development.

Ridley, C. R. (1995). *Overcoming unintentional racism in counseling and therapy: A practitioner's guide to intentional intervention.* Thousand Oaks, CA: Sage Publications.

Sue, D. W., & Sue, S. (1990). *Counseling the culturally different* (2nd ed.). New York: Wiley.

INTERNET RESOURCES

Websites

The Multicultural Pavilion <curry.edschool. virginia.edu/go/multicultural>

The Anti-Racism Resource Web Site <darkwing. uoregon.edu/~dennisw/race.html>

Multicultural Links and Resources <curry.edschool. virginia.edu/go/multicultural/sites1.html>

Pathways to Diversity: Resources from University of Southern California <www.usc.edu/Library/ QF/diversity/index.html>

Race and Ethnicity On-line Resources: American Studies Web at Georgetown University <www.georgetown.edu/crossroads/asw/ race.html>

REFERENCES

American Counseling Association. (1991, September/ October) [Special issue].

American Psychological Association. (April, 1993). White American researchers and multicultural counseling [Special issue]. *Counseling Psychologist, 21*(2).

American Psychological Association. (1995, January). Culture and Counseling [Special issue]. *Counseling Psychologist, 23*(1).

American Psychological Association. (1996, April). Multicultural challenges [Special issue]. Theory, evaluation, and training. *Counseling Psychologist, 24*(2).

Arredondo, P., & D'Andrea, M. (1995). AMCD approves multicultural counseling competency standards. *Counseling Today, 37*(9) 28–32.

Atkinson, D. R., Morten, G., & Sue, D. W. (1993). *Counseling American minorities* (4th ed.). Dubuque, IA: William C. Brown Communications.

Atkinson, O., Thompson, C., & Grant, S. (1993). A three-dimensional model for counseling racial/ ethnic minorities. *Counseling Psychologist, 21*(2), 257–277.

Belkin, G. (1984). *Introduction to counseling*. Dubuque, IA: Brown.

Cheatham, H. E., Ivey, A. E., Ivey, M. B., & Simek-Morgan, L. (1993). Multicultural counseling and therapy: Changing the foundations of the field. In A. E. Ivey, M. B. Ivey, and L. Simek-Morgan, *Counseling and psychotherapy: A multicultural perspective* (3rd ed.). Boston: Allyn & Bacon.

Corey, M. S., & Corey, G. (1992). *Becoming a helper*. Pacific Grove, CA: Brooks/Cole.

Das, A. K. (1995). Rethinking multicultural counseling: Implications for counselor education. *Journal of Counseling and Development, 74,* 45.

Das, A. K., & Littrell, J. M. (1989). Multicultural education for counseling: A reply to Lloyd. *Counselor Education and Supervision, 29,* 7–15.

Fukuyama, M. A. (1990). Taking a universal approach to multicultural counseling. *Counselor Education and Supervision, 30,* 6–17.

Heath, A. E., Neimeyer, G. J., & Pedersen, P. B. (1988). The future of cross-cultural counseling: A Delphi poll. *Journal of Counseling and Development, 67*(9), 27–30.

Ivey, A. E., Ivey, M. B., & Simek-Morgan, L. (1993). *Counseling and psychotherapy: A multicultural perspective* (3rd ed.). Boston: Allyn & Bacon.

Jackson, M. L. (1987). Cross-cultural counseling at the crossroads: A dialogue with Clemmont E. Vontress. *Journal of Counseling and Development, 66*(9), 20–23.

Katz, J. H. (1985). The social–political nature of counseling. *The Counseling Psychologist, 13,* 615–624.

Kim, S., McLeod, J. H., & Shantzis, C. (1992). Cultural competence for evaluators working with Asian American communities: Some practical considerations. In M. Orlandi and R. Weston (Eds.), *Cultural competence for evaluators* (pp. 203–260). Rockville, MD: U.S. Department of Health and Human Services.

Lee, D. (1984). Counseling and culture: Some issues. *Personnel and Guidance Journal, 62,* 592–597.

McAdoo, H. P. (Ed.). (1993). *Family ethnicity: Strength in diversity.* Newbury Park, CA: Sage.

Ohlsen, M. (1983). *Introduction to counseling.* Itasca, IL: Peacock.

Paniagua, F. A. (1994). *Assessing and treating culturally diverse clients: A practical guide.* Thousand Oaks, CA: Sage.

Parham, T. (1993). White researchers conducting multicultural research: Can their efforts be "mo betta"? *Counseling Psychologist, 21*(2), 250–256.

Parker, W. M. (1987). Flexibility: A primer for multicultural counseling. *Counselor Education and Supervision, 26*(3), 176–180.

Patterson, C. H. (1996). Multicultural counseling: From diversity to universality. *Journal of Counseling and Development, 74,* 227.

Payne, R. K. (1995). *A framework for understanding and working with students and adults from poverty* (Rev. ed.). Baystown, TX: RFT Publishing.

Pedersen, P. (1991). Multiculturalism as a generic approach to counseling. *Journal of Counseling and Development, 70*(1), 6–12.

Pedersen, P. (1994). *A handbook for developing multicultural awareness.* Alexandria, VA: American Association for Counseling and Development.

Pedersen, R., & Marsella, A. (1982). The ethical crisis for cross-cultural counseling and therapy. *Professional Psychology, 13*(4), 492–500.

Ponterotto, J. G., Alexander, C. M., & Grieger, I., (1995). A multicultural checklist for counselor training programs. *Journal of Counseling and Development, 23*(1), 11–20.

Ponterotto, J. G., & Benesch, K. F. (1988). An organizational framework for understanding the role of culture in counseling. *Journal of Counseling and Development, 66*(1), 237–240.

Ponterotto, J. G., & Casas, J. M. (1991). *Handbook of racial/ethnic minority counseling research.* Springfield, IL: Charles C. Thomas.

Ridley, C. R. (1995). *Overcoming unintentional racism in counseling and therapy: A practitioner's guide to intentional intervention.* Thousand Oaks, CA: Sage.

Rogers, C. (1979). Groups in two cultures. *Personnel and Guidance Journal, 58,* 11–15.

Sabnani, H. B., Ponterotto, J. G., & Borodovsky, L. G. (1991). White racial identity development and cross-cultural counselor training: A stage model. *The Counseling Psychologist, 19,* 76–102.

Speight, S. L., Myers, L. J., Cox, C. I., & Highlen, P. S. (1991). A redefinition of multicultural counseling. *Journal of Counseling and Development, 70,* 29–36.

Sue, D. W. (1981). *Counseling the culturally different: Theory and practice.* New York: Wiley.

Sue, D. W. (1992). The challenge of multiculturalism: The road less traveled. *American Counselor, 1*(1), 7–14.

Sue, D. W., Bernier, T. E., Durran, A., Feinberg, L., Pedersen, P., Smith, E. T., & Vasquez-Nuttall, E. (1982). Position paper: Cross-cultural counseling competencies. *Counseling Psychologist, 10*(2), 45–52.

Sue, D. W., & Sue, S. (1990). *Counseling the culturally different* (2nd ed.). New York: Wiley.

Wehrly, B. (1995). *Pathways to multicultural counseling competence: A developmental journey.* Pacific Grove, CA: Brooks/Cole.

Wilkinson, C. B. (1986). Introduction. In C. B. Wilkinson (Ed.), *Ethnic psychiatry* (pp. 1–11). New York: Plenum.

chapter 19

focus on

ASSESSMENT OF INDIVIDUALS

- What do tests have to do with counseling?
- Can assessment be fully objective?
- How can assessment and diagnosis be harmful?
- How do cultural issues affect diagnostic decisions?

Assessment, the testing and evaluation of clients, is one of the most controversial topics in the field of counseling. For clients, it can mean being observed, appraised, analyzed, and labeled in some way. For members of minority groups, it can mean being subjected to culturally biased tests. For counseling students, it can mean taking courses that are heavily laden with mathematical and statistical concepts.

We believe that a full understanding of assessment concepts and practices is necessary whether or not counselors choose to use tests and other diagnostic instruments. It is necessary to communicate with those who do use these tools in case conferences, referrals, and correspondence, as well as to understand the professional literature. This chapter outlines the general background, philosophy, and principles of the assessment and diagnosis of individuals. Assessment approaches are presented from different theoretical views, followed by descriptions of instruments and techniques. Finally, basic guidelines for the process and practice of assessment and diagnosis are presented.

BACKGROUND

Assessment has been part of the field of counseling from the very beginning. Vocational counselors early on used a variety of instruments to help clients match personal and job characteristics. The administration of tests and interpretation of test results have been major activities of the school counselor for decades. Nevertheless, counselors and the U.S. society in general have had mixed attitudes toward assessment and assessment processes. There has been much concern about the possible negative effects of testing. Some cities, including Los Angeles, have restricted the use of intelligence tests in their schools. Among the ranks of counseling professionals, there also has been a great deal of controversy related to the nature and appropriateness of assessment and diagnosis. In 1972 Leo Goldman, an expert in the use of tests in counseling, stated that "there is increased feeling that the use of tests in counseling has been on the whole a sad disappointment and that in recent years matters have actually become worse" (p. 213).

Sugarman (1978) reports that there have been objections to the use of assessment and appraisal techniques on five different grounds:

1. It is reductionistic, reducing the complexity of the person into diagnostic categories.
2. It is artificial.
3. It ignores the quality of the relationship between the examiner and the test taker.
4. It judges people, casting a label on them.
5. It is overly intellectual, relying on complex concepts, often at the expense of a true understanding of the individual.

Additionally, there is evidence that gays and lesbians, African Americans, ethnic minorities, women, and nontraditional men (e.g., men who choose to participate in activities historically viewed as women's work) are disproportionately diagnosed with certain disorders or misdiagnosed altogether (Enns, 1993; Paniagua, 1994; Ridley, 1995; Robertson & Fitzgerald, 1990; Sinacore-Guinn, 1995). Also, culturally appropriate behaviors that do not meet Western standards of behavior often are viewed as pathological (Draguns, 1989; Mwaba & Pedersen, 1990; Sinacore-Guinn, 1995).

In 1972 the National Education Association (NEA) advocated a moratorium on the use of standardized tests. At least two states have laws regulating the use of tests (Zytowski, 1982); however, such movements have not significantly curtailed the use of tests. Engen, Lamb, and Prediger (1982), reporting on the results of test use in secondary schools, found that schools continued to give tests and would do even more testing if more funds were available. The current pursuit of excellence in schools appears to have resulted in increased emphasis on testing in the schools, with a particular focus on competency testing. In 1985 the NEA reversed its earlier position and announced support for competency testing for teachers as well. In 1997 President Clinton advocated increased testing of students to determine levels of student achievement.

Businesses and industries have used tests and inventories for many years, primarily as aids in the selection of job candidates. Testing has been and continues to be a generally accepted function in mental health centers, state employment offices, and other private and public clinics and agencies. It has even become part of the counseling profession itself. Individuals seeking to become Nationally Certified Counselors (NCC) have to successfully pass a multiple-choice test.

Tests and their use have not changed significantly since objections were raised in the 1970s and earlier. Basically, what seems to have changed is the overall attitude of people toward tests. Recent Gallup polls of the U.S. population indicate a general acceptance of the use of standardized tests. Assessment procedures of all types are now an accepted part of contemporary society.

PURPOSES OF INDIVIDUAL ASSESSMENT

In studying the assessment process, first the process is defined and then the purposes for using assessment procedures are explained. Also noted is the context in which assessment procedures are generally found.

Definition and Purposes of Assessment

"**Problem assessment** consists of procedures and tools used to collect and process information from which the entire counseling program is developed" (Cormier & Cormier, 1985, p. 146). Following are some of the purposes of assessment:

- To obtain information on the client's presenting problem and other related problems.
- To identify the controlling or contributing variables associated with the problem.
- To determine the client's goals and expectations for counseling outcomes.
- To gather baseline data that will be compared with subsequent data to assess client progress and the effect of treatment strategies. This helps the practitioner decide whether to continue or modify the treatment plan.
- To educate and motivate clients by counselors' sharing their views of the problem with them, by increasing their receptivity to treatment, and by contributing to therapeutic change through reactivity. **Reactivity** refers to behavior change that is a consequence of the assessment procedure rather than the result of a particular change strategy.
- To use the information obtained from the client to plan effective treatment interventions and strategies. The information obtained during the assessment process helps to answer the following question: "What treatment, by whom, is most effective for this individual with that specific problem and under which set of circumstances?" (Cormier & Cormier, 1985, pp. 146–147)

The study of individual assessment is not a course in statistics. Many counseling students have approached courses in this area with trepidation and have, in their own minds, labeled courses in tests and measurements or individual appraisal as statistics. Mathematical and statistical terms are involved in the study of assessment techniques, but a basic awareness of such concepts does not constitute an in-depth study of statistics.

The use of mathematical concepts, however, may be enough to unnerve some students who may have been attracted to the field of human services largely because of its relative freedom from mathematics. Generally speaking, there is not a significant emphasis on mathematical concepts in most counseling and consulting work. It is necessary, however, for professionals in the field to know and to understand the technical aspects of the field, even if a counselor or consultant does not regularly use assessment instruments. As practitioners in the counseling field strive to make the profession more scientifically based, one must consider that there will be an increasing amount of rigor in terms of assessment, diagnosis, and research. Suggested guidelines for professional preparation in assessment include a basic course in measurement and evaluation; because such a course does not emphasize statistics, there should also be a course in basic statistics. These courses should be followed by the supervised administration of assessment instruments during practicum and internship courses (Loesch, 1984).

DIAGNOSIS

An ongoing concern in counseling and psychotherapy is whether to make routine, formal diagnoses of every client. Unlike the field of medicine, for which such a question would be considered unthinkable, there is a concern in the field of counseling as to the validity of such a practice. In counseling and psychotherapy, there are at least four different points of view, or models, that describe the causes of mental disorders and the use of diagnosis. These include the medical model and three nonmedical models, which are the behavioristic, the humanistic, and the human services.

The Medical Model

The concept of disease or illness is fundamental to the **medical model.** In the practice of medicine, a clinical diagnosis of the illness is made, which includes classifying and labeling the disorder. A treatment plan is then formulated and implemented to cure the patient by dealing with the bacterial, viral, or genetic factors that have been scientifically determined to be the causative agents.

Historically, a distinction has been made between two types of disorders. **Organic disorders** are caused by physical abnormalities of the brain, nervous system, and other internal systems. **Functional disorders** are those caused by psychological factors operating within the individual, such as poorly controlled drives and impulses, unrealistic ideas, and unresolved conflicts. The current view of many adherents of the medical model is that "all mental and emotional disorders are organic" (Albee & Ryan-Finn, 1993, p. 117).

Once a diagnosis has been made and the patient's condition has been labeled, a number of treatment modalities are possible. These include drug therapy to control emotions and behavior. Drugs used may include tranquilizers and antidepressants. Other medical treatments include electroconvulsive, or shock, therapy and psychosurgery (e.g., a lobotomy, the severing of nerve fibers connecting the frontal lobes from other parts of the brain). The use of tranquilizers has dramatically reduced the need for the number of lobotomies in recent years. Rehabilitation psychotherapy, occupational therapy, and psychotherapy are also used as part of the therapeutic process.

The medical model has been strongly criticized for some time now. In his book *The Myth of Mental Illness* (1973), Szasz maintains that most of what adherents of the medical model call mental illnesses are not illnesses at all, but actually are problems in living manifested by deviations from moral, legal, and social norms. He holds that this medical approach is a form of persecution in the guise of treatment that can have the effect of excluding undesirable people from society even though they have committed no crime. Further, to label persons "sick" removes from them the responsibility for their behavior, with the result that they have little chance of recovery. In fact, they may accept the label, consider themselves sick and helpless, and continue life as a mental patient.

In addition to the social control of which Szasz speaks, Kovel (1980) states that what is left out of the assessment process using the medical model is the effect of environment and society. People are affected by conditions such as poverty, unemployment, lack of opportunity, and crime. If a person with deviant behavior is treated and cured, have we just made him or her acceptable for what may be, in fact, a sick society?

Diagnosis is also seen as a dehumanizing process. The diagnostic label becomes the identity of the person. These labels can actually be harmful to people, affecting their interpersonal relationships, employment opportunities, and even their civil rights. People who have been labeled *psychotic* may, in some states, be hospitalized against their will and lose their legal rights in the process.

Many counselors have felt that they would be "losing some of their hearts or perhaps selling their souls to incorporate diagnosis into their practice" (Carlson, Hinkle, & Sperry, 1993, p. 308). This is particularly a problem in marriage and family counseling, since the categories in the *Diagnostic and Statistical Manual (DSM)* that apply directly to family problems are usually not covered by third-party payments. To qualify for third-party payments in a family counseling situation, practitioners have to diagnose one of the family members with a malady that is covered. Carlson, Hinkle, and Sperry (1993) maintain that this can be done with integrity and that doing so may, in fact, be quite desirable as part of developing a treatment approach for a family. Albee and Ryan-Finn (1993) are particularly critical of the medical model, since it ignores compelling evidence that social factors play a significant role in the etiology of mental disorders and is focused, therefore, almost exclusively on remediation with little or no concern about prevention. Ridley (1995) believes that the lack of focus on the social conditions that cause distress is especially harmful to minorities.

Nonmedical Model Approaches to Assessment and Diagnosis

A number of nonmedical approaches share the following strategies: (1) avoiding medical terminology, such as *patient, diagnosis, symptom, pathology, mental illness, treatment,* and *cure;* (2) focusing on factors other than biological ones, such as environmental factors; and (3) keeping a significant amount of the responsibility for change with the client.

The following are three nonmedical approaches and their views of the etiology of maladaptive behaviors:

1. *Behaviorism:* Inappropriate behavior is learned and can be unlearned.
2. *Humanism:* Abnormal behavior is the result of a lack of self-acceptance and esteem, ill-defined or unrealistic personal goals, and a failure to accept responsibility for inappropriate behaviors (Bootzin, 1980).
3. *Human Services:* Society's failure to provide basic needs sometimes results in maladaptive behavior on the part of the deprived.

There are great areas of conflict between the adherents of the medical and the nonmedical approaches. These areas of conflict involve issues of power and turf. Who can do what in the field of human services? Who can receive third-party payments? Who can be licensed by governments or governmental agencies? At present, psychiatrists, who invariably follow the medical model, have the broadest scope of power and territory in the field of human services; however, in varying degrees in different states, other professionals and even paraprofessionals are increasingly able to participate more fully in the field.

Formal diagnosis with the medical approach, therefore, is not a regular practice for all professionals in the counseling field. For example, behaviorists, who do not expect to receive third-party payments, generally do not make diagnoses using the diagnostic guidelines in the *Diagnostic and Statistical Manual of Mental Disorders,* 4th edition (American Psychiatric Association, 1994), more commonly referred to as the *DSM-IV.* Behaviorists focus on behaviors that need to be changed, and a mutual contract might be made between the client and the counselor to modify a given behavior. On the other hand, the use of the

DSM-IV as a diagnostic tool is routine in agencies that require a formal diagnosis and when third-party payments are involved. Behaviorists expecting third-party payments also need to make a formal diagnosis. At present, insurance companies and government agencies usually do not make payments for services when a formal diagnosis using the *DSM-IV* has not been made. A controversial aspect of this practice is that governmental agencies and insurance companies are dictating what the actual practices of helping professionals are. An additional concern is that third-party providers have access to the records of their clients to monitor diagnoses, treatment plans, and other records, thus jeopardizing the confidential nature of the therapeutic relationship. Only professionals who work with clients who pay their own bills may be able to avoid this dilemma.

Ideas in action Assume that you are having a difficult time with your studies. You've gone to a medical doctor and have been found to be in sound physical shape, yet you are having difficulty communicating and getting your homework done on time.

You decide to see a counselor but you don't have the resources to pay for what might be an unknown number of sessions. You do have insurance coverage, however.

The counselor's receptionist tells you that to go through the insurance company, a diagnosis will have to be made—one that is acceptable to the insurance company (they are selective). Furthermore, the insurance company may restrict the number of sessions that it will cover. In addition to being diagnosed (having a label of being treated for mental illness), the insurance company will have access to your records since it paid for treatment (the records won't be confidential).

Do you continue or not?

With your classmates discuss the position such a client is put in.

The DSM-IV *Multiaxial Assessment*

The fourth edition of the *Diagnostic and Statistical Manual of Mental Disorders (DSM-IV)*, published by the American Psychiatric Association in 1994, is the basic instrument used by mental health practitioners in making and reporting formal diagnoses. A counselor must be aware of the system and the vocabulary that the majority of practitioners working in the field use, even if one does not use them in practice.

The *DSM-IV* has evolved from a relatively simple approach of applying to a given condition a one- or two-word label to the present system, which requires consideration of a client in several dimensions. The current diagnostic system is considered to be multiaxial, because there are five different axes, or areas of functioning, that can be considered when making assessments:

> Axis I: Clinical syndromes and conditions not attributable to a mental disorder that are a focus of attention or treatment

Axis II: Developmental disorders and personality disorders
Axis III: Physical disorders and conditions
Axis IV: Severity of psychosocial stressors
Axis V: Global assessment of functioning (GAF)

Extensive descriptions of each syndrome or disorder are provided along with decision trees, which help the practitioner select or rule out possible disorders. The major advantage in using this multiaxial classification system is that it "ensures that attention is given to certain types of disorders, aspects of the environment, and areas of functioning that might be overlooked if the focus were on assessing a single presenting problem" (American Psychiatric Association, 1987, p. 15).

In addition to diagnosing the client as to mental health, personality disorders, and physical condition, scales have been developed to help the clinician make consistent determinations of the severity of the psychosocial stressors (Axis IV) and the global assessment of functioning (GAF) (Axis V). When using the GAF on Axis V, the clinician should record a current determination and an estimate of the highest GAF for the past year.

Thus, rather than give a one- or two-word label to a diagnosed person, such as "depressive neurosis," as was the practice prior to the adoption of the *DSM-III* (1980), the practitioner now can come up with a diagnosis such as the following:

Axis I: 296.24 Major depression, single episode; severe without psychotic features
Axis II: 301.60 Dependent personality disorder
Axis III: Diabetes
Axis IV: Psychosocial stressors: separated from spouse; conflicts with children;
  Severity: 3—Moderate
Axis V: Current GAF = 44
Highest GAF past year = 55

Ideas in *action*

DSM-IV is not only bigger than ever but has its own set of accessories—a "library" that includes a casebook, five projected volumes of research reports, several volumes describing clinical interviewing techniques, a study guide, a glossary, a computerized version of the manual, and more. We doubt that the road to continued success for psychiatry is a series of manuals, each in a new color coordinated with accessories, each bigger than the last, and each with built-in obsolescence that insures demand for the next model.

Kutchins & Kirk (1995, p. 4)

DSM-IV may appear somewhat quaint and primitive once we understand more deeply the nature and causes of psychiatric disorders, but it will have fulfilled its intended function by facilitating the growth of that understanding.

Frances, First, & Pincus (1995, p. 4)

What is your reaction to the above quotes? Look at Table 19.1. Which arguments are strongest? How do you feel about making a diagnosis using the *DSM*?

TABLE 19.1   Arguments for and against the use of the *Diagnostic and Statistical Manual (DSM).*

For the *DSM*	Against the *DSM*
Provides a common language for discussing diagnosis	Assessing a diagnosis to a client is uncomfortable to many counselors
Increases attention to behaviors	Promotes a mechanistic approach to mental disorder
Facilitates the learning of assessment	
Provides a diagnosis for clients with insurance coverage	Creates a false impression that the understanding of mental disorders is more advanced than is actually the case
Helps inform clients if their symptoms will be covered by insurance	Has an extensive focus on signs and symptoms of mental disorders to the exclusion of a more in-depth understanding of the client's problems
Assists with accountability, record keeping, and treatment planning	
Identifies clients with issues beyond counselor's areas of expertise	Medical model ignores prevention
	Ignores social conditions that contribute to client's problems
Information helpful in research in which associations may be found between factors on various axes	Harmful to women and culturally different groups
Symptoms that commonly occur together are grouped in order to facilitate research and education	Labels people and excludes people from society
	Insurance companies are dictating how *DSM* will be used
Classifications, criteria, and descriptions meant to be used as guidelines and not applied mechanically	Third-party providers have access to clients' records, thus jeopardizing confidentiality
Will eventually be superseded as new knowledge is acquired through neuroscience and clinical research	Does not provide a definition that clearly distinguishes mental disorders from normality and that works in every clinical situation
	Term "mental disorder" implies a mind–body dualism
	Overly complex with built-in obsolescence

DIFFERENT THEORETICAL APPROACHES TO ASSESSMENT

As noted in chapters 10 and 11, the approaches of practitioners to the use of assessment tools vary significantly with regard to theoretical stance. The following are descriptions of how practitioners from different theoretical outlooks approach client assessment.

Psychodynamic

Assessment and diagnosis play major roles in the work of psychodynamic therapists. Such therapists are generally psychiatrists who are fully trained diagnosticians. They may use a variety of objective measures in the assessment process but tend to focus on more of the subjective types of measurement. They believe that conscious data do not tell the real story. Psychoanalysts assess the client's unconscious by techniques such as free association, dream analysis, and the use of projective instruments, such as the Rorschach and the

Thematic Apperception Test (TAT). Psychoanalysts make inferences, interpretations, and diagnoses from these data and then make interventions in line with the theoretical guidelines they follow.

Projective techniques, such as the Rorschach Diagnostic Test, require that clients respond to ambiguous stimuli such as an inkblot. These instruments are presented with their basic purpose deliberately concealed from the client. The presupposition is that if the client is able to respond without being defensive, the responses that emerge can reveal unconscious aspects of the personality. The responses are then interpreted by the clinician.

Cognitive–Behavioral Assessment

Cognitive–behavioral practitioners use a variety of assessment procedures. There are the very explicit behavioral descriptions used by strict behaviorists, and then there is the strategy of assessing client characteristics, behaviors, and traits and making diagnoses on the basis of such data.

> Ways in which behavior may be measured directly include situational behavior sampling, both verbal and nonverbal, and the physiological measurement of emotional reactions. In behavior sampling, the emphasis is on detailed information concerning the onset, magnitude, and duration of the behaviors of interest and the circumstance of their occurrence. The subject himself may supply this information through various self-report techniques such as daily records, lists of problematic situations, or responses on preset survey scales (schedules). (Mischel, 1971, p. 200)

A variety of checklists or survey instruments may be used in this approach, but there is rarely any use of standardized or projective tests. The counselor and the client record change of certain thoughts and behaviors often in the form of a contract.

Humanistic–Transpersonal Assessment

In the humanistic–transpersonal view, the clients are considered to be their own best assessors. Research indicates that self-assessment has yielded predictions as accurate as those from more sophisticated personality tests, combinations of tests, clinical judgments, and complex statistical analyses. People may be good predictors of their own behavior for such diverse outcomes as success in college, jobs, and psychotherapy (Mischel, 1971, p. 221).

In this approach, which includes person-centered and Gestalt therapies, there is no systematic formal testing or other external measurement. There is no formal diagnosis per se. There is no attempt to learn about the client through paper and pencil tests or other external methods. There is, however, an attempt to work with the client directly. Through the exploration and understanding of the client's perceptions of problems, a mutual diagnosis is reached at which both the client and the counselor acknowledge what the problem really is.

This does not preclude the use of test instruments or other devices. In discussing the client-centered approach to assessment, Patterson and Watkins (1981) suggest that when there is information the client needs and wants that might be provided by a test, tests are introduced and the client is encouraged to participate in the selection of appropriate instruments. Any assessment instruments might be used as needed. Test result data are presented as completely and as objectively as possible by the humanistic or transpersonal counselor. The client is to make the interpretations and personally ascribe any meaning to the results. The object is to keep the **locus of evaluation**—the place in which judgments are made—with the client. This process is more likely to result in material that is understandable and usable to the client in the pursuit of personal change.

Human Services Assessment

The first step in working with the human services approach is not a diagnosis but "an assessment of the victim's life situation with a view to discovering what needs are not being met" (Schmolling, Youkelles, & Burger, 1993, p. 145). The person may be lacking in terms of adequate diet, housing, medical care, or even social interaction. Once the assessment is made, practitioners work to help clients find the resources to meet their needs.

ASSESSMENT TECHNIQUES

As noted in the discussion of the different approaches, assessment takes place at different levels and with different methods. The following is an overview of basic techniques used in the field of mental health.

Nonstandardized Assessment Techniques

Counselors use a variety of techniques and procedures in the process of gathering data. Some can be highly structured and designed so that each time a procedure is used the process is exactly the same. This is called using a **standardized format.** A less rigorous but also important way of obtaining information is through the use of **nonstandardized instruments.** Such tools may be idiosyncratic, specific only to a given client or set of circumstances, with a minimal chance for replication. A brief description of some nonstandardized formats follows.

Observation
The casual observation of human behavior is one of people's most popular pastimes. Many people describe themselves as people watchers, and it is perhaps as a result of this that many enter the field of human services. Observation is the most fundamental assessment procedure. Highly developed skills in the use of other assessment tools are negated if the powers of observation are not well developed. Gibson and Mitchell (1981) describe casual observation and two higher levels in their discussion of the levels of observation:

> *First Level: Casual Information Observation:* The daily unstructured and usually unplanned observations that provide casual impressions. Nearly everyone engages in this type of activity. No training or instrumentation is expected or required.
>
> *Second Level: Guided Observation:* Planned, directed observations for a purpose. Observation at this level is usually facilitated by simple instruments such as checklists

or rating scales. This is the highest level used in most counseling programs. Some training is desired.

Third Level: Clinical Level: Observations, often prolonged, and frequently under controlled conditions. Sophisticated techniques and instruments are utilized, with training usually at a doctoral level. (p. 111)

Problems with Observation.   Because people do something all the time, it does not necessarily mean that they do it well. The process of observation is no exception to this rule. That is why awareness and training are necessary for people to be more effective observers. People need to be aware that their observations of a person or situation may be different from those of others viewing the same scene. Movies like *Rashomon* have demonstrated how this phenomenon can work. Also, observation can be taken too casually, and when a person may really need a particular piece of data, it isn't always available. For example, a person may not know the name of a particular street that is crossed regularly.

> Behavioral observation is common to all psychological approaches. It is the use that is made of the data that distinguishes between approaches. In the psychodynamic orientation behaviors serve as indirect signs of hypothesized underlying dispositions and motives. Behavioral approaches treat observed behavior as a sample, and the focus is on how the specific sample is affected by variations in the stimulus conditions. (Mischel, 1971, p. 200)

As noted in chapter 6, more than half of the message that a client communicates is nonverbal. Counselors should be attuned to all of the nonverbal cues available and note the discrepancies and inconsistencies between these and verbal messages. Specific areas to focus on are listed in chapter 6. The senses are the best tools available and include "listening with your eyes," "seeing with your ears," "sensing with your entire body," and "listening with the third ear" (Reik, 1948, p. 1). To supplement your personal tool collection and your self as instrument, the following are descriptions of a number of paper and pencil instruments.

Observational Instruments

Formats have been developed to provide assistance in making and recording observations, checklists, rating scales, and anecdotal reports. Each of these instruments makes the observations more systematic and provides a record from which changes can be measured.

Checklists.   The purpose of a checklist is to focus the observer's attention to the presence or absence of predetermined characteristics. A simple check mark or "yes" or "no" indicates whether the characteristic is observed. Characteristics may include the following:

1. Is punctual
2. Is able to carry on a sustained conversation

Rating Scales.   A rating scale is a special kind of checklist on which the observer can note not only the presence of a given characteristic or attribute but also the degree to which it manifests itself. Rating scales can be particularly helpful in making observations of individuals when they are in a natural setting: at school, at work, or playing in a team sport. Below is an example of an item from a rating scale used in an office setting:

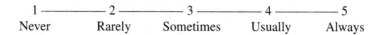

The benefits of rating scales and checklists include having an easy to use approach for making objective observations of selected characteristics. They also offer the possibility of comparing the observations of more than one observer using identical criteria. There are also some limitations in the use of such instruments, including (1) often poor and unclear directions for the scales' use; (2) a failure to define terms adequately; (3) limited scales for rating; (4) items that tend to prejudice how one responds; (5) overlapping items; and (6) excessive length (Gibson & Mitchell, 1981, p. 118). Additional limitations include ratings made without sufficient observations; giving higher ratings than may be accurate; middle rating, which means playing it safe by giving a middle or average rating to everyone on every item; and biased ratings, in which an observer's bias on one item may affect the observer's responses on other items. In addition to being used as instruments for recording ongoing observations of clients, counselors can use checklists and rating scales for making recommendations, such as indicating a student's potential for success in graduate school, and as part of evaluations, such as rating a counselor's ability to work with adolescent clients. This format is also used in certain types of measures of client attitudes and interests.

Anecdotal Reports.   Anecdotal reports are subjective descriptions of a client's behavior at a specific time or for a specific situation. These reports generally start out by noting the time, date, and place. These are followed by a general description of the event and the manner in which the client participated in it. The report ends with observer comments that may be evaluative in nature.

Anecdotal observations made over a period of time can be helpful in providing a fuller picture of a client's behavior than can responses on a checklist or rating scale. Because of its subjective nature, however, observer bias can be an important factor and needs to be noted and acknowledged. The more the observer is trained to note and record specific behaviors and to keep the reporting of behaviors separate from interpretations, biases, and evaluations, the more valuable the anecdotal observations.

Self-Report Instruments

In making an assessment of an individual, the most direct source of information is the client. More systematic forms of obtaining information other than simply letting the clients tell stories include questionnaires, structured interviews, open-ended questions, autobiographies, and self-descriptions.

Questionnaires.   Questionnaires are a common type of nonstandardized instrument used for data gathering. They can be short enough to be filled out by a client a few minutes before the first visit to a counselor and can be designed to provide a variety of data. Questionnaires can be used to collect vital information to determine the counseling or consulting needs of groups or organizations. This information seeking is often included as part of a larger process called a needs assessment. With a needs assessment the desired objectives or goals of a person, group, or organization are determined. Questionnaires can also be used to obtain feedback on the results of counseling and consulting. A special form of the questionnaire format consists primarily of incomplete sentences that the client is expected to complete. The sentences can be designed, for example, to bring out affective responses, such as "When I get angry, I…" or "People can tell when I am happy, because…." Responses to such questions help a counselor compare observations with client statements and can lead to other productive areas, such as dealing with the inability to communicate emotions directly or difficulty in handling negative feelings.

Structured Interviews.   A structured interview is a form of questionnaire that is read to a client by a counselor. The client is encouraged to respond as directly as possible to all questions, and the counselor has the opportunity to ask for clarification or elaboration of any question. Such an interview may be required of all first time clients by a mental health agency as part of a case management process. One purpose is to assign the client to the staff member or program that best meets the needs of the client. Another type of structured interview focuses on a specific issue or syndrome, such as depression or alcoholism, and the questions are designed to highlight related aspects of behavior. Careful records, including tape recordings, are generally made in the case of structured interviews to be sure that all comments are noted and that nonverbal behaviors are also included.

Personal Essays and Autobiographies.   More extensive written material, such as having a client write a personal essay on a given topic (for example, "the kind of job that I believe I would enjoy the most"), is another way to gather useful data in a short time and can be given as a homework assignment. A more elaborate version of the personal essay is to have the client write an autobiography. The type of material included as well as the areas not covered can provide significant data to work with in a counseling relationship.

Journals.   Having a client keep a journal on a regular basis and noting new issues and changes provides another method of obtaining self-report data on an ongoing basis. A journal is more than a diary or log of daily events. It is an opportunity to record thoughts and feelings, make sketches, doodle, and write poems without having to worry about being evaluated. A client can share all or part of a journal at various times during therapy. Major advantages to having clients keep journals are that it helps them become better observers of their own behavior and better communicators about issues of concern. A specialized version of the journal is a dream journal, which can be used as material to explore during a counseling session.

These types of assessment procedures are all nonstandardized. A number of techniques are included that are idiosyncratic and unsystematic. The same person using any one of these techniques would quite likely not use the technique exactly the same way each time.

Standardized Assessment Techniques

There is also a need for assessment devices that can be administered in a consistent manner to a wide variety of people. Many different tests, usually published instruments, are standardized. A **standardized test** is one that has detailed, specific directions for the administration of the instrument, including the exact words with which to introduce the instrument to the client and any time limits. The procedures for scoring are also specifically detailed so that all people scoring a given test will record results in the same manner. There are two basic categories of standardized tests: norm-referenced and criterion-referenced tests.

Norm-Referenced Tests

Another characteristic of most published instruments is that they have norms to which test scores can be compared. **Norms, or normative tables,** are generally included in the manual accompanying published tests. These tables provide data on the performance of various groups of people taking the same instrument during the period of time when the test was being developed. The results of a newly administered test can be compared immediately to those of a peer group (for example, ninth-grade boys). Norm groups are often nationwide samples, but they can also be regional or local. A great deal of time and effort goes into the preparation of published standardized instruments. Test items are carefully tested and analyzed before being included in the final instrument. The **reliability,** or consistency, of scores and the instrument's **validity,** the ability of a test to measure what it purports to measure, are also determined, with related data included in the manual of the published instrument. Finally, many tests are the subjects of research projects and related evaluative studies that often lead to revised editions after a period of time.

Criterion-Referenced Tests

Whereas the results of a norm-referenced test allow counselors to compare a client's score with an appropriate norm group, the results give little information with regard to a specific skill level. A **criterion-referenced test** is a test that is "used to ascertain an individual's status with respect to a well-defined behavioral domain" (Popham, 1978, p. 93). "A domain of behaviors consists of a set of skills or dispositions that examines display when called on to do so in a testing situation. For example, a behavioral domain in the field of mathematics might consist of an individual's ability to solve a certain class of simultaneous equation problems" (p. 94). A well-constructed criterion-referenced test yields a clear description of what a client can or cannot actually do. Properly constructed competency or achievement tests can serve as examples of criterion-referenced tests. A test can be both criterion- and norm-referenced.

Types of Standardized Instruments

Assessment instruments have been developed to measure virtually all aspects of humans. Published standardized instruments are generally catalogued and reviewed in a series of volumes entitled the *Mental Measurement Yearbook* (Buros, 1989). In this yearbook, critical reviews of the various instruments are published along with a description of each instrument. Some of the basic standardized assessment instrument classifications are achievement and aptitude (intelligence) tests, personality inventories, attitude questionnaires, interest inventories, and projective techniques.

Achievement Tests.   Achievement tests are designed to assess what a person has learned in a given subject, such as music, mathematics, or German, as a result of specific curricular experience. The instrument can be designed for one subject or can include a variety of subjects. Examples of the latter type of instrument are the Iowa Tests of Basic Skills and the Metropolitan Achievement Tests.

Aptitude (Intelligence) Tests.   A test used as a predictor of some future performance is called an aptitude test (Thorndike & Hagen, 1977). Aptitude tests are designed to measure the propensity to perform certain tasks that may not already be a part of a person's repertoire. Aptitude tests can be considered a form of ability testing, measuring the potential ability that a person has in a specific area. Intelligence tests can be considered measures of general ability. As discussed in chapter 17, there is no generally agreed-on definition of intelligence; however, most intelligence tests are designed to be indicators of the ability to be successful in school.

Some examples of aptitude tests are the Differential Aptitude Test (DAT), the Aptitude Classification Test (ACT), and the Scholastic Aptitude Test (SAT), which was renamed the Scholastic Achievement Test in 1993. Examples of intelligence tests include the Stanford-Binet Intelligence Scale and the Wechsler Adult Intelligence Scale-Revised (WAIS-R).

Personality Assessment Instruments

Even though a person's personality includes everything about that person, distinctions have been made so that assessing human abilities such as aptitude and intelligence has been distinguished from the study of other dimensions of the personality. Thorndike and Hagen (1977) describe several characteristics of personality other than abilities that can be identified and assessed, including temperament, character, adjustment, interests, and attitudes:

- *Temperament* refers to an individual's characteristic mood, activity level, excitability, and focus of concern. It includes such dimensions as cheerful–gloomy, energetic–lethargic, excited–calm, introverted–extroverted, and dominant–submissive.
- *Character* relates to those traits to which definite social value is attached. They are the "Boy Scout" traits of honesty, kindliness, cooperation, industry, and so on.
- *Adjustment* indicates how well the individual has been able to make peace internally and with the surrounding world. Individuals are considered well-adjusted to the extent that they can accept themselves and to the extent that their way of life does not get them in trouble with their social group.
- *Interests* refer to tendencies to seek out and participate in certain activities.
- *Attitudes* relate to tendencies to favor or reject particular groups of individuals, sets of ideas, or social institutions. (Thorndike & Hagen, 1977, pp. 394–395)

Many different approaches have been created to assess each personality characteristic or dimension described. A brief description of some of these approaches follows.

Attitude Questionnaires.   Attitude questionnaires are designed to assess the intensity of a person's sentiments with regard to a specific subject such as women's liberation, abortion, or gun control. Attitude questionnaires are relatively easy to create and as a result are probably encountered more often by the general public than are most other assessment devices. Politicians, for example, often use questionnaires to determine voter sentiment toward political issues. The Gallup research organization regularly surveys the general public on a variety of issues, and the results are often published in newspapers and journals. An attitude questionnaire generally takes the form of a series of statements related to a given topic to which the respondent is to make one of five choices: strongly agree, agree, strongly disagree, disagree, or undecided. The respondent may be asked the questions orally or may respond on paper to a written series of statements (see Figure 19.1). A major limitation of questionnaires is their low reliability. The responses people make to the statements on a questionnaire may not correspond to their actions. For example, students in a school may indicate a favorable attitude toward counseling, and yet there may be very few self-referrals. Questionnaires can be useful research tools with the caveat that the responses given are those the respondents are willing to share at the time (Thorndike & Hagen, 1977).

Interest Inventories. Instruments designed to determine patterns or tendencies that an individual has with regard to personal interests are called interest inventories. Interest inventories can be designed for almost any purpose—to determine interest in music, art, or athletics, for example. Many inventories have been designed for use in counseling and, in particular, for use in helping clients make career choices.

Interest instruments are usually constructed in the form of checklists or forced choice questions, on which the client has to select a preference from a choice of activities. For example, "Would you rather hang wallpaper, sing in a choral group, or teach young children?" One of the more popular inventories, the Strong-Campbell Interest Inventory, allows for the comparison of client interest patterns with those of people in various occupations.

Having an interest response pattern similar to that of architects, for example, does not necessarily mean that a client should pursue such a career. The client may, in fact, have no direct interest in architecture. Further, there is generally a very low correlation between interest and ability, so having an interest in an area does not guarantee success in it. The reverse is also true. Having a high degree of ability in an area does not guarantee that a person will be satisfied with a career in that area. A person might have musical ability, for example, but may not wish to pursue a career in the field of music. Interest inventories, then, are useful to help a client become aware of current areas of interest. Such findings in the area of career counseling, for example, can provide the basis for continued exploration on the part of the counselor and the client to determine reasonable career alternatives, combining perceived interests and abilities.

Personality Inventories. A number of self-report instruments have been developed that are related to personal adjustment and temperament, such as the Guilford-Zimmerman

---

Attitude Toward Counseling

Read each statement. Then circle the symbol that best represents your reaction to the statement according to the following scale:

> A — Strongly agree with the statement
> a — Tend to agree with the statement
> ? — Undecided. Neither agree nor disagree
> d — Tend to disagree with the statement
> D — Strongly disagree with the statement

A a ? d D   1. If I had a personal problem that I wanted to talk about with someone, I would go to the school counselor.

A a ? d D   2. Counselors can be helpful to me when I need to make important decisions in my life, such as what to do after graduation from high school.

FIGURE 19.1   Example of an attitude questionnaire.

Temperament Survey and the Minnesota Multiphasic Personality Inventory (MMPI). After responding to such instruments, clients receive results related to such characteristics as sociability, emotional stability, and masculinity. The validity of such instruments, in general, is low. These instruments involve reading and understanding the material presented and the ability to objectively relate the material to personal behavior. They also require frank and honest answers (Thorndike & Hagen, 1977). Thorndike and Hagen (1977) conclude that in view of the facts that scores can be distorted and that there is limited validity to instruments of this nature, they should be used "very sparingly…and only as an adjunct to more intensive psychological services" (p. 434).

Cultural Issues Related to Assessment

One of the major areas of concern related to testing and evaluation has been the issue of cultural differences. Cultural differences can affect diagnostic decisions as well as counseling interventions and outcomes. Diagnostic systems such as the *DSM-IV* are not readily transferable to other cultures. They may not even be appropriate for all subcultures within U.S. society. For example, the early editions of the *DSM* classified homosexuality as a mental illness. Even the later editions are still criticized as ignoring specific cultures and lacking "adequate sensitivity to value judgment and to cross-cultural and cross generational mores" (Klerman, Vaillant, Spitzer, & Michaels, 1984, pp. 542–543). It was not until the 1994 edition that there was any mention of spiritual issues (American Psychiatric Association, 1994).

With regard to testing, there is an ongoing debate over the degree to which various tests and other psychological instruments are culturally biased; for example, the SATs have been criticized for years as being biased against women, particularly on the mathematics portion of the test. For over a quarter of a century various minority groups have challenged almost all achievement and aptitude tests as being culturally biased and leading, among other things, to the placement of exceptionally high proportions of minority students in special education classes in public schools.

The best assessment instruments, however, will not do their job if they are not properly administered. There are very specific guidelines for the routine administration of tests. There are also guidelines for dealing with exceptional cases. Elmore, Ekstrom, and Diamond (1993) surveyed counselors regarding the extent to which they incorporated principles of good testing practices in their work. They found that more than half of the counselors surveyed do not routinely make appropriate modifications to administration procedures when testing individuals with disabilities.

These concerns need to be addressed by all practitioners from the very beginning of their careers. All counselors need to make the following assessment guidelines and standards part of their professional approach to counseling.

ASSESSMENT GUIDELINES

Practitioners should be aware of the basic issues involved in the use of assessment and appraisal procedures.

1. Each person's uniqueness is to be valued. Appropriate use of individual assessment and appraisal procedures acknowledges this uniqueness.
2. Variations exist within individuals as well as between individuals.
3. Appropriate assessment procedures require the direct participation of the individual in the assessment process. Federal regulations also require that assessment procedures be modified to appropriately allow the abilities of individuals with disabilities to be fully appraised (U.S. Department of Health, Education, and Welfare, 1977).
4. Accurate appraisals are limited by both instruments and personnel. All tests, for example, have some error of measurement so that any label or other diagnosis must be qualified.
5. If there are serious implications, both positive and negative data need to be evaluated and multiple sources of data used. For example, if a client earns an IQ of 80 on the single administration of an intelligence test, it is imperative that both environmental and testing conditions be evaluated. Multiple sources of assessment need to be used, including a second administration of the original instrument, before the label "mentally retarded" is applied.
6. In each assessment case, there are specific ethical guidelines to be followed (see Appendix B).

There are also specific guidelines for counselors published in documents called the Responsibilities of Users of Standardized Tests (RUST) (American Association for Counseling and Development & Association for Measurement and Evaluation in Counseling and Development, 1989) and the Code of Fair Testing Practices in Education (Joint Committee on Testing Practices, 1988).

Using a humanistic approach, Fischer (1985) offers six interrelated principles as guidelines for an individualized approach to assessment:

1. *Be descriptive.* Observe behavior and provide descriptions of samples of the client's behavior "along with their meaning to the assessor" (p. 46).
2. *Be contextual.* Descriptions of behaviors, both in the assessment session and outside of it, need to include contextual circumstances. To paraphrase Fischer, contexts include the physical setting, the location within a period of time, the assessor's relation to the client, and what the assessor perceives as the meaning of the situation for the client. For example: "At first she smoothed the fresh paper, lined up the two pencils, and leaned back expectantly, reminding me of a student with new supplies" (p. 46).
3. *Be collaborative.* The client must be encouraged "to be an informed, active participant throughout the assessment, and to comment on any written document. As a co-assessor, the client is acknowledged as partly responsible for his or her past and future and as capable of participating in his or her development" (p. 47). Assessment is not a secret mystical process that is done to a client. The process is used to acquire the best possible understanding of the individual, and this can be done only with direct input from the individual.
4. *Be interventional.* Assessment of any type always has an impact on the client in both positive and negative ways. It is important that interventions be made as constructive as possible. "These interventions into the client's ways of moving through situations are intended both to evaluate the client's current possibilities and to try out different ones" (p. 47). Assessment can be an isolated process; however, with a properly developed

therapeutic relationship and active client involvement, much positive therapeutic growth can occur.

5. *Be structural.* Behavioral events are described fully in terms of observed data in a given context and how they came into being. "What?" refers to when and how, as seen through some particular behavior. The question "why?" is not usually addressed, as it generally applies to causation, which is not observable or operationally described.

6. *Be circumspect.* Conditions do not always allow for full assessment. Assessment instruments all have errors of measurement, and assessors have personal, professional, theoretical, historical, and cultural limitations. All of this does not negate the value and meaning of the assessment process, but it is important to remember these factors in order that results may be kept in proper perspective.

PROFESSIONAL ORIENTATION

Students and practitioners with a particular interest in the area of measurement and individual assessment may join the Association for Assessment in Counseling (AAC) (formerly the Association for Measurement and Evaluation in Counseling and Development), a division of the ACA. It publishes a quarterly journal, *Measurement and Evaluation in Counseling and Development.*

SUMMARY

A description of the background, philosophy, principles, and techniques of individual assessment has been given, beginning with the idea that such a study is not the same as a course in statistics. The study of individual assessment merely uses measurement and statistical terms to understand individual differences and to facilitate communication among professionals. Even though some type of assessment and diagnosis occurs in almost every counseling relationship, there is no universal agreement as to what assessment criteria and techniques should or should not be used. The use of tests and other diagnostic procedures has been criticized on a number of grounds, in particular for possible harmful effects.

Four approaches to diagnosis have been described: the medical, the behavioristic, the humanistic, and the human services models, each having a different focus in assessing a client's problem. A comparison of the relationship of diagnosis and assessment to different theoretical approaches to counseling has been presented.

The importance of formal diagnosis as a requirement for payment of services by insurance companies and governmental agencies has been noted as a trend that may make most discussions of diagnosis and assessment purely academic for most practitioners. A description has been given of the diagnostic system of the American Psychiatric Association, *DSM-IV,* a system almost universally used by mental health practitioners who make and report formal diagnoses. Diagnoses made with this system are designed to give information on five different dimensions rather than just provide a simple label as required in previous systems.

Specific assessment techniques have been described in two basic categories: nonstandardized and standardized approaches. Nonstandardized approaches include observation, checklists, rating scales, anecdotal reports, questionnaires, and structured interviews. Standardized techniques include achievement and aptitude tests, and attitude, interest, and personality inventories.

Cultural, ethical, and administrative issues have been discussed and a set of humanistically oriented guidelines for use in the assessment process has been presented.

QUESTIONS AND ACTIVITIES

1. Consider the theoretical stance you have tended to favor since reading chapters 10 and 11. What assessment and diagnostic approaches would be included as part of this theoretical approach? How comfortable are you with the idea of using these assessment materials?

2. Arrange to take a battery of tests. Include an intelligence or aptitude test, a personality inventory, and an interest inventory. Be aware of your attitudes and emotions as you prepare for and take the tests, and then again when you receive your results.

   a. How different might your feelings be if you were to take these or other instruments under different circumstances, such as in a psychiatrist's office after suffering the loss of a parent?

   b. Review the results of your tests. How accurate do they seem? Were you able to interpret the results yourself or did you receive assistance from a counselor? In what ways was the counselor's behavior helpful? In what ways are the results helpful to you?

3. Assume that you had to be clinically evaluated because of a severe emotional disturbance. How would you react to being diagnosed as manic-depressive, or as a borderline personality? What would your reaction be once you realized that these labels would probably follow you the rest of your life and would even influence your children's lives? What alternatives might there be to using such labels?

4. What is your stand with regard to the fact that insurance companies and government agencies may dictate to you what diagnostic approaches and even perhaps what types of clinical interventions you might use in a given case? Check with other classmates and find out how many others share your views.

5. How would you strive to be sure that you would be sensitive to cultural differences while using assessment instruments and diagnostic classifications?

RECOMMENDED READINGS

American Association for Counseling and Development & Association for Measurement and Evaluation in Counseling and Development. (1989, May). Responsibilities of users of standardized tests. *Guidepost, 33,* 12, 16, 18, 27, 28.

American Psychiatric Association. (1994). *Diagnostic and statistical manual of human disorders* (4th ed.). Washington, DC: American Psychiatric Association.

INTERNET RESOURCES

Websites
Association for Assessment in Counseling
   <www. uc.edu/~wilson/aac/index.htm>
Assessment and Evaluation on the Internet
   <ericae2.educ.cua.edu/intass.htm>

Clinical Psychology Resources: Assessment and Classification   <www.psychologie.ini-bonn.de/kap/links/ii_clas.htm>
DSM-IV   <indy.radiology.uiowa.edu/Providers/ClinRef/FPHandbook/15.html>

DSM-IV (The Merck Manual Section 12: Psychiatric Disorders) <www.merck.com/ !!rsTh200SyrsThp13dm/pubs/mmanual/html/ mpnjkhdb.htm>

ERIC/CASS Assessment Digests <www.uncg.edu/ ~ericcas2/assessment/toc_assessment.htm>

Ethical and Social Issues in Testing <www. counseling.org/enews/volume_1/0107C.htm>

FAQ (Frequently Asked Questions) on Psychological Tests <www.apa.org/science/test.html>

REFERENCES

Albee, G., & Ryan-Finn, K. (1993). An overview of primary prevention. *Journal of Counseling and Development, 72*(2), 115–123.

American Association for Counseling and Development & Association for Measurement and Evaluation in Counseling and Development. (1989, May). Responsibilities of users of standardized tests. *Guidepost, 33,* 12, 16, 18, 27, 28.

American Psychiatric Association. (1980). *Diagnostic and statistical manual of human disorders* (3rd ed.). Washington, DC: American Psychiatric Association.

American Psychiatric Association. (1987). *Diagnostic and statistical manual of human disorders* (3rd ed., Rev). Washington, DC: American Psychiatric Association.

American Psychiatric Association. (1994). *Diagnostic and statistical manual of human disorders* (4th ed.). Washington, DC: American Psychiatric Association.

Bootzin, R. (1980). *Abnormal psychology* (3rd ed.). New York: Random House.

Buros, O. R. (Ed.). (1989). *The tenth mental measurement yearbook.* Lincoln, NE: University of Nebraska.

Carlson, J., Hinkle, J. S., & Sperry, L. (1993). Using diagnosis and *DSM-III-R* and *-IV* in marriage and family counseling and therapy: Increasing treatment outcomes without losing heart or soul. *The Family Journal, 1*(4), 308–312.

Cormier, W. H., & Cormier, L. S. (1985). *Interviewing strategies for helpers.* Monterey, CA: Brooks/Cole.

Draguns, J. (1989). Normal and abnormal behavior in cross-cultural perspectives. In J. Berman (Ed.), *Cross-cultural perspectives* (pp. 235–278). Lincoln, NE: University of Nebraska Press.

Elmore, R., Ekstrom, R., & Diamond, E. (1993). Counselors' test use practices: Indicators of the adequacy of measurement training. *Measurement and Evaluation in Counseling and Development, 26,* 116–124.

Engen, H. B., Lamb, R. R., & Prediger, D. J. (1982). Are secondary schools still using standardized tests? *Personnel and Guidance Journal, 60,* 287–290.

Enns, C. (1993). Twenty years of feminist counseling and therapy: From naming biases to implementing multifaceted practice. *The Counseling Psychologist, 21,* 3–87.

Fischer, C. (1985). *Individualizing psychological assessments.* Monterey, CA: Brooks/Cole.

Frances, A., First, M., & Pincus, H. A. (1995, June 1). *DSM-IV:* Its value and limitations. *Harvard Mental Health Letter, 11,* 4.

Gibson, R., & Mitchell, M. (1981). *Introduction to guidance.* New York: Macmillan.

Goldman, L. (1972). Tests and counseling: The marriage that failed. *Measurement and Evaluation in Guidance, 4,* 213–220.

Joint Committee on Testing Practices. (1988). *Code of fair testing practices in education.* Washington, DC: Author. (ERIC Document Reproduction Service No. ED 301 574)

Klerman, G., Vaillant, G., Spitzer, R., & Michaels, R. (1984). A debate on *DSM-III. American Journal of Psychiatry, 14*(2), 539–553.

Kovel, J. (1980). The American mental health industry. In D. Ingleby (Ed.), *Critical psychiatry* (pp. 72–100). New York: Pantheon Books.

Kutchins, H., & Kirk, S. (1995, May 1). *DSM-IV:* Does bigger and newer mean better? *Harvard Mental Health Letter, 11,* 4.

Loesch, L. (1984). Professional preparation guidelines: An AMECD imperative. *Measurement and Evaluation in Counseling and Development, 17*(3), 153–157.

Mischel, W. (1971). *Introduction to personality.* New York: Holt, Rinehart & Winston.

Mwaba, K., & Pedersen, P. (1990). Relative importance of intercultural, interpersonal, and psychopathological attributions in judging critical incidents by multicultural counselors. *Journal of Multicultural Counseling and Development, 18,* 107–117.

Paniagua, F. A. (1994). *Assessing and treating culturally diverse clients: A practical guide.* Thousand Oaks, CA: Sage.

Patterson, C. H., & Watkins, C. E. (1981). Some essentials of a client-centered approach to assessment. *Measurement and Evaluation in Guidance, 15*(1), 102–106.

Popham, W. J. (1978). *Criterion-reference measurement.* Englewood Cliffs, NJ: Prentice-Hall.

Reik, T. (1948). *Listening with the third ear.* New York: Farrar, Strauss.

Ridley, C. R. (1995). *Overcoming unintentional racism in counseling and therapy.* Thousand Oaks, CA: Sage.

Robertson, J., & Fitzgerald, L. F. (1990). The (mis)treatment of men: Effects of client gender role and lifestyle on diagnosis and attribution of pathology. *Journal of Counseling Psychology, 37,* 3–9.

Schmolling, R., Youkelles, M., & Burger, W. (1993). *Human services in contemporary America.* Pacific Groves, CA: Brooks/Cole.

Sinacore-Guinn, A. (1995, September 1). The diagnostic window: Culture- and gender-sensitive diagnosis and training. *Counselor Education and Supervision, 35,* 18–27.

Sugarman, A. (1978). Is psychological diagnostic assessment humanistic? *Journal of Personality Assessment, 42,* 11–21.

Szasz, T. (1973). *The myth of mental illness* (Rev. ed.). New York: Harper & Row.

Thorndike, R., & Hagen, E. P. (1977). *Measurement and evaluation in psychology and education* (4th ed.). New York: Wiley.

U.S. Department of Health, Education, and Welfare. (1972). Nondiscrimination on the basis of handicap. *Federal Register, 42,* 22676–22702.

Zytowski, D. (1982). Assessment in the counseling process for the 1980s. *Measurement and Evaluation in Guidance, 15*(1), 15–21.

chapter 20

focus on

RESEARCH AND EVALUATION IN COUNSELING

- Why can't I just counsel and let someone else worry about doing research?
- Does research show that psychotherapy works?
- Does professional training actually make therapists more effective?
- What is essential for a research study to be considered valid?

No research without action, no action without research.

Kurt Lewin in Yalom (1995, p. 487)

The hallmark of a professional counselor is that the work performed has a sound theoretical and research base. This means that decisions can be clearly supported by the research literature and, as needed, could be communicated to clients, supervisors, colleagues, insurance companies, and even in court. The research does not have to be based solely on the results of what other practitioners have done. In fact, the codes of ethics of the American Psychological Association (APA) and the American Counseling Association (ACA) state that practitioners have a responsibility to improve their profession through research. Leading figures in the field have been urging more research in counseling and psychotherapy for many years (Rogers, 1963; Vacc & Loesch, 1984; Muro, 1984; Remer, 1981; Heppner, Kiviglighan, & Wampold, 1992).

The field of counseling is quite young and is still developing its necessary scientific base. Ongoing research is needed to continue to measure the effects of counseling. Which counseling skills and theories produce desirable results? How and with what type of clients? Research helps us understand how counseling works and helps us find the best ways to improve therapeutic procedures. Research can help eliminate many of our biases, prejudices, and outdated ideas so that we can perceive what we do more clearly and objectively. Research also is needed in order to help us keep pace with modern technology and use it effectively. Knowing how to read, interpret, and conduct research can help stimulate the creative juices necessary for ongoing professional growth and to further the development of the field. These skills also provide you with the confidence to try approaches new to you in your work. You will become a scientist–practitioner (Heppner, Kiviglighan, & Wampold, 1992).

Also, in an age of accountability, it is essential that counselors evaluate the effectiveness of the approaches and resources used. This chapter provides a general overview of research and evaluation methodology. The problems of counseling research are examined, followed by proposals for both increasing the amount of research conducted and for using the results of research.

TYPES OF COUNSELING RESEARCH

Research in counseling can examine either the process of counseling, the outcomes of counseling, or both.

Process Research

Process research refers to behavior that occurs within and outside of the counseling session. It measures how change occurs during counseling as opposed to what results from counseling. It attempts to uncover how counseling works and what factors are associated with improvement or deterioration. Process research can observe counselor behaviors, client behaviors, or the interaction between the two.

An example of process research would be having trained observers use a coding system to make notations on counselor and client communication patterns. Such a system might then prove useful in suggesting specific interventions for specific therapeutic outcomes. Such a system might also be used to investigate the effects of silence with clients from different ethnic groups, or the effects of counselor self-disclosure at different stages of the counseling process.

Outcome Research

Outcome research is concerned with whether therapy works and how the various approaches compare. It assesses what has occurred as a result of counseling. Outcome research is difficult and expensive to conduct. Process research questions tend to be more amenable to research than outcome questions. The results of outcome research are confounded by problems in the selection of measures and subjects.

Outcome research originally focused largely on confirming the legitimacy of psychotherapy. In the early 1980s there was more or less a consensus that psychotherapy, as a generic treatment process, was demonstrably more effective than no treatment (Goldenberg & Goldenberg, 1991). Since then researchers have focused on comparative outcome studies looking at the relative advantages and disadvantages of alternative treatment strategies for clients with various kinds of problems. An example of outcome research is the YAVIS syndrome referred to in chapter 1, which Schofield (1964) used to describe successful clients: young, attractive, verbal, intelligent, and successful. That study concluded that counseling was most successful with clients who were most like their counselors. Other examples are studies indicating results of different approaches used in working with depression or psychosomatic disorders.

METHODS OF RESEARCH

Many research methods are available to counselors. Each method of research has its own strengths and limitations. Which method should be used is determined by the particular research question raised. As you review each of the four basic types of research methodology (descriptive, experimental, evaluative, and historical), try to formulate possible research questions for each type that you might be interested in investigating as a practitioner in the field.

Descriptive Research

Descriptive research is concerned with items that currently exist, such as techniques, relationships, attitudes, values, beliefs, and trends. There are several methods of conducting descriptive research. One method is **survey research,** which is used mostly to collect data in order to gain factual information. Surveying is done through the use of questionnaires or interviews on a representative sample of some population. Survey literature is used to learn about preferences, attitudes, and behaviors of groups of people (La Fleur, 1983); someone conducting a study on the effects of child abuse later in life might survey members of a survivors' support group. School counselors investigating the relevance of counseling services would survey the students in their particular schools. Usually this type of research gathers information that helps counselors plan and evaluate services and contributes to the understanding of the particular population being studied. There are a number of considerations to be aware of in survey research, including the size of the population sample being studied, the wording of questions, item selection and sequencing, the spacing of questions, and the percentage of questionnaires returned. A return of at least 70% is needed for data to be usable.

The case study is one of the earliest forms of counseling research. Much of Freud's writings consisted of client case studies. The **case study** examines how information collected on one unit, such as the individual, family, or group, changes over time. Case study results cannot readily be generalized to other units. They can, however, help in developing questions, hypotheses, and generalizations for further investigations using different methods (La Fleur, 1983).

Other methods of descriptive research include **content analysis,** in which the investigator systematically examines transcripts or documents in order to use the data according to some previously established criteria, and **participant–observer research,** in which the counselor is both the researcher and a participant in the counseling. The latter approach is used to evaluate ongoing counseling services and to conduct longitudinal and developmental studies.

Further examples of descriptive research include follow-up studies that track individuals after they leave counseling or counseling students after they graduate.

Experimental Research

Experimental research involves the description, comparison, and analysis of data under controlled conditions (Pietrofesa, Hoffman, & Splete, 1984). It attempts to hold some variables constant and manipulate others to predict results in controlled conditions. Experimental research uses laboratory studies, hypothesis testing, and well-controlled experimental designs. This research approach is usually used to answer questions dealing with cause and effect relations such as which treatment approaches might work better with certain types of clients. Thus, a researcher may randomly assign these clients to different types of treatments and possibly maintain a control group for whom treatment is delayed. The groups receiving the different approaches would then be compared with each other and with the control group (Gelso & Fretz, 1992). The major limitation of experimental research is the difficulty in the control of variables. A high degree of control is needed to permit the counselor to make cause and effect conclusions about the data gathered (La Fleur, 1983). For example, in order to control all variables, experiments are performed in a laboratory in which simulated counseling situations are set up. Because this type of study is done in a laboratory setting, it is often difficult to generalize anything about the way clients behave in real life (Goldman, 1976). An example of an experimental research study is an analysis of the effect of counselor-offered facilitative conditions on the depth of client self-disclosure in initial interviews (Kottler & Brown, 1985).

Historical Research

Historical research collects and examines existing information (La Fleur, 1983). Its goal is to develop future perspectives based on the examination and analysis of past information. It is often concerned with trends, causes, and effects. An example of historical research is how federal and state governments have helped mold the practice of counseling (Brown & Pate, 1983).

Evaluative Research

Evaluative research is usually done in the field. It involves delineating, obtaining, and providing useful information in order to make judgments on the merits or performances of various counseling programs or procedures. This research approach is used to help improve decisions about competing methods or treatments (Kottler & Brown, 1985), as well as to justify the use of resources (Blocher, 1987). It should be based on specific, understandable goals and objectives in order to be meaningful. It also should use valid measuring criteria once the goals are clearly defined. These criteria are then dependent on their valid application. Finally, meaningful evaluation requires feedback, follow-through, and planned continuous process (Gibson & Mitchell, 1990). Examples of evaluative research are an analysis of the effect of group counseling on the self-concept and school behavior of low-achieving adolescents (La Fleur, 1983) and evaluation of a community mental health counseling program.

Ideally, evaluative studies should be an integral part of a counselor's or agency's regular practice so that they are viewed as a natural, ongoing part of the work of a professional counselor, rather than something "that really should be done if I/we ever get around to it." Well-designed and executed evaluation studies can generally have more immediate impact on the work of the counselor than other types of research (Burck & Peterson, 1975).

Ideas in action   How do you feel personally about being a researcher as well as a practitioner? As a prospective counselor, are you willing to make a commitment to conduct research as part of your professional obligations? Which type of research would you be most interested in learning how to conduct? Why?

Alternative Research Methodologies

In recent years there has been increasing dissatisfaction with traditional approaches to counseling research. In chapter 12 the tension between first-order and second-order cybernetics was examined. First-order cybernetics contends that there can be objective observers who can conduct impartial research into a reality governed by universal laws. Second-order cybernetics, following postmodern–constructivist and general systems theory views, contends that knowledge is relative and dependent on context; there is no fixed truth or objective reality that can be discovered and observed. There are only subjective, multiple realities. Even the researcher is not seen as an outside observer who is able to discover truths. Rather, the researcher is seen as a part of the observing system and also a creator of the reality being observed; therefore, researchers cannot be separated from what they observe.

Qualitative Versus Quantitative Research

Quantitative research is seen as following the first-order cybernetic model. Observations are transformed into numbers and expressed mathematically, and results are analyzed statistically. **Qualitative research** is often defined by contrasting it to quantitative research, in that its findings are not arrived at by statistical or other quantification procedures (Hanna & Shank, 1995). Research in the qualitative mode is conducted within a phenomenological framework and takes into account the subjectivity of human experience by seeking underlying, subjective meanings. Observations are made verbally and linguistically. Qualitative research examines broad, general patterns as opposed to specific and precise behavior. Rather than seeking to control variables that may interfere with validity of research design, all variables are viewed as part of the context and included in the investigation.

Quantitative research isolates variables, imposes categories, and interferes with natural behavior. Qualitative research examines natural behavior and events in natural settings without trying to impose categories or disrupt natural behavior. Additionally, the researcher seeks to avoid personal biases by making as few assumptions as possible. In the qualitative mode, hypotheses are not tested but are formed in a discovery-oriented process. The data and interpretations are valid only under the unique conditions of a particular project at a particular time and place (Becvar & Becvar, 1996).

Both qualitative and quantitative research can advance knowledge in the field. The approach to be used will be determined largely by the research questions the investigator seeks to answer.

PROBLEMS AND ISSUES IN RESEARCH

Although a practitioner may not be able to cite a specific reference, most practitioners' graduate school training was likely based on a tremendous amount of research data, all the way from personality theory to intervention strategies. The accumulation may be slow, but the data eventually advance our working knowledge of the field (Heppner & Anderson, 1985, p. 545).

In fact, many of the numerous citations in almost every chapter of this book are derived from research. When one considers that counseling research has had an extremely brief history with the most important empirical findings only appearing since the 1960s, a great amount has been accomplished. Considering all the various issues and conflicts in the field of counseling and among counseling theories, it is not surprising that issues and conflicts must be faced in counseling research. Future professionals can view the present state of the profession with excitement and challenge. With this idea in mind, we now look at the problems and issues in conducting research in the field of counseling.

Practitioners' Antipathy toward Conducting Research.   Originally, counseling research and counseling practice were considered to be separate disciplines and were performed by different professionals. This did not prove desirable, and mental health professionals were urged to integrate the two roles, thus creating the scientist–practitioner (Howard, 1985). This concept of the scientist–practitioner has become complex and difficult to implement and leads to numerous problems.

Few counselors engage in research or use research findings in their practice (Howard, 1985; Vacc & Loesch, 1984; Muro, 1984; Gelso, 1979). In fact, many practitioners find that research has little relevance to their practice (Minor, 1981; Larson & Nichols, 1972; Goldman, 1976; Howard, 1985; Heppner & Anderson, 1985). Research is read mostly by other researchers rather than by practitioners (Goldman, 1976).

Counseling students, counselors, and counselor educators generally view their major role as that of helping people (Muro, 1984; Vacc & Loesch, 1984) and place a lower priority on research. Many counseling students are intimidated by the thought of having to take a research course. Winfrey (1984) reported that beginning master's level students resent having to use their credits on a research or statistics course rather than on a course in their specialty.

Ideas in action   What kind of priority do you believe counselors should place on research and evaluation? Are there research courses in your counseling program? If so, what are your thoughts and feelings about taking them? Are you intimidated by the idea of learning how to do research? If so, what are your concerns? What can you do about them?

The Belief That Counseling Is More of an Art Than a Science.   Some counselors believe that the effective ingredients of counseling are such factors as faith, hope, expectation, and motivation, which cannot be empirically defined or researched because of their complexity.

Those who believe that counseling is a science maintain that counseling is a predictable and logical process and can be researched. They are primarily concerned with controlled experimental research rigorously conducted in laboratories (quantitative research). The core values for these scientific researchers are that only those data that can be observed, measured, studied objectively, and replicated are considered the proper data of social science (Woolsey, 1986). As a result, researchers have dismissed persons' inner experiences as subjective, private, and not meeting core values.

Relevance Versus Rigor.   Even if the more subjective factors of counseling such as persons' inner experiences could be researched, how much rigor would they have? Gelso (1985) hypothesizes that the more rigorous the research, then the less relevance it will have to practice. Therefore, any attempts to solve problems of high relevance create problems such as low rigor. He called this the **bubble hypothesis.** Some critics, such as Howard (1985), believe that studies can be designed that are both relevant and rigorous. Heppner and Anderson (1985) and Gelso (1985), for example, call for a balance of rigor and relevance.

Difficulty Researching Counseling Theory.   Hill (1982) believes that counseling is still in too early a stage of development for researchers to be testing counseling theories. Counseling theories confound the matter by not using universally agreed-on operational definitions for variables. This results in duplication among researchers with little communication among them. Other problems in communication include the use of jargon and highly specialized language that builds a semantic wall between researchers and practitioners (Heppner & Anderson, 1985). For example, in describing the data of counseling, researchers speak with terms such as *perceived self-efficacy, cognitive expectancies and attributions, reward–cost balancing, conceptual self-systems,* and *factors in counselor–client interactions.* Practitioners refer to the same phenomena with such phrases as *the will to power, the true self, the I–Thou versus the I–it relationship, authentic versus inauthentic self, being there,* and *being present* (Woolsey, 1986, p. 90).

Drawing Conclusions.   Goldman (1976) reports that it is extremely difficult for studies to be done in such a way as to permit any firm conclusions. The few studies that do usually permit little generalization beyond the setting in which they were conducted and the samples that were studied. Heppner and Anderson (1985) find that because results from counseling research are presented in small pieces over time, many articles on a topic are necessary before there is enough information to be of use to counselors. Further, a considerable amount of time is necessary to synthesize the information.

Counselors and researchers, however, are continually pressed for certainty. Politicians and interest groups want to know causes and solutions for many problems as well as the value of present programs. Counselors need to pursue the determination of the value of counseling work and continue to strengthen the theoretical and methodological bases but also need to educate the public on the present limits of counseling research technology (Becvar & Becvar, 1988).

RESEARCH INTO COUNSELING EFFECTIVENESS

Recently, with the pressures from managed care and other economic factors, there has been much debate taking place over the effectiveness of counseling and psychotherapy, especially in Internet newsgroups, e-mail lists, and conferences. The issue is of special significance to the approximately 16 million people a year who use counseling and other mental health services in the United States. An estimated 24 million more are in need of assistance, though many of them find help outside the mental health system through their religious places of worship, friends, support groups, and self-help books. The issue of how to pay for needed counseling services is far from settled.

Counseling Does Not Help

In a thorough review of the literature on studies of counseling effectiveness done since 1979, Christensen and Jacobson concluded that the outcome of therapy is not enhanced by training, education, or years of experience (Rutter, 1994). They found that in many cases paraprofessionals did as well or better than licensed professionals. They also found that self-administered treatments worked just as well as those delivered by live therapists in certain cases. Computerized treatments have been shown to work for obesity, phobias, and depression. Additionally, they reported that psychotherapy as well as drug therapy show disappointingly low success rates for treating marital distress, agoraphobia, and children's disorders, among others.

Counseling Helps

An article in *Consumer Reports* (1995) looked at whether people have actually been helped by mental health care, specifically psychotherapy. Based on the results of a candid, in-depth survey of its readers, it was found that among the 4,000 respondents who had actually sought help for psychological problems, 9 out of 10 felt that their condition had improved significantly after psychotherapy treatment, and that the longer they stayed in therapy, the more they improved. The National Mental Health Association, a mental health lobby, reported that mental health professionals have an 80% success rate in treating depression (Rutter, 1994). Smith, Glass, and Miller (1980) found that the average client who received therapy was better off at the end of treatment than were the 80–85% of comparable clients who did not receive such treatment.

Counseling Can Help and Hurt

Back in chapter 1 the issue was raised that there is research evidence supporting that all helping relationships may be for better or for worse, and that the results depended upon the counselor's level of skills in facilitating the client's progress toward goals. Harmful effects can be accounted for largely by the levels of functioning of the helpers in various interpersonal dimensions.

Yalom (1995) urges us not to expect more from psychotherapy research than it can deliver. He believes that it is unlikely that psychotherapy research will effect any rapid major change in practice. He argues that one major reason for this is resistance by practitioners who have often spent years in training and apprenticeship learning one major approach. Those practitioners often cling stubbornly to what they have learned and will only change slowly if substantial evidence supports a change. Also, actively practicing therapists cannot afford to wait for science to validate what they do while their clients suffer. The economics of the marketplace can also have a strong impact on research. With the pressure of managed care pushing the field toward brief therapy, research into long-term therapy will not be funded even if there is a consensus that such research is important. Finally, Yalom points out that because psychotherapy is both an art and a science, most aspects of psychotherapy inherently defy quantification.

ENCOURAGING THE USE AND DEVELOPMENT OF COUNSELING RESEARCH

The solution to the problems of counseling research begins with the graduate student, who must become an active agent in making research a workable tool for the counseling profession. The first step involves the development of a spirit of inquiry. Gelso (1985) suggests that students and practitioners actively seek answers to the question, "How do these partic-ular findings relate to my practice?" whenever encountering research studies. Goldman (1976) suggests the question, "To what populations, settings, and variables can this effect be generalized?" Nejedlo (1984) advocates asking probing questions "about the process of change, the development of potential students' programmatic needs, and the resolving of problems from the context of individuals in the societal environment in addition to an indi-vidual in his or her own environment" (p. 150). Barkley (1982) proposes six research-related competencies that graduate students should have:

1. The ability to pose good research questions.
2. The ability to use clear definitions of terms.
3. An understanding of sources of confusion and ambiguity and how they may be controlled.
4. Awareness of problems associated with observation and measurement.
5. An understanding of the importance of documentation in the literature.
6. Knowledge about the process of research and the motivation to learn more about it throughout one's professional life.

As a counseling student, in addition to mastering the six competencies listed here, you should make it a part of your professional approach to the field to learn to read and under-stand the scientific counseling literature in original sources (see Table 20.1 for guidelines for reading a research article and Appendix C for a list of professional journals).

Questions should be raised in every course about the nature and quality of research and the support of facts and theoretical positions presented in textual material or in classroom presentations. When class projects are assigned, use such occasions as opportunities to develop research skills. For example, learn how to retrieve sources of information from psy-chological indexes, computer databases such as *Psychlit,* and from the Internet, becoming skilled at reading research articles, conducting a survey, doing structured interviews, or writing a case study. Consider courses in statistics and research design as excellent oppor-tunities to develop your skills as a scientist–practitioner rather than obstacles to be endured (be aware that computers have helped significantly to reduce the amount of drudgery often associated with the conduct of research). Whenever the opportunity should present itself, participate as a subject in a study or as part of a research team that a faculty member, for example, might create.

When doing research of any kind, develop it so that it might be acceptable even in abstract form for a professional newsletter or journal or for a presentation at a professional

---

TABLE 20.1   The evaluation process.

- Develop a needs assessment: What needs to be improved?
- Identify goals and performance objectives to be assessed.
- Develop an evaluation plan with valid measuring criteria.
- Apply the evaluation plan.
- Utilize the findings. Revise and improve the program.
- Follow up.

convention. Graduate student research is encouraged by a number of professional organizations, and the publication of articles is an excellent way to begin the development of your professional resume.

Finally, many master's level students often decide to pursue doctoral degrees, and a determining factor for entrance into many advanced degree programs is the quality of the student's statistical research background. Most universities will not accept doctoral candidates in counseling or clinical psychology programs who don't have statistics and research courses as well as a master's thesis or equivalent. As should be obvious from your readings in this book, you are encouraged to develop all of your skills and abilities related to your chosen profession. There is simply no way of predicting what opportunities might develop for you.

NEW PARADIGMS IN COUNSELING RESEARCH

In 1976 Leo Goldman wrote an article calling for a revolution in counseling research. Numerous others have echoed his sentiments (Elmore, 1984; Gelso, 1985; Howard, 1985; Keeney & Morris, 1985; Vacc & Loesch, 1984; Woolsey, 1986). They have initiated a movement in counseling that attempts to create alternatives to traditional research methods in order to make counseling research more relevant.

Elmore (1984) advocates an entirely new formulation for counseling research that is not based on research paradigms of physical science, but on a wholistic model incorporating physical, mental, and spiritual development of persons to meet the demands of advanced technology and cultural diversity. A new paradigm in counseling has emerged, derived from quantum physics, and based upon a general systems view of life. The principles of this new paradigm are complementary to qualitative research methods. They emphasize relationships rather than isolated parts, inherent dynamics of relationships, process thinking, wholistic thinking, subjectivity, and autonomy. Rather than using the metaphor of a machine composed of separate entities into which it may be reduced and studied, this new paradigm views the universe as an indivisible whole composed of dynamic relationships including those of observers who cannot be separated from what they observe. Becvar and Becvar (1988) state that

> observer and observed influence each other, and the activity of scientific study changes what is being studied. This position seems to reflect the essence of Einstein's statement that the theory decides what we can observe. In other words, what we can see and what is "out there" is decided by the paradigm we have in our heads. . . . we are looking in a mirror and what we see is our own reflection looking at us looking in a mirror. (p. 296)

An example of this phenomenon is reported by Ivey, Ivey, and Simek-Morgan (1993). They cite a series of studies reporting that the way a client (Gloria) interacted with three famous therapists (Carl Rogers, Fritz Perls, and Albert Ellis) in the film series *Three Approaches to Psychotherapy* was a function of the therapist she was with, although she was the same person in each interview. It is possible that prior knowledge of each theory, or what was in Gloria's head, influenced how she behaved. There also seemed to be a process in which Gloria and her therapist influenced each other and reinforced each other's behaviors.

Inherent in this movement to evolve a new paradigm is the need to view research from a much broader perspective than the paradigms of physical science. Goldman (1976) states that "this obsession with the values and standards of the physical sciences has led us away from more meaningful, though admittedly cruder, studies of human beings and of counseling processes" (p. 545). Goldman promotes the following changes:

1. *Use macroscopic rather than microscopic research.* Microscopic research focuses on very narrow topics. It examines individuals under a microscope (and in effect supports the status quo). Macroscopic research examines the whole functioning human being, dealing with broader areas of human functioning; in other words, the researcher is working with a whole client who comes from a family, community, and economic and cultural background. The boundaries of the research problem should be expanded to encompass the whole life of the client as much as possible and the framework of belief expanded to encompass more pieces of the systemic whole.
2. *Conduct field rather than laboratory research.* Field-based research examines people's lives where and as they live them. It is research done in real situations such as the counseling office, people's homes, or in the workplace.
3. *Study individual cases rather than average changes in groups of persons.* Combining data from groups of people usually reveals how several factors play a part in certain situations but does not help to understand the individual. For example, Goldman (1976) notes that correlations between personality measures and underachievement might reveal that social activity, excessive anxiety, or low achievement motivation play a part. However, if one were working with an individual client, the data would not deal with the complexity and interaction among these factors within the client.
4. *Maintain an open arrangement with persons whose behavior is being studied.* This prevents subjects from being treated as objects and encourages an openness in the researcher–subject relationship similar to the desired openness in counselor–client relationships.
5. *Conduct more applied evaluation of programs in field settings.*

Keeney and Morris (1985) suggest doing research from a cybernetic review of science advocated by Gregory Bateson in his rules of thumb for conducting research. These rules of thumb include thinking esthetically (visualizing, analogizing, comparing, and looking for patterns and configurations); living with your data (being a detective, mulling, contemplating, inspecting, and thinking about, through, and beyond); being as precise as possible without closing off possibilities; looking to growing systems and configurations for your explanations; and aiming for catalytic conceptualizations (e.g., warm ideas are contagious).

Ideas in action   Using Goldman's suggestions and Bateson's rules of thumb, choose an individual with whom you can spend some time to study as a participant–observer. Find out everything you can about this person. Include the larger systems, such as the individual's family, work, and community. Inform this individual about what you will be doing. Do not interview this individual by asking questions, but draw your inferences from observations and responsive listening. At the conclusion of your study, check out your results with this individual. What did you discover?

Keeney and Morris also suggest using research designs other than sociological, statistical experimental designs including cybernetics, etiology, anthropology, and sociolinguistics. Winfrey (1984) suggests using research techniques from business and industry. For example, business uses marketing techniques in studying consumers, which would be applicable to counselors studying their clients.

Students, as they progress through their course of study, should familiarize themselves with these alternative approaches. These approaches make research in counseling more relevant and at the same time offer great possibilities for advancing the profession. Ideally, students should do various types of research as an integral part of their education and in the process recognize that conducting research is a stimulating and challenging endeavor. Perhaps, one day, if not now, you might be able to agree with Heppner, Kiviglighan, and Wampold (1992) when they say, "Research can be fun" (p. 2).

SUMMARY

The importance of research and evaluation in terms of strengthening and furthering the counseling profession has been stressed in this chapter. The two basic types of counseling research, process and outcome, have been described along with four major methods of conducting research: descriptive, experimental, evaluative, and historical.

The issues in research have been explained, and from the perspective of a new paradigm, a number of alternatives have been offered to encourage more research in counseling and to make the results more relevant. In the final analysis, any student in the field must make a commitment to becoming fully involved in the vital research component of the profession and strive to become a scientist–practitioner.

QUESTIONS AND ACTIVITIES

1. Read a research article on some aspect of counseling that is of interest to you. How relevant is the article to the actual practice of counseling? In what way is it relevant? What would have made it more relevant for you? Discuss your findings in class.

2. Are you approaching counseling as an art or a science? What is the implication of your answer for counseling research? Would your bias, whatever it is, affect your approach as you read about as well as conduct research?

3. Would you consider a counselor who did not become involved in conducting research to be a complete professional? Can counselors be considered ethical if they employ certain techniques without having them empirically validated? What are some ways that counselors can remain informed on the latest research in the field?

4. How do you feel about becoming a scientist–practitioner? What would it take for this stance to be workable for you?

5. Survey your classmates regarding some item of interest to you and share the results with the class and instructor.

6. Look back at your own life. How would information collected about you have changed over time? What questions, hypotheses, and generalizations for further investigation can you draw?

7. Alternatives to the traditional scientific research paradigms are often viewed as less than scientific. The traditional model is widely accepted and has much credibility in U.S. society. Would it be more expedient to use the traditional model to serve the political purpose of advancing the field of counseling or

to risk using the new paradigm, which might eventually become the predominant view?

8. Choose a topic in the field that is of interest to you, such as counselor self-disclosure or countertransference. See how many recent journal articles you can find on your topic by searching *ERIC/CAPS* (resources in education), *Psychological Abstracts, Current Index to Journals in Education,* or *Social Sciences Index* in your library. Obtain two or three of the journal articles that sound most interesting and read them.

9. From those articles that you have read in various professional journals, select the two that you believe to be the most valuable. Make a separate report for each of the two articles using the following guidelines (see Table 20.1):

On a 4 × 6 card, with your name and date in the upper left-hand corner, include the following:

a. Author(s), date, title, journal, volume number, issue, pages.

b. What was the main message that this article held for you?

c. How much confidence do you have in the conclusions in light of the manner in which the information was collected and reported?

d. What cautions must you be aware of in applying the conclusions to future real-life situations?

e. How relevant is the article to the actual practice of counseling? In what way is it relevant? What would have made it more relevant for you?

RECOMMENDED READINGS

Goldman, L. (1976). A revolution in counseling research. *Journal of Counseling Psychology, 23,* 543–552.

Howard, G. S. (1985). Can research in the human sciences become more relevant to practice? *Journal of Counseling and Development, 63,* 539–554.

INTERNET RESOURCES

Websites—Researching on WWW

The Internet contains its own researching tool kits called search engines. If you enter a word or phrase in the search "query," it will return all the websites that contain that word or phrase. This can be a frustrating effort if you have chosen a very common word, such as "counseling" or "psychology," that appears on several hundred thousand websites. Each search engine has information on how to narrow your search to a specific subject. Some of the popular search engines are the following:

Lycos   <www.lycos.com>
Excite   <www.excite.com>
Open Text Index   <www.opentext.com/omw/
   f-omw.html>
Alta Vista   <altavista.digital.com>
Infoseek   <www.infoseek.com/>
HotBot   <www.HotBot.com>

These search services find every page on the Web that contains your search request (often thousands of pages).

Usually you still have to spend time narrowing your search to fit your needs.

Yahoo   <www.yahoo.com>

This organizes the Web into a format that is based on subject categories rather than individual words. It is similar to the card catalog headings in a library and is the easiest way to find websites on very general topics, such as education, mental health, travel, and sports.

Inference   <m5.inference.com/ifind/>

This is a parallel search engine that will eliminate duplicate listings of URL sites for your particular topic.

Websites—Research Directories

Argus/University of Michigan
   Clearinghouse   <www.clearinghouse.net>
The Awesome Lists   <www.cais.com/makulow/
   awesome.html>
World Wide Web Virtual Library   <www3.org/pub/
   DataSources/bySubject/Overview.html>

Thor: The Virtual Reference Desk   <thorplus.lib. purdue.edu/reference>

Websites—Standard Research Sites
National Institute of Mental Health   <gopher:// gopher.nimh.nih.gov>
ERIC (Educational Resources Information Center)   <ericir.syr.edu>
ERIC/CASS (Counseling and Student Services)   <www.uncg.edu/~ericcas2/>

Websites—Commercial Databases
Most offer free bibliographic searches but charge for sending you the actual article.

CARL/UnCover   <www.carl.org/carlweb>

This is a comprehensive database of more than 17,000 journals offering one hour delivery on many journal articles, via fax or e-mail.

NlightN   <www.nlightn.com>

This on-line service is provided by the Library Corporation. Its database includes the American Psychological Association's PsycINFO® and the subset PsycLIT®.

The Electric Library   <www.elibrary/com>

The database includes journal articles from the American Counseling Association's *Journal of Counseling*

and Development and from journals published by ACA divisions.

Websites—National Clearinghouses and Government Resources
ERIC: Celebrating 30 Years   <www.aspensys.com/ eric/>
U.S. Department of Health and Human Services   <www.os.dhhs/gov>
National Clearinghouse for Alcohol & Drug Information
National AIDS Clearinghouse
National Institute of Mental Health   <gopher:// gopher.nimh.nih.gov/>
National Institute on Drug Abuse
National Institute on Alcohol Abuse and Alcoholism   <www.niaaa.nih.gov/">
ERIC/AE (ERIC Clearing House on Assessment and Evaluation)   <www.cua.edu/www/eric_ae/>
National Mental Health Services Knowledge Exchange Network
(ERIC/CASS) Educational Resource Information Center/Counseling and Student Services   <www.uncg.edu/~ericcas2/>

REFERENCES

Barkley, W. M. (1982). Introducing research to graduate students in the helping professions. *Counselor Education and Supervision, 21*(4), 327–331.

Becvar, D. S., & Becvar, R. J. (1988). *Family therapy: A systematic integration.* Boston: Allyn & Bacon.

Blocher, D. (1987). *The professional counselor.* New York: Macmillan.

Brown, J., & Pate, R. (1983). *Being a counselor: Directions and challenges.* Monterey, CA: Brooks/Cole.

Burck, H., & Peterson, G. (1975). Needed: More evaluation, not research. *Personnel and Guidance Journal, 53,* 563–569.

Elmore, T. M. (1984). Counseling as research: On experiencing quality. *Measurement and Evaluation in Counseling and Development, 17,* 142–148.

Gelso, C. J. (1979). Research in counseling: Methodologic and professional issues. *The Counseling Psychologist, 8*(3), 7–35.

Gelso, C. J. (1985). Rigor, relevance, and counseling research. On the need to maintain our course between Scylla and Charybdis. *Journal of Counseling and Development, 63*(9), 551–553.

Gelso, C. J., & Fretz, B. R. (1992). *Counseling psychology.* Fort Worth, TX: Harcourt Brace Jovanovich.

Gibson, R. L., & Mitchell, M. H. (1990). *Introduction to counseling and guidance* (3rd ed.). New York: Macmillan Publishing Company.

Goldenberg, I., & Goldenberg, H. (1991). *Family therapy: An overview* (3rd ed.). Pacific Grove, CA. Brooks/Cole.

Goldman, L. (1976). A revolution in counseling research. *Journal of Counseling Psychology, 23,* 543–552.

Hanna, F. J., & Shank, G. (1995). The specter of metaphysics in counseling research and practice: The qualitative challenge. *Journal of Counseling and Development, 74*(9), 53–56.

Heppner, P. P., & Anderson, W. P. (1985). On the perceived nonutility of research in counseling. *Journal of Counseling and Development, 63,* 545–547.

Heppner, P. P., Kiviglighan, D., & Wampold, B. (1992). *Research design in counseling.* Pacific Grove, CA: Brooks/Cole.

Hill, C. (1982). Counseling process research: Philosophical and methodological dilemmas. *The Counseling Psychologist, 10*(4), 7–20.

Howard, G. S. (1985). Can research in the human sciences become more relevant to practice? *Journal of Counseling and Development, 63,* 539–544.

Ivey, A. E., Ivey, M. B., & Simek-Morgan, L. (1993). *Counseling and psychotherapy: A multicultural perspective* (3rd ed.). Boston: Allyn & Bacon.

Keeney, B. P., & Morris, J. (1985). Implications of cybernetic epistemology for clinical research: A reply to Howard. *Journal of Counseling and Development, 63*(9), 548–552.

Kottler, J. A., & Brown, R. W. (1985). *Introduction to therapeutic counseling.* Monterey, CA: Brooks/Cole.

La Fleur, K. N. (1983). Research and evaluation. In J. A. Brown & R. H. Pate (Eds.), *Being a counselor* (pp. 147–172). Monterey, CA: Brooks/Cole.

Larson, J., & Nichols, D. (1972). If nobody knows you've done it, have you? *Evaluation, 1,* 39–44.

Mental health: Does therapy help? (1995). *Consumer Reports, 60,* 734–739.

Minor, B. J. (1981). Bridging the gap between research and practice. *Personnel and Guidance Journal, 59*(8), 485–486.

Muro, J. J. (1984). Counselor education—Quo Vadis? *Measurement and Evaluation in Counseling and Development, 17,* 137–138.

Nejedlo, R. (1984). The counselors of tomorrow and research. *Measurement and Evaluation in Counseling and Development, 17,* 149–152.

Pietrofesa, J., Hoffman, A., & Splete, H. (1984). *Counseling: An introduction* (2nd ed.). Boston: Houghton Mifflin.

Remer, R. (1981). The counselor and research, Part I. *Personnel and Guidance Journal, 59*(9), 621–627.

Rogers, C. (1963). Psychotherapy today or where do we go from here? *American Journal of Psychotherapy, 17*(1), 5–16.

Rutter, V. (1994). Oops! A very embarrassing story. *Psychology Today, 27,* 12.

Schofield, W. (1964). *Psychotherapy: The purchase of friendship.* Englewood Cliffs, NJ: Prentice-Hall.

Smith, M. L., Glass, G. V., & Miller, T. I. (1980). *The benefits of psychotherapy.* Baltimore: Johns Hopkins University Press.

Vacc, N. A., & Loesch, L. C. (1984). Research as an instrument of professional change. *Measurement and Evaluation in Counseling and Development, 17,* 124–131.

Winfrey, J. K. (1984). Research as an area of renewal for counselor educators and supervisors. *Measurement and Evaluation in Counseling and Development, 17,* 139–141.

Woolsey, L. K. (1986). Research and practice in counseling: A conflict in values. *Counselor Education and Supervision, 12,* 84–94.

Yalom, I. D. (1995). *The theory and practice of group psychotherapy* (4th ed,). New York: Basic Books.

Epilogue

HOW DOES ALL OF THIS MATERIAL FIT TOGETHER?

We live in a time of rapid change in our society and throughout the world. Counselors face many new and exciting challenges as a result of these changes. They need to be prepared to work in a wholistic way with their increasingly diverse clientele.

Who the counselor is, what the counselor can do, and what the counselor knows provide the foundation for becoming creative counselors prepared for working cooperatively and energetically to meet these challenges in the twenty-first century. These creative counselors will be increasingly involved in the preventive and developmental aspects of counseling, and with groups, institutions, and communities in a consulting mode. They will develop a greater interest in the spiritual and transcendental aspects of life and will be more actively involved in causing societal change.

This chapter briefly reviews our journey through the field of counseling, indicating how the various topics relate to the process of becoming a professional counselor. Because the field of counseling is in a process of constant growth, we also note the stance the professional counselor needs to take for the future.

This text approaches counseling from a wholistic, systems conceptualization. Such a conceptualization views the field of counseling as interconnected with a broad spectrum of related content areas. Each component is a whole in itself as well as being part of the greater totality that includes those who are effective counselors. Likewise, each chapter of this text is a whole in itself as well as being part of a section and of the total book. This approach views effective counselors as more than just being knowledgeable, skillful, or nice individuals who want to help. These effective counselors have to be creative and open to looking at new ways of conceptualizing problems and working to bring about change.

In essence, the field of counseling has been presented here in terms of the primary agent, the counselor: the counselor's knowledge, skills, and being.

WHO THE COUNSELOR IS

The self of the counselor is an integral part of the counselor–client–environment system. Any counseling, whether individual, group, or family, involves an interpersonal interaction between at least two people. The counselor greatly affects the counseling. As Satir (1987) points out, this involvement of the counselor's self occurs regardless of, and in addition to, the treatment philosophy or the approach.

Chapter 1 emphasizes that there is a definite correlation between the functioning level of counselors and effective counseling. The functioning level includes counselors' mental and physical well-being, belief systems, and specific qualities such as empathy, respect, congruence, and acceptance of self and others.

Counselors may not be able to help anyone get beyond the point that they themselves have attained. Therefore, counselors have a responsibility to monitor and evaluate their own self-actualization efforts in order to help others in their quest for self-actualization. As a major part of this process, counselors need to learn how to deal with stress and prevent burnout so that they cannot only be present and effective models for their clients but also lead fully functioning lives. Chapter 2 presents the acronym BE NATURAL (breathing, exercise, nourishment, attitude, time management, uniqueness, relaxation, association, and laughter) to serve as a strategy to ensure the development and retention of approaches for dealing with prevention and burnout.

Counselors also need to be aware of their professional attitude and their responsibilities to their clients and to society. Counselors must be aware of their power and not use it in ways that will harm their clients or that will develop dependency relationships. Satir (1987) states that it is the therapist's responsibility to create a context in which people feel and are safe, and this requires sensitivity to one's own state.

WHAT THE COUNSELOR CAN DO

Chapters 7–8 especially focus on counseling skills. It is not enough to have fine personal qualities or to be knowledgeable. Counselors also must be able to apply these components in an ethical manner in their work with clients.

The most effective counselors are those who have the widest repertory of responses and can use them in a socially intelligent manner. Such a repertory enables them to respond spontaneously to the wide variety of client needs. Counseling is for the client; it is not a virtuoso performance by the helper. (Egan, 1986, p. 57)

It is through practice and experience that these skills are learned. Initially, counselor trainees often feel self-conscious and awkward. As the skills are internalized, counselor trainees feel more spontaneous and natural. They are able to put the skills together smoothly and work effectively with their clients.

WHAT THE COUNSELOR KNOWS

Chapters 9–20 provide a broad overview of knowledge in the field of counseling, including foundation and specialty areas, human growth and development, multicultural and assessment issues, and research and evaluation considerations. Our objective has been to provide an extensive coverage of major content areas related to the field of counseling.

The content areas are those covered in most master's level programs, as well as on the examination used for certifying counselors. We hope that the knowledge and experience gained as a result of your involvement with the materials presented here will enable you to make an informed decision about whether to continue your education in the field of counseling. If you do decide to continue, this book will provide a basic resource for future studies.

In today's information age, we never seem to have enough knowledge. No matter how large the book or how extensive the degree program, there will always be something additional that could have been included. What we include in this volume can be considered the basics that, if internalized, will provide you with a broad framework of knowledge for further learning and a repertoire of responses applicable to a wide variety of circumstances. We stress the importance of this approach because virtually every contact with a client brings with it the possibility of a counselor's being confronted with content for which there was no specific course.

The elements of this foundation include having the knowledge of the characteristics necessary for establishing an effective therapeutic relationship; the knowledge and ability to provide a broad variety of appropriate responses; the knowledge and ability to grasp the personal meanings of another person, including meanings that are cultural in nature; the knowledge of social and political issues; the knowledge of ethical practices and the principles on which ethical decisions are made; knowledge of the full range of human development necessary to deal with issues of a developmental nature; awareness of a broad variety of theoretical approaches, with an emphasis on the wholistic, systems approach; and an awareness of the importance of preventive counseling.

Counselors, now and in the future, will face issues and problems for which they were not specifically trained. They need to know their own ethical limitations; how to find resources, including referral sources; and how to attain specialized training if desired. It is important for counselors to know that the general principles and practices espoused in this volume are applicable when the counselors initially confront such issues as AIDS, gay/lesbian concerns, adult children of alcoholics, sexual dysfunction, child abuse, and other current or future issues. Counselors also need to know that much additional education and experience are necessary for them to be deemed competent in working in-depth in any of these areas. As the range and scope of issues that counselors deal with continue to expand, counselors must be continually open to change and willing to examine their values and beliefs. The obvious conclusion emerges: learning about this field is a lifelong pursuit. As Hershenson and Power (1987) state,

> When a physician graduates from medical school, that physician is not immediately qualified as a neurosurgeon. Further specialized learning and experience are required. Similarly, no counselor fresh out of a graduate program is an expert, advocate, consultant, or counselor. (p. 380)

Counseling is a young, vital, and dynamic field filled with countless stimulating challenges for working with the human condition in a variety of ways at a number of different levels. We hope that, no matter what way you choose to use the facts and ideas presented here, you have been enriched by this orientation to the field of counseling.

REFERENCES

Egan, G. (1986). *The skilled helper* (3rd ed.). Pacific Grove, CA: Brooks/Cole.

Hershenson, D., & Power, J. (1987). *Mental health counseling.* New York: Pergamon.

Satir, V. (1987). The therapist story. In M. Baldwin & V. Satir (Eds.), *The use of self in therapy* (pp. 17–25). New York: Haworth.

appendix A

AN EXAMPLE OF A COUNSELOR FUNCTIONING IN A COUNSELING RELATIONSHIP

The following excerpts are from an actual counseling session. The counselor, Elaine Cole, demonstrates how all three dimensions—who the counselor is, what the counselor can do, and what the counselor knows—come into play when working with a client. Cole is working with Edward, a 58-year-old man in cardiac rehabilitation as a result of a major coronary suffered two years prior to beginning counseling. At first Edward is depressed and out of touch with many of his feelings regarding his heart attack. The following dialogue is from the fourth session (Boy & Pine, 1982, pp. 150–161).

CLIENT: Down deep I think—there's a little jealousy in me about the human race. That is—I've got to come down and face facts and look at it that way. I've had a heart attack. I look at the other person. If I'm trying to walk and carry something—that's really difficult. If you ask me to pick up this chair and carry it across the hall—that's a strain. I know it and I see people with packages in their hands and they walk and walk. I'm a little envious of that. I used to do it. I've lost all this. To me it's natural to feel the way I do. I had this strength and now it's gone.

COUNSELOR: Uh-huh.

What the counselor can do: verbal following/attending

CLIENT: Well—my down days--I do get them. It's so odd because I question myself--how come you're down? I try to blame it on other things like the weather.

COUNSELOR: Sounds to me like you realize you feel a lot of anger, disappointment, and jealousy about the fact that *this had to happen to you.*

What the counselor can do: reflection of feeling—empathizing

CLIENT: Well, this is what I think "down days" are really about.

COUNSELOR: Why me?

CLIENT: Yeah, why me, Lord? But I also look around and know a lot of people who haven't made it. So there's a bright side and a low side and sometimes I'm thankful.

COUNSELOR: So, I can look at my heart attack and say—there are people who aren't as well off as I am, but still, there is always that feeling there are a lot of people better off physically than I am—they can carry bags and lift chairs and damn, I wish I were one of them again.

What the counselor knows: the importance of staying with the client's negative feelings. People often think that negative feelings like anger, disappointment, and jealousy get worse if we direct the client's attention to it, without any hope or reassurance. The opposite seems to be the case. Staying with a negative feeling allows the client to access it and then move from it, as Edward begins doing in the subsequent responses.

What the counselor can do: reflection of content—meaning

CLIENT: Yes—Yes! If people only knew how valuable life is—how valuable that "ticker" is, they wouldn't waste life!

COUNSELOR: It makes you so angry when you see people not appreciating life.

What the counselor can do: reflection of feeling—empathizing

CLIENT: Yes—if they could only learn to appreciate, I never appreciated life as I do now...I want to live life fully. I don't just want to be forgotten. When you asked me, "Are you afraid to die?" possibly this is my answer: I am afraid to die before I leave my mark. I'm afraid to live—but, yes, I'm also afraid to die. So what is there to be contented with?

COUNSELOR: It's good to hear you say that you are afraid to die. When we started our sessions four or five weeks ago you repeated quite often, "I'm not afraid to die, Elaine. I've almost been there and it's not scary. It's just that I don't want to leave what's here."

What the counselor can do: self-disclosing, summarizing how client has changed

CLIENT: I ask myself, have I given enough to this life? I've got too much to share. I want to share it with people.

COUNSELOR: I deeply want to leave something of myself to people.

What the counselor can do: reflection of content

CLIENT: If I keep everything to myself—this is not love and I love people. If you love people you want to give them something. I've got knowledge.

COUNSELOR: And I want to share it. That means a lot to me—*that* will make my life worthwhile—give it meaning. I can't work at my old job anymore, but if I can share part of *me* with other human beings—that will make the rest of my days really meaningful.

What the counselor can do: personalizing the meaning of the client's remark, reflecting client's goal. This interchange is a good example of how the client moves from considering the situation he is in to deeper considerations.

CLIENT: This may be the goal I'm after. Of course you may think I'm an oddball.

COUNSELOR: I think you are just a beautiful person, Edward, and I get such wisdom from you. You're right—you have a great deal to give people.

What the counselor knows: Understanding the client's frame of reference brings about this change in focus toward more outwardly directed goals.

Self-disclosure—feedback

[As the session continues, Edward shares the insight that he felt weak and rejected after being turned down for military service because of shortness of breath. He realizes that he has spent his whole life trying to get over this rejection.]

CLIENT: I'm tying all this together now, and when you say, "Ed, are you afraid to die?" I'm tying all this in— and possibly I have a reason to say that. From then on [time of rejection from army] I *realize* now that I over- worked my body.

COUNSELOR: I was so angry about being rejected I overworked my body to show people, "See, I'm not weak."

Reflection of feeling and content

CLIENT: Yes, yes.

COUNSELOR: I'm just as good a man as anyone else.

Further reflection of content

CLIENT: I think now this is exactly what I was doing.

COUNSELOR: I was trying to prove to myself and the whole world that I was strong.

Further reflection of content— serves to reinforce and clarify original client statement

CLIENT: Umm—that gave me the spirit of fighting back.

COUNSELOR: I was angry.

What the counselor can do: reflection of feeling implied in client's statement

CLIENT: Rage! More than anger!

COUNSELOR: Real rage!

What the counselor can do: more accurate reflection of feeling: What the counselor knows: The importance of staying with a nega- tive feeling

CLIENT: Right....

[Later in the session]

CLIENT: I feel pretty good about coming here.

COUNSELOR: I'm glad you do because I certainly gained a lot from our times together.

Who the counselor is: authentic and open; what the counselor can do: use of appropriate self-disclosure

CLIENT: I'm glad, because I don't believe that when I'm over here and you're in that chair that I have to put you up on a pedestal.

COUNSELOR: I hope you don't!

Who the counselor is: authentic and open

CLIENT: This is what I'm learning—I've got something to give, too.

COUNSELOR: I don't feel inferior to people anymore because I'm valuable in my own way.

What the counselor can do: reflection of meaning

CLIENT: Yes, I'm valuable and it's good to feel that way.

COUNSELOR: Good for you! Sounds like it's going well. Looks like our time is up for today—but you're working through a lot, Edward, and I want to encourage that, because you are getting in touch with your feelings and sharing them, and that's a good thing. It's great! You're putting a lot of pieces of the puzzle together.

Who the counselor is: caring, encouraging; What the counselor can do: summarizing progress

CLIENT: Yes—I really think that.

COUNSELOR: See you next time. I look forward to our getting together again.

Self-disclosing

Note how Cole integrates her skills, personal characteristics, and knowledge so expertly and fluently. She allows Edward to deal with material that is most meaningful to him and demonstrates a positive regard for his ability to change and grow. Although Cole's responses seem on the surface to be effortless and simple, in practice such counselor responses are difficult because they require a very strong belief in clients' capacities to work things out for themselves.

As counseling continues, Edward gets more and more in touch with his feelings that he has formerly repressed. He terminates counseling after the eighth session with a new zest for life and newly recognized goals and aspirations. "Counseling provided Edward with the courage to reach forward and emerge as a freer, more spontaneous, more authentic person who could deal with himself, others, and the various dimensions of his coronary" (Boy & Pine, p. 150).

From *Client-centered counseling: A renewal,* by A. V. Boy and G. J. Pine, 1982, Boston: Allyn and Bacon. Copyright © 1982 by Angelo V. Boy. Reprinted with permission.

appendix B

CODE OF ETHICS AND STANDARDS OF PRACTICE OF THE AMERICAN COUNSELING ASSOCIATION

(4th Revision)

CODE OF ETHICS*

Preamble

The American Counseling Association is an educational, scientific, and professional organization whose members are dedicated to the enhancement of human development throughout the life span. Association members recognize diversity in our society and embrace a cross-cultural approach in support of the worth, dignity, potential, and uniqueness of each individual.

The specification of a code of ethics enables the association to clarify to current and future members, and to those served by members, the nature of the ethical responsibilities held in common by its members. As the code of ethics of the association, this document establishes principles that define the ethical behavior of association members. All members of the American Counseling Association are required to adhere to the Code of Ethics and the

Standards of Practice. The Code of Ethics will serve as the basis for processing ethical complaints initiated against members of the association.

Section A: The Counseling Relationship

A.1. Client Welfare

a. Primary Responsibility. The primary responsibility of counselors is to respect the dignity and to promote the welfare of clients.

b. Positive Growth and Development. Counselors encourage client growth and development in ways that foster the clients' interest and welfare; counselors avoid fostering dependent counseling relationships.

c. Counseling Plans. Counselors and their clients work jointly in devising integrated, individual

*From *Ethical Standards of the American Counseling Association* (4th ed.), by the American Counseling Association, 1995. Available: www.counseling.org/ethics.htm. Reprinted with permission. No further reproduction authorized without written permission of the American Counseling Association.

counseling plans that offer reasonable promise of success and are consistent with abilities and circumstances of clients. Counselors and clients regularly review counseling plans to ensure their continued viability and effectiveness, respecting clients' freedom of choice. (See A.3.b.)

d. Family Involvement. Counselors recognize that families are usually important in clients' lives and strive to enlist family understanding and involvement as a positive resource, when appropriate.

e. Career and Employment Needs. Counselors work with their clients in considering employment in jobs and circumstances that are consistent with the clients' overall abilities, vocational limitations, physical restrictions, general temperament, interest and aptitude patterns, social skills, education, general qualifications, and other relevant characteristics and needs. Counselors neither place nor participate in placing clients in positions that will result in damaging the interest and the welfare of clients, employers, or the public.

A.2. Respecting Diversity

a. Nondiscrimination. Counselors do not condone or engage in discrimination based on age, color, culture, disability, ethnic group, gender, race, religion, sexual orientation, marital status, or socioeconomic status. (See C.5.a., C.5.b., and D.1.i.)

b. Respecting Differences. Counselors will actively attempt to understand the diverse cultural backgrounds of the clients with whom they work. This includes, but is not limited to, learning how the counselor's own cultural/ethnic/racial identity impacts her or his values and beliefs about the counseling process. (See E.8. and F.2.i.)

A.3. Client Rights

a. Disclosure to Clients. When counseling is initiated, and throughout the counseling process as necessary, counselors inform clients of the purposes, goals, techniques, procedures, limi-

tations, potential risks, and benefits of services to be performed, and other pertinent information. Counselors take steps to ensure that clients understand the implications of diagnosis, the intended use of tests and reports, fees, and billing arrangements. Clients have the right to expect confidentiality and to be provided with an explanation of its limitations, including supervision and/or treatment team professionals; to obtain clear information about their case records; to participate in the ongoing counseling plans; and to refuse any recommended services and be advised of the consequences of such refusal. (See E.5.a. and G.2.)

b. Freedom of Choice. Counselors offer clients the freedom to choose whether to enter into a counseling relationship and to determine which professional(s) will provide counseling. Restrictions that limit choices of clients are fully explained. (See A.1.c.)

c. Inability to Give Consent. When counseling minors or persons unable to give voluntary informed consent, counselors act in these clients' best interests. (See B.3.)

A.4. Clients Served by Others

If a client is receiving services from another mental health professional, counselors, with client consent, inform the professional persons already involved and develop clear agreements to avoid confusion and conflict for the client. (See C.6.c.)

A.5. Personal Needs and Values

a. Personal Needs. In the counseling relationship, counselors are aware of the intimacy and responsibilities inherent in the counseling relationship, maintain respect for clients, and avoid actions that seek to meet their personal needs at the expense of clients.

b. Personal Values. Counselors are aware of their own values, attitudes, beliefs, and behaviors and how these apply in a diverse society, and avoid imposing their values on clients. (See C.5.a.)

A.6. Dual Relationships

a. Avoid When Possible. Counselors are aware of their influential positions with respect to clients, and they avoid exploiting the trust and dependency of clients. Counselors make every effort to avoid dual relationships with clients that could impair professional judgment or increase the risk of harm to clients. (Examples of such relationships include, but are not limited to, familial, social, financial, business, or close personal relationships with clients.) When a dual relationship cannot be avoided, counselors take appropriate professional precautions such as informed consent, consultation, supervision, and documentation to ensure that judgment is not impaired and no exploitation occurs. (See F.1.b.)

b. Superior/Subordinate Relationships. Counselors do not accept as clients superiors or subordinates with whom they have administrative, supervisory, or evaluative relationships.

A.7. Sexual Intimacies With Clients

a. Current Clients. Counselors do not have any type of sexual intimacies with clients and do not counsel persons with whom they have had a sexual relationship.

b. Former Clients. Counselors do not engage in sexual intimacies with former clients within a minimum of two years after terminating the counseling relationship. Counselors who engage in such relationships after two years following termination have the responsibility to examine and document thoroughly that such relations did not have an exploitative nature, based on factors such as duration of counseling, amount of time since counseling, termination circumstances, client's personal history and mental status, adverse impact on the client, and actions by the counselor suggesting a plan to initiate a sexual relationship with the client after termination.

A.8. Multiple Clients

When counselors agree to provide counseling services to two or more persons who have a relationship (such as husband and wife, or parents and children), counselors clarify at the outset which person or persons are clients and the nature of the relationships they will have with each involved person. If it becomes apparent that counselors may be called upon to perform potentially conflicting roles, they clarify, adjust, or withdraw from roles appropriately. (See B.2. and B.4.d.)

A.9. Group Work

a. Screening. Counselors screen prospective group counseling/therapy participants. To the extent possible, counselors select members whose needs and goals are compatible with goals of the group, who will not impede the group process, and whose well-being will not be jeopardized by the group experience.

b. Protecting Clients. In a group setting, counselors take reasonable precautions to protect clients from physical or psychological trauma.

A.10. Fees and Bartering
(See D.3.a. and D.3.b.)

a. Advance Understanding. Counselors clearly explain to clients, prior to entering the counseling relationship, all financial arrangements related to professional services including the use of collection agencies or legal measures for nonpayment. (See A.11.c.)

b. Establishing Fees. In establishing fees for professional counseling services, counselors consider the financial status of clients and locality. In the event that the established fee structure is inappropriate for a client, assistance is provided in attempting to find comparable services of acceptable cost. (See A.10.d., D.3.a., and D.3.b.)

c. Bartering Discouraged. Counselors ordinarily refrain from accepting goods or services from clients in return for counseling services because such arrangements create inherent potential for conflicts, exploitation, and distortion of the professional relationship. Counselors may participate in bartering only if the relationship is not exploitative, if the client requests it, if a clear written contract is established, and if such arrangements are an accepted practice among professionals in the community. (See A.6.a.)

d. Pro Bono Service. Counselors contribute to society by devoting a portion of their professional activity to services for which there is little or no financial return (pro bono).

A.11. Termination and Referral

a. Abandonment Prohibited. Counselors do not abandon or neglect clients in counseling. Counselors assist in making appropriate arrangements for the continuation of treatment, when necessary, during interruptions such as vacations, and following termination.

b. Inability to Assist Clients. If counselors determine an inability to be of professional assistance to clients, they avoid entering or immediately terminate a counseling relationship. Counselors are knowledgeable about referral resources and suggest appropriate alternatives. If clients decline the suggested referral, counselors should discontinue the relationship.

c. Appropriate Termination. Counselors terminate a counseling relationship, securing client agreement when possible, when it is reasonably clear that the client is no longer benefiting, when services are no longer required, when counseling no longer serves the client's needs or interests, when clients do not pay fees charged, or when agency or institution limits do not allow provision of further counseling services. (See A.10.b. and C.2.g.)

A.12. Computer Technology

a. Use of Computers. When computer applications are used in counseling services, counselors ensure that (1) the client is intellectually, emotionally, and physically capable of using the computer application; (2) the computer application is appropriate for the needs of the client; (3) the client understands the purpose and operation of the computer applications; and (4) a follow-up of client use of a computer

application is provided to correct possible misconceptions, discover inappropriate use, and assess subsequent needs.

b. Explanation of Limitations. Counselors ensure that clients are provided information as a part of the counseling relationship that adequately explains the limitations of computer technology.

c. Access to Computer Applications. Counselors provide for equal access to computer applications in counseling services. (See A.2.a.)

Section B: Confidentiality

B.1. Right to Privacy

a. Respect for Privacy. Counselors respect their clients' right to privacy and avoid illegal and unwarranted disclosures of confidential information. (See A.3.a. and B.6.a.)

b. Client Waiver. The right to privacy may be waived by the client or his or her legally recognized representative.

c. Exceptions. The general requirement that counselors keep information confidential does not apply when disclosure is required to prevent clear and imminent danger to the client or others or when legal requirements demand that confidential information be revealed. Counselors consult with other professionals when in doubt as to the validity of an exception.

d. Contagious, Fatal Diseases. A counselor who receives information confirming that a client has a disease commonly known to be both communicable and fatal is justified in disclosing information to an identifiable third party, who by his or her relationship with the client is at a high risk of contracting the disease. Prior to making a disclosure the counselor should ascertain that the client has not already informed the third party about his or her disease and that the client is not intending to inform the third party in the immediate future. (See B.1.c and B.1.f.)

e. Court-Ordered Disclosure. When court ordered to release confidential information without a client's permission, counselors request to the court that the disclosure not be required due to potential harm to the client or counseling relationship. (See B.1.c.)

f. Minimal Disclosure. When circumstances require the disclosure of confidential information, only essential information is revealed. To the extent possible, clients are informed before confidential information is disclosed.

g. Explanation of Limitations. When counseling is initiated and throughout the counseling process as necessary, counselors inform clients of the limitations of confidentiality and identify foreseeable situations in which confidentiality must be breached. (See G.2.a.)

h. Subordinates. Counselors make every effort to ensure that privacy and confidentiality of clients are maintained by subordinates including employees, supervisees, clerical assistants, and volunteers. (See B.1.a.)

i. Treatment Teams. If client treatment will involve a continued review by a treatment team, the client will be informed of the team's existence and composition.

B.2. Groups and Families

a. Group Work. In group work, counselors clearly define confidentiality and the parameters for the specific group being entered, explain its importance, and discuss the difficulties related to confidentiality involved in group work. The fact that confidentiality cannot be guaranteed is clearly communicated to group members.

b. Family Counseling. In family counseling, information about one family member cannot be disclosed to another member without permission. Counselors protect the privacy rights of each family member. (See A.8., B.3., and B.4.d.)

B.3. Minor or Incompetent Clients

When counseling clients who are minors or individuals who are unable to give voluntary, informed consent, parents or guardians may be included in the counseling process as ap-

propriate. Counselors act in the best interests of clients and take measures to safeguard confidentiality. (See A.3.c.)

B.4. Records

a. Requirement of Records. Counselors maintain records necessary for rendering professional services to their clients and as required by laws, regulations, or agency or institution procedures.

b. Confidentiality of Records. Counselors are responsible for securing the safety and confidentiality of any counseling records they create, maintain, transfer, or destroy whether the records are written, taped, computerized, or stored in any other medium. (See B.1.a.)

c. Permission to Record or Observe. Counselors obtain permission from clients prior to electronically recording or observing sessions. (See A.3.a.)

d. Client Access. Counselors recognize that counseling records are kept for the benefit of clients, and therefore provide access to records and copies of records when requested by competent clients, unless the records contain information that may be misleading and detrimental to the client. In situations involving multiple clients, access to records is limited to those parts of records that do not include confidential information related to another client. (See A.8., B.1.a., and B.2.b.)

e. Disclosure or Transfer. Counselors obtain written permission from clients to disclose or transfer records to legitimate third parties unless exceptions to confidentiality exist as listed in Section B.1. Steps are taken to ensure that receivers of counseling records are sensitive to their confidential nature.

B.5. Research and Training

a. Data Disguise Required. Use of data derived from counseling relationships for purposes of training, research, or publication is confined to content that is disguised to ensure the anonymity of the individuals involved. (See B.1.g and G.3.d.)

b. Agreement for Identification. Identification of a client in a presentation or publication is permissible only when the client has reviewed the material and has agreed to its presentation or publication. (See G.3.d.)

B.6. Consultation

a. Respect for Privacy. Information obtained in a consulting relationship is discussed for professional purposes only with persons clearly concerned with the case. Written and oral reports present data germane to the purposes of the consultation, and every effort is made to protect client identity and avoid undue invasion of privacy.

b. Cooperating Agencies. Before sharing information, counselors make efforts to ensure that there are defined policies in other agencies serving the counselor's clients that effectively protect the confidentiality of information.

Section C: Professional Responsibility

C.1. Standards Knowledge

Counselors have a responsibility to read, understand, and follow the Code of Ethics and the Standards of Practice.

C.2. Professional Competence

a. Boundaries of Competence. Counselors practice only within the boundaries of their competence, based on their education, training, supervised experience, state and national professional credentials, and appropriate professional experience. Counselors will demonstrate a commitment to gain knowledge, personal awareness, sensitivity, and skills pertinent to working with a diverse client population.

b. New Specialty Areas of Practice. Counselors practice in specialty areas new to them only after appropriate education, training, and supervised experience. While developing skills in new specialty areas, counselors take steps to ensure the competence of their work and to protect others from possible harm.

c. Qualified for Employment. Counselors accept employment only for positions for which they are qualified by education, training, supervised experience, state and national professional credentials, and appropriate professional experience. Counselors hire for professional counseling positions only individuals who are qualified and competent.

d. Monitor Effectiveness. Counselors continually monitor their effectiveness as professionals and take steps to improve when necessary. Counselors in private practice take reasonable steps to seek out peer supervision to evaluate their efficacy as counselors.

e. Ethical Issues Consultation. Counselors take reasonable steps to consult with other counselors or related professionals when they have questions regarding their ethical obligations or professional practice. (See H.1.)

f. Continuing Education. Counselors recognize the need for continuing education to maintain a reasonable level of awareness of current scientific and professional information in their fields of activity. They take steps to maintain competence in the skills they use, are open to new procedures, and keep current with the diverse and/or special populations with whom they work.

g. Impairment. Counselors refrain from offering or accepting professional services when their physical, mental, or emotional problems are likely to harm a client or others. They are alert to the signs of impairment, seek assistance for problems, and, if necessary, limit, suspend, or terminate their professional responsibilities. (See A.11.c.)

C.3. Advertising and Soliciting Clients

a. Accurate Advertising. There are no restrictions on advertising by counselors except those that can be specifically justified to protect the public from deceptive practices. Counselors advertise or represent their services to the public by identifying their credentials in an accurate manner that is not false, misleading, deceptive, or fraudulent. Counselors may only advertise the highest degree earned which is in counseling or a closely related field from a college or university that was accredited when the degree was awarded by one of the regional accrediting bodies recognized by the Council on Postsecondary Accreditation.

b. Testimonials. Counselors who use testimonials do not solicit them from clients or other persons who, because of their particular circumstances, may be vulnerable to undue influence.

c. Statements by Others. Counselors make reasonable efforts to ensure that statements made by others about them or the profession of counseling are accurate.

d. Recruiting Through Employment. Counselors do not use their places of employment or institutional affiliation to recruit or gain clients, supervisees, or consultees for their private practices. (See C.5.e.)

e. Products and Training Advertisements. Counselors who develop products related to their profession or conduct workshops or training events ensure that the advertisements concerning these products or events are accurate and disclose adequate information for consumers to make informed choices.

f. Promoting to Those Served. Counselors do not use counseling, teaching, training, or supervisory relationships to promote their products or training events in a manner that is deceptive or would exert undue influence on individuals who may be vulnerable. Counselors may adopt textbooks they have authored for instruction purposes.

g. Professional Association Involvement. Counselors actively participate in local, state, and national associations that foster the development and improvement of counseling.

C.4. Credentials

a. Credentials Claimed. Counselors claim or imply only professional credentials possessed and are responsible for correcting any known misrepresentations of their credentials by others. Professional credentials include graduate degrees in counseling or closely related mental health fields, accreditation of graduate programs, national voluntary certifications, government-issued certifications or licenses, ACA professional membership, or any other credential that might indicate to the public specialized knowledge or expertise in counseling.

b. ACA Professional Membership. ACA professional members may announce to the public their membership status. Regular members may not announce their ACA membership in a manner that might imply they are credentialed counselors.

c. Credential Guidelines. Counselors follow the guidelines for use of credentials that have been established by the entities that issue the credentials.

d. Misrepresentation of Credentials. Counselors do not attribute more to their credentials than the credentials represent, and do not imply that other counselors are not qualified because they do not possess certain credentials.

e. Doctoral Degrees From Other Fields. Counselors who hold a master's degree in counseling or a closely related mental health field, but hold a doctoral degree from other than counseling or a closely related field, do not use the title "Dr." in their practices and do not announce to the public in relation to their practice or status as a counselor that they hold a doctorate.

C.5. Public Responsibility

a. Nondiscrimination. Counselors do not discriminate against clients, students, or supervisees in a manner that has a negative impact based on their age, color, culture, disability, ethnic group, gender, race, religion, sexual orientation, or socioeconomic status, or for any other reason. (See A.2.a.)

b. Sexual Harassment. Counselors do not engage in sexual harassment. Sexual harassment is defined as sexual solicitation, physical advances, or verbal or nonverbal conduct that is sexual in nature, that occurs in connection with professional activities or roles, and that either (1) is unwelcome, is offensive, or creates a hostile workplace environment, and counselors know or are told this; or (2) is sufficiently severe or intense to be perceived as harassment to a reasonable person in the context. Sexual harassment can consist of a single intense or severe act or multiple persistent or pervasive acts.

c. Reports to Third Parties. Counselors are accurate, honest, and unbiased in reporting their professional activities and judgments to appropriate third parties including courts, health insurance companies, those who are the recipients of evaluation reports, and others. (See B.l.g.)

d. Media Presentations. When counselors provide advice or comment by means of public lectures, demonstrations, radio or television programs, prerecorded tapes, printed articles, mailed material, or other media, they take reasonable precautions to ensure that (1) the statements are based on appropriate professional counseling literature and practice; (2) the statements are otherwise consistent with the Code of Ethics and the Standards of Practice; and (3) the recipients of the information are not encouraged to infer that a professional counseling relationship has been established. (See C.6.b.)

e. Unjustified Gains. Counselors do not use their professional positions to seek or receive unjustified personal gains, sexual favors, unfair advantage, or unearned goods or services. (See C.3.d.)

C.6. Responsibility to Other Professionals

a. Different Approaches. Counselors are respectful of approaches to professional counseling that differ from their own. Counselors know and take into account the traditions and practices of other professional groups with which they work.

b. Personal Public Statements. When making personal statements in a public context, counselors clarify that they are speaking from their personal perspectives and that they are not speaking on behalf of all counselors or the profession. (See C.5.d.)

c. Clients Served by Others. When counselors learn that their clients are in a professional relationship with another mental health professional, they request release from clients to inform the other professionals and strive to establish positive and collaborative professional relationships. (See A.4.)

Section D: Relationships With Other Professionals

D.1. Relationships with Employers and Employees

a. Role Definition. Counselors define and describe for their employers and employees the parameters and levels of their professional roles.

b. Agreements. Counselors establish working agreements with supervisors, colleagues, and subordinates regarding counseling or clinical relationships, confidentiality, adherence to professional standards, distinction between public and private material, maintenance and dissemination of recorded information, workload, and accountability. Working agreements in each instance are specified and made known to those concerned.

c. Negative Conditions. Counselors alert their employers to conditions that may be potentially disruptive or damaging to the counselor's professional responsibilities or that may limit their effectiveness.

d. Evaluation. Counselors submit regularly to professional review and evaluation by their supervisor or the appropriate representative of the employer.

e. In-Service. Counselors are responsible for in-service development of self and staff.

f. Goals. Counselors inform their staff of goals and programs.

g. Practices. Counselors provide personnel and agency practices that respect and enhance the rights and welfare of each employee and recipient of agency services. Counselors strive to maintain the highest levels of professional services.

h. Personnel Selection and Assignment. Counselors select competent staff and assign responsibilities compatible with their skills and experiences.

i. Discrimination. Counselors, as either employers or employees, do not engage in or condone practices that are inhumane, illegal, or unjustifiable (such as considerations based on age, color, culture, disability, ethnic group, gender, race, religion, sexual orientation, or socioeconomic status) in hiring, promotion, or training. (See A.2.a. and C.5.b.)

j. Professional Conduct. Counselors have a responsibility both to clients and to the agency or institution within which services are performed to maintain high standards of professional conduct.

k. Exploitative Relationships. Counselors do not engage in exploitative relationships with individuals over whom they have supervisory, evaluative, or instructional control or authority.

l. Employer Policies. The acceptance of employment in an agency or institution implies that counselors are in agreement with its general policies and principles. Counselors strive to reach agreement with employers as to acceptable standards of conduct that allow for changes in institutional policy conducive to the growth and development of clients.

D.2. Consultation (See B.6.)

a. Consultation as an Option. Counselors may choose to consult with any other professionally competent persons about their clients. In choosing consultants, counselors avoid placing the consultant in a conflict of interest situation that would preclude the consultant being a proper party to the counselor's efforts to help the client. Should counselors be engaged in a work setting that compromises this consultation standard, they consult with other professionals whenever possible to consider justifiable alternatives.

b. Consultant Competency. Counselors are reasonably certain that they have or the organization represented has the necessary compe-

tencies and resources for giving the kind of consulting services needed and that appropriate referral resources are available.

c. Understanding With Clients. When providing consultation, counselors attempt to develop with their clients a clear understanding of problem definition, goals for change, and predicted consequences of interventions selected.

d. Consultant Goals. The consulting relationship is one in which client adaptability and growth toward self-direction are consistently encouraged and cultivated. (See A.1.b.)

D.3. Fees for Referral

a. Accepting Fees From Agency Clients. Counselors refuse a private fee or other remuneration for rendering services to persons who are entitled to such services through the counselor's employing agency or institution. The policies of a particular agency may make explicit provisions for agency clients to receive counseling services from members of its staff in private practice. In such instances, the clients must be informed of other options open to them should they seek private counseling services. (See A.10.a., A.11.b., and C.3.d.)

b. Referral Fees. Counselors do not accept a referral fee from other professionals.

D.4. Subcontractor Arrangements

When counselors work as subcontractors for counseling services for a third party, they have a duty to inform clients of the limitations of confidentiality that the organization may place on counselors in providing counseling services to clients. The limits of such confidentiality ordinarily are discussed as part of the intake session. (See B.1.e. and B.1.f.)

Section E: Evaluation, Assessment, and Interpretation

E.1. General

a. Appraisal Techniques. The primary purpose of educational and psychological assessment is to provide measures that are objective and interpretable in either comparative or absolute terms. Counselors recognize the need to interpret the statements in this section as applying to the whole range of appraisal techniques, including test and nontest data.

b. Client Welfare. Counselors promote the welfare and best interests of the client in the development, publication, and utilization of educational and psychological assessment techniques. They do not misuse assessment results and interpretations and take reasonable steps to prevent others from misusing the information these techniques provide. They respect the client's right to know the results, the interpretations made, and the bases for their conclusions and recommendations.

E.2. Competence to Use and Interpret Tests

a. Limits of Competence. Counselors recognize the limits of their competence and perform only those testing and assessment services for which they have been trained. They are familiar with reliability, validity, related standardization, error of measurement, and proper application of any technique utilized. Counselors using computer-based test interpretations are trained in the construct being measured and the specific instrument being used prior to using this type of computer application. Counselors take reasonable measures to ensure the proper use of psychological assessment techniques by persons under their supervision.

b. Appropriate Use. Counselors are responsible for the appropriate application, scoring, interpretation, and use of assessment instruments, whether they score and interpret such tests themselves or use computerized or other services.

c. Decisions Based on Results. Counselors responsible for decisions involving individuals or policies that are based on assessment results have a thorough understanding of educational and psychological measurement, in-

cluding validation criteria, test research, and guidelines for test development and use.

d. Accurate Information. Counselors provide accurate information and avoid false claims or misconceptions when making statements about assessment instruments or techniques. Special efforts are made to avoid unwarranted connotations of such terms as IQ and grade equivalent scores. (See C.5.c.)

E.3. Informed Consent

a. Explanation to Clients. Prior to assessment, counselors explain the nature and purposes of assessment and the specific use of results in language the client (or other legally authorized person on behalf of the client) can understand, unless an explicit exception to this right has been agreed upon in advance. Regardless of whether scoring and interpretation are completed by counselors, by assistants, or by computer or other outside services, counselors take reasonable steps to ensure that appropriate explanations are given to the client.

b. Recipients of Results. The examinee's welfare, explicit understanding, and prior agreement determine the recipients of test results. Counselors include accurate and appropriate interpretations with any release of individual or group test results. (See B.1.a. and C.5.c.)

E.4. Release of Information to Competent Professionals

a. Misuse of Results. Counselors do not misuse assessment results, including test results, and interpretations, and take reasonable steps to prevent the misuse of such by others. (See C.5.c.)

b. Release of Raw Data. Counselors ordinarily release data (e.g., protocols, counseling or interview notes, or questionnaires) in which the client is identified only with the consent of the client or the client's legal representative. Such data are usually released only to persons recognized by counselors as competent to interpret the data. (See B.1.a.)

E.5. Proper Diagnosis of Mental Disorders

a. Proper Diagnosis. Counselors take special care to provide proper diagnosis of mental disorders. Assessment techniques (including personal interview) used to determine client care (e.g., locus of treatment, type of treatment, or recommended follow-up) are carefully selected and appropriately used. (See A.3.a. and C.5.c.)

b. Cultural Sensitivity. Counselors recognize that culture affects the manner in which clients' problems are defined. Clients' socioeconomic and cultural experience is considered when diagnosing mental disorders.

E.6. Test Selection

a. Appropriateness of Instruments. Counselors carefully consider the validity, reliability, psychometric limitations, and appropriateness of instruments when selecting tests for use in a given situation or with a particular client.

b. Culturally Diverse Populations. Counselors are cautious when selecting tests for culturally diverse populations to avoid inappropriateness of testing that may be outside of socialized behavioral or cognitive patterns.

E.7. Conditions of Test Administration

a. Administration Conditions. Counselors administer tests under the same conditions that were established in their standardization. When tests are not administered under standard conditions or when unusual behavior or irregularities occur during the testing session, those conditions are noted in interpretation, and the results may be designated as invalid or of questionable validity.

b. Computer Administration. Counselors are responsible for ensuring that administration programs function properly to provide clients with accurate results when a computer or other electronic methods are used for test administration. (See A.12.b.)

c. Unsupervised Test Taking. Counselors do not permit unsupervised or inadequately supervised use of tests or assessments unless the tests or assessments are designed, intended, and validated for self-administration and/or scoring.

d. Disclosure of Favorable Conditions. Prior to test administration, conditions that produce most favorable test results are made known to the examinee.

E.8. Diversity in Testing

Counselors are cautious in using assessment techniques, making evaluations, and interpreting the performance of populations not represented in the norm group on which an instrument was standardized. They recognize the effects of age, color, culture, disability, ethnic group, gender, race, religion, sexual orientation, and socioeconomic status on test administration and interpretation and place test results in proper perspective with other relevant factors. (See A.2.a.)

E.9. Test Scoring and Interpretation

a. Reporting Reservations. In reporting assessment results, counselors indicate any reservations that exist regarding validity or reliability because of the circumstances of the assessment or the inappropriateness of the norms for the person tested.

b. Research Instruments. Counselors exercise caution when interpreting the results of research instruments possessing insufficient technical data to support respondent results. The specific purposes for the use of such instruments are stated explicitly to the examinee.

c. Testing Services. Counselors who provide test scoring and test interpretation services to support the assessment process confirm the validity of such interpretations. They accurately describe the purpose, norms, validity, reliability, and applications of the procedures and any special qualifications applicable to their use. The public offering of an automated test interpretations service is considered a professional-to-professional consultation. The formal responsibility of the consultant is to the consultee, but the ultimate and overriding responsibility is to the client.

E.10. Test Security

Counselors maintain the integrity and security of tests and other assessment techniques consistent with legal and contractual obligations. Counselors do not appropriate, reproduce, or modify published tests or parts thereof without acknowledgment and permission from the publisher.

E.11. Obsolete Tests and Outdated Test Results

Counselors do not use data or test results that are obsolete or outdated for the current purpose. Counselors make every effort to prevent the misuse of obsolete measures and test data by others.

E.12. Test Construction

Counselors use established scientific procedures, relevant standards, and current professional knowledge for test design in the development, publication, and utilization of educational and psychological assessment techniques.

Section F: Teaching, Training, and Supervision

F.1. Counselor Educators and Trainers

a. Educators as Teachers and Practitioners. Counselors who are responsible for developing, implementing, and supervising educational programs are skilled as teachers and practitioners. They are knowledgeable regarding the ethical, legal, and regulatory aspects of the profession, are skilled in applying that knowledge, and make students and supervisees aware of their responsibilities. Counselors conduct counselor education and training programs in an ethical manner and serve as role models for professional behavior. Coun-

selor educators should make an effort to infuse material related to human diversity into all courses and/or workshops that are designed to promote the development of professional counselors.

b. Relationship Boundaries With Students and Supervisees. Counselors clearly define and maintain ethical, professional, and social relationship boundaries with their students and supervisees. They are aware of the differential in power that exists and the student's or supervisee's possible incomprehension of that power differential. Counselors explain to students and supervisees the potential for the relationship to become exploitive.

c. Sexual Relationships. Counselors do not engage in sexual relationships with students or supervisees and do not subject them to sexual harassment. (See A.6. and C.5.b)

d. Contributions to Research. Counselors give credit to students or supervisees for their contributions to research and scholarly projects. Credit is given through coauthorship, acknowledgment, footnote statement, or other appropriate means, in accordance with such contributions. (See G.4.b. and G.4.c.)

e. Close Relatives. Counselors do not accept close relatives as students or supervisees.

f. Supervision Preparation. Counselors who offer clinical supervision services are adequately prepared in supervision methods and techniques. Counselors who are doctoral students serving as practicum or internship supervisors to master's level students are adequately prepared and supervised by the training program.

g. Responsibility for Services to Clients. Counselors who supervise the counseling services of others take reasonable measures to ensure that counseling services provided to clients are professional.

h. Endorsement. Counselors do not endorse students or supervisees for certification, licensure, employment, or completion of an academic or training program if they believe students or supervisees are not qualified for the endorsement. Counselors take reasonable steps to assist students or supervisees who are not qualified for endorsement to become qualified.

F.2. Counselor Education and Training Programs

a. Orientation. Prior to admission, counselors orient prospective students to the counselor education or training program's expectations, including but not limited to the following: (1) the type and level of skill acquisition required for successful completion of the training, (2) subject matter to be covered, (3) basis for evaluation, (4) training components that encourage self-growth or self-disclosure as part of the training process, (5) the type of supervision settings and requirements of the sites for required clinical field experiences, (6) student and supervisee evaluation and dismissal policies and procedures, and (7) up-to-date employment prospects for graduates.

b. Integration of Study and Practice. Counselors establish counselor education and training programs that integrate academic study and supervised practice.

c. Evaluation. Counselors clearly state to students and supervisees, in advance of training, the levels of competency expected, appraisal methods, and timing of evaluations for both didactic and experiential components. Counselors provide students and supervisees with periodic performance appraisal and evaluation feedback throughout the training program.

d. Teaching Ethics. Counselors make students and supervisees aware of the ethical responsibilities and standards of the profession and the students' and supervisees' ethical responsibilities to the profession. (See C.1. and F.3.e.)

e. Peer Relationships. When students or supervisees are assigned to lead counseling groups or provide clinical supervision for their peers, counselors take steps to ensure that students and supervisees placed in these roles do not have personal or adverse relationships with peers and that they understand they have the same ethical obligations as counselor educa-

tors, trainers, and supervisors. Counselors make every effort to ensure that the rights of peers are not compromised when students or supervisees are assigned to lead counseling groups or provide clinical supervision.

f. Varied Theoretical Positions. Counselors present varied theoretical positions so that students and supervisees may make comparisons and have opportunities to develop their own positions. Counselors provide information concerning the scientific bases of professional practice. (See C.6.a.)

g. Field Placements. Counselors develop clear policies within their training program regarding field placement and other clinical experiences. Counselors provide clearly stated roles and responsibilities for the student or supervisee, the site supervisor, and the program supervisor. They confirm that site supervisors are qualified to provide supervision and are informed of their professional and ethical responsibilities in this role.

h. Dual Relationships as Supervisors. Counselors avoid dual relationships such as performing the role of site supervisor and training program supervisor in the student's or supervisee's training program. Counselors do not accept any form of professional services, fees, commissions, reimbursement, or remuneration from a site for student or supervisee placement.

i. Diversity in Programs. Counselors are responsive to their institution's and program's recruitment and retention needs for training program administrators, faculty, and students with diverse backgrounds and special needs. (See A.2.a.)

F.3. Students and Supervisees

a. Limitations. Counselors, through ongoing evaluation and appraisal, are aware of the academic and personal limitations of students and supervisees that might impede performance. Counselors assist students and supervisees in securing remedial assistance when needed, and dismiss from the training program supervisees who are unable to provide competent service due to academic or personal limitations. Counselors seek professional consultation and document their decision to dismiss or refer students or supervisees for assistance. Counselors ensure that students and supervisees have recourse to address decisions made to require them to seek assistance or to dismiss them.

b. Self-Growth Experiences. Counselors use professional judgment when designing training experiences conducted by the counselors themselves that require student and supervisee self-growth or self-disclosure. Safeguards are provided so that students and supervisees are aware of the ramifications their self-disclosure may have on counselors whose primary role as teacher, trainer, or supervisor requires acting on ethical obligations to the profession. Evaluative components of experiential training experiences explicitly delineate predetermined academic standards that are separate and do not depend on the student's level of self-disclosure. (See A.6.)

c. Counseling for Students and Supervisees. If students or supervisees request counseling, supervisors or counselor educators provide them with acceptable referrals. Supervisors or counselor educators do not serve as counselor to students or supervisees over whom they hold administrative, teaching, or evaluative roles unless this is a brief role associated with a training experience. (See A.6.b.)

d. Clients of Students and Supervisees. Counselors make every effort to ensure that the clients at field placements are aware of the services rendered and the qualifications of the students and supervisees rendering those services. Clients receive professional disclosure information and are informed of the limits of confidentiality. Client permission is obtained in order for the students and supervisees to use any information concerning the counseling relationship in the training process. (See B.1.e.)

e. Standards for Students and Supervisees. Students and supervisees preparing to become

counselors adhere to the Code of Ethics and the Standards of Practice. Students and supervisees have the same obligations to clients as those required of counselors. (See H.1.)

Section G: Research and Publication

G.1. Research Responsibilities

a. Use of Human Subjects. Counselors plan, design, conduct, and report research in a manner consistent with pertinent ethical principles, federal and state laws, host institutional regulations, and scientific standards governing research with human subjects. Counselors design and conduct research that reflects cultural sensitivity appropriateness.

b. Deviation From Standard Practices. Counselors seek consultation and observe stringent safeguards to protect the rights of research participants when a research problem suggests a deviation from standard acceptable practices. (See B.6.)

c. Precautions to Avoid Injury. Counselors who conduct research with human subjects are responsible for the subjects' welfare throughout the experiment and take reasonable precautions to avoid causing injurious psychological, physical, or social effects to their subjects.

d. Principal Researcher Responsibility. The ultimate responsibility for ethical research practice lies with the principal researcher. All others involved in the research activities share ethical obligations and full responsibility for their own actions.

e. Minimal Interference. Counselors take reasonable precautions to avoid causing disruptions in subjects' lives due to participation in research.

f. Diversity. Counselors are sensitive to diversity and research issues with special populations. They seek consultation when appropriate. (See A.2.a. and B.6.)

G.2. Informed Consent

a. Topics Disclosed. In obtaining informed consent for research, counselors use language that is understandable to research participants and that (1) accurately explains the purpose and procedures to be followed; (2) identifies any procedures that are experimental or relatively untried; (3) describes the attendant discomforts and risks; (4) describes the benefits or changes in individuals or organizations that might be reasonably expected; (5) discloses appropriate alternative procedures that would be advantageous for subjects; (6) offers to answer any inquiries concerning the procedures; (7) describes any limitations on confidentiality; and (8) instructs that subjects are free to withdraw their consent and to discontinue participation in the project at any time. (See B.1.f.)

b. Deception. Counselors do not conduct research involving deception unless alternative procedures are not feasible and the prospective value of the research justifies the deception. When the methodological requirements of a study necessitate concealment or deception, the investigator is required to explain clearly the reasons for this action as soon as possible.

c. Voluntary Participation. Participation in research is typically voluntary and without any penalty for refusal to participate. Involuntary participation is appropriate only when it can be demonstrated that participation will have no harmful effects on subjects and is essential to the investigation.

d. Confidentiality of Information. Information obtained about research participants during the course of an investigation is confidential. When the possibility exists that others may obtain access to such information, ethical research practice requires that the possibility, together with the plans for protecting confidentiality, be explained to participants as a part of the procedure for obtaining informed consent. (See B.1.e.)

e. Persons Incapable of Giving Informed Consent. When a person is incapable of giving informed consent, counselors provide an appropriate explanation, obtain agreement for

participation, and obtain appropriate consent from a legally authorized person.

f. Commitments to Participants. Counselors take reasonable measures to honor all commitments to research participants.

g. Explanations After Data Collection. After data are collected, counselors provide participants with full clarification of the nature of the study to remove any misconceptions. Where scientific or human values justify delaying or withholding information, counselors take reasonable measures to avoid causing harm.

h. Agreements to Cooperate. Counselors who agree to cooperate with another individual in research or publication incur an obligation to cooperate as promised in terms of punctuality of performance and with regard to the completeness and accuracy of the information required.

i. Informed Consent for Sponsors. In the pursuit of research, counselors give sponsors, institutions, and publication channels the same respect and opportunity for giving informed consent that they accord to individual research participants. Counselors are aware of their obligation to future research workers and ensure that host institutions are given feedback information and proper acknowledgment.

G.3. Reporting Results

a. Information Affecting Outcome. When reporting research results, counselors explicitly mention all variables and conditions known to the investigator that may have affected the outcome of a study or the interpretation of data.

b. Accurate Results. Counselors plan, conduct, and report research accurately and in a manner that minimizes the possibility that results will be misleading. They provide thorough discussions of the limitations of their data and alternative hypotheses. Counselors do not engage in fraudulent research, distort data, misrepresent data, or deliberately bias their results.

c. Obligation to Report Unfavorable Results. Counselors communicate to other counselors the results of any research judged to be of professional value. Results that reflect unfavorably on institutions, programs, services, prevailing opinions, or vested interests are not withheld.

d. Identity of Subjects. Counselors who supply data, aid in the research of another person, report research results, or make original data available take due care to disguise the identity of respective subjects in the absence of specific authorization from the subjects to do otherwise. (See B.1.g. and B.5.a.)

e. Replication Studies. Counselors are obligated to make available sufficient original research data to qualified professionals who may wish to replicate the study.

G.4. Publication

a. Recognition of Others. When conducting and reporting research, counselors are familiar with and give recognition to previous work on the topic, observe copyright laws, and give full credit to those to whom credit is due. (See F.1.d. and G.4.c.)

b. Contributors. Counselors give credit through joint authorship, acknowledgment, footnote statements, or other appropriate means to those who have contributed significantly to research or concept development in accordance with such contributions. The principal contributor is listed first and minor technical or professional contributions are acknowledged in notes or introductory statements.

c. Student Research. For an article that is substantially based on a student's dissertation or thesis, the student is listed as the principal author. (See F.1.d. and G.4.a.)

d. Duplicate Submission. Counselors submit manuscripts for consideration to only one journal at a time. Manuscripts that are published in whole or in substantial part in another journal or published work are not submitted for publication without acknowledgment and permission from the previous publication.

e. Professional Review. Counselors who review material submitted for publication, research, or other scholarly purposes respect the confidentiality and proprietary rights of those who submitted it.

Section H: Resolving Ethical Issues

H.1. Knowledge of Standards

Counselors are familiar with the Code of Ethics and the Standards of Practice and other applicable ethics codes from other professional organizations of which they are members, or from certification and licensure bodies. Lack of knowledge or misunderstanding of an ethical responsibility is not a defense against a charge of unethical conduct. (See F.3.e.)

H.2. Suspected Violations

a. Ethical Behavior Expected. Counselors expect professional associates to adhere to the Code of Ethics. When counselors possess reasonable cause that raises doubts as to whether a counselor is acting in an ethical manner, they take appropriate action. (See H.2.d. and H.2.e.)

b. Consultation. When uncertain as to whether a particular situation or course of action may be in violation of the Code of Ethics, counselors consult with other counselors who are knowledgeable about ethics, with colleagues, or with appropriate authorities.

c. Organization Conflicts. If the demands of an organization with which counselors are affiliated pose a conflict with the Code of Ethics, counselors specify the nature of such conflicts and express to their supervisors or other responsible officials their commitment to the Code of Ethics. When possible, counselors work toward change within the organization to allow full adherence to the Code of Ethics.

d. Informal Resolution. When counselors have reasonable cause to believe that another counselor is violating an ethical standard, they attempt to first resolve the issue informally with the other counselor if feasible, providing that such action does not violate confidentiality rights that may be involved.

e. Reporting Suspected Violations. When an informal resolution is not appropriate or feasible, counselors, upon reasonable cause, take action such as reporting the suspected ethical violation to state or national ethics committees, unless this action conflicts with confidentiality rights that cannot be resolved.

f. Unwarranted Complaints. Counselors do not initiate, participate in, or encourage the filing of ethics complaints that are unwarranted or intend to harm a counselor rather than to protect clients or the public.

H.3. Cooperation With Ethics Committees

Counselors assist in the process of enforcing the Code of Ethics. Counselors cooperate with investigations, proceedings, and requirements of the ACA Ethics Committee or ethics committees of other duly constituted associations or boards having jurisdiction over those charged with a violation. Counselors are familiar with the ACA Policies and Procedures and use it as a reference in assisting the enforcement of the Code of Ethics.

STANDARDS OF PRACTICE

All members of the American Counseling Association (ACA) are required to adhere to the Standards of Practice and the Code of Ethics. The Standards of Practice represent minimal behavioral statements of the Code of Ethics. Members should refer to the applicable section of the Code of Ethics for further interpretation and amplification of the applicable Standard of Practice.

Section A: The Counseling Relationship

Standard of Practice One (SP-1): Nondiscrimination. Counselors respect diversity and must not discriminate against clients because of age, color, culture, disability, ethnic group, gender, race, religion, sexual orientation, marital status, or socioeconomic status. (See A.2.a.)

Standard of Practice Two (SP-2): Disclosure to Clients. Counselors must adequately inform clients, preferably in writing, regarding the counseling process and counseling relationship at or before the time it begins and throughout the relationship. (See A.3.a.)

Standard of Practice Three (SP-3): Dual Relationships. Counselors must make every effort to avoid dual relationships with clients that could impair their professional judgment or increase the risk of harm to clients. When a dual relationship cannot be avoided, counselors must take appropriate steps to ensure that judgment is not impaired and that no exploitation occurs. (See A.6.a. and A.6.b.)

Standard of Practice Four (SP-4): Sexual Intimacies With Clients. Counselors must not engage in any type of sexual intimacies with current clients and must not engage in sexual intimacies with former clients within a minimum of two years after terminating the counseling relationship. Counselors who engage in such relationships after two years following termination have the responsibility to examine and document thoroughly that such relations did not have an exploitative nature.

Standard of Practice Five (SP-5): Protecting Clients During Group Work. Counselors must take steps to protect clients from physical or psychological trauma resulting from interactions during group work. (See A.9.b.)

Standard of Practice Six (SP-6): Advance Understanding of Fees. Counselors must explain to clients, prior to their entering the counseling relationship, financial arrangements related to professional services. (See A.10.a.–d. and A.11.c.)

Standard of Practice Seven (SP-7): Termination. Counselors must assist in making appropriate arrangements for the continuation of treatment of clients, when necessary, following termination of counseling relationships. (See A.11.a.)

Standard of Practice Eight (SP-8): Inability to Assist Clients. Counselors must avoid entering or immediately terminate a counseling relationship if it is determined that they are unable to be of professional assistance to a client. The counselor may assist in making an appropriate referral for the client. (See A.11.b.)

Section B: Confidentiality

Standard of Practice Nine (SP-9): Confidentiality Requirement. Counselors must keep information related to counseling services confidential unless disclosure is in the best interest of clients, is required for the welfare of others, or is required by law. When disclosure is required, only information that is essential is revealed and the client is informed of such disclosure. (See B.1.a.–f.)

Standard of Practice Ten (SP-10): Confidentiality Requirements for Subordinates. Counselors must take measures to ensure that privacy and confidentiality of clients are maintained by subordinates. (See B.1.h.)

Standard of Practice Eleven (SP-11): Confidentiality in Group Work. Counselors must clearly communicate to group members that confidentiality cannot be guaranteed in group work. (See B.2.a.)

Standard of Practice Twelve (SP-12): Confidentiality in Family Counseling. Counselors must not disclose information about one family member in counseling to another family member without prior consent. (See B.2.b.)

Standard of Practice Thirteen (SP-13): Confidentiality of Records. Counselors must maintain appropriate confidentiality in creating, storing, accessing, transferring, and disposing of counseling records. (See B.4.b.)

Standard of Practice Fourteen (SP-14): Permission to Record or Observe. Counselors must obtain prior consent from clients in order to record electronically or observe sessions. (See B.4.c.)

Standard of Practice Fifteen (SP-15): Disclosure or Transfer of Records. Counselors must obtain client consent to disclose or transfer records to third parties, unless exceptions listed in SP-9 exist. (See B.4.e.)

Standard of Practice Sixteen (SP-16): Data Disguise Required. Counselors must disguise the identity of the client when using data for training, research, or publication. (See B.5.a.)

Section C: Professional Responsibility

Standard of Practice Seventeen (SP-17): Boundaries of Competence. Counselors must practice only within the boundaries of their competence. (See C.2.a.)

Standard of Practice Eighteen (SP-18): Continuing Education. Counselors must engage in continuing education to maintain their professional competence. (See C.2.f.)

Standard of Practice Nineteen (SP-19): Impairment of Professionals. Counselors must refrain from offering professional services when their personal problems or conflicts may cause harm to a client or others. (See C.2.g.)

Standard of Practice Twenty (SP-20): Accurate Advertising. Counselors must accurately represent their credentials and services when advertising. (See C.3.a.)

Standard of Practice Twenty-One (SP-21): Recruiting Through Employment. Counselors must not use their place of employment or institutional affiliation to recruit clients for their private practices. (See C.3.d.)

Standard of Practice Twenty-Two (SP-22): Credentials Claimed. Counselors must claim or imply only professional credentials possessed and must correct any known misrepresentations of their credentials by others. (See C.4.a.)

Standard of Practice Twenty-Three (SP-23): Sexual Harassment. Counselors must not engage in sexual harassment. (See C.5.b.)

Standard of Practice Twenty-Four (SP-24): Unjustified Gains. Counselors must not use their professional positions to seek or receive unjustified personal gains, sexual favors, unfair advantage, or unearned goods or services. (See C.5.e.)

Standard of Practice Twenty-Five (SP-25): Clients Served by Others. With the consent of the client, counselors must inform other mental health professionals serving the same client that a counseling relationship between the counselor and client exists. (See C.6.c.)

Standard of Practice Twenty-Six (SP-26): Negative Employment Conditions. Counselors must alert their employers to institutional policy or conditions that may be potentially disruptive or damaging to the counselor's professional responsibilities, or that may limit their effectiveness or deny clients' rights. (See D.1.c.)

Standard of Practice Twenty-Seven (SP-27): Personnel Selection and Assignment. Counselors must select competent staff and must assign responsibilities compatible with staff skills and experiences. (See D.1.h.)

Standard of Practice Twenty-Eight (SP-28): Exploitative Relationships With Subordinates. Counselors must not engage in exploitative relationships with individuals over whom they have supervisory, evaluative, or instructional control or authority. (See D.1.k.)

Section D: Relationship With Other Professionals

Standard of Practice Twenty-Nine (SP-29): Accepting Fees From Agency Clients. Counselors must not accept fees or other remuneration for consultation with persons entitled to such services through the counselor's employing agency or institution. (See D.3.a.)

Standard of Practice Thirty (SP-30): Referral Fees. Counselors must not accept referral fees. (See D.3.b.)

Section E: Evaluation, Assessment and Interpretation

Standard of Practice Thirty-One (SP-31): Limits of Competence. Counselors must perform only testing and assessment services for which they are competent. Counselors must not allow the use of psychological assessment techniques by unqualified persons under their supervision. (See E.2.a.)

Standard of Practice Thirty-Two (SP-32): Appropriate Use of Assessment Instruments. Counselors must use assessment instruments in the manner for which they were intended. (See E.2.b.)

Standard of Practice Thirty-Three (SP-33): Assessment Explanations to Clients. Counselors must provide explanations to clients prior to assessment about the nature and purposes of assessment and the specific uses of results. (See E.3.a.)

Standard of Practice Thirty-Four (SP-34): Recipients of Test Results. Counselors must ensure that accurate and appropriate interpretations accompany any release of testing and assessment information. (See E.3.b.)

Standard of Practice Thirty-Five (SP-35): Obsolete Tests and Outdated Test Results. Counselors must not base their assessment or intervention decisions or recommendations on data or test results that are obsolete or outdated for the current purpose. (See E.11.)

Section F: Teaching, Training, and Supervision

Standard of Practice Thirty-Six (SP-36): Sexual Relationships With Students or Supervisees. Counselors must not engage in sexual relationships with their students and supervisees. (See F.1.c.)

Standard of Practice Thirty-Seven (SP-37): Credit for Contributions to Research. Counselors must give credit to students or supervisees for their contributions to research and scholarly projects. (See F.1.d.)

Standard of Practice Thirty-Eight (SP-38): Supervision Preparation. Counselors who offer clinical supervision services must be trained and prepared in supervision methods and techniques. (See F.1.f.)

Standard of Practice Thirty-Nine (SP-39): Evaluation Information. Counselors must clearly state to students and supervisees in advance of training the levels of competency expected, appraisal methods, and timing of evaluations. Counselors must provide students and supervisees with periodic performance appraisal and evaluation feedback throughout the training program. (See F.2.c.)

Standard of Practice Forty (SP-40): Peer Relationships in Training. Counselors must make every effort to ensure that the rights of peers are not violated when students and supervisees are assigned to lead counseling groups or provide clinical supervision. (See F.2.e.)

Standard of Practice Forty-One (SP-41): Limitations of Students and Supervisees. Counselors must assist students and supervisees in securing remedial assistance, when needed, and must dismiss from the training program students and supervisees who are unable to provide competent service due to academic or personal limitations. (See F.3.a.)

Standard of Practice Forty-Two (SP-42): Self-Growth Experiences. Counselors who conduct experiences for students or supervisees that include self-growth or self-disclosure must inform participants of counselors' ethical obligations to the profession and must not grade participants based on their nonacademic performance. (See F.3.b.)

Standard of Practice Forty-Three (SP-43): Standards for Students and Supervisees. Students

and supervisees preparing to become counselors must adhere to the Code of Ethics and the Standards of Practice of counselors. (See F.3.e.)

Section G: Research and Publication

Standard of Practice Forty-Four (SP-44): Precautions to Avoid Injury in Research. Counselors must avoid causing physical, social, or psychological harm or injury to subjects in research. (See G.1.c.)

Standard of Practice Forty-Five (SP-45): Confidentiality of Research Information. Counselors must keep confidential information obtained about research participants. (See G.2.d.)

Standard of Practice Forty-Six (SP-46): Information Affecting Research Outcome. Counselors must report all variables and conditions known to the investigator that may have affected research data or outcomes. (See G.3.a.)

Standard of Practice Forty-Seven (SP-47): Accurate Research Results. Counselors must not distort or misrepresent research data, nor fabricate or intentionally bias research results. (See G.3.b.)

Standard of Practice Forty-Eight (SP-48): Publication Contributors. Counselors must give appropriate credit to those who have contributed to research. (See G.4.a. and G.4.b.)

Section H: Resolving Ethical Issues

Standard of Practice Forty-Nine (SP-49): Ethical Behavior Expected. Counselors must take appropriate action when they possess reasonable cause that raises doubts as to whether counselors or other mental health professionals are acting in an ethical manner. (See H.2.a.)

Standard of Practice Fifty (SP-50): Unwarranted Complaints. Counselors must not initiate, participate in, or encourage the filing of ethics complaints that are unwarranted or intended to harm a mental health professional rather than to protect clients or the public. (See H.2.f.)

Standard of Practice Fifty-One (SP-51): Cooperation With Ethics Committees. Counselors must cooperate with investigations, proceedings, and requirements of the ACA Ethics Committee or ethics committees of other duly constituted associations or boards having jurisdiction over those charged with a violation. (See H.3.)

RECOMMENDED READINGS

The following documents are available to counselors as resources to guide them in their practices. These resources are not a part of the Code of Ethics and the Standards of Practice.

American Association for Counseling and Development & Association for Measurement and Evaluation in Counseling and Development. (1989). *The responsibilities of users of standardized tests* (Rev.). Washington, DC: Author.

American Psychological Association. (1985). Standards for educational and psychological testing (Rev.). Washington, DC: Author.

American Rehabilitation Counseling Association, Commission on Rehabilitation Counselor Certification, & National Rehabilitation Counseling Association. (1995). *Code of professional ethics for rehabilitation counselors.* Chicago, IL: Author.

American School Counselor Association. (1992). *Ethical standards for school counselors.* Alexandria, VA: Author.

Joint Committee on Testing Practices. (1988). *Code of fair testing practices in education.* Washington, DC: Author.

National Board for Certified Counselors. (1989). *National Board for Certified Counselors code of ethics.* Alexandria, VA: Author.

Prediger, D. J. (Ed.). (1993, March). *Multicultural assessment standards.* Alexandria, VA: Association for Assessment in Counseling.

appendix C

PERIODICALS IN THE FIELD OF COUNSELING

An important way for students to become aware of the nature and scope of a field is through the various publications within the field. Many of the periodicals listed below may be found in college and university libraries. Student subscriptions may be available for some journals, usually after you become a member of the sponsoring organization.

The following list of periodicals is intended to indicate the extensive nature of the field encompassed by the counseling profession and is not intended to be complete.

ACAE News: Send message "subscribe" to counseling.org/enews/subscribe
Alcohol Health and Research World
American Counselor
American Journal of Drug and Alcohol Abuse
American Journal of Orthopsychiatry
American Journal of Psychiatry
American Journal of Psychotherapy
American Psychologist
American Vocational Journal
AMHCA Journal (American Mental Health Counselors Association)
Annual Handbook for Group Facilitators
APA Monitor
Biofeedback and Self-Regulation
Common Boundary Between Spirituality and Psychotherapy
Corrective and Social Psychiatry

Counseling and Human Development
Counseling and Values
Counseling E-zine: www.gate.net/~rational/ezine0198.htm/
Counseling Psychologist
Counselor Education and Supervision
Developmental Psychology
Educational and Psychological Measurement
Elementary School Guidance and Counseling
Family Process
Family Relations
Family Therapy Networker
Gerontologist
Gestalt Journal
Gestalt Newsletter
Group and Organization Studies
Group Process
Hispanic Journal of Behavioral Sciences
Human Development
Human Relations
Human Resource Management
International Journal for the Advancement of Counseling
International Journal of Family Counseling
International Journal of Group Psychotherapy
International Journal of Social Psychiatry
Journal of Abnormal Psychology
Journal of Alcohol and Drug Education
Journal of Applied Behavior Analysis
Journal of Applied Behavioral Science

Journal of Applied Psychology
Journal of Black Psychology
Journal of Clinical Psychology
Journal of College Student Personnel
Journal of Consulting and Clinical
  Psychology
Journal of Counseling and Development
Journal of Counseling Psychology
Journal of Cross-Cultural Counseling
Journal of Employment Counseling
Journal of Family Counseling
Journal of Group Psychotherapy, Psychodrama,
  and Sociometry
Journal of Humanistic Education and
  Development
Journal of Humanistic Psychology
Journal of Marriage and the Family
Journal of Multicultural Counseling and
  Development
Journal of Occupational Psychology
Journal of Offender Counseling
Journal of Personality
Journal of Personality Techniques and Personality
  Assessment

Journal of Psychology
Journal of Specialists in Group Work
Journal of the National Association for Women's
  Deans, Administrators, and Counselors
Journal of Transpersonal Psychology
Measurement and Evaluation in Counseling and
  Development
Occupational Outlook Quarterly
Occupations
Organizational Behavior and Human Decisions
  Processes
Organizational Dynamics
Personnel Psychology
Psychiatry
Psychological Bulletin
Psychological Reports
Psychology in the Schools
Rehabilitation Counseling Bulletin
School Counselor
Small Group Behavior
Social Psychology
Training and Development Journal
Transactional Analysis Journal
Vocational Guidance Quarterly

AUTHOR INDEX

Please note, italic page numbers indicate bibliographic references, and page references followed by *f* or *t* refer to figures or tables respectively.

SUBJECT INDEX